DATE DUE			
MAY 9			
NOV 7			
MAR 28			
APR 23			
FEB 10			
FEB 24			
MAR 10			
MAR 24			
APR 15			
APR 29			
MAY 14			

INTERNATIONAL POLITICS *IN A* REVOLUTIONARY AGE

INTERNATIONAL POLITICS *IN A* REVOLUTIONARY AGE

BY

W·W·KULSKI

SYRACUSE UNIVERSITY

J·B·LIPPINCOTT COMPANY

New York AND *Philadelphia*

Library of Congress Catalog Card Number 64-12758
PRINTED IN THE UNITED STATES OF AMERICA

TO

THE MEMORY OF

THOSE WHO HAVE FALLEN VICTIMS

OF NATIONAL HATREDS

AND IDEOLOGICAL FANATICISMS

Preface

This book on contemporary international politics is intended to provide those who are not specialists in the field with a guide for a better understanding of our international environment. Its contents are not woven around any of the current theories of international relations, as valuable as these are for the advancement of research. These theories are new; they are not yet fully and convincingly tested; and they usually stress one particular aspect of international politics or one particular theme (decision-making, conflict, the game approach, the communication factor) to the prejudice of other aspects or themes. They do not yet offer a foolproof and all-embracing explanation of international phenomena and cannot provide total guidance for an examination of international politics.

The formulation of a comprehensive theory of international relations whose fixed laws would make it possible to predict the behavior of states must overcome three difficulties. First, human actions are not always rational and hence predictable; moreover, what is rational for one man may not be rational for another. Secondly, decisions in international affairs are choices between two or more apparently rational courses of action; this freedom of choice introduces a considerable factor of chance which cannot be defined in advance. Thirdly, international phenomena of a similar kind, those which may be grouped together in one class, do not amount to large numbers; yet the calculus of probabilities works with large numbers. The demographic statistics for the advanced countries are reliable, are founded on great numbers, and have been kept for generations. Prior to 1940 it seemed that these vital statistics offered excellent material for the forecast of future birth and death rates. These predictions were "safely" grounded in the extrapolation of long-term trends which had been emerging for many decades from the vital statistics. The sudden and unexpected reversal in the forties of the declining trend in the Western birth rate disproved the prewar predictions. This reversal not only pointed to the need for even greater amounts of data but also demonstrated the role of chance (free choice) in human affairs. These three preliminary difficulties, which plague attempts at a general and coherent theory of international politics, can be summed up in the well-known dictum: "It takes an infinity of cases to prove a proposition, and only one to disprove it."

The familiar image of chess is more misleading than helpful in illuminating the nature of international politics. At the international chessboard, not two, but well over a hundred players (states) sit, each moving his own figure according to his own best judgment. Each move represents a challenge to all or at least several other players and brings about a chain of multiple responses. In deciding how to shift the position of his own figure, each player must study and anticipate the moves of a hundred other players. The value of each figure is relative and depends on the position occupied by individual players; a pawn for one player might be a tower for another. The stakes are not defined in the same terms for all the participants in the international game, and the players are not bound by any universally accepted rules. For all these reasons the game is infinitely more complex than chess.

It is hoped that an eclectic approach will make this book useful to nonspecialists and perhaps also to diplomats and other practitioners who need from time to time to cast a global glance at the stage on which they exercise their profession.

The author has relied heavily on his knowledge of the history of international relations but has not burdened the text with historical references which might not be understood by nonspecialists. The modern patterns of international politics have been described whenever states have behaved similarly in similar circumstances often enough to warrant the induction of general conclusions from particular events. Above all, the main trends of our time have been delineated, those trends which make us live in a rapidly changing world. Revolutionary in the full sense of the word, these trends compel the present generation, as they will also compel later generations, to live a dangerous life in an international environment which our fathers or grandfathers would have called abnormal but which we must accept as normal for our time. The nuclear and outer-space revolutions in military technology, with their terrible sanction for mistakes in international behavior, cannot be unmade. The political emancipation of formerly dependent peoples cannot be ignored, and the desire of the underdeveloped countries for economic and social modernization cannot be suppressed. The so-called population explosion has not only increased the population of the less developed areas of the world relative to that of the advanced countries but has also had a profound effect on economic and social conditions within these areas. The "Third World" (the underdeveloped countries) has become the huge stage of revolutionary change and of its concomitant, political instability. The ideological strife which separates the West from the Communist states and which has repercussions in the "Third World" contributes its share to the unsettled and hazardous condition of our time. All these revolutionary trends, each having worldwide significance, coincide in our time and make it an era of truly profound change. No previous historical period can be legitimately invoked as a precedent for our time; no previous era of change was plunged in the throes of several revolutionary trends, and none knew a human universe so tightly integrated by technology that each part was influenced by changes taking place in all the other parts.

Because our world is radically different from the one which existed prior to 1914, a book on international politics must adjust its perspective to new circumstances. Specifically, it can no longer be West-centered. Although the present book has been written primarily for Western readers, a glance at the table of contents will indicate that considerable space has been given to the study of environments that are relatively unfamiliar to these readers, namely to the underdeveloped countries and the Communist states. The West comes into its own, however, in discussions of its internal problems, such as NATO or the European Community, and in the analysis of its relations with the other two sides of the international triangle—the Communist states and the "Third World" of the underdeveloped countries.

The author does not claim to be a "realist"; anyone who writes about international politics can only describe his own image of "reality." His image will not—and could not—coincide exactly with the images of others, since no two human minds or human lives are identical. Only in the sense that everyone has an equal right to call his image the reality does the author claim to be a realist.

This book is the fruit of many years of research and teaching and of a long diplomatic career. Both academic and practical experiences have influenced its tenor.

My acknowledgements begin by the expression of a deep gratitude which I owe to my beloved wife, faithful companion and friend. This book would not have been written but for her help and encouragement.

I also owe a debt of gratitude to Syracuse University for its generous policy of leaves of absence and for its financial assistance. My warm appreciation is due to Dr. William P. Tolley, the enlightened Chancellor of Syracuse University, to Dr. Frank Piskor, Vice-President for Academic Affairs, and to Mr. Harlan Cleveland, Assistant Secretary of State and former Dean of Maxwell Graduate School.

I wish to express my grateful thanks to the Social Science Research Council for a grant which enabled me to make a study of the problems of underdeveloped countries, a study which has proved very useful for my better understanding of contemporary trends in international politics.

Last but not least, I express my warm appreciation to J. B. Lippincott Company for their friendly co-operation, and in particular to Mr. Alex Fraser, who greatly helped in the publication of this book, and to Mr. Tom Abrams, who edited the manuscript.

W. W. Kulski

Syracuse, New York
November, 1963

Contents

CHAPTER I: INTRODUCTION

CHAPTER II: THE NUCLEAR REVOLUTION AND THE PROBLEM OF WAR

CHAPTER III: MASS NATIONALISM

CHAPTER IV: THE THIRD WORLD—POLITICAL EMANCIPATION

CHAPTER V: THE THIRD WORLD—THE REVOLUTION OF MODERNIZATION

CHAPTER X: DIPLOMACY

INTERNATIONAL POLITICS *IN A* REVOLUTIONARY AGE

CHAPTER I

Introduction

THE STATE

International politics is the study of relations between states, each of which holds the power of ultimate decision concerning its foreign policy. This power includes the choice of objectives to be pursued in relation to other states and the choice of means to be used in order to attain these objectives. The magnitude of this discretionary power can be appreciated if one remembers that each state has the right to possess armed forces and remains the ultimate judge of their use. It can at any time decide to use its armed forces if not deterred by international prohibitions against the use of force or by fear of retaliation.

A closer look at these awe-inspiring actors on the international stage, the sovereign states, reveals, however, that they are only puppets operated by human beings, the state agents. The state is nothing but a concept corresponding to a certain type of organized human relations. The individuals who are the subjects of these relations constitute the only living reality. The state does not exist outside their minds and has no intellect or will of its own. It can be described as the image of an organized group of individuals who live on a definite territory and are collectively responsible for the acts of their government, which claims their supreme allegiance and the right to speak on their behalf in relation to other states. The government is composed of individuals whose decisions are, by a legal fiction, deemed to be those of the state. Thus, a number of individuals, constitutionally authorized to do so, substitute their own intellects and their own wills for the nonexistent intellect and will of the state. Their commissions and omissions are attributed to the state, i.e., engage the collective responsibility of all the citizens. This convention of imputing the decisions of state agents to the state itself lies at the root of international relations and forms the foundation of national collective responsibility. The action undertaken by a president, a prime minister, a foreign secretary is no longer his own but becomes that of the state, which legally is the subject of international relations.

Yet the concept of the state cannot be equated with either the state agents or even the total number of citizens living at a given moment. The state agents feel that they act on behalf of a social entity whose image is present in their minds. The total number of citizens living at a given time is not a fixed notion. Each day some of them die and some others are born. The word *state* evokes in their minds the continuity of their organized group. The concept of the state extends into the remote past and seems to reach far into the indefinite future. It includes the historical legacy left by preceding generations and the future of generations yet unborn. The living citizens are the products of the heritage accumulated by their ancestors; the moment they think of the future of their own children, they project the concept of the state into the future. The image of the state is thus the image of a continuous social phenomenon whose "life" seems almost eternal if measured by the short span of human life. By the same token, the state seems to detach itself from the individuals who compose it. It acquires its own interests which can no longer be equated with the sum total of individual interests of its citizens. The state agents are expected to take care of these collective interests, which transcend the present moment and reach into the future. The dictum "To govern is to foresee" reflects this notion of the continuity of state interests, which can be well served only by those state agents who foresee the distant effects of their decisions.

The state agents whose acts are imputed to the state are numerous and occupy positions of varying importance. Beginning with the heads of state and of government and foreign ministers and ending with a minor official who makes decisions by virtue of delegated powers, all of them engage the collective responsibility of all their countrymen both living and yet unborn. Whether their interpretation of what is good for the collective interests of the state is right or wrong, the agents of foreign states have no choice but to impute their decisions to the whole national community.

National collective responsibility for the acts performed by state agents rests on the assumption that all the citizens must be held answerable either because they have endowed the state agents with the mandate to speak on their behalf or at least because they have done nothing effective to disavow them and to replace them with other state agents. This assumption inculpates all citizens, those who are interested in public affairs as well as those who are not, those who have voted for the elected state agents as well as those who have voted against them or have abstained from voting, and also those citizens of authoritarian states who are prevented by their system of government from influencing the choice of their rulers or the selection of national policies. The consequences of collective responsibility in international politics may seem cruel and unjust, but governments have no choice in the matter. They must accept the acts of agents of foreign states as those of the whole national community or the relations between states would become impossible. There are no other spokesmen who could with authority substitute their voice for that of the official state agents and who wield control over the national armed forces. International politics are, in fact, the relations between state agents whose acts have repercussions across international boundaries.

Collective responsibility is fully revealed after each major war. The victors call to account the whole defeated nation. The pro-Nazi, anti-Nazi, and politically indifferent Germans were equally affected by the Allied occupation of their country, by the reparations, by the territorial amputations, and by the division of Germany into two states. The same was true of the Japanese. The individual responsibility of the Nazi and Japanese leaders and war criminals before the tribunals of the victorious powers was superimposed on collective responsibility but did not replace it. Collective responsibility is evident in a less dramatic way in day-to-day international relations. A faulty foreign policy on the part of state agents results in a steady deterioration of the external situation of the whole national community, while an intelligent policy benefits the whole nation.

The rapid rate of change, characteristic of our historical period, makes it even more obvious that the fate of the common man is being greatly, if not decisively, affected by decisions made on his behalf and in his name. He might not be interested in international politics, but they are interested in him as one who will pay his share of the national penalty.

THE ELEMENT OF CHANCE IN INTERNATIONAL POLITICS

If we remember that the acts of states in their mutual relations are in fact decisions made by state agents, we will realize the qualitative difference between international politics, as an academic discipline, and the natural sciences. This difference consists in the existence of human free will. Of course, there are many external limitations on the exercise of this free will, such as the power of other states. But the fact remains that any two individuals faced with identical circumstances do not necessarily choose the same course of action. Each situation usually offers or seems to offer a choice of two or more courses of action. The political decision consists in choosing one course of action rather than another. The existence of this choice makes for an element of chance in international relations.

Two scientists, accepting the same scientific hypothesis valid at a given time and using the same standards for the evaluation of their findings, will agree that the same causes invariably produce, under identical circumstances, the same results. Hence they are able to predict these results. But two specialists in international politics are not placed in the same favorable position. They cannot predict with certainty that the same causes will always produce the same governmental decisions, and they might differ widely in their predictions of probable international developments.

There are other factors unknown to the natural sciences which enhance the role of chance in international politics. Very many facts of international life are jealously kept secret by governments, and other governments must make decisions in ignorance of these facts. No mortal is able to know all the facts which are necessary for a full understanding of the actions undertaken by governments; therefore, any analysis of an international problem can be vitiated by this element of the unknown.

The well-known facts in international politics are not the same as facts in the sciences. The human mind simultaneously perceives and interprets social facts. They can be understood only if related to the frame of reference of the individual observer, but this frame of reference varies from one individual to another. Hence, what we call a social fact is never exactly the same fact for any two individuals, each of whom is interpreting its meaning according to his own values and interests.

This problem is even more complex in the case of international events. The mental image of these events is colored not only by individual beliefs and interests but also by group subjectivity. Human beings are the children of their various national environments and inherit from them their standards of judgment, their self-evident truths, and their conception of national interests. Hence, the same international event will be seen in a different light by two men belonging to different nationalities. Compulsory education, which exalts national values and promotes national self-evident truths, has in our time greatly intensified this national subjectivity. Pascal said: "Truth on this side of the Pyrenees, untruth on the other side." The "self-evident" truth on this side of the Pyrenees or of the Atlantic will color the interpretation of international events differently from another and possibly opposite but equally "self-evident" truth on the other side. The past and present experiences of any two nations are never identical; their scale of fundamental values and their standards of judgment cannot be identical either.

If one realizes the bearing of national subjectivity on the evaluation of international events, he is prompted to eliminate one misleading and often-used word from the vocabulary of international politics. This word is *objectivity.* No human being can become so entirely divorced from his national environment or at least his ideological group and their self-evident truths as to have the right to sit in judgment and proclaim the only true version of international life. When someone claims to take an objective stand on an international matter, he implies that his own version of the facts, or at best the version current in his country or in his ideological camp, is the only true one for the whole of mankind. This is the summit of individual or national presumption. Objectivity, in the sense of an interpretation of events which should be acceptable to all reasonable men, is unattainable in this diversified world.

However, objectivity should not be confused with intellectual honesty. Intellectual honesty is necessary for an intelligent understanding of international events. It presupposes the greatest possible effort to learn all the accessible facts and to eliminate from one's mind all prejudices which are not held to be self-evident truths. The meaning of intellectual honesty can be illustrated by the method which a foreign service officer should follow. He will gather all the accessible data, not excluding those facts which are unpleasant from the point of view of his national interests or which contradict his wishful thinking. He will accept as a fact that foreign nations have their own self-evident truths which may be at variance with those of his own country. He will therefore realize that many events have a different meaning for another nation from the meaning which he and his countrymen attach to them. He should be able to interpret these events not only from the point of view of his own country but also from that of other nations. If he is familiar with the self-evident truths and the concept of national interests of a foreign country, he will be able to understand, without sharing it, the interpretation which that country attaches to a sequence of international events. Only then will he discover the full divergence between his own national interpretation and that adopted by a foreign government. This in turn will help him to determine whether this divergence can be bridged by some sort of accommodation. If the same man insisted that his national interpretation of events is objective, i.e., universally valid, he would never be capable of understanding the reactions of other nations and would supplant this understanding with a moral indignation at foreign iniquity, an indignation ridiculous in foreign eyes and useless for his own country.

The realm of chance in international relations is further enlarged by human folly. Men are no mere rational machines. Emotions interfere with our judgments. A government might decide quite unexpectedly on a course of action which is harmful to its own national interests and could not have been rationally foreseen by outside observers.

The factor of chance deprives the academic science of international politics of the hope of ever becoming an exact science which could be reduced to mathematical formulae or claim to have discovered unalterable laws of human behavior. International politics can, however, deduce certain clues from the rich history of international relations which can serve as useful signposts for future action. It is true that history never repeats itself, but analogous situations do occur. Whenever history confronts us with several analogous situations, we can ask why certain men succeeded while other men failed under similar circumstances. We thus can learn from the experience of former ages. For instance, history invariably teaches us that coalitions are bound together only by the existence of a common threat to the vital national interests of the members of the coalition. We thus can expect that any coalition will tend to become weaker if its members begin to disagree about the seriousness or imminence of that threat. We will not be surprised if the coalition disintegrates soon after the elimination of the common threat, as after the victorious termination of a war against the common enemy. History also tells us that whenever an irreconcilable conflict arises between the self-evident ideological truths cherished by a nation and its most vital national interests, the most probable choice will favor national interests at the expense of self-evident truths.

The factor of chance is further enhanced in international politics by the fact that all politics, including international politics, require not only knowledge but also art. The political talent which is needed for a successful foreign policy cannot be precisely defined and has been variously called a knack, a political flair, or intuition. Its meaning can be better understood by analogy with other arts. Several men can be trained in the knowledge of music; yet after a time one of them will become a distinguished composer, another will reach fame as a celebrated soloist, a third will teach music or be a member of an orchestra, while still another's performance will be endured only by his own family. The same is true of politics. It is political talent that enables a man to make a decision which will be acclaimed by future generations as wise and farsighted, while perhaps his knowledgeable expert advisers confront him with persuasive arguments in favor of other courses of action. But political talent is of no avail if no historical opportunity offers itself for its display. Machiavelli rightly said: ". . . They [the statesmen] owed nothing to fortune but the opportunity which gave them matter to be shaped into what form they thought fit; and without that opportunity their powers would have been wasted, and without their powers the opportunity would have been in vain." What can the most talented man do if he guides the destinies of a weak nation and is confronted by a coalition of hostile great powers bent on the destruction of his country? By the same token, a politician without political gifts will miss the most conspicuous opportunity, and his country will pay the bill.

WISHFUL THINKING

One among many typical errors in thinking about international affairs deserves special mention at this point, the error of wishful thinking. It consists in an irrational optimism which implicitly assumes that one's own nation has a compact with history which protects it against disasters. Events of the present, if not propitious, are bound eventually to be shaped by providence or history in a way which will redress the situation. However, the historical record is there to tell us that no people has ever had a compact with destiny. Even such an imposing structure as the Roman Empire was eventually reduced to ashes which served as a cultural fertilizer for new social structures. The future is molded by the efforts of all countries, but the international struggle frequently opposes the effort of one nation to that of another. One does not need to be a pessimist to realize that:

A. Human progress is a highly relative notion and its meaning varies in time and from one country or ideological group to another. A Westerner would see progress in a course of events that married the prosperity of his nation with the universal triumph of democracy; a Russian would see progress in a different development, one that would culminate in a no less happy marriage between the prosperity of his country and the universal victory of Communism. The future cannot simultaneously fulfill these contrary expectations and confirm these conflicting interpretations of human progress.

B. Whatever the meaning attached to human progress, there is no necessary connection between it and the international situation of a particular country. For instance, the universal victory of Communism might not entail at all the dominant position of Russia in the world but might spell out the rise of several rival centers of power.

C. Human progress, whatever its definition, does not unfold along an ever-ascending curve. The history of our own civilization demonstrates that the curve of human destiny has sometimes gone up to wonderful heights, as during the Greek classical period, and has plunged at other times to a barbarian level, as during the Dark Ages. Who can tell whether the curve will now continue to go up or take a plunge into the abyss?

Wishful thinking may result in two attitudes. First, it may lead to a perilous relaxation of national effort and an underestimation of the gravity of international problems. It surely inclines toward an underestimation of the actual and potential strength of other nations, especially unfriendly ones. Secondly, it may result in an overestimation of the power of one's own country and in the assumption that one's own government can do anything it wants if it only has the will-power. Foreign problems, unlike domestic ones, cannot be solved by the fiat of any one government, which, however powerful the state it represents, must nevertheless maneuver among many contending nations, some of them also powerful.

Wishful thinking has produced certain comforting but false clichés. One of them is the belief that the virtuous cause must finally win out.

This assumption raises the question of what is a virtuous cause in international politics; each of the contending nations usually firmly believes in the righteousness of its cause and is no less profoundly convinced that the opposing nation espouses an evil cause. Assuming the impossible, namely that most of mankind would be able to agree on what standpoint reflects the requirements of pure virtue, there would still remain the risk that future history would reverse the verdict. The history of international relations is not exactly a record of virtuous conduct; moreover, the applause of historians is seldom a tribute paid to the moral virtue of statesmen but rather to their political virtue, a quality which Machiavelli called *virtù*. This political virtue is not a moral notion but a purely political one and synonymous with prudence, i.e., the capacity of clearly defining the objectives of foreign policy and of carefully balancing these objectives with the available means. A politically virtuous man may sometimes use means which could be questioned from the point of view of moral virtue. Most historians will nevertheless acclaim him for his success in achieving his objectives and leaving a lasting imprint on the historical record. Moreover, history is usually written from the point of view of the victors. Their cause, therefore, looks retrospectively virtuous, even in the moral sense, to their spiritual descendants. Several successive generations of European school boys have been elated by the victory of Roman virtue over Carthaginian wickedness; they have inherited the Roman legacy and look at ancient history from the Roman point of view. If Carthage had not been defeated and wantonly destroyed by the Romans, if instead it had been victorious, the Europeans would probably have been its spiritual heirs and would have rejoiced over the triumph of Carthaginian virtue without deploring the destruction of Rome.

The Czechs enshrined an optimistic motto in their national coat of arms: "Truth shall win." They could see the bitter irony of this optimism when the German troops were occupying Prague in 1939 and again when their democracy was ended in 1948 by a Communist coup.

DOMESTIC AND FOREIGN POLICIES

There exists no Chinese wall to separate domestic politics from foreign policy. The two are entangled. The self-evident truths, the degree of readiness to uphold national independence against an external threat, the intensity of social solidarity, the scope and gravity of internal divisions and social conflicts, the pool of knowledge and skills, these and other domestic factors determine the choice of foreign policies and also their efficacy. The form of government, the strength and representativeness of interest groups, the criteria of recruitment of national elites, extend or narrow down the range of people who influence in varying degrees the formulation of foreign policy. Domestic politics are reflected in the foreign policy of each country as in a mirror.

In the same way, foreign developments influence domestic politics. An external threat may generate an outburst of passionate nationalism with its clamor for conformity and its witch-hunt of nonconformists. A depression in one country may have grave repercussions in several other countries. Western, notably American, living standards have forced the Soviet leadership into a competition which has caused a steady rise of Soviet living standards. The emancipation of several African peoples stimulates American Negroes in their struggle for equality. A revolution in one country may have repercussions well beyond its national boundaries. The Russian October Revolution has changed the ways of life of one-third of mankind and is affecting the lives of the remaining two-thirds. The Cuban revolution is a factor of importance for the whole of Latin America. All the underdeveloped countries are fascinated by the alluring image of the advanced countries, an image which beckons to them from the end of the long and arduous road of modernization. The European ideologies, whether democratic or totalitarian, influence their elites and compel them to re-examine traditional self-evident truths. Conversely, neither the West nor the Communist bloc can remain indifferent to the revolutionary change that is taking place in the underdeveloped countries. The direction which this domestic change will take is perhaps more important for the two rival blocs than the present foreign policy of the underdeveloped nations.

Domestic and international politics serve as frameworks for each other. However, except for the very weak and in fact dependent countries, each nation has an incomparably greater leeway in formulating her domestic policies than in determining her foreign policy, which is criss-crossed by the foreign policies of other states. Freedom of decision in international politics is strictly limited even for the great powers.

THE ERA OF RELATIVE STABILITY

The contrast between the political nineteenth century (1815-1914) and our own time enables one to gauge more accurately the nature of the historical period in which we live. After the French Revolution and Napoleonic wars international politics returned to "normalcy." This relative stability was not, of course, a sort of immobility, because human actions never allow for the maintenance of an undisturbed status quo. Many aspects of the international situation were altered throughout this period between 1815 and 1914, but the basic framework withstood the test of new developments until the outbreak of the First World War. The general peace lasted throughout these hundred years. The rate of change was slow by comparison to our own time in spite of the various social forces which were undermining the status quo. For instance, the national movements greatly modified the status quo as it had been fixed by the Congress of Vienna, but their effects were limited to Europe, actually only to parts of Europe (Germany, Italy, the Low Countries, the Danubian and Balkan regions), and never caused a general war in which all the great powers became involved.

Why was it that our ancestors were able to live in a world of relative stability? First of all, the problems of international politics were simplified by the fact that the main stage was limited for almost the whole period to Europe only. The main actors, the great powers, were exclusively European until the rise of the United States in the last decades of the nineteenth century. The admission of the United States to the great powers' club did not greatly alter the situation because of American isolationism, which precluded an active participation in great-power politics. As long as the European great powers respected the Monroe Doctrine, accepted their political exclusion from the Western Hemisphere, and took into consideration the American voice in Far Eastern affairs, they enjoyed a free hand in the Eastern Hemisphere. The admission of Japan to the same club in 1905 heralded the advent of a new era, but Japan, like the United States, was content to limit her interests to one region, the Far East.

The great powers with truly universal interests, or at least with interests centered around the main stage of Europe, were five in number: Britain, France, Russia, Prussia, which was later replaced by a unified Germany, and the steadily declining but still strong Austria, to be known after 1867 as Austria-Hungary. The relations between these five powers created the framework within which smaller states took care of their own interests. Italy, although admitted to the club after its unification, was never a true great power in its own right but enjoyed a rank and influence much greater than its power warranted, thanks to the fluidity of nineteenth-century politics; the great powers sometimes needed Italian support in their never-ending maneuvers with regard to each other.

The men who made decisions on behalf of the great powers (sovereigns, ministers, diplomats, and those members of the upper and middle classes who exerted an influence on the formulation of foreign policies) were much less numerous than now. Basically, foreign policy was the monopoly of the sovereign and his government, while the role of advisers and implementing agents was largely confined to professional diplomats. Depending on the domestic regime, a varying number of members of parliament, scions of aristocratic families, important businessmen, influential publicists, and others exerted an influence on the formulation of foreign policy. The very air of international stability did not stimulate many people even among the upper and middle classes to be intensely and steadily interested in foreign affairs. This in itself facilitated diplomatic transactions.

The people who formulated or influenced foreign policy had a common cultural and social background. All of them Europeans, they shared the same cultural values. They frequently differed on the merits of one or another form of government: some of them preferred autocracy to representative government, others believed in the parliamentary system, still others in some sort of intermediate system. But they were content to uphold their favorite system of government in their own country and felt no urge to extend it to foreign lands. The social beliefs of people who "counted" were practically identical. It was the era of the dominance by the upper and middle classes, who had no interest in questioning the principle of private ownership of the means of production or the concept of profit as the legitimate reward for the owner of those means. Private property was truly "sacred" for them. It was considered self-evident that the expropriation of that property by any government should remain an exceptional measure and should call for adequate compensation. The socialist movement with its heretical views was, it is true, gradually gathering momentum, but no government was socialist. All the governments protected the interests of the upper and middle classes, although the rise of the lower classes caused a number of them to pay increasing attention in the second half of the period under consideration to the needs of the workers. The political and social emancipation of the common man was clearly beginning.

THE BALANCE OF POWER

The great powers had a mutual understanding about how international problems should be handled. This understanding consisted in their acceptance of a political system called the balance of power. This system is probably as old as the history of international relations and reappears whenever the stage is occupied by more than two powers if they are uncommitted to each other. It amounts to a maneuvering among the three or several powers with one main objective in mind, to prevent any of them from dominating the others. The king of Persia played this game during the Peloponnesian War whenever he tried to keep the balance between Athens and Sparta, the two enemies, by throwing his support to the weaker side. The Italian principalities and cities of the fifteenth and sixteenth centuries fully mastered the art of the balance of power, effectively preventing by their shifting combinations the unification of Italy under one ruler; eventually they prepared their own disaster by inviting the intervention of non-Italian powers in order to uphold their domestic balance of power. Henry VIII was fully aware of the rules of the game in his maneuvering between two continental and contending great powers: the Hapsburg Empire and the French Kingdom. The seventeenth and eighteenth centuries lived under the auspices of the balance of power.

Napoleon was defeated by the ultimate weapon of this political system—a coalition of all great powers to stop the dangerous expansion of one of their peers.

The balance of power requires for its operation the existence of certain conditions:

A. There must exist a multistate international stage shared by great powers of roughly comparable strength. Thus, the triumph of the Roman Empire within the world of the Hellenistic civilization precluded balance-of-power politics for lack of actors.

B. The great powers must accept the main principle of the system, namely the moderate nature of their foreign objectives. These objectives must remain reasonably limited and thus compatible, after a process of diplomatic adjustment, with the equally limited objectives of other great powers.

C. The great powers must respect the right of each of them to model its domestic regime as it likes. Ideological conflicts and missionary zeal are incompatible with the system because they cannot be reconciled with limited objectives in international affairs.

D. Since the strength of the great powers must be roughly comparable, the system requires for its operation a slow rate of change in the distribution of power. The nineteenth-century technology of war changed very slowly by our standards. Industrialization progressed at a moderate rate. The great powers were not afraid that one of them would suddenly surpass the others in the technological quality of its armed forces and thus basically affect the distribution of power. This distribution could be calculated by using fairly simple indexes, such as the total number of the population, the economic potential, the size of armed forces, and the quality of armaments. The secrecy peculiar to the present-day totalitarian regimes was unknown, and information was rather easily accessible.

E. The system can best operate if all the great powers remain mutually uncommitted and enjoy considerable latitude in their maneuvering to prevent the rise of one of them to a position of hegemony. But the minimum condition is that at least one great power of considerable strength remain uncommitted and the others be kept in line by the potential sanction of its throwing its weight on the scale of the weaker group against the stronger. This power plays the role of the balancer, i.e., of the state that keeps the balance in the distribution of power among the other contending states. As long as contending powers neutralize each other by their equal force, the balancer can stay aloof; if one of them or a group of them appears to overtake the rivals, the role of the balancer consists in stepping in diplomatically or even militarily to restore the balance by adding its power to that of the weaker side.

The role of balancer was played in the nineteenth century by Great Britain. For several decades of that century it was not difficult to play this role. As long as the continental great powers had a strength of comparable magnitude and thus were able to neutralize each other and as long as they were preoccupied with their own competition, Great Britain did not need to take sides. She could afford to enjoy her "splendid isolation." The superior financial and naval strength of Great Britain helped her in acting on the continent as a sort of "disinterested" arbiter whose main interest in Europe was to watch over the maintenance of the balance of power. Her paramount political position was generally, if sometimes grudgingly, accepted until the rise of a unified Germany.

F. The balance of power entails another important condition, namely that none of the great powers intend to undermine the status quo. This is the other facet of the moderation of foreign objectives. The great powers in the nineteenth century observed this important rule. It did not mean that the status quo, as the Congress of Vienna had determined it, remained unaltered, but its modifications were usually accepted by all the great powers, often by common agreement, even if one or another of them gave its assent only reluctantly. These changes were not considered to have a drastic effect on the distribution of power. Of course, the judgment of the time could now be challenged. For instance, the unification of Germany under Prussian aegis modified the basic distribution of power in Europe, but this was not realized at the time.

The extra-European expansion gave rise to political disputes but eventually resulted in accommodations between the great powers concerned. These deals, consisting in the "fair" distribution of colonial spoils, could be concluded because the people most concerned, Asians and Africans, had no voice in the matter.

This system began to fail in providing a feeling of security to the great powers once one of them, a unified and fully industrialized Germany, had overtaken its continental peers and become the leading military power; moreover, Germany also aspired to be the leading naval power and a colonial power as well. The German-Austrian alliance started a series of commitments among the great powers which culminated in 1907 in the completion of two rival blocs, the Triple Alliance facing the Triple Entente. With Britain, the balancer, committed to the Triple Entente, freedom of maneuvering was gone. The system of the balance of power did not function any longer, and its failure was brought into the open by the outbreak of the First World War, which marked the end of an era.

The governments which hurled Europe into that war could not possibly foresee in 1914 that this time it was not to be just another European military contest of limited significance. Yet this gigantic inter-European struggle was to culminate in an ideological split into two hostile camps and the termination of a long period of uncontested dominion by the white man over the "colored" peoples.

It is tempting to look back at the nineteenth century with nostalgia and see in it a period which was more moral than ours. This flattering image is partly true. First, that century gave the world a hundred years of peace, which was in itself a political but also a moral achievement. Secondly, in their international relations in the nineteenth century, Europeans never sank to the moral debasement of their descendants in this century. Due process of law and respect for human dignity were generally observed. Of course, several European nationalities lived under the foreign rule of other European nationalities and their aspirations were stifled by the status quo. But they were not threatened at that time with gas chambers, concentration camps, and mass deportations.

However, this retrospectively rosy picture is Europe-centered. The same century firmly believed in the division of the world into "civilized" and "uncivilized" peoples. Only Europeans and their descendants overseas were civilized; all other peoples, even those belonging to venerable though non-European civilizations, were lumped together as a barbarian or semi-barbarian multitude in need of being civilized. The Europeans were convinced that they had the right and even the duty to shoulder this "white man's burden" and take care of these colonial or semicolonial wards; it was taken for granted that the wards should generously pay for their "education" at the European colonial school. Colonization was conceived of as a lofty mission for which colonial peoples were expected to be grateful. The profound difference between the European outlook of that time and the prevailing view in our era can be gauged by the following quotation from the writings of a great French liberal, Ernest Renan:

> The conquest of a country of inferior race by a superior race, which settles there to govern it, is not shocking at all. England practices this kind of colonialism in India with great benefit to India, to mankind in general, and also with benefit to herself. . . . While conquests between equal races should be condemned, the regeneration of inferior or degenerate races by a superior race is a part of the Providential order for mankind. The common man in our country is almost always a "declassé" nobleman; his heavy hand is built for handling a sword rather than a servile tool. He prefers to fight rather than to work, i.e., he wants to return to his original condition. *Regere imperio populos:* this is our vocation. . . . Nature has created a race of workers, i.e., the Chinese race, which combines a marvelous manual dexterity with an almost total lack of honor; rule them with justice, while making them pay for the benefits which your government bestows on them and let them provide the conquering race with an ample dowry. They will be satisfied with this arrangement. The Negro race is a race of workers of the soil; be good and humane to

them, and everything will be fine. The European race is that of masters and soldiers.[1]

Even a reactionary of today would not dare to write these lines which a liberal of the nineteenth century considered axiomatic. The conviction that European civilization was superior made possible the co-existence of an authoritarian colonial regime for non-Europeans and the gradual extension of electoral franchise for the European common man. It was perfectly moral for the European governments to extort from an ignorant African chieftain his assent to a treaty whereby he accepted foreign rule but to feel a genuine indignation if the same chieftain or his descendants later realized the mistake and revolted in violation of a "valid" treaty. The Asians and Africans of today would not concur in the opinion that Europe in the nineteenth century was particularly moral.

THE REVOLUTIONARY ERA

The inter-war period was one of a great illusion. It seemed to many that the world was returning or was about to return to pre-1914 conditions of "normalcy." But after the Second World War no one could possibly doubt that the international world prior to 1914 was gone forever. The shape of the new world, which is only emerging, is yet unknown. We are only in the initial or middle course of a historical crisis which is giving birth to this new world. We know, however, what are the great contemporary trends which are shaping the face of this coming world. We also know that these trends, while they cannot be reversed, can be channelled in various directions depending on the choices made in this generation and in future generations.

One of the great trends of our time is the vertiginously rapid progress of the science and technology of war. The rate of this progress makes the computation of the distribution of power liable to revisions at short intervals and also much more complex than in former times. The nuclear stalemate seems to ensure a certain stability, but if either of the nuclear powers were able to master the means of an effective active defense or to make another decisive breakthrough, the very notion of nuclear stalemate would dissolve into thin air.

Nuclear weapons of mass destruction have radically modified the conditions of international politics by enormously increasing the risks. The nuclear powers are confronted by the alternatives of causing nuclear catastrophe through political miscalculation or being gradually defeated because paralyzed by the fear of assuming risks. Since the highest stake in present international relations is the annihilation or at least the crip-

[1] Ernest Renan, *Oeuvres Complètes,* Vol. 1, p. 390. Paris: Calmann-Lévy, 1947.

pling of whole nations, nuclear weapons have had a paradoxical political effect. The nuclear powers, which have at their disposal destructive weapons of a magnitude unknown to former ages, are compelled by the very existence of these weapons to tread on the international stage with an infinitely greater caution than was required of great powers in pre-nuclear times. The risks of using force are great even in relation to small nations, because this use might lead to direct conflict between the nuclear powers themselves. This consideration, as well as the hostility between the two rival blocs, has endowed smaller countries with a vicarious power which allows them to speak more loudly, to maneuver among the great powers more freely, and to reap in the process more benefits than could have been gained by states of that rank in the pre-nuclear age. Their diplomatic power is out of proportion to their feeble military power.

The stage of international relations has been widened to encompass the whole globe. Europe is no longer the center of international politics, although it remains a very important part of the global stage. The continental European powers have been relegated to the position of regional powers and no longer monopolize the global decisions. The two greatest powers of today are non-European (the United States) and only partly European (the U.S.S.R.), while new centers of power are emerging in other continents, notably in Asia. Non-European problems, which were solved by the nineteenth-century powers in terms of their own interests, have now acquired an independent life and in turn influence the fate of Europe. This universalization of international politics complicates by itself the relations among states. The balance-of-power system was operated by a small number of great powers. Now the great powers are at odds, and the role of over a hundred large and small states located all over the globe is not, therefore, to be discounted.

This century has brought about the awakening of national aspirations in Asia and Africa and the political self-assertion of Latin America. This has completely transformed the status quo as it existed in 1939. European control of Asia is ended; Africa progresses rapidly toward political emancipation. A new multistate system has emerged.

The statesmen of the nineteenth century were seldom of unusually great stature but enjoyed the advantage of having inherited from their national environment a long tradition of active international politics. They were used to the global perspective; it is true that it was easier to master this perspective at that time because it was mainly limited for practical purposes to Europe. The politicians who are at the helm of the newly independent states are inclined to look at international problems from the point of view of their regional interests and are not yet accustomed to a global frame of reference. The parting of ways between their peoples and the colonial powers has been on the whole rather peaceful; their independence was not bought at a high price in human blood.

This often inclines these politicians to underestimate the role of material power in international relations and to overestimate the actual weight of their own states.

There is today no power which has the required strength for the role of balancer of power. Even if all the uncommitted nations could form a united front, their combined strength would be too small to affect seriously the distribution of power between the great powers. The present centers of significant strength are all committed to one or the other of the two rival blocs, and flexibility in diplomatic maneuvering is gone. Since the destructive capacity of the nuclear powers is equal and since the strength of the uncommitted states makes no real difference, the coalition, this ultimate instrument for preventing the hegemony of one great power, has become unusable. Present-day coalitions have a different purpose, namely to increase the strength of the two rival centers and thus to maintain a precarious equilibrium. It is true that the quarrels within the opposite blocs, if they persisted and culminated in open breaches between allies (between Russia and China, for example), might lend greater flexibility to international diplomacy (see Chapter 2, "Alliances").

The governing elites no longer share a common cultural and social background. Communists and non-Communists are poles apart, and it is more difficult to find a common denominator between statesmen who belong to different civilizations than it was to find common ground between the European politicians of the past century.

The national awakening of non-European continents, combined with the Western colonial retreat, has resulted in the multiplication of centers of decision. The number of states whose actions and reactions must be taken into consideration is constantly increasing without any assurance that all of them have a reasonable chance of surviving the test of domestic and foreign challenges. Their national self-assertion, helped by the propitious circumstances which the rift between the great powers has created, includes the determination to become, as far as possible, economically independent. Since this self-assertion comes in the wake of the gradual termination of Western dominance, it is another facet of the Western retreat and unavoidably has anti-Western undertones. The new relationship gradually emerging between the West and the peoples whom the West had for centuries dominated politically and economically is inevitably marred by conflicts over how the past should be liquidated.

Yet the same national self-assertion might not forever favor the Communist opponent of the West. For the time being, the Communist powers can reap benefits from the disputes between the West and the underdeveloped countries by playing the role of the counterbalancer of the West. If the West and the underdeveloped countries eventually find a new *modus vivendi*, the same national self-assertion will find it difficult to accommodate itself to the Communist ideological crusade and its goal, the conversion of the world to the Communist self-evident truths and ways of life. Nationalism is equally suspicious of any foreign dominance. Moreover, the stronger Russia and China become, the more difficult it will be for weaker nations to live undisturbed in their neighborhood.

This century has brought back the ideological conflicts waged by states themselves. It belongs in this respect to earlier eras, such as the time of the Peloponnesian War, the era of the Christian-Moslem struggles, or the period of the Religious Wars, eras marked by the opposition of two hostile ideological camps. The Communist states are officially committed to an ideology which they want to extend to the whole world. Hence, they are by definition inimical to the present political, economic, and social status quo in the non-Communist states. A government convinced of its moral duty to convert foreign peoples cannot accept the concept of limited goals which is fundamental to the balance-of-power theory. The conflicts of national interests, inherent in the multistate system, are today aggravated by the "religious" war fought between hostile ideologies.

The attitude of states toward the international status quo divides them into two categories, revolutionary powers and status-quo powers. A revolutionary power is a state which not only wants to upset the status quo but is prepared to assume the risks of actions directed toward this end. A status-quo power is a state which either feels satisfied with the status quo or is reluctant to face the risks of attempting to modify it.

Psychologically, it is understandable that a revolutionary power is better conditioned for taking in stride the instability of international politics and actually welcomes it as a necessary condition to the success of its own efforts to overthrow the status quo. A status-quo power is more bewildered by this instability and would prefer nothing more than a stabilization of international relations in an atmosphere of general relaxation. The two mentalities are so different that it is very difficult for a status-quo power to understand the psychology of the leaders of a revolutionary power. The former power is inclined to assume that, despite appearances, the revolutionary power pursues in fact only limited objectives which leave enough room for a mutual accommodation and a lasting *modus vivendi*. Public statements by the government of the revolutionary power, if they refer to goals of almost unlimited scope, are dismissed as destined for home consumption. This interpretation was often attached by Britain and France to Hitler's speeches. However, a speech for domestic consumption (whether the "consumers" are the speaker's countrymen or his ideological followers) might be more revealing of the truth than remarks made in conversation with a foreigner, whether a prime minister, a journalist, or an intellectual. A leader who addresses his own countrymen or ideological followers intends to rally their support for his foreign policy and makes public commitments from which he cannot easily retreat for fear of losing prestige.

The importance of the psychological factor in international politics is manifest whenever a country suffers setbacks which are not caused by the lack of its actual or potential power. The successes of one state and the corresponding setbacks of other states, if unrelated to the actual distribution of power, are due to one or all three of the following causes: the winner's superior adroitness in foreign policy, superior will-power, or superior ability to understand the mentality of the opponent. International politics is, therefore, a contest in which the material power of states is not the only factor. It is a competition of intellect and will. It is inaccurate to say that a nation's military and material power is the inflexible limit of its foreign policy. This limit can be, at least to some degree, pushed further away by an intelligent foreign policy or by the errors committed by the opponents. Actually, opportunity in foreign affairs is often created by the errors of other nations.

The Western powers could have checked the Japanese imperialist venture in its first stage, at the time of the military seizure of Manchuria. At that time Japan was not yet allied to Germany, which was neither Nazi nor fully re-armed. Yet the United States, Great Britain, and France, the three status-quo powers in the Far East, preferred to wait and hope that Japan pursued only limited objectives which did not seriously affect their own vital interests. The rapid rise of Nazi Germany could have been halted in the first years of the Third Reich. In particular, the military occupation of the Rhineland in March, 1936, provided Britain and France with an opportunity to accept the challenge and thus to cripple the Nazi regime. The German army, one year after the introduction of military conscription, was in the process of reorganization and unable to match the Western forces. The Western powers had a legal title to intervention in the Versailles Treaty and the Locarno Pact. They preferred, however, to trust in the Nazi assurances of the limited nature of their foreign objectives. Eventually they were confronted with the German-Japanese alliance and an overwhelming danger both in Europe and in the Far East. But for the later military intervention of the United States and the Soviet Union, not only France but probably Britain as well would have been defeated.

Soviet political successes in Eastern Europe and the Communist revolution in China were taking place in the forties at a time when the United States temporarily occupied a paramount position in the world. The U.S. had an atomic monopoly, and if its conventional armed forces had not been drastically demobilized, it could have had an imposing superiority in these as well. Other great powers were either incapacitated by the last war or immensely weakened. The Soviet Union was bled white by the war with Germany. Russia's successful resistance to the onslaught of German might was bought at the price of unbelievably great human and material losses. For several years after the war it was incapable of facing again any major contest of strength; this, in fact, reduced its negotiating ability. Yet during the forties it firmly consolidated its zone of influence in Eastern-Central Europe, while the Chinese revolution gave it an ally in the Far East. The impressive Soviet successes in the forties were divorced from the actual distribution of power. The United States hoped at that time that a further expansion of Soviet influence would be checked on an imaginary line of political and military containment, that the Soviet dynamic resolve would be undermined by a process of attrition due to the lack of new successes, and that eventually a mutually agreeable and stable *modus vivendi* could be found. In the meantime, the temporary paramountcy of the United States was ended in the fifties by the rehabilitation of the Soviet Union and its acquisition of nuclear weapons. The nuclear stalemate became a reality.

The rapid expansion of Soviet political influence in all non-European continents, a process which has been taking place in the fifties and sixties, has been due to the historical opportunity in the underdeveloped countries which the Soviet leaders have discovered and have exploited with great ability. But again, this expansion has not reflected the actual international distribution of power. The Western power potential is still much greater than that of the Communist bloc, but it is not translated into immediately usable power. It is a paradox that the West complains about its conventional armed forces being inadequate to repel a Soviet attack in Europe or a Communist intervention in the peripheral areas, while the Soviet Union, much poorer than the West, is able to maintain large and up-to-date conventional forces and at the same time keep abreast with nuclear weapons.

The history of the inter-war and postwar periods indicates that the West has a defensive attitude. This might be due to several reasons. The Western nations have reached the stage of the harvest, i.e., of the welfare state. The present generation can at last taste the fruits of prosperity, and all social classes partake, for the first time in human history, of this feast of prosperity. The Western peoples have every reason to feel satisfied with their present domestic lot and do not want to be disturbed by external ventures. Satisfied at home, they have great difficulty in understanding other people who are discontented with their lot (the underdeveloped countries) or who are interested in foreign ventures because they want to upset the status quo (the Communist leaders).

The democratic ideology is no longer expansionist as it was at the time of the French Revolution and thereafter. Its most dynamic idea, equality before the law, swept the legal privileges of the aristocracy into the dustbin of history and thus removed the legal obstacles to social mobility. It spent its appeal by being generally accepted. The present social problem is how further to increase social mobility and equal opportunity. This problem has two facets. Equal opportunity for human beings in the underdeveloped nations requires, first of all, the modernization of their countries. Until the completion of this process, an individual in those countries will not have an equal opportunity in life with his fellow-man who is fortunate enough to live in a developed country. The other aspect of the same problem is of interest to all nations, developed and under-developed. It consists in an equal opportunity at the start in life, i.e., an equal opportunity of access to education at all levels regardless of the financial position of parents. Whether one looks at the one or the other facet of equal opportunity, he discovers that the Communists are in true competition with the West in offering their own programs for equal educational opportunity and for the modernization of underdeveloped countries. If extending equality of opportunity is the essence of social progress in our time, the West no longer has a monopoly, as it did in the nineteenth century, on the recipes for progress; it has a rival in the Communist ideology.

The democratic ideology links progress with individual freedom. It offers a more noble but also a more arduous road toward a world of greater social opportunity. However, its regime of political democracy cannot be easily transplanted to unprepared soil. Democracy cannot be exported and implanted by bayonets. The Communists also offer equality of opportunity but combined with a totalitarian regime which is easy to export and can be operated by a strong-willed and well-organized minority. Because its exportation does not wait upon the conversion of a majority, the Communist ideology is dynamic.

Toleration is the essence of democracy. Tolerant of different views at home, a democrat is inclined to acknowledge that his truth might not be the truth for other people. Used to compromises as the heart of domestic politics, he assumes that all foreign peoples can be persuaded by rational arguments that compromise is superior to an unyielding struggle. His mood is not militant. Moreover, a democratic state, unlike a Communist one, cannot possess an official doctrine of ideological beliefs and hence cannot propagandize them to foreign populations. The very idea of using force to spread democratic ways of life contravenes the democratic principle of voluntary acceptance. The Communist, intolerant of domestic differences of opinion, takes the same view of foreign peoples whom he wants to transform in his own image. He believes that he holds absolute truth concerning the meaning of history and the nature of social relations and that he possesses an infallible formula for human happiness. Unrestrained by doubt or scepticism, he is zealous in his endeavors to impart his ideological truth to other people. He is a missionary by definition.

Whatever the reasons for the defensive posture of the West, they do not prejudge its future policies. The two world wars proved that a democratic society, if fully aware of the challenge, is able to mobilize its resources and to make the necessary sacrifices. The projection of defensive attitudes into a distant future can be entirely mistaken. This error cost the Third Reich its existence and reserved for the Communist powers a surprise in Korea, where the American military reaction in 1950 was not expected. A democratic power would commit a no less serious error if it believed that it would always have time to wake up to external threats.

Political competition in the underdeveloped countries is more difficult for the West than for the Communist bloc. The past has heavily mortgaged the relations of the underdeveloped countries with the Western powers. The revolution of modernization is the revolt of peoples disinherited by history. It amounts to a claim by those who have been left behind by modern progress to an equality of status with the advanced nations. This equality can be achieved only by their becoming modern or, in other words, like the advanced countries. This requires a radical transformation of social institutions as well as economic, technological, and scientific development. These transformations can only be achieved over a long period of painful transition during which two or three generations will have to shed obsolete customs, work hard, and sacrifice their immediate well-being for the sake of their descendants. This process of modernization is a revolution the like of which mankind has never known before, not only because it will affect every aspect of the social life of the vast majority of mankind but also because its far-reaching repercussions will be felt by the advanced countries as well. The greater power of the latter countries will be reduced because of the rise of new centers of power among the present underdeveloped peoples, and the present international division of labor, which favors the advanced countries, will be radically modified. One of the most important questions of our time is what types of governments will carry out this revolution of modernization; the answer to this question might decisively tilt the balance in favor of either bloc.

The Communist ideology has the advantage of appealing to the discontented who abound in the underdeveloped countries. It promises sweeping changes. It seems to carry the torch of hope for those who feel despair. But the West has many untapped resources which can be used in this competition. Unlike the Communist states, it is not faced with the problem of industrialization, which consumes so much national effort in the European and Asian Communist states and which is truly completed only in Russia and Czechoslovakia. Its prosperity allows it to render much greater economic assistance to the underdeveloped countries than the Communist nations can afford in view of their low living standards. The tide of the revolution of modernization does not decisively favor either of the contending blocs.

THE TRIANGULAR SHAPE OF CONTEMPORARY INTERNATIONAL POLITICS

The national self-assertion of the non-European continents and the ideological conflict between the West and the Communist powers have given a triangular shape to contemporary international relations. The underdeveloped countries form the main battlefield for the two contending blocs, whose competing influences can move forward or retreat only in this gray area of political fluidity.

The triangle is formed by three types of relationships: between the states belonging to either bloc, between the two contending blocs, and between either bloc and the underdeveloped and non-Communist states which Frenchmen rightly call the "Third World." The bipolar image of contemporary international politics is false except for the bipolarity of the nuclear stalemate. Since there are only two powers with a fully developed means of delivery of nuclear weapons and hence with the capacity for intercontinental mass destruction, the political problems relating to the nuclear stalemate are of direct concern to the United States and the Soviet Union only. As co-monopolists of intercontinental power, they could govern the world by mutual agreement. Since they are divided by a deep conflict, their opposing nuclear forces neutralize each other and do not unduly hinder the freedom of maneuvering enjoyed by other states. Nuclear bipolarity is destined to disappear in time. Other nations will acquire nuclear stockpiles, and, after a time, those of them endowed with the required economic, scientific, and technological potential will come into possession of an intercontinental system of delivery. That distant day will mark the end of nuclear bipolarity and also a decline in the relative power positions of both the United States and the Soviet Union.

The present dominant position of these two powers will suffer a gradual decline for other reasons as well. If the European community develops successfully and, even more, if it is strengthened by the adhesion of several other European states, it will become a political and economic organization with a combined power equal, if not superior, to America or the Soviet Union. China will in due time attain the same rank. Economic development will elevate the presently underdeveloped countries to a much higher power level than they occupy today. A few of them have a reasonable chance of becoming great powers. Japan, if fully rearmed, and Germany, if unified, will win back their ranks as great powers. Gradually, the world will again become a constellation of great powers of roughly comparable strength.

Even now the other nations have great freedom to maneuver between the two contending nuclear powers. The policy of non-commitment, which attracts a steadily increasing number of states, is proof in itself that the world is not bipolar, for if it were, all countries would have been committed either to the United States or to the Soviet Union.

Even the triangular image fails to reflect all the complexities of international politics. Actually, there are as many aspects of these politics as there are states. The foreign policy regarding any state must be shaped with due regard both to the triangular shape of international politics and to that state's own problems; it cannot be deduced simply from one single general formula. The situation in each underdeveloped country, in spite of certain common characteristics, is different—the forms of government, the social institutions, the degree of national homogeneity, the level of economic underdevelopment, the importance of its strategic location, the nature of its foreign policy, the caliber of its elites, vary from one country to another.

The concept of the bloc is not so simple as it might appear, because either rival bloc is composed of several distinct states. China is not Bulgaria and is fully independent of Russia. Since the Twenty-second Congress of the Soviet Communist party in October, 1961, it has been obvious that Russia and China differ on foreign policy and ideological problems. Their different geographical locations and their different levels of economic development provide those two Communist powers with different perspectives. The degree of autonomy of Eastern European countries varies, although all are dependent on the Soviet Union. Only Albania is favored by its isolated geographical location, which has allowed it to demonstrate publicly its insubordination to the Soviet Union and its preference for China. One sweeping formula could not represent the complex relations between the members of the Communist bloc, and the same is true of the Western bloc. The national interests of the component states of the latter bloc are not and cannot possibly be identical.

The triangular image of contemporary international politics reflects the main factor in these politics, the battle between the West and the Communist countries for influence in the underdeveloped Third World. However, as noted earlier, this image should not be taken to suggest that any of the three sides of the triangle represents a monolith. Both the Western countries and the Communist countries are divided among themselves by divergent national interests (see Chapter 2, "Alliances"; Chapter 7, "Proletarian Internationalism"; and Chapter 9, "European Integration"), while the underdeveloped countries do not form a political bloc. Yet all the Communist countries profess the same ideology in spite of their discordant interpretations of that ideology, all of them wish to expand the realm of their system, and none of them would welcome the collapse of a Communist regime anywhere. The West is for all Communist parties the bastion of the opposite ideology although they differ on how the bastion should be stormed. The Western countries quarrel over the inner structure and external policies of NATO, but are nevertheless bound together by ties of mutual defense, by a common ideology, and by the similarity of their economic and social regimes. None of them would wish a territorial expansion of the Communist realm. The members of neither rival bloc follow a co-ordinated policy toward the members of the opposing bloc, but both groups of states agree in regarding the underdeveloped Third World as the political "soft belly" in their international competition. It is there that the two ideological groups are confronting each other with direct and open hostility. The Third World is itself rent by divergent national interests. Yet its members are united by their common desire to gain international status and to become modernized economically and socially.

Since the bipolarity of international relations is a misleading image, a grave error would be committed by either of the nuclear powers if it concentrated its attention on relations with the other nuclear power. Each can greatly influence the power position of the other by the policies followed in relation to the other states of the world. The Soviet Union has not achieved anything spectacular in direct negotiations with the United States, but its great effort since 1955 to extend its influence to the underdeveloped countries has created new and serious problems for the United States. Soviet policy is certainly not bipolar.

The two-world picture is as inaccurate as the bipolar. According to this picture, the globe is divided into two political worlds, the Communist world and the "free" world. The free world includes all the non-Communist states as though all of them were free in the sense of being democratic, which is patently untrue of many of them, and as though all of them were firmly committed to the West. In fact, the world of today is not neatly divided into two camps separated by an imaginary boundary line. This image is only an obsolete reflection of a reality which no longer exists. It implies that the Communists are masters in their part of the globe and that the West controls the other part. Yet the Western retreat from former colonial possessions and the political emancipation of the non-European continents have radically changed the international situation. The Western governments were able before the Second World War to decide alone how and for what purpose the resources of India, Pakistan, Ceylon, Burma, Indochina, Indonesia, Africa, the Near East, and several other non-European areas would be used. Hundreds of millions of people were their political subjects. Now these countries are independent and formulate their own foreign policies. They can choose commitment to the West, a policy of aloofness, or even a flirtation with the enemies of the West. The word of the United States carried, before the last war, decisive weight in the Western Hemisphere. This is no longer generally true. Cuba is politically committed to the Communist bloc, and a trend toward noncommitment is coming to the surface in a few other Latin American countries.

In short, the former Western zone of influence has been emancipated. The Third World is wide open to the conflicting influences of the contending blocs. But neither bloc can deeply affect conditions within the other bloc. The use of force for this purpose would carry with it almost the certainty of nuclear war.

Western subversion within the Communist bloc would be blunted by totalitarian censorship, domestic surveillance, and repressive measures. The Soviet success in suppressing the revolt in East Berlin and the Hungarian insurrection has proved that popular discontent does not result in the fall of a Soviet-supported regime. Judging from the history of totalitarian regimes, only the following three developments could bring about a weakening of the Communist bloc or the fall of a Communist regime: an external catastrophe (the Nazi regime fell only after Allied occupation of German territory), a disintegration of the ruling party (this took place in Hungary but had no lasting effect because of Soviet intervention), or the defection of one of the members of the bloc, such as took place in Yugoslavia in 1948. The nuclear stalemate makes unrealistic any expectation that military defeat could terminate the existence of the Communist bloc. The disintegration of the Communist party in Russia or in China does not appear probable, while the same process in a small Communist country would be remedied by the intervention of either Communist great power. Defection from the bloc could be effectively prevented by the same intervention, as it was in 1956 in Hungary, unless the defecting country were, like Yugoslavia in 1948, protected by its favorable location. Of the present members of the bloc only Albania has no common frontier with other bloc members. This geographical safety allowed it to challenge the Soviet Union publicly and to manifest its ideological preference for China. A decisive weakening of the bloc could come only from an open rupture of the Soviet-Chinese alliance. If this rupture materialized, it would probably cause a general international realignment. The NATO states would then be faced with the possibility of a more friendly policy toward one of the Communist great powers in order to isolate the other. It is far from certain that all of them would be inclined to make the same choice. Thus, the West cannot unleash a nuclear war to weaken or destroy the opposite bloc or do anything effective to precipitate its internal disintegration.

The Communist bloc is in the same position regarding the NATO bloc. It cannot use force against this bloc for the same reason of nuclear stalemate. The two blocs touch each other directly, without being separated by the underdeveloped countries, only in Europe. The boundary line is there buttressed on both sides by the fear of nuclear war. Communist subversion in the advanced countries of the West is as ineffective as any Western attempt to undermine the Communist bloc by the same process. The Western attachment to individual freedom and the prosperity shared by all social classes offer the same protective shield against subversion as censorship, surveillance, and repression do for the Communist camp.

While neither bloc can do much within the realm of the other, the vast non-Communist underdeveloped areas have become an open field for battle between the two influences. It is not the Communists who have forced the door of the Third World to other than Western influence. This has been achieved by the Western colonial retreat and the political emancipation of peoples formerly dominated by the West. The concept of containment is unrealistic if it means excluding the political influence of the other bloc from the gray areas of the Third World. If the Communist bloc tries to shape events beyond its own frontiers by military action or by assistance supplied to one of the factions fighting a civil war, the policy of containment can be applicable provided the West has the means of counteraction and the will to use them. The Korean War proved that this was not impossible. Events in Laos demonstrated that the West might lack the military means appropriate for intervention or the will to assume the risks or that local conditions might be adverse to a Western military action. But political containment in the sense of barring underdeveloped areas to Communist influence has been proved unrealistic by developments in the fifties and sixties. The West cannot stop the government of an underdeveloped but independent state from entering into friendly relations with the Communist bloc in search of an alternative source of military supplies and of economic and technical assistance or in quest of political support needed to counterbalance Western pressure. This has been amply demonstrated in Asia, the Near East, Africa, and Latin America. The countries of India, Indonesia, the United Arab Republic, Iraq, Guinea, Mali, and Cuba come immediately to mind, and others could be cited. Containment in this sense is unrealistic; the battlefield of the Third World is wide open to both blocs whose competition there will be balanced in various ways by the governments of the underdeveloped countries themselves. This is why the shape of contemporary international relations is triangular; the song is sung by a trio, not by a duet.

CONTEMPORARY CONTRADICTIONS

Our time is characterized by many contradictions. One of these has already been mentioned, namely between the power of mass destruction possessed by the nuclear powers and the political caution which the same power imposes on them. Several other contradictions of our time deserve mention:

A. Moral standards, if measured by the yardstick of the nineteenth century, have deteriorated. Never before in history has cruelty had such handmaidens as the administrative and technological efficiency of the modern state and hence acquired such a capacity for mass destruction and torture. The Nazi persecutions of the Jews and other nationalities could be considered an unusual aberration if imprisonment and torture as instruments of policy were unique to the Nazi regime. It suffices to glance at the other totalitarian and authoritarian regimes to become convinced that the Nazi mentality was not an isolated phenomenon of our time. Those persecuted or exterminated by the Nazi regime were not victims of anger, vengeance, or mob fury, nor were they granted any alternative to persecution or death. Extermination was carried out by a modern and efficient state administration according to a coldly conceived plan. The victim of Roman persecutions or of the Inquistion could save himself by abjuring his Christian, Jewish, Moslem, or heretical faith, but the Nazi victim, earmarked for death because of his "race," could not appease his tormentors with conversion or abjuration. Modern technology, including rapid means of transportation and the gas chambers, permitted the extermination of millions at a rate inconceivable in a prescientific age. A nineteenth-century European could not have imagined that his descendants would be morally capable of carrying out the destruction of human beings on this gigantic scale.

Rapid scientific progress has offered mankind for the first time in history the instruments for its own self-destruction. Nuclear, chemical, and bacteriological weapons provide man with the means of obliterating populations of any size he wants. The most ominous paradox of our time is that technological progress has been accompanied by moral regression.

B. This imbalance is further aggravated by the intensity of ideological fanaticism. Cold reason indicates that it is safer to let foreign peoples believe what they want than to be pushed by a fanatical zeal for forcible conversion to the brink of a general disaster for the whole of mankind, including fanatics. Yet this rational attitude does not seem to prevail.

Fanaticism is no invention of the twentieth century. In all ages those who have believed that they held the keys to absolute truth, and hence to human happiness or salvation, have immolated their fellows who refused to be converted on the altar of what they thought was the collective good of mankind. Fanatics of all times have distinguished between their collective image of the human species, which they intended to make happy, and the individual human beings whom they killed or made unhappy for the sake of this image. While this attitude is not historically new, the risks involved in attempting forcible conversions are now immensely greater than ever before. Today mankind could perish in the name of its brighter future. Moreover, the emotional excitement caused by the ideological struggle transforms important international issues into symbols of moral courage or moral surrender. It is difficult for the parties to an ideological war to examine these issues on their intrinsic merits. These parties, in their desire to uphold their moral rectitude and their faith in the cherished self-evident truths or in their fear of being denounced by their followers for a moral betrayal, might unintentionally carry the bluff of brinkmanship too far and find themselves in a situation from which there might be no retreat.

C. The Western colonial retreat and the emancipation of the "colored" peoples contrast with the triumphant infiltration of other civilizations by the European civilization which the "white" man has created. This civilization, which extends from the Pacific coast of the Western Hemisphere to the Pacific coast of Russia, carries its modern message to the underdeveloped countries under the mutually hostile flags of the West and the Soviet Union. But the message of modern society, originally conceived in the womb of European civilization, is in many respects the same whether its political formulation is democratic or Communist. The standard-bearers of European civilization are themselves engaged in a bitter civil war over their ideological principles but remain nevertheless the children of the same civilization. They "Europeanize" the non-European continents by spreading the concepts of modern industrial society. For the first time in history, mankind, rent by ideological strife originating in Europe, is nevertheless acquiring a common cultural denominator which is European.

D. The process of national self-determination is bringing about the disintegration of multinational empires and the proliferation of medium-sized or small states. However, power and prosperity in our time go to the huge concentrations of populations on large territories well supplied with economic resources. A numerous population provides the large market needed for rapid economic growth. A large territory often means a greater and more diversified pool of natural resources; it also offers a better chance of survival in a nuclear war. A large population economically developed can master the costly and intricate techniques required for modern military power, and influence in international politics usually goes hand in hand with power. National self-determination entails a process of fragmentation, while the objectives of power and prosperity militate in favor of large state units or unions of smaller states.

E. The rise of the common man is a general phenomenon in all advanced countries and is a foreseeable development in the underdeveloped countries. Governments can no longer ignore the material needs and aspirations of the masses. Social mobility in modern society implies that the children of common men have access to the highest rungs of the national ladder. The power elites are being increasingly recruited independently of family background. At the same time, this is also the era of totalitarian regimes in which common men, even if ruled by people of the same social extraction, are tightly regimented and have nothing to say about the domestic and foreign policies of their countries. Totalitarian regimes seek to oblige the common man in a different way. They acknowledge his yearning for material well-being and for equality of opportunity for his children. They flatter his ego through mock elections that cultivate an illusion of citizen participation in political affairs and by showing him his magnified reflection in the symbol of the state or of the toiling masses in whose name he has been refused any effective political role.

DEFINITION OF TERMS

Certain terms constantly recur in discussions of international politics. It is useful to define these terms at the outset. The foreign policy of every country exists to serve *national interests*. National interests are fluid; they change from one historical period and from one country to another. Schematically, national interests are the self-evident truths, the ways of life, and the well-being of a nation. They concern foreign policy insofar as they have to be promoted or protected in relation to other nations. But this schematic definition immediately raises the question of what a nation understands at a given moment of its history by its self-evident truths, its ways of life, and its well-being. The national elites provide the answer which fills the framework of the schematic definition with a concrete meaning. This answer, i.e., the current interpretation of national interests, is never of permanent validity.

A domestic revolution which brings to power a new elite, inspired by a militant ideology, might result in a reinterpretation of national interests which calls for the conversion of other nations to the same ideology. A notable accretion in national power, due to rearmament, the rapid growth of economic strength, or scientific and technological progress, might result in a reinterpretation of national interests which enlarges their scope. A relative decline in power, due to a corresponding rise in power of other states, might compel a government to restrict the scope of national interests by cutting down its foreign commitments.

One nation considers that the protection of national interests requires only freedom from foreign interference and a reasonable expectation that other countries will not commit an aggression or will be defeated if they are tempted to do so. Another nation might think that its security cannot be ensured unless its neighbors are reduced to the status of satellites or altogether conquered. A defensive or aggressive interpretation can be attached to the concept of national interests.

In the course of its history the same country revises the meaning of national interests in the light of changing domestic and external circumstances. American national interests, as reflected in the Monroe Doctrine, did not exceed the limits of the Western Hemisphere. Today, some one hundred and forty years later, the exclusion of the United States from the affairs of the Eastern Hemisphere would be considered calamitous for national interests.

Economic well-being might be equated with the protection of the domestic market, might mean a search for foreign economic and technical assistance, or might include the exploitation of foreign natural resources and a quest for foreign markets. The preservation of national ways of life, including the self-evident truths and the political, economic, and social structure, acquires a meaning only after the elucidation of what a nation considers at a given moment to be the desirable ways of life. The Western societies of the nineteenth century would have been horrified if the concept of what we now call the welfare state were included in the national ways of life to be preserved. Today the West would be equally horrified if it felt that a foreign threat could undermine its economic system on which the welfare state is founded. The same nation might at one time cherish an authoritarian form of government as the best and at another time hold democracy to be the ideal form of political life. One country might consider that its ways of life are not for export and that it can exist although other nations believe in different self-evident truths and wish to have different ways of life. Another country might feel that its ways of life and self-evident truths have a universal validity or that the survival of different self-evident truths is a perpetual menace to its own ways of life.

The term *national interests* should be used in the plural, because the singular form produces the false impression that there exists one monolithic interest to be protected. In fact, there are always several interests. The external promotion of one of them might endanger another. This possibility of conflict between particular national interests calls for the careful elaboration of a hierarchy of interests, the lesser ones to be sacrificed, if necessary, for the sake of the more important.

If the interpretation of national interests were always defensive, it could be compressed into a simple formula of protecting national independence and territorial integrity against all external threats. National independence implies a free choice of self-evident truths and ways of life, while the nation, a territorial unit, can enjoy this free choice only on a definite territory enclosed within state boundaries. However, national interests are quite often given an offensive meaning and then cannot be fitted within the framework of a simple defense of national independence and territorial integrity. The power elite of a country might believe that the national self-evident truths should be extended beyond national borders or that the well-being of their countrymen requires an expansion of national territory or encroachment on the economic independence of other countries. National interests would then be equated with a threat to the territorial integrity and national independence of other states.

The definition of national interests implies what the general *objective* of foreign policy should be. *Objectives* are images of the future condition of foreign affairs which the government considers desirable and attainable by the means at its disposal. The *general* objective is the future condition of all foreign affairs of concern to a given state which this state deems desirable. The *particular* objective is the desirable settlement of one international issue of concern to a given state. The total of particular objectives should fit within the framework of the general objective, i.e., the gradual achievement of particular objectives should eventually result in the attainment of the general objective.

These images of the desired future serve as signposts for the foreign policies of states. The image held by one government might be the opposite of the image held by another; their foreign policies will clash with each other. The images of the future entertained by two governments might just as well largely coincide; these two governments will be able to co-operate. Hence, the objectives of a state, whether general or particular, cannot be realistically defined without a knowledge of the objectives of other states. This knowledge will indicate the amount of foreign opposition or co-operation which a nation will encounter in the pursuit of its objectives. The power of a nation, as compared to the power of other nations, will offer the answer to the last question, namely, whether or not the images of a desirable future are realistic and attainable by the means at the state's disposal. If they are not, the objectives must be reduced and modified accordingly.

Power is the capacity to influence human behavior. Power in international politics is therefore the capacity of a state to influence the behavior of other states. Power might mean either the total capacity of acting in this sense or only the sum of *tangible* assets which a state possesses and can use for this purpose. Tangible assets are those which can be computed exactly and then compared to similar assets at the disposal of other states. These assets include, among others, military forces in being; total population, its age-composition, skills, and knowledge; economic, scientific, and technological strength, and its rate of growth; geographical location; and wealth and variety of natural resources. All these assets, if known to foreign states, can be computed and compared with the tangible assets of other states. The comparison finally allows for the estimation of the relative tangible power of each state. The difficulty consists in collecting all the data necessary for computation and comparison. A number of these data are classified as state secrets and withheld from public knowledge.

The total capacity to influence the behavior of other states also includes *intangible* assets, which cannot be precisely measured but which nevertheless remain very important elements of national power. These intangible assets include the quality of foreign policy; the appeal for foreign peoples of national self-evident truths and ways of life; the moral stamina and national solidarity of the population; and the political talents and characters of the governing elite.

There is an interdependence between the tangible and intangible elements of national power. A timid nation or a timorous leadership, afraid to assume risks in foreign affairs, might eventually become the loser in the game of international politics in spite of great material power. Lenin and his colleagues were not the first or the last leaders to prove that a nation or regime could survive the hostility of much stronger states thanks to political acumen and strength of character; it certainly was not the tangible power of Soviet Russia which enabled the Bolshevik regime to withstand foreign intervention and the assault of domestic enemies. Nevertheless, a weak nation, whatever its intellectual and moral qualities, can be overwhelmed by the crushing material superiority of a great power.

The interaction of ideologies and material power has often been illustrated throughout the history of great ideological movements. It is true that ideas know no frontiers and that they can overcome great material power by a process of gradual infiltration. Christianity eventually conquered the Roman Empire, and the ideas of the French Revolution seduced the nations which had defeated the French army at Waterloo. But material power helped in the expansion of Christianity in the later Roman and Medieval periods; the balance of material power eventually traced the frontiers between Christianity and Islam. It was not Soviet material power which was the decisive factor in the pro-Soviet orientation of the Cuban regime but the attraction of Communist ideology superimposed on hostility toward the United States. The ideological community of the various Communist parties makes them so many assets to the foreign policy of the Communist powers. Nevertheless, the international Communist movement would probably have been of minor significance but for the fact that it is supported by the impressive array of material power possessed by the bloc of Communist states, notably the U.S.S.R.

As the sum of the available means for influencing the behavior of other states, power is neither moral nor immoral per se. The objectives for which it is used can be evaluated, however, by the yardstick of one's self-evident truths and in consequence declared moral or immoral.

The objectives of foreign policy must be carefully balanced with the available national power. But this power can be increased by one or all of the following methods:

A. A better and wider mobilization of national human and material resources. Usually foreign states cannot prevent a nation from undertaking a more strenuous effort at home and might be unable themselves to keep the pace.

B. A combination of national power with that of other states which pursue similar objectives. Such combinations are usually brought about through an alliance between two or more states.

C. Supplementing national power which falls short of desirable objectives with a skillful foreign policy. If international circumstances are propitious, the conflicts of interests between the members of an enemy coalition or between the great powers can be exploited in order to divide other countries or to play one of them against the other. This method provides a nation, which otherwise has inadequate national power, with a vicarious, diplomatic power derived from counterbalancing the power of other states. The power of these states is mutually neutralized by their own rivalries and conflicts of interests; the nation which knows how to derive an accrued capacity for diplomatic action from these circumstances has, in effect, increased its means.

If the means cannot be increased in any way, the objectives must be reduced to avoid the imbalance.

National power does not need to be used to serve as an argument in international transactions. Its very existence is an asset. For instance, nuclear power is not principally destined for actual use but to serve as a deterrent against a surprise attack and also as a reminder to the other nuclear power that it should carefully calculate the risks of each important foreign move which might affect the vital interests of the other holder of strategic nuclear weapons.

International politics are often defined as a struggle for power. This definition makes power an end in itself. It is true that the holder of power, whether an individual or a state, wants to have power, but this begs the question of why the power is sought. If power is the capacity to influence human behavior, it is devoid of meaning unless one knows *how* he desires to mold the behavior of others. One must have an objective for which power is to be used; an image of the desired future behavior of other men must be present in the mind of the holder of power.

Power is, therefore, nothing but a means for achieving the desired objectives; it can never be an end in itself.

There is another reason why international politics cannot be epitomized as a struggle for power, namely that a large part of international relations takes the form of co-operation between governments whose actions are directed toward the same objectives. Practically all states co-operate in concerted action against certain evils of universal concern such as epidemics, the illicit trade in harmful drugs or opium, or the trade in women and children. The Universal Postal Union unites states which might otherwise be divided by their political and ideological conflicts. A nation which extends its economic and technical assistance to another co-operates with the recipient state. The very fact of international conflict presupposes co-operative alliances formed against a common enemy.

Two authors who cannot be suspected of a moralistic approach to politics, Machiavelli and Lenin, both knew that politics were much more than a struggle for power. The means which Machiavelli recommended to his ideal Prince were not particularly moral by traditional standards, but he neither forgot the co-operative aspect of political life nor overlooked the objective to be served by the Prince's accumulation of power. He knew that the Prince could not rule by coercion only and advised him to win over the allegiance of his subjects. He placed before the Prince an objective which had supreme importance for him, the unification of Italy and the expulsion of foreign powers. Power was for him only a means.

As a Marxist, Lenin fully realized the importance of the co-operative factor in politics. He stressed the factor of struggle within the capitalist society, but the class solidarity of the proletariat was to offer a way out and to lead toward a new society where social co-operation would be the heart of human relations. His teachings revolved around the central theme of the seizure of power, and he certainly did not underestimate power as a factor in politics. But power was for him only a means in the process of a universal socialist revolution. His hero, the Communist, like Machiavelli's Prince, was not to be a creature perpetually seeking greater power for its own sake but a man in quest of power as the key which was to open the door to a happy future for mankind. Power was to be the servant of the idea.

The tendency found among a number of Western writers to equate international politics with a struggle for power (power frequently means in this equation material power only) has its opposite error in the tendency of the underdeveloped countries to underestimate the importance of power in international relations. The newly acquired independence of these nations has usually been won at a relatively low cost; the Western colonial retreat has been peaceful for the most part and has seldom been conditioned on a protracted or intense armed struggle. The policy of nonalignment can strengthen this tendency to underestimate the importance of power. The uncommitted nations may ascribe their security to the wisdom of their neutralist policies or to the moral virtues of their leaders, but it rests mainly on the balance of power between the two rival blocs.

An uncommitted nation, a bystander in the dangerous game of international politics, might be inclined to overestimate the value of the verbal assurances of friendship which are contained in international treaties and communiqués. Indian-Chinese relations provide a pertinent illustration. The Indian government for several years trusted the Chinese assurances which found their formal expression in the Indian-Chinese treaty on the five principles of peaceful co-existence, signed in 1954 (see Chapter 7). Frequent Indian statements of the time unhesitatingly recommended Communist China to other states as a reliable and trustworthy partner. The discovery, made since, of the Chinese military occupation of parts of the Indian Himalayan territory taught the Indian government a lesson which it is not likely to forget.

Power is unevenly distributed among the states. This is why it is more correct to speak of the international distribution of power than to speak of the balance of power; the latter term should, for the sake of clarity, be reserved for the political system which has been described above.

One can look at the international distribution of power from various perspectives. These perspectives include the distribution of power between any two states (bilateral), between all the states located within a geographical area (regional), or between all the states of the world (global). Great powers with worldwide interests are primarily interested in the global distribution of power, in particular between themselves. But the regional distribution of power is never without significance for the global distribution. If a relatively small state, friendly to a great power, becomes much stronger than its neighbor, which is less friendly, this change in the regional distribution of power will be of interest to that power and, by repercussion, to other great powers. By the same token, small states situated in the same region are usually preoccupied with the regional distribution of power, but their relations are also influenced by the great powers. Hence, they cannot lose sight of the global distribution of power between the great powers.

However, the inclination of great powers to concentrate on the global distribution and that of smaller states to concentrate on the regional distribution can result in rather serious misunderstandings. A great power might want to increase its power vis-à-vis another great power by concluding an alliance with a smaller state located in a strategic area. In consequence it will supply arms to its ally and thus upset the regional distribution of power by making the ally stronger than before. Other states in the same area might resent this policy of the great power and remain unconvinced by its arguments that it acted as it did in order to improve the global distribution of power in relation to another great power but did not intend to tilt the regional distribution in favor of its ally. The American policy of including Pakistan within the Baghdad and SEATO arrangements was motivated by the desire to strengthen the United States in relation to the Soviet Union and China. Because it necessitated the shipment of American arms to Pakistan, it embittered India for whom the regional distribution of power was all-important.

The foreign image of the power of a nation may be distorted by inadequate information. For instance, many people in the West overestimated Soviet power in the years immediately following the last war. Impressed by spectacular Soviet victories, they overlooked the cost of those victories and their crippling effect on Soviet power. Other Westerners made the opposite mistake of underestimating Soviet capacity for postwar rehabilitation and for the acquisition of nuclear weapons; they were therefore surprised by the rapid increase in Soviet power throughout the fifties.

A time lag often occurs in the realization of a rise or decline in the power of a state, especially if it is a great power. A declining great power, unless defeated in war, is usually credited with power it no longer possesses, while the strength of a rising great power is for a time underestimated.

For all these reasons the real distribution of power may differ at times from contemporary estimates of it. This may cause gross political miscalculations. Unnecessary concessions may be made when the power of another nation has been overestimated or foolish risks assumed when it has been underestimated.

Prestige is the respect which a country enjoys abroad. A nation can be respected for various reasons. It might be an important cultural or ideological center to which foreign multitudes are harking for guidance and enlightenment. Its policy might have the reputation of being invariably prudent and wise. Its people might have earned respect for never being a nuisance to neighboring nations. However, most of the time foreign respect is caused by the tangible power which a nation possesses. This kind of prestige is the privilege of great powers, which owe their rank to their material strength. Great powers rise and fall on the battlefields, where the contest of force makes or unmakes them. The prestige of a great power is, first of all, a shadow of its material strength. But this prestige might be enhanced for reasons unrelated to tangible power—by the quality of its foreign policy, for instance, or the appeal of its national culture; it can be reduced if foreign nations feel that the great power pursues an unwise policy or lacks will-power, i.e., the capacity to assume risks commensurate with its relative material strength.

In our time of ideological competition the prestige of a nation might also stem from the attraction of its ways of life as a model of "the best society." For many countries, the best society might not be the society where the individual is freest but the one which is most efficiently organized for economic growth and scientific and technological progress.

Whatever the reasons for prestige, it is as great an asset in foreign policy as the reputation for solvency is in business. In this sense it is in itself an element of national power. The foreign image of the strength of a nation might be true or false; in either case it is a fact of international politics, because foreign governments will base their calculations on this image until such time as they discover that the prestige with which they have credited a nation is either too high or too low. In the meantime the diplomatic position of that nation will be unduly enhanced or no less unduly impaired.

A *commitment* is an express obligation undertaken by one state toward another to act or not to act in a stipulated manner. The usual form is a written treaty. Commitment limits the freedom of future action and should not, therefore, be lightly assumed. This formal limitation of future freedom of decision carries with it the risk of a radical change in circumstances which might make the fulfillment of a commitment much more onerous than originally expected. Usually international commitments are founded on an exchange of somewhat comparable advantages.

A *policy* is an external action undertaken to achieve a particular objective. *Foreign policy* is the total of those actions, all of them aiming at a general objective, i.e., the desirable international situation.

Principles are the self-evident truths which a nation holds at a given time to have universal validity, i.e., to be applicable to all nations and all human beings. *Morality* is a complex of such principles, usually deemed applicable to the relations between nationals of the same country as well as to the relations between individuals of different nationalities. An *ideology*, i.e., a system of ideas concerning the arrangement of the best society, is usually held to be of universal validity; people who believe in it rarely restrict its validity to their country only.

If certain moral or ideological self-evident truths are considered, whether rightly or wrongly, to be of universal validity, the nation professing these truths should be expected to adhere to a foreign policy consistent with them. It might, however, find such adherence detrimental to its national interests. A conflict then arises between these professed self-evident truths and national interests. History is only too rich in examples of such conflicts. Governments, however, disclaim ever having been faced with a conflict of this sort, for they invariably assert that their national interests coincide with their professed self-evident truths; they are no less inclined to accuse unfriendly governments of constantly violating moral and ideological principles. The ordinary mortal loves his own country and is rarely able to concede that his government could have made a foreign move which is hard to reconcile with the principles in which he, his government, and his countrymen sincerely believe. It is easier for him to acknowledge that his government has committed a political error; moral blemishes are conceivable in the record of other nations only. These attitudes make the discussion of conflicts between self-evident truths and national interests embarrassing when one's own country is the subject or intellectually useless and bordering on xenophobia when the subject is another country.

However, no country has been able to escape the dilemma. The young United States was compelled to face it in 1793 when it had to make a choice between the observance of its word (the French alliance) and its own survival through neutrality in the European war. India has been independent for less than two decades; yet its record already supplies illustrations of the problem. Has it not denounced the use of force for the settlement of international problems? Did it not use force in order to annex Portuguese Goa?

The less stable a historical period is and the higher the stakes are of international politics, the more often conflicts will arise between national interests and self-evident truths. Morality requires that one remain faithful to his word; domestic law duly acknowledges the sanctity of contracts; yet our own time has witnessed international behavior flagrantly inconsistent with these dictates. The troops of Germany, one of the co-signatories and co-guarantors of the treaties on the permanent neutrality of Belgium and Luxemburg, in 1914 invaded the territories of these two states, because the German government felt that this was demanded by the highest national interests. During the Second World War, the Nazi and Soviet governments violated several treaties of nonaggression. In 1941, the United Kingdom and the Soviet Union occupied neutral Persia in open violation of international law because they thought this occupation essential in the war against Germany. The Yalta Far Eastern Agreement of 1945, which granted several concessions to the Soviet Union at the expense of China, was contrary to the Treaty of Washington of 1922 whereby the signatories, including the United States and Great Britain, had assumed the obligation of respecting the territorial and administrative integrity of China. Pledges to hand over the administration of the Manchurian railroads to the U.S.S.R., to recognize special Soviet rights in the commercial port of Dairen and the right of the U.S.S.R. to erect its naval base in Port Arthur, and to acknowledge the final detachment of Outer Mongolia from China could hardly be reconciled either with the Treaty of Washington or with the moral precept that a friend should not be sacrificed for the sake of one's own interests. The need, felt at that time, to obtain a formal Soviet promise to enter the Far Eastern war against Japan proved to be stronger than other considerations. National interests prevailed as usual. The German Chancellor said in August, 1914, with a brutal frankness: "Necessity knows no laws." Other statesmen have not been so outspoken. Yet few politicians would contest the Roman maxim: *"Salus Reipublicae suprema lex esto."* (The salvation of the Republic shall be the supreme law.) This maxim, if followed in international politics, means that national interests should prevail over other considerations if there is or seems to be no other course to follow.

Their professed ideologies do not prevent strange bedfellows from consorting together in disregard of conflicting self-evident truths. Nazi Germany and the Soviet Union co-operated in 1939-41 and found this, for a time, a very profitable business. The Western democracies were very glad to have the Soviet Union as an ally against the Axis powers, and the Soviet Union was no less happy to receive lend-lease supplies from the capitalist United States. In the postwar years, the democratic and antitotalitarian United States has co-operated with Communist Yugoslavia and Fascist Spain only because both have been unfriendly to the Soviet Union. The Soviet government did not hesitate to supply arms to the Egyptians, to offer them credits, and to underwrite their costly Aswan Dam project, because Egypt was at odds with the West; this aid was given in utter disregard of the fact that the Egyptian and Syrian Communists, ideological brethren of the Soviet Union, were pitilessly and brutally persecuted by President Nasser's government.

Previous periods of international stress and crisis were not more moral in this respect than our own time. The sixteenth century was the stage of a bitter political rivalry between the two Christian monarchies, the Hapsburg and the French. It was also a time when the ideological opposition between Christians and Moslems seemed as irreconcilable as the present opposition between Communists and democrats. However, Francis I, the king of France, did not scruple to conclude an anti-Hapsburg alliance with the Sultan of Turkey, who had no more qualms of conscience in allying himself with an infidel. The Hapsburg emperor, another Christian sovereign, riposted by forming an alliance with the Moslem Shah of Persia. Christians and Moslems crossed ideological lines in deference to what we now call national interests. The Thirty Years War, a religious war between Catholics and Protestants, provided another occasion for the sacrifice of ideological convictions on the altar of state interests. Two cardinals of the Catholic Church, Richelieu and Mazarin, who guided French policy during that war, gave political and financial support to the German Protestant princes and to the Protestant leader, King Gustavus Adolphus, in their bitter struggle against the Catholic Hapsburg emperor. The *raison d'état* proved to be stronger than religious preferences. The British, for whom the parliamentary system of government was a political dogma, led the coalitions against Revolutionary France, while their allies were all absolutist monarchies; the national interests of Britain were more important than its aversion to the domestic regimes of its allies.

In our own time the impact of national interests can be measured by the Chinese claim in March, 1963, regarding the validity of frontiers founded on the so-called unequal treaties. (These are the treaties which the great powers imposed in the nineteenth century on a weak China.) The Chinese press was replying to the Soviet jibe that China patiently tolerated the existence of two imperialist enclaves, British Hong Kong and Portuguese Macao, while it denounced as cowardice the Soviet removal of offensive weapons from Cuba. The Chinese answered that the Russians should be more cautious in raising the problem of unequal treaties to which Hong Kong and Macao owed their existence. The present Russian-Chinese frontiers, they said, were also due to the unequal treaties which Russia imposed in the nineteenth century on China. This potential claim to the Soviet (formerly Chinese) Far Eastern territories could not be squared with "proletarian internationalism," which should have made politically irrelevant the frontiers within "the fraternal family of socialist nations." Prodded by the bitter polemic with the Soviet Party, the Chinese Communists disclosed that their nationalism could at times prevail over their Communist ideology. One can be no less sure that the Soviet Communists are not inclined to abandon any part of Russian territory in order to please their Chinese or other fellow-believers.

The conflict between principles and national interests is so frequent a feature of international politics that to ignore it out of moral squeamishness amounts to an unrealistic blindness regarding the importance of the *raison d'état* as the determining factor in the formulation of foreign policies. The usual silence on this subject is not infrequently due to hypocrisy. If hypocrisy is the tribute paid by vice to virtue, the propensity to pay this tribute is much stronger in international relations than in personal relations.

The first and last thing to remember about international politics is that they are relations between living men and hence never static. This is self-evident if one looks at the pages of history. The names of actors have changed or the roles assigned to them have become more or less important; past settings seem almost unreal they were so different from the present one; many of the problems which then haunted mankind now seem insignificant. It is almost incomprehensible that while the whole of Europe was in a ferment before 1914 about the Russian-Austrian rivalry in the Balkans today many people do not even remember the name of Austria-Hungary. Preoccupied with Communism, we forget that Nazism was in 1933-45 the main threat to the future of mankind. It is more difficult to realize that present international conditions are no more eternal than past ones. Yet in a few decades the actors on the stage will not all be the same as today; those who occupy the forefront will be compelled to share it with new stars; some of the actors will be dropped from the cast; the decors will be of a different design; and the themes of the diplomatic dialogues will rarely be the same as those which arouse such passionate interest today. Like former generations, our own is moving into an unknown international future. We cannot stop the march of mankind, but we can influence the choice of the road along which it will continue to progress.

CHAPTER II

The Nuclear Revolution and the Problem of War

WAR AS AN INSTRUMENT OF FOREIGN POLICY

General Von Clausewitz wrote: "War is regarded as nothing but the continuation of state policy with other means." In pre-nuclear days, this famous statement was considered so true and quoted so often that it finally became a cliché. But the invention of nuclear weapons seems to have deprived this dictum of any meaning; a war which can end in the extinction of the belligerents, including the policy-makers, can hardly be deemed a continuation of state policy.

This complete denial of the political sense of wars and of the use of force in general in contemporary international politics is, however, too sweeping and calls for several reservations. First, there are two schools of thought regarding the probable effects of an all-out nuclear war. One accepts the view that the use of all the available means of mass destruction would end in a catastrophe equally fatal for both belligerents. The other, that of the "broken-back war," holds that the belligerents would not exhaust their combative strength during the stage of mutual nuclear attacks but would still be left with the capacity for waging a protracted war until one of them achieved a victory as meaningful as that won by the victors of earlier wars. Secondly, if one of the nuclear powers could accomplish a technological breakthrough which would make possible an effective neutralization of the enemy's retaliatory force, its nuclear first strike would also be the last and decisive. Since it could win the war at a relatively small risk, nuclear war would have for this power a definite political meaning. Thirdly, both nuclear powers might in time develop their active and passive defenses to such a degree of efficiency that nuclear weapons could no longer cause an irreparable calamity. Finally, the nuclear age does not rule out the use of conventional weapons and the limited application of force in general. In Korea the United States, a nuclear power, deliberately conducted a war with non-nuclear means. The French war in Indochina was another proof that hostilities in our time are not necessarily nuclear. Conventional weapons continue to be the regular instruments of politics in civil wars and colonial uprisings, as witnessed by the guerrilla operations in Malaya and Algeria and the civil wars in China and Cuba. The feasibility of a limited use of force was amply demonstrated by the Soviet Union in Hungary, by Britain and France in Egypt, and by India in the former Portuguese Goa.

Clausewitz's dictum retains its validity in the nuclear age although it might have lost its meaning regarding an all-out nuclear war. Insofar as the use of force does not amount to the collective suicide of both belligerents, the decisions to use force presupposes the preliminary formulation of political objectives.

However, it would be senseless to deny that the existence of nuclear weapons has brought about a revolution in international politics. The very fact that they *could* be used, with consequences which no one can predict with certainty, has immensely raised the risks involved in a faulty foreign policy. The area of national survival, within which external policies must revolve, has been radically reduced.

At the same time, the ultimate decision as to the continuation of foreign policy by other means, i.e., by force, paradoxically continues to reside with each independent state. At least theoretically, a nuclear power is as free to unleash nuclear catastrophe as a pre-nuclear great power was to begin conventional hostilities. Nowadays, however, the sovereign freedom of the state implies the freedom to annihilate its own and the enemy's population and perhaps bring unmitigated calamity on the whole of mankind. Non-nuclear states also retain the freedom to use force at their own pleasure. The use of force has remained, as our ancestors would have said, the last argument of kings. The events of the postwar period proved more than once that the prohibition of force, enshrined in the Charter of the United Nations, did not prevent the member states from "continuing their state policies with other means."

Now as before the use of force and military victory cannot be ends in themselves. Clausewitz said it clearly: "The subordination of the political point of view to the military would be unreasonable, for policy has created the war; policy is the intelligent faculty, war only the instrument, and not the reverse. The subordination of the military point of view to the political is, therefore, the only arrangement possible." This simple truth was sometimes forgotten by the belligerent governments. Fascinated by the prospect of military victory, they planned their military strategy only with the view to achieve victory as rapidly and as fully as possible. They lost sight of the true end of hostilities, namely a postwar distribution of power in which their country's share would compare desirably with that of all the countries affected by the war, including not only the defeated enemy but also wartime allies and neutrals. Clausewitz was right in insisting that insofar as possible military strategy should be conceived with a view to its ultimate effect on all the nations concerned: the enemy, the allies, and the neutrals.

The question of why states have had recourse to war as "another means" of conducting their policies has been answered in many ways. Some of these answers have been quite primitive, like the one which sought to discover *the* reason for wars in the profiteering of armaments manufacturers. Why, then, did the Soviet Union attack Poland and Finland in 1939, or why did China commence armed hostilities against India in 1962, if all industries, including armament-producing industries, had been nationalized in these Communist states? Another answer of a rather low intellectual caliber assigns the cause of wars to the pugnacious instincts of man. This explanation overlooks the fact that the same "pugnacious" men who fight international wars very seldom make domestic revolutions. If a feeling of national solidarity and the existence of a state monopoly on the use of power are usually sufficient to prevent human pugnacity from subverting domestic public order, then the pugnacious instincts of man can hardly be so overpowering as to account for the frequent, long, and bloody wars of history.

More serious views ascribe the reasons for war to such phenomena as overpopulation and the need for more land to accommodate a fast-growing population; a search for foreign markets, raw materials, and places for capital investment; a missionary zeal to convert other nations by force to a new ideology; and so on. Most of these theories contain a grain of truth but stress only one aspect of the question and fail to provide a sufficiently general answer.

One of these theories deserves particular attention because it has become a major issue between the Soviet and the Chinese Communist parties. Lenin believed that the true cause of wars was modern imperialist capitalism. This fully developed capitalism was no longer able to find a sufficient outlet for its expanding production in the capitalist country itself. The capitalist governments were driven to wars by the dire necessity to fight for markets and for access to raw materials and places where surplus capital could be invested. This necessity was said to explain the wars between capitalist states themselves (for example, the First World War) and their wars of conquest against the underdeveloped countries. The other reason for capitalist wars was an undying hostility toward the socialist states, which represented a permanent challenge to the survival of capitalism. Lenin's conclusion was that wars were inevitable as long as imperialist capitalism existed and could be eliminated only by the universal triumph of socialism.

This deterministic view was abandoned by the Soviet Communist party at its Twentieth Congress in 1956. The party declared that Lenin was right in his time but that he could not possibly foresee the new developments which were making wars avoidable though still possible. These new developments were (1) the invention of nuclear weapons that will inevitably make any major war uncontrollably destructive; and (2) the postwar growth of peace-loving forces (the socialist states, the unaligned states, and the peaceful elements in the imperialist countries) which are strong enough to prevent the imperialists from unleashing a major war.

The Chinese do not deny that an all-out nuclear war would be terribly destructive, but they add that, if the imperialists were to initiate this war, the final result would be the destruction of the capitalist system and the final triumph of socialism. They might, in fact, accept the prospect of the nuclear destruction of the main belligerents, the United States and its Western allies as well as the Soviet Union, because socialism would survive in China, left alone by the nuclear powers and able afterwards to ensure the triumph of socialism in other countries. In any case, they are more sceptical than the Russians concerning the possibility of restraining the imperialist powers from playing the game of "nuclear blackmail" and consider that the socialist states should not be unduly afraid of nuclear risks and should not "capitulate" before that blackmail. They say that the imperialist states, first of all the United States, are domestically rotten because they represent a decaying social and economic regime. They are "paper tigers," and their existence should not paralyze the socialist states, which must boldly support every Communist revolution and every struggle of the underdeveloped countries against the imperialists. The Soviet Communists reply that the "paper tigers" have "nuclear teeth" and that this forces the U.S.S.R. to calculate the risks carefully.

These two points of view boil down to a different evaluation of the risks which the socialist states can safely assume. Both parties are willing to support "just wars," such as colonial uprisings, the struggle of an underdeveloped country against a Western power, or the exertions of a "progressive" party in a civil war, but they do not agree on the risk of escalation.

At any rate, the Leninist equation of imperialist capitalism with the causes of wars is no longer upheld by the Soviet party and most of the other Communist parties.

The causes of war may be summed up in the following two considerations:

1. As long as states have in their hands the ultimate decision concerning the use of force, war is always possible. However, the existence of nuclear weapons is a powerful deterrent to a nuclear war and also an incentive to calculate carefully the risks of escalation which are involved in any minor war.

2. States have had recourse to war for all sorts of reasons, but all these reasons can be classified under the general heading of national in-

terests, if the term *national interests* is interpreted flexibly (see Chapter 1). Governments which have initiated hostilities have always done so in the belief that this was the most effective way of reaching their objectives. The decision was made within the framework of the interpretation of national interests which a given government adopted at the time. The "moral obligation" to use force in spreading the ideology dominant in a given state or to protect co-believers in a foreign country; a preoccupation with the maintenance of a favorable distribution of power; the alleged need to win foreign lands for an expanding population; the desire to seize control over alien territories in order to increase the might of the state or to ensure additional markets, sources of raw materials, and places for capital investment; the belief that "racial superiority" gives a nation the "right" to rule alien peoples; the intention of preventing another power from unleashing war at a time of her own choice; the ambition to unite all people of the same nationality under one government or to overthrow alien control; the urge to acquire "better" frontiers or to conquer strategic locations; an attempt to settle outstanding disputes with an enemy state; the search for greater security to be obtained by the weakening of a rival state; and so on, all these reasons for war were dictated by what national interests seemed to require and by the interpretation of national interests which the government concerned adopted as its own.

THE TOTAL WAR

The First World War was the first to be retrospectively called *total*. Measured by the suffering and destruction which it caused, the Second World War merited this appellation even more. The image of a nuclear war gives the fullest meaning to those awe-inspiring words, *total war*.

Total wars can be waged only by the "advanced" nations having at their disposal all the means of destruction which an industrialized economy and an efficient science can devise and manufacture. Total wars are therefore a concomitant of modern progress.

The totality of modern wars is reflected in the following features. First, the whole population of the state is called upon to participate in the war effort. The integration of modern man within his national society makes him feel that the war of his state is his own war. Wars are no longer fought by professional armies, as in previous ages, but by armed forces recruited through compulsory and universal military service. Almost every family has at least one representative in the ranks of combatants and therefore its emotional involvement in the war is greatly enhanced. Civilians, whether industrial workers, farmers, technologists, scientists, state officials, or others, are engaged in work which is related either directly to the war effort or to the more or less normal functioning of the society despite the war emergency. Except for children and the elderly, every citizen, man or woman, contributes to the national struggle against the foreign enemy. Whole nations are in arms, and the dividing line between actual combatants in uniform and civilians becomes very thin. From the point of view of the enemy this line tends to disappear for two reasons. The devastation of the opponent's homeland with its concomitant, the destruction of civilians, becomes a "legitimate" military operation because it reduces the enemy's economic and military potential and thus hastens the end of military resistance. For the belligerent it is at least questionable which is more effective—to kill armed soldiers or to exterminate the civilians whose daily productive work enables the armed forces to fight. Moreover, devastating attacks on the enemy homeland can undermine the will to resist not only among the civilians but also among members of the armed forces who might collapse morally at the news of the destruction of their families and friends, their homes and cities. If the means of attack are powerful enough, the enemy can destroy the social fabric of the opponent and thus reduce him to defeat by undermining his capacity and will to fight. Thus, wholesale destruction of enemy civilians can always be justified on the grounds that it shortens the war, spares the lives of one's own countrymen, and hastens military victory.

The blockade of enemy commerce, which amounts in our time to an attempt at stopping all supplies, even those having no direct military usefulness, is bound, as the experience of the two world wars proved, to inflict privations, including food shortages, on the civilians rather than the military personnel, who enjoy priority over the civilians. The dropping of the two atomic bombs on Japan was considered justified as a means of shortening the war, but the victims were civilians living in the open cities.

The vast range of destructiveness of modern weapons makes it impossible to limit devastation to purely military targets, which in modern societies are situated in or close to densely populated urban centers. Much of the indiscriminate devastation of modern warfare results less from human cruelty than from the cruelty inherent in modern weapons. For instance, a submarine under orders to harass enemy commerce, can neither give a warning to commercial vessels, for that warning would reveal the submarine's position to enemy warships and planes, nor accommodate within its narrow space the survivors of a ship that has been sunk.

The war is total by the global nature of the war effort which, if time allows, consists in an utmost mobilization of manpower and economic resources. It is also total because of the full emotional involvement of the belligerent populations, who feel that they are fighting for a common national cause and that they are the targets of enemy operations. Hatred for the enemy grows in intensity; the spectacle of the enormous human and material losses which the country suffers at the hands of the enemy makes the population feel that victory should reduce the adversary to a total and unconditional surrender. The war objectives, which might have been limited at first, tend to become unlimited.

The dividing line between civilians and combatants may disappear for other reasons. The enemy may invade and occupy all or part of the national territory; if the civilian population believes that its own armies or its allies may eventually change a temporary defeat into a final victory, they may continue the struggle by other means. Especially if the enemy has installed a ruthless regime of occupation that makes no real distinction between the guilty and the innocent, a resistance movement will develop, involving guerrilla warfare, terroristic attempts on the lives of enemy soldiers and officials, sabotage, and other acts of violence. The enemy ripostes with a reign of terror, and the ensuing struggle is frankly between civilians, if occasionaly armed, and the enemy armed forces and police. This struggle is in itself a new source of mutual hatred.

The total war leaves only a slim chance that the belligerents will observe the international rules of war. These rules, as they emerged during the nineteenth and early twentieth centuries, were intended to achieve two results—to spare unnecessary cruelty to the combatants, and to protect civilians from the effects of warfare. The cruelty of modern weapons and the deep involvement of civilians in the war effort make it almost impossible to abide by these rules today. The emotional upheaval caused by modern warfare does not incline the belligerents toward respect for international law. However, there are two restraints. If both belligerents fear retaliation, they will probably refrain from certain forms of hostilities. Thus, chemical warfare was avoided by all belligerents during the Second World War because both sides were fully prepared to wage it. Secondly, those rules which can be observed without seriously hindering the war effort (for instance, the decent treatment of prisoners of war) have a reasonable chance of being respected in the reciprocal interest of the belligerents.

The totality of modern wars is reflected in a second feature; not only do these wars tend to involve the whole population of warring countries, but they tend to involve all the great powers and most of the smaller states, as shown in both world wars. The interests of modern states, in particular of the great powers, are so interlocked that once an armed struggle is joined the great powers, and after them the smaller states, are drawn into the vortex. When all the great powers are committed, the stakes become so high that the position of neutrals is constantly imperilled. These neutrals are too weak to protect their rights as guaranteed by international law or even their status of neutrality. The history of the two world wars provides only too many illustrations of the hapless situation of neutral nations. The blockade always interferes with neutral commerce. A neutral placed in dangerous proximity to a powerful belligerent might be forced, as Sweden was during the last war, to buy noninvolvement in actual hostilities at the price of violating international law by rendering unneutral services, such as allowing the transport of belligerent troops through its territory or restricting supplies of strategically vital goods to one belligerent only. The status of neutrality, even if formally acknowledged by both belligerents, does not provide any foolproof guarantee against a sudden invasion if one of the belligerents feels that this is vital to the success of its military operations. The list of neutrals who learned this lesson during the two world wars is long—Belgium, Luxemburg, Norway, Denmark, Holland, Yugoslavia, Greece, Rumania, Hungary, Persia, and others. If Switzerland fared better it was not because the belligerents respected its right to neutrality but because they considered its neutral status to be in their own interests. The possession of Swiss territory was not deemed vital to the pursuit of hostilities, while the existence of this small neutral country allowed the belligerents to reap certain benefits of equal value to both, to mention only the services which the International Committee of the Red Cross, located in Switzerland and composed of Swiss citizens, rendered to both camps by ensuring the proper treatment of prisoners of war. A country which chooses neutrality in the twentieth century can never be sure that its rights will be respected by the belligerents and that its territory will escape the horrors of war. In this respect, total war means that every country is in peril of being dragged into the struggle.

It would be idle to speculate on the value of neutrality in an all-out nuclear war. If the war lasted for only a short period of time, during which the nuclear belligerents concentrated on destroying each other, the third states would have a chance of surviving and eventually emerging stronger because of the mutual annihilation of the belligerents. At the worst, the short duration of hostilities would allow the nuclear powers to drag with them into the abyss only those third states on whose territory vital enemy bases were located. If, as some think more probable, the war were prolonged, the neutrals would fare no better than in the two world wars. If one of the nuclear powers, favored by an unexpected technological breakthrough, suddenly became capable of wiping out the other nuclear power without suffering unbearable losses, this power could impose its will on all states, committed or uncommitted.

The deep emotional involvement of the belligerent populations does not leave much room for any true sympathy for the cause of neutrals whose peaceful and prosperous existence seems almost inexcusable against the background of general suffering. There is likely to be an outcry of moral indignation if neutral rights are trampled under foot by the enemy but no protest if this is done by one's own government.

Modern wars are total in still another sense. The emotional intensity generated by a total war is heightened by war propaganda which represents the enemy as the very incarnation of the devil. Thus, a war fought for national objectives begins to appear as a moral crusade for a better world and for the conversion of the enemy to a higher morality and a better form of government, both of these objectives to be imposed by force of arms. The First World War was allegedly fought to "end all wars" and to "make the world safe for democracy." The Second World War was labelled a struggle either against Fascism or against "the decadent democracies, the Jews, and Bolshevism." A future war may be represented as a moral crusade against capitalism or totalitarianism.

This ideological aspect of modern wars makes them pitiless, because the belligerents feel that they are fighting not only for their status as great powers or for national independence and territorial integrity but also for their form of government, their ways of life, and their most cherished national "self-evident" truths. Defeat in a total war entails the right of the victor to impose on the vanquished his own type of government and his own patterns of social life. The war is fought for the highest stakes. No wonder that the aftermath of war leaves little room for anything but a Draconian settlement of accounts, possibly moderated by discords among the victors themselves.

When whole populations wage a global war for global objectives, the war and its aftermath are bound to have unforeseeable consequences. War is the *last* argument of kings because, as Clausewitz said, it is "the province of chance." Thucydides, the witness of one of the greatest wars in antiquity, said: "War is certainly not one of those things which follow a fixed pattern." No one can predict the military outcome of a major war just as no one can forecast its political, economic, and social consequences for the victors and the vanquished alike. This truth is amply proved by the two world wars. Would the governments of the great powers have decided on war in 1914 if they had known the final outcome of that war and could have foreseen the decline in the relative power of Britain and France in spite of their victory, the collapse of the imperial regime in Germany, the irremediable loss by Germany of its former status as a world power, the disintegration of Austria-Hungary, and the social revolution in Russia? Would Hitler, Mussolini, and the Japanese leaders have decided on the course which led their countries to the Second World War if they had known that utter defeat awaited them and their nations, that Germany would be deprived of large territories and be quasipermanently divided into two states, that Japan would lose all its overseas possessions, and that Italy would be reduced to the status of a secondary power? Would the initial belligerents in both world wars have rejoiced at the prospect that the main but unexpected beneficiaries of these two gigantic convulsions would be the United States and the Soviet Union?

The ideological conflict of our time and the existence of nuclear weapons have made the outcome of future major wars even more unpredictable. Would Communism or democracy survive a nuclear conflict?

Whatever the fate of their regimes and ideologies, would the citizens themselves of the belligerent nations survive a nuclear holocaust?

THE NUCLEAR REVOLUTION

Marx said that a great quantitative change becomes a qualitative one. This is certainly true of the change in military technology due to the invention of nuclear weapons. The result is stupendous; war no longer involves limited risks such as a partial loss of national territory, a temporary enemy occupation, reparations or a war indemnity, or, in the worst cases, the loss of national independence and total annexation by a foreign state. It may now entail the risk of an almost total extermination of the belligerent population or at least of human losses of a magnitude never before recorded in history and possibly accompanied by the collapse of the social fabric. Stratospheric fallout, a concomitant of nuclear hostilities, would be a lethal threat to all countries, belligerent and neutral alike.

The debate concerning the extent of devastation which a nuclear war would cause revolves around the question whether the human and material losses thus inflicted would be bearable for the belligerents or not. But certainly no one denies the great magnitude of those losses. The estimates of hypothetical losses vary. In June, 1959, for instance, the Office of Civil Defense and Mobilization told a Joint Congressional Atomic Energy subcommittee that a nuclear attack, in which 224 military and civilian (cities) targets would be hit by 263 thermonuclear bombs with a total force equal to 1,446 million tons of TNT, would result in about 20 million killed, another 22 million fatally injured, and over 17 million injured but able later to recover. These figures did not include people contaminated by radioactive fallout. Another calculation assumes that a successful attack on fifty of the largest metropolitan areas in the United States would expose to its direct effects 40 per cent of the American population and 75 per cent of American industries. Total casualties, including the victims of radiation, would range from 40 to 80 million people. These and other estimates can be erroneous even at the time of their publication and are of uncertain future value because of the constantly increasing destructive power of nuclear weapons and also because of a possible breakthrough in the realm of active defense. But they are useful in giving an idea of the revolution brought about by nuclear weapons. This revolution can also be measured by comparing modern weapons with those used in the Second World War. The largest bomb produced during the Second World War had an explosive capacity of 20 tons of TNT. The atomic bomb that was dropped at Hiroshima was a thousand times more powerful; it had an explosive equivalent of 20,000 tons of TNT. Since that time hydrogen bombs have been tested with an explosive power which is three thousand times greater than the atomic bomb dropped on Hiroshima. While atomic bombs were measured only in kilotons (thousands of tons of TNT), thermonuclear bombs are measured in megatons (millions of tons of TNT). Both nuclear powers have in their possession nuclear bombs measured in tens of megatons. In 1961, the Soviet Union tested a bomb of explosive capacity higher than 50 megatons. A bomb in the range of 100 megatons is within the realm of technological feasibility. Since the production of fissionable bombs is relatively cheap and their size and weight have been greatly reduced, there is no necessary limit to the explosive capacity of megaton bombs. The technological problem is of a different nature, namely whether it is more practical to drop one big megaton bomb or two or more smaller ones; the extent of destruction does not increase in strict proportion to the size of the bomb. Moreover, there is eventually a "rational" upper limit to the size of megaton bombs, namely the explosive power which is needed to devastate a target (for instance, a metropolitan area); additional explosive power would be wasted.

A 10-megaton bomb represents five times the explosive power of all the bombs dropped on Germany in five years of the last war. Rear Admiral Lewis L. Strauss, then Chairman of the Atomic Energy Commission, declared after the test of a 15-megaton bomb carried out by the United States on March 1, 1954, on the Bikini Atoll, that one bomb of this size would wipe out the largest city in the world. It was later learned that the same test produced an unexpectedly large amount of radioactive debris which was deposited as fallout of dangerous intensity over thousands of square miles and up to the distance of 200 miles or more downwind from zero ground. Professor Edward Teller disclosed in 1958 that the lethal effects of radiation caused by the same explosion extended to a distance of thirty miles; an unprotected person standing at that distance would not have been hurt by blast or fire but would have been killed by radiation within a matter of minutes after the beginning of the fallout.

Nuclear bombs cause losses not only by the effect of blast and of a fire storm but, unlike conventional bombs of the pre-nuclear age, also by the radioactive fallout. Fallout is of two types: local and stratospheric. Local fallout (tropospheric) originates in that part of the atmosphere that lies below 35,000 to 45,000 feet above the ground. Its effects last no longer than one month; it covers no more than a few hundred square miles from zero ground. Of course, several simultaneous or almost simultaneous explosions in the megaton range would blanket a very large territory with local fallout. For instance, a few hundred bombs of megaton range with a total yield of two to three thousand megatons could blanket half the United States with a lethal or near-lethal local fallout. Local fallout produces immediate acute effects such as death, radiation sickness, skin burns, and other damage to the human body depending on the size of the dose. It can also cause chronic effects such as bone cancer, leukemia, or premature aging. Because of its limited range, local fallout represents a danger only to the nuclear belligerents.

Stratospheric fallout originates above the 35,000 or 45,000 feet level, has a much wider range, and is of incomparably longer duration than local fallout, lasting from five to ten years. The radioactive debris which the explosion catapults into the stratosphere gradually descends to the earth, mainly with rainfall. Stratospheric fallout travels over thousands of miles and is unevenly disseminated over the world. It escapes human control and has chronic effects. Since it is released by tests involving explosions in the megaton range, stratospheric fallout is also a threat in peacetime. The danger to human beings comes from the two elements disseminated by stratospheric fallout, Cesium 137 and Strontium 90, especially the latter, which is easily dissolved in water. Strontium 90 is absorbed by plants. Hence, human beings can be contaminated by eating plants and meat or drinking milk (cattle graze on the plants). Strontium 90 accumulates in the bones, affects the marrow, and causes bone cancer and leukemia. Cesium 137 causes genetic mutation with long-term effects for future generations.

The existence of the stratospheric fallout with its worldwide and unpredictable effects makes all-out nuclear war a threat to all countries, including the nonbelligerents. It also creates a legitimate interest for all states in the nuclear tests of megaton range.

The invention of nuclear weapons of the megaton range has simplified the problem of delivering the means of destruction to enemy territory. In the Second World War it was necessary to make 1.4 million bomber sorties over a period of four years to produce telling effects on Germany. Today much more devastating results could be achieved within one or a few days.

The casualty rate would be much higher in nuclear warfare than in conventional bombing not only because of the much greater explosive power of nuclear weapons but also for other reasons. The warning time would be much shorter because of the greater speed of modern planes and the existence of missiles with nuclear warheads. The warning time for intercontinental missiles is no longer than fifteen minutes and will be increased at the most to thirty minutes by the use of warnings supplied by orbiting satellites. The shelters of the last war usually offered adequate protection. For effective protection in nuclear warfare, the civilian population would need very deep shelters impervious not only to the fire storm, which would claim a much higher number of casualties than the blast itself, but also to local fallout. These shelters would have to provide their occupants with oxygen, food, light, and heat for the duration of local radioactivity. Their cost might be prohibitive. Panic induced by the huge explosion of only one bomb and by the ensuing fire storm, by the shocking sight of immense material and human destruction, and by the lingering fear of another attack could further reduce the effectiveness of passive defense. The enemy could intensify this panic by dropping bombs which only simulate the effects of nuclear bombs (a violent detonation, brilliant mushroom cloud, etc.).

A fact commonly omitted from popular discussions of modern war is that other than nuclear means of mass destruction exist, such as the chemical and bacteriological weapons which could be combined with intercontinental and intermediate missiles. Nuclear attacks could be accompanied by chemical and bacteriological assaults which would destroy human life directly or threaten it by the destruction of crops, the poisoning of water and food, or the killing of domestic animals.

The so-called neutron bomb will have no other effects than the local radiation which is popularly named death rays. The uncontrollable stratospheric fallout, the blast, and the fire storm, which damage material property, would be eliminated. The local radiation would instantly destroy all life within the perimeter of the effectiveness of the bomb. At first glance, it would seem that the belligerent who possessed a monopoly on neutron bombs or warheads would also possess a great advantage over his adversary. He could exterminate the enemy population without exposing his own to the effects of stratospheric fallout and could become the master of enemy territory materially undamaged by his attacks although depopulated. However, he could not prevent the enemy, if able to retaliate, from using bombs of the present type, that is to say, causing stratospheric fallout and material damages. It seems that the neutron bomb would not basically modify the main problem of the nuclear age, namely whether a surprise attack would leave to the enemy enough of his nuclear retaliatory power to enable him to inflict unbearable losses on the aggressor.

The vulnerability of economically advanced countries to the effects of nuclear warfare is due to the concentration of their populations and industries in several metropolitan and urban areas. The number of those areas of vital importance for the economic potential of the United States or the Soviet Union does not exceed two hundred in either case. The leading fifty-four American metropolitan areas contain over 60 per cent of the national industrial capital and a population of some 70 million, including a high proportion of the people whose skills are associated with large-scale production. The total number of 170 metropolitan areas represents 75 per cent of industrial capital and 55 per cent of the total population. By far the greater part of these metropolitan areas are situated in the eastern and especially northeastern regions of the United States where even the nonurban population would be exposed to the overlapping effect of local fallout. In the Soviet Union, population and industrial capital are concentrated in the western parts of the country. Moreover, the metropolitan areas in both countries are also the centers of political, administrative, economic, and intellectual life. Their destruction could result in the disruption of organized social life.

In the absence of any past experience of an all-out nuclear war there is no conclusive argument in the debate between the two schools of thought regarding the ability of modern societies to survive the impact of nuclear warfare and to continue hostilities with the means still left. Every argument in this debate is hypothetical and revolves around a human faculty which cannot be measured in advance of the actual test, the power of psychological resistance to misfortune. There are Western and Soviet supporters of the concept of a "broken-back" war that would follow the nuclear stage of hostilities. As a matter of fact, this was the official Soviet position according to which a nuclear war would be an unprecedented calamity for mankind but would, nevertheless, end in the victory of Communism over capitalism. Assuming that this official view was seriously held (this is far from certain), it presupposed that mankind would be only moderately afflicted by the accumulation of radioactive ruins and would retain enough zest for building a worldwide Communist society in the midst of these ruins. The main argument advanced by Western commentators who favor the view that war would continue after the exchange of nuclear bombings rests on the Soviet experience in the last war. The initial German victories in 1941 deprived the Soviet Union of 40 per cent of its population, 40 per cent of its grain production, approximately 60 per cent of its coal, iron, steel, and aluminum production, and 95 per cent of certain key military industries, such as the ball-bearing output. They lost 4 million soldiers, dead, wounded, or captured. Yet the Soviet Union was able to rebuild its industrial production, to pour new divisions into combat, and eventually to win the war. Assuming that the first stage of the most intense nuclear attacks would result in comparable losses for the belligerents, would they not retain the same capacity to recover and to continue hostilities?

This argument overlooks a few points. No one can be sure in advance that nuclear devastations would not exceed the proportions of the Soviet losses in 1941. The German advance was rapid but extended nevertheless over several months; the Soviet government had time to evacuate most of its vital industries which were soon able to resume production in the unoccupied parts of the U.S.S.R. The economic losses were partly compensated by American lend-lease supplies. Moreover, the Soviet population in the unoccupied regions and the Soviet armies could reasonably hope to recover the population left on German-occupied territory; this population was alive, even if temporarily ruled by the enemy. The psychological shock would have been different had the same 40 per cent of the national population been exterminated. Finally, nuclear devastations would not be limited to a definite part of the national territory but would be widespread, thus making it difficult to sustain a "normal" organized life in other parts of the same territory; the Soviet government enjoyed in 1941-42 the advantage of being able to maintain "normal" national activity on the whole unoccupied territory.

The theory that a war could continue after the initial stage of all-out nuclear attacks rests on two very broad assumptions. It presupposes that the capacity of both belligerents to deliver nuclear blows would terminate at the same time and with comparably indecisive results. It also assumes that modern armies and navies would not only retain the will to fight after the widespread destruction of their homelands and families but could somehow operate while their bases, ports, communication centers, and sources of supplies (factories and depots) were in large part reduced to radioactive rubble.

The analogy with the Soviet experience in the last war seems for all these reasons ill-founded. The theory of a protracted war between the nuclear powers would be convincing only if they acquired a means of active defense so effective that human and material losses could be reduced to a bearable level, i.e., would not endanger the survival of an organized modern social life. Such defenses may be developed sooner than expected, or they may never be developed at all if the offensive weapons of mass destruction continue to evolve more rapidly than the means of active defense. In the present condition of the lack of any balance between the destructive power of offensive weapons and the means of active defense, one can legitimately raise the question whether eminently urban and highly organized modern nations could withstand nuclear war and be able to continue hostilities. The modern society is highly dependent upon communications, the distribution of essential supplies, transportation, and urban community relationships. The simultaneous destruction of most of the major population centers would probably create problems of catastrophic proportions. These problems, coupled with the psychologically debilitating effects of radioactivity and with widespread panic, might swamp the capability of the government to maintain some semblance of public order. It is also hard to imagine such fortitude on the part of the surviving population that they would concentrate their effort on the continuation of a war of attrition rather than on the rebuilding of an organized social life from the shambles of their former existence. Would they not be discouraged by the prospect that their eventual "victory" would be Pyrrhic?

This last question raises the whole problem of the political sense of a nuclear war. As long as the nuclear powers have no effective means of active defense, they must expect tremendous mutual devastations. They would probably be able to knock each other out of the ring of great powers either forever or for a long time to come. Their places would automatically be taken over by other states which did not participate in the war. Is it in the American or the Soviet interest to enfeeble each other by nuclear hostilities and thus make room for others, whether China, India, or Western Europe?

Some people entertain the optimistic view that an all-out nuclear war would consist in a duel between the two strategic forces. The belligerents would spare each other's cities and civilian populations. The power finally outmatched and left with a hopelessly crippled nuclear force would hasten to acknowledge its defeat; the war would end at this point. However, technological progress makes the strategic force steadily less vulnerable as a result of better dispersal, mobility, and protection. One can foresee the time when the nuclear powers will become technologically incapable of destroying or even seriously impairing the enemy massive deterrent. They will then be left with no choice but either to refrain from nuclear war or to turn the whole fury of their mutual nuclear attacks on the only really vulnerable targets—the open cities and the civilian populations.

If, in the absence of an effective active defense, nuclear war would be calamitous for such large countries as the United States and the Soviet Union, it would be even more calamitous for the smaller nations. A people of a few millions, who live on a compact territory, could be totally exterminated. Seven or eight large megaton bombs would probably paralyze such countries as Great Britain or France or West Germany. The only chance for those nations with relatively small territories would be that their major allies or enemies, the United States and the Soviet Union, would be so preoccupied with their mutual destruction that they would have no time to spare for eliminating the smaller belligerents.

The problem can best be illustrated by the example of Great Britain. Its whole territory, including the six counties of Northern Ireland, comes to just over 94,000 square miles, an area smaller than Oregon. Over 50 million people live in this small area. Moreover, this population is concentrated in a few urban areas such as London, the Midlands, and Glasgow. The scale of urban concentration can be gauged by the fact that about one-fifth of the total population resides in the London metropolitan area. The picture which *The Economist* painted on January 21, 1956, of the effects on London of the explosion of one 10-megaton bomb is not very cheerful. Everything would be destroyed within four miles of the center of the fireball. The greater part of London County would be damaged beyond repair. The fire tempest, generated by the explosion, would start a ring of fires extending for ten miles into the suburbs. Sixteen miles away from zero ground, people would be blistered by heat and the buildings severely damaged by blast. The radioactive dust would float for 200 miles beyond the sight or sound of the explosion. This picture may be exact or exaggerated; regardless, there is no certainty that two 10-megaton bombs instead of one would not be discharged on London in case of a nuclear war. The problem of countries with large urban concentrations and a relatively small territory can be summed up in two points. First, only a small number of megaton bombs would be needed to wipe out the population and cover the whole territory with an overlapping blanket of local radiation. Secondly, the smallness of the territory would not allow for a meaningful dispersal of the population and other targets.

England also provides a telling example of the impact of progress in war technology on the security derived from geographical location. It was for almost a thousand years effectively protected by the Channel and its naval defenses. The two world wars disclosed its vulnerability to submarine warfare and air attacks. D-Day proved that an amphibious operation across the Channel was technically feasible. If it could be carried out from England to the continent, it could take place in the opposite direction as well. Nuclear weapons have completed the process of dismantling the insular security of Britain by suspending over British heads the question of their biological survival in an all-out war.

Countries with old cultures face another aspect of the problem of nuclear war. Cities are for them much more than political and economic centers; they harbor treasures of historical and artistic value which embody the past of the nation. Apartment houses and factories could be rebuilt, but the irreplaceable treasures of national culture, which many generations have accumulated, would be lost forever.

It is self-evident that countries with smaller territories would be repelled by the prospect of nuclear war even more than the United States and the Soviet Union. This fact would necessarily affect their foreign policy by inclining them to avoid great risks. By contrast, China with its 680 million population and a very high natural increase could assume the risk of losing many millions. If China should one day achieve a nuclear parity with the present nuclear powers, it would feel safer than the United States and the Soviet Union. Assuming that all three states had equal nuclear power, China would enjoy a greater freedom to assume risks. One hundred million killed in a nuclear war would be a major calamity for the United States and the Soviet Union but would be a bearable loss for China, a hundred million amounting to about one-seventh of the Chinese population. However, this argument could be carried too far. With the present large nuclear stockpiles, the ever better means of delivery, the existence of deadly chemical and bacteriological weapons, and the certain prospect of an ever-increasing capacity for mass destruction, even China could not escape the twin risks of either unbearable human losses, too great even for a population of its size, or the collapse of its regime in the ruins of an organized urban society.

No one can anticipate the capacity of a population to sustain the psychological impact of nuclear warfare and its ability to reorganize its social life from the shambles left by enemy attacks. It would be groundless to predict that the Americans or the Russians, the British or the Chinese, would bear the brunt of nuclear warfare most successfully. Perhaps none of these nations could avoid a breakdown in morale. But the existence of nuclear weapons has introduced a new factor which cannot be disregarded in the evaluation of national morale in peacetime. This new element is the fear of nuclear war. A government whose people are terrified at the prospect of such a war can pursue only a timid foreign policy. The role of this fear in a given country can be evaluated in the light of several questions: Has the population a sufficient knowledge of the perils involved in nuclear warfare? Has it enough imagination to comprehend the problem? Has it had actual experience in a major modern war (devastations of the national territory, enemy occupation, and other effects of direct involvement in total war), and is it therefore able to imagine the horrors of a nuclear war? Is it so much affected by the fear of nuclear war that it loses sight of the fact that such a war would be equally perilous to the enemy and that its population is gripped by the same fear? In other words, has it retained enough self-control to realize that the nuclear risk limits the freedom of international action of all states, not just of one's own country? Or is the average man sheltering behind the screen of escapism and not much affected by the fear of nuclear war simply because he tries not to remember the existence of the problem?

THE SURPRISE ATTACK

It seems at first sight that the overwhelming destructive power of modern weapons has supplied a *rationale* to the concepts of the surprise attack and the lightning war. In the past both concepts have had a great attraction for militarists, because they promised a quick victory at a cheap price for the victor. The Japanese twice attacked by surprise, once in 1904 and again in 1941. In both cases they won an initial, though not decisive, advantage. The victory over Russia was secured by subsequent naval and military successes; Pearl Harbor commenced a series of events which ended in the unconditional surrender of Japan. In both cases the surprise attack could not bring about an immediate victory because it did not deprive the enemy of the means of effective defense.

The German *blitzkrieg* was calculated to secure a quick victory by combining the factor of surprise (the opening attack coming from an unexpected direction) with the concentration of a powerful force at the point of attack. Like the surprise attack, the lightning war would have made political sense if it had decided the outcome of the war. Germany tried twice and twice failed to secure the final decision through this sort of strategy. The German Von Schlieffen Plan, elaborated several years before the outbreak of the First World War, called for a lightning campaign against France. The plan was to move the right wing of the German army swiftly against France from an unexpected direction, through permanently neutral Belgium, to strike at and destroy the left wing of the French army, to cut off France from the Channel and Britain, to impose a separate peace, and then to turn full force against the French ally, Russia, and defeat this country in turn. The plan miscarried in 1914 because the Russian offensive against East Prussia caused the Germans to divert a part of their western task force for defense in the east. The battle of the Marne turned into a French victory, and the war, planned to be short, was protracted. The same plan was carried out successfully in 1940, but this time Germany was unprepared for the next logical move, an amphibious operation against Britain. In both world wars the *blitzkrieg* ended in the defeat of Germany.

The pre-nuclear concepts of the surprise attack and the lightning war were premature, because the then existing military technology was inadequate for the wresting of a quick and decisive victory from an adversary of comparable strength. Only the invention of nuclear weapons and ballistic missiles seems to have given these concepts a political meaning. If a nuclear power were able to take the enemy by complete surprise and to wipe out his retaliatory force or at least destroy his will-power by the appalling devastations of his homeland and the subsequent collapse of his social fabric, the enemy would be reduced in a matter of hours to the mercy of the victor. Even if the enemy were still left with the remnants of a crippled retaliatory force, his counterblow would be too feeble to change the outcome of the war, would inflict on the aggressor only bearable losses, and would not much delay the unavoidable surrender.

The nuclear concept of surprise attack rests on the following assumptions: (1) that an accurate knowledge is possible of the location of enemy targets, in particular the location of his retaliatory forces; (2) that enough technical accuracy can be achieved in the attack to eliminate most, if not all, of the crucial targets; (3) that the effectiveness of surprise would not leave the enemy time to disperse his retaliatory forces and take other measures for defense; (4) that the assailant can achieve dominance in nuclear striking power and the ability to deliver further attacks, if necessary, to complete the destruction of the enemy's nuclear power and to proceed with the devastation of his cities; this remaining capacity would serve as a warning that further resistance by the enemy would be futile; and (5) that a counterblow by the enemy would not cause more damage than could be borne by the aggressor and repaired within a reasonable period of time.

All these assumptions carry with them a high degree of uncertainty. Knowledge of enemy targets might prove to be unobtainable or inexact. The nuclear forces now have a growing capacity for mobility and dispersal. The airfields could be destroyed, but it is unlikely that a surprise attack could disable all the long-range planes, many of which are constantly air-borne. Missile-launching submarines could not be easily detected. Missile launching pads could be mobile, could be placed on railroad cars or on barges, or could be hardened. If hardened, only pinpointed and very accurate direct hits could wreck them. The accuracy and effectiveness of a surprise attack could not be guaranteed. The enemy active defense might prove to be stronger than expected; the number of bombers and missiles hit before reaching the targets might be larger than planned. The technical "perfection" of the ballistic missiles could be marred by defects in their launching, by a mistake in the computation of the trajectory or in the keying of guidance instruments, by an erroneous calculation of the location of enemy targets due, for instance, to enemy deception, to various unexpected interferences such as magnetic anomalies, meteoric dust, or various forms of radiation, to the malfunctioning of one of thousands of delicate component parts, or to all sorts of other defects which might affect any complex engine. The effect of the surprise will eventually be reduced by orbiting satellites which will provide a warning of the attack by missiles at the moment of their launching; the enemy would thus have about half an hour for alerting his retaliatory force.

In short, the surprise attack does not promise an immediate and decisive victory. It does not protect the aggressor against a telling counterblow which could cause unbearable losses. The only advantage of the first strike is the certainty that it would at least reduce the enemy retaliatory force and thus also the amount of damage this force could inflict, but the scale of damage could very well remain unbearable.

The government planning a surprise attack would secure an additional advantage if it proceeded with the evacuation of its major cities before launching the attack. It would thus reduce in advance the human losses likely to result from the enemy counterblow. But this evacuation would also serve to warn the enemy and cancel the effect of surprise unless the major cities were periodically subjected to evacuation as a routine exercise and the true evacuation prior to the surprise attack were taken by the enemy for another routine exercise.

A totalitarian state would have two advantages in planning a surprise attack. First, the decision to launch the attack could be kept secret much more effectively than in a democratic state. Secondly, knowledge of the location of the critical targets could be secured more easily from a democratic state than from a totalitarian one. A large amount of information, including military information, is accessible in a democratic society through direct observation or through the careful perusal of newspapers and technical journals. The press gives wide publicity to the existence or planning of new weapons as well as the location of missile sites, radar-warning installations, air-defense facilities, and naval communication centers. The advantages of totalitarian secrecy will be at least partly nullified by the orbiting reconnaissance satellites which will send back photographs taken over any territory of the globe.

Soviet doctrine developed in the fifties the concept of the pre-emptive attack. This attack is a nuclear first strike triggered by reliable information that the enemy himself is intending to attack in the immediate future. The pre-emptive attack would transform the enemy surprise attack into a counterblow. The Soviet concept seems unrealistic. The speed with which a nuclear attack can be launched makes it improbable that the other state would have enough time for a pre-emptive action. The theory of the pre-emptive attack would in practice amount either to a retaliatory counterblow in response to an enemy surprise attack or to a preventive surprise attack against a state only suspected of planning to unleash a nuclear war at some unspecified future time. The Soviet theory carries with it the risk of ordering a pre-emptive attack on the basis of false information concerning the enemy's intentions.

THE NUCLEAR STALEMATE

The nuclear stalemate is a situation in which the nuclear powers have the capacity to inflict on each other unbearable damage in response to a surprise attack. In this situation no nuclear power can risk unleashing a nuclear war for fear of being crippled, in retaliation, beyond the hope of recovery.

The nuclear stalemate could exist between more than two nuclear powers, but the powers who uphold the stalemate must all have reached the point of nuclear saturation. This point is attained when a power has accumulated a nuclear stockpile and developed an intercontinental means of delivery sufficient to inflict a crippling counterblow. For the time being, only two powers have reached this point, the United States and the Soviet Union. The nuclear stockpiles and the means of delivery which Britain and France possess are inadequate to qualify them for any important role in maintaining the stalemate which rests on the balance of forces between the United States and the U.S.S.R.

Sir Winston Churchill told the Commons on March 1, 1955: "Then it may well be that we shall, by a process of sublime irony, have reached a stage in the story where safety will be the sturdy child of terror, and survival the twin brother of annihilation." He was saying that the two great powers, having acquired an equal capacity for destroying each other, may unintentionally have provided for themselves and for all other nations a guarantee against an all-out war by turning that war into a politically senseless venture. For the first time in history military technology itself has become a deterrent to war.

The nuclear stalemate will endure as long as both parties maintain this parity in the power of destruction. If one of them achieved a spectacular breakthrough in military technology and thus acquired a fair chance of inflicting unbearable losses on the enemy without exposing itself to unbearable damage in return, the nuclear stalemate would cease to exist on the same day. This stalemate depends on a more or less parallel scientific and technological progress in the main nuclear powers.

The stalemate offers safety against all-out nuclear wars; it does not provide any guarantee against other wars or other uses of force. It certainly does not necessarily perpetuate the international status quo, which could be undermined by the use of force short of nuclear hostilities and by nonmilitary means. It is untrue to say that the stalemate leaves no alternative to a nuclear war on the one hand and a general acceptance of the status quo on the other. Perhaps just the opposite is true. The fear of nuclear catastrophe might incline the great powers to accept piecemeal modifications of the status quo more readily than in the pre-nuclear age when their sharp reactions to international events did not involve this terrible sanction.

This "balance of terror" has introduced a new factor in the calculation of risks. On the one hand, if a nuclear power were to take an action detrimental to the most vital interests of the other power and thus compel the opponent to choose between the acceptance of a major defeat without war and the horror of a nuclear war, there would be no certainty that the state thus challenged and driven to despair would not decide to use strategic nuclear weapons. Never before has the miscalculation of one power regarding the reactions of another been pregnant with such dire consequences. The risks involved in every major international decision must nowadays be calculated with an infinitely greater caution than ever before. On the other hand, a nuclear power could become so fearful of inviting a nuclear reaction from another power that it would not dare to assume even slight risks. It would then be deprived by the nuclear stalemate of all initiative and would be led by gradual stages to a complete political defeat. It would know of no answer to the initiative of its nuclear peer but retreats, each of which would seem preferable to the slightest risk of nuclear conflagration; in time, these retreats could irremediably alter the international situation. For the first time in history the formulation of foreign policy must tread cautiously between this Scylla of gradual political defeat and this Charybdis of foolishly running the risk of a nuclear war.

The nuclear stalemate thus offers a risky premium to those who are willing to assume the initiative in the piecemeal changing of the status quo. It is risky in that one nuclear power can always err in its calculation of what another nuclear power will tolerate. The initiative consists in a move that results in a limited and local change in the status quo but does not visibly entail a major loss for the other nuclear power. The opposing power is not pushed back to the point where it must choose between a visible unacceptable degradation of its international position and recourse to nuclear war. The secret of the political offensive in the nuclear age consists in marching forward by measured steps, none of which taken separately represents a major challenge to the other nuclear power. The receding power is confronted at each step with the embarrassing choice of either accepting a retreat which seems to be of only local significance and appears to have no political connection with other local retreats which took place before, or else reacting apparently out of proportion to this local and limited challenge and thus possibly inviting, through miscalculation, a nuclear catastrophe. Each time the retreat seems wiser; each time the power which has assumed the initiative in this piecemeal alteration of the status quo scores another success. A series of these successes could eventually amount to a radical modification of the international status quo.

The nuclear stalemate favors the revolutionary power, for it is this power which wants to change the global status quo and is thus constantly impelled to assume the initiative in international politics. It is on the move because its objectives are dynamic. The revolutionary power knows that its opponents do not want to have recourse to the ultimate weapon any more than it does. It expects them to retreat in every situation which does not visibly involve their global international position. The use of this technique requires great skill. The pressure exerted against the status-quo power must be carefully measured; the receding power should never feel that it is being gradually pushed along a road of continuous and never-ending concessions. It must not be forced to conclude that its concessions would not buy a stable *modus vivendi*. Each initiative of the revolutionary power should seem to qualify as an issue to be determined on its own merits only, not as a link in the chain of a general political offensive. The concession expected from the status-quo power should be acceptable per se.

The status-quo power should remember, in planning its own defense against tactics of this sort, that nuclear weapons are equally dangerous to its opponents, that they know it, that they cannot escape the grip of nuclear fear and cannot, in the last analysis, assume too great risks. In measuring the risks of initiative, each power must include in its calculations the degree of psychological resistance it expects to encounter in the other nuclear power. If this resistance seems to be too stiff, the initiative might be abandoned for fear of serious consequences out of proportion to the expected gain. It is difficult for the status-quo power to use the tactics of piecemeal advance, because the nature of its quiet policy does not stimulate such a power to assume the initiatives which would confront the revolutionary power with the same dilemma of gradual and local retreats or a nuclear war.

The crisis which broke out in October, 1962, over the installation of Soviet offensive weapons (intermediate missiles and planes capable of carrying nuclear warheads) in Cuba, at a distance of a hundred miles from the American coast, which was there unprotected by a warning system, illustrated the possibility of a serious miscalculation. The Soviet

Union probably did not expect a sharp reaction. The naval blockade ordered by the President placed the U.S.S.R. before a most unpleasant dilemma of either retreating or responding by force to the use of force by the United States Navy against Soviet vessels which would have refused to be searched on the high seas. The two countries were placed on nuclear alert. For a short time it was unknown whether a chain of events would not end in the catastrophe which neither power desired. Then the Soviet Union retreated and consented to withdraw its weapons. It suffered a humiliating setback all the most visible because it backed down in fear of nuclear war and in spite of the fact that the American blockade, extended in peacetime to ships of all nations, was questionable from the point of view of international law.

This miscalculation proved once more that a nuclear power should never challenge a peer in the zone of its immediate and most vital national interests, such as the Carribean area is for the United States. By contrast, the United States refrained in an analogous situation from interfering within the Soviet zone at the time of the Hungarian uprising. For this reason the political offensive usually, though not always, develops on the battlefields of the gray areas of the Third World located between the two rival blocs.

The nuclear stalemate has produced another political consequence regarding the same areas. A great power which intends to use force outside its own sphere of most vital interests in order to settle a dispute with a smaller nation situated in the gray area where the interests of both nuclear powers intermingle must take into consideration the risk of a reactive intervention by the other nuclear power. Ordinarily this risk is not high because neither nuclear power would be quick to risk a nuclear war for the sake of its influence in the gray area, but it exists nevertheless. Hence, the freedom to use force against a small nation outside the zone of the other great power's most vital interests is now restricted by lingering uncertainty concerning the reaction of that power and by the possibility of a direct clash which could end in nuclear war.

By contrast, a nuclear power continues to have the freedom to use force in dealing with smaller nations located within the zone of its own most vital interests. Its nuclear opponent cannot openly interfere because this would amount to a direct challenge to the nuclear power which the latter might answer by using all the means at its disposal. The United States refrained in 1956 from any interference with the Soviet military repression of the Hungarian revolution precisely because it was not sure that the Soviet Union would not decide to defend its Eastern European zone of influence by nuclear means if necessary. If in 1961 the United States had undertaken a direct military action against Cuba, it is more than probable that the Soviet Union would have abstained, for the same reasons, from any effective interference.

The balance of terror has fundamentally modified the problem of security for both nuclear powers. The former security of the United States, due to the barrier of the two oceans, and the relative security of the Soviet Union, due to its immense territory, are both gone. Space has become an insufficient protection. The time required for the full mobilization of human and material resources is no longer available to either power. The other very important source of American security in the past, the balance of power among the great powers of the Eastern Hemisphere, disappeared a long time ago, actually prior to 1914.

THE MASSIVE DETERRENT

The nuclear stalemate is founded on the possession by both the United States and the Soviet Union of strategic (megaton) nuclear weapons which are often called the massive deterrent. The existence of this deterrent provides a reasonably solid guarantee against nuclear war but offers no guidance for foreign policy. The massive deterrent means that a nuclear power has the capacity to annihilate itself together with its rival. If only one great power had the nuclear monopoly, its massive deterrent would have an altogether different meaning, for it would have the capacity to destroy its opponent without endangering its own national life. But in the present situation the influence of the massive deterrent on international developments is rather sharply circumscribed. Its potency depends on the calculation of the adversaries. If they truly believe that the massive deterrent would be used in certain circumstances, it really deters. If they have at least some lingering doubt about it, the massive deterrent can still exercise a restraining influence. If they think that it would be foolish on the part of the other power to have recourse to nuclear weapons, the massive deterrent becomes a useless instrument for prevention.

There is not the slightest doubt that nuclear weapons would be instantly used by either nuclear power in defense against a nuclear attack on its own national territory. All cases below the level of this obvious form of self-defense are tainted with varying degrees of uncertainty. The person or persons who would have to make the deadly decision would measure the stakes to be defended with strategic nuclear weapons against the obvious consequences for the national homeland. No one can tell with perfect assurance whether any stake, short of national defense against a direct nuclear attack, would be deemed worth the consequences of unleashing an all-out nuclear war. Which ally or which foreign territory would be considered so vital as to induce the decision to use the massive deterrent? Possibly none. At any rate, a nuclear power must possess other means of action than the use of the massive deterrent; otherwise, it might be pushed by its exclusive reliance on the massive deterrent toward a choice between annihilating itself and the rival power or doing nothing.

In the last analysis, the massive deterrent provides an absolutely necessary guarantee against a nuclear attack on the national territory but very little besides. A nuclear power relying only on its massive deterrent would be practically disarmed in all or most of the cases where its own territory would not be attacked.

Reluctance to use the massive deterrent in cases other than self-defense could be strenghtened by personal considerations, by the realization that this time the government would truly be in the same boat as the whole population. The personal safety of members of governments and their families was usually not endangered in former wars, at least not by enemy action. They resided in the safe hinterland, far from the battlefields. Their greatest personal risk was that of losing power or being punished by their own countrymen, after the defeat. The trials of the political and military leaders of the Axis powers following the Second World War added a new political risk. The suicide of Hitler and the assassination of Mussolini threw a new light on the problem of the personal safety of national leaders in case of defeat in a total war. But nuclear weapons would pose a direct threat to this safety from the very moment of the beginning of hostilities. They would certainly be used against the national capital and the temporary residence of the enemy political and military leaders; they and their families would be exposed to danger almost as much as ordinary citizens.

The political effectiveness of the massive deterrent is proportionate to the degree of probability which the adversary attaches to its use under certain circumstances. This calculus of probabilities is full of uncertainties. The past behavior of a nuclear power is not necessarily a safe guide for making predictions about its future behavior. It is true that the United States was unwilling to use nuclear weapons during the period of its monopoly. The Soviet Union exploded the first atomic bomb in 1949 and the hydrogen bomb in 1953. Only in the fifties did it begin to develop a means of intercontinental delivery (first, long-range planes and later, about 1957, ballistic missiles of intercontinental range). Taking into account this Soviet time-lag in the acquisition of an atomic stockpile and the means of delivery, it can be said that the United States had a nuclear monopoly between 1945 and perhaps as late as the middle fifties. During those years the United States was the paramount power; it had the nuclear monopoly and hence its geographical security was yet impregnable, and it had at its disposal all the time that would be needed to mobilize its vast resources. The Soviet blockade of Berlin in 1948 supplied a test of American intentions. The United States responded to the challenge by the airlift but did not try to send an armed convoy through the Soviet lines. If it had sent a convoy, the Soviet Union would probably have backed down rather than face a protracted war which would have exposed its homeland to American nuclear attacks and which did not promise to end in a Soviet victory. This restrained American reaction to the Soviet challenge in Berlin seemed to prove beyond any doubt that the United States was most reluctant to create a situation which might have led to hostilities even at a time when it possessed most of the assets. However, a hasty conclusion would not have been warranted. The same president of the United States who did not send an armed convoy to Berlin in 1948 had not hesitated in 1945 to order the dropping of atomic bombs on the cities of a nearly defeated Japan and in 1950 made the rather unexpected decision to oppose by force the invasion of South Korea. As a matter of fact, the Soviet Union does not seem to be sure that the United States would be unwilling to use nuclear weapons except in self-defense; Soviet policy usually stops short of the brink of subjecting American will-power to a severe test.

The Cuban crisis in 1962 demonstrated American readiness to face all possible risks in the event of a direct threat to the safety of the United States, and the Soviet reluctance to move to the brink of catastrophe.

The Soviet Union has a psychological edge on the United States. The difficulty of preventing press leaks in a democratic society, as well as the need to prepare public opinion for any vital executive decision, stand in the way of a sudden and unexpected use of strategic nuclear weapons. These conditions do not exist in a totalitarian regime, whose intentions are always veiled in complete secrecy. It does not consult its population beforehand but musters popular support after its policies have already been implemented. The totalitarian regime enjoys the advantage of leaving its foreign opponents in the dark and widely guessing concerning its willingness or unwillingness to use nuclear weapons under certain circumstances. By keeping foreign governments ignorant of its true intentions, the totalitarian regime can manipulate the fear of nuclear war, making this fear a tool of pressure in international affairs.

The massive deterrents form together a sort of nuclear umbrella under whose protection a nuclear power can make use of conventional force, short of challenging directly the most vital interests of the other nuclear power. If the two nuclear powers have visibly unequal conventional forces in being, the stronger one might be tempted to undertake a local military operation. The stronger power would expect that its nuclear rival would not dare to riposte by unleashing an all-out nuclear war and, unable to cope with the local challenge by conventional means, would be compelled to accept the accomplished fact. The effect of the nuclear stalemate might well be to give a marked advantage to the nuclear power which has superior conventional forces; the existence of this conventional superiority against the background of nuclear parity provides an asset in diplomatic transactions, because it widens the range of the means of pressure. The opponent is aware that the hand of the other nuclear power is strengthened by its superiority in conventional arms whose use seems more probable than that of nuclear weapons.

The nuclear parity has created a situation in which the massive deterrents cannot play any active role in international politics. Their role is the passive one of neutralizing each other. However, the balance of terror does not altogether preclude the possibility of a nuclear war. This possibility exists in the following cases:

A. If a nuclear power were convinced that it alone had solved the problem of "bearable" losses and that its surprise attack would force the enemy to surrender immediately.

B. If a nuclear power were misled by a false alarm and were to start nuclear hostilities in the belief that they are only a counterblow against a presumed enemy attack. Error in the warning system is not out of the question, and the newest weapons might preclude a useful correction of the error. Manned planes can, of course, be recalled from their punitive mission, but missiles, once launched, cannot be stopped on their way to enemy targets.

In the past a country was forewarned of invasion not only by the increasing tension in relations with an opponent but also by the mobilization of enemy forces and their concentration on the frontiers. (It is true that the latter forewarning was peculiar to land forces. A naval or air attack could come as a surprise even in the pre-nuclear age, as evidenced by the Japanese actions in 1904 and 1941.) Today, international tension is a daily fact of life; the government planning a surprise attack would, if anything, attempt to lull the adversary by a sham effort to reduce tension. Modern strategic forces need not be mobilized; they are always ready to strike. The enemy cannot be sure what the intentions are of merchant ships possibly armed with intermediate ballistic missiles or that missile-armed and undetected submarines do not take battle stations off his coasts or that camouflaged launching sites are not about to strike or, in the near future, that an orbiting bomber-satellite will not discharge its deadly warheads. This perpetual feeling of insecurity and the parallel need to be constantly on the alert create a tense atmosphere in which a fatal mistake could be committed in "retaliating" against a supposed enemy attack erroneously signaled by radar confused by meteors or other celestial phenomena.

C. If one nuclear power were unwise in encroaching on the most vital interests of the other power and thus made it feel that it must use its massive deterrent or else be compelled to surrender without war. This possibility is rather unlikely because neither nuclear power is eager to test the will-power of the other in this way.

As pointed out before, the use of the massive deterrent is completely certain only in the event of a nuclear attack on the national territory. In all other cases unusual fortitude would be required to plunge one's country into an all-out nuclear war with its unpredictable scale of destruction. Crucial questions hang over all alliances entered into by the nuclear powers: Would all these commitments be honored or only those deemed of the greatest possible importance to the major ally, and if honored, would only conventional weapons be used for fear of provoking a nuclear retaliation? As a result of the nuclear parity, for the first time in history the full implementation of a mutual assistance treaty threatens the survival of the major ally.

Western Europeans wondered during the period of American nuclear monopoly whether Americans were trigger-happy and would unleash a general war without any pressing reason. Their fears proved to be utterly ill-founded. They now wonder whether Americans might not be so reluctant to use nuclear weapons that they would rather see Western Europe occupied by Soviet troops than expose their own cities to destruction. The American protective nuclear shield, which had been the guarantee of Western European security, was dented by the Soviet acquisition of nuclear parity.

If the Soviet-Chinese inter-allied problems were discussed as freely as the NATO problems are, we should probably learn that the Chinese are haunted by the same doubt as to whether their major ally would stand by them at the risk of the destruction of his own cities. The nuclear parity poses the same problems for the two rival blocs, except for the additional problems created for NATO by the inferiority of its conventional forces. This inferiority makes it doubtful whether a conventional Soviet advance into Western Europe could be effectively warded off by conventional or even tactical nuclear means of defense. Western European thinking tries to escape the dilemma by ruling out the possibility of any conventional warfare in Europe which would not immediately become a full-scale nuclear war. However, Western Europe cannot be completely sure that the United States would use its massive deterrent against Soviet territory in order to repel any Soviet attack even if this attack had a limited objective such as the occupation of West Berlin. This uncertainty regarding American intentions compels a growing number of Western Europeans to think of a nuclear force independent of American veto, either a national force (the British and French way of trying to solve the dilemma) or a collective Western European force equally free of American control. The British possession of nuclear weapons is of little comfort for the continental countries who know the British vulnerability to nuclear warfare and would not expect Britain to use these weapons except in strict self-defense.

The present insecurity of Western Europe is due not only to uncertainty about the American decision in the event of a Soviet invasion, but also to two other factors. First, even the largest continental nations have no massive deterrent of their own and must rely on the United States.

Secondly, they are unable or unwilling to redress the imbalance in conventional forces and thus preclude the success of a Soviet conventional attack.

The problem of the allies of a nuclear power is twofold: they cannot be sure that their powerful ally will use nuclear weapons when these are necessary to defend them against enemy attack, and at the same time they cannot be sure that he will refrain from using such weapons at a time or place deemed unnecessary by the allies. The exceedingly short period of time which the ballistic missiles allow for any warning system raises one of the most important questions of our era. The head of government of a nuclear power would have barely half an hour for receiving the report of an impending enemy attack, convincing himself that the report is most probably correct, alerting the retaliatory force, and finally ordering the counterblow. He would know that his decision is irreversible. This short period would leave no time for consultation with allies; yet their fate would also be vitally affected. As a matter of fact, the head of government would have no time to consult anyone, including other members of his government.

In other cases where the massive deterrent could conceivably be used, i.e., for the defense of an ally or of a territory strategically or economically vital to the alliance, the nuclear power would have more time to consult its friends. The reaction would not be automatic, as it would be in the event of an enemy nuclear attack on the national territory, and it would probably follow a thorough examination of the case. It is also probable that all or some of the allies would be asked to give their advice. But sufficient time for consultation does not solve the problem of who would be entitled to make the decision to use the massive deterrent or not to use it. Most probably the nuclear power would never delegate this power of decision to any allied body, because its territory would be the first target of retaliation. If it delegated powers of decision to an allied body, would the decision be made unanimously or by some specified majority and would the nuclear power retain the veto that could cancel the collective decision? The present distribution of intermediate missiles with American control over the nuclear warheads does not revoke the American monopoly of the ultimate decision. The transfer of a part of the American massive deterrent to NATO would not change the essence of the present situation if the order to use this NATO nuclear force could come only from an American general in his capacity as NATO supreme commander, because understandably he would never issue this order without permission from the president of the United States. If the supreme commander were a European general and had to follow the instructions of a collective NATO body in which the American veto would not operate, it is not very probable that the thirteen European NATO governments would have the time to consult fully and, if they had, that they would agree among themselves. The distribution of nuclear weapons to each of the NATO allies would make all of them masters of the fateful decision, but the risk of an error in the warning system or of a politically unwise decision to unleash nuclear war would be multiplied by fifteen. This is probably one of the reasons why the Soviet Union has not distributed nuclear weapons to its allies; another may be its limited trust in their loyalty.

Another possible solution for the American allies in Europe is to build up a joint European nuclear deterrent founded on their own production of warheads and means of delivery and independent of American control. If Britain and France pooled their nuclear resources, they could, together with other European NATO countries, create a European collective massive deterrent. However, they would first have to solve the very formidable problem of contriving a joint authority which would have the right to use the European nuclear force in those cases of extreme urgency which would allow no time for consultation among the allies.

THE NUCLEAR CLUB

Any nation which was formerly one of the dominant powers in the world cannot help feeling humiliated and insecure because of its dependence on a nuclear ally. The decisions of the nuclear power escape its control, and the interests of the two countries coincide (they are allies for this very reason) but can never be identical. The security of the non-nuclear ally rests, in the last analysis, on the massive deterrent of the nuclear ally, who may always elect not to use it. This dependence on the major ally inevitably restricts the freedom of the non-nuclear party to the alliance in the formulation of its foreign policy. This is the problem which exists, actually or potentially, in the relations between the United States, on the one hand, and the senior NATO allies such as Britain, France, and Germany, on the other. It probably poisons Soviet-Chinese relations. It is not surprising that the desire for greater independence from the major ally takes the form, among others, of an ambition to become a nuclear power and thus the master of one's national destiny. Sir Winston Churchill tactfully but clearly expressed these feelings in a speech on March 1, 1955, in the House of Commons. Explaining the reasons for the British decision to acquire nuclear weapons, he said:

> Unless we make a contribution of our own—that is the point which I am pressing—we cannot be sure that in an emergency the resources of other powers would be planned exactly as we would wish or that the targets which would threaten us most would be given what we consider the necessary priority, or the deserved priority of such cardinal importance that it would really be a matter of life or death for us.

General De Gaulle advances the same argument in favor of the French acquisition of nuclear weapons. At the present time there are four nuclear powers—two with a complete nuclear arsenal, Britain short of fully adequate means of delivery, and France, which began its nuclear career only recently. The existence of three nuclear Western powers will complicate the Soviet computation of risks. The calculus of probabilities regarding Western reactions to Soviet initiatives which would seriously affect the West will become even more difficult than it is now. It will not be enough to guess correctly the possible reaction of the United States if two other Western powers can independently decide to use their own massive deterrents. The security of the NATO area will be increased in proportion to Soviet uncertainty regarding Western reactions.

However, the multiplication of centers of nuclear power increases the risks of nuclear conflagration. Judged by the experience of postwar years, neither the United States nor the Soviet Union is trigger-happy with nuclear weapons. Both Britain and France are status-quo powers, and the nature of their foreign policies does not warrant any fear that either of them would unleash nuclear hostilities. But can one be sure that other governments, when they acquire their own nuclear arsenals, will be equally prudent? Common sense would offer a reassuring answer. The threat of retaliation should restrain all future nuclear powers as much as it does the present ones from foolishly playing with nuclear fire. Unfortunately, governments are not always guided by common sense.

This argument is usually advanced to explain the American refusal to share nuclear secrets with the NATO allies. It might be the reason for the Soviet reluctance to help China in acquiring nuclear weapons. Another reason for the American and Soviet unwillingness to assist their major allies in becoming nuclear powers might be the realization that this would notably reduce their dependence on Washington and Moscow respectively.

The problems facing an advanced nation which intends to join the nuclear club are best understood in the light of discussions between the proponents and opponents of the French national nuclear force. According to the plans of the French government, this force should consist in the late sixties of supersonic planes armed with atomic bombs; it should reach its full development in the seventies when it is expected to include nuclear-powered submarines, land-based launching sites, and missiles armed with nuclear warheads.

Those Frenchmen who advocate the acquisition of a nationally controlled nuclear force argue as follows:

1. A nuclear power has a greater weight in international politics and a stronger voice in inter-allied discussions.

2. The major ally might decline to use its nuclear force in certain cases where the vital interests of non-nuclear allies would be involved.

Dependence on the nuclear shield provided by an allied but foreign nation results in political dependence.

3. Modern armed forces are of no use if they are not armed with nuclear weapons, in particular tactical weapons. An army or a navy armed only with conventional weapons gradually becomes obsolete or must rely even for tactical nuclear weapons on supplies controlled by the nuclear ally.

4. Nuclear research and the production of nuclear weapons stimulate scientific and technological progress and the development of certain key industries, such as electronics, as well as plants for the industrial use of atomic energy. A non-nuclear nation is doomed to lag behind the technological and industrial progress of the nuclear powers.

The arguments advanced by the opponents can be summarized as follows:

1. The cost of nuclear armaments is prohibitive and nations less rich than the United States and the Soviet Union cannot reasonably hope ever to become the peers of those two principal nuclear powers. The effort required from a nation which aspires to membership in the nuclear club entails, first, covering the road of scientific exploration and industrial production along which the United States and the Soviet Union have already traveled for several years. Even if the aspiring nation, at the price of great financial sacrifices, achieved nuclear parity with the two principal powers, it would have to continue to spend great sums of money in order to stay in the ever-continuing and costly race. If it could not afford to spend as much as the United States and the Soviet Union, out of its much smaller national budget, all its financial sacrifices might result in the acquisition of a nuclear force which would be inadequate to deter a major nuclear power. In the process, it might run a serious risk of neglecting its conventional armed forces and endangering its social welfare, since a great percentage of its over-all budget would be absorbed by nuclear expenditures.

2. A country with a relatively small territory, like France or any other European country, would always remain in a position of inferiority vis-à-vis another nuclear power which is endowed with a very large territory. Its population could be swiftly obliterated by a small number of multimegaton bombs. Hence, its nuclear deterrent would have less value psychologically.

3. The use of nuclear weapons against a small nation, or the threat of their use, could be prevented by a major nuclear power if the latter wanted to interpose its protective shield in defense of the small nation. The example of Britain in November, 1956, is a case in point. According to one view, Britain, a nuclear power, did not dare to use the nuclear threat against Egypt, allegedly for fear of a Soviet retaliation.

It is interesting to note that those Frenchmen who oppose a French nuclear force do not argue against it on humanitarian grounds but propose alternative solutions which they deem more practical than the acquisition of a national nuclear force. They propose as an alternative a collective nuclear deterrent which would be placed under either a joint NATO control or a combined Western European administration.

Whatever view one prefers to take of the matter, there is no existing force that could indefinitely restrict the nuclear club to its present four members. The peaceful use of atomic energy, which will eventually become worldwide, will help in the accumulation of materials, such as plutonium, which are required for the production of nuclear weapons. Nuclear know-how will become universal. Even if it were politically feasible, an agreement between the present nuclear powers could not effectively shut the door of the nuclear club to the new candidates. The three original signatories of the treaty on the prohibition of nuclear tests (the United States, the Soviet Union, and Britain) are unable to enforce the ban on nations which refuse to accede to the treaty. It is inconceivable that the three powers would act in concert against their allies (France, for example, or China) and jointly undertake a punitive action to compel them to refrain from acquiring a nuclear stockpile and the means of delivery.

Sooner or later, perhaps earlier than generally expected, new members will force the door open and will enroll themselves in the nuclear club. Those countries which are highly industrialized, like France, or in the process of rapid industrialization, like China, will in due time reach the point of nuclear saturation and become members of the senior club which now counts two eminent members, the United States and the Soviet Union. Others will be capable of joining only the junior club of those nations whose nuclear arsenal would be inadequate to threaten the great powers with obliteration.

An increase in the membership of the senior club will mark the date of the final disruption of the present basically bipolar nuclear system with its two dominating centers, the United States and the Soviet Union.

THE LIMITED USE OF FORCE

Force can be used, without involving the belligerents in an all-out nuclear war, in the following cases: (1) a *limited war* in which both nuclear powers would directly participate but would refrain, by a tacit or formal agreement, from attacking each other's homeland and would thereby limit the zone of combat to the third countries; (2) a *peripheral war* in which neither of the nuclear powers, or only one of them, would take part openly but in which both would be vitally interested; (3) a *local war* fought between small countries without undue interference, direct or indirect, by the nuclear powers; (4) *the use of force*, or the threat of its use, by a nuclear or other great power *against a small country* without interference by the other great powers; (5) *the domestic use of force* (a coup, a revolution, a civil war, a colonial insurrection). This domestic use of of force can be of international concern because of its possible repercussions on the vital interests of the great powers.

The concept of a *limited war* is founded on several assumptions:

1. It is assumed that this type of war would be fought by the nuclear powers for vital stakes, such as Western Europe or the Near East, but less vital than the defense of their own national territory.

2. Since the stakes are less than national self-preservation, the nuclear belligerents would tacitly or otherwise agree to refrain from using strategic nuclear weapons and to limit the hostilities to the use of other weapons, possibly including tactical nuclear weapons.[1]

3. The concept of the limited war assumes that neither belligerent would pursue unlimited goals such as the unconditional surrender of the enemy. Obviously, unlimited war aims call for defense by all available means without restriction.

4. It must be assumed that the allies of the nuclear belligerents would consent, or submit, to the use of their territories as the battlefields of this limited war.

5. The last and most pervasive assumption is that, through the entire course of the war, the political and military leaders and the populations of the belligerent countries would remain impervious to strong and irrational emotions and would refrain from using strategic nuclear weapons even when the alternative is certain, if limited, defeat. Both the governments and the populations concerned would have to show an unprecedented degree of self-control and moderation.

The limitation of weapons implies a limitation of war aims. Yet it does not signify that such a war would necessarily end in the restoration of the *status quo ante bellum*. It would be absurd for a nuclear power to start a limited war or to create a situation leading to its outbreak without any desire to modify the status quo. If it were lucky in its "limited" warfare, it would impose its terms on the defeated enemy. This raises the question of which "limited" losses would be considered limited by the vanquished party. Would the loss of oil-bearing fields in the Near East or of continental Western Europe or of Eastern Europe be deemed preferable to the prospect of a desperate recourse to strategic nuclear weapons? Which "lesser" losses, for instance that of West Germany, Yugoslavia, Czechoslovakia, East Germany, or Iraq, would be acceptable for either nuclear power? No one can answer these questions with any certainty.

If the nuclear power which had not started the war were to prove the

[1] Strategic (megaton) weapons are those which are destined to be used for the destruction of the enemy's weapons (his massive deterrent) and/or his human and economic potential. Their use would be considered the decisive factor in winning the war. Tactical nuclear weapons, measured in kilotons or their fractions, would be used in winning battles but would not be considered promptly decisive for the outcome of the war.

superiority of its arms, it would probably not be content to re-establish the *status quo ante bellum*. It would avail itself of the victory obtained in the limited war to impose on the aggressor limited changes in the status quo. Of course, there exists a third possibility—a limited war could be fought to a standstill and end in the restoration of the status quo or in its equivalent.

Total nuclear war could be unleashed by one nuclear power, but a limited war could be fought only with the assent of both powers. A limited war can be waged if both parties have adequate military forces for this sort of combat; if one of them is capable of waging a major war only with the full use of strategic nuclear weapons, the other might move swiftly in attaining its limited objectives and leave to its enemy the choice of either retaliating by a strategic attack on the aggressor's homeland or accepting the loss of important assets without fighting. The capacity for a limited war (and also for a peripheral war) is composed of two elements: (1) The presence within or close to the area to be contested of sufficient ground troops to resist the initial attack, or the capacity to transport them very rapidly to the theater of operations. Otherwise the aggressor might move swiftly to create a *fait accompli* which could not be negated by limited warfare. (2) An economic and industrial potential sufficient to maintain the forces deployed in a limited or peripheral war (if the latter were to drag on).

The capacity of the NATO and associated powers to raise and supply forces capable of fighting limited or peripheral wars is potentially much superior to that of the Soviet Union and its own allies (except for Chinese manpower). The United States, the United Kingdom and the European-populated members of the Commonwealth, and the European NATO countries, represent together approximately 500 million people and at least two-thirds of the industrial output of the world. The Soviet and Eastern European populations together comprise some 315 million against the aggregate population of the NATO countries, North America and Europe, amounting to 450 million. The Soviet bloc, including China, accounts for a billion people but also for a much smaller accumulation of scientific and technological skills and for less than one-third of the industrial output of the world. It would appear that the Western bloc could easily afford all three capabilities—strategic nuclear weapons, tactical nuclear weapons, and conventional armaments, the latter two supported by any required amount of military manpower. If the Soviet Union enjoys a notable superiority in the ground forces which face each other in Europe, this superiority is not related to the statistical data of the problem.

The vital areas for which the nuclear powers could conceivably wage a limited war are located in the Eastern Hemisphere. Hence, a land power located in that hemisphere would enjoy a logistic superiority over a naval power situated in the Western Hemisphere. The land power could wage a limited war relying on its own and other continental communications and supplies. The sea power must move troops and supplies across the ocean and cope with the enemy's submarine and air threat to its communications. The underlying assumption of a limited war is that only the homelands of the nuclear powers would be exempt from strategic enemy attacks, not their navies and merchant marine. This technological problem of the naval power simply illustrates the old truth that power loses effectiveness as the distance between its sources and the theater of operations increases. This truth suffers one modern exception—strategic nuclear weapons which can be delivered almost instantly over great distances. However, the logistic problem of the sea power was twice solved in the world wars. Moreover, Soviet and, much more, Chinese land transportation facilities are still inadequate for modern purposes and stretch tenuously over enormous territories. The heavy demands placed on Soviet railroads (about 83 per cent of all transportation) have not yet been met with a rail network comparable to that of the United States or Western Europe. The density of hard-surface roads in the Soviet Union is much lower than in the West, and water transport accounts for only 12 per cent of the freight turnover and 3 per cent of passenger traffic. Thus, the Soviet and Chinese logistic asset of inland transportation is not so great as might be imagined from a quick glance at the map; their transportation difficulties would be greater in Asia than in Europe. Finally, the concept of the limited war rules out attacks on the homelands of nuclear powers but not on their inland transportation in other countries.

The limited war could be fought with either conventional or tactical nuclear weapons. However, the modernization of the armed forces of nuclear powers and their main allies suggests that tactical nuclear weapons will finally form an integral part of the usual armaments. Perhaps no future major war (the limited one would be a major war) will be fought without the use of these weapons.

The current definition of tactical weapons in kilotons is not very meaningful. There is a tremendous difference between a fraction-of-a-kiloton shell fired from a bazooka and a several kiloton bomb of the size of the one dropped on Nagasaki. Would the belligerents be willing to restrict the caliber of tactical weapons and forego the military advantages of the use of larger weapons because their allies would want them to spare the cities and civilians? The distinction between the strategic and tactical use of nuclear weapons on the basis that troops and military installations are the only legitimate targets for tactical weapons does not make much sense in heavily populated countries where the military targets (depots, freight yards, bridges, docks, etc.) are frequently located close to civilian targets. Hence the political problem: would the countries to be protected by the use of tactical weapons consent to risk their own destruction rather than be subjugated by the enemy? They would probably prefer to hold this vital decision in their own hands. For those countries which are destined to become the battlefields of limited wars the graduated deterrent of these wars would seem, in effect, not very different from the massive deterrent.

There is an additional risk that the nuclear powers, protected by their agreement to grant each other immunity in their respective homelands, might eventually be tempted to use megaton weapons on each other's military targets located in the third countries, with foreseeable results for the latter countries.

To take Western Europe as an illustration, an all-out nuclear war fought for its sake would entail the devastation of both the United States and the Soviet Union, while Western Europe itself would have a chance of escaping nuclear destruction. This eventuality holds little appeal for the nuclear powers. A *limited* war fought for the same stake would guarantee the United States and the Soviet Union immunity from nuclear devastations; their national territories would enjoy the status of sanctuaries inaccessible to strategic weapons. But Western Europe, the battlefield of this limited war, would pay the price of vast destruction due, among other causes, to the use of large tactical nuclear weapons. This consummation has little to commend itself to the Western Europeans. Of course, the Eastern Europeans would be equally exposed to the fury of the limited war. The "best" solution for all concerned would be to wage the limited war with conventional weapons, if the modern technology of war had not advanced to its present stage.

Limited war carries with it the constant danger of escalating into an all-out war. First, a belligerent, unwilling to accept a limited defeat, might decide to use its last card and to attack the source of the enemy's power, its homeland. Secondly, an error in the warning system, more likely to occur in wartime and more likely to be credited then, could become the signal for an all-out war.

Tactical weapons would so far increase the firepower of modern armies that a limited war could be fought only with maximum mobility and speed and a minimum concentration of troops. It would be a mistake to think that the use of tactical nuclear weapons would reduce the need for a large ground force, a deficiency in manpower supposedly being offset by high firepower. Assuming that both opponents would be equally well armed with tactical nuclear weapons, their losses would be comparable and would probably be very high. In fact, the use of tactical nuclear weapons presumes the existence of a very large trained manpower. One cannot exclude the possibility that the high rate of casualties would force the belligerents to build deep shelters and eventually to resort to a static warfare of attrition.

Whatever the disadvantages of large-caliber tactical nuclear weapons to the countries which would serve as battlefields, these weapons might eventually become "conventional" armaments, just as firearms replaced the bow. The desire to have greater firepower for less money will accelerate this process.

The third possible form of international war is the *peripheral* war.

It would be fought with limited weapons and for limited objectives and would not directly involve *both* nuclear powers. Either one or both of them would wage it by proxy, i.e., by supplying and financing the belligerents. The fact that both of them would not be openly engaged and would not face each other on the battlefields presupposes that the stakes would be less vital than those of a limited war. The danger of the peripheral war escalating into an all-out war between the nuclear powers would be much less than in a limited war in which both of them would be actual belligerents. The peripheral war need not be a petty affair, suggested by its other name, the brushfire war. It could be protracted and costly, as the Korean War was. Tactical nuclear weapons could be used in the peripheral war especially if one of the nuclear powers directly participated in the hostilities. The peripheral war could be waged without the direct participation of the nuclear powers, which would then finance the war effort of their respective friends and supply them with war materiel.

The fourth kind of war is a *local* one fought by two or several smaller nations without support from the great powers. Such a war would be conceivable only if the great powers thought that its outcome would not substantially affect their own important interests.

Force could be used under still different circumstances. A strong state, faced with a threat by a weaker state to its unimpeded access to vital resources or to its international prestige, might be strongly tempted to use force. The only effective restraint would be the fear of intervention by another great power on behalf of the small country. The natonalization of the Suez Canal was interpreted by the British and French governments as a menace to their vital supplies of Near Eastern oil. After an abortive invasion, however, they desisted from a further use of force against Egypt under combined American-Soviet pressure. The Soviet Union simultaneously used force in Hungary where a revolution had challenged its political, ideological, and military position in Eastern Europe. Since no complication arose in relation to the other nuclear power, the Soviet use of force was entirely successful.

The United States compelled the Soviet Union to liquidate its offensive military installations in Cuba by the threat of the use of naval force against Soviet shipping in the Caribbean. India forcibly expelled Portugal from Goa and was in turn confronted with the Chinese attack on her northern borders. These and other postwar events indicate that resort to force has been rather frequent in our nuclear age though always on a limited scale.

Finally, force can be used domestically but with possible international repercussions. A regime or government friendly to one rival bloc could be confronted with a civil war or actually overthrown in a coup or revolution; this domestic use of force could end in the establishment of a new regime or government friendly to the opposite bloc. If this reversal threatened to affect important interests of the former bloc or of one of the great powers belonging to that bloc, or to initiate a chain reaction in neighboring countries, the bloc or great power concerned might intervene by force to restore its former influence and to reinstall a friendly government. This is what the Soviet Union succeeded in doing in 1956 in Hungary and what the United States failed to achieve in 1961 in Cuba.

The modern great power might be faced with a type of warfare for which usually its armed forces are the least ready, namely guerrilla warfare. This type of warfare is not peculiar to our time. Napoleon was confronted with it in Spain and Russia. It would be a great mistake to view guerrilla warfare as a purely military problem which could be solved by the proper training of regular troops to be used against the guerrillas. The secrecy and ubiquity of guerrilla operations are unthinkable without the complicity of the local population who, some through conviction and others through fear of reprisals, assist the guerrillas by providing them with shelter, food, intelligence information, and recruits. Because of these grassroots contacts, the guerrillas can operate by night and hide by day, often camouflaged as innocent civilians. Foreign regular troops fight under very difficult conditions. They might not elicit any notable support from the local population. Of a different ethnic stock, they can be detected immediately, while the guerrilla fighter can easily lose himself in a crowd of his countrymen.

The political problem consists in finding native supporters and recruiting them for anti-guerrilla operations and generally attracting the population to one's side. If the native government, opposed by the guerrillas, is inefficient, corrupt, or blind to the need for social reforms, the powers which support it might be fighting a losing battle. Their support will be interpreted, not only by hostile propaganda but also by public opinion back home, as help extended to the reactionary forces. Foreign assistance might prove futile, if native soldiers, fighting for the official government and armed by the supporting great power, see no valid reason why they should risk their lives in combating their fellow-countrymen, the guerrillas. Direct intervention by the armed forces of the great power concerned is possible, but its success depends largely on winning the sympathy of the local population.

The British were able to eliminate guerrilla warfare in Malaya by effecting a large-scale resettlement of the population in the areas concerned. The French failed in Indochina, where eventually they faced regular insurgent armies, and in Algeria. But for general support by the Algerian Moslems, it would be difficult to understand why the French army, half-a-million strong, was not able, after seven years of insurrection, to destroy guerrilla detachments that were, according to all accounts, numerically rather feeble. The unlucky landing in Cuba in 1961 failed because it did not evoke any visible response from the Cuban population.

Guerrilla warfare aims at exhausting the power of resistance of the adversary and compelling him to accept his defeat.

THE FORCES IN BEING AND THE POTENTIAL

Tangible power is usually divided into two categories: the military forces in being, which can be used immediately, and the power potential, i.e., those national resources which can be mobilized in time of war and thus determine the eventual strength of the fully mobilized national power. This distinction was very important in past, conventional wars. A great power usually had the time required to mobilize fully its resources in manpower and economic capacity and to shift its production to war purposes. Rarely was there a danger of its being overrun quickly by enemy armies and thus prevented from fully mobilizing its power potential. Nuclear weapons have changed this situation. It now seems possible that a total surrender could be imposed on a nation as soon as its forces in being have been destroyed and before its power potential can be mobilized. It also seems possible that the power potential itself could be destroyed irreplaceably.

An all-out nuclear war would have to be fought with the forces in being, i.e., such military manpower, such strategic nuclear weapons, and such means of delivery as would be ready in peacetime. For those who believe in the theory of a "broken-back" war, the power potential would retain its importance even in an all-out nuclear war. The nuclear hostilities would open the war but would be accompanied by other military and naval operations; this first stage would be followed by a period of possibly protracted military, naval, and air hostilities presumably supported by whatever means of strategic nuclear warfare survived the first stage of mutual nuclear destruction. This rather optimistic version of an all-out war does not underestimate the crucial importance of nuclear forces in being. If these forces were inadequate for an immediate and crippling counterblow, the war would be decided in the first stage because there would be for the vanquished party no choice but to surrender or suffer the penalty of a complete devastation of its territory, now wide-open to further nuclear attacks. Those who do not believe in the theory of the "broken-back" war have to deny the possibility of mobilizing the power potential in an all-out war, which would be consumed during the stage of mutual nuclear attacks. In both versions the forces in being have acquired an importance incomparably greater than they ever possessed before.

The same could be said of the conventional armed forces. If two hostile powers possess equal nuclear forces—so that both are deterred from initiating nuclear hostilities—but unequal conventional forces, the power with superior conventional forces might be tempted to use them for a military advance of regional significance; it would then expect that its nuclear adversary would be unable to strike back with adequate conventional forces and would not dare to use its nuclear massive deterrent.

This greatly enhanced importance of the forces in being has produced a situation in which a country with a lower potential (for instance, a lower industrial output) would have to be considered an equal of another state with a higher potential if only its forces in being capable of waging strategic nuclear warfare have reached the saturation point, i.e., have the capacity to destroy the rival state's retaliatory forces. This same position of nuclear equality would be achieved by the state whose massive deterrent could effectively disrupt the social fabric of the rival state even after the latter had delivered a surprise attack. The relative nuclear power of two states is not necessarily proportionate to the relative size of the two national potentials. Two nuclear powers who have reached the point of saturation are equals despite discrepancies in their potentials. This does not mean, of course, that they have become peers in any respect other than their equal power of nuclear destructiveness.

The forces in being have the following functions:

1. To deter an enemy attack on the national territory with the threat of an immediate and effective retaliation.

2. To provide the time necessary for the mobilization of the national potential (a function ruled out in an all-out nuclear war but still valid in other wars).

3. To allow for choice between the various conceivable types of modern wars—all-out, limited, and peripheral.

They can perform all three functions on the condition that a great power make the necessary sacrifices, such as allocating resources to military production that would otherwise be allocated to consumer production, making military service compulsory in order to supply enough personnel for all military assignments, diverting a considerable share of the available technological and scientific talent to military research and development, and gearing the educational system to supply the necessary number of trained scientists and technologists.

In one version of the nuclear war the national potential remains important in peacetime but loses its significance with the outbreak of hostilities, which presumably would destroy it. In the other version it retains its significance after the first, nuclear stage of war and is expected to sustain the national war effort in the later stages. However, the peacetime relation between the potentials of the two prospective belligerents might become meaningless in both versions of nuclear war. The initial, nuclear stage of a "broken-back" war would destroy a considerable share of these potentials. No one can forecast what share would remain intact after this stage. Would the two belligerents suffer comparable losses or would one of them be much luckier than the other? Nuclear war would carry with it, as any war, the factor of chance.

Despite all these considerations it would be foolish to write off the importance of the power potential. It determines in peacetime the size and quality of the forces in being, including the mass deterrent. Only a country with vast economic resources and an up-to-date scientific knowledge can afford to have a true mass deterrent. Only a major and expanding economy has so far been able to forge ahead in the scientific and technological progress which determines the future quality of the forces in being. The power potential would play its traditional role in the limited and peripheral wars which offer the time and opportunity for its full mobilization. Finally, the power potential is basically the economic and scientific capacity of a nation; it traces the limits within which a country can exercise an economic and technological influence on other countries, especially in the form of economic and technical assistance extended to the underdeveloped nations.

If the definition of power potential were enlarged to include not only the human and economic resources which can be mobilized but also all other factors which influence the national capacity for waging war, the expanded definition would include the following elements:

1. The size, location, and topography of national territory.

2. The size, age composition, demographic trends, labor productivity, and morale of the population.

3. The volume and variety of foodstuffs and raw materials produced on the national territory, the known reserves of raw materials, and the capacity to import them, if necessary, in peacetime and in wartime; under this same heading should be included the volume of output and the reserves of the sources of energy as well as the capacity to import them from abroad.

4. The total industrial capacity, the types of goods produced in peacetime (especially the respective proportions of capital and consumer goods), and the rate of growth of productive capacity.

5. The national capacity in land, maritime, and air transportation.

6. The human and material resources in science and technology and the related problem of the nature of the educational system.

7. The efficiency of the administrative and managerial staffs.

8. The quality of national leaders and elites.

The mere enumeration of all these factors indicates the extreme difficulty of comparing the power potentials of any two nations of similar strength. Much of the pertinent information is inaccessible, especially in the totalitarian states. Certain factors are so complex that a comparison of them is almost impossible. For instance, the morale of a population and the ability of military leaders can truly be tested only in war. Yet some rough comparisons of national potentials are necessary, because the power of any country is not an absolute notion and acquires meaning only when compared with that of another country of similar strength.

The total size of the national territory has always been important because it has determined the ability of a nation to prolong resistance in war and to make use of calculated retreats. Charles XII, Napoleon, and Hitler learned this the hard way during their military campaigns in Russia. Today, total size is equally important, for it determines the ability of a nation to disperse its resources for waging war and, generally, to absorb nuclear attacks. Geographical location is also important. Britain was, and the United States still is, sea-protected against an invasion; American invulnerability in this respect has been to some extent reduced by the possibility of air-borne operations against exposed parts of the national territory, such as Alaska. The insular or quasi-insular location is certainly better than the continental one, but it offers no protection against air attacks by long-range bombers and ballistic missiles, and by missile-carrying submarines operating against the coastal areas. On the other hand, a country protected by the sea against an invasion is hindered in its overseas operations by the problem of logistics, including the threat of submarines. Mountain chains do not ensure any safety against air attacks but represent a certain obstacle for ground forces; the air-borne invasion could, however, help in overcoming this geographical obstacle. Climate is another important factor because it might be a hindrance to military operations.

The total size of the population determines the size of manpower available for national production and for the forces in being. The same total size indicates the proportion of human losses which a country can "afford" without being disabled or destroyed. This consideration is especially important in our nuclear age. The actual size of the civilian and military manpower is also determined by the age composition of the population (the proportion of able-bodied people to children, old people, and other dependents) and the rate of natural increase (see Chapter 6). Two countries with populations of the same size and of a similar age structure might show considerable differences in their per capita productivity because of differences in living standards, technological skills, the length of the workday, the attraction of leisure time, and so forth. To take living standards as an example, a labor force accustomed to high standards will require that a considerable share of the nation's capacity for production be invested in the output of consumer goods, with the result that a smaller share of the nation's resources will be available for the production of capital goods and military materiel. On the other hand, a labor force accustomed to much lower standards might be less productive per capita because of inadequate material incentives or because of fatigue resulting from poor nutrition, substandard housing, overcrowded commuter transportation, or other unfavorable conditions.

From the purely military point of view, other considerations are important, such as the number of trained reserves and military cadres (officers and noncommissioned officers) who represent the nucleus of both existing and future armed forces. From a more general point of view, equally important are per capita labor productivity and the amount and variety of scientific and technological skills. Labor productivity, measured by man-hours spent in the production of the total national product, depends not only on the morale of the labor force but also on the technological facilities, the quality of productive organization, the amount of available per capita energy, and so forth. Automation will gradually shift the problem of labor productivity from human effort to the quality of equipment, while atomic energy will eventually open the possibility of an unlimited supply of energy.

Morale rests, in the last analysis, on social solidarity, and may be equated with patriotism. Basically, it is the capacity of the individuals who compose a nation to make sacrifices for the sake of the national community. The degree of social solidarity depends on the civic ideals which parents, friends, neighbors, and teachers inculcate and which are further strengthened or weakened by the mass media. The degree varies with the nature and the strength of external challenges.

Morale is, in other words, the capacity to face external dangers. Without it, a nation will collapse if confronted with a truly serious threat, such as an enemy invasion or a powerful air attack. Morale includes today the capacity to endure the everpresent risk of nuclear devastations without losing the will to assume limited risks in international politics. Any foreign policy will fail that is not rooted in national fortitude equal to the risks of policy; morale is the ultimate frontier of any foreign policy.

Important as it is, it cannot be safely measured in advance of the actual tests of life. One learns about the morale of a population by observing its behavior in the face of actual danger, and then the knowledge comes too late. Past behavior may offer misleading indications of future attitudes. For instance, no one who had witnessed the heroic endurance of Frenchmen during the First World War would have believed that they would quickly collapse in 1940; the Russians collapsed in 1917 but resisted admirably during the Second World War, which exacted greater sacrifices. A careful observation of the daily attitudes of a population toward their social duties might be useful in predicting their behavior in the face of an external threat. However, those predictions are liable to error, because nations, like individuals, tend to behave differently under normal conditions and in the hour of danger. Danger might undermine the stamina of a respectable citizen but evoke heroism in an inconspicuous or unruly individual.

The economic life of any modern nation is inconceivable without at least a certain amount of imported foodstuffs, raw materials, sources of energy, and such manufactured goods as are not produced at home or produced in insufficient quantities. However, those countries which must depend for their survival on imported goods are incomparably more vulnerable than others which are nearly self-sufficient. Britain and Japan are obvious examples of such vulnerable countries because a fully successful blockade would make them helpless. Western Europe, which imports 19 per cent of foodstuffs, 70 per cent of raw materials, and almost all its oil, also needs to maintain vital ties with the outside world. Even the United States increasingly relies on the importation of certain raw materials. This dependence of the advanced countries on raw materials and fuel produced in the underdeveloped areas of the Third World indicates the importance of these areas for the security and prosperity of the West.

Reliance on foreign imports of essential goods becomes hazardous in case of war for two reasons: (1) the risk that maritime transportation will be disrupted by enemy blockade, in particular by enemy submarines; and (2) the need to divert a sizable part of national effort to the production of export goods in order to pay for vital imports. These imports can also be paid for by the liquidation of assets which the country possesses abroad; by the same token, a part of its external political influence is also liquidated.

Wartime dependence on vital imports can be lessened in advance by stockpiling the most important raw materials and fuel. Also, substitutes can be manufactured; in wartime their cost of production becomes a minor consideration. Agricultural imports can be reduced by better techniques in national production and by rationing, i.e., by reducing consumption. Eventually, the imports of certain foodstuffs which are not indispensable to the national diet can be discontinued completely. No modern nation can survive without imports of oil, except the United States and the Soviet Union.

A nation which depends on foreign imports must maintain an efficient transportation system and be able to protect this system in wartime.

Another component of the power potential is the total capacity of industrial production and its rate of growth. This capacity determines the ultimate size and quality of the nuclear and other forces in being. It is also important for other reasons. It is the foundation of national ability to provide economic assistance to other countries. It is an essential component of the total national product of any advanced country. If it were to grow more slowly than the population (its rate of growth being less over a number of years than the rate of natural increase), eventually the living standards would begin to decline. Yet the level of living standards is an important asset in the competition between the countries whose economies are founded on the private ownership of the means of production and the other countries with fully nationalized means of production. Another consideration also relates to international competition; if the underdeveloped countries were to detect, over long periods of time, that a totally nationalized economy grows more rapidly than any other, they would become convinced that the future, in particular their own future, is tied up with this sort of economy and this kind of politcal regime. Finally, a rapidly growing economy usually goes hand in hand with rapid technological progress, which in turn influences the quality of armaments. It would be a fatal mistake for a nation to allow its rate of economic growth to fall below that of other nations, especially unfriendly nations.

The total industrial output of a nation can be usefully subdivided into the production of military hardware, capital goods, and consumer goods. The greater the share of industrial output that a nation reserves for consumer goods, the less the share that it can reserve for military equipment and for the capital goods which are an investment in future production.

Flexibility in industrial production depends largely on output of the machine-tool industry. The latter factor determines the capacity for shifting quickly from one type of output to another. A nation with a large and comparatively inexpensive output of machine tools is able to play an important role in the industrial development of other countries. Hence, automation is crucial in this particular industry.

The nation's future also depends on its ability to integrate new inventions into its productive system. Automation, which will lead to increased output but may also lead to the social disaster of widespread unemployment, is typical of the inventions which will test the ability of advanced nations to integrate them into their production.

Another important consideration is the length of time required between the appearance of a new concept of weaponry and its actual integration within the armaments of the forces in being. This lead-time might last from five to ten years. Its length depends, among other factors, on the rapidity of governmental decisions, on the ability to concentrate effort on one project and not disperse it among several projects of a similar nature, and on the managerial and industrial capacity of the nation. The choice between various projects might be that between a less refined system which can be produced quickly and a better system which would require a longer time to produce. The totalitarian regime offers certain advantages in this respect. Decisions can be made quickly; projects can be initiated, accelerated, or discontinued without fear of a public discussion; national resources can be commandeered with great ease because of the nationalization of all the means of production; specialists and skilled workers can be ex officio assigned; and budgetary allowances can be fixed without public protest.

Modern military technology places such a high premium on new inventions and discoveries and on the ability to incorporate them into actual production that national power directly relates to the level of science and technology, the nature of education, and the size and diversity of industrial plant. The sequence begins with the educational system, which determines the quantity and quality of the scientists, technologists, industrial managers, and other specialists. International competition for influence and status among nations is waged, first of all, in the classrooms, from the secondary to the postgraduate level. Assuming that a country has solved this preliminary problem of education, the next stage is to provide adequate financial support for pure research in mathematics and the sciences. It is impossible to be sure in advance that each research project will eventually have a practical application, and yet pure research is the precondition of progress in the applied sciences and technology. The third stage is that of deducing practical conclusions from the scientific research, making a selection among many possible projects, and translating the chosen projects into feasible blueprints. Last comes the stage of producing weapons from the blueprints.

The government intervenes at each stage since it has the greatest financial resources for promoting the required type of education, encouraging research, and financing the actual production. The politicians of today must have a minimum of familiarity with scientific and technological problems in order to judge the relative merits of competing projects despite the often conflicting views of experts.

The educational system has two aspects which are important for international competition: the quality of the civic training of the youth, and the quality of the knowledge disseminated, especially scientific and technological knowledge. The former aspect molds national morale. The latter determines the total annual supply of future scientists and other specialists, their caliber and skills, the resulting capacity of the nation to meet international competition in peaceful and military inventions (usually the two cannot be separated), and its ability to provide technical assistance to other countries in the form of expert services and training. If one nation requires more years of education than another to graduate full-fledged scientific, technological, and managerial specialists, there is probably, at some level of schooling, a waste of too many precious hours on nonscholarly pursuits. Another possible waste in the educational system is the failure to tap all potential talents for higher education. If school fees bar the gifted children of poorer parents from the university, their talents will remain unproductive and the nation will be handicapped in international competition. The full mobilization of all potential talent would require the elimination of university fees and/or the granting of liberal scholarships to all deserving students, two practices followed in the Soviet Union. A related problem is the need to develop a system of selection which, on the basis of talent and industry alone, would limit the number of university students to the available human(faculty) and material(labs, libraries) resources. If the competition among nations is ultimately a contest of individual abilities, success in international competition requires that all the talented young individuals of a nation have free access to a university education of high quality, and this cannot be provided without some system of selective admission.

Finally, transportation capacity is another important element of the national power potential. Highways, waterways, railroads, air transport, and maritime transportation are equally important in peacetime and wartime. This capacity helps to overcome the distance which separates the country from its foreign sources of supply and foreign markets and also from the theaters of military operations. In peacetime the distance between the sources of fuel (coal, oil) and raw materials, on the one hand, and the industrial centers, on the other, is an important factor in the cost of production, because it determines how much of the energy available for all purposes must be spent on transportation. Although distance ordinarily reduces the effectiveness of military power because a part of the national effort must be invested in transportation instead of armaments, this is almost untrue of the nuclear-powered submarine, the future nuclear-propelled airplane, or the long-range ballistic missile, because of the high energy of the nuclear power which propels them and the immense destructiveness of the nuclear weapons which they transport.

A GLANCE AT THE MODERN ARSENAL

Even a most detailed review of the weapons now available to advanced nations is of doubtful value because of the fantastically rapid rate of change. Every year opens new vistas which surpass in audacity anything that Jules Verne could have imagined. An up-to-date survey becomes obsolete after the lapse of a fairly short period of time. Moreover, no survey could be complete because of the large amount of information which is classified.

If a glance at what is known today has any usefulness, it is to prove the growing vulnerability of all countries, including the most powerful, and perhaps of our civilization itself, to the threat represented by the modern weapons of mass destruction. Hence, the enormous risks which contemporary international politics involve.

Nuclear weapons (bombs, warheads, shells) can be delivered to their targets by various means: manned aircraft, unmanned but guided and air-breathing missiles, ballistic missiles, medium-range missiles launched by manned planes from a distance of several hundred miles, naval torpedoes, submerged submarines, and, on the battlefields, as shells and short-range rockets fired by the artillery and infantry. An outer-space satellite will become another means of delivery.

Long-range missiles have not made the airplane obsolete. The handicap of the modern jet plane is its need for very long runways and hence for big airfields, which are "ideal" targets for long-range ballistic missiles. However, a good portion of the aircraft forming the strategic retaliatory force can remain air-borne and thus escape destruction. Moreover, the future nuclear-powered plane will be able to remain in flight for very long periods of time (its uninterrupted flight capacity may reach 25,000 miles) and cruise over enormous distances without refuelling.

Although more vulnerable than the missiles (it is incomparably easier to hit an airfield than a launching pad), planes offer definite advantages which the present-generation missiles cannot provide. They can perform reconnaissance missions to locate enemy targets and report on the results of bombing; this task will be taken over in due time by the orbiting satellite of the type of the Samos. They can be recalled home while flying on a retaliatory mission if the government realizes that it reacted to a false alarm. If sent on a bombing mission, they can search for targets, including mobile targets such as moving launching pads, submarine and surface vessels, and troops. The plane can be armed not only with bombs but also with various missiles: air-to-ground, air-to-air, and guided. It can deliver its nuclear weapon from a distance of several hundred miles and therefore from a position of relative security. While it now can find the target in any weather and by day or night, the cost of the sortie has become almost negligible because of the vast destructiveness of the several-megaton bomb capable of destroying the largest city and carried by a single plane. The speed of a plane cannot stand comparison with that of a ballistic missile but is being constantly increased and should not be underestimated. It now exceeds 1,000 miles per hour and might reach 2,000 miles in the near future. As long as a missile cannot perform all the functions which require human judgment, the manned plane will retain its military usefulness although some of its tasks are, or will be, taken over by the missile and the satellite.

Ballistic missiles are of various ranges: short-range of a few hundred or less miles for tactical use on the battlefields, intermediate (IRBM) with a range up to 1,700 miles, and intercontinental (ICBM) with a range of from 5,500 to 10,000 miles. The missiles with the maximum range could be launched from any point on the earth to any other point, thus threatening the enemy from all the directions of the compass. Their speed is between 15,000 and 18,000 miles per hour. This speed reduces the warning time, for the United States and the Soviet Union, to less than fifteen minutes; the permanently orbiting satellites of the type of the Midas, which could detect a missile at the time of its launching, will increase the warning time to half an hour. The missile obviously has an all-weather capacity. Its accuracy at intercontinental distances may reach the probability of error of about half a mile from zero ground. However, if it carried a megaton warhead and were fired against an urban agglomeration, an error of even a few miles would make no practical difference. The present-generation missiles are inferior to bombers in both accuracy and destructive power. One should not forget, however, that the largest rockets, which are being used for the launching of the heaviest satellites, have the capacity to deliver several-megaton warheads over intercontinental distances.

The territories of the Soviet Union and its allies would be vulnerable to intermediate ballistic missiles launched from American overseas bases located in the Eastern Hemisphere and from American submarines hiding under the ice-sheet of the Arctic Ocean. The American coastal areas could be hit by intermediate Soviet missiles fired from submarines, while missiles of the same range launched from the territories of the Communist countries could reach England and Western Europe, the Near East, Japan, Taiwan, and some other areas of importance to the United States. The mutual threat is not confined to the intercontinental missiles.

The missile seems at first sight to offer a great advantage to the aggressor. He could launch a surprise attack from all the directions of the compass, thus reducing the effectiveness of active defense. He would be favored by the shortness of the warning time. However, the retaliatory force would enjoy the same advantages. Launching pads are incomparably less vulnerable than airfields and have a reasonable chance of escaping the effects of surprise attack. They can be hardened or made mobile. In other words, the missile has not necessarily increased the prospect of success of a surprise attack.

There are several weaknesses in the present-generation ballistic missiles. They have, like artillery shells, a fixed trajectory and thus are vulnerable to defensive antimissile missiles in spite of their velocity. They cannot hit moving targets such as surface or submarine ships or the missile-launching platforms moving on rails or rivers. They cannot provide post-bombing reconnaissance reports, and they cannot be recalled once launched. Some of these defects will be obviated in the future. The trajectories will be changeable by remote control, and detection by enemy radar will be made more difficult by antiradar shielding and a variety of decoys and jamming devices.

The liquid propellent requires at least fifteen minutes for the launching operation, an important defect for a nation responding to an enemy attack. When solid fuel is used, the size and weight of the missile can be reduced and it can be launched from submarines and mobile land platforms (railroad trucks or barges). The time for launching is one or two minutes and allows for an almost instant retaliation. The liquid-fuel missiles require stable and sizable launching sites which can be hardened (placed underground and armored) but which can be located by the enemy well in advance of his attack and destroyed by direct and powerful hits. Solid fuel made possible the Polaris with its range of 1,200 miles; the submarine has therefore become a menace to land areas. The solid-fuel, land-based Minuteman can be launched almost immediately.

The victorious outcome of all major wars fought by England since it became a dominant naval power (except for the American war of independence) could lead to the hasty conclusion that the naval power has a natural superiority over the land power. It should be remembered that England won its wars against the land powers because it was always able to find allies among other land powers which took care of neutralizing the English foes in land warfare. Moreover, its own homeland was secure behind the natural barrier of the Channel. Finally, its naval supremacy remained unchallenged as long as the land powers could not afford to spend money on land and maritime armaments simultaneously and had not discovered an effective and practical sea weapon. This weapon was finally invented; the submarine revolutionized the strategy of war. Twice, the German submarine blockade very seriously threatened to disrupt what the British called during the last war the Atlantic lifeline. The modern submarine, nuclear-powered and armed with the IRBM which can be launched while the submarine is submerged, has become a deadly weapon. The difficulty of detecting a submarine at a great depth and over the vast expanses of the oceans provides this instrument of war with two qualities very important in a nuclear age, mobility and the capacity for dispersal. Because it can cover 120,000 miles without refuelling, the nuclear-powered submarine can be easily concealed. It can stay submerged while cruising because it extracts oxygen from the sea water and does not need to surface periodically. The nuclear engine does not need oxygen to function. The submarines of this type are perpetually moving bases for both attack and retaliation; they reduce the need for bases on foreign territory and have the obvious advantage of being under exclusive national control.

Nuclear-powered submarines are a far greater threat to surface vessels than conventional submarines were though these were a very serious menace. They can disrupt the trade of the enemy and his supplies to troops fighting overseas. Their existence enormously complicates the problem of logistics in a limited or peripheral war which a naval power must fight across the ocean. The ability of the United States, for instance, to conduct such a war depends on the effective control of the Atlantic and Pacific oceans. Hence, one of the most urgent problems of the naval powers is to develop an adequate means of combating submarines, such as depth charges and sonar devices. When it is recalled that they can also launch missiles against coastal areas, it becomes apparent that nuclear submarines have virtually equalized the land and sea powers.

Submarines have other missions, including that of destroying other submarines. Along with other instruments of war they have made the large aircraft carrier extremely vulnerable. Enemy planes can hit these vessels from a distance of several hundred miles. The light cruiser, which in past wars was hopelessly outgunned by the aircraft carrier in close-range battle, has now become a dangerous enemy that can launch its missiles from a safe distance. The aircraft carrier is, however, a sort of constantly moving airfield, its mobility giving it great superiority over land-based airfields.

One of the crucial goals of the current arms race is to develop a reasonably effective means of *active defense*. The nation which could outdistance its adversary by securing these means would suddenly place itself in the position where a surprise attack would become a "reasonable" proposition. The problem of active defense consists in finding effective countermeasures against submarines, long-range planes, and, above all, missiles; in the future it would include the problem of defense against attack from outer space. Ground-to-air guided missiles, antiaircraft artillery, and interceptor planes could inflict great losses on enemy bombers; however, the surviving bombers, even if few, could still cause enormous damages due to the high destructive capacity of a hydrogen bomb. Antimissile missiles might attain an efficiency which would allow them to hit oncoming enemy missiles at a safe distance. Nuclear depth charges and sonar devices might provide an answer to the submarine threat. The same scientific and technological progress which solves the present problems of active defense will create new problems by bringing improvements in existing offensive weapons and forming the basis for new ones. For instance, the trajectory of the ballistic missile will eventually be liable to deviations imparted by remote guidance. Competition between offensive and defensive weapons, in which the former have so far been several steps ahead of the latter, might never result in a balance. This competition revolves around electronics, which has become one of the most crucial elements in modern armaments (for such purposes as air navigation, bomb-aiming, missile guidance, detection and interception of enemy planes and missiles, etc.). Electronic devices can be jammed or otherwise interfered with by other electronic devices. The arms race is partly a duel in perfecting electronic devices.

Passive defense calls for the deep shelters which could protect the population during a nuclear attack. These shelters must have the capability not only of withstanding the blast and the fire storm caused by a nuclear explosion but also of insulating the occupants from the effects of local fallout and also of the chemical and bacteriological attacks which the enemy might deliver simultaneously. The occupants, cut off from the outside world for the duration of the radioactive emergency, must be able to breathe and eat. The shelters would have to be provided with mining equipment for blasting an exit through the ruins which would accumulate on the surface. Presumably, they would have to accommodate a thousand persons each and be easily accessible within less than half an hour. The number of shelters near the center of metropolitan areas would have to be greater than the size of the population there would indicate, to accommodate commuters from the suburbs.

Moreover the population saved by shelters must be able to rebuild its life and resume productive work. This calls for the safe storage of foodstuffs, industrial tools, especially machine tools, and other implements, raw materials, gasoline, and means of transportation, notably trucks. It seems probable that no modern nation could afford the cost of a passive defense which could both save its population and enable it immediately to resume modern life and production. This argument does not deny the usefulness of any passive defense which would at least contribute to reduce the losses.

The dispersal of the national economy and the replacement of large metropolitan areas by many small urban centers are forms of passive defense. However, this dispersal goes against the grain of modern development, and its cost would be prohibitive. It would be wise to promote the dispersal of new industries; by the same token, the less developed areas of advanced countries would benefit by the dispersed building of new industries. The foundation of new industrial centers in the Asian provinces of the Soviet Union and in the inland provinces of China might be due, among other causes, to this consideration.

The conquest of outer space has opened unprecedented vistas not only for scientific but also for military progress, the two being interlocked. The rapidity of this progress, since the placing in orbit of the first satellite and the successful launching of astronauts, is so amazing that estimates of future military implications can become obsolete in a short time. Only one thing is certain. A power which could win control of outer space would also win control of the air space which envelops the earth and hence would become the master of our globe.

Outer-space satellites could perform various functions of military significance:

1. They could reconnoiter by taking photographs in orbit. These photographs, despite the high altitude of the satellite, can now attain a precision of detail equal to what the human eye can see at a distance of a hundred feet. The photographs can be radioed back to reveal the "secrets" of the whole surface of the earth, thus ending the "privacy" of all countries, including the so-called closed societies. This method of reconnoitering will place the democratic and totalitarian states on an equal footing with regard to the knowledge each has of the location of the surface targets of the other.

The reconnaissance mission could be performed after a nuclear attack to report the kind and amount of destruction inflicted on the enemy. In this respect, the satellite would become a complement of the ballistic missile.

2. They could perform a warning mission by detecting the exhaust fumes of missiles. The satellite can report the launching of the ICBM at the moment of their being fired. The warning time is thus extended almost to the whole period of time which the ICBM needs to cover the distance between its launching site and the target.

3. The satellite could become either a link or an obstacle in telecommunications. It could serve, for example, as a powerful transmitting device

for television. It could also be used for jamming electronic communications.

4. It could help in maritime and air navigation by determining the exact location of aircraft, surface vessels, and submarines. This would greatly assist in the precise bombing of enemy targets from aircraft, surface warships, and submarines.

5. It will assist in making long-term and precise forecasts of weather, a task having military significance.

6. The satellite could be used as an orbiting launching platform for missiles. These outer-space bombing platforms will constitute a threat beyond the reach of active defense until such time as man can invent a device for destroying the satellites themselves.

These and possibly other functions of the satellites give only a foretaste of the military implications of the further exploration of outer space. No doubt the race for interplanetary exploration is not motivated by scientific interest alone. There is no limit to the human search for more powerful weapons of destruction. Unfortunately, the human imagination is much less fertile in finding techniques for peace.

While people talk seriously about manned platforms installed on the moon, one can ask whether military bases located on foreign territory have not become obsolete. The security of the United States, like that of the Soviet Union, requires a maximum dispersal of the retaliatory force, the quickest warning system possible, and the most reliable intelligence network. For the time being, the American bases overseas help in achieving all three objectives. The United States can launch its planes not only from the airfields located on its own territory but also from the far-flung bases situated in a ring around the Soviet Union and much closer to the Soviet vital centers than the American-based airfields. The IRBM, posted on the launching pads which are built on the territories of friendly states, can reach the U.S.S.R. and its allies, while they would have been of no use if the launching sites were located on American territory. However, the growing fleet of nuclear-powered and nuclear-armed submarines has given the United States an advantage which foreign bases with the American IRBM cannot provide, namely dispersal, greater immunity to destruction, and mobility. This explains the new trend in the military policy of the United States of withdrawing its IRBM from foreign bases and assigning the same protective function to the Polaris-armed submarines. The bases render other important services: they are an extension of the American warning system; some of them can serve as naval or military bases (a vital consideration in wars other than all-out nuclear); they can help in tracing the effects of nuclear, missile, and outer-space experiments and tests; and, if they are located close to Soviet territory, they are ideal sites for the electronic collection of intelligence.

The ring of overseas bases surrounding Soviet territory has provided the United States with an obvious asset, namely the ability to strike from all possible directions of the compass, thus greatly complicating the Soviet problem of active defense. This asset will lose its value as the Soviet Union develops greater capacity in the ICBM and in the IRBM launchable from submarines; these weapons and the global-range nuclear-powered planes which the Soviet Union may some day perfect will also make American territory vulnerable to attacks from all directions.

New techniques will gradually reduce the importance of foreign bases and eventually eliminate them altogether. On the day when the security of the United States will be adequately guaranteed by a large fleet of nuclear-powered and nuclear-armed submarines and by a network of solid-fuel ICBM (Minutemen) capable of being fired almost immediately and placed in well-protected, underground launching sites, the need for foreign bases for IRBM will disappear. The orbiting satellites might successfully take over the warning and intelligence missions. An expanded capacity and security of overseas maritime and air transportation will eliminate the need for military depots and bases on foreign territory.

However, for the time being, the overseas bases continue to be very useful in spite of the political problems which they entail. A change in the foreign orientation of the host country can force the United States to liquidate a base. A domestic revolution might have the same result. The existence of the base is frequently a cause of friction with the government or the population of the host country. The latter country might be alarmed by Soviet threats to launch nuclear attacks against all overseas American bases in the event of a Soviet-American conflict. It might be frightened by this threat into requesting the liquidation of the base. The liquidation of a base before the expected time entails the loss of a heavy financial investment which could have been used for other military purposes. Militarily, a far-advanced base is vulnerable to Soviet ground attack and to destruction by Soviet planes and IRBM. All those political and military risks do not yet outweigh the advantages of overseas bases.

However, the technology of war points to developments which will finally allow the United States to dispense with foreign bases and thus free itself from this alien mortgage on its own security.

ALLIANCES

The purpose of the alliance (treaty of mutual assistance) is to combine the power of the allies against their common enemy. The allies are expected to provide either additional military strength and additional economic, scientific, and technological potential or facilities on their territories which will make the power of the other party to the alliance more effective (for instance, military, naval, air, or intelligence bases).

The hoped-for effects of the alliance are two, preventive and repressive. The allies sign the treaty of mutual assistance in the expectation that their combined power will compel the adversary to make concessions without war or will deter him from opening hostilities against any of them. If the alliance fails to have this preventive effect and the adversary is not deterred from attacking one of the allies or from undertaking political actions which they cannot tolerate, the second objective of the alliance is to confront the common enemy with the combined military counteraction of all the allies. These two objectives are implied in every alliance whether it is offensive or defensive. An offensive alliance aims at the modification of the status quo by the co-ordinated political or military action of the allies; a defensive alliance functions to uphold the status quo.

The alliance can be concluded for additional reasons. It may be the price which a great power must pay for installing on the territory of a weak state a military, naval, or air base or the listening devices which increase the range of the great power's warning system against a surprise attack. It may be designed to provide a great power with a legal pretext for intervening in the affairs of a smaller state in order to protect its own interests. By intervening directly or by supplying equipment or advisors, a great power may be able to preserve the friendly government of a smaller state from external attack or internal subversion. The great power is in a better position to justify its intervention if it can invoke a former commitment to the friendly government. This commitment might be a treaty of alliance or a unilateral guarantee like the one extended by the signatories of the SEATO treaty to South Vietnam, Laos, and Cambodia. Of course, a legal title to intervene can be provided, without any former treaty or guarantee, by a request for help addressed to the great power by the threatened government. The great power which is determined to uphold the status quo without worrying about an adequate justification for its action can intervene without invoking any legal title or can manufacture this title at the last minute. The Soviet Union twice demonstrated this technique. After its armed attack on Finland in 1939, the Soviet Union quickly formed behind the lines of its troops a rival Finnish government which was presided over by a Soviet citizen of Finnish descent and which requested the Soviet Union to assist it against the other Finnish government that continued to reside in Helsinki and quite successfully resisted the Soviet offensives. This "government" set up by the Soviet Union was disbanded on the conclusion of the Soviet-Finnish peace treaty in March, 1940. The Soviet Union used the same technique more successfully in November, 1956, at the time of its armed intervention in Hungary. It improvised a rival Hungarian government which requested the Soviet Union *ex post facto* to help it in the "civil war" against the Hungarian government established in Budapest. The subterfuge was in both cases too obvious to convince anyone; the military success of the two operations was more effective in making the third states accept accomplished facts.

A French general ruefully observed during the First World War that Napoleon had not been, after all, an exceptional military genius, because he had been lucky in fighting against a coalition. He was right in saying by implication that it is not easy for a coalition to achieve a truly co-ordinated policy. The allies have different national interests, and each of them has its own hierarchy of international problems. Their different geographical locations alone give them different perspectives on international events. Their co-ordinated policies have to be leveled down to the lowest common denominator or the achievement of co-ordination on a higher level involves a certain amount of friction. A minor ally with geographically limited interests might be inclined to minimize the importance of issues in a distant area, but the same issues might be of vital concern to the major ally with worldwide interests. The over-all solidarity of the allies does not make their interests identical; these interests might continue to be in conflict in the areas of their traditional competition. The main question constantly facing every alliance is to what extent the allies really acknowledge the importance of common interests, which the existence of the same enemy has created, and the superiority of these common interests over their other interests which have remained divergent. They should consult on matters of common concern, but the allies might have different views on what is or is not a matter of common concern. They should follow a co-ordinated policy on those matters; this is, however, one of the most difficult tasks in foreign policy. If they fail to co-operate and work instead at cross-purposes, their common adversary will certainly exploit their quarrels and will try to weaken them all by splitting their united front.

The two opposite coalitions, NATO and the Communist bloc, have entered a period of internal stress. The main reasons for this parallel development in the two coalitions are political and economic. The nuclear stalemate, achieved by the two major allies, the United States and the Soviet Union, has generated a sense of a greater security among the junior allies. An open aggression against a junior ally by the opposite principal nuclear power seems to be a very remote possibility. In consequence, the feeling of dependence on the major ally is lessened. The junior allies consider that they now have an opportunity to assert their own national interests whether or not these are consistent with the interests of the major ally or other junior allies. The fear that the opposite coalition might benefit from the quarrels among the allies does not seem to act as an effective deterrent. Since the members of a coalition can never have identical interests and since the solidarity of an alliance decreases with any apparent decrease in the imminence and gravity of an external threat, there is nothing surprising in the crisis which has developed within both coalitions. The misunderstandings between the United States and Britain, on the one hand, and France and, to a lesser degree, Germany, on the other, characteristically parallel the rift between Russia and China.

The other factor is economic. The time when Western Europe needed the Marshall Plan for its recovery is gone. The economic expansion of Western Europe at a rate higher than that of the United States has given the European allies a feeling of self-confidence which they did not have in the forties. The American need for Western European co-operation in maintaining the exchange rate of the dollar contrasts with the former period when Western Europe suffered from the dollar shortage. The distribution of economic power within the Western coalition has been modified. The European allies claim, therefore, a bigger share of influence within NATO. What they want is to replace American leadership with a partnership which would give them a greater voice in NATO policies. The value of NATO is not contested. The problem between the United States and Western Europe consists in the need to find a new form of co-operation which would not involve subordination to the major ally.

One of the main aspects of the Soviet-Chinese dispute is also economic but its nature is different. A developed Russia faces an underdeveloped China. Formulated in Communist ideological language, their problem is whether or not all the Communist states should enter the Communist stage of development at the same time. "Communist stage" here means the stage of full economic development and high living standards. The practical issue centers in the Chinese claim that their economic development should be underwritten by Russia and the Eastern European countries even at the price of a much slower economic expansion of the European Communist states and at the risk that they may be unable to catch up with the capitalist West in the foreseeable future. China, like Western Europe, complains of not having a sufficiently equal voice with the major ally in the policies of the coalition (see Chapter 7).

CHAPTER III

Mass Nationalism

TERMINOLOGY AND DEFINITIONS

Nationalism is one of the revolutionary trends which are reshaping our international environment. It was born as a mass phenomenon out of the emancipation of the common man whose national and other feelings have gradually become, since the French Revolution, a factor of immense importance in the political life of mankind. It is much older than the other revolutionary trends of our era, having left its indelible mark on the political history of Europe in the nineteenth century. It has been radically transforming the political map of the world for the last one hundred and seventy years. It has been gaining in importance as a factor in social solidarity because of the simultaneous weakening of other social ties such as those of the family, the church, and the local community.

Yet this social phenomenon, so familiar to modern man, has been subjected to a great variety of conflicting interpretations and exposed to confusing and equivocal semantics. The same words, used in reference to nationalism, often have two different meanings. *Nation* is currently a synonym of the *state* and of the *nationality. Nationality* may mean either a distinct social group or be the synonym of *citizenship*. In both English and French the adjective *national* may refer to the nationality, as in the expressions *national culture* and *national language*, or to the state, as in the expressions *national museum, national currency*, and *national debt*. The word *nationalism* itself has acquired in this century a tone of opprobrium; hence it is often reserved to designate the feelings of foreign nationalities, while these same feelings at home are designated by the old-fashioned word *patriotism* or by more detached phrases such as "loyalty to the Queen" or "loyalty to country." This game of words allows a great many people to feel indignant if accused of a lack of loyalty to their own country and at the same time to castigate the nationalism of foreign peoples not only if this nationalism happens to be rabid and full of hatred for other nationalities but also if it disturbs the status quo or conflicts with one's own national interests. Yet this social phenomenon is basically the same whatever its external manifestations and its names might be.

The nationalities which for centuries have had their own state tend to confuse the idea of nationality with the idea of the state. While the word *nation* may refer to both ideas, loyalty to the state and allegiance to the nationality are not necessarily synonymous; they have often been entangled in open and bitter conflict.

Nationality is a complex phenomenon because its characteristics vary widely with time and place. It defies all attempts at a perfect and all-embracing definition. Yet it is tangible enough to be distinguished from other social groups which share with it one or more characteristics. Like the members of a nationality, the members of an ideological organization (such as a church or the international Communist movement) might share a belief in a common past, a faith in the same self-evident truths, and a will to retain their distinct identity as a group, but an ideological organization does not claim a part of the globe as its own, although it might venerate certain places as holy because of a historical association; the nationality, moreover, is not organized unless through the intermediary of its own nation-state. Labor unions and other professional organizations are functional but not territorial. A province, a city, or another territorial unit of public administration might elicit local patriotism but, unlike the nationality and the state, does not claim the supreme loyalty of modern men. Moreover, two cities or two provinces inhabited by the same nationality have the same cultural patterns, unlike any two nationalities.

How do the social phenomena of the nationality and the state differ from each other? A nationality is a group of people who believe that they share a common past, who claim a territory as their own, who share a faith in the same self-evident truths, and who want to maintain the distinct identity of their group. The state is also a territorial group but is organized under a government that claims supreme jurisdiction over its nationals.

The state and the nationality might be practically equal in extent if the population of a state belongs entirely or almost entirely to one nationality. In any case, there are certain similarities between the two social groups. Both are territorial groups; each state exercises its jurisdiction over a definite territory, and each nationality considers a part of the earth as its own. Both claim from the individual his supreme allegiance. The individual is usually born as a citizen (subject, national) of a state and as a member of a nationality. The number of naturalized state citizens or of people who have opted in their own conscience for a nationality different from that of their parents is small in relation to the total population of the world. A person born of the nationals of a given state (*ius sanguinis*) or on its territory (*ius solis*) is claimed as its citizen. The legal procedure of expatriation (the renunciation of citizenship) and naturalization (the acquisition of another citizenship) requires not only an act of will on the part of the individual concerned but also the assent of the naturalizing state and often that of the state of former allegiance. The transfer of loyalty from one to another nationality consists in an act of individual will; it takes place within the conscience of the person concerned.

There are notable differences between the state and the nationality. The state is organized; the nationality has no general organization of its own except when it possesses a state which it controls. A particular organization might pretend to express the opinions and aspirations of the whole nationality, but it always falls short of controlling all the members of the nationality. Since the state is an organized social group with a government which claims supreme jurisdiction and which has the power to enforce this claim, the ties between the individual and the state are legal. The ties between the members of the same nationality are emotional and are focused in their national consciousness, an inner conviction of belonging to the same nationality. However, if a nationality possesses a state of its own, its members include the state in their emotional attachment to the nationality. In this case, the state may be called a *nation-state*.

Because the nationality is not legally organized, the national consciousness of each individual is the determining factor. If he feels that he is a member of a given nationality, he is. The nationality exists only in the consciousness of its members. This consciousness integrates the various elements of a nationality, such as a belief in a common past, the concept of a national territory, common "self-evident" truths and ways of life, and the determination to preserve the distinct identity of the group. Other elements may be integrated in the national consciousness, such as a common language or a common religion, factors which both unite the nationality and make it different from other nationalities. It is characteristic of national consciousness that it gives the members of the same nationality a feeling of affinity with one another and at the same time a feeling of alienation from other nationalities. The national consciousness makes of another man either a countryman or a foreigner. If language is added as a distinguishing factor, it enormously fortifies these two feelings.

The discussion of nationalism is further confused by the fact that national consciousness is a matter of highly intimate and subjective feelings which cannot be easily tested and by the fact that this consciousness does not possess the same intensity in all individuals or all social classes. This intensity has also varied from one historical period to another.

A HISTORICAL SURVEY

There are two reasons why it is not possible to give a full account of the history of nationalism during the thousands of years prior to the emergence of the common man as a full-fledged citizen. First, insufficient records are available; since the nationality or similar ethnic group did not claim supreme allegiance during this period, the phenomenon of nationalism did not attract the attention it has received during the last two centuries. The second difficulty, well known to historians, is that of interpreting former ages in the light of contemporary concepts. Yet this does not authorize the thesis that nationalities and national consciousness were unknown to previous historical periods. This thesis, sometimes propounded, is an emotional reaction to the ravages caused in this century by nationalistic excesses and to the instability of our time which is partly due to the national self-assertion of formerly colonial or semicolonial peoples. It is imbued with wishful thinking. It amounts to saying that, if national feelings are of a fairly recent origin, they have no deep roots and can be exorcised from human hearts. If they disappear as suddenly as they made their appearance, mankind will recover its mental stability. This thesis errs by grossly underestimating one of the most powerful factors in international politics and the probability of its remaining powerful for a long time to come. It glosses over the many proofs of the existence of national feelings of varying intensity in former ages.

A social phenomenon must exist prior to its description and analysis by doctrine. The doctrine of nationalism and nationalities is not older than the eighteenth century, but common sense indicates that it could not have been elaborated without the prior existence of the facts themselves—nationalities and national feelings. What is truly new in the era that followed the French Revolution is not the nationality as a distinct social group but the articulate mass expression of national feelings, *mass nationalism*. As long as the masses were deprived of political rights, the upper and ruling social classes could ignore the feelings of the masses as politically inconsequential. This does not prove that the masses had no consciousness of belonging to a nationality; as a matter of fact, they sometimes demonstrated this consciousness in a spontaneous hostility to the foreign invader. The progressive political emancipation of the common man, ushered in by the French Revolution, compelled the ruling groups to heed the feelings of the common man. Universal education made these feelings articulate. The political, economic, and cultural integration of the common man within the national society made him more keenly aware of his nationality. Public education, the press, radio, television, urbanization, and the nation-state, with its powerful means of imposing uniform ways of life, have brought the intensity of national feelings to a level never experienced in previous historical eras. Mass nationalism, a phenomenon now easy to observe, has become a regular feature of international life.

The thesis that national feelings were insignificant in previous ages does contain a grain of truth, the truth that national allegiance has not always been supreme over other human loyalties. Mankind has known various social groups, territorial and otherwise, which have claimed at various times the supreme loyalty of individuals. While the nationality and the state nowadays present conflicting or mutually supporting claims to the supreme loyalty of men, the city-state, the empire, the tribe, the organized religion, the feudal lord, have at various times made the same claim. The city-state was usually the center of the highest loyalty in the ancient Hellenic world. At least this was true of free citizens; we can doubt whether this feeling was shared by the slaves, who were usually of foreign descent. Socrates expressed this deep city patriotism, which overrode all other considerations, in the Platonic dialogue which protrays him on the eve of his execution. In the *Crito* his friends plead with him to escape from the Athenian prison, but he refuses. His noble argument throws a revealing light on the center of Greek supreme loyalty. He protests that he has been reared since birth under Athenian laws, that he has benefited from them, and that he cannot suddenly, in his old age, disobey them because they have been applied against him. If Socrates and his Greek contemporaries had been the patriots not of one city-state but of the whole Hellenic community, he would have felt that it was his patriotic duty to continue to teach Greeks in the other cities in defiance of the verdict of his native Athens.

The Roman Empire substituted a different supreme loyalty, a loyalty to the whole Empire composed of various linguistic and ethnic groups but unified by the common Hellenistic culture, by the state administration, and by the general use among educated people of the Latin and Greek languages. This overriding loyalty was strongly felt, especially after A.D. 212, the year of the Edict of Emperor Caracalla, who extended Roman citizenship to all free inhabitants of the Empire. One can measure the intensity of this feeling by the pride which the Apostle Paul displayed in his Roman citizenship, even though Paul was an avowed nonconformist. Rutilius Namatianus, a Gallo-Roman poet, expressed this supreme loyalty to the Roman Empire in his famous incantation to Rome: ". . . Thou hast merged together the most diverse nations into one single Fatherland. . . . Thou hast offered to the vanquished peoples participation in thy civilization and hast made one city of what was the universe."

The Germanic tribes which overran the Western Roman Empire owed their supreme allegiance to the tribe and the war leader or chieftain but had no visible feeling of mutual solidarity. The Middle Ages witnessed the conflicting claims to supreme allegiance made by the Western Church, the emperor, the king, and the feudal lord.

The object of supreme loyalty has varied through the ages. This does not mean that no national feeling could co-exist with a supreme loyalty that was reserved for a social group other than the nationality. The Bible makes clear that the ancient Jews had a clear consciousness of being a distinct nationality united by the same religion, the same conviction of being the chosen people, the same language of their holy scriptures, and the myth of a common racial descent. The ancient Greeks, despite their supreme loyalty to the city, had a consciousness of belonging to a cultural and linguistic group which bore many resemblances to what is now called a nationality. They clearly distinguished between a Hellene and a barbarian (a stammering man, i.e., one who speaks a non-Greek language and belongs by implication to a different culture). A feeling of common bonds, uniting all the Greeks, manifested itself during the wars against the Persians. After the Macedonian conquest the Greeks asserted their solidarity in supporting Alexander the Great in his conquest of foreign lands in the East; this was for them the triumph of the Greek over the barbarian. Later, they acted in the whole Mediterranean world as eager apostles of the Hellenistic civilization which they themselves had created. Not only the Greeks but also the Medes, the Persians, the Egyptians, the Phoenicians, the Gauls, and the Latins were in pre-Roman antiquity distinct ethnic and cultural groups. They recognized themselves and were recognized by others as being different from other such groups. Probably the Egyptians had as strong a national consciousness as the ancient Jews; their pride in their distinct identity was pride in their great culture, in their religion, and in their glorious history.

The Middle Ages were the cradle of modern European nationalities even though national consciousness was rather weak for several reasons: the feudal structure that fragmented the linguistic groups, the supreme loyalty claimed by the Church, the use of Latin as the *lingua franca* of the educated people, changes in the political boundaries which were often due to dynastic considerations, such as royal marriages, but never to ethnic or linguistic considerations. Temporal attachments could not flourish at a time when the supreme loyalty was thus defined in 1095 by Pope Urban: "Let no attachment to your native soil be an impediment, because, in different points of view, all the world is exile to the Christian, and all the world his country." Local loyalties, strengthened by the isolation of the medieval man from other regions, loyalties to the native province, to the feudal lord, to the city, also stood in the way of a larger national solidarity.

Yet we have several proofs of the existence of a national consciousness, usually submerged but sometimes brought to the surface by hostile contact with another national group. The medieval Roman Empire became an essentially German empire after the election of Henry I as Emperor in 919. This fostered national pride among the Germans but inclined other nationalities, such as Englishmen, Frenchmen, and Poles, to assert their independence of the Empire. The Crusades stimulated national consciousness by bringing crusaders of various nationalities into daily contact. Because national consciousness includes a sense of alienation from other nationalities, it is not surprising that it was often clarified by conflict with another nationality. The Hundred Years War acted as a final catalyst for both Englishmen and Frenchmen; they took full cognizance of their own national identity by opposing each other. That this clarification was not limited to the upper classes is proved by the fact that the French leader, Joan of Arc, was a girl of humble social origin. Her famous battle cry "Drive the Englishmen from France" sounds like a modern nationalistic slogan. The struggle against the Moslems helped the Castilians, the Catalans, and the Portuguese of the Iberian Peninsula to take stock of their national feelings. German expansion toward the east stimulated national consciousness among the western Slavs. The constant menace of invasions from Asia crystallized the Russian national consciousness as early as the eleventh century. The *Tale of the Host of Igor*, dating from the twelfth century, is clearly imbued with a pronounced national feeling.

When Edward I appealed in 1295 to the Model Parliament to defend England against the aggressive designs of the French king, he used an argument that sounded modern, namely that the French king intended to erase the name of the English from the face of the earth. In 1362 English began to replace Norman French as the language of Parliament and of the courts. The process of taking cognizance of national feelings was accelerated in England, perhaps by its isolated geographical position. Numerous European visitors to medieval England noted the contempt for aliens displayed by the English people. The history of England which Matthew Paris wrote in the thirteenth century shows a great dislike for continental Europeans; more interesting, those Europeans were for him Frenchmen, Germans, Italians, distinct from each other as though the French kingdom of his time united all French-speaking lands and Germany and Italy were unified under one central government. The same process was slower in France. During the Hundred Years War the French-speaking Guyenne and Gascony were mostly pro-English and the French-speaking Burgundians were the sworn enemies of the French king. Yet several speakers at the French Estates General in 1484 voiced a quasi-modern concept when they spoke of French unity as superior to all provincial loyalties.

Examples multiply in the fifteenth century. The emergence of large unified states out of the feudal fragmentation helped to clarify the national consciouness because those states were usually founded on the linguistic unity of at least the dominant section of the population. The king personified the nation-state and was its living symbol. Nationalities, ruled by a foreign sovereign, sometimes revolted. The Swedes rose up against their Danish king in 1434 and elected a native nobleman as their ruler. It is interesting that the revolt had begun among the Dalarna district miners, who again in 1521 supported their countryman, Gustavus Vasa, in his claim to the Swedish throne; for the Swedes, Gustavus Vasa was *their* king who was to take the place previously held by a foreigner, the king of Denmark.

Students at the medieval universities were divided into "nations," but the term then had a different meaning. A nation included students from one province only or from several linguistic groups; it was basically a geographical subdivision of the student body. However, students at the Prague University were, after 1400, mainly Czechs and Germans, and their co-existence was no longer facilitated by the presence of large groups of students of other nationalities. In 1409 King Wenceslaus gave three votes to the Czech "nation" and only one to the German "nation." The German students withdrew in protest and in the same year founded a rival university at Leipzig. Czech national sentiment was fortified not only by opposition to the large German minority in their own country and by the official use of their language as the state language since the reigns of Charles IV and his son Wenceslaus, but also by the reformation movement of John Huss, who recommended to his countrymen the cultivation of their native tongue. Since the Germans remained Catholics throughout the fifteenth century, the Hussite Czechs opposed them for both religious and national reasons. Czech dissatisfaction with foreign sovereigns led them in 1458 to elect a countryman as king, George Podiebrad. At the same time, the Hungarians elected their countryman Matthias Hunyadi for the same reason.

The Council of Constance (1414-18), which terminated the Great Schism in the Western Church, was rent by rivalries between the dominant nations of the time—the Germans, the French, and the English. The eventual choice of an Italian, Martin V, as Pope was a sort of compromise. The same Council witnessed an acrimonious dispute between the Poles and the German Teutonic order. Nevertheless, the picture was not yet modern. The prelates attending the Council were divided into four and later five "nations." Although the Spanish and Italian "nations" roughly corresponded to our ethnic and geographical notions, the other three included more than one nationality in our sense of the word. Thus, the English nation counted among its members Scandinavian prelates as well as French-speaking prelates from those large parts of France which were then held by the English crown; the German nation included Czech, Polish, and Hungarian prelates; and the French nation did not embrace the whole French-speaking clergy.

In Italy the feeling of over-all national community was submerged by strong local loyalties. Yet this feeling of cultural unity was not absent, as evidenced by Dante, who wrote in Italian (the thirteenth and fourteenth centuries), by Francesco Petrarca (the fourteenth century), who expressed his Italian feelings in the famous poem *Italia Mia*, and by his contemporary, Cola di Rienzi, who unsuccessfully planned to unite Italy under Roman leadership and to extend Roman citizenship to all Italians. *The Commentaries* (Memoirs) of Pope Pius II, which cover the years between 1405 and 1464, abound in proofs of the contemporary existence of an Italian national feeling, too weak however to overcome the bitter rivalries among the Italian princes and cities. Pius II also frequently refers to similar feelings in several other European countries. The French invasion in 1494 by Charles VIII prompted Niccolo Machiavelli to write *The Prince* with the purpose of offering practical if ruthless political advice to a providential prince who would unite Italy and expel the foreigner. It would be arbitrary to consider these individual cases as inconsequential; men are in each epoch the products of their environment and can reflect only the feelings which exist in their time. It can be said, however, that such individual voices as those of Rienzi and Machiavelli magnified the weaker national sentiments of their Italian contemporaries.

Even the medieval national saints evidenced the existence of nationalities; had national feelings been negligible in the Middle Ages the Church would not have felt the need to bestow patron saints on the various nations, such as St. Denis for France, St. Boniface for Germany, St. Patrick for Ireland, St. Stanislaus for Poland, St. Wenceslaus for Bohemia, St. Stephen for Hungary, and so on.

The Scottish wars with England and the Welsh revolts against English rule also prove that national feelings were not unknown in the Middle Ages. After the last Welsh revolt in 1400 Henry IV tried to stamp out national resistance by forbidding Welshmen to bear arms, to own castles, or to hold office. Mary, the daughter of Charles the Bold of Burgundy, had to promise that her subjects' languages would become the languages of state administration and that her officials would be recruited only among the natives.

By the end of the Middle Ages the European nationalities were fully formed. Pope Pius II, who had tried in vain, after the Turkish conquest of Constantinople in 1453, to unite Western Christendom for a crusade against the Moslems, exclaimed: "There are so many different nations, and who could shepherd such a mixed flock? Who has the command of the multitude of tongues they speak, or is able to deal with men of such widely different manners and characters? Where is the mortal man that could bring England into accord with France, or Genoa with Aragon, or conciliate Germans, Hungarians, and Bohemians in their disputes?"

In retrospect, it is difficult to say whether the linguistic community of the population helped in the building of large unified states during the later part of the Middle Ages, or whether the formation of those states promoted the feeling of national solidarity. Probably both assumptions are true.

During the three centuries which intervened between the decline of the Middle Ages and the French Revolution the feeling of attachment to one's country was reflected in loyalty to the sovereign, who personified the nation-state. There were several such states, each with its dominant ethnic-linguistic group: England, France, Spain, Portugal, Holland, Denmark, Sweden, Poland, Russia. Of course, the lack of universal education, of general military conscription, and of cheap newspapers, as well as the subdued position of the lower classes, prevented the development of a heightened national consciousness.

The royal government had a practical interest in favoring the official use of the language that was spoken by the majority of the population or by its most influential section. French was declared the official language of the courts in 1539 in spite of the protests of the Provençals against the exclusion of their language. Philip II made Spanish the official language of his kingdom.

The Renaissance, with its exaltation of the Greco-Roman virtue of patriotism, also contributed to the stimulation of national feelings. The discovery in 1455 of the only copy of Tacitus' *Germania* caused the German humanists to take great pride in the Teutonic virtues which Tacitus had extolled. This national sentiment later declined in Germany as a result of the Thirty Years War that divided the country; it revived in force only in reaction to the Napoleonic invasion. A lively English patriotism can be seen in Shakespeare's royal dramas (the dying John of Gaunt's praise of England, King Henry V's address before the battle of Agincourt, for instance). The puritanic belief that Englishmen were a chosen people further fortified national pride.

The Thirty Years War was for the Germans a civil war fought between Catholics and Protestants. Its opening stage in Bohemia was, however, marked by an outburst of national feelings. The Bohemian Diet passed in 1615 (almost on the eve of the War) a statute against the employment of officials who did not know Czech and ordered all aliens (in fact Germans) who resided in Bohemia to teach Czech to their children; it debarred those who did not know the Czech language from the privileges of the aristocracy and the urban patriciate. For the Czechs, the War was not only for freedom of conscience but also against the German Hapsburgs.

The foundation of national Protestant churches intensified national feelings, for the church came to be identified with the nationality because of its use of the vernacular language and because its clergy were independent of Rome.

However, the revolt in the sixteenth century against Spanish rule demonstrated the uncertainty of national feelings in the Low Countries. Catholic Flemings eventually preferred, for religious reasons, to remain under Spain together with the Catholic but French-speaking Walloons. The Protestant Dutchmen, who spoke at that time practically the same language as the Flemings, broke with Spain for both national and religious reasons. However, the Portuguese insurrection against Spanish rule in 1640 was certainly not due to religious motivation, since both peoples were Catholic.

The eighteenth century, therefore, did not mark the beginning of national consciousness but laid the cornerstone for modern mass nationalism. It stimulated national consciousness through its intense interest in the national cultural past, folklore, and language. The French Revolution opened the gates of political life to the common man by eliminating aristocratic privileges, by proclaiming the principle of equality before the law, and by transferring power to the bourgeoisie. The nineteenth century completed the process through the gradual extension of the electoral franchise and the no less gradual expansion of the school system. The Industrial Revolution made its own contribution by further enabling the common man to become politically articulate; it accelerated the process of urbanization that created politically alert populations, and it encouraged the spread of literacy through techniques of printing.

The eighteenth and early nineteenth centuries abound in manifestations of national feelings. When Joseph II tried to introduce German as the official language in the public administration and schools of his hereditary lands, he met with fierce resistance, especially in Hungary. Danish became the official language of Denmark in the second half of the eighteenth century, replacing German for army use. In 1771 Gustavus III told the Swedish parliament of his pride in having been born a Swede and of his love for the native country. In 1766 the French statesman Turgot sounded a modern note in a letter in which he cautioned against confusing the nation with the state and defined the nation as a community of language. The French Revolution completed the process by eliminating the king, the symbol of national loyalty, and by transferring allegiance directly to the French nation.

Thus, in the eighteenth century the men who, like Johann Gottfried Herder (1744-1803), began to shape the literature on the problem of nationalities and national feelings did not create a social phenomenon but only took cognizance of it and hence contributed to its future growth.

The national feelings of the modern period are distinguished from those of preceding centuries mainly by their greater intensity, an intensity made possible by the participation of the common man in the affairs of his country. The difference can be measured by the abandonment in the early nineteenth century of the earlier and not infrequent practice of hiring foreigners as diplomats. The previous assumption was that professional loyalty would prove stronger than attachment to the native country. The Emperor of Russia made an anachronistic gesture by offering to Bismarck, then the departing Prussian ambassador, a post in the Russian diplomatic service. Bismarck expressed the spirit of the time by declining the offer.

As noted earlier, the French Revolution marked the beginning of a new era, that of European mass nationalism. Its wars were fought by common men, who proudly called themselves citizens but no longer subjects. Its flags were deployed not only in the name of freedom and equality but also for "the sacred and inalienable rights of nations." The common man was entering on his new political career not only as a citizen but also as a patriot. The French example of a genuine mass patriotism was contagious for the whole continent. Mass nationalism was beginning its triumphant march across Europe, from Spain to Russia. The concept that men owed their highest allegiance to their nation was taking hold of all European peoples.

It is interesting to note that the French troops were repaid in their own patriotic coin in Spain (1808-14) and in Russia (1812-13), where they were harassed by peasant guerrillas. Evidently national consciousness was not limited to the upper classes, for the Spanish or Russian peasant did not come out against the foreigner to defend his vested interests, which were nonexistent. He was a serf and knew that he would remain a serf whether under foreign or national rule.

The Congress of Vienna (1814-15) seemed to mark a sudden halt in the progress of mass nationalism. The statesmen assembled in Vienna considered the French revolutionary and imperial era as an abnormal interlude and tried, as far as possible, to restore the *status quo ante bellum.* They were guided in their political and territorial decisions by two ideas. One was the idea of legitimacy, i.e., the principle that sovereigns and dynasties had a right to recover territories which they had lost during the French wars. The other was the concept of the balance of power, which inclined the Congress in favor of distributing provinces among the victors according to a careful evaluation of the size of each territory and the number of its population. The new frontiers were traced with due respect for both principles, especially the second. Millions of people were placed under alien rule. The aspirations of the populations concerned were completely ignored, except for those treaty provisions which guaranteed a certain autonomy to the Poles.

However, the march of nationalism could not be halted for long. The political map of Europe, as traced in Vienna, was gradually changed by national aspirations which were summed up in the desire of people speaking the same language to be united in one state of their own. The ideal of the nation-state profoundly influenced the events of the nineteenth century. The revolts and policies inspired by this ideal transformed the continent from the European frontiers of the Ottoman Empire up to the Low Countries. Paradoxically, European control over alien peoples in Asia and Africa was, during this same period, extended and consolidated. The so-called Augustan period of European colonialism contrasted with the triumphs of nationalism in Europe itself.

The Greeks rose up in arms in 1821 against Turkish rule, and several years later their independent state was internationally recognized. The other Turkish-controlled Christian populations followed the Greek example. During the period between 1821 and 1913 several Balkan and Danubian nations emerged as new independent nation-states: Greece, Rumania, Serbia, Montenegro, Bulgaria, and finally Albania. The Turkish state, an imposing if decrepit empire in 1815, was eventually able to retain only a small territory in Europe.

The Belgians, placed by the Congress of Vienna under the sovereignty of the Dutch crown, revolted in 1830; their independence was recognized in 1831 by the European great powers. The Poles twice fought against Russia for the recovery of their independence (1830-31 and 1863-64), but were defeated both times. Fear of Polish aspirations was the main reason for close co-operation between the partitioning powers (Russia, Austria, and Prussia, later the German Empire) for several decades of the nineteenth century. The nationalities of the Austrian Empire began to stir. The Hungarian insurrection in 1848-49 was suppressed by Austrian armies which Russia assisted with its expeditionary corps. This insurrection was not, however, fruitless; in 1867 the Austrian emperor conceded to the Hungarians an equal partnership in the control of the Empire, which was transformed into the Austro-Hungarian Dual Monarchy. The fact that the Dual Monarchy was henceforth ruled by Austrians and Hungarians further embittered the other component nationalities; their discontent was growing deeper with the passage of each decade.

A powerful movement toward unification within one state was taking hold of Italians and Germans. The small Kingdom of Piedmont and Sardinia assumed the mission of uniting all Italians under one government. Austria, the only foreign power to control large Italian-speaking provinces, was proclaimed the main enemy. It was defeated, with French military help, in the war of 1859-60. At that time Austria lost Lombardy, and in 1866 the province of Venice. Gradually the small Italian states, including most of the Papal states, were annexed by the Kingdom of Piedmont and Sardinia, which in 1861 was renamed the Kingdom of Italy. Finally, a united Italy ended the temporal rule of the Popes and in 1870 proclaimed Rome its national capital.

Prussia, which had taken the lead in the process of German unification, defeated its rival Austria in 1866, and after its victory over France, the only great power which could have opposed the German integration, the unified German Empire was proclaimed in 1871. This event radically modified the distribution of power in Europe.

The force of nationalism was fully understood by the two belligerent coalitions during the First World War. The Germans and the Austro-Hungarians appealed to the nationalities controlled by their enemies, in particular by Russia. Britain, France, and Italy directed their propaganda to the restive nationalities of Austria-Hungary. Britain instigated the Arab revolt against the Turks. The temporary weakness of Russia, due to the war and the revolution, gave various non-Russian nationalities an opportunity to assert their will to become independent. President Wilson included among his war aims the liberation of oppressed nationalities. It was understood, however, that this liberation could take place only at the expense of the enemies (Germany, Austria-Hungary, Turkey, and Bulgaria) and also of Bolshevik Russia. It was impossible to extend the principle of national self-determination to the populations controlled by the Allies.

Military defeat in the fall of 1918 brought about a spontaneous disintegration of Austria-Hungary, one of the oldest European great powers. The existence of that imposing empire, which had for centuries withstood the assaults of time and the adversities of history, was terminated, not by the decree of the Allied victors, but by the will of its several component nationalities, each wishing to take its own separate way. On the ruins of the Austrian-Hungarian and Russian empires new states arose: Finland, Estonia, Latvia, Lithuania, Poland, and Czechoslovakia. Other states, which had existed prior to 1914, greatly expanded their territories by including provinces where the majority of the population spoke their language. Italy, Rumania, and Greece were the main beneficiaries of this process. Serbia united within one state, now called Yugoslavia, almost all southern Slavs (principally Serbs, Croats, and Slovenes), who had been ruled by Austria-Hungary prior to 1918.

The Paris Peace Conference (1919-20) acknowledged the territorial changes that had already taken place and redrafted the frontiers mainly according to the principle of nationality. Ideologically, it took a stand opposite to the Congress of Vienna. Linguistic statistics were carefully consulted, and in a few cases plebiscites were held to ascertain the wishes of the populations concerned. The price of this vast operation of redrafting the map of Europe, which the Paris Peace Conference undertook, was paid by the defeated nations—Germany, Austria, Hungary, Turkey, and Bulgaria. The political face of Central and Eastern Europe was drastically modified.

Three great powers were bitter about these changes. Germany lost large territories to Poland, France, and Denmark. Russia, renamed the Union of Soviet Socialist Republics, was stripped of the Tsarist provinces which now became the independent states of Finland, Estonia, Latvia, Lithuania, and Poland, and of another province annexed by Rumania. The third great power which was dissatisfied with the postwar status quo was Italy, one of the victorious Allied nations. The Italians thought that Britain and France had given them—in Europe, the Near East, and Africa—less than their legitimate share of the spoils of victory.

Opposition to the status quo for territorial and other reasons eventually brought about the German-Italian Axis and the temporary German-Soviet co-operation in 1939-41.

Mass nationalism gave rise after the First World War to new political movements which can be called by their generic name of Fascism, Italian Fascism having been the first of its kind. They were new in one sense, namely that the administrative machinery of the modern state, along with modern mass media of information, made possible the perfecting of age-old authoritarian forms of government, tyrannies and dictatorships; the masses could at last be tightly controlled by a single political organization brooking no opposition.

The principal reasons for the success of Italian Fascism and German National-Socialism were:

1. Widespread national frustration due to the outcome of the First World War.

2. Unsettled economic conditions (inflation, impoverishment of large sections of the middle and lower-middle classes, unemployment).

3. The fear of Communism.

4. Disappointment with the parliamentary regime and loss of confidence in the ability of parliamentary politicians to cope with the principal problems of the day.

5. Disunity and lack of resolution among the political parties and other organizations which were opposed to the Fascist or the Nazi movement.

Both movements were unorthodox; their ability to govern was not yet tested; their opposition to the existing governments and parliamentary parties was forceful and uninhibited; their aggressive nationalism could not be equalled by other parties; they seemed to many to be the saviors of the country and the messiahs of a great national future.

It is difficult to speak seriously of the Fascist ideology. Unlike political democracy and Communism, Fascism had no universal ideology—no coherent complex of ideas concerning the arrangement of "the best society"—which all the Fascist parties would have called their own. The only permanent ingredients in the Fascist "ideology" were an exalted and aggressive nationalism and the government of the state by one single party. Fascism everywhere was principally a parasite that throve on frustrated nationalism. Except for these two ingredients, Fascism took various shapes and adopted various views regarding social problems, depending on the conditions and traditions of the country concerned.

Mussolini did not hide the lack of any coherent Fascist doctrine when he said in 1919: "Facts are our doctrine." He added in 1924 that the only permanent component of Fascism was the Italian nation. In 1929-30 the Italian Fascists tried to construct a doctrine around the concept of the corporate state, but even this doctrine was not considered a dogma. Hitler refused in 1933 to present an ideological program, saying that all such programs were irrelevant and that only human will counted. His *Mein Kampf* was not written until after the first Nazi attempt to seize power in 1923; it was an autobiography and a passionate appeal to action rather than a presentation of coherent doctrine. Both movements proudly displayed their contempt for "cold rationalism." Whatever "doctrine" the two movements produced in the later stages of their history was principally a motley of irrational myths and signposts for political action. Both "doctrines," if divorced from nationalism, would have been empty shells.

The generic name of Fascism is used not because Fascists of various nationalities shared the same coherent political and social philosophy, but because all Fascist movements had certain common features. These features derived from the political tactics used by the Fascist party to seize and hold state power.

1. Both movements fully exploited the national feelings of their countrymen, and both whipped these feelings up to a frenzy. Both identified the nation with the state, and both subordinated everything, individuals and social groups, to an omnipotent state controlled by the monopolistic party. Mussolini said in 1925: "Everything within the state; nothing outside it." Hitler claimed that the state was "an immanent conscience of the nation." Both movements equated the will of the state with that of the party, and the will of the party with that of its supreme leader. The deification of the nation-state justified complete state control over all human activities and all social organizations, which became obedient subsidiaries of the state and the party.

2. Both movements openly believed that the means were sanctified by the end, which was the greatness and might of the nation. The brutal suppression of Italian domestic opposition and the external conquests, the Nazi concentration camps, gas chambers, foreign wars, brutal treatment of populations in the occupied countries, were all justified by the superior interest of the Italian or German nation.

3. Both exploited the fear of Communism and both masqueraded as socialist. Their "true socialism" was opposed to liberal economies and to Communism. This "true socialism" was to reconcile social classes by enlisting them in a common service of the nation-state. In fact, neither movement did anything spectacular for the working people, and both were supported by big business and large landowners who regarded them as bulwarks against Communism. Both drew their recruits from the frustrated elements in all social classes, including the workers. The picture of Fascism and Nazism as having been movements followed and supported only by the rich and by the petty bourgeoisie finds no justification in the statistical data concerning the social distribution of their membership. It is unfortunately true that both movements had a large popular appeal for all sorts of reasons, such as their rabid nationalism, their ability to whip up collective hysteria by demagogic slogans, attractive symbols and mass meetings, and their myths, which, like all myths, had the magnetism of the irrational (a myth, accepted on faith, liberates the believers from the burden of critical thinking and provides them with a sense of intellectual security).

These myths were woven around the nationalist theme. The Italians were told that they were the legitimate heirs of the glories of the Roman Empire and that they were destined to rebuild a new empire around the Mediterranean Sea, which was called *Mare Nostrum* (Our Sea). The Germans were assured that they belonged to a superior biological race, the incarnation of Aryanism, and that this gave them the right to rule other peoples, who were inferior by definition because they were not Germans. The myth of German racial purity demanded the protection of this purity; anti-Semitism was the logical consequence. However, Fascism does not necessarily include anti-Semitism; the Italian Fascists did not practise anti-Semitism until the last phase of their history when they were reduced to the subservient position of German satellites.

4. Both movements were unconditionally subordinated to their respective charismatic supreme leaders, the *Fuehrer* or the *Duce*. Both believed that the leader was anointed by destiny for his mission and was endowed with supernatural powers of will and intellect. Hitler said that he acted as "a catalyst of national energy." His followers of whatever rank were expected only "to believe, obey, and fight." Italian Fascists owed the same blind obedience to their *Duce*.

It is, however, uncertain whether the dogma of the supreme leader is a necessity for any Fascism or whether an oligarchic committee could preside over the destinies of the party and the state. In the known cases of recent European history the strong personality of the leader did not provide an opportunity for the question to arise.

5. Both movements emphatically rejected democratic ideals. They opposed political equality, which they contemptously equated with the blind law of numbers. Hitler said: "History is made by minorities." Both considered that the nation-state should be ruled by a political elite, but neither was specific about how these elites should be selected for their supposedly superior political wisdom.

The elitist principle, founded on the concept of a noncompetitive power elite, led logically to the conclusion that only one political organization should be allowed to exist, the Fascist or the Nazi; its opponents were naturally excluded from the power elite and not permitted to organize or to express their views. Individual freedoms were meaningless, for they were a denial of the concept of society founded on blind obedience to a single party and its supreme leader.

This total power over the state and all social organizations and this total control over all citizens, both vested in a single party, are a common feature of Fascist and Communist regimes. For this reason, both are usually called totalitarian. However, this should not blind one to other and profound differences between the two types of political societies.

Not all authoritarian regimes of recent times should be identified with the Fascist type; many of them have belonged to the old type of military dictatorship and other kinds of nondemocratic government and have not had the effective and total control over political and social activities which the Fascists and Nazis exercised. However, the single-party regimes which have been emerging in several underdeveloped countries (for instance, in the United Arab Republic and in Ghana) bear a resemblance to the Fascist concept of government.

Is European Fascism a dead movement? The survival of Fascist groups is an obvious denial. No one can say what its future might be if circumstances were again to favor its growth. It is also impossible to say what the "doctrine" of neo-Fascism would be in any given country. It could be a composite of all sorts of ingredients, but any Fascism is unthinkable if divorced from an aggressive nationalism, antidemocratism and anti-Communism, and a single-party elitist concept.

The history of European nationalism in the nineteenth and twentieth centuries has amply proved that nationalism can co-exist with any ideology. It has been liberal-democratic in several Western countries where national traditions and popular attachment to democratic ideals have precluded the rise of Facism as an important movement. In other countries nationalism prospered under all sorts of authoritarian or Fascist regimes. Communist Russia and China have wedded their nationalism to the Marxist-Leninist ideology although this ideology originally was truly cosmopolitan. This ability of nationalism to cohabit with any political ideology which happens to prevail in a given country demonstrates the tremendous vigor of national feelings among modern men.

It was an optimistic error on the part of several intellectual leaders of European nationalism in the first half of the nineteenth century to believe that nationalism necessarily was joined to the liberal and progressive ideas of the time and that the triumph of national self-determination would bring about a happy community of satisfied nation-states which would no longer have any reason to quarrel. The reality proved to be less beautiful than they had expected.

Another error frequently committed in our time is to believe that only Fascist nationalism is aggressive. Any nationalism can become imperialist and disregard the aspirations of alien peoples. The colonial history of liberal Britain, France, Holland, and Belgium, as well as the historical record of the Soviet Union and Communist China, prove that the desire to expand at the expense of other peoples is not the monopoly of any kind of regime. On the other hand, modern mass nationalism is not necessarily aggressive, as the examples of such countries as Sweden, Norway, Denmark, and Switzerland prove.

Summing up this brief historical outline confined to Europe, it may be said that national feelings have undergone many fluctuations. The question is not whether they existed at all in former centuries but how strong they were in relation to other loyalties.

It would be wrong to assume that national consciousness in Asia and the Near East made its first appearance in this century. Although the historical records are inadequate, they afford glimpses of remote periods when national feelings rose to the surface, alternating with long periods when they were submerged beneath other loyalties. A few examples will illustrate this statement.

The Arabs did not consider all other Moslems as their equals during the Omayyad Caliphate which was a predominantly Arab empire. The hostile reaction of non-Arab Moslems contributed to the fall of this Caliphate and the rise of the cosmopolitan Abbassyd Caliphate, in which loyalty to Islam took precedence over other loyalties and in which the national descent of the Moslem faithful lost its importance. This same religious loyalty to the Caliph was the essence of the Turkish Empire. The millet autonomy conceded to other denominations made it easier for the Balkan Christian subjects of the Empire to preserve their identity. Those Balkan Christians who were not Greeks (Serbs, Bulgarians, Rumanians, and others) eventually asserted their nationhood in a dual revolt—against Turkish political rule, and against the Greek domination of their national churches.

In ancient India we find an interesting written testimony of the reaction against foreign conquest. Kautilya, the preceptor of one of the Indian princes, Chandragupta Maurya, wrote his famous classic *Arthasastra* in the fourth century B.C. In its recommendation that political objectives be pursued ruthlessly, this collection of political advice reminds one of Machiavelli's *The Prince;* both authors were reacting to a foreign invasion—Kautilya to the Greek irruption into northern India under Alexander the Great, and Machiavelli to the French invasion of Italy. As clearly as Machiavelli, Kautilya expressed his hatred of foreign rule. Many centuries later, in the seventeenth and the eighteenth centuries, the Hindu Maratha movement bore all the marks of a mass national revolt against Muslim rule and the Moghul Empire. It had purely Indian roots, its spiritual and military leaders owing nothing to the European concepts of national self-determination, concepts which were to develop in Europe at a much later date.

There are few examples of such a stubborn survival of national consciousness after many centuries of alien rule as the one offered by the Annamites (Vietnamese). Their country was incorporated at the beginning of our era into the Chinese Empire. It remained a part of this empire for nine hundred years. The Chinese have shown many times over their talent for absorbing conquered peoples into their own nationality by slowly infusing them with the Chinese national consciousness. The Annamites, however, resisted assimilation. After Annam had recovered its independence, its people were not Chinese but still Annamites, although their culture has since had a strong Chinese coloration.

Resistance to foreign conquest and rule during the four centuries of European colonialism probably sprang from a variety of causes, such as religious or cultural antipathy, economic exploitation, or the injustices of colonial administrations. It is possible that one of these causes was sometimes an inarticulate national reaction against foreign domination.

CONFLICT OF LOYALTIES

The opposition between two social loyalties has been a frequent occurrence in every society. When the conflict involves two supreme loyalties, it becomes a very serious matter and can cause deep emotional disturbance for the individual concerned. The monotheistic Jews and early Christians were faced with this conflict because the cult of the Roman emperor was for them a sacrilege, while other Roman citizens saw in it a symbol of imperial loyalty. The conversion of Constantine ended this conflict for the Christians. The medieval struggles between the popes and the emperors and kings created a similar problem for the individual who had to make a choice between the two allegiances, both claiming to be supreme, one to the temporal sovereign and the other to the Church. In modern times the main conflict of supreme loyalties is between the state and the nationality if the two do not coincide. Since both claim supreme loyalty, the individual is compelled to make a choice, and regardless of which claim he chooses to honor, the penalty is the same—to be declared a traitor, either by his state or by his nationality. There are many examples in this and former centuries of persons who have conspired against their state in order to liberate their nationality from alien control; often they were executed as traitors but proclaimed by their nationality as its heroes. Other persons, who have placed state allegiance above loyalty to the nationality and collaborated with state authorities against their rebellious countrymen, have been praised by the state as patriotic citizens and stigmatized by the nationality as contemptible traitors. The tragedy of these conflicts of conscience and their political importance can escape the attention of those whose two supreme loyalties coincide within the nation-state. Yet it should be remembered that the powerful movement toward self-determination is the expression of a deep desire to eliminate this tragic conflict of loyalties. Those who want to throw off foreign rule and form a state of their own nationality simply desire to put an end to the situation in which loyalty to one entity entails disloyalty to the other.

Another conflict of loyalties arises in a time of intense ideological struggle if this struggle transcends national boundaries. Then men are confronted with the choice between loyalty to their state and loyalty to their ideology. The Peloponnesian War was only partly a conflict of interests between the Greek city-states; it was also a struggle between the two ideologies of democracy, centered in Athens, and oligarchy, represented by Sparta. Citizens of the warring cities were often divided by their ideological differences, and ideological fifth columns were well-known. The same was true during the Religious Wars; a Catholic or a Protestant was often compelled by his own conscience to make a choice between loyalty to a sovereign who professed the other religion and loyalty to his own religious cause even though it was defended by a foreign sovereign. The same conflict has reappeared in our time. The pro-Nazi fifth columns during the last war placed their anti-Semitism and their preference for the totalitarian form of government above loyalty to their own nation. A Communist considers that his allegiance to the international Communist movement is more important than loyalty to his national government. His ideological creed makes him think that he is actually a better and more farsighted patriot than most of his own countrymen; it teaches him that he works, not for a foreign government, but for a better future for his own people. If he undermines the present political structure of his country and does it in step with the actions of the Communist states, he hopes to redeem his people from the shackles of a regime which is, according to his convictions, doomed by history; he thereby prepares the ground for a better regime, the Communist. Our historical period thus knows three supreme loyalties which are often in conflict—loyalty to the nationality, to the state, and to the ideology and its own organization.

THE ELEMENTS OF NATIONAL CONSCIOUSNESS

National consciousness cannot be created by fiat. People feel that they belong to the same nationality only if they share certain beliefs; these beliefs do not need to be scientifically correct as long as they are held to be true. To begin with, members of every nationality believe that they have a moral right to a part of the earth which they deem to be "their own." Their claim may clash with that of another nationality, since the two images of national *territory* may intrude upon each other. The members of the nationality usually inhabit the territory which they claim although members of another nationality might live there as well. However, the Jewish community, dispersed throughout the world, was able to preserve its cohesion and identity, among other means, by nurturing the image of the ancestral home as the predestined land of Israel during the two millennia which preceded the rebirth of the Jewish state and during which only a small fraction of the Jewish people actually lived in Palestine.

The image of the national territory is formed in modern times by school maps. This image is an abstract concept; members of the nationality do not actually know the territory they cherish, only fragments of which are truly familiar to them. Whenever they think with deep emotion about their country, they evoke in their imagination the landscapes which they have actually seen and which bring back memories of their own lives. It does not matter that the national territory in its entirety remains unknown to them. They are ready to defend the known and unknown parts of that territory with equal stubbornness against foreign encroachments.

Language is another factor which contributes to national solidarity. It is the most powerful bond for the self-evident reason that it is the means of human communication. The mere fact of speaking the same language can make strangers feel closer, but the stranger with whom we cannot converse seems all the more alien and remote. The Greeks expressed this feeling in their word *Barbaros,* which originally probably meant a stammering person, and the Slavs in the word *Nemcy,* derived from the Slavic word for a mute man; the Slavs bestowed this name on their western neighbors, the Germans.

While a common language has certainly been one of the most important factors in the rise of national consciousness (especially in Europe), two or several nationalities often use the same tongue, such as the English- and Spanish-speaking nationalities whose evolution into separate nationalities was due to historical and geographical reasons. By the same token, a nationality may be multilingual if its national consciousness is composed of other elements strong enough to provide the members of the nationality with a feeling of belonging together and being set apart from other national groups. It is, for instance, an open question whether the bilingual Belgians and Canadians, the Swiss with their four spoken languages, the multilingual Indians and Pakistanis, are bound together only by loyalty to the same state or form single nationalities composed of two or more linguistic groups. In any case, the other factors which make up the national consciousness (for instance, a common historical past, the same self-evident truths and ways of life, the will to preserve the identity and cohesion of the national group) must be strong enough to withstand the pressure of possibly divergent aspirations and interests of the component linguistic groups. The differences in cultural characteristics between the linguistic groups are unavoidably deepened by the existence of distinct literatures corresponding to the different languages. Assuming that not only multilingual states but also multilingual nationalities can exist (the Swiss seem to offer the best proof), it must be conceded that their problem of national cohesion is much more difficult than that of unilingual nationalities. The frictions between the English- and French-speaking Canadians, the English- and Afrikaans-speaking white South Africans, the French- and Flemish-speaking Belgians, the numerous linguistic groups of India, and the Urdu- and Bengali-speaking Pakistanis, to mention only these cases, suffice to demonstrate the problem. If this friction were to increase in intensity, each linguistic group would develop into a separate nationality.

As powerful a factor as language is in the formation and preservation of national consciousness, it would be erroneous to consider it an absolutely indispensable element to the existence of a nationality or to the determination of the nationality to which an individual belongs. The Jews did not lose their national identity after adopting Aramaic as their spoken language. The Irish did not lose their national consciousness after adopting English as their spoken language. The plebiscites which were held after the First World War in Central Europe disclosed that many persons voted against the wishes of the nationality whose language they used at home. Finally, language is no criterion of national consciousness for the people who are bilingual by birth, as some may be if their parents are of different nationalities.

Language was the main factor in building national consciousness in Europe. In this respect, it is interesting to compare the histories of Western and Eastern Christendom. The Eastern churches used the local languages or at least an archaic form of these languages in their religious services and thereby helped certain nationalities to preserve their identity in spite of centuries of foreign domination. The Greek, Armenian, Serb, and Rumanian churches are examples. The clarification of national consciousness was, on the other hand, retarded in the Western countries by the ritual use of Latin in the Middle Ages, especially since the same language was also used in general intellectual intercourse. The rise of vernacular literatures had the opposite effect of deepening the differences between the various linguistic groups, including their educated elites. This new trend, which favored the literary use of vernacular languages and which began in the later Middle Ages (Dante and Chaucer are the medieval protagonists of national languages), gathered full momentum in the sixteenth century. In their efforts to "purify" Latin, the humanists turned it into a truly dead language by extirpating the medieval alterations which had made it a malleable and living instrument of expression for medieval man. They unintentionally increased the attraction of the vernacular literature. During the Reformation, vernacular translations of the Bible further popularized the national languages. The invention of printing ensured a wide circulation of the vernacular literature. The literate people became even more conscious of the ties uniting them to other people who spoke the same language.

The national leaders of today fully realize the importance of language as a common bond, as shown by the modern revival of Hebrew in Israel and of Gaelic in Ireland, as well as by the efforts of newly independent multilingual communities in Asia to institute, by decree so to speak, a national language (India, Indonesia, and the Philippines, for example).

Those who now consider themselves Arabs are of a most diversified ethnic origin. They acquired a feeling of community, which has survived to the present time, after the conquering Arabs had converted them to

Islam and imposed on them the vernacular use of the sacred language of the Koran, Arabic.

Even the script used by a nationality is not without its importance. The Serbs and the Croats, who speak the same basic language, divided centuries ago into separate and rather antagonistic nationalities after the Serbs were converted to the Greek-Orthodox religion and the Croats to the Catholic religion; the religious and cultural differences that developed as a result were accentuated because the Serbs necessarily adopted the Eastern Cyrillic alphabet and the Croats the Western Latin alphabet.

The Soviet government attaches great importance to this matter of alphabet in its policy toward the Central Asian non-Russian nationalities of the U.S.S.R. Intending to cut them off from their linguistic cousins across the borders (the Turks and the Iranians), it compelled them in the late twenties to replace the Arabic script with the Latin; this was also a means of undermining their knowledge of the sacred language of Islam, the religion of their ancestors. After the Turks had themselves adopted the Latin script, the Soviet government imposed in the thirties the use of the Russian script instead of the Latin. At the same time the Soviet government has been working incessantly to spread among the non-Russian nationalities of the U.S.S.R. the knowledge of the Russian language, which was proclaimed officially in 1956 "the second *native* language" of Soviet citizens who are of non-Russian descent. Moreover, the same government has been proceeding with a gradual revision of the vocabulary of Central Asian nationalities by coining new words from Russian roots in order to replace native words of Arabic, Persian, or even local origin.

The concept of language involves its continuity. The continuity of its language clarifies the continuity of the nationality itself. The image of the nationality always embraces past and future generations. Past generations seem to live on in the cultural heritage which they accumulated and which molds the mentality of the living generation. Future generations are included in the national consciousness because this consciousness cannot exist without the will to preserve, eternally as it were, the identity of the nationality. The members of a nationality can enliven their sense of national continuity by referring to the continuity of the language which was spoken by their ancestors and will be spoken by their descendants. Yet this image of linguistic continuity is, strictly speaking, as inaccurate as the belief that all the present members of the nationality use exactly the same language. The language spoken by remote ancestors would be hardly understood by their heirs, the vocabulary and the grammar having in the meantime greatly evolved. Variations in speech can be considerable among regional dialects and between social classes. A London cockney certainly speaks a different English from Sir Winston Churchill's, in pronunciation, grammar, and vocabulary. However, a concept which people take for true is a social fact in spite of its inaccuracy. If a man believes that he speaks the same language as his ancestor who lived several hundred years ago or the same language as his uneducated countryman, this belief in itself strengthens his national consciousness. Of course, there is a residual truth in this belief, which is fortified by the existence of the national literature, one of the heirlooms of every nationality.

Members of the same nationality usually share another belief, namely in their *common descent.* This belief is also inaccurate; all nationalities are mongrels, the fusion of several races, owing to human migrations throughout the ages. Although actual intermarriage is usually limited to members of the same nationality, the concept of common descent is as mythical as that of racial purity. While it has little biological meaning, a belief in common descent does have an important cultural meaning. All the people who feel that they belong to the same nationality consider its former generations to be their spiritual ancestors although some of these people well know that their physical forebears came from another country. This can be observed in the countries which have absorbed large foreign immigrations. The descendants of these immigrants hark back to the former generations and to the heroes long dead of their present nationality and do not feel emotionally related to the nationality of their physical ancestors.

While belief in a common ethnic descent strengthens the national consciousness, national solidarity is weakened by any social segregation within the national group. The feeling of belonging together is inevitably undermined when a portion of the population is discriminated against. The caste system in India, legally outlawed but socially persistent, and color segregation in South Africa and in the South of the United States certainly hinder national cohesion. In South Africa, in fact, the policy of *Apartheid* excludes the colored majority of the population from what could be considered a South African nationality; dissension between the English- and the Afrikaans-speaking sections of the white population makes it seem doubtful whether even the whites form one nationality.

Religion has often played an important role in providing a sense of community by differentiating a nationality from its neighbors. The ancient Jews were able to preserve their identity, despite many historical vicissitudes, because their monotheistic religion separated them from other peoples of antiquity. The theological disputes among the Eastern Christians, which divided the Egyptians, Syrians, and Mesopotamians from the Orthodox Greeks, often had an undertone of national friction. This antipathy felt for the Greeks made it easier for the Arabs to conquer the Near Eastern provinces of the Byzantine Empire and to convert the inhabitants to Islam. The millet system of autonomy helped the Christian communities to preserve their national identity within the Turkish Empire. As noted before, the Hussite movement was also a national movement for the Czechs. Religion separated the Serbs from the Croats, and the Flemings from their linguistic brethren the Dutchmen. Islam was the main factor in consolidating the Ottoman Empire whose Sultan-Caliph acted as the secular and religious leader of all Moslems. It retarded the national self-assertion of the ethnic divisions of the Arab and later Turkish empires by becoming itself the object of supreme loyalty for the faithful. After the victory in 1908 of the Young Turks with their promotion of purely Turkish patriotism, the other Moslem nationalities of the Empire, such as the Arabs and the Kurds, lost the feeling of being equal subjects of the Sultan; Islamic unity was broken, to be gradually replaced by separate national movements. Religion helped the Catholic Irishmen to preserve their nationality under the rule of Protestant Englishmen, while Protestantism fortified the solidarity of the English during their struggles against Catholic Spain and France. In recent times religion has proved an important common tie for various Asian nationalities: Islam for Indonesia, Pakistan, the Malays, and the Arabs; Buddhism for Burma, Thailand, Cambodia, and Ceylon. Even within the last fifty years religion has been used as a determinant of nationality. In the exchanges of population transacted between Turkey, Greece, and Bulgaria after the First World War, the religion confessed was considered more important than the language spoken at home; thus Bulgarian- and Greek-speaking Moslems were exchanged for Turkish-speaking Christians (Greek Orthodox).

The impact of religion on the national consciousness can be fully appreciated only if it is realized that religion signifies in this context not only a set of beliefs but also distinct cultural patterns and ways of life. For instance, it is in this wide sense that religion divided India into two main communities, the Hindu and the Moslem, each having its own diametrically different philosophy of life and habits of daily existence. If theological differences alone were sufficient to account for this split within the Indian subcontinent, there would exist a sort of Islamic nationality much larger than the present Pakistan and embracing all the Moslems of the world, which is patently untrue. The two main communities of the subcontinent had different customs and traditions and were separated by several centuries of mutual animosity. In 1947 the Moslems were confronted with the prospect of cohabitation with the Hindus in one state despite different ways of life and past resentments, and they were alarmed at the possibility of becoming a minority discriminated against by the Hindu majority. The much-debated question whether the Moslems of India formed a religious community but were a part of the Hindu nation, as the leaders of the Congress Party believed, or whether they were a separate nationality, was decided by the partition. The very existence of the Pakistani state can only deepen the feeling among the Pakistanis of being a distinct national community which can never be merged with the Hindu nation.

With its declining influence on modern life, religion plays a minor, perhaps negligible, role in the national consciousness of advanced peoples. It is obvious that a modern nationality remains cohesive despite the variety of religions professed by its members and the existence of agnostics and atheists. This is true of all the peoples belonging to the realm of European civilization, including the Western Hemisphere and Russia, but is becoming true of other peoples as well. For instance, Christian Arabs greatly contributed to the renaissance of modern Arab nationalism, while a Christian or agnostic Hindu does not renounce his Indian nationality.

Religion has exerted another kind of influence on modern nationalism. The latter has borrowed from religion certain external means for the promotion of the feeling of kinship. National anthems, flags, festivals, heroes, and national sacred documents bear the distinct mark of religion, with its prayers, visible symbols, saints, and sacred scriptures. These symbols and ceremonies help to make the nationality, which is, after all, only a concept in human minds, seem palpable.

Latin American history proves that a national consciousness can originate for reasons other than linguistic and cultural similarity. Except for Brazil and Haiti, all Latin Americans (excluding the nonassimilated Indians) speak Spanish. They inherited the Spanish culture at the time of their independence. Yet *geography* (natural obstacles to continental communication) divided the Latin Americans into several nationalities; colonial administrative subdivisions were another factor. The separate national consciousness was strengthened with the lapse of time by the existence of several states, each of which demanded the supreme loyalty of its citizens and, like states on the other continents, confined the life of its population mainly within its own boundaries. Linguistic and cultural affinity could not prevail against these centrifugal factors, just as it failed to maintain the national unity of the English-speaking overseas possessions of Britain.

Scandinavian history offers an earlier illustration of the role of geography in the emergence of separate nationalities. The Scandinavians spoke the same language until approximately A.D. 1000, but a mountain range divided the Swedes from the Norwegians, and the Danes were separated from both by the sea. The linguistic and other differences which developed within these geographical barriers resulted, during the later Middle Ages, in the emergence of the three Scandinavian nationalities.

The description of the mentality or character of a nationality is at best always a difficult task, because it involves of necessity sweeping generalizations about a great multitude of individuals who are obviously not identical. To guard against false generalizations it is useful to know the civic ideals which are promoted by the schools, to discover the virtues and vices which are singled out as desirable or undesirable qualities in a citizen. The civic education, even if only partly successful, inevitably leaves its mark on the mentality of the people. The upper classes and the educated strata play an important role in this respect, because their values and their behavior are the models which the rest of the population tends to imitate. Thus, civic education and social imitation instill the habits which become the ways of life of a given nationality.

Prejudices and popular clichés are frequently the source of false images of other nationalities. It is tempting to attribute to a foreign nationality which one dislikes certain hateful or contemptible traits of character and to assert that these traits have recurred throughout its long history. However, the characteristics of a nationality, which seem at first to be immutable, do change, although slowly. For instance, English self-control is a fairly new characteristic of which one finds no trace in the dramas of Shakespeare. From the fifteenth to the seventeenth century the Czechs appear to have been an inflammable nation apt to take to arms without fear of heavy odds and ready to face great risks. After their defeat by the Hapsburgs in the Thirty Years War and the destruction of their educated upper classes mainly through the process of Germanization, the Czechs suffered a long period of national eclipse. Following the cultural and political revival in the eighteenth century, the reborn Czech nation seemed to have acquired a new mentality; though stubbornly determined to preserve their national identity, the Czech people had become more circumspect and were more disposed to calculate the risks calmly. The Frenchmen of this century hardly bear any resemblance to their ancestors who in the time of Louis XIV or of Napoleon were a turbulent and recurring menace to the security of their neighbors. Alteration in the mental and moral characteristics of a nationality may be due to a variety of causes, such as economic and social evolution or the dramatic impact of foreign defeats or victories.

The great variety among the nationalities precludes any rigid definition of this real but very elusive phenomenon. This is why the Communist definition is inadequate. It lists four factors which must all be present to validate the claim of a social group to be a nationality:

1. One common language.
2. A definite territory where the nationality forms the majority of the population.
3. A community of economic life.
4. A common culture.

This definition arbitrarily settles the controversial question of bilingual or multilingual communities and denies by implication that the Indians, the Pakistanis, the Belgians, the Swiss, or the Canadians are nationalities. The second prerequisite, a territory inhabited in the majority by the same nationality, has been invoked by the Soviet government in its refusal to acknowledge the Soviet Jews as a nationality and to grant them the right to preserve their cultural identity. A nationality is usually a community of economic life, but this rule suffers exceptions. The Poles led three separate economic lives during the long period after the Partitions when they were the subjects of three foreign states. The Germans of today live under two diametrically opposed economic systems. However, even a Communist would not deny that the Poles were a nationality in the nineteenth century or that the Germans are a nationality today. The fourth factor listed in the definition is noncontroversial, since the nationality cannot exist without a common culture. Yet the notion of a common culture should not be oversimplified. The national culture is unequally shared depending on the degree of education; there is, however, a residue of cultural traditions which binds together the whole nationality and forms the essence of national consciousness.

THE FUTURE?

What is the future of mass nationalism? Are we nearing the time when a new loyalty will emerge superior to national loyalties? Only a prophet could answer this question for the remote future. As for the next few decades, however, if the trends of the last two hundred years and of our own time provide any guidance, mass nationalism will continue to be the principal source of social solidarity even though it fragments mankind into many groups often inimical to one another. This century has witnessed an intensification of nationalism—its savage outburst in Nazi Germany, its marriage to Communism in Russia and in China, and its rapid extension to the non-European continents. There are several reasons why conditions in our time are more propitious than in former centuries for the flowering of the mass nationalism which binds the individual to the chariot of his own country.

The most interesting phenomenon in the advanced and democratic countries is the social and economic integration of the common man within his nation-state. He has the ballot and his interests are defended by various professional and other organizations. His aspirations cannot be ignored by the governments elected by universal suffrage. Unlike his ancestor in former centuries, he considers himself a citizen and has truly become an integral part of his nation. He has broad access to education. He receives at school an image, however primitive it may be, of the national history, culture, and territory, and his steadily improving living standards make him think that he has a stake in the modern welfare state which protects him against economic hazards. The small farmer or industrial worker has found his fatherland. He is more a part of it than ever before. The warmth of his national feeling is revealed in times of stress when an external threat imperils the security of the country which he calls his own. Universal military service and what it eventually entails—the duty to fight together with other members of the same nationality—strengthen the feeling of national solidarity.

The well-being of the nation is a matter of common concern. Tariffs and immigration restrictions are viewed as barriers against invasion by cheap foreign goods or by undesirable aliens who might accept work at low wages and ultimately undermine by their mass influx the cultural unity of the nation.

Modern technology and universal education promote the reign of uniformity within the nationality. In former ages the illiterate peasants who formed the bulk of the population lived in isolated villages; their outlook was parochial but could not be, for the same reason, uniform throughout the national territory. They could learn about events which occurred outside their own rural community only from occasional visitors to their village. Today the citizen of an advanced country is literate. This does not necessarily mean that he is more intelligent than his forebear, but he has access to information about world events. He receives this information at school in his early years, later from newspapers, radio, and television, rarely from books but more often from a public speaker. An illiterate person in the underdeveloped countries now has a device for transcending the horizon of his native village, the radio, which has become the newspaper of the illiterates.

The abundance of means for transmitting information is so impressive that one could jump to the conclusion that modern man is truly enabled to form an independent opinion about everything. Yet all these means of information are national in character. The average man understands only his own language; hence foreign newspapers, periodicals, radio broadcasts, and television are closed to him. He could listen to foreign broadcasts in his own language, but this would entail buying a more expensive receiver, and, more important, he is wary of foreign "propaganda," which, he typically assumes, can never attain the level of "objectivity" of his national sources of information. He is daily bombarded by information which his own countrymen pour out for his benefit. These countrymen might differ widely in their interpretation of domestic issues but are usually in basic agreement on the foreign problems which they think might affect the future of their country. The mass media tend to offer a basically uniform interpretation of foreign events. Deviations are rare. The common man has no way of forming independent views on international issues because he lacks sufficient knowledge for a critical appraisal of the picture built up by the national media of information. The very fact that two men who live hundreds or thousands of miles apart but within the same country, who have never seen each other, nevertheless share the same reactions to foreign events creates an additional bond between them and all other members of the same nationality.

The evolution of modern societies does not lead to the breakdown of boundaries but, on the contrary, toward the enclosure of the individual life within the invisible intellectual frontiers traced by the nation-state. This in turn creates a stronger feeling of "togetherness," of belonging to the same nationality. There is a paradoxical contrast between this growing national uniformity and the ever-increasing rapidity of international transportation. A distant country can now be reached in several hours, while the same journey, in a not too remote past, took several weeks. But the rapidity of the plane is counterbalanced by governmental control over foreign travel; the refusal of a passport or a visa is a more effective barrier than the ocean was for the traveler of a bygone age. It would be bold indeed to claim that modern man can wander the world as freely as a medieval student or artisan did while searching across Europe for knowledge and skill. The modern separation of men by the frontiers of nation-states encourages the substitution of "My country, hence it is always right" for the more humble "My country, right or wrong."

The great success of the movement for self-determination constantly widens the circle of uniform societies, because the once common antinomy between the nationality and an alien state is being eliminated and replaced by nation-states. Populations that were once colonial are now acquiring their own states, along with the economic, educational, social, and informational means for molding national opinion. If it was never easy to be a nonconformist, it has become even harder in the new as well as the old nation-states. Urbanization, universal education, and the technology of mass information do not favor nonconformity.

Another factor that tends to strengthen national allegiance is the gradual erosion of other loyalties. Yet man is a social animal and cannot invest his own life with a satisfactory meaning except by placing the interests of a social group above his own. Society, in turn, cannot survive unless it places the collective interests above those of the individual. However, modern ways of life are weakening family ties; wives and mothers take jobs outside the home to help in earning the family living and have social interests that reach beyond the family circle, and children feel emancipated at a much earlier age than in the past. The church allegiance is not as strong as before. Civic organizations are meaningless unless, as the word *civic* implies, their goals are related to the welfare of the larger national society. Professional associations cannot capture deeply emotional loyalties. The little homelands—the city, the village, the province—stir less emotion in an age when mobility makes so many citizens only short-term inhabitants of any place. Gone are those intense loyalties which linked the individual to the city in ancient Greece or in the Middle Ages. International groups, except for the Communist organization, have proved unable to elicit allegiances stronger than national ties. The dismal failure of the Second International at the outbreak of the First World War demonstrated that the "proletariat" and their leaders had fatherlands, contrary to what Marx had believed. Actually, the two world wars proved that modern men did not hesitate to favor the nationality above all other loyalties. Two men in different uniforms could have been bound by the same religion, the same political or social convictions, even by personal friendship; yet they were suddenly mortal enemies and only because of their divergent national loyalties. With the weakening of other loyalties, the attachment of the individual to his nationality has become increasingly important as a means of withstanding the strain of social disorganization. This consideration is especially relevant for the underdeveloped countries, which must achieve an unusual degree of social solidarity to survive the hazardous and difficult period of modernization. National loyalties will continue to be important until mankind forms other, equally strong attachments.

It is an observable fact that national feelings reach the zenith of their intensity at a time of external danger. All nationalities live now in an epoch of a deep crisis. They sense it and realize that they cannot entirely control the march of events, which are directed by one's own country but also by all other countries. The external world, which seems so full of menace, has the face of the foreigner. Hence the natural reaction to close ranks around the national flag.

The force of national feelings has also been demonstrated by the policies of the Soviet and Chinese Communist parties. These, like other Communist parties, began their careers as sections of an international movement which placed its ideology above national loyalties. The Soviet party started in the thirties to promote Russian nationalism, used it as a powerful instrument for rallying the Russian people to the defense of their country during the last war, and has since continued to make domestic appeals in which a hardly disguised Russian nationalism is skillfully blended with ideological doctrine. The Chinese party follows a similar pattern in which a forceful xenophobia is interwoven. The disciples of the true internationalists Marx, Engels, and Lenin have been compelled to discover that the deepest feelings of modern men can be stirred by an appeal to patriotism and have not neglected to exploit this source of social energy.

A GOOD OR BAD SOCIAL PHENOMENON?

The truth about nationalism lies somewhere between the exalted praises of the extreme nationalists and the anathemas of their opponents. Like all ideological mass movements which mobilize the emotions of vast multitudes nationalism has produced its saints and heroes as well as its inquisitors and hangmen, self-denial and the spirit of sacrifice as well as a ruthless fanaticism, love of one's country as well as hatred of other nationalities, constructive effort by the national community as well as persecution of nonconformists and the butchering of foreign "enemies." It can be turned to many uses, but it is not a utilitarian movement. A numerically small nationality could benefit by adopting the language of another nationality which opens the door to a richer vocabulary and a greater wealth of ideas and knowledge; yet it will cling to its own tongue as the most cherished heirloom. National consciousness always entails the will to preserve the identity of the group.

The main virtue of nationalism is that it constitutes a powerful factor in creating social solidarity. It helps to integrate the individual socially by providing him with a sense of belonging to a group and by offering him the feeling of security which results from his vicarious participation in the power of the group. National emotions can be mobilized for great domestic tasks which demand self-denial for their accomplishment. As a matter of fact, the welfare state in its present and only known form would have been inconceivable without the consciousness of national solidarity which impels those who can to aid their less fortunate countrymen. Of course, there were other reasons for the emergence of this concept, such as the fear of a social revolution and the growing influence of working-class organizations, but the modern feeling of social obligation toward all classes has developed within the boundaries of the nation-state and has been stimulated in its growth by the consciousness of belonging to the same nationality.

A nationality subject to the foreign rule recovers its self-respect in the struggle for freedom. Its members assert their own personal dignity in refusing to take orders from a foreign government and from administrators who usually have neither affection for nor interest in their colonial subjects. The individual who revolts against foreign domination casts off the feeling of inferiority which is inherent in his being a part of the subject nationality.

National differences are the source of cultural variety and hence contribute to the enrichment of mankind. For instance, Europe was not culturally impoverished by the rise of its numerous nationalities. Each produced its own interpretation of the common European civilization, and all contributed to a common cultural treasury. It is diversity, not uniformity, which nourishes human culture, whether this diversity is due to national or other causes. Culturally, the Greek period of antiquity was incomparably more creative than the subsequent Roman period; one of the reasons for the "Greek miracle" was the keen intellectual competition between the independent cities. The cultural history of the Roman Empire, on the other hand, ended in intellectual sterility. However, the same Greek cities which founded our civilization were constantly embroiled in quarrels and struggles which culminated in the disaster of the Peloponnesian War, while the Roman Empire bestowed a rare and precious gift on the Mediterranean world—*Pax Romana.*

The same two facets are evident in nationalism. The existence of numerous nationalities stimulates intellectual competition and diversity but has also been the source of many cruel wars. Like other mass movements, nationalism can be harnessed to destructive purposes. It can be shaped into a force bent on aggression, territorial expansion, and the subjugation of other nationalities. The nation may be deified and this divinity manipulated by its high priests, the national leaders, while the rank and file are turned into blind and fanatical worshippers. The Nazi period in Germany offers the most recent and most horrible example of the degeneration of nationalism into a macabre folly of hatred. This was a repulsive spectacle of human beings who became slaves of their national passions, who blindly sacrificed their own individual freedom and human dignity on the altar of what their leaders had persuaded them to be the national interest, and who marched abroad to make slaves of foreign nationalities.

Ethnocentrism is a frequent symptom of nationalism. It consists in viewing one's own country as the center of the world and as the only measure of the accomplishments and failures of foreign nations. It amounts to a naive belief that one's own nationality is necessarily intellectually and morally superior to other nationalities and that it has discovered the only true "self-evident truths" and the secret of "the good life." It overlooks the fact that national values are always the product of national histories and that these histories are different from one another. It cannot accept the view that the values cherished by one nationality are true for it but that other values might be equally true for another nationality which has lived in different historical circumstances. The ethnocentric nationalist measures foreign nations by the yardstick of his own national values and adjudicates them in consequence good or evil, respectable or contemptible, likable or ridiculous. The ethnocentric attitude precludes any effort to discover why a foreign country preserves its own "self-evident truths" and abides by its own customs; it denies in advance even a relative value to those alien beliefs and ways of life which are markedly different from national ones. Foreign nations, if they are very different from one's own, cut the contemptible figure of evil, backward, or unenlightened communities. The ethnocentric approach to international problems precludes any realistic foreign policy, because it amounts to an incapacity for understanding the motivations which guide other countries.

The ethnocentric bias is very difficult to overcome in our era of ideological conflict, because to admit that one's "self-evident truths" do not need to be self-evident to foreign peoples looks almost like a betrayal of these cherished truths. A Communist will have great difficulty in placing himself in the position of a Western democrat, in trying to understand his motivations, and in admitting that democratic values might not only be self-evident to the democrat but also not necessarily dictated by the desire for material profit. He is in danger of underestimating the power of resistance of Western democracies if he believes that material considerations are their only motivation. At the same time, the Westerner places individual freedom at the top of his hierarchy of values. This does not help him to understand that other peoples, to whom history has left a different legacy and who face different problems, might give priority to other values. For instance, Communism, which horrifies the Westerner as a threat to his individual freedom, can lure a great many non-Westerners with its promise of greater social mobility than they now enjoy and with its methods of rapid modernization, including techniques for accelerated economic development. If an Asian peasant, starving and underemployed, often landless and exploited by his landlord and the moneylender, were by a miracle transported to a Soviet collective farm and had to live there the life of the Soviet collective farmer, he might discover that it would be worthwhile to accept the strict Soviet discipline of labor and Communist ideological conformity as the price for never going hungry and for having the opportunity to send his children to school. But an American or European small farmer would be repelled by the same experience. The American coal miner would be appalled by the living and working conditions of the Soviet coal miner, but a Bolivian tin miner would probably find life in the Soviet *Donbas* very attractive. The Western ethnocentric belief that the whole of mankind is unknowingly but inexorably marching toward the universal fulfillment of democratic ideals is as fallacious as the belief that all human beings will become Christians or Communists.

One of the symptoms of national or cultural ethnocentrism is the frequent tendency in the West to use terms borrowed from the familiar political vocabulary for the interpretation of events which take place in non-Western countries. These terms, once they are transplanted to a different soil, acquire a new meaning which is conditioned by the local history and social situation. For instance, *democracy* traditionally means for the Westerner a regime founded on the individual freedoms, the existence of competing political parties and interest groups, and free elections. He might misunderstand the meaning of the same word when used by a Communist, for whom *democracy* means the total nationalization of the means of production, the elimination of private profit, the enforcement of social mobility, and the rule by one party which claims to represent the interests of the whole population. The term *parliamentary democracy* has a definite sense in the West but can acquire an altogether different meaning in an underdeveloped country where the term can be used to camouflage a regime in which illiterate voters, manipulated by the upper classes, elect a parliament which is the instrument of the same classes and which cannot claim to represent the whole nation; or the same term can refer to another regime in which one party dominates the parliament and in fact uses arbitrary means to prevent the opposition from ever becoming an alternate government. This semantic problem is politically important, because national ethnocentrism tends to give a universal meaning to the terms which originated in one's own country or civilization. This might result in a confused and mistaken interpretation of events in foreign countries.

Another word in common use throughout the world can further illustrate this semantic problem. For the Westerner, *liberation* means not only the termination of alien rule but also the end of any native system of government which is not founded on the consent of the governed. Thus, the slogan "Liberation of Eastern Europe" conveyed to Westerners who treated the slogan seriously the image of two objectives—the termination of Soviet control over the Eastern European nationalities, and the end of the native Communist regimes and their replacement by democratic regimes. The citizen of an underdeveloped country usually understands by the same word the termination of foreign rule or predominant influence—the process which is now called *decolonization*—but not necessarily the establishment of a native democratic system of government. The Communist interprets *liberation* to mean not only the end of Western colonial rule but also the elimination of the native social and economic regime, which he calls *feudal* or *capitalist* and considers obsolete, and its replacement by the Soviet type of socialist regime.

Cultural empathy is the opposite of national ethnocentrism. It is an intellectual curiosity which seeks to understand foreign values and their historical and other sources, as well as the capacity to concede to other nationalities the right, which one claims for his own country, to possess their own "self-evident truths" and ways of life.

NATIONAL SELF-DETERMINATION

National self-determination is the freedom of a nationality to determine its own political fate and to manage its own affairs. Its second meaning is the aspiration to unite all members of the same nationality within their own nation-state. It can be implemented in various ways, from the achievement of political autonomy within a larger, multinational state to the formation of an independent nation-state. It is fulfilled in the second sense when international frontiers are modified to incorporate in one territory people of the same nationality.

The triumph of national self-determination does not necessarily entail that members of the nationality which has won its own state will enjoy the democratic freedoms. National self-determination for one nationality may mean a deterioration in the situation of another nationality or community. The formation of a new nation-state liberates the subject nationality from foreign rule, but those members of the formerly ruling nationality who reside in the same territory and elect to stay rather than emigrate to their original homeland are suddenly scaled down from the position of a privileged minority to the status of equality or perhaps of a group discriminated against. Such was the fate of the German and Hungarian minorities in the nation-states formed or enlarged after the First World War, and such is the present problem of the European minorities who refuse to emigrate from the territories which only recently were colonial dependencies of their own country. For an Englishman in the British East and Central Africa or for a Frenchman in North Africa, the equality of treatment in a newly independent state is a change for the worse compared with his privileged position under the colonial administration. The colonial power frequently favored a native minority in its colonial dependency and thus sought to buy its co-operation against the majority. The day of independence might then mark the beginning of discrimination and persecution which the government of the triumphant majority inflicts on the minority. Moreover, in the new and old nation-states the temptation is great to discriminate against all national minorities who by their very existence blur the picture of national homogeneity. In other words, minorities, national or otherwise, do not necessarily have cause to rejoice in the self-determination of the majority of the population and might look back with nostalgia on the period of rule by a foreign power which had no reason to discriminate against them.

The process of self-determination has its own ironies. A colonial people feel indignant when the colonial power resists their demand for political emancipation. Once victorious and masters of their own independent state, the same people feel no less indignant when a minority of the population, who have a different national consciousness and do not feel happy under the new government, claim the benefit of self-determination in the form of secession. The newly independent state is usually adamantly opposed to the application of self-determination against itself.

The triumph of self-determination is not an unmixed blessing. The new state may find it difficult for a time to replace foreign administrators with its own people if the native trained personnel is in short supply, may have to face economic difficulties after having severed ties of allegiance to the colonial power, or may face expenditures formerly borne by the colonial power, such as the cost of maintaining an army and a diplomatic service. It is not always true that a native government ensures better living conditions than a colonial administration. If one were to compare the conditions before 1935 (the Italian conquest) in independent Ethiopia with those of the Gold Coast, the result would very much favor the British administration. Yet the Ethiopians fought desperately in 1935-36 against the Italian invaders. The future president of an independent Guinea, Sékou Touré, told President De Gaulle what was the usual choice of subject peoples in these proud words: "We prefer poverty in freedom to wealth in servitude." His own people shortly afterwards confirmed the truth of his words by voting almost unanimously for independence in spite of the French threat to cut off all assistance. Moreover, the postwar history of newly independent states proves that native governments are now much more aware of the urgent need for economic and social development in their countries than colonial administrations were before the Second World War.

National self-determination is not a legal right which is adjudicated by a supranational tribunal. Taking into account its popularity in our time, it might be called a moral right. If it were a moral right, the question would arise whether all subject nationalities may avail themselves of this right. Is there an objective criterion by virtue of which this right may be granted to certain nationalities and refused to others?

The conservative bias of mind, which tends to respect situations of long standing but to abhor the disturbances that always accompany change, implicitly approves of the existing nation-states but notes with suspicion and disfavor the clamor of unredeemed nationalities for their own states. Yet there is no valid statute of limitation. If a period of thirty years were specified as prerequisite to the legitimate existence of states, a multitude of states in Asia, the Near East, and Africa would have to be disqualified. If the requisite period were 150 years, a great many European states would have no right to exist, including Germany, Italy, Belgium, and several states in Eastern Europe. If it were 200 years, the legitimacy of all states in the Western Hemisphere would be questioned. After all, all existing states were new at one time.

Numerical strength or territorial extent are no better criteria in view of the existence of many robust yet small states of old lineage. Economic self-sufficiency would militate against the independent existence of practically all states.

The political maturity of the population is an arbitrary criterion whose contents depend on the values of the individual observer. For a democrat a nation is mature if it practises political democracy, but for a Communist only a country ruled by the Communist party is truly mature, while a Fascist would supply a still different definition. Asians and Africans can ask some very indiscreet questions about the political and moral maturity of white men. Was it not white men who caused the slaughter of many millions, mainly their own racial brethren, and the vast destruction of wealth and of historical and artistic treasures in the two world wars? Was it not they who combined technological efficiency with cruelty in inventing concentration camps and gas chambers and who inflicted tortures as a part of judicial and administrative investigations in the very twentieth century which is still their century? If the white man were to retort by pointing to the Japanese wartime record, the present ruthlessness of the Chinese regime, or the cruelties committed by Asians and Africans in former historical periods, this sort of debate would end in a draw.

The problem of whether a nation is mature enough to govern itself politically can be reduced to the practical question of whether it has enough trained personnel to run a modern state. This question, however, leads to a vicious circle. The colonial administration is in no great hurry to train its native successors because it dislikes the very idea of having successors. Usually a country ruled by foreigners has little chance of training its own native elites. This in itself constitutes a powerful argument in favor of self-determination. The record of the colonial powers of the nineteenth century and the first several decades of this century is not very inspiring in this respect. Even now it is not brilliant although both Britain and France, unlike Portugal and Spain, have made a much greater effort since the last war. Colonial history does not prove that a native educated elite would emerge more rapidly under paternalistic colonial rule than in response to the actual and pressing need of an independent state.

There exists, moreover, a solution to this problem of qualified personnel. It consists in hiring competent aliens as civil servants. These aliens perform two functions: they act as advisory and implementing senior officials and as teachers who train their native successors. If the colonial power withdraws in good grace, its own nationals, often former colonial administrators, are hired to ensure the smooth functioning of the new state during the interim period. If the parting of ways is not so friendly or if the government of the newly independent state does not trust the loyalty of foreign civil servants who are all of the same nationality, it will hire specialists of various nationalities. In either case, the activities of these expatriates, as the English call them, are controlled by the native government which formulates the policies that the aliens have to implement. Of course, this provisional solution has its own difficulties. Serious friction may occur between the native ministers and their foreign aides. The newly independent country may feel that it can become completely independent only by removing all aliens from its public administration and the armed forces. Finally, there may not be enough candidates for service in a formerly colonial country; prospective candidates may be deterred by an unhealthful climate, by poor housing, or by the consideration that their stay abroad will not contribute later to their professional advancement in their own country.

In any event, the movement toward self-determination has been so rapid that the issue of political maturity has become irrelevant. What objective criterion would explain why the Algerians were considered unfit for self-government while the Libyans, who, unlike the Algerians, had practically no educated elite, were given an independent state; or why is it that the Africans of Southern Rhodesia should be held immature and fit only to be governed by a European minority while other Africans have achieved their independence? The answers fall short of providing any criterion. It was politically convenient for the Western powers to forestall Soviet interference through the machinery of the United Nations; hence, they elected to make Libya independent, at least nominally, rather than place it under a trusteeship, although Libya at that time had only sixteen persons with university degrees. It was fairly easy for Britain and France to concede independence to West Africa where settlers were few, but it was difficult to withdraw from Central Africa or Algeria where Europeans were numerous and very vocal.

History has amply proved that the fate of nationalities is decided by factors which have little to do with the notion of equal justice for all. The nation-states have owed their birth in past centuries and in the present century to two factors: the will of the nationality to win the battle for its self-determination, and propitious external circumstances. When either factor has been lacking, the movement for self-determination has failed. The autonomous Breton movement collapsed miserably in spite of the frantic efforts of a small group of Bretons during the inter-war period; it never found mass support among the population of Brittany, who considered themselves French. Unfavorable external circumstances might prevent a nationality with a strong national consciousness from winning its independence. The Poles and Czechs have illustrated this principle in a past which ended as recently as 1918. Either the controlling foreign nationality consents to withdraw for its own reasons (the British withdrawals from Asia and West Africa exemplify the process), or it is compelled to do so either by a successful insurrection of the controlled nationality, which it is unable to quell by force (for instance, the Belgian uprising against the Dutch king in 1830), or by defeat in a foreign war (the Austrian-Hungarian Empire collapsed following its military defeat in 1918, and neither the Austrians nor the Hungarians were able to hold together the other nationalities of the Dual Monarchy).

Thus, national self-determination is not a simple exercise of a right but is an aspiration whose fulfillment depends on the distribution of power both within the controlling state and on the international level. This was convincingly illustrated by the events which followed the First World War. The defeat of Germany, the disintegration of Austria-Hungary, and the temporary weakening of Russia allowed several nationalities in Eastern Europe to acquire their own nation-states or to unite their linguistic brethren, formerly the subjects of one of these three empires, within already existing states of their own (Italians, Poles, Czechs, Slovaks, Yugoslavs, Rumanians, Albanians, Lithuanians, Latvians, Estonians). The international distribution of power was unusually favorable for these nationalities. The victorious powers generally sympathized with their aspirations, which could be satisfied entirely at the expense of the defeated enemies or of Bolshevik Russia. The same distribution was unfavorable for the Arabs. It is true that their former sovereign, Turkey, was defeated, but the victors, Britain and France, hastened to divide among themselves the Arab lands taken away from Turkey. The principle of national self-determination was a moral issue for President Wilson who represented a power without political or territorial ambitions in the Near East. Britain and France made use of the principle in an effort to undermine the unity of their enemies, Austria-Hungary and Turkey. Rejecting it as a generally valid concept, they did not intend to apply it to their own colonial possessions. Then and now, the problem of national self-determination is not a moral issue which the various chanceries debate on its own merits in each particular case.

There is no guarantee that the present popularity of self-determination will last forever. A different distribution of power might favor a new imperialism and the reversal of the present trend. Moreover, this trend is not universally successful even at the present time. The Russians do not seem to be disturbed in their control over the non-Russian nationalities of the U.S.S.R., nationalities which form 40 per cent of the total population. The Chinese have tightly fastened their own control over alien national groups which probably amount to over 40 million. Only recently they added conquered Tibet to their dominions. It has always been a common illusion, however, that contemporary trends will persist forever and cannot be reversed.

The problem of national self-determination is complicated by the fact that not all populations which make a bid for their own state are nationalities in the unequivocal European sense. Are the Arabs one nationality because they speak the same language, most of them profess the same religion, all have cultural roots in the Islamic civilization, and hark back to the glories of the Arab Caliphates, or are they Iraqis, Syrians, Lebanese, Egyptians, Tunisians, Moroccans, Algerians, and so on? The present record is confusing in this respect. When an African population of many tribes, languages, and religions, initially grouped together within a single colony by a European power, claims the right to self-determination, it is not a nationality in the European sense. This population is bound together not by a common national consciousness but by the same aversion to foreign rule exercised by an alien race and by a relatively short period of common life under the same colonial administration. The new state which succeeds to an artificially created colonial possession is plagued by the centrifugal loyalties felt by the population for the tribe or the religious or linguistic community. It can survive only by eliciting a supreme loyalty superior to all other allegiances. This problem does not exist for a true nationality, which simply envelops its new state in its own supreme loyalty.

Whenever a nationality wants to conquer its own nation-state or to enlarge the territory of its existing state by including a neighboring population which it claims as a part of its own family, international tension follows, because another state and another nationality must pay the cost of the operation. A change in the political map of the world might bring about the union of several smaller states; this was the result of the German and Italian unifications. Usually the success of self-determination ends in the fragmentation of a multinational state or of a colonial empire, as evidenced by the collapse of Austria-Hungary and of the Ottoman Empire and more recently by the steady disintegration of the European colonial empires.

FRONTIERS

An impartial tracing of frontiers between two nation-states would in most cases leave unredeemed national minorities on both sides of the boundary line. This is the consequence of the intermingling of national and linguistic groups all over the Eastern Hemisphere where migrations have been taking place throughout millennia. The era of mass nationalism therefore brings in its wake the problems of frontiers and of national minorities.

Boundary lines are usually the visible results of a power struggle between states. Whenever a frontier has been contested between two states, force rather than a peaceful negotiation has decided whether it would remain unchanged or be modified in favor of the victor. Natural obstacles such as rivers or mountains often attracted attention as lines of defense and became in the imagination of a nation "the natural frontiers" of its habitat. Today, when geographical barriers can easily be crossed and when a country can conceivably be defeated by air assaults without an army having to cross its boundaries, natural frontiers have lost the military meaning they often had in the past. They can, however, retain a sentimental value in the national imagination as desirable landmarks for denoting the extent of the national territory.

History has proved time and again that the tracing of contested frontiers can be achieved in one of the following ways:

1. By a negotiated bilateral agreement if the two states concerned find this arrangement agreeable. For the most part, small boundary rectifications have been made in this peaceable manner.

2. By the decision of the great powers imposed on a small country. Thus, at Munich in 1938 Britain, France, Germany, and Italy imposed the cession of the Sudetenland by Czechoslovakia.

3. By the unilateral decision of a victor who dictates territorial conditions of peace to a defeated foe.

The major territorial changes have been habitually realized in the last way and have been due to the preponderance of power that favors one state over another. Power considerations, more than anything else, have also determined the territorial decisions of the great powers. The problem of the Sudetenland, for instance, was not discussed on its merits. Britain and France agreed with the German claim in order to avoid a war with Germany for which they were unprepared.

Since power is the decisive factor in the modification of frontiers, the various ethnic, linguistic, historical, economic, and strategic arguments, which the two parties to a territorial dispute carefully devise, are largely irrelevant except insofar as these arguments serve to justify to the public a decision actually determined by the distribution of power. In fact, neither great powers nor small nations have ever abandoned any territory under the influence of the most persuasive arguments; they have done so when faced with superior power.

Since the nationality and the state are territorial concepts, the loss of a part of the national territory is felt as painfully as the amputation of a part of the human body. The territorial provisions of a peace treaty are longer and more bitterly resented by the defeated nation than all other concessions.

Theoretically, the fairest solution to a territorial dispute would be a decision founded on the freely expressed will of the population concerned, who would be asked to vote in a plebiscite. The popular referendum is conceivable in one of two situations: either the two states concerned agree on this procedure, as France and Sardinia did regarding Savoy and Nice, or the plebiscite is imposed on the parties by the great powers. The popularity of self-determination towards the end of the First World War decided the victorious great powers to hold plebiscites in several, though not all, contested areas of Central Europe. In all these cases the problem was that of frontiers between a defeated foe and a small ally and was not of the utmost importance to the great powers themselves. Whenever their own vital interests were involved, the same great powers refrained from consulting the populations concerned (the distribution of the German colonies, the fate of the Arab-populated provinces of Turkey, and the French reannexation of Alsace-Lorraine).

If the plebiscite is decided upon, the first difficulty consists in finding truly neutral personnel for the temporary administration of the contested territory and for the supervision of the referendum. If the great powers with global interests or the states of the same geographical area provide the troops and the administrative personnel, their sympathies and interests might favor one party over the other. This was actually demonstrated on the occasion of the plebiscites which followed the First World War; the sympathies of the victorious great powers did not coincide and were manifested in clashes of opinion within the allied personnel assigned to the contested territory. The second difficulty consists in determining who has the right to vote: should this right be confined to the population actually residing in the area on the day of the referendum, or should emigrants be allowed to participate in the vote if the composition of the population has changed noticeably during the preceding decades owing to voluntary or compulsory migrations? If the outside great powers do not want or for some reason cannot impose the plebiscite, the two parties or one of them can prevent it, as proved by the stubborn Indian rejection of all suggestions to settle the Kashmir dispute with Pakistan by a referendum.

Generally speaking, the state which holds the contested territory, remains impervious to arguments and refuses territorial concessions as long as it feels that it has the power to resist the claims of the other party or is protected by the strength of a great power which wants to maintain the status quo for its own reasons.

The territorial changes that followed the Second World War were dictated to the defeated enemies and to weaker allies by the victorious great powers, who made no attempt to consult the populations concerned. Germany, Japan, Hungary, Rumania, and Finland lost large territories, while the U.S.S.R. and smaller allies were the main beneficiaries. The United States gained control over several Pacific islands.

NATIONAL MINORITIES

The term *national minorities* is rather loosely used. A national minority might actually be a minority in the total population of a given country but might at the same time form the majority in a particular province. In the recent colonial past a foreign-controlled nationality could hardly be called a minority if the controlling nationality were numerically much smaller; thus the Indians and Pakistanis, controlled by the much smaller British nationality, or the Indonesians, governed by the Dutch, could hardly have been considered minorities. Could the various nationalities of Austria-Hungary be called minorities in spite of the fact that none of them formed the majority of the population and that the ruling Austrians and Hungarians were only two among several pluralities?

If the term is strictly limited to those national groups which are truly minorities in the total population of the state, a politically significant distinction should be made between two different kinds of minorities: first, a national minority may represent the bulk of a given nationality which as a whole is concentrated within the frontiers of one state only; secondly, a national minority may be a portion of a much larger nationality which controls the neighboring nation-state. The first kind of minority can have only two aspirations, either to secede and form its own independent state, or to seek political autonomy and equal treatment within the existing state. The second type of minority usually prefers to have the international frontiers changed in order to become citizens of their own nation-state. Also, the neighboring state is emotionally attracted to the national minority beyond the border and is inclined to believe that the best solution would be the annexation of the territory inhabited by that minority. The difference between the two cases has an influence on the choice of policies open to the state where the minority lives. In the first case, it can make a genuine effort to satisfy the aspirations of the minority by granting it autonomy and equal treatment; the minority might then become convinced that its will to preserve its cultural identity and its aspirations for self-government have been satisfied short of secession. In the second case, the most tolerant and benevolent treatment can be of no avail because the minority might prefer, beyond the possibility of compromise, to live under the rule of its own countrymen and continue to clamor for a modification of frontiers.

A national minority can be assimilated and eventually diluted by the majority of the population if the following conditions are fulfilled:

1. Both the majority and the minority do not object to intermarriage, and their biological merger is possible.

2. The members of the minority, if they act as loyal citizens of the state, are treated as equals of the members of the majority of the population and are not made to feel like second-rate citizens.

3. The minority weakens in its will to preserve its cultural identity, loses the hope of successfully retaining its distinctive cultural features, and yields to the process of assimilation by the majority.

Successful assimilation ends in the extinction of the nationality as a distinct group, as it did with the Provençals and the Bretons in France. The secessionist aspiration of the minority (the desire to form a separate state or to join the ethnic-linguistic brethren across the boundary line) *ipso facto* precludes not only assimilation but any lasting *modus vivendi* with the majority.

This century has seen various methods of treating national minorities and alien nationalities. One of them is assent by the state concerned to outright secession. The controlling state might have come to this decision for various reasons: the weakening of its own power and its reduced ability to maintain its rule in the face of the growing opposition of the controlled nationality; its inability to assume the financial burden of the government of the dependent territory when the population insists on the need for great outlays for economic development; pressure by foreign powers; or a costly uprising by the colonial population which cannot be quelled. Whatever the reasons in each particular case, thc United Kingdom assented to the secession of several territories in Asia and Africa, as did France in Morocco, Tunisia, Algeria, Indochina, and Tropical Africa, Holland in Indonesia, and Belgium in the Congo.

The other solution is that of granting to the controlled nationality the satisfaction of its claims and thus dissuading it from secession. The classical example is the Austrian-Hungarian agreement of 1867 which gave the Hungarians political equality with the Austrians and made them co-masters of the Dual Monarchy. The same Hungarians who had revolted against Austria in 1848-49 proved their complete loyalty between 1867 and 1918, the date of the disintegration of the common empire due to factors beyond the control of both Austrians and Hungarians.

The nationality which has obtained its independence might still wish to retain intimate ties with the formerly dominant power. This has been the case, with few exceptions, among the former British dependencies which chose to stay within the Commonwealth of Nations. The French policy of decolonization in sub-Saharan Africa and Madagascar has proceeded in this same direction and has been generally successful in safeguarding between France and its former colonies closer relations than between the latter countries and other states.

A policy which acknowledges the aspirations of the controlled nationality usually promises greater rewards than an open persecution and discrimination which provoke a counterreaction in the form of greater cohesion and resistance on the part of the oppressed nationality.

The aftermath of the First World War was marked by an attempt to solve the problem of national minorities by the regime of toleration. Practically all of Eastern Europe, from Finland in the north down to Greece and Turkey in the south, was compelled by the allied great powers to accept definite international obligations regarding the treatment of its minorities (national, racial, linguistic, and religious). This was effected either by special treaties signed by the states concerned and the allied great powers or by a series of equivalent declarations which other Eastern European states had to make as a condition of their admission to the League of Nations. The substance of these international obligations was as follows:

1. The minorities were to be assured of equal treatment with the the respective majorities, no discrimination being allowed because of nationality, race, or religion.

2. The minorities were to be given facilities—for instance, state subsidies for their own schools—to preserve their culture and language.

3. Any individual or any organization could advise the League of Nations of the violation of these obligations.

4. The Council of the League could issue, in the event of a violation, injunctions and recommendations to the governments concerned which were designed to eliminate the wrongs done to the minority.

This system worked until the decline of the authority of the League of Nations in the late thirties; the minorities certainly fared better than they would have without international protection, although the treaty provisions were not very strictly observed. The same system was weakened by certain inherent defects. Because it was imposed from without, the system was often resented by the states concerned. It was limited to Eastern Europe; hence, states which were forced to accept it felt that they were discriminated against, because no other state, including the colonial powers, was subjected to the same or similar regime of international control. The minorities themselves continued to long for another solution, namely for reunion with their countrymen in the neighboring nation-state. The discussions in the League of Nations, brought on by complaints from the minorities, were exploited by these neighboring states as the occasion for propaganda tending to prove the ineffectiveness of international protection and the need for the revision of frontiers. As a result, no one was satisfied, neither the minorities, nor the state which controlled them on its territory, nor the state across the border. This system collapsed with the outbreak of the Second World War.

The provisions in the peace treaties of 1947 had a different aim, namely to guarantee fundamental human rights to the whole population of the defeated states. But these provisions would also have benefited the national minorities insofar as their equal treatment was concerned. The peace treaties did not foresee any role for the United Nations as a factor in enforcement. In any event, the human rights provisions have become a dead letter because the Soviet Union has resisted their application to the territories of the signatory states which have since become its allies.

Other methods for dealing with national minorities have been used in this century. Nazi Germany tried radically to solve the problem of the ethnic groups which it considered inferior by wholesale extermination in concentration camps. This policy was supplemented by the mass expulsion of non-Germans from their native territories to make room for German settlers. If the Nazis had been victorious or had had more time to carry out their policy, the ethnic map of Central Eastern Europe would have been radically changed. Not only would the European Jews have been completely expunged, but various Eastern European populations would have been greatly reduced and their educated classes probably exterminated. The Romans used a similar method when they conquered the rival city of Carthage, razed this cultural center, and either massacred its inhabitants or sold them into slavery.

A relatively more humane but nevertheless ruthless policy was applied by the Soviet government to several numerically small nationalities of the Soviet Union. Accused of disloyalty during the last war, several small nationalities like the Volga Germans, the Crimean Tartars, and various Moslem populations of the Caucasus were deported wholesale from their homelands and scattered over the immense Soviet territory. This dispersal would have been successful in obliterating national consciousness in the descendants of the deportees, because they would have lived in small clusters among different nationalities and would eventually have been assimilated. This policy of forced dispersal was reversed a few years after Stalin's death, and the survivors of the mass deportations were allowed to go back to their ancestral homelands.

Another method consists in the cultural obliteration of the educated class and the reduction of the nationality to the level of an inarticulate mass deprived of cultural leadership. This was the Hapsburg policy toward the Czechs after the Thirty Years War; the Czech upper classes succumbed to the forced Germanization. The same policy was at various times followed by the Soviet government whenever it "purged" the ranks of the intelligentsia of non-Russian nationalities under all sorts of pretexts but usually because of their "bourgeois nationalism." The deportations or exterminations of large numbers of that intelligentsia during the Stalinist period and their replacement by Russian immigrants weakened several Soviet nationalities.

Another policy makes use of state-sponsored vast internal migrations which gradually build up an ever-increasing number of islands of settlers of the dominant nationality within the homeland originally populated by another nationality. This policy has been applied on a gigantic scale in the Soviet Union. Whatever the motivation, economic or national or both, Soviet economic growth has been constantly accompanied by vast migrations of Russians and Ukranians, who have been settled in outlying Soviet areas hitherto mostly populated by other nationalities. The settlers went there as public administrators, party officials, industrial managers, engineers, other specialists, workers, or even ordinary peasants to help in the realization of various economic projects. The result is that several nationalities, especially in Central Asia, have in their midst an ever greater percentage of Slavs, mostly Russians. In two cases, those of the Kazakhs and the Kirghizs, the natives have already become minorities in countries where their ancestors fairly recently formed the majority of the population. This policy may eventually reduce all smaller nationalities of the Soviet Union to the position of national minorities in the literal sense of these words. Since their Communist revolution, the Chinese have practiced the same policy, sending millions of Chinese to provinces inhabited by non-Chinese nationalities. The vast number of Chinese and the relatively small number of the non-Chinese populations (about 6 per cent of the total) make it certain that every province of China will acquire in due time a Chinese majority.

Another radical policy consists in the total expulsion of an alien population from the state where they have lived. Nazi Germany used this method on a large scale in Eastern Europe. After the German defeat the three allied powers decided at the Potsdam Conference in 1945 to underwrite a mass expulsion of Germans from Poland, from the Polish-administered former German territories east of the Oder-Neisse, from Czechoslovakia, and from Hungary. These expellees, together with the German refugees who fled from the same territories before the advancing Soviet troops, exceed ten million in present-day West Germany. The U.S.S.R. proceeded with its own expulsion of Germans from the northeastern part of East Prussia, which it had annexed in 1945. This sort of mass expulsion effectively solves the problem of national minorities but is not only inhumanly cruel but also liable to a new turn in fortune's wheel. If the distribution of power were to change, the expellees or their descendants might come back and expel the new settlers.

The exchange of minorities is a less barbarous method, because it is founded on an agreement freely negotiated between the two governments concerned. It involves, however, the uprooting of a great number of individuals, who are compelled to leave the country of their ancestral residence and to settle in another country because such is the will of the two governments. This kind of exchange took place during the inter-war period between Greece and Turkey; Greeks from Turkish Asia Minor were exchanged for Turks from Greece. The resulting radical reduction in the numbers of the two minorities (certain categories of Turks and Greeks were exempted from the exchange) led the two countries to accept their frontiers as really final and therefore helped to end or greatly lessen the animosity which had divided the two nations for several centuries. This political result was bought at the price of privations inflicted on millions of individuals who were uprooted from their ancestral homes. At least the two nations could not denounce each other, because the policy of exchange was devised by their own governments without any external pressure. Similar exchanges of population took place at the same time between Turkey and Bulgaria, but much smaller numbers were involved.

CHAPTER IV

The Third World— Political Emancipation

TERMINOLOGY

The concepts and terminology of nationalism have been forged in Europe out of the raw materials supplied by its own history. However, both Western observers and educated non-Europeans are inclined to apply these concepts and terms mechanically to the non-European areas where a powerful movement toward self-determination (i.e., against foreign rule or influence) has been gathering momentum since the beginning of this century. This indiscriminate use of European notions and vocabulary is understandable. No other concepts are readily available for the analysis of a social phenomenon which, if not identical, is nevertheless similar to European nationalism. Moreover, the movement toward self-determination having been inspired and led by persons educated in the West or at schools operating according to Western patterns, the intellectual tools of this movement have necessarily been limited to the European concepts of nationalism.

There are, at any rate, two similarities between national self-determination in Europe and in the non-European areas. First, in both cases a community has sought to throw off control exercised by an alien government. Secondly, the self-assertion of the community has been due to an unfriendly confrontation with this alien government and what it represents, a foreign nationality and race; this confrontation has helped the insurgent community to discover its own distinct identity. In Europe or elsewhere, the movement for political emancipation has always had its roots in the interdependent feelings of estrangement from outsiders and solidarity within the insurgent community.

Much more evidence and study are needed to be sure that the European notions can be transferred to the non-European areas and, if they can be, how they should be adapted to different circumstances. The differences are numerous. All European nationalities belong to the same civilization; however, their linguistic differences, strengthened by other factors, have prevented them from considering themselves members of one closely knit group. India or China is itself a civilization. Is India also one nationality in the European sense in spite of its division into a multitude of linguistic groups? The secular trend in Europe greatly reduced the role of religion as a factor in national consciousness; religion is still an important factor in certain non-European nationalisms, such as the Pakistani, the Arab, and the Indonesian.

As pointed out before, the truly difficult problem exists in sub-Saharan Africa where the strength of the self-determination movement can no longer be questioned but where the European concepts are hardly applicable. Precolonial Africa knew only tribal loyalties, on which sometimes a higher allegiance to a native "empire" of several tribes was superimposed. The colonial powers traced the boundaries of their African possessions according to their own convenience, disregarding tribal loyalties. Each African colony included not only several tribes and fractions of tribes, not only several linguistic groups, but usually more than one religion, the result of Christian and Moslem proselytism and of the survival of "pagan" cults. Now the same territory, arbitrarily carved out by a colonial power, becomes an independent state which inherits this mosaic of disparate groups. If a tribe or a linguistic group has a lively sense of its own identity and is cut into two or more fragments by political frontiers, it may develop an irredentist movement comparable to those which Europe has known. For instance, the Ewes, who form one linguistic group, were divided after the First World War by the new boundary line that cut through the former German Togoland. Now, the Ewes of British Togoland live in Ghana to which this British-mandated territory was joined, and the Ewes of French Togoland are citizens of the now independent Republic of Togoland. The Somalis inhabit independent Somalia (formerly the Italian and British Somalilands), French Somaliland, Ethiopia, and Kenya.

The movement for self-determination, directed against European rule, provided the initial unifying factor for those African populations otherwise divided by their tribal, religious, and linguistic loyalties. Since it was directed against the colonial power, this movement had to develop within the political framework of the colonial possession. However, after the retreat of the colonial power and the establishment of an independent state, what remains is a population composed of tribes often traditionally hostile to each other, of a number of detribalized individuals, of various religious and linguistic groups, all of them no longer united by opposition to the European rulers. This is not a nationality in the European sense. However, there are three unifying factors: a background of African culture transcending tribal or other frontiers, a remembrance of the common colonial past which was the period of growing political consciousness, and a new state inherited from the colonial power. Out of these factors may develop a supreme loyalty to the state. Throughout history, social groups other than the nationality have been able to attract and hold the supreme loyalty of individuals. When it is recalled that the antiquity of our own civilization knew supreme loyalties other than to the nationality, it can be readily conceded that the population of a new African state may eventually find a strong bond of community in allegiance to a state which is not a nation-state.

IMPERIALISM AND COLONIALISM

For convenience we will use the word *nationalism* in discussing non-European areas, inexact as this application of the word may sometimes be. Nationalism owes its origin in these non-European continents to the impact of the European civilization[1] and to the revolt against European colonial rule or political and economic domination. The recent colonial or semicolonial experience of Asia and Africa explains why nationalism is there so strongly colored by anticolonialism, which often amounts to anti-Westernism.

The terms *imperialism* and *colonialism*, which often recur in modern political parlance, require some clarification, because their actual meaning varies with political convenience or ideological context. *Imperialism* is a policy which aims at the political, economic, or cultural domination of one social group by another. *Colonialism* is the name for the resulting domination. These two terms may be used in reference to other historical epochs but it should be remembered that the social groups concerned are different in each epoch. Thus, we may speak of the imperialism and colonialism of a tribe which conquers and then assumes control over another tribe. The ancient Assyrians, the Athenians at the time of their hegemony over the so-called allied cities, the Greeks during the conquest of western Asia and Egypt under Macedonian leadership, the subsequent post-Alexandrine monarchies, and the Romans, could all be said to have acted as imperialists and colonialists. However, the modern use of the same terms should refer to the contemporary concepts of nationality and the nation-state. *Imperialism* in this modern sense is a policy which aims at fastening the control of one nationality upon another nationality, an alien race, or a foreign ethnic group. *Colonialism* is the actual control exercised by a nationality over alien nationalities, races, or ethnic groups.

History has known four types of imperialism: political, economic, cultural, and assimilative. Political imperialism, if successful, results either in

[1] For a definition of the term *European civilization*, see Chapter 5.

the annexation of the territory inhabited by the subjugated population and the establishment of direct government by the conquering nationality (colonial conquests in Asia and Africa provide an abundance of examples) or in the extension of indirect political control over a foreign state (open or disguised protectorates). For instance, the Nazi-occupied European countries were placed either under a direct German administration or under an open or disguised German protectorate. The Communist states of Eastern Europe (except for Yugoslavia and Albania) are under a hardly disguised Soviet protectorate which controls their foreign and military policies and also their ways of life (political, economic, and social regimes).

Economic imperialism is more subtle because it avoids imposing an open political control but subordinates the economic life of one country to the needs of another. These needs might be for raw materials (including strategic materials), agricultural products, cheap labor, markets for manufactured goods, or opportunities for profitable capital investments. It can be called imperialism if it results in the economic dependence of one state on the other. For instance, if one state has in fact a monopoly on the purchase of the bulk of staple exports from another state and thus exercises control, through its purchases and the prices it pays, over the balance of payments and indirectly over the economy of the other state, the latter country is placed in a position of economic but also, by repercussion, political dependence. The same is true if the economy of one state vitally depends on the supplies of raw materials from another state which has a factual monopoly of these supplies; this is essentially the situation of Eastern Europe whose industrial production depends on the Soviet supplies of certain raw materials such as iron ore.

Cultural imperialism is the most subtle of all and also the most irreversible in its results if successful. It involves an effort by one nationality to impose its own "self-evident truths" and ways of life on other nationalities. One can talk of cultural imperialism only if the nationality which is subject to the foreign cultural influence has not willingly invited it. There is no trace of any imperialism by other countries in the process of Westernization which Peter the Great carried out in Russia and Kemal Atatürk in Turkey. European civilization cannot be accused of imperialism at the present time, for the Asians and Africans who want to modernize their countries have themselves decided to adopt certain of the European ways of life.

Cultural imperialism takes place only if the "conversion" to alien values is forcibly imposed. This was the case during the Christian and Moslem expansions in the early Middle Ages when force was often used to convert non-Christian or non-Moslem peoples. Insofar as the Soviet Union and China openly acknowledge that they are determined to extend their creed and ways of life to foreign nations, they exhibit an attitude which can be described as cultural imperialism. This Soviet or Chinese cultural imperialism amounts to the intention of remodeling the whole world on the image of Russia or China.

If successful, cultural imperialism is the most effective kind of imperialism because it transforms the culture of one people in imitation of the culture of another people.

Assimilative imperialism consists in the attempt to change the national consciousness of individuals by shifting their inner allegiance from one nationality to another. It works by persuasion and social pressure. If it is successful, the individual begins to feel that he no longer belongs to the nationality of his forebears but to another nationality. This is the process referred to in what has been called the Germanization of the Slavs, the Russification of non-Russian nationalities, the Turkification of the Kurds, and so on. The process is invisible because it takes place in the hearts of individuals. What is visible are the means of persuasion and social pressure which are used to convince the individual that he should abandon his present nationality and rally to the other nationality. Eventually, the statistics of nationalities and spoken languages may reveal a noticeable shift in the numbers of the two nationalities.

Force is often the instrument of imperialism. Territorial annexation or the fastening of indirect political control is usually conditioned on the threat of force or its actual use. The preponderant military power of a state might be the decisive factor in securing economic concessions or in imposing cultural and political values on an alien nationality. The attraction of superior military and economic power might persuade an individual to shift his inner allegiance from his present nationality to the stronger one.

In actual practice these various forms of imperialism are not necessarily divorced from one another. Economic imperialism can be the prelude to or the consequence of political imperialism. Political imperialism, if it results in a long period of control, creates conditions which favor the expansion of cultural influence.

Modern imperialism and colonialism are usually associated with the West and with expansion to overseas territories. From a political point of view, however, the geographic factor of the seas that divide the controlling state from the subject alien population is meaningless. A population can as easily be conquered overland and ruled by a continental neighbor. Actually, the cultural and assimilative imperialisms are made easier by direct overland contact. For instance, the immigration by settlers of the conquering nationality into the homeland of the conquered is cheaper and easier than overseas emigration. The constant growth of islands of alien settlers, whose immigration is promoted by the dominant state, disrupts the ethnic and cultural homogeneity of the subject population and prepares the ground for its cultural and national assimilation. The Western colonial powers have been able to implant fairly sizable European settlements in parts of Africa, but they have been incomparably less successful in creating large alien enclaves within the native population than the Russians have been in Central Asia, which is not divided from Russia proper by any sea.

The Arabs, the Turks, the imperial Chinese, the Germans, and the Russians extended their rule over other ethnic groups usually by overland routes. The Western Europeans did it by crossing the seas. The location of the conquering nationality determined the mode of expansion.

It is no more true that only Asians and Africans fell victim to foreign (European) imperialism than to say that imperialism was a European monopoly. Actually, no race has been guiltless. The Mongols imposed their rule on such different ethnic communities as the Chinese, the Near Eastern peoples, and the Russians. Europeans often subjugated other Europeans; Poland, for instance, was partitioned among the Germans, the Austrians, and the Russians. Europeans were also conquered by non-Europeans, as evidenced by the Arab conquest of Spain and the Turkish conquest of the Balkan and Danubian areas. The imperial Chinese, who never accepted the concept of the equality of states, founded their foreign relations on the fact, or fiction, that their protectorate was extended to other states which had to pay a tribute, at least a symbolic one. Chinese claims included Tibet, Outer Mongolia, Korea, Burma, Thailand, Vietnam, Laos, Cambodia, Malaya and parts of Indonesia, Nepal, Sikkim, and Bhutan; Chinese suzerainty in these areas was either actual for periods of time or nominal. At times, Indian cultural influence extended deeply into Southeast Asia.

Imperialism and colonialism have been practised by all the principal races. The determining factors were two: the unequal distribution of power between the two groups concerned, and the conquering impulse of one of them. Today especially, in view of the steady and general Western retreat from Asia and Africa, imperialism and colonialism cannot be identified exclusively with Western policies. This retreat stands in sharp contrast with the undisturbed Russian control over those 40 per cent of the Soviet population who are of non-Russian descent and with the Soviet position of a protecting power in Eastern Europe. It was not the West but China that carried out the most recent annexation by force of an alien nationality (the Tibetans); India has its own protectorates—Sikkim and Bhutan—while all Asian states harbor large national minorities which are often roughly treated or discriminated against.

There is a remarkable contrast between the political emancipation of some 900 million people in Asia, Africa, and the Near East, including the populous countries of India, Pakistan, and Indonesia, and the political subjection during the same period of approximately 100 million people in Eastern Europe who either lost their independence or were subjected to foreign control. Asians and Africans typically overlook the Soviet annexation of Estonia, Latvia, and Lithuania, or the Soviet domination of several Eastern European nationalities. However, the West retreated from colonial possessions in Asia and Africa, while the Soviet Union, almost at the same time, expanded its territory or its control over foreign nations.

This contrast does not greatly impress Asians and Africans for several reasons. Except for the Central Asians, they have never experienced Russian colonialism but have preserved a vivid memory of the Western colonial rule which ended only recently in Asia and still survives in large parts of Africa. Soviet imperialism has been directed against white people, again with the exception of Central Asians, while Asians and Africans associate colonialism with the racial problem (white control over the colored people). Western colonialism is familiar to them, but the Soviet policy toward non-Russian nationalities and toward Eastern Europe is not; the sources of information are limited and always suspected of being anti-Soviet in intent. Their own self-determination movement was directed against the West. Hence, colonialism and imperialism remain associated with the West only. The Asian and African outlook cannot be understood without attention to this anticolonialist ingredient.

THE BALANCE SHEET OF WESTERN COLONIALISM

The Westerner tends on his part to be self-righteous and either to forget the colonial era or to look upon his colonial rule as a benevolent and beneficient, though paternalistic, government. He thinks of himself as the guardian of individual freedom and of respect for human dignity; but he played a different role in his colonial possessions. A balance sheet of the evils and benefits of the colonial era may help to explain the resentments which survive in Asia and Africa.

The great maritime voyages at the end of the fifteenth and throughout the sixteenth centuries opened the era of One World in which all the continents and islands of the globe were compelled by the Europeans to take cognizance of one another. For the next four centuries the Europeans, who had previously clashed with other civilizations only across the Mediterranean and then never decisively, were able to assert their supremacy over other civilizations and other peoples. Whatever the reasons for this supremacy, the European became the master of the world. He controlled the seas and worldwide commerce; his increasingly rapid progress in science and technology provided him with superior military and naval techniques and made opposition to his rule futile; he opened vast areas to his settlement and other areas to his profitable economic ventures; he exported his religious and other ideas; he imposed his rule over alien peoples although his race represented a minority of mankind; and he made Europe *the* stage of international politics where he reached decisions affecting the fate of other continents. For four centuries, every major war between the European nations had immediate repercussions elsewhere by shifting the control of non-European areas from one European state to another. The operation of the complex balance-of-power mechanism in Europe was often facilitated by the so-called policy of compensation carried out at the expense of non-European peoples.

This policy of compensation consisted in a settlement between two or more great powers whereby each of them acquired territorial accretions, zones of influence, or other assets of equivalent importance (hence the term *compensation*). These simultaneous and equivalent gains, which were expected not to alter the distribution of power among the great powers concerned, were always made at the expense of other peoples too weak to resist the enforcement of the deal. The carving out of sub-Saharan Africa was a means of economic expansion often concerted between the European powers, who avoided mutual disputes by agreeing on the zones reserved for each of them. Whether the European powers were able to agree or failed to do so, it always remained true that the Africans had no voice in the matter. The Anglo-French agreement of 1904 and the Anglo-Russian agreement of 1907, which were the cornerstones of the Triple Entente, were concluded at the expense of Egypt, Morocco, and Iran. The Anglo-French agreements of the First World War concerning the division of spoils in the Near East were paid for by the Arabs. The last agreement of this sort was the Yalta Far Eastern Agreement of 1945 which made China (neither present at Yalta nor consulted beforehand) pay the cost of Soviet participation in the Far Eastern War.

However, it should be recalled that agreements of this kind were also concluded at the expense of Europeans; Asians and Africans were not the only victims. The partitions of Poland were the typical compensation deal among the partitioning powers. The sacrifice of Czechoslovakia at Munich was meant to buy "peace in our time" for Britain and France.

European colonialism reached its apogee in the years between 1815 and 1914 (this period should be extended for Africa to include the interwar period between 1918 and 1939). This was also a time of rapid economic development for most of the colonial powers (except for Spain and Portugal), of a no less rapid population increase in Europe (except in France), and also of the final colonial partition of those areas of Asia and Africa which had until then escaped European political domination. The industrialization of Europe, achieved during this period (much earlier in Britain), and the absence of a similar economic development in the European colonial possessions and in other non-European countries, which were reduced to semicolonial dependence, are the main sources of the present glaring contrast between the advanced and the underdeveloped areas. At the beginning of the European expansion (the sixteenth century), the differences in economic and technological development between Europe and such civilized countries as China and India were not noticeable; after the Industrial Revolution an abyss opened. Economic and demographic expansion in the nineteenth century offered Europe powerful incentives to extend and tighten its political and economic control over Asia and Africa.

During this same period between 1815 and 1914 a paradox developed. The colonial powers, which dominated their overseas possessions by virtue of superior skill and strength, derived a considerable part of their strength from these same possessions. Colonial raw materials, markets in the colonies for manufactured goods, and cheap native labor played an important role in the economic prosperity of the colonial powers. Colonial soldiers fought in the wars waged by these powers and maintained public order in the colonies. The colonial territory often served as a base from which the colonial power extended its influence. Thus India, with its vast storehouse of manpower and resources, made it possible for Britain to become and for a long time to remain the dominant power in Asia. From its base in India, Britain extended its influence to the Far East, Southeast Asia, and the Persian Gulf. The cost of military expeditions was debited to India. Without India as an axis to the vast British imperial system in Asia, it would not have been possible for an island off the northwestern corner of Europe to control for so long the destinies of a vast continent stretching from the Chinese coast to the Arabian Desert between Baghdad and Damascus.

That the period of European mastery lasted for four centuries is much more surprising than that it has finally come to an end. The non-Europeans, even those in Asia who were highly civilized, were for centuries unable to borrow from the European the techniques and knowledge which made him powerful and efficient. These secrets were not wrested from Europe until the second half of the nineteenth century when Japan voluntarily became a disciple of the West in science, technology, military art, and modern state structure. At that point two historical epochs began to co-exist. The Augustan Age of European colonialism, when political and economic control over non-European lands was tightened and colonial rule was extended to parts of Asia and Africa previously left undisturbed, coincided with a period of slow awakening in Asia, a period that saw the first, modest national movements. The dormant peoples were beginning to rise from their slumber, awakened by the European ideas of equality, freedom, and national self-determination which were the very negation of the colonial system. The anticolonial revolt of Asia and later of Africa had its origin in the very period when the European colonial mastery seemed to be unchallengeable. But the first rumblings of Asian national movements before 1914 failed to impress Europe where few people suspected that the era of the European dominion was slowly coming to an end. The Japanese rise in 1905 to the status of a great power was generally considered a freak, not a sign of things to come.

Now, when European colonialism is obviously ending, it is possible to look at the record.

COLONIAL EXPLOITATION

It cannot be denied that the period of European mastery was also one of economic exploitation of non-European peoples. It is a cold moral comfort to say that the exploitation of the conquered by the victors is the usual consequence of an undisputed superiority in power. The temptation to exploit the weak has proved too great for all races. Looking only at the history of European civilization, it is clear that the ancient Greeks considered the Mediterranean lands, populated by the "barbarians," as a *res nullius* where the Greeks could come, repulse the natives from the coast and evict them from the fertile land, and found their own settlements, as their spiritual descendants did later in the Western Hemisphere. Carthage lived on the forced labor of North African natives. The Phoenician and Greek trade drained wealth from the "barbarian" countries, which at that time were non-Phoenician and non-Hellenic Europe and North Africa. The "barbarian" slave supplied the productive energy of a nonmechanical age. At the time of its greatness, Athens, the motherland of democracy, probably had a number of slaves equal to half its population. Its economic life was unthinkable without their labor. Rome, in turn, lived on slave labor and the exploitation of the economic resources of conquered lands. The medieval German drive toward the East was more a conquest of land for settlement than a Christian missionary venture.

After the conquest of the Americas the Europeans looted the treasures accumulated by the Incas and the Aztecs and proceeded to exploit the gold and silver mines and organize plantations. The Indians, who in North America were partly exterminated to make room for European agricultural settlements, were reduced in South America to the position of human chattel forced to work on the plantations and in the mines. Soon after, another form of forced labor was imported, African slaves. It is a paradox of history that Christianity, which had contributed so much toward the abolition of slavery of the white man, did not prevent Christian Europeans from restoring this institution for a more efficient economic exploitation of the Americas. This time it was the colored man who became the slave. It is estimated that about 15 million Africans were made slaves in the Western Hemisphere. The actual loss for Africa may have been three times this number because of the high mortality rate on the ships which transported captured Africans across the Atlantic and also because of great human losses from the intertribal wars waged by the Africans themselves for the purpose of selling captives to the European traders. The slave trade not only contributed to the exploitation of the resources of the Americas but also yielded tremendous profits which were then invested in the economic development of Europe. For instance, the returns from this trade were a factor in the growth of Liverpool from a village into a city. The African slave trade, in which several European nations took part and which had its parallel in Arab slave-hunting expeditions in the same continent, lasted for two and a half centuries. It certainly disorganized and weakened the African populations.

At the time when this trade was coming to an end in the nineteenth century, Europeans needed cheap labor for their colonial plantations and mines as well as for the building of colonial railroads. They turned to manpower that was readily available and inexpensive. Indians were transported to Africa and the Caribbean area, Africans were subjected to the regime of forced labor, and Chinese were encouraged to emigrate to other parts of Asia. Beginning in 1847, Chinese laborers, in spite of the protests of their government, were illegally shipped to overseas mines and plantations. The transportation conditions caused an extremely high mortality rate among the Chinese laborers. This illegal exportation of Chinese coolies was contemptuously referred to as the "pig trade."

Immigration from India to East, Central, and South Africa was also encouraged as a means of getting cheap labor, particularly for the building of railroads. The descendants of Indian laborers now form Asian minorities in these parts of Africa and earn their living as retail traders, white-collar workers, or professional men. Trapped as they are between the white man's racial discrimination and the African's distrust, their situation is far from enviable.

There are other examples of this previous tendency among Europeans to look upon non-Europeans as cheap labor and a source of profit but not as fellow-men. The various trading companies which were founded in Europe for the purpose of trade with, and economic exploitation of, the newly discovered continents, combined, in virtue of charters granted by their governments, political and economic powers. They were sovereigns in the conquered lands, but they were also employers. This combination of economic and political powers, somewhat similar to what now exists in the Communist countries because of the nationalization of the means of production, delivered the native to the company. The company could make him work under any conditions and enforce *criminal* sanctions against him if he disobeyed. This situation was fully exploited by the Dutch United East India Company which mercilessly extracted the highest profits from its plantations in Indonesia and at the same time represented the highest authority to which the native laborers could appeal. The profits were exported to Holland.

The Dutch company was replaced by direct rule in 1798. In the 1830's the Dutch government introduced the so-called cultivation system, which was gradually abolished between 1877 and 1915. This system obligated the Indonesian peasant to plant a large portion of his fields with commercial crops which were then delivered to the government to be sold for export. Under this system the peasant was often left with crops inadequate for the support of his family. At the same time, the government granted the Chinese various monopolies on the sale of certain commodities of general consumption and entrusted them with levying several taxes; this further increased the misery of the peasant.

After the cultivation system had been abolished, the policy of the colonial administration favored European enterprise over the native producer. During the Great Depression, for example, the Dutch-owned rubber plantations were protected against the effects of the fall in demand on the international market by a policy that discriminated against the native producers. Native output was held in check by various administrative measures such as low production quotas and high taxation. As a result of the colonial policy, most of the wealth fell into Dutch and Chinese hands.

Although its regime was incomparably more humane, the British East India Company added a black page to the history of European colonialism. The European trade with China was for many years a one-sided affair, the Chinese exporting silk, tea, and rhubarb, and the Europeans exporting bullion in payment. The growing popularity of opium attracted the attention of the company despite the Chinese prohibition in 1729 of the trade in opium. In 1773 the company secured a monopoly on the trade of opium, and in 1797 a monopoly on its manufacture in India. Opium produced in India and illegally exported to China became a source of considerable profit and a means of maintaining a balance of payments between the company and China. In the sixteen years between 1818 and 1833 opium jumped from 17 to 50 per cent of the total value of British imports into China. Opium was smuggled through Canton, the only port open to foreign trade, by shippers to whom the company paid large bonuses for engaging in this illicit traffic. The Chinese government protested and appealed, over the head of the company, to the British government which controlled the company, but to no avail. The British Cabinet and Parliament did not intervene for fear of depriving the company of an important source of revenue which was invested in Britain. In 1839 the Chinese government, disregarding its military weakness, took the forceful measures of blockading foreign commercial establishments in Canton and destroying their stocks of opium. Britain responded with a declaration of war on China. The main purpose of this war of 1840 was to compel China to open other ports to foreign trade. To the present day the Chinese refer to it as "the Opium War," for which their ancestors had to pay by ceding the island of Hong Kong. The second British war in 1860, also motivated by the desire to throw China open to foreign economic penetration, was marked by the conquest of Peking and the senseless burning of a historical and artistic monument, the Imperial Summer Palace. This act of vandalism is not forgotten in the anti-Western propaganda of the Chinese Communist Party.

A knowledge of the history of the nineteenth century and the first decades of this century makes it easier to understand the anti-Western sentiments of the Chinese and their inclination toward xenophobia. China, once an empire that had refused to deal with foreign countries on an equal footing, was subjected during this period to the most humiliating treatment by the European powers. European settlements such as the International Settlement in Shanghai, founded between 1860 and 1880, were foreign enclaves where the Chinese authorities did not function, where the Chinese courts had no jurisdiction even over the Chinese, where Chinese laws did not apply, and where the Chinese themselves were looked upon as an inferior race. The Chinese coast lay defenseless before European fleets which, at no risk to themselves, could support what was aptly called gunboat diplomacy. In the last decade of the past century, China was in fact parcelled out into zones of influence, each zone reserved for the political and economic activities of a foreign power (Britain, France, Germany, Russia, and Japan). Its territory was thrown wide open to foreign imports when it was compelled to adopt a tariff that placed a duty of only 5 per cent on all foreign goods. As a result, China was unable to develop its own industries. The unequal treaties which China had to sign were not formally abrogated until 1943.

The decisions concerning each colony were made by the local administration, which was composed of nationals of the colonial power, and by the government of that power. It was quite natural that both the colonial officials and the members of the government felt duty-bound to administer the colonial possessions, first of all, from the point of view of the interests of their own country. The economic interests of the colonial population were subordinated to those of the colonial power. This outlook persisted until the Second World War, except in India where the British policy had to be modified after the First World War under the pressure of the growing Indian national movement. After the Second World War it was no longer possible to ignore the economic aspirations of colonial peoples. The colonial regime has ceased to be a one-sided, profitable venture; this is one of the reasons for the Western colonial retreat.

During the early colonial era the Europeans determined the conditions of trade with the colonial territories, deriving large profits, among other means, from the resale of colonial products on European markets. It is interesting, in this connection, to note a chronological coincidence. The Industrial Revolution took place in Britain at the same time that Britain extended its control over India after the battle of Plassey (1757); as a result of this coincidence, profits drained from India could be invested in the industrial development of Britain.

After the European Industrial Revolution the profits of colonialism multiplied. The colonial powers followed a system which exploited to the fullest the economic possibilities inherent in colonialism. The extraction of raw materials and the production of expensive agricultural products were concentrated in the hands of European corporations, which found it profitable to invest capital in overseas territories where the income was higher than in Europe but where the security of investments was as great owing to the protection provided by the colonial administration. These raw materials and agricultural products were supplied, first of all, to the domestic market of the colonial power; the surpluses were then sold to other industrial nations. Shipping, banking, insurance, and other services related to the economies of the colonial possessions were monopolized by the corporations of the nationality of the colonial power. The colonial market, where the development of native industries was discouraged, was reserved for manufactured goods produced by the colonial power. This system was safeguarded not only by customs duties on imports from other industrial nations but also by such measures as excise duties on manufactured goods (mainly textiles) produced in the colony. The purpose was to eliminate foreign competition on the colonial market but also to discourage the growth of native industries and thus keep the territory dependent on manufactured goods imported from the colonial power. This system certainly did not stimulate the economic development of the colonial dependencies. Whatever development did take place was distorted because the colonial power and the private corporations were interested in developing only those branches of production which supplied goods for which there was a demand either on the domestic market of the colonial power or on the markets of other industrial nations.

The economic advantages of a modern colonial empire in recent decades (after the First World War) can be summed up as follows:

1. The power of modifying the rate of exchange between the metropolitan country and the dependency in any way judged profitable by the colonial power.

2. The protection of the colonial market against imports by other countries and thus the reservation of this market for imports from the metropolitan country. Usually, this benefit was partly compensated by offering to the dependency a preferential entry for its raw materials and foodstuffs. The currency regulations were in this respect often more effective than the customs duties; these regulations compelled the colonial possession to buy within the monetary zone of the colonial power, i.e., on its market. Cheaper goods produced in a different monetary zone could not be bought because of the refusal by the colonial power to supply the needed foreign currency.

3. The accumulation of hard currencies paid by other countries for exports from the colony. These reserves of hard currencies were used to back up the currency of the metropolitan power and to finance its own purchases abroad. Exports of Malayan rubber and tin, for example, helped Great Britain to replenish its dollar reserves.

4. An unimpeded access to the raw materials of the colonial possessions.

5. The transfer of a large share of the profits made in the dependency by the corporations of the nationality of the colonial power for investment in the latter country.

6. The profits made for rendering various services to the colonial possession such as banking, shipping, and insurance.

Moreover, it was generally understood until after the Second World War that the colonial possession should remain financially self-sufficient and should not cause any expenditure from the colonial power.

To take one example at random for the illustration of an earlier practice, the Lancaster cotton industry enjoyed in India the security of a vast market; its competition ruined the native rural handicraft industry. The rise of the local textile industry was hampered by an excise duty. Railroad construction was in the hands of the British corporations; their minimum interest on the invested capital was guaranteed by the government. The British large-scale plantations of tea, rubber, coffee, and indigo were promoted by governmental control over the discipline of native labor and by the allocation of land. Banking, shipping, and insurance were in British hands. The British government began to show a true interest in the economic problems of India itself only after the First World War.

A similar situation in the Dutch East Indies survived until the Second World War. The economic life of the Belgian Congo was entirely controlled until the day of independence by Belgian corporations which, with interlocking interests, were mainly concerned with the exploitation of mineral resources and related industries. These corporations, in which capital other than Belgian also participated, had enough power to determine the Congolese policies of the Belgian government, which itself held a large share of their stock. The corporations naturally thought, first of all, of their own profits and the demands of the international market rather than of a balanced development of the colonial territory. These examples can be multiplied. The essence of the problem was that the native populations had until recently no way of protecting their own interests and no pressure groups in the parliaments of the colonial powers to voice their own aspirations. They were, so to speak, absent from the stage of politics of the metropolitan countries; the absent are always wrong.

The colonial regime in sub-Saharan Africa had as its objective the exploitation of natural resources. The practical problem was to secure African labor for the European plantations and mines. Since the era of slavery had ended, other means had to be used to force the native out of his village. Various means were employed—land alienation, cash taxation, and forced labor. In East and Central Africa where the climate did not discourage white immigration, the land was taken away from the African, who was then left with three choices: to crowd into the reservations endowed with poor land, to squat on the white estates as agricultural laborers, or to emigrate and seek work in the mines or in the European-founded cities. The alienation of land for the benefit of the European mining corporations had the same effect. Compelled to pay the newly instituted cash taxes, the African was in this way forced to seek employment for cash wages. The remaining needs for manpower were met by ordering the tribal chieftains to conscript their young men either for work on the plantations and in the mines or for public works, in particular for the building of roads and railroads. Not until 1930, in the Geneva Convention on Forced Labor did the colonial powers agree to abandon this form of recruitment of African manpower.

Land alienation and racial discrimination have been the main sources of African bitterness. The European, so respectful of private property in his own country, did not scruple to seize native property that had been alienated in fraudulent deals with ignorant tribal chieftains or by the decisions of the colonial administration. The legal sense of the whites was appeased by the fact that the natives could not produce written deeds and that their confiscated property had usually been communal property which the colonial government hastened to proclaim Crown or state property and hence alienable to whom the colonial administration thought fit. Whenever land was needed for the European mining corporations or for the white settlers, the native was expelled and herded into the reservation. West Africa was at least protected by its climate and its malaria-bearing mosquito against white immigration. But East and Central Africans had two masters—the colonial administration and the white settler.

The classical example was that of the Kenya Highlands with their healthy climate and fertile soil. Sixteen thousand square miles of the Highlands were reserved for the whites, who numbered in Kenya, all occupations included, only about 60,000 as against 5.5 million Africans. The displaced tribes were left with 52,000 square miles of inferior land. The situation of the Africans can be gauged by the density of the population in the Kikuyu Reserve; it is 414 persons to the square mile, while the average density in British East Africa is only 32.5 and the density in the most fertile areas in West Africa only infrequently reaches 300 persons, a figure high for sub-Saharan Africa.

The white settlement in East and Central Africa has created a bitter racial conflict and has made the European disengagement much more difficult than in West Africa or in those parts of East Africa where the white settler never came in large numbers. The problem is basically the same as it was in Algeria, where the European settlers formed over 10 per cent of the total population. The comparative figures of the white and African populations indicate to whom the future belongs. Most of the 5 million Europeans in Africa were concentrated, as recently as 1962, at the two poles—Algeria and the Union of South Africa.[1] In between these two large concentrations, the whites form in East and Central Africa islands of population that are numerically feeble but politically and economically dominant. In the Central African Federation, where the whites were as recently as 1961 strongly entrenched in power, Africans form over 96 per cent of the total population of more than 7 million. The Europeans are a minority of 3.5 per cent; the remaining fraction is made up of Asians. Only in Southern Rhodesia do the whites attain the relatively high proportion of the 7.7 per cent of the total population. But this white portion of the population owns over half the land in Southern Rhodesia. Out of this vast acreage of 48.6 million acres only about 28 million acres are actually cultivated; the rest are kept in reserve for future assignment to white settlers. The Africans resent the existence of these unused reserves of land more bitterly then they do the alienation of land in favor of those Europeans who actually make use of it. The land distribution between the two races and the open racial discrimination in Southern Rhodesia explain the strong opposition of the Africans of Nyasaland and Northern Rhodesia to the continued existence of the Central African Federation, which for them represents ruthless domination by the white man.

The African, faced with white supremacy, invokes the European principle—one man, one vote. He wants to be master in his native country. The law of numbers favors him, as does the movement toward self-determination which has already largely emancipated his race.

European investors and the colonial administration in Tropical Africa were interested in developing the type of production that was assured of a steady demand on the Western markets. As a result, active and relatively prosperous enclaves emerged within an otherwise stagnant economy. A striking example of this lopsided development is the Copperbelt of Northern Rhodesia with its only railroad joining it to its outlet in the south. The only modern townships and the only hard-surface roads lie along the railroad, which is flanked by a narrow belt of European and African cash-crop farming. The bulk of the country is left in its original primitive condition and is being drained of its best manpower by the attraction of the mining centers.

The existence of these enclaves in Africa has another effect. The mines and subsidiary industries owned by the European corporations have at their disposal a large pool of unskilled laborers who come from the native villages and reservations. When the employer has selected the fittest laborers, the less fit are rejected back to their native village, which is thus bereft of its most active elements. The migrant labor, floating between the mines and the native villages, cannot organize itself effectively and is

[1] Approximately 80 per cent of the Europeans left Algeria in the last stage of the war and since independence. Those who have chosen to stay now number less than 200,000.

unable to acquire any collective bargaining power. The worker can accept less than a full living wage because his family is left behind and somehow subsists in its usual rural misery. When he falls ill, is unemployed, or reaches old age, he goes back to his village; the employer is free from any social security obligation. But this same system offers no incentive for acquiring a higher industrial skill, for increasing labor productivity, and for staying permanently on the job.

RACIALISM AND THE DENIAL OF EQUALITY

All the resentments which have their source in the colonial period will die out, healed by the lapse of time. One is bound to survive longest and to poison the relations between the West and the Afro-Asian nations for many years to come. This is the resentment caused by the racial discrimination of the colonial period.

There is hardly a trace of the racial complex in the European mentality of precolonial history. The ancient Greeks felt superior to other peoples only because of their pride in the Hellenic civilization; not only colored men but other white men were "barbarians." The Romans did not make distinctions among the racial stocks of their citizens; men of various racial origin ascended the imperial throne. The medieval European felt superior to a Moslem only for religious reasons and was repaid by a corresponding sense of superiority in the Moslem, whose culture was in fact superior to that of Western Europe for a long period during the Middle Ages. Marco Polo's description of his travels in Asia bears no trace of a sense of superiority on his part but is instead characterized by admiration for other civilizations, notably the Chinese.

The new attitude toward other races was slow to develop. As late as the Elizabethan period it was natural for Shakespeare to write about a mixed marriage, and the African Othello is not pictured as an inferior human being. The new attitude was probably due to several causes, not least of which was the slave trade; the helpless Africans could be treated as chattel only because of the implicit assumption of their inferior human status. A second reason was the ease with which the Europeans, small in number, conquered and controlled vast populations. The image of small bands of intrepid conquerors, armed with primitive firearms and imposing their will on the Aztec and Inca empires and the vast populations of Asia, was not forgotten for a long time by the descendants of the conquerors and of the conquered alike, to whom it seemed strong proof of the "intrinsic" superiority of the white man.

A third reason was political. Only by cultivating an awed respect for his race could the European maintain his mastery without great and constant military exertions. The ruled populations had to believe that it was impossible to overturn the mastery of the white man. Respect for the white man was inculcated by racial discrimination against the natives who in this way were daily reminded of their inferior status, an inferiority which was due to nature and hence irremediable. This sense of racial superiority affected in various degrees the outlook of the home populations of the colonial powers. Even now, at the time of the colonial retreat, the immigration of colonial subjects to the territory of the colonial power is creating racial problems in Europe itself. Race riots in England have their counterpart across the Channel in the animosity which the French working class feels toward the immigrant Algerian workers. Whatever the reasons for the racial resentments of our time, a different color of skin or different facial features serve as a focus for the discontent of the lower-class whites. In the colonies themselves a sense of racial superiority was felt by both colonial officials and white settlers, especially those of the lower social position. If he resided in a colony, a white man who felt socially inferior to other Europeans could compensate by feeling racially superior to the colonial subjects and by acting accordingly.

Color discrimination is the worst of all possible forms of discrimination. If a man is discriminated against because of his convictions or because of his nationality, he has a way of escape. He can, under pressure, change his opinions or his national allegiance or simulate the change. The price he has to pay is injurious to his human dignity but, as a convert to a different ideology or nationality, he wins for himself an equality formerly denied. This is why Soviet discrimination against religious groups in the U.S.S.R. and not infrequently against the non-Russian nationalities of the U.S.S.R. is incomparably less humiliating than the color bar, which has never existed in Russia either before or after the October Revolution. But the man who is singled out for systematic abuse only because of his physical features or the color of his skin has no way to regain equality or to secure himself against persecution. He is branded forever as an inferior human being *for reasons entirely independent of his will*; he can do nothing about it. This is the tragedy of color discrimination, as it was the tragedy of the Nazi racial persecutions. The European Jews were being exterminated, not because of their convictions, but because of their "racial" descent. The bitter humiliation suffered in consequence of color discrimination cannot be easily forgotten and has created a sort of antiwhite complex which continues to be nourished by such current developments as the *Apartheid* policy in South Africa. This complex is not necessarily limited to Asia and Africa; it should not be forgotten that most of the Latin American countries have mixed populations.

Colonial racial discrimination was a twofold insult to human dignity because it was inflicted by foreign intruders entirely alien to the local native society. It sometimes produced paradoxical situations when superimposed on a local pattern of discrimination. In India and in Ceylon a high-caste man, who looked with contempt upon his own countrymen of lower caste, felt outraged by the European sense of superiority which relegated him to an inferior status within the hierarchy of colonial society.

However, in spite of castes and classes the members of the native society were prodded by European racial discrimination into an awareness that they were all being treated as second-class human beings because of certain external characteristics which they all had in common. This realization contributed greatly to the emergence of a feeling of community which was to become an important factor in the growing hostility to colonial rule.

Racialism inevitably resulted in a double standard; policies which were unthinkable with respect to another white man were considered suitable for a colored man because he was colored. This double standard, the negation of the equality dear to Europeans in their mutual relations, was reflected in various colonial practices. In French Africa, with few exceptions, the Africans were not citizens but subjects deprived of all political rights until after the last war. They were responsible for a number of offenses defined by administrative regulations and punished according to administrative procedure. Their compulsory military service was longer than that of Frenchmen. The native conscripts were divided into two contingents, one for military service and the other for work on public projects. Native labor was also conscripted through tribal chieftains for the building of roads. Even after French citizenship was extended in 1946 to all overseas subjects, the natives did not acquire electoral rights equal with Frenchmen residing in the colonies. However, they were freed from forced labor and assured of court trial in all criminal offences.

Until the last war the colonial administrations in Africa used conscripted manpower for the building of major roads and railroads. While the shortage of volunteer labor may have made conscription the only practical solution to the problem of developing a network of transportation (outside of importing cheap labor from Asia), the concept of forced labor would have been at that time unthinkable in Western Europe.

Certain criminal procedures, also unthinkable in Europe of the nineteenth and twentieth centuries, were considered by European colonial administrators to be quite suitable for the "natives," presumably because of their inferior place in the scale of human kind. Until very recently corporal punishment was used in the British and, to a lesser extent, in the French and Belgian colonies. It was a mark of great progress when the whip, made with hippo-hide (the traditonal instrument of slave-traders), was eventually replaced for this judicial purpose by the cane. Collective punishment was considered the best way of maintaining public order in an emergency situation. As late as the fifties the British authorities in Kenya responded to the Mau-Mau movement by punishing the Kikuyu tribesmen collectively;

within two years they confiscated from them more than 10,000 head of cattle, 12,000 sheep, and 5,000 goats.

Criminal sanctions for the breaches of labor contracts would also be unthinkable in modern Europe although, it is true, they were included in Soviet labor legislation during the period between 1940 and 1956. In South Africa criminal penalties are attached by law to labor offenses committed by Africans, such as the failure to appear for work, absence without leave, intoxication during working hours, careless work, and damaging the employer's property. The laws in Southern Rhodesia, although less severe than in South Africa, also penalize Africans for breaches of labor contracts. Portuguese legislation in Angola and Mozambique punishes breaches of labor contracts or damage to the employer's property with imprisonment.

Laws regulating passes reflect the same racialist mentality because they apply only to Africans. In the Union of South Africa the native is required to carry a pass which serves as a kind of personal record; the bearers of the passes are fingerprinted by the police. In Southern Rhodesia the natives are also subjected to a pass system although it is less rigid than in South Africa.

In the nineteenth century the British rule in India was founded on a frank racialism. No Indian could hold a King's commission in the Indian Army and none was promoted to the higher positions in the Indian Civil Service. European hotels and clubs were closed to Indians. Actually, the Britisher lived in his own Anglo-India, and the Indians in their native India. The two seldom met socially. Dutchmen and Frenchmen similarly relied in their Asian possessions on the racial prestige of the white man. The Asian discovered that Europeans of differing nationalities, not always friendly to one another in Europe, formed a solid front against the Asians. The white clubs, hotels, and schools were closed to Asians but open to all Europeans whether they belonged to the ruling nationality or not. The same was true in semicolonial China where the Europeans formed a united front of privileged aliens.

For both Asians and Africans the color bar meant not only an inferior social status but also limited economic opportunities; the best paid administrative and business positions were in fact reserved for the whites. The bitter resentment of natives who were discriminated against in their own country was bound to grow in intensity with the rise of a new class of Western-educated natives whose career prospects were dimmed only because of their color. Asians and Africans who succeeded in acquiring a Western education and Western manners were resented by white men who considered them out of place in the colonial world.

For instance, Indonesians with a Western education were either unable to obtain government- or Dutch-controlled business employment in their own country or were given posts inferior to their educational qualifications or were paid salaries lower than Europeans of the same rank. School fees were required of Indonesian children, while European students, unless their parents were well-to-do, were enrolled without fees.

If colonial racialism belongs in Asia to the pre-independence past, it is still a shocking reality in various parts of Africa. This means in practice that the African is barred from the better official and private-enterprise jobs, that he is paid lower wages than white employees, that the better land is reserved for the white settler, that school facilities are unequal, that the African is subject to segregation in housing and in public transportation, and that he is required in some areas to have a pass for urban residence and in others a pass for after-curfew circulation in the cities.

The torrent of self-determination has swept away racial discrimination in those parts of Africa where independent states have supplanted French, Belgian, and British colonies. But racialist regulations survive in Southern Rhodesia and in South Africa, and the regime of inequality still reigns in the Portuguese possessions. Only the so-called *assimilados*—i.e., Christian Africans with a minimum of formal education—are recognized as equal Portuguese citizens. Out of the total of over 10 million Africans in Angola and Mozambique only about 35,000 have reached this status. Postwar white immigration, encouraged by the Portuguese government, has complicated the racial problem, because land in certain areas is reserved for white settlers and the increase in the number of whites leads to unofficial segregation in hotels, restaurants, and theaters. The Portuguese school system is calculated to restrict the number of *assimilados*; it requires the native child to attend a three-year rudimentary preparatory school before admission to the elementary school. When he is ready to enter high school, the native student, who necessarily spent the first three years of his education in the preparatory school, may be refused admission on the grounds that he is older than the maximum age limit.

The solidarity of the working class does not exist in a society divided along color lines. The European labor unions in Southern Rhodesia and in South Africa support the racial discrimination which results in much higher wages for the European worker. The wide gap between the earnings of Africans and white workers is due not only to different wage scales but also to the exclusion of the Africans from the skilled jobs. A Moslem in Algeria had an average income amounting to one-tenth of that received by the Algerian European. His living standards were those of an Iranian or Iraqi peasant. It is unrealistic to expect him to feel much admiration for the French "civilizing mission" which produced these results after one hundred and thirty years of French rule. In general, the European settled in colonial Africa had, or still has, a higher living standard than his social counterpart in Europe. It is not surprising that it is the white people of the lower classes who most vigorously supported racial discrimination in Algeria and who still support it in those parts of sub-Saharan Africa which are not yet emancipated.

In the nineteenth century racial discrimination was justified by the argument that the nonwhites were incapable of reaching the European level either because of their lack of inborn aptitudes (Africans) or because of the debilitating influence of the climate or of their obsolete civilizations (Asians). These rationalizations have been replaced in this century in Africa by a new theory which argues that the African cannot usefully acquire modern knowledge and techniques because of the retarding effect of his backward native environment. This theory has been refuted by the many Africans who have achieved high efficiency in intellectual pursuits though their parents or grandparents had lived a tribal existence.

Racial resentment has been intensified in Africa by an uneven political development which has enabled certain areas to achieve full independence and left other areas in their position of colonial dependence. The Algerian war between the two races, racial discrimination in Southern Rhodesia and in South Africa, and the rumblings of revolt in Angola unpleasantly remind the independent African of his own recent past and of his relations with the white man.

The racial problem is also aggravated by another fact, namely that the underdeveloped nations are mostly colored while the advanced nations are almost all white. It is true that Japan is an advanced nation and that most of the Latin American countries, including those with white majorities, as well as large areas in Eastern and Southern Europe, must be included within the semi- or underdeveloped world. But basically the two worlds, the rich and the poor, are separated from each other by a color line.

THE COLONIAL REGIME AND MINORITIES

The colonial powers certainly did not create the problem of minorities in Asia and Africa, but they aggravated it by their policies. They brought European and Asian minorities to Africa and either encouraged or tolerated large alien immigrations into their Asian possessions. The colonial regime pursued three policies which undermined the homogeneity or the social solidarity of the native societies. It accorded preferential treatment to certain minorities in order to rely on their gratitude and loyalty for a more effective control over colonial majorities; it promoted the migration of cheap labor from one colonial possession to another and even from foreign countries to colonial possessions; it tolerated spontaneous and large immigrations which were attracted by the new opportunities created by the orderly colonial administration and by the prospect of finding jobs in the colonial territory. The very fact that different countries found themselves ruled under the same flag made possible a fairly easy migration of individuals of one ethnic group into territory inhabited by another group. This was particularly true of the Indians who migrated in search of work to various parts of the British Empire in Asia, Africa, and the Caribbean area. Today, Indian overseas settlements exist not only in Southeast Asia but also in East, Central, and South Africa, British Guiana, Trinidad, and Jamaica.

The policy of favoring certain groups can be illustrated by the three cases of Burma, India, and Indonesia. Aware of the danger of a revival of militant Burman nationalism (the Burmans had a keen national consciousness, stimulated over many centuries by their being placed between two powerful neighbors, the Indians and the Chinese), the British colonial government encouraged the development of separate ethnic identities among the Chins, the Kachins, the Karens, and the Shans. Their differences from the Burmans were stressed and their racial and other affinities ignored. The teaching of Burmese was forbidden at the Chin schools until 1941. This policy, aided by conversions to Christianity, proved most successful with the Karens, with whom independent Burma has had no end of difficulties. The British regiments in Burma were recruited among the Chins, Kachins, and Karens but not among the Burmans.

In India, Britain relied mostly on the Hindus after the Great Mutiny of 1857, and later, after the rise of Hindu nationalism, on the Muslims. Of course, the colonial power did not create the animosity that exists between the Hindus and the Muslims. The Hindus remembered the several centuries of Muslim oppression and discrimination under the Moghul Empire; the Muslims could hardly forget the powerful Hindu revolt, the Mahratta movement, which precipitated the ruin of the declining Moghul Empire. But the estrangement between these two groups, separated not only by religion but also by their entirely different cultural and social concepts, was aggravated by the British decision in 1907 to institute separate electorates for the Hindus and the Muslims in the whole Indian territory. This decision of the viceroy of India, Lord Minto, was taken in the full knowledge of its significance as a means of further alienating the Muslims from the Indians and thus better securing British rule. The system of separate electorates provided that Muslims should be represented only by Muslims. The Muslims thus became a political entity that was officially separate from the Hindus. Muslim-elected representatives were thereby guided toward thinking in terms of their own religious and cultural community rather than of all-Indian interests. This separation of the two communities certainly contributed to the later Muslim movement for a separate Pakistani state, although the insistence of the Congress Party on Hinduism was another reason, not to mention other historical and cultural cleavages between these two sections of the population of the subcontinent.

The origin of the strong economic position of the Chinese minority in Indonesia goes back to the policy of the Dutch East Indies Company which relied heavily on Chinese assistance in the economic exploitation of the archipelago. As intermediaries between the Company and the native population, they were able to monopolize the domestic trade. After the replacement of the Company by direct Dutch rule, the colonial administration continued to favor the Chinese to whom it leased monopolies on the collection of certain taxes and the sale of certain commodities of general consumption. Not until the end of the nineteenth century were these monopolies entirely terminated.

The consistent though unsuccessful French policy of pitting the Berbers against the Arabs in North Africa is another example, among many more, of the divisive effects of colonial favoritism.

The city of Singapore and Malaya provide an illustration of the mingling of various ethnic stocks which was promoted or made possible by colonial rule. Economic opportunities attracted such large Chinese and Indian immigrations that the Malays now form barely half the population of their own country, the Chinese and Indian pluralities combining to form the other half, while Singapore, built up under British dominion, is a Chinese city.

The large Tamil minority in Ceylon, currently struggling against the supremacy of the Sinhalese majority, owes its origin only partly to the pre-British invasion by the Tamil conquerors of northern Ceylon. A much greater number of Tamils immigrated to work on the British plantations at the time when both India and Ceylon were governed by the United Kingdom.

Finally, Europeans saddled large areas of Africa with their own and Asian minorities.

The Asians frequently mention another factor which tends to disrupt the cultural unity of their peoples, namely the Western missionary activities which produced native Christian minorities within societies formerly dominated by Hindu, Moslem, or Buddhist cultures. This problem is, however, a minor one because of the relatively small numbers involved.

COLONIAL RELUCTANCE TO TRAIN NATIVE ELITES

The colonial educational policies in Asia ranged between the two extremes represented by the achievements of the British administration and the United States, on the one hand, and the deliberate failure of the Dutch to train local elites in Indonesia, on the other. After the British had left the Indian subcontinent only 10 per cent of civil servants (Britishers) were withdrawn; the new Indian and Pakistani governments were able to carry on with the existing native personnel and after only minor adjustments. The same was true in the Philippines and to a lesser degree in Burma and Ceylon.

In Indonesia, where the Dutch administration had trained only a small number of lower public officials, the independent native government had to build from the ground up. The Dutch policy deliberately did not provide opportunities for the education of local elites (in public services, business, and other walks of life). Only after the First World War were three higher professional schools (technology, law, and medicine) founded in Indonesia, but in 1940, the last year before the Japanese occupation, only 637 Indonesians attended those schools while only 37 were graduated in the same year. As late as 1938-39 only 204 Indonesians were graduated from high schools as against 457 Europeans and 116 Chinese. The Europeans were a small minority, the Chinese numbered about 2 million, but the total population was at that time around 70 million. This policy failed dismally to achieve its purpose, for it did not prevent a numerically small elite from leading an anticolonial revolt and achieving independence. But Indonesia had to begin its independent existence with an inadequate supply of university-educated personnel. This policy explains in part why the Dutch are still denounced in Indonesia, while Great Britain now enjoys a high respect in its former Asian dominions.

The colonial record in Africa was not, until very recently, much different from the Dutch record in Indonesia. The colonial powers were caught unprepared by the swift political awakening, which they had not anticipated before 1939. They had looked upon the Africans as culturally immature wards who should be fed only small doses of education. Even as late as 1948 a United Nations survey revealed a dismally low proportion of African populations attending any school. Granted that the organization of a widespread network of schools has been hampered by the underdevelopment of Africa, the fact remains that Africans have manifested in the last decades a great eagerness to provide their children with educational opportunities and, by implication, with a chance to become equals with the Europeans. Before 1939 the colonial powers were not very keen on hastening this process, and some, like Portugal, continue to feel this way.

It is admittedly difficult to assign priorities to any of the three levels of education (primary, secondary, and higher) when one is faced with an illiterate population and a great shortage of trained elites. The best solution consists in striking a balance by extending elementary education while simultaneously training university-educated elites who will be able to take over the government of their own country. The colonial powers were usually reluctant to provide the latter opportunity, fully realizing that this opportunity would eventually spell the end of their own rule.

The Belgians were interested in extending primary and trade education in order to augment the Congolese skilled manpower which they needed for the exploitation of local natural wealth, but they failed to provide opportunities for higher education. The founding of the university in Leopoldville took place shortly before the concession of independence. The Belgian policy proved as futile in delaying political emancipation as the Dutch policy had been in Indonesia. However, the chaos in the Congo which followed the Belgian withdrawal was due in large part to the absence of a native university-trained elite (the total number of university graduates was said to have been ten persons for the whole country) and the lack of experience in self-government.

France made less effort in primary education but allowed young Africans to attend its own universities; it thus produced a sizable African elite with French intellectual equipment. But in Algeria only one-sixth of the Arab children were enrolled in schools, a surprisingly low percentage after one hundred and thirty years of French administration.

The Portuguese record in Africa is the worst. As mentioned before, the school system in Angola produced approximately 30,000 *assimilados* for over 4 million of the total population and less than 5,000 in Mozambique, which numbers 5.8 million of the total population. In other words, several centuries of the Portuguese "civilizing mission" failed to make any inroads on the illiteracy of African natives. It is probable that this policy will be no more successful than the Dutch and Belgian policies in arresting the movement toward self-determination, but it will have a detrimental effect for many years on the future of Mozambique and Angola after they have reached independence.

The neglect of proper school facilities for the Africans in the Central African Federation stands in contrast with an honest effort in Uganda and Tanganyika. The British Commission on Higher Education for Africans in Central Africa reported as late as 1954 that the public libraries were either closed to Africans because of the color bar or charged an admission fee which Africans could not afford.

ANTI-WESTERNISM

All these shortcomings of past and present colonial policies have caused the Asian and African nationalisms to be permeated with a strong anticolonialist feeling which amounts to the conviction that no people can trust another to take care of their interests. This anticolonialism has a great many anti-Western connotations. Among Africans still living under the colonial system anti-Western feelings are manifested in a revolt against racial discrimination, the white settler, and the white administration. With other Africans and with Asians it takes the form of a bitter realization that they have emerged from the colonial period as economically backward peoples, the pariahs of the modern world. Nor do they lose sight of the fact that the white tenth of the world population has an 80 per cent share in the total world income.

The Western retreat was not always a peaceful parting of the ways, as the Indonesians and the Vietnamese know. There is nothing that unites Asians and Africans culturally, but two circumstances unite them emotionally: both were dominated for years by the white man, and both belong to the economically submerged majority of mankind. The emotions aroused by these two circumstances pit the nonwhites against the whites.

The leaders of now independent countries continue to harp on the theme of anticolonialism. They do it for various reasons in spite of the Western retreat. One reason is that this retreat has not yet been completed, and there is a lingering suspicion that Western imperialism might be revived in another form. Then, too, these leaders have only recently taken part themselves in the struggle against colonial rule and have spent a good part of their lives in colonial prisons; it would be hard for them under any circumstances to forget this unpleasant past overnight, but they now have a political interest in reminding their followers of the heroic record of their leaders. Moreover, anticolonialism has now acquired a new meaning; it now implies a determination to achieve greater economic independence from the West. Finally, anticolonialism helps to promote national unity; the image of Western colonialism or imperialism serves as a rallying banner for the newly independent countries which are still deficient in national solidarity.

Anti-Western feelings are nourished by the survival of colonial rule in parts of Asia and Africa. The problems of West Irian and of Algeria acted as irritants, not only in the relations between Indonesia and Holland and between France and the Arabs, but more generally in the relations between Asians and Africans, on the one hand, and the West, on the other. The same is still true of the Portuguese colonies in Africa and of white dominance in Southern Rhodesia.

The nature of these anti-Western resentments can be illustrated by many examples. The Arab case is as telling as any other. The history of Arab grievances against the West begins with the First World War and in a few instances with the nineteenth century. The Arabs feel that their own divisive local loyalties owe their origin or their strength to European interference. Although the medieval Arab empire disintegrated owing to its own centrifugal forces and to the Turkish conquest, the Arabs point to more recent developments: the French rule in Algeria, Tunisia, and Morocco; the Italian in Libya; the British in Egypt and the Sudan; the British and French in the mandated countries of the Near East; and the British protectorates over the small Arab areas in the Persian Gulf region. They claim that these various political entities now have strong local loyalties because they were either created or maintained by European politics.

The Near Eastern Arabs begin their indictment of the West by citing Britain's violation of its pledges given in the 1915 correspondence between Sir Henry MacMahon, the British High Commissioner for Egypt and the Sudan, and Emir Hussein, the Sherif of Mecca. While the Sherif clearly promised to support British military operations against his sovereign the Turkish Sultan by encouraging a revolt among the Arab subjects of the Ottoman Empire, Sir Henry made somewhat ambiguous promises concerning the postwar British espousal of Arab national aspirations. The correspondence was couched in uncertain terms, and no map was attached. However, certain points were clear: the promise of self-government for the various Arab provinces of the Turkish Empire in the form of several separate states subject to the over-all British protectorate; the reservation of Lebanon and the Syrian coast for the French zone of influence; and no mention of any Jewish home in Palestine, at that time a part of the Turkish province of Syria. One cannot deny that Britain violated these pledges in its Balfour Declaration of November 2, 1917, on the Jewish home and in the secret British-French treaty signed on May 16, 1916, by Sir Mark Sykes and Georges Picot. The latter treaty assigned to France not only what had been reserved for it in the MacMahon-Hussein correspondence but also the inland provinces of Syria. On April 24, 1920, the Inter-Allied Conference at San Remo ratified the division of Arab lands between the British and French mandates. The British-sponsored Jewish immigration to Palestine greatly increased the percentage of this population, which had amounted in 1918 to 10 per cent of the total.

The Arabs also blame the West for the formation of the independent state of Israel and for the nonenforcement of the boundary lines which the United Nations had recommended in 1947; they forget that they themselves rejected these boundary lines by unleashing a war against Israel in 1948. They are inclined to ascribe to the West the responsibility for the survival of Israel and for the existence of almost a million Arab refugees from Israel; they also resent the Tripartite Declaration which the United States, Britain, and France adopted in May, 1950, against any forcible change in the Arab-Israeli frontiers. They added in 1956 another grievance, the British-French co-operation with Israel in the attack on Egypt. All these resentments have been grafted on the still lingering Islamic animosity toward Europeans.

It is not very surprising that Arab or other Afro-Asian leaders, if placed in opposition to one or another Western power, are tempted to follow the age-old maxim that "the enemy of my enemy is my friend." This enemy of the West is the Communist bloc, which seems to offer a desirable counterbalance. If they are told that a great weakening of the Western bloc may make it possible for Russia and China to begin their own imperialist drive, they are inclined to answer that the troubles of each day suffice and that it is too early to worry about potential dangers. An African still smarting under colonial rule and racial discrimination might go further and answer that there is no point in warning a man who tries to escape from a burning house that he might freeze outside.

THE BENEFICIAL RESULTS OF COLONIALISM

If political passions did not demand all-black or all-white pictures, the debit side of the colonial ledger would be set off against the credit side. It is undeniable that the colonial system brought with it certain benefits for the colonial populations. Some of these benefits were intended by the colonial administration and some were merely fortuitous, but the results are felt to the present day.

First of all, colonialism brought to certain areas the political and administrative unity which became the foundation of newly independent states, and modern patterns of state administration which had been unknown before. In Africa the very concept of the state was introduced by the Europeans whose creature, the colony, has been gradually transformed since the Second World War into independent states. The colonial period in Africa, despite all its shortcomings, was a time of transition from tribal existence to the modern state. India had never been united under one central government; neither the native Hindu kingdoms nor the Moghul Empire ever extended their rule over the whole subcontinent. The British *raj* was the first government to exercise its control (direct over British India and indirect over the princely states) over the whole subcontinent. This enabled India to emerge for the first time in its history as one state which unites all Hindus except those who live in Pakistan. Ceylon also owes its political unity to British rule. The Dutch colonial administration was the first to weld together the peoples of various tongues and cultures who populated the archipelago. The ancient empires of Java and Sumatra had never ruled over the whole of Java, let alone the numberless islands of what is now known as Indonesia. Subjects of the same European power, 90 per cent confessing the same Islamic faith, able to communicate through a Malay *lingua franca,* the Indonesians eventually discovered that they formed one nationality. It is probable that Asia and Africa would now be fragmented into many small independent states if the colonial powers had not laid the foundations of the larger, unified structures of the present day.

Secondly, the colonial populations benefited by the economic development, however lopsided it may have been, which took place under foreign rule. Although the colonial powers did not devote any thought, until after the Second World War, to the balanced economic growth of their dependencies, they opened up the exploitation of local natural resources by bringing in their investment capital and their managerial and engineering skills, and in several cases they founded local processing industries if this was warranted by the prospect of high profit. Of course, the scope of this economic development varied from one dependency to another, but often the outline of an economic substructure was filled in. Roads and railroads, postal services, telecommunications, modern harbors with shipping lines leading to other continents, a public health system, schools—all these form the legacy of colonialism. The so-called population explosion (in less dramatic words, the sharp reduction in the mortality rate) in the former colonial countries is initially due to the colonial administration and its health services. The growth of modern cities, such as Bombay, Calcutta, Madras, Shanghai, Tientsin, Singapore, Colombo, and Jakarta, was also due to European organizational skill and to the European concept of the modern city. These great economic and cultural centers with their concentration of educated classes have played an extremely important role in setting the countries concerned on the road to modernization. Western economic concepts and techniques influenced the more enterprising elements of the colonial population and helped in the rise of a middle class.

Thirdly, European law with its social implications acted as a stimulus of social change. The colonial powers eliminated certain native institutions and customs which were deemed barbaric by European standards. Such age-old Indian customs as human sacrifice practiced among the Kapalikas, the burning of widows on their husbands' funeral pyres (*suttee*), the dedication of women to temples, and infanticide were forbidden by the East India Company. The Great Mutiny of 1857-58 made the British administration more cautious about tampering with local customs; for instance, the custom of marrying girls before puberty continued to be respected. The British reforms were all the more meritorious in view of the great difficulties which an alien administration had to face in trying to alter the patterns of an old society in which all aspects of life were regimented by time-honored customs. The other colonial powers were also breaking down obsolete institutions which were hampering social mobility and modernization. These reforms could be carried out more easily if they were supported by the native educated classes, as they were in India in this century. It was in the inter-war period that the British administration, in co-operation with the Central Indian Legislative Assembly, enacted two notable laws: the Age of Consent Act, which raised the minimum marital age for girls to fourteen, and the Civil Marriage Act, which made the first breach in the caste system by validating marriages between persons belonging to different castes.

Above all, the Europeans introduced the concept of equality before the law. It is true that they claimed for themselves in China, Turkey, and several other non-European countries the privilege of exemption from local laws and jurisdiction and that they often applied different laws to themselves if residents in the colonies and to the native inhabitants. But their colonial subjects were *inter se* treated as equals before the law. This was often a complete innovation. In India, for instance, a Brahmin could not be convicted on the evidence of a lower-caste Hindu, punishments varied in severity depending on the caste status of the defendant, and the Muslim courts did not accept the testimony of a non-Muslim against a Muslim. The concept of equality before the law presupposed the equal right of all human beings to personal dignity. The natives discovered in this principle of equality a powerful weapon against racial discrimination and generally against European rule. Equality before the law started another process, the emancipation of women, a process which can no longer be halted.

Throughout the nineteenth century the European judiciary system was introduced. A modern system of taxation was established. In other words, the colonial powers were laying the cornerstones of modern societies where they had found archaic or primitive ones.

It is impossible to deny that Britain and later France, once convinced of the inevitability of the evolution toward self-government, have done much to ensure an orderly transition from the colonial status to that of independence. The Indochinese and Algerian wars should not make one forget the assent of the French Fifth Republic to a rapid and peaceful transition of Tropical Africa to the status of independence. Britain should be credited with having set the first example in India where the Western colonial retreat began. In 1917 Britain promised to lead India gradually toward the self-governing status of a Dominion. Certainly, few in Great Britain expected at that time or before the Second World War that the new evolution, acknowledged by Britain, would end so soon in complete independence; it was generally hoped that a slow and gradual development would be eventually crowned by Dominion status. Whatever the expectations were, Britain honestly trained India throughout the inter-war period for its future career as a self-governing entity. Provincial governments responsible to elected provincial legislatures were given authority over a large number of subjects though still under over-all British control. Indians became the holders of several portfolios in the central government of India although the most sensitive posts were reserved for British nationals. Indians were offered an opportunity to practice parliamentary government. This was not yet true self-government but a preparation for it. A new economic policy was inaugurated in the same period; tariff protection was given to Indian industries which could at last develop unhampered by competition from British industries. As a result, investment capital was attracted to Indian manufactures. The Indian Armed Forces and the Indian Civil Service were increasingly staffed with Indian higher personnel. Officer's commissions and the higher administrative posts were thrown open to Indians who thus were enabled since the First World War to build up their own personnel for running a modern state. The smooth transition to independence in India and Pakistan as well as in Ceylon was in no small degree due to British policy. British fears (or hopes) that an independent India would mean chaos and that the British presence would remain the ultimate guarantee of order were quickly proved groundless, thanks in part to this groundwork laid by Britain itself. If the mutual Hindu and Muslim massacres were the price of the partition, all other apprehensions about the difficulty of absorbing the princely states and of consolidating a state inhabited by so many linguistic groups and religious sects were allayed by an orderly transition to independence.

Perhaps the greatest boon conferred by colonialism, although not always intentionally, was the infiltration of European concepts of modern society. This infiltration began in the nineteenth century and continues to the present day. At that time, the tightening of the colonial administration, the geographical extension of colonial rule, the more intense economic exploitation, brought Asia and Africa closer to Europe. These two continents were compelled to face the European cultural challenge; the shock treatment administered by European imperialism and colonialism made it impossible to ignore the ideas of the European intruders. The Asians in the past century and the Africans in this century began their quest for European knowledge. The revolution of modernization, which today fascinates Asia and Africa, has its intellectual roots in the Augustan period of colonialism.

Finally, nationalism, the revolt against European political and economic dominance, was inspired by European ideas, was formulated by Western-educated native elites, and received its strength from growing impatience with Western rule. If Asians and Africans believe that nationalism is a beneficial phenomenon, they cannot deny that they took over its intellectual concepts from Europe and that they did it during the colonial period.

THE WESTERN COLONIAL RETREAT AND THE RISE OF NON-EUROPEAN NATIONALISM

Beginning with the second half of the nineteenth century, the main vehicle of the European cultural influence was the school. Those who could afford it went to the European schools, usually those of the colonial power. Others enrolled in such schools of Western type as were available in their own countries. The network of schools which offered a Western type of education was first organized by the colonial administration and by European and American missions. The first generation of Asians and Africans to become acquainted with Western ideas and techniques were graduates of these schools. They were attracted to European knowledge for various reasons. Some were stimulated by sheer intellectual curiosity; others hoped to advance their careers in the colonial administration or in European business enterprises; still others wanted to enhance their social status by achieving intellectual equality with the Europeans. But another important motivation was the desire to wrest from the Europeans the secret of their superior power, which was their knowledge. The second half of the nineteenth century witnessed the rise of a class of Western-educated Asians whom colonial officials contemptuously referred to as "Wogs" (Westernized oriental gentlemen) but who were destined to lead the awakening of their countries. The same process has been taking place in Africa in this century.

The European ideas of equality before the law, of national self-determination as manifested in the German and the Italian unifications and in the Eastern European struggles for independence, of government by consent, contrasted strangely for these Western-educated Asians and Africans with actual European practice in the colonial dependencies. They could see through the European claim to superiority by noticing the human shortcomings of Europeans observed at close range in their own homelands where these Asians and Africans lived as students. They could discover the contradiction between Christian teachings and actual European behavior. European prestige, carefully cultivated in the colonial and semicolonial countries, was gradually being shattered in the minds of Asians and Africans who had mastered European knowledge; they were, by contrast, regaining their own self-confidence. Many of them were attracted by the European doctrine of Marxism, perhaps because it was a challenge to the social and economic premises of European societies. The European literature on nationalism supplied them with intellectual tools for the clarification of their own group consciousness.

European education was leading not only to revolt against European political dominance but also to a re-examination of inherited Asian or African values. These Western-educated Asians and Africans were to replace the former traditional elites (the mandarines, the priests, the nobility, the tribal chieftains) who had proved unable to cope effectively with European dominance.

There is no end of examples proving this influence of Western education on the rise of Asian and African self-assertion. The first national organization in India, the Indian National Congress, was founded in 1885 by Western-educated Indians. All the successive leaders of the Congress, including Mahatma Gandhi and Jawaharlal Nehru, were trained in the West. The founder of the Pakistani state, Jinnah, was a British-educated lawyer. Dr. Sun Yat-sen, the father of the Chinese Revolution, the Indonesian and the West Indian leaders, the African protagonists of self-government such as Dr. Nnamdi Azikiwe, Obafemi Awolowo, Abubakar Tafawa Balewa, Kwame Nkrumah, Tom Mboya, Julius Nyerere, Leopold Senghor, Felix Houphouet-Boigny, and a host of others were all products of Western education. Modern Arab nationalism owes its intellectual origin to Christian Arabs educated or influenced by Western missionary schools. If the same movement was later stimulated by the reaction of both Moslem and Christian Arabs to the Young Turkish nationalism, the latter nationalism itself had been inspired by Western ideas.

The Asians and Africans who wished to attend Western schools had to acquire the knowledge of a European language, usually that of the colonial power; the nationals of independent states such as Japan, China, or Thailand had a choice and usually opted for English. Whatever the European language selected, it served as a key to European knowledge and, in addition, played the important role of *lingua franca* in multilingual communities such as India and various African territories. For instance, the present political unity of India is due in no small degree to Lord Macaulay's plan of 1832 to provide the Indians with educational opportunities in English. If the British administration of the time had decided to promote education in the many vernacular languages of India, the European influence would have infiltrated Hindu civilization at a slower pace, because a much smaller number of Indians would have been able to read English, and the awakening would have come much later. The graduates of vernacular-language schools would have been segregated into separate and not necessarily friendly groups without any linguistic medium of communication. India would probably have become a replica of Europe: one civilization but divided into many rival states and nationalities, each founded on its own linguistic identity. The English-educated Indians formed an all-Indian elite who eventually ensured the transition to an independent and united India. If the African states have been able so far to preserve the territorial unity of the former colonies, this is also due to the unifying influence of the *lingua franca* supplied by the colonial power. Otherwise these former colonial dependencies would probably have experienced insurmountable difficulties in maintaining some cohesion in the face of several political elites, each knowing only its own vernacular language. Moreover, the process of modernization would have been greatly delayed for lack of easy access to the European knowledge which only a European language can provide.

It is Western technology that has supplied the Western-educated elites in Asia and Africa with the means of reaching their illiterate countrymen, namely radio and motion pictures, while the literate but less educated can be reached with another European invention, the cheap newspaper and pamphlet.

The national reaction against European colonialism had to be combined with an assertion of the homogeneity of the colonial population and its cultural worth. The leaders of colonial revolts had to turn to the precolonial past of their countries to find there the historical justification for their claim to independence. The Asians referred to the records and the archeological relics of the former glories of their countries; the Africans sought to define the concept of the African "personality." The Asians were greatly helped in their quest by the Western scholars who had developed oriental studies, who had unearthed the relics of the precolonial past in their archeological explorations, and who had initiated historical research founded on European methods. The colonial administration often took measures to preserve historic monuments, the landmarks of former Asian glories. This is a debt owed by Asian nationalism to the West even though European scholars were motivated by intellectual curiosity, not by the desire to provide raw materials for a revival of oriental nationalism.

In Africa other Western scholars helped by their studies to clarify the contours of this African personality which now fascinates the African elites. The process of urbanization, begun by the Europeans, helped the Africans to develop a sense of community larger than tribal allegiance. Living together under deplorable conditions in the segregated housing districts and brought into close urban confrontation with the white man and his claim to superiority, they gradually acquired a feeling of solidarity that transcended tribal and linguistic differences. Education on the European model also helped the African to rise above his tribal allegiance and to visualize the future in terms borrowed from Europe, in terms, that is, of a modern state and perhaps a federation of such states. The same education was also a step in achieving equality of status with the European and eventually winning an independent state.

The Western retreat from Asia and Africa, which few would have predicted before 1914 and not many expected before 1939, is due to two causes: changes which affected the colonial powers, and the awakening of the colonial and semicolonial populations. The two wars reduced the strength of the colonial powers and confronted them with the ideological challenge of Communist anticolonialism, a challenge backed up by the power of the Communist bloc. The awakening of the colonial populations made it much more difficult than before to maintain colonial control. The new Western concept of the welfare state could hardly be reconciled with a complete indifference to the fate of the colonial common man, but large expenditures would have been required for the economic development and social welfare of the colonial populations. As a matter of fact, after the Second World War the colonial powers, especially Britain and France, began a planned development of their overseas territories. These plans placed great emphasis on the welfare of the natives, in particular their education and public health. The colonial powers soon discovered that they would have to face large expenditures not only to build the social substructure but also to maintain the social services already established. It is costly to build a school or a hospital but it is also costly to keep it in operation. In other words, after the last war the colonial venture was becoming a financial burden instead of the profitable enterprise it had once been. It was becoming increasingly difficult to rely on the armed forces, police, and minor officials, recruited among the colonial subjects, to maintain public order against nationalist opposition. The rule by sheer force would still have been possible in the less populated colonies but would have antagonized the newly independent states of Asia and Africa which are important pawns in the competition between the Western and Communist blocs.

Whatever the causes of the decision by the Western powers to terminate their colonial rule, they did it only when confronted by the awakening of Asia and Africa. This awakening was gradual and due to many reasons. Once the process had begun, the rumblings of discontent of one colonial population had a contagious effect on the others, and the success in achieving independence by one colony encouraged the others in the struggle for their own self-government. The British retreat from India, Ceylon, and Burma in 1947 certainly precipitated the retreat of Britain and other colonial powers from their possessions in Asia and Africa.

By historical coincidence the second half of the nineteenth century marked the beginning of two conflicting developments. On the one hand, not until the middle of the last century did the Asians begin to feel acutely the heavy hand of European imperialism, after the British war of 1840 against China and after the tightening of the British administration in India following the Great Mutiny of 1857. It was in the second half of the same century that Indochina became a French colonial possession (1863-74) and that Thailand lost a part of its territory to Britain and France. Africa was finally carved up among the European powers in the same period.

On the other hand, an event took place in the middle of the century which caused the first Asian reaction of self-defense. On July 8, 1853, Commodore Perry appeared before the shores of Japan with his warships and gave that country a choice between opening trade with the United States or suffering the consequences implied by the presence of his naval squadron. When he came back next year with a stronger naval force, the Japanese yielded as the Chinese had done before them. Japan, opened to Western commercial penetration, seemed destined to become another China. But the Japanese were the first non-Europeans to decide to wrest from Europe the secret of its power. During the short period between 1868 and 1893, Japan was modernized and enabled not only to defend its independence but to deal with the West on a footing of equality. This feat, which seemed at that time a spectacular exception to the general rule of Asian helplessness, attracted the attention of many Asians. Then another event shook Asia. An Asian power, armed with Western know-how, proved in 1904-05 that it was able to inflict a crushing defeat on a European great power, itself a busy colonizer in Central Asia and an active participant in the general process of carving up the Chinese Empire. The Japanese victory over Russia was the first proof, since Vasco da Gama's ships appeared in Asian waters, that Europeans were not invincible. The white man could be beaten at his own game. For a time Japan became an inspiration to many Asians. Students flocked to Japanese schools, and Japan encouraged the emerging nationalist movements.

In Canton in 1905 the Chinese used the weapon of the weak by instituting a boycott of American goods in reprisal for the treatment of their countrymen in the United States. In 1908 they used the same weapon against the Japanese who had been attracted in the last decade of the nineteenth century by the prospect of getting their share in China. The progress of the Indian national movement, the gradual reawakening of China, and the national self-assertion of the Turks had repercussions elsewhere. The first nationalist organization in Indonesia, Budi Utomo, was founded in 1908 to be followed in 1912 by a much stronger Sarekat Islam. In 1909 the Indians made a boycott campaign against British cottons. In 1911 the Chinese revolted against the debilitating rule of the Manchu Dynasty, which had proved its incapacity to stem the menacing tide of European and Japanese encroachments. In 1916 the Indian Congress and the Moslem League, founded in 1906, made a joint declaration in favor of self-government. The Arabs began to stir in response to the disruption of Moslem solidarity by the Young Turkish nationalism. Asia was awakening, but the process was greatly accelerated by events which were taking place in 1914-18 in Europe itself.

The First World War, the first civil war within the European civilization to affect other continents, shattered the prestige of the white man. The Europeans, who had seemed to rally together against the Asians and Africans whenever their colonial interests had been involved, were now engaged in a mortal struggle with one another. They needed Asian and African soldiers and workers for the war effort. The war not only weakened the power of Europe but also undermined the self-confidence of Europeans. They began to doubt whether it was the manifest destiny of Europe to be the main stage of international politics and to remain the master of other peoples and races. They were unable to decide the outcome of their fratricidal struggle without the intervention of the United States; only ruins remained of the balance of power.

The new outlook was reflected in the European attitude toward India and China. Britain promised India in 1917 a gradual evolution toward self-government, and China began to be treated with greater consideration. Tariff autonomy was restored to China, and gunboat diplomacy ceased to be fashionable.

Even though President Wilson's doctrine of national self-determination was mainly intended to benefit the nationalities controlled by the defeated Germany, Austria-Hungary, and Turkey, its message sent a thrill over Asia. It was natural for an Asian, as it was later natural for an African, to ask the question whether all the peoples of the world had the same birthright to self-government.

Much more important in its consequences was another event of the

First World War, the October Revolution in Russia. The European civilization, already rent by a gigantic military conflict over competing national interests, was suddenly split by a great schismatic movement that challenged the validity of political and economic dogmas formerly accepted by all governments. The challenge was no longer launched by private Marxist groups but by the government of a European great power. Two ideologically hostile camps took the place of what had been the official political-social unity of outlook among the European governments. The October Revolution had a message specifically addressed to the colonial and semicolonial peoples. It asked them to rise up against their masters, the European powers, and to unite with European Communists in a struggle against "imperialist capitalism" as Lenin called it. For him, this was a way of hastening the downfall of capitalism. For the Asians and Africans his message had a different meaning; it meant that a new ally had been acquired in the struggle for independence from the West.

This cleavage within the European civilization gave the colonial peoples the assurance that Europe would not be united against them as it used to be. Increasingly the energy of the West was to be absorbed by the struggle with the schismatic Europeans of the Soviet Union and was becoming less available for the exercise of government in the non-European lands.

The anticolonialist platform of the Soviet and affiliated Communist parties compelled the progressive and socialist parties in Western Europe, where an anticolonialist element had always been represented, to face the issue of colonialism with a greater sense of urgency. The nationalist-minded Asians and Africans were finding friends not only among the Communists but also among the socialists of Europe. This was especially true in Britain where the growing influence of the Labor Party and its increasingly sympathetic stand in favor of colonial aspirations, certainly prepared the psychological ground for the great colonial retreat.

The October Revolution presented the colonial nationalist movements with a dilemma. Formerly, their leaders thought of the independent future of their countries in the terms of Western liberalism. Now they were offered the alternative of modernization according to the Soviet pattern which was receiving increasing attention after the success of the first Five Year Plan. The concept of planned progress was taking root in many minds and was replacing the Western model of economic development founded on private initiative. The former Western monopoly of intellectual influence was being broken by the new Marxist-Leninist teachings emanating from Moscow. This intellectual rivalry between the two sections of the European civilization quickened the pulse of Asian and African thought.

The appearance of the Communist parties in the colonial and semicolonial countries had a twofold significance. The other nationalist organizations were forced to intensify their struggle against colonial domination because they were faced with a native competitor who did not mind outbidding his opponents. The same competitor, by offering his own social program, also compelled them to examine the whole problem of the future economic and social transformation of their societies.

The impact of the October Revolution can be measured by the reaction of Dr. Sun Yat-sen, a man who had before firmly believed in Western liberalism. Discouraged by the Western policies toward republican China, he turned to Moscow as a new ally. In his manifesto to the Chinese people of July 25, 1919, he said: "If the Chinese people wish to be free, like the Russian people, and be spared the lot prepared for them by the Allies at Versailles . . . let it be understood that its only allies and brothers in the struggle for national freedom are Russian workers and peasants of the Red Army." In 1925 in a letter addressed to the Soviet government shortly before his death, he again affirmed his faith in the country which he preferred to the West: "You are at the head of the Union of Free Republics, the heritage left to the oppressed peoples of the world by the immortal Lenin. With the aid of that heritage the victims of imperialism will inevitably achieve emancipation. . . . Taking leave of you, dear comrades, I want to express the hope that the day will come soon when the U.S.S.R. will welcome a friend and ally in a mighty and free China, and that in the great struggle for the liberation of the oppressed peoples of the world both those allies will go forward to victory hand in hand." Dr. Sun Yat-sen was expressing these confident feelings despite the fact that his new ally had moved troops into Outer Mongolia, continuing in this respect the imperial policy inaugurated in 1911 of detaching this province from China, and had reasserted the claim to a joint administration of the Manchurian railroads, another Tsarist heritage. A good number of other Asian nationalist leaders, particularly in French Indochina, were inclined to look at Soviet Russia as he did; some of them went much further and embraced the Leninist doctrine.

The impact of the October Revolution is far from exhausted to the present day; certainly the continuation of the civil war within the European civilization is helping the non-Europeans in their self-assertion in world politics.

The mutually stimulating effect of nationalist movements was illustrated, among hundreds of other examples, by the spectacle of Atatürk's Turkey, which not only emerged successfully from a trial of force with the Western powers in the years following the First World War but also carried out a bold program of Westernization. This achievement had an electrifying effect on other Moslem lands from North Africa to Indonesia. The Western universities were in this century a sort of meeting ground for young people coming from the various non-European countries. These Asian and African students, living and working together at the British, French, American, and other Western universities, were attracted to one another not only by their common venture of discovering the strengths and weaknesses of the West and of penetrating into the treasure-house of European ideas but also by their similar aspirations to liberate their peoples from Western dominance. Their anti-Western feelings, strengthened by oft-encountered Western racialism, inevitably produced the conviction that Asians and Africans shared a community of interests. Students from the same country or the same area, facing a totally different Western environment, were acquiring a stronger sense of belonging to the same ethnic or cultural group. They could realize, surrounded by foreigners, that their own differences, which seemed so important back home, were almost insignificant if compared with what divided them from their Western colleagues. Thus, Indians from various castes and linguistic groups discovered in the Western cities that they were members of the same family, as did Indonesians born on widely different islands, Arabs from lands distant from each other, and Africans speaking entirely different languages.

The inter-war period that witnessed the rise of Asian nationalism also witnessed the first symptoms of a similar phenomenon in Africa. The African self-assertion was due not only to the impact of Western education and not only to the contagious Asian example but also to the Pan-African movement. This movement, stimulated by the American and Caribbean Negro intellectuals who contacted Western-educated Africans, rendered one principal service to Africa: it helped to eliminate the sense of inferiority that inhibited educated Africans. The first Pan-African Congress, held in Paris in 1919, was organized by Dr. W. E. B. DuBois, the founder of the American National Association for the Advancement of Colored People. The program was modest and consisted in the request, addressed to the Paris Peace Conference, for a better protection of African interests in the colonial territories and for native participation in the colonial administration. The participants in the Congress were Negro intellectuals from the Western Hemisphere and Africa, as were the delegates to the Second Congress held in London in 1921. This Second Congress protested against racial discrimination. The Third and Fourth Congresses, which met in 1923 in London and in 1927 in New York, were again confined to intellectuals. The Fifth Congress, in 1945, was more significant because it was attended by new political leaders from Africa, such as Kwame Nkrumah and Jomo Kenyatta who were soon to acquire great stature in their native lands of Ghana and Kenya. The participants were not only intellectuals but also African leaders drawn from the ranks of political, trade-union, and peasant movements, as well as African students studying in the West. At that Congress the Africans asserted themselves; it became obvious that they no longer needed the prodding of Negroes from the Western Hemisphere. Since 1945 it has been evident that the racial solidarity among the Negroes from the two parts of the world can no longer conceal their divergent aspirations.

The Negroes from the Western Hemisphere are interested in ending racial discrimination, but the countries where they reside are their own countries which they share with the white majorities. Culturally, they are not Africans and would be strangers in the continent of their ancestors. Their solidarity with the Africans is tenuous and probably would not survive the end of racial discrimination. The Africans, on the other hand, are interested in becoming the masters of their own countries where they form the crushing majority of the population. For them, Pan-Africanism means the co-operation and perhaps eventually the union of independent African states.

For a short time after the First World War, Britain and France entertained the illusion that their colonial empires were expanding instead of verging on disintegration. Their rule was extended to the Arab Near East where the third rival, Russia, was for a time eclipsed. Yet the nationalist movements, which before 1914 had been confined mainly to the educated classes, began to exert an influence on the attitudes of the masses. Mahatma Gandhi discovered the weapon of the weak, civil disobedience. It was particularly effective in India where a small nucleus of British administrators relied on the co-operation of Indians in maintaining British rule. The Indian civil service, the army, and the police could not operate without the assistance of the Indians who formed their ranks and who began to occupy higher positions as well. If the Africans in Southern Rhodesia and in South Africa were better organized, the same weapon of civil disobedience could prove quite effective in furthering their cause since they provide the manpower indispensable to the white economy.

The Second World War further precipitated the colonial retreat. Japanese victories over the Western powers shattered what remained of white prestige. Vast colonial territories were occupied by Japanese troops. Although the Japanese intended to replace Western colonialism with their own, they encouraged the local nationalists, prodded their anti-Western feelings, and, once faced with the prospect of their own defeat, helped in building independent governments and, after their surrender, left arms to the native troops. This was particularly true of Indochina and Indonesia. If the Asian nationalist leaders turned, as they did in Burma, against the Japanese, they did so to assert their aspirations before the Europeans would have time to come back.

Europe was further weakened by the war and eclipsed by the rise of the two powers, the United States and the Soviet Union, neither of which had any sympathy with European colonialism. Exhausted by the war, the colonial powers had neither the material strength nor the moral fiber to resist the tide. The retreat from Asia began with its electrifying effect on Africa.

Postwar events contributed to the subversion of Western prestige. France was defeated in 1954 by the Vietnamese Communist armies at Dien-Bien-Phu. It was tempting for Asians to forget the various reasons which had prevented the United States from deploying its full strength against China on the Korean battlefields. What most impressed them was the standstill to which the Chinese forces seemed to compel the Americans and the undecisive outcome of the Korean War.

The political retreat of the Western powers seldom means the end of their influence as was the case of Holland in Indonesia or of France in Guinea. The ties of past association are usually too strong to be broken overnight. These ties are of various kinds. The governing elites of the newly independent states are usually familiar with only one European language, that of the former colonial power, and feel at ease in the cultural atmosphere to which that language belongs. The linguistic bond ties them to the information media, especially the press agencies, of the former colonial power. The students who have learned its language at home are sent to its universities rather than elsewhere. The country remains within the monetary zone of the former colonial power, and its trade continues to flow toward and from its market. In the case of the former British and French colonial possessions, the continuation of intimate economic relations is promoted not only by the monetary zone but also by the preferential treatment reserved for the commodities exported from these Asian or African territories. Capital invested in colonial enterprises by corporations and individuals of the colonial power usually remains invested. The newly independent territory still uses the banking, insurance, transportation, and other services which the former colonial power continues to provide. Even military materiel might be bought from the same power. In turn, the colonial power is often inclined to supply its economic and technical assistance to the emancipated colonies in order to preserve its political influence and to protect its investments against the threat of expropriation. The loans and grants are the price of its continued presence.

The colonial retreat means even less a sudden disappearance of the West. Western powers other than the former colonial power appear on the stage of the emancipated states with their own political and economic influence. It would be a gross misconception to think that the emancipation has resulted in the expulsion of all Western influence and in the opening of the gates to the Communist bloc, which can assert its influence there without fear of competition from the West. But the end of colonial dominion does not mean that the change is more legal than real. The ultimate decision concerning the domestic and external policies of the newly independent country is now vested in its own government. It can send its students in spite of the linguistic difficulties to universities other than those of the former colonial power; it can promote investment by other countries; it can seek other markets; and it can counterbalance the influence of the former colonial power by accepting economic aid from other Western countries and from the Communist bloc. These and other steps have in fact been taken by former colonial possessions to loosen the ties of past association. In other words, the surviving influence of the former colonial power does not cancel the effects of the political emancipation. This fact is evident in the difference between the political orientation of the former colonial powers, all of which are committed to NATO, and of the former colonial possessions, most of which follow a policy of non-commitment.

Even if the relations between the two countries remain cordial, the former colonial power is confronted with the problem of resettling a sizable number of its citizens who had resided in the colonial territory as officials, private businessmen, professional men, skilled workers, or agriculturists. They had belonged to a privileged minority that was seldom popular; they might have no choice but to go back to their own country which then has to find jobs for them.

THE PROBLEM OF NATIONAL INTEGRATION

The trend in Europe has been toward the consolidation of existing nation-states, or the emergence of new ones, which have largely homogeneous populations or at least a clear predominance of one nationality united by language and by a distinct national consciousness. This process of national integration is being furthered by the concept of the welfare state in which each social class has its obvious economic stake in the existence of the nation-state. In Europe the problems of national integration arose gradually and were solved gradually, over a period of centuries. The newly independent states of Asia and Africa are facing these problems only now and facing them all at once. Most of the Latin American countries have not yet solved the same problems; their Indians, *mestizos,* or Negroes usually live on the margin of the national culture and are only partly or not at all assimilated. The disappointing experience of Mexico after the Revolution of 1910 proves that the solution of this problem will be neither quick nor easy. One of the goals of that revolution was to end the political rule by the small white upper class and to integrate the *mestizos* and the Indians politically and culturally within one Mexican nation by agrarian and educational reforms and by developing a new foundation for Mexican culture which would fuse the Spanish and Indian elements. Yet several decades later it cannot be said that this process of integration is close to successful completion.

The Arabs face a different dilemma, namely whether their national integration will take place within the existing states or within a unified Arab state. The movement toward unification is hindered by the different histories of the various Arab populations and hence by their cultural differences. An educated Arab of the North African Maghreb has been influenced by French culture, his fellow-Arab in Egypt or Iraq by English culture, and their reminiscences of the times prior to Western colonialism are markedly different. If the Pan-Arab movement were finally to prevail over local loyalties to Egypt, Iraq, Syria, and other existing political entities, would its territorial extension include only the Arab Near East or also the Sudan and the Maghreb?

The factors which militate in favor of Pan-Arabism are as follows: Islam conceived not only as a religion but also as a culture; a common language; anti-Western resentments originating in the colonial period; the shared ambition to become modern and economically developed; the image of the glories of the medieval Arab Empire, especially of the Omayyad Caliphate when Calish Omar was reported to say of the Arabs that they were "the substance of Islam"; and, last but not least, the hostility toward Israel which unites the Near Eastern Arabs. If the Pan-Arab movement were eventually to fail in uniting all the Arabs under one state flag, it might still be the source of solidarity with respect to the non-Arab world unless even this solidarity were neutralized by the rivalries between the various Arab states.

These rivalries are due to the following reasons:

1. The economic conflict between the oil-producing countries, often socially backward and having small populations but a very large income derived from oil royalties, and other Arab countries which are poorer and overpopulated but socially more advanced. The most obvious contrast is between the United Arab Republic (Egypt) and the various small but oil-rich sheikdoms of the Persian Gulf. If the U.A.R. were able to extend its control over these sheikdoms, the oil revenue would be diverted toward capital investment in Egyptian economic development instead of being invested in London banks.

2. Competition for the political leadership which usually divides Egypt from Iraq, Syria, and Saudi Arabia. The smaller Arab countries fear that they will be swallowed up by the larger Arab states during the process of unification.

3. The vested interests of the ruling groups in the existence of the present Arab states. This factor also hindered the movement toward the German and the Italian unifications. The merger of several smaller states necessarily reduces the number of available high national posts; this personal consideration is not unimportant.

4. The sentimental attachment to the existing states, i.e., the local nationalism.

The various attempts to establish a federated Arab state in the Near East serve as a warning against hasty judgments. The union of Egypt and Syria (the United Arab Republic) collapsed in 1961, shortly after its foundation, as a result of the Syrian revolt. The more ambitious scheme, outlined in 1963, to federate Egypt, Syria, Iraq, and later Yemen within one state under the same name of the United Arab Republic might or might not be successful and enduring. The Maghrebian Arabs either do not intend to join or have adopted a wait-and-see attitude toward the Near Eastern attempts to federate the Arab states.

The multilingual communities in Asia and Africa face the most difficult problems of national integration. The issue before them may be summed up in the following alternative: either each linguistic group places its own aspirations above the over-all loyalty to the state or the linguistic groups evolve a supreme loyalty to the state which they have inherited from the colonial administration. European history does not offer an encouraging precedent. The European tendency to equate the community of language with the nationality is evidenced not only by the existing nation-states but by present problems such as the ever-recurring quarrel between the French-speaking Walloons and their Flemish-speaking neighbors who are citizens of the same Belgium.

India is a major example of the problem, a very important one because India is the largest non-Communist state and viewed, rightly or wrongly, as a Chinese competitor for Asian leadership. China, however, is a homogeneous state, while the unified state of India does not antedate the British conquest. Its component regions, if they wanted to hark back to the past glories of the pre-British period, would each locate their "golden" eras in a different century. The grand total of languages spoken in India amounts to more than two hundred, but the major linguistic areas are ten. None of the linguistic groups represents the majority of the Indian population. The largest, Hindi, amounts to 31 per cent of the population and, if the Urdu (a language derived from Hindi but having a large admixture of Persian and Arabic words) and the Punjabi groups are included, it still does not exceed 46 per cent. Its designation in the Indian Constitution as the official language might eventually become meaningless because of widespread opposition from other linguistic groups. The other major linguistic groups are large both in percentages and in total figures. They amount to the following percentages of the total population: Telugu, 10; Marathi and Tamil, 8 each; Bengali, 7; Gujarati, 4.6; Kannada, 4.1; Malayalam, 3.8; Oriya, 3.7; Assamese, 1.4. The four major southern languages (Telugu, Tamil, Kannada and Malayalam), unlike Hindi, do not stem from the Sanskrit but form together the Dravidian family of languages. Many southerners who speak these languages have strong antinorthern feelings; they are descendants of the natives whom the northern Arians conquered thousands of years ago. To them, the national pre-eminence of Hindi symbolizes the continued domination of the North. The claim of Hindi as the national language is not strengthened by the fact that some of the other languages, such as Bengali, Tamil, and Marathi, have produced richer literatures and by the fact that Hindi is not yet developed enough to serve readily as a modern vehicle of communication.

The opposition to Hindi is also due to utilitarian reasons. English continues in fact to be the national language and serves as the medium of civil service and army examinations. Indians of all languages are thus placed in a position of equal opportunity, all of them facing the exams in an acquired language. But if Hindi were to replace English, the northerners, for whom Hindi is the native language, would be *ipso facto* favored over the others, who would rarely be able to manipulate Hindi with equal ease. The northerners would figure in the federal administration out of proportion to their numbers. This development would multiply the present complaints that the national government and the leadership of the ruling Congress Party are dominated by Hindi-speaking people, in particular those from the Uttar Pradesh state.

The unity of the Indian state has so far been guaranteed by the existence of an educated elite bound together by the English language. The present trend toward the growing predominance of the various regional languages in education and in local politics might eventually undermine the role of English as the *lingua franca*. If fluency in English were to decline at the secondary school level, local languages might eventually become the vehicle of university education. Then the present all-Indian elite would gradually be replaced by several regional ones, fluent in their own languages but imperfectly versed in English. Would it be possible to maintain the present unified framework of the civil service and of the army if the admission and promotion examinations were to be conducted in several regional languages instead of English?

The strength of regional languages is bound to grow because of the expansion of literacy. At the primary level, instruction must be provided in the mother tongue. The ever-increasing mass of literates will have only primary education and can be reached only in their native language. This promises a great future for the vernacular press and for such means of mass communication as radio, television, and motion pictures, which cannot transmit their message to the literates who know only their native tongue and to the illiterates, except through the intermediary of the vernacular language. This unavoidably growing significance of the vernacular tongues might generate strong local patriotisms. Would it result in a hiatus between national and provincial politics? Already the pressure by the linguistic regions has compelled the national government to rearrange the administrative division of India by making the provincial boundaries conform more closely to the frontiers between the major linguistic groups. This concession has not stopped other similar claims, as evidenced, among other examples, by the Sikh agitation for their own state. It is interesting that the Indian Communist party has usually supported the aspirations of the linguistic groups to their own statehood within the federal state and openly considers these groups to be separate nationalities.

India faces another formidable obstacle not only to full national integration but also to social mobility, the condition of a truly modern society.

Hindu society is composed of some 3,000 subcastes, which are the subdivisions of the four main castes. Born in his subcaste, a man is confined by immemorial custom, strengthened by religious sanctions, to live and die within his caste. He should exercise the profession of his subcaste, cannot marry outside this group, and should not share his meals with members of other subcastes. Hence, social and economic status is rigidly determined by birth. This system is infinitely more subdivided than the premodern European structure of estates and professional guilds and is a greater hindrance to social mobility. European modernization began with the abolition of all legal distinctions between the estates (equality before the law) and with the breaking down of the professional monopoly of the guilds. The caste system should be gradually abolished to enable India to make full use of the capabilities of its citizens and also to ensure its national unity.

Below the thousands of subcastes are the Untouchables, whom Hinduism places beyond the pale of its society. The "unclean" occupations, such as scavenging, are reserved for this group. No social contacts are permitted by Hindu tradition between them and the caste Hindus however low their caste may be.

It is true that members of the Indian elite have been making great efforts in this century to loosen the hold of this archaic social system, that they have tried especially to improve the lot of the Untouchables and to reintegrate them into the national society, that the caste system is not legally enforceable, and that the Constitution has formally abolished Untouchability. But a social institution which is rooted in an immemorial past and which can claim religious sanction cannot be expected to yield overnight to legislative fiat and to thc most earnest campaign of the intellectual elite. The process of urbanization should help in progressively undermining the caste system, which can be enforced with ease in the villages but much less easily in the large cities.

The Untouchables, the outcastes, represent almost 15 per cent of the Indian population. The depressed subcastes at the bottom of the social structure were officially numbered in 1953 at 116 million. The problem is aggravated by the fact that the subcaste, which is a socially self-contained group, does not overlap linguistic lines but is a part of the linguistic group. Thus, two similar subcastes, which should have a feeling of social solidarity across the whole breadth of the national territory, are in fact estranged from each other by linguistic differences. Each linguistic region contains its own subcaste structure which, with local variations, reflects the over-all structure of the Hindu system.

The system is so deeply rooted in Indian soil that it refuses to disintegrate rapidly. In the cities members of the same subcaste and the same linguistic group tend to congregate and to move upward collectively as a social unit. The subcaste thus becomes a pressure group, especially in provincial politics where political parties, including the Communists, have little choice but to seek the support of certain subcastes rather than others. A rapid and complete elimination of castes would cause a major social upheaval. Hinduism is the unifying factor in India, but, whether it is understood as a religion or as a way of life, it has prevented the fusion of Hindus and Moslems into one nation. If it is true that the caste system is an integral part of Hinduism (the future might disprove this proposition), is there a contradiction between Hinduism and modern society with its inherent element, unrestricted mobility?

The past has left to India another legacy—the Moslem minority which includes about 10 per cent of the population and whose national integration is not made easier by their entirely different ways of life and the existence on the same subcontinent of a Moslem state. Numerically, India contains the third largest Moslem population after Pakistan and Indonesia.

Pakistan faces an equally difficult problem of integration, aggravated by the division of the country into two parts separated from each other by a thousand miles. The Western Pakistanis are in the main the descendants of the Muslim conquerors from Central Asia and traditionally have had cultural contacts with the Moslems of Western Asia. The Eastern Pakistanis (Bengalis), who form 56 per cent of the total population, are probably the descendants of native Indians who were converted to Islam. The Pakistani and the Indian Bengalis would have formed one nationality in the European sense if they were not divided by religious differences. They speak the same Bengali language and share many customs. United by religion to the Western Pakistanis, the Bengali Pakistanis differ from them in language, ethnic composition, and ways of life. Political power has been mainly concentrated in Western Pakistan, a fact that does not please the more numerous East Pakistanis. West Pakistan is in turn divided into five linguistic groups: the Punjabi, the Pushtu which is also spoken by a large number of Afghans on the other side of the frontier, the Sindhi, the Urdu, and the Baluchi. Fortunately, Urdu is the *lingua franca* of Western Pakistan. Urdu and Bengali are constitutionally recognized as the two official languages, while English remains the working language of the state. Hindus represent a 13 per cent minority.

The Philippines has selected one of its vernacular languages, Tagalog, as the national one. Indonesia did the same by elevating one of the Malay dialects, the Bahasa Indonesia, to the status of a national language. There is no simple solution for the Federation of Malaya where three groups form major pluralities, none of which can claim the numerical majority. The distribution in 1952 was as follows: out of the total of 5.5 million the Malays numbered 2,716,000 persons; the Chinese, 2,092,000; and the Indians, 617,000. The future of this composite community is uncertain, especially since the Chinese might be pulled away in their loyalty by the attraction of their own country and by the fact that they number 850,000 people in the neighboring Singapore against only 130,000 Malays and 80,000 Indians.

All Asian countries are beset by the problem of their national, linguistic, or religious minorities, who complicate the process of national integration. Ceylon has a Tamil minority that makes up 23 per cent of the population and claims linguistic equality with the Sinhalese majority. About 25 per cent of the Burmese population are non-Burmans such as Arakanese, Karens, Shans, Chins, Kachins, Indians, and Chinese. There are about 600,000 Moslem Malays in the four southern provinces of Buddhist Thailand; there exists a sizable Cambodian minority in Vietnam, and a Vietnamese minority in Cambodia; Thais live not only in Thailand but also in China, Cambodia, Laos, and Vietnam. Indian minorities are to be found in Burma, Malaya, and Ceylon. The Ambonese, the Eurasians, and the Arabs in Indonesia, the Moslems (Moros) in the Philippines, a great many aboriginal and unassimilated tribes throughout South and Southeast Asia, and other minorities add to this mosaic of languages and races.

Politically, however, the main problem is that of the Chinese minorities to be found in large numbers in Southeast Asia. This part of Asia is underpopulated by Asian standards except for the island of Java, Central Luzon in the Philippines, lower Thailand, lower Burma, the Red River delta in Vietnam, and the lower Mekong River area. The total population of some 185 million people face three demographic giants: China with 700 million, India with 450 million, and Japan with 90 million. Japan was once attracted by the raw materials and the *lebensraum* in Southeast Asia. China may also be when it stands on its own feet as an industrialized giant. This is why the problem of some 13 million Chinese settlers in the area is potentially very important. They number about 2.5 million in Indonesia and approximately 3 million in Thailand; they form the great majority of the population of Singapore and the second plurality in Malaya; they reach a million in Vietnam (both states included); and they are to be found in considerable numbers in all the countries of the area. They are usually reluctant to succumb to assimilation, and the local majorities, with whom they are not popular, have not encouraged them to become assimilated. They maintain their cultural identity by supporting their own network of Chinese schools and by sending their children to the schools on Taiwan or on the mainland, by their own associations, and by their local Chinese-language press. They usually occupy an important position in the economic life of their country of residence, often controlling retail and wholesale trade. Both the Nationalist and the Communist Chinese governments consider the overseas Chinese an integral part of the Chinese nation. The Communist government displays a great interest in them and in 1959-60 risked a deterioration in its relations with Indonesia by trying to intervene on their behalf because of Indonesian discrimination and persecution. The hostility of the newly independent states, which contrasts with their privileged position under the European administrations which had no reason to discriminate against them, and their own will to retain their cultural identity might make these Chinese minorities look increasingly toward China, whatever their feelings for the Communist regime might be. The growing power of the country of their ancestors provides them with a feeling of vicarious strength and a compensation for the unfriendliness of the local environment.

Western Asia is no more free of minorities. Turkey, Iran, and Iraq are saddled with the problem of large Kurdish minorities which several times in this century have reminded the world of their existence by revolting against one or another of the three states. All the Near Eastern countries have religious minorities. Lebanon is a country of religious and national pluralities, none of which forms a majority; Maronite Catholics, members of the Greek Orthodox Church, Sunnite and Shiite Moslems are the major groups. The Shiite majority of Iraq is usually subject to the political dominance of the Sunnite minority; the same majority controls Iran, but Persians do not form more than two-thirds of the population, the remaining one-third being Kurds, Turkmen, and Arabs. Afghanistan is divided into the Sunni majority of 80 per cent and the remaining Shiite minority, but only half of its population speaks Pushtu, the other half being divided between Tadjiks and Hazaras.

The problem of minorities in Asia, as anywhere else, is usually complicated by the fact that their fate might interest foreign states, particularly immediate neighbors of the same ethnic stock, religion, or language.

The linguistic complexity which hinders national integration in Asia is an infinitely more serious problem in Africa. Scholars vary in their estimates of the total number of African languages. Whether 1,000 or 700 is closer to the truth, the fact remains that Africa, in proportion to its population, has the greatest number of languages of all the continents. This diversity of languages stands in the way of the national integration of the sub-Saharan states, which are all multilingual, and does not augur well for the realization of an African union. The use by educated Africans of the European *lingua franca* is the saving device, but it requires that school instruction at the secondary and higher levels be continued in the tongue of the former colonial power. Another drawback is that the English-, French-, and Portuguese-speaking Africans will perpetuate the present divergence in cultural orientation.

The other disadvantage, inherent in the process of learning in a foreign language, is that time must be spent in mastering the language before knowledge can be assimilated. Not many individuals can learn to express their thoughts and feelings as easily in a foreign language as they can in their own. Each language is fraught with the cultural history of the ethnic group that created it. Thus, a man born in a different culture finds it difficult to express the patterns of thought of his native environment in a foreign tongue which is for him almost a dead language.

A monolingual society engaged in learning the ideas and methods of modern Europe need not adopt a European language as its language of instruction, but may imitate the Japanese of the period of Westernization and enrich its own vocabulary to cope with the notions introduced by European knowledge. If one of the native languages truly becomes the *lingua franca* of the country, as seems to be the case in Indonesia, the same solution will be adopted. But in a multilingual society which for one reason or another cannot make one of its languages the true *lingua franca* there is no way to escape the need for instruction in a European language at the secondary and higher levels. It is irksome to national pride and it erects a barrier between the educated elites and the masses, but it is a means of holding the elites together and therefore essential to the survival of the state.

The sub-Saharan communities are heterogeneous not only linguistically and in their tribal allegiances but also religiously. Although certain territories are predominantly Moslem, Christianity and Islam co-exist in sub-Saharan Africa with the pagan cults (fetishist and animist) which remain the religion of the majority. Islam is more successful in its proselytism than Christianity, probably because it is not a European religion and has not been associated with racial discrimination and because its dogmas and its ritual are much simpler than those of Christianity. The center of Moslem missionary activity is the Al-Azhar University in Cairo.

The complexity of the African situation can be illustrated by a few examples which demonstrate the whole difficulty of social integration of the newly independent states or of the territories which will eventually become independent. The African population of Portuguese Mozambique is composed of two major groups: the Swahili-speaking northerners who are mainly Moslems, and the pagan central and southern populations who include a small Christian minority and who speak various Bantu languages. The tribes extend into other colonial territories. The Tsougas of southern Mozambique live also in Southern Rhodesia and South Africa; the Ndjans inhabit both central Mozambique and Southern Rhodesia. This division of tribes by international frontiers will be the headache of independent states, as already proved by the quarrels between Guinea and Sierra Leone or between Ghana and Togoland, each pretending to unite the tribes by annexing a part of the neighboring state.

Nigeria, the largest sub-Saharan state, is the home of 248 distinct linguistic groups, of which the major groups are only the largest pluralities. Yorubas in the western region represent only 16.6 per cent of the total Nigerian population; Ibos in the eastern region, 17.9 per cent; Hausa in the northern region, 18.2; and Fulanis in the same region, 9.9. It is true that the major linguistic groups dominate in their own regions, but this neither reduces the discontent of smaller linguistic groups nor helps to eliminate the rivalry between the regions. The northern region, which includes 60 per cent of the total population, is predominantly Moslem and on this score feels superior to the other two regions; the latter regions, which have been more receptive to the European cultural influence, have their own feeling of superiority. In Ghana the strong Ashanti tribe resents the political domination by coastal politicians. In Liberia the 15,000 to 20,000 descendants of freed American Negroes rule rather despotically over one or one and a half million native Africans. Similar stories could be told about other areas.

The western Nigerian leader Obefemi Awolowo was not excessively pessimistic in 1947 when he said: "Nigeria is not a nation. It is a mere geographical expression. There are no 'Nigerians' in the same sense as there are 'Englishmen,' 'Welsh,' or 'French.' The word 'Nigerian' is merely a distinctive appellation to distinguish those who live within the boundaries of Nigeria from those who do not." He fully realized that Nigerians or, as a matter of fact, almost all sub-Saharan populations of the former or present colonial possessions are not nationalities in the European sense. Yet Nigeria and several other colonial entities are now independent states. Their most immediate problem is to substitute a strong loyalty to the inherited state for a nonexisting allegiance to the nationality.

The African problem of integration is certainly not made easier by the existence of white and Asian minorities. Judged by the general trend toward the termination of the white man's supremacy, the battle of the white settlers is a losing battle. France has recognized political defeat after seven years of war against Algerian self-determination. The numerical reality of 9 million Moslems versus 1 million Europeans has proved to be stronger than the French army of half a million men who could not subdue the Arab guerrillas. Britain has acknowledged the same reality in East and Central Africa except for Southern Rhodesia. There is not much chance that the white minority in Southern Rhodesia, where it amounts to 8 per cent of the total population, should prove more successful in its defense of white supremacy than the European minority in Algeria, which both proportionately and numerically was much larger.

The problem of South Africa stands apart, because the whites form there the largest white portion of the population in the whole of Africa and because the Union is an independent state where the colored people have no appeal to a higher authority in Europe. The proportions are as follows: about 3 million whites, almost 10 million Africans, 1 million "Coloreds" (the descendants of early Dutch settlers and native women), and about half a million Asians whose forebears were imported from India as cheap labor. The whites, even though basically united against the non-Europeans, are split into two sections which are not very friendly to each other: the Afrikaans-speaking (60 per cent) Europeans and the English-speaking (40 per cent) Europeans. About 3 million Africans live among the whites as industrial labor, the rest in the native reservations. The potential strength of the Africans lies not only in their numbers but also in the fact that their work is the condition of the white men's prosperity. The policy of *Apartheid* directed against all nonwhites, entails for the Africans the deprivation of political rights, wages much lower than those of the white workers, prohibitions against their own labor unions and exclusion from the white unions, housing in segregated townships, passes for residence and for circulation outside the native reservations, inferior and inadequate educational facilities, and criminal responsibility for so-called "statutory offences," i.e., breaches of the discriminatory laws applicable only to the Bantu majority (offenses against pass regulations are an example).

Several Latin American countries, which belong economically to the Third World, are culturally unintegrated societies where the European ways of life and often the use of the European language (Spanish) have not yet been extended to the Indian populations or where the *mestizos* (*cholos*) or Negroes have not yet been fully absorbed in the national life and fully accepted as equal citizens. There are large Negro populations in Brazil and in the Caribbean islands. The Indians (without counting the *mestizos*) represent very large percentages, sometimes majorities, in other Republics, as illustrated *exempli modo* by the following figures: Mexico, 28 per cent; Peru, 47; Bolivia, 57; Guatemala, 67; Ecuador, 58; El Salvador, 40; Honduras, 40; Paraguay, 65; Nicaragua, 24. These figures do not include all the Republics and are given only as an indication of the importance of the problem. They vary from one specialist to another either because the criteria for including an individual within one or another racial group are not always the same or because Latin American statistics are often unreliable. But whatever the percentage of Indians, it is always impressively high.

In the racially mixed Latin American countries race tends to coincide with social class. The social differences, which are already serious because of the very uneven distribution of national income, are aggravated by the fact that the better off and politically dominant class is white or near white, while the poor tend to be colored (Indians, Negroes) and the intermediate position is occupied by the *mestizos* or mulattoes. In those Latin American countries where the nonwhites represent the majority of the population or a very large minority the whites and near whites dominate the national life because they possess wealth and political power, occupy the crucial social positions, are literate, and are concentrated in the urban centers. The Indians are usually illiterate and are poor *campesinos* (peasants) who quite often do not even know the language of their political masters. In the cities with racially mixed populations it is the whites who live in the better districts and the dark-skinned people, whether *mestizos*, Negroes, or Indians, who are crowded in the slums. The whites and near whites usually predominate in the secondary schools and universities.

While Latin American social history is reflected in this coincidence of social status and color of skin, the present dividing line is not rigid. An Indian or Negro who has mastered Spanish or Portuguese, who dresses in European clothes, and who earns a decent living is *ipso facto* considered "white," i.e., a member of the upper or middle class.

The process of modernization cannot be fully implemented and a truly democratic system of government cannot function in a country where two distinct societies co-exist: the white or white-*mestizo* which rules the country and beneath it the Indian and/or Negro society which is underprivileged and culturally unassimilated. Sooner or later the very process of modernization will demand the cultural integration of nonwhites who in turn will begin to exert a true political influence. The recent Bolivian revolution indicates the future trend with its recognition of the Indian majority as true citizens.

In the Western Hemisphere and elsewhere the unresolved problem of social integration complicates the process of modernization which is a Herculean task even in the racially and linguistically homogeneous countries. Yet no country can become economically and socially modern while it relegates a large proportion or the majority of its population to a marginal role in the national life.

Nationalism is a powerful but neutral social force. It can be harnessed to any program that the national elites want to formulate on the condition that this program finds popular support. Once they have received their independence, the non-European peoples must decide which domestic and external objectives they want to pursue and how they intend to utilize the immense reservoir of social energy represented by nationalism or a similar feeling of social solidarity.

The pre-independence stage was relatively easy. A people took cognizance of their collective identity as a reaction to alien rule. The objective was simple—to get rid of alien dominance. Once this has been achieved, the much more complex question arises as to what should be done next. Dr. Kwame Nkrumah rightly said at the Gold Coast Parliament in 1953: ". . . self-government is not an end in itself. It is a means to an end."

The passage from one stage to the other is not easy. During the struggle against colonial rule the singleness of purpose made the image of an independent future so attractive that it seemed that all problems would find their magical solution on the day of independence. The differences of opinion and of interest could be readily subordinated to that single purpose of independence. After the retreat of the colonial power, there is no way of escaping the problem that the end of self-government must be defined in a program of practical policies.

Almost unanimously, the elites of the newly independent states have defined the end of self-government as the modernization of their societies. But independence brings with it other problems to be solved. There is the problem of national integration which must be solved concurrently with the process of modernization. There is the problem of defining the national territorial aspirations: will the independent state be content with the present territory usually delimited by the colonial powers or will it claim slices of neighboring territories? If the decision is in favor of the latter course, conflicts will ensue with other states. The rather short record in this regard of the newly independent states or of states which have emerged from semi-colonial status is no better than the European record. The Chinese print maps which include large portions of foreign territories claimed as parts of China. They contest in particular the Chinese-Indian borders in Kashmir and Assam and do not seem to recognize the dominant Indian position in the Himalayan states of Nepal, Sikkim, and Bhutan. The Afghans claim that the 5 million Pushtu-speaking Pathans of Western Pakistan should be united with their fellow Pathans of Afghanistan or form an independent state. Cambodia fears the territorial ambitions of Thailand and Vietnam. The territorial claims of new African states clash at several points.

Another question is that of defining the role of religion in the official life of the state. This is an important question for the Asian countries where religion is closely interwoven with the ways of life, as in Pakistan, Indonesia, the Arab countries, and the Buddhist states of Cambodia, Laos, Thailand, Burma, or Ceylon. The modernized elites may face conflicts between the requirements of economic and social progress and the retarding influence of archaic institutions and customs sanctified by religion.

The multilingual societies will have to decide whether the language of the former colonial power or one of the vernacular tongues should serve as the national language.

The materials of a common precolonial past will have to be used to strengthen the feeling of social solidarity by providing an image of glories and miseries shared in the remote past, an important element in the national consciousness. These materials are readily available in the Near East and in Asia but not in Africa where folklore must be substituted for history as a link with the past.

Finally, the most difficult problem facing the underdeveloped countries, whether they are newly independent or not, is to create an original synthesis of their own values with those which they intend to borrow from the European civilization in the process of modernization. Even if they wanted, they could not become exact replicas of the countries which are members of the European civilization. They cannot retain all their traditional values, some of which cannot be reconciled with the modern concept of progress. The process of forging a new hierarchy of values will be difficult and long.

All these grave problems besetting the underdeveloped countries of Asia, the Near East, Africa, and Latin America will have to be solved one way or another by the university-educated elites. It is this intelligentsia that is playing and is destined to play the most crucial role in the period of social and economic transformation and modernization. The intelligentsia, whose only common bond is their higher education, are neither a social class with definite collective interests nor a compact ideological group with one philosophical outlook. Their education confers on them the distinction of being the section of society most apt to handle general and abstract ideas; this distinction divides them into ideological factions often hostile to one another. The present government, as well as the "next" government which a revolution or a coup or simply an ordinary political crisis might bring to power, finds its members, leading supporters, and also its main enemies within this intelligentsia.

Those of the intelligentsia who possess the political power and formulate the national policies can adopt various attitudes toward the problem of social and economic development. They might oppose this development while paying lip service to its necessity, because they fear the loss of power as the final result of social renovation. They might be afraid that modernization would bring new elites to the fore and that their own political influence would be reduced by the rise of the common man. If they draw their main income from land, they might oppose agrarian reform as subversive of their wealth and influence whatever the economic or social justification might be for splitting up large estates. Yet the process of modernization seems to be inevitable and the open or disguised resistance of the upper classes can only delay it. A negative or helpless attitude on the part of the present governing groups would sooner or later result in their being overthrown and replaced by a new governing group which might be Communist or non-Communist.

The alternative for the present governing groups is to assume the leadership in the process of modernization; the only way of avoiding a revolution is to meet it halfway. Even a reformist policy of the present governing group and their willingness to make sacrifices out of their own vested interests cannot prevent an unavoidable consequence of the process of modernization, namely the rise of new elites. The modernization of an undeveloped country brings in its wake social mobility and new ways of earning money; consequently, new elites are bound to rise from among the lower social classes. The choice for those social groups who now hold power in the underdeveloped countries is between sharing power with the social newcomers or losing it altogether in a political upheaval.

The process of modernization in Japan was guided by a farsighted section of the upper class who overcame the resistance of other sections. In Russia and China the former governing groups were forcibly ejected and replaced by new ones who assumed the responsibility for the development of their countries.

The choice open to the current governing groups in the underdeveloped countries has its international aspects. The advanced countries cannot substitute themselves for the local government and its supporters in the formulation of domestic policies. The economic and social structure of an underdeveloped country can be changed only by domestic processes. Except for their economic and technical aid, the advanced countries play only one important role—and that an unintentional one—in the domestic life of the underdeveloped countries; the image which they project of modern society serves as a yardstick for measuring the progress or stagnation of other countries. This image fascinates the progressive elites in underdeveloped countries, dispels apathy, and evokes a desire to become modern which will not allow an archaic society to remain quietly somnolent. But no foreign government, whatever the amount of its economic assistance, can step into the shoes of the local governing group and make the necessary political choices for it. However, these choices have a bearing on the international distribution of power. If the existing ruling group fails to shoulder its historic responsibility, is swept away by a revolution, and is replaced by a new governing group recruited from among the more farsighted or bolder section of the intelligentsia, the new government might introduce a completely new orientation in foreign policy and thus affect the international distribution of power. The Cuban revolution offered an illustration of how domestic developments in an underdeveloped country can affect the distribution of power between the United States and the Soviet Union.

A member of the intelligentsia, whether he supports the present ruling group or belongs to the opposition, is usually a half-stranger in his own country if he is progressively minded and revolts against the status quo. His ambition to remold his own people in the image of the advanced peoples makes him an enemy of the obsolete institutions which his own countrymen may cherish. In Asia and Africa his education of the European type cuts him off from the illiterate masses or at least makes it difficult for him to communicate with them intelligibly. His views may differ from those of the older generation and of the uneducated people on many topics, including the merit of social customs sanctified by religion or by time immemorial. He may place the over-all interests of the national community over those of his tribe or caste, he may claim the right to choose his wife outside his own social group, he may be a fervent partisan of land reform carried out at the expense of the vested interests of his own father and his social class, or he may find the dietary customs of his religious community absurd. He may be resented as a half-stranger and feel himself to be a half-stranger especially if he has had the personal experience of living in a modern society.

If he is not discouraged, he may be tempted to break down by force resistance to the reforms which he deems salutary for his people and to favor the authoritarian form of government as the precondition of modernization. He might lean toward this type of government for other reasons as well. The centrifugal tendencies of the diverse ethnic, tribal, linguistic, or religious factions of the population might compel him to believe that the only way to safeguard the unity of the exising state is to govern without seeking popular approval. If he holds power, he might discover that the masses have expected the termination of colonial rule to usher in an immediate and visible improvement in their daily existence. Since no government, even the most eager to carry out the process of modernization and the most sensitive to social justice, can perform the miracle of creating a welfare state out of an economically underdeveloped society, the disappointed masses may become restless. Authoritarian government may then appear to be the only way of maintaining public order. The fact that a growing proportion of the intelligentsia in the underdeveloped countries are enticed by the image of the modern society does not necessarily mean that they are attracted by the democratic form of government (see Chapter 5).

The intelligentsia have been influenced in their thinking by many ideas indigenous to the European civilization, such as nationalism, economic growth, scientific and technological progress, the welfare state, the labor movement, Marxism or Marxism-Leninism, modern state organization, and so on. At the same time, the environment where they live and act is backward or archaic by modern standards. In 1956 the Indonesian novelist Takdir Alisjahbana gave the following picture of the contrast between intellectual concepts borrowed from abroad and surrounding conditions:

"Asia is living in thirty centuries at one and the same time. The Stone Age lives alongside the Machine Age, medieval feudalism and mysticism battle modern democracy and rationalism, and communalism and economic planning jostle each other daily."

If adapted to local conditions, this statement could be applied to Africa, the Near East, and large parts of Latin America.

The Russian ideological schism and the Western re-examination of traditional values have undermined the prestige of Western social concepts. But the intelligentsia of the underdeveloped countries have not yet been able to construct for themselves their own version of modern society, a version that would reflect the economic and social advances of Europe and yet answer to the peculiar needs of their own peoples. Mr. Nehru referred to this intellectual confusion when he wrote in 1956: ". . . this [former] faith in Western thought is itself being shaken, and so we have neither the old nor the new, we drift not knowing whither we are going." This uncertain state of mind, compounded of the loss of faith in the traditional native values and of the new scepticism regarding the validity of Western values, hinders the intelligentsia in providing a leadership sure of its ideals and long-term objectives.

Two sections of the intelligentsia merit special mention. One of these is composed of the military officers. Their training familiarizes them with modern techniques, the concepts of modern organization, and the decision-making process. They form a sort of modern enclave in a retarded country and may be tempted to use their military power in an emergency created by the failure of the civilian government. Often the sons of lower-class families, these officers may be more ready to carry out radical social reforms than a civilian government intimidated by vested interests. If they assume power, they usually govern in a sort of coalition with other sections of the intelligentsia such as civilian experts and those intellectuals who are willing to supply an ideology as a *raison d'être* of the economic and social reforms.

The other section is composed of the university students, who are apt to play a more important role in an underdeveloped country than in an advanced country. The university student has the prestige of his education in a predominantly illiterate country. Young and open to new ideas, he is deeply affected by the winds of modernization. The usual opposition between the two generations acquires a much deeper significance in an underdeveloped country, where it is often a conflict between the young who boldly look forward to a modern future for their country and their parents who are kept back by old habits and vested interests. The discontent which often prevails among the students originates not only in their revolt against the status quo but also in uncertainty about their own personal future in a backward country which might be unable to give them jobs consistent with their academic qualifications. Their university studies familiarize them with the outside world; they are able to gauge the gulf which divides their own country from the advanced nations but also to understand how this gulf could be bridged. If allied with other forces, these young people may become an important factor in the molding of national destinies.

Asia and Africa are such a mosaic of diverse nationalities and religious and linguistic groups that the image of an Asian and even more of an Afro-Asian unity is false. Culturally, a fundamental unity underlies the European civilization which extends from the Pacific coasts of the Western Hemisphere to the Pacific coasts of Russia and includes the whole of Europe. But Asia alone is the home of several distinct civilizations—e.g., the Far Eastern, the Hindu, the Moslem—as well as of several great religious-philosophical systems, such as Buddhism, Hinduism, Islam, Confucianism, each very different from the others. What is culturally common between a Japanese and an Arab, a Filipino and a Ceylonese, an Indonesian and a Nigerian, a Chinese and an Ethiopian? If they do have something in common, it is that modern element in their cultures which all have borrowed from the European civilization. Prior to the colonial period these various peoples had only haphazard relations with one another or no relations at all. During the colonial period their closest relations were with one or another European power rather than with each other. Politically they are as much divided as the Europeans. The Chinese and the Indians quarrel openly over their frontiers, the Pakistanis and the Indians look upon each other as enemies, the Arabs are unable to find a common political language, the young African governments eye with suspicion the ambitions and motives of their neighbors. Basically, Asia and Africa are only geographical expressions in spite of the display of Afro-Asian unity at the Bandung Conference in 1955. Even at Bandung they were divided into three groups: the uncommitted nations, those committed to the West, and the Communist countries. The Declaration which the Conference adopted was of necessity composed of the usual international platitudes except for one principle which was meaningful to all the participants: "Recognition of the equality of all races and of the equality of all nations, large and small."

However, when Asians and Africans speak of Afro-Asian solidarity, they refer to something more than a slogan. First, they share the bitter memory of the colonial or semicolonial past and hence a residue of anti-Western resentment of varying degrees of intensity. Secondly, the past and present behavior of white men makes all of them very sensitive to racial discrimination. Thirdly, several of them still face unresolved disputes with one or another Western nation, such as the disputes over the British protectorates in the Persian Gulf and the unredeemed African colonies. Finally, all of them and most of the Latin American countries form together the economically underdeveloped Third World beset with the same or similar problems. For the time being, the countries of the Third World are able to forget the forces that divide them when they are confronted with such problems of common interest as colonialism, racialism, and the need for foreign aid.

CHAPTER V

The Third World—the Revolution of Modernization

THE UNDERDEVELOPED WORLD AND THE INTERNATIONAL DIVISION OF LABOR

Economically, the world can be divided into three parts: the developed countries (the Western nations, Japan, the Soviet Union, and a portion of Communist Central Eastern Europe); the semideveloped or unevenly developed countries (the remainder of Central Eastern Europe and a few Latin American countries such as Argentina, Mexico, or Uruguay); and the underdeveloped countries (Portugal, Spain, Greece, the southern area of Italy, Communist China, North Vietnam, North Korea, Mongolia, as well as non-Communist Asia, the Near East, Africa, and most of Latin America). This division of the world into levels of economic development does not coincide with the political division. Countries committed to the West, uncommitted countries, and Communist countries can be found in each of the three economic subdivisions.

Approximately 60 per cent of mankind live in the underdeveloped countries, 10 per cent in the semideveloped, and 30 per cent in the developed.

The advanced countries derive most of their national income from the secondary (manufacturing) and tertiary (services) industries, while the underdeveloped countries rely for their national income on the primary industries (agriculture and extraction of raw materials). In the non-Communist world, the present international division of labor is reflected in the trade between the advanced nations and the underdeveloped countries.

Considering the different nature of their domestic production, it is not surprising that the mutual trade consists mostly in the exchange of manufactured goods produced by the advanced nations for the primary commodities (raw materials and agricultural products) exported by the underdeveloped countries. This pattern of trade does not favor the underdeveloped countries for several reasons:

1. The steady decline over the last several decades in the price of primary commodities compared with the price of manufactured commodities makes international trade increasingly more costly for the underdeveloped countries. Table 1 shows how many units of manufactured goods could be purchased at various times by the same quantity of primary commodities.

TABLE 1

Period	Units
1876-1880	100
1881-1885	102.4
1886-1890	96.3
1891-1895	90.01
1896-1900	87.1
1901-1905	84.6
1906-1910	85.8
1911-1913	85.8
1921-1925	67.3
1926-1930	73.3
1931-1935	62.0
1936-1938	64.1
1946-1947	68.7

The prices varied duc to changes in the economic situation of the advanced countries, but the secular trend in the steady decline of prices for primary commodities has remained the same.

2. Primary commodities as the main or only output are the symptom of a backward economy with a very low per capita national income. This in turn implies a very weak international bargaining position.

3. The international market in primary commodities is highly uncertain. Sudden fluctuations in price and in demand and supply have immediate and serious repercussions on the vulnerable economies of underdeveloped countries. A depression in the advanced countries causes a significant fall in demand; the appearance of a new producer of the same commodity brings an unwelcome increase in the supply. In both cases, the volume of exports or the level of prices or both are adversely affected.

4. The protectionism of the advanced countries usually extends to those raw materials and agricultural products which they produce them-

selves. This further restricts the foreign markets to which the underdeveloped countries export their primary commodities. The preferential treatment accorded by some advanced countries to certain underdeveloped countries collides with the interests of other underdeveloped countries which produce the same commodities and which are excluded partly or completely from a foreign market by such practices. British preferential tariffs in favor of the other members of the Commonwealth and French preferential treatment of imports from former French colonies are examples of this privilege bestowed for political reasons on certain underdeveloped countries at the expense of others.

5. The demand for primary commodities is vulnerable to the effects of technological progress in the advanced countries. A substitute might replace a natural product previously imported (synthetic rubber and fiber are good examples), or improved techniques may make it profitable to exploit domestic mineral deposits of lower quality which were once considered unprofitable. This prospect of substitutes or of improved techniques for the exploitation of minerals of lower quality casts serious doubt on the proposition that the international market for primary commodities will expand at the same pace as the industrial output of the developed countries.

6. This same proposition is undermined by two other considerations. The advanced countries are shifting their industrial expansion from the light industries, which are heavy consumers of raw materials per unit of production, to the heavy industries, such as the engineering and chemical industries, which require a much smaller proportion of raw materials. Moreover, their economic development is characterized not only by the constant growth of secondary industries but also by the rapid expansion of the tertiary (services) industries which create no demand for raw materials.

7. A rapid increase in the demand for raw materials is also checked by the economies in industrial production which are made possible by modern technology; the systematic recovery and reprocessing of metals is an example.

8. The rise in the living standards of the industrial nations means an ever-increasing demand for manufactured consumer goods and services rather than for a greater quantity or even a greater diversity of agricultural products. Moreover, certain countries with very high living standards, such as the United States, Canada, and Australia, and semideveloped Argentina increasingly export their foodstuffs and compete on the international market.

9. If all these uncertainties of the international market did not exist, the demographic pressure (a rapid increase in population) would in any case compel the underdeveloped countries with rural overpopulation to develop industries and thus to provide nonagricultural jobs for the expanding populations.

The present international division of labor is in itself a challenge to the underdeveloped countries. For this and several other reasons they aspire to transform their economies and abandon their present role of producers of primary commodities and importers of manufactured goods. For them, economic modernization means that the present division of the world into industrial and agricultural countries will eventually be abolished.

If and when most of the present underdeveloped countries realize their dream of becoming economically advanced, will the result be beneficial or disastrous for the present industrial nations? The answer to this question is implied in Table 2.

TABLE 2

INTERNATIONAL EXPORTS IN 1957 WITHIN THE NON-COMMUNIST WORLD[1]

Total of International Exports	100
Exports of Industrial to Nonindustrial Countries	26
Exports of Nonindustrial to Industrial Countries	22
Exports of Industrial Countries to One Another	43
Exports of Nonindustrial Countries to One Another	9

The twenty industrial nations of the non-Communist world are each other's best customers, while the more than one hundred non-industrial countries, inhabited by two-thirds of the population of the same world, have very little trade with each other. The industrial nations export to each other almost twice as much as to the nonindustrial countries. The latter countries export to the industrial nations two-and-a-half times more than to each other. The main reason for this situation is self-evident: countries with the highest purchasing power (the highest per capita national income) are necessarily the best mutual customers. They are not only the great consumers but also the great producers, representing 90 per cent of the industrial output and 80 per cent of the total production of the non-Communist world. Over 90 per cent of the total investment within the same area takes place in the industrial nations.

This short analysis suggests that the industrialization of the present underdeveloped countries should result in a great expansion of international trade and should stimulate economic activity in the present industrial countries. The process can be visualized in three stages.

The first stage will be characterized by the tendency in the underdeveloped countries to export semifinished goods rather than raw materials (flour instead of grain, crude metal instead of ore, cellulose and paper instead of wood, refined oil instead of crude oil, and so on) and to import an increasing volume of capital goods required for the equipment of their new domestic industries. Already capital goods comprise almost half the total imports of these countries from the industrial nations. While the

[1] Reproduced from Nurkse, Ragnar. *Patterns of Trade and Development.* Stockholm: Almquist and Wiksell, 1959. p. 21.

advanced countries export manufactured goods mostly to each other, in the capital-goods category their exports go mostly to the less developed countries. A hundred years ago the trade between these two types of countries consisted predominantly of an exchange of textiles for foodstuffs and fibers; it is now increasingly composed of capital goods from the advanced countries and minerals from the underdeveloped countries.

The second stage of development, i.e., when a developing country acquires more of its own manufacturing industries, will continue to call for great quantities of imported capital goods.

In the third stage, when most of the present underdeveloped countries will become industrial, their trade with one another and with the advanced countries will be stimulated by the growing purchasing power which now stimulates trade between the industrial nations. This stage will probably be marked by an equitable division of labor founded on a more pronounced specialization of each country in its industrial exports but no longer on the division of countries into the present two categories of producers of either primary commodities or manufactured goods.

In all three stages the growing purchasing power of the underdeveloped countries should enable the advanced nations to increase their exports and hence to sustain full employment and prosperity at home. The underdeveloped countries are now important to the economies of the advanced nations as suppliers of raw materials, but in the future they should also become important as expanding markets.

This hope that international trade will expand concurrently with the economic development of the present underdeveloped countries will be frustrated if these countries choose to follow the example of the Communist countries and, for political and ideological reasons, restrict their trade with the West to an unavoidable trickle.

Will the progressive industrialization of the underdeveloped countries increase the competition for raw materials, and will the present advanced nations find it more difficult and more expensive to purchase the raw materials indispensable to their own production? No certain answer can be given now. At first glance, it seems obvious that an increase in the demand for raw materials should cause a rise in prices and that the secular trend of declining prices should therefore be reversed. This might be the picture of the future. However, the ratio of imports of foreign raw materials to the gross national product of advanced nations has been decreasing during the last several decades. It is impossible to predict to what extent the future demand for raw materials will be compressed by yet unknown technological developments such as new substitutes, the extraction of domestic lower-grade ores, and so on.

Only one thing is certain—that the process of economic development of the underdeveloped countries cannot be stopped and that it will revolutionize the present pattern of the international division of labor.

THE CRITERIA OF UNDERDEVELOPMENT

The underdeveloped countries differ from each other. Hence, no description of their conditions and problems in general will apply in every particular case.

The concept of underdevelopment implies a comparison; the yardstick is the economic and social condition of other countries which are considered advanced in the same historical period. Thus, England was an underdeveloped country until the fifteenth century when it switched from exporting wool for further processing in the Low Countries to its own production of woolen textiles; it was underdeveloped by comparison with the Low Countries of the time. After the British Industrial Revolution the continent of Europe remained underdeveloped until the completion of its own industrialization. A country is economically underdeveloped if it does not use its available human and natural resources to the extent permitted by contemporary technology. Economic underdevelopment is caused by and in turn causes social underdevelopment, the survival of a society which is archaic by the yardstick of contemporary advanced nations.

The usual features of underdevelopment are as follows:

1. An extremely high natural increase in population resulting from a high birth rate and a rapidly declining mortality rate. The proportion of dependents (those below the age of fifteen or above the age of sixty-five) in the total population is much higher than in the advanced countries; in other words, the social burden of dependents is much heavier (see Chapter 6).

2. Unsatisfactory conditions of public health, sanitation, and housing.

3. The inferior status of women.

4. Child labor.

5. Malnutrition caused by a diet that is low in calories and deficient in proteins.

6. Low per capita productivity due, among other reasons, to inadequate equipment, undernourishment, the frequency of debilitating and endemic diseases, insufficient material incentives, and ignorance of effective production techniques. The United States, with a population smaller than that of Latin America, produces six times as much.

7. A high rate of illiteracy, which frequently reaches or surpasses 80 per cent of the total population.

8. A paucity of skilled manpower, including managerial and technological personnel, and generally a small proportion of university graduates.

9. Low geographical and social mobility. Individuals are confined to the place of residence and social class of their parents much more than in the advanced countries.

10. A lack of national integration. The individual is not yet certain

whether he owes supreme allegiance to his nationality and his state or to his ethnic, linguistic, religious, racial, or tribal group. Communal solidarity competes with national solidarity. Moreover, two "nations" co-exist politically and culturally within the same nation. In Asia and Africa a European-educated elite with a modern outlook confronts an illiterate majority, and in several Latin American countries a culturally European population confronts the socially submerged and culturally alien Indian peasants (see Chapter 4).

11. The slight impact of mass communication media. The average man is not reached by the printed word and not often by the radio.

12. A lack of motorized vehicles, telephones, and other modern devices which are normal features in the life of the advanced countries.

13. A basically agricultural economy, although there might be some extracting industries which produce for the developed nations. Exports include foodstuffs and raw materials.

14. Too many people for the number of available jobs. Rural overpopulation conceals the unemployment or underemployment of a large section of the peasant population.

15. A low per capita consumption of energy.

16. In consequence of several of the symptoms cited above the per capita national income is very low. Hence, the underdeveloped country does not accumulate savings sufficient for the investment which its economic development requires.

Their per capita national income provides one of the clearest indexes of the economic situation of the underdeveloped countries. Of course, this average index yields only a rough outline of the contrast between the rich and the poor nations. The per capita income does not reveal the co-existence in the same country of a small wealthy class with the poor masses. For instance, the United Nations statistical survey of national incomes in 1949 placed Venezuela in the category of countries with a relatively high average of between $450 and $600 per annum, even though Venezuela was an economically underdeveloped country with a very poor population; its reliance on the extractive industries such as oil and iron ore supplied a very high income to a fraction of the population, concentrated in Caracas. The average for sub-Saharan Africa was at that time below $50, but low incomes were the lot of Africans while the white settlers enjoyed high living standards. To take one example, the African average in 1953 was $50 in Southern Rhodesia, but the national average was $170; this striking contrast was due to the high incomes of the European corporations and the white settlers. The same United Nations survey placed South Africa in the category between $200 and $300, but these figures did not disclose the fact that the whites received average wages four times higher than those received by the native workers, who were usually confined to the unskilled jobs.

The average figure of the per capita national income also fails to show what portion of this income is distributed to individual citizens as their personal income and what portion is spent on state expenditures, such as on national defense, or is ploughed back in capital investment. For instance, the Soviet Union shows a rather high per capita national income, but this does not mean that the living standards are high, because a large share of national income is reinvested each year in further economic growth. A relatively low average does not necessarily indicate that a country is underdeveloped and has few industries. Japan is the only fully industrialized nation in Asia, but its rather low living standards were reflected in the 1954 per capita national income of $200.

As a general proposition, however, it can be said that a very low per capita national income reflects the economic underdevelopment and poverty of the population. The average for the underdeveloped countries is usually under $150, mostly below $100, not infrequently around $50. These countries represent almost two-thirds of mankind and include non-Communist and Communist countries alike. The Asian average is $55. The Near Eastern average ranges from $50 to $150. The contrast with the advanced nations emerges sharply when these figures are compared with those of the developed nations. In 1954 the United States had a per capita national income of $1,850, Britain of $850, France of $700, Italy of $300 (this latter figure reflects underdevelopment in southern Italy). At the other extreme, the average in the same year was $58 in Bolivia, $44 in the Philippines, $30 in Indonesia, $55 in Kenya, $51 in Uganda, and $20 in Nyasaland. The average for Latin America varied between $250 for semi-developed Argentina and $100 for Brazil.

These figures set the United States, Canada, most of the non-Communist countries of Europe, Australia, and New Zealand, with their general prosperity, against Asia, Africa, the Near East, and most of Latin America, where living standards are low and often miserable. All in all, only one-tenth of mankind enjoy a per capita national income higher than $500.

Asia, with over half of the world's population, produces 10 per cent of the world's income. Asia, Africa, and Latin America (68 per cent of the population of the world, and a population growing at a rapid pace) produce together only about 15 per cent of the total income of the world. The United States and Canada (7 per cent of the population of the world) produce 40 per cent of the world's income. The remaining areas (the Soviet Union, Europe, and Oceania), with 25 per cent of the population of the world, account for 45 per cent of the income of the world. These approximate figures reveal the true meaning of the present international division of labor.

The figures for the consumption of raw materials disclose the same picture. The United States consumes 50 per cent of the total production of raw materials in the world; other developed countries, 45 per cent; the underdeveloped countries, only 5 per cent.

Their low living standards are reflected in the number of calories consumed in the underdeveloped countries. While 3,000 calories per day are considered necessary for human well-being, this figure is reached or surpassed only in the advanced countries. The average for Asia is 2,000 or less. It is 1,850 in India, 1,940 in Ceylon, 1,960 in the Philippines, and 1,900 in Peru. Moreover, the diet is deficient in proteins, such as meat, fats, oil, milk, butter, and cheese, and in fruit and vegetables. It consists mainly of cereals and starch supplemented whenever possible by fish. The low incomes compel the average person in the same countries to spend most of his income on food.

Good health is one of the preconditions of a widespread initiative, of an active participation in community affairs, and of a determination to improve the environment. Yet health conditions in the underdeveloped countries are deplorable: undernourishment reduces physical resistance, housing is deficient, and public sanitation and medical facilities are grossly inadequate. These conditions account for a mortality rate, especially an infant death rate, which is much higher than in the developed countries, for a low life expectancy, and for a very low labor productivity. Slum cities co-exist with primitive villages. There is an alarming shortage of hospitals, doctors, trained nurses, dentists, and pharmacists.

Illiteracy is another plague. It is an obstacle on the road to modern life since an illiterate person cannot easily assimilate new ideas and can hardly be employed as a skilled worker. Another endemic weakness is the reliance of the underdeveloped country on one or a few staple products for its exports and for the upholding of its balance of payments. The situation of Latin America is illustrative (see Table 3).

Only Argentina, Mexico, and Uruguay had a more varied composition of exports; even so, the Argentinian and Uruguayan exports were in large part (40 per cent for Argentina and 58 per cent for Uruguay) made up of related articles: wool, meat, hides, and skins. More than half of Mexican exports consisted of five articles: cotton, lead, coffee, copper, and zinc.

Undiversified exports make the balance of payments highly vulnerable to variations in demand and price on the international market. They also create an economic dependence on the main importers, a dependence which becomes very marked if only one country is the main importer. The data for 1952 disclose the following distribution of Latin American exports: to the United States and Canada, 62 per cent; to Latin America, 8 per cent; to the sterling area, 6 per cent; to Western Europe, 19 per cent; to the rest of the world, 5 per cent. Their imports were similarly distributed: from the United States and Canada, 61 per cent; from Latin America, 7 per cent; from the sterling area, 9 per cent; from Western Europe, 21 per cent; and from the rest of the world, 2 per cent.

Many other underdeveloped countries are in the same vulnerable position. Ghana, with two-thirds of its exports consisting of cocoa, is not an

TABLE 3

PERCENTAGES OF TOTAL EXPORTS FOR LATIN AMERICA IN 1952

Country	Percentage of exports
Bolivia	Tin, 59; tungsten, 10; zinc, 9; lead, 8
Brazil	Coffee, 74
Chile	Copper, 63; nitrate, 13
Colombia	Coffee, 82; petroleum, 16
Costa Rica	Bananas, 59; coffee, 34
Cuba	Sugar, 85
Dominican Republic	Sugar, 45; coffee, 23; cacao, 13
Ecuador	Bananas, 27; cacao, 22; coffee, 26
El Salvador	Coffee, 88
Guatemala	Coffee, 82
Haiti	Coffee, 66
Honduras	Bananas, 66; coffee, 26
Nicaragua	Coffee, 51; cotton, 18
Panama	Bananas, 38
Paraguay	Cotton, 34; quebracho, 18
Peru	Cotton, 34; sugar, 14; lead, 11; zinc, 6; copper, 6
Venezuela	Petroleum, 95

exception in Tropical Africa. Eighty per cent of Egyptian exports are made up of cotton; and 53 per cent of Turkish exports, of tobacco and fruits. In South and Southeast Asia each country relies on a few products as the main articles of export. Several Near Eastern countries depend mainly on oil for their exports, while a few others, such as Egypt and Syria, bolster their balance of payments with profits derived from the trans-shipment of oil through their territories (the Suez Canal or pipelines).

The consequences of this lopsided foreign trade are obvious. First, if the main article of export is principally purchased by one country, economic dependence on that foreign market follows. The exporting country may try to shake off this dependence by finding supplementary or alternative markets. The Communist bloc sometimes offers, for its own reasons, new markets that help to offset the preponderant Western position. Secondly, a country which has only a few articles to sell is in a weak position for negotiating commercial agreements with a highly developed state which can threaten to shift its purchases to another country. Thirdly, a technological change abroad (for instance, the invention of a substitute raw material), sudden new competition from another underdeveloped country (for instance, the rising African production of coffee, which competes with the Latin American output), a crop failure, a fall in prices on the international market, overproduction that brings surpluses and lower prices, stiff competition by a developed country which for domestic reasons subsidizes the production and export of the same commodities (for instance, the protection by the United States and European countries of beet sugar in spite of the fact that cane sugar is more cheaply produced in the underdeveloped countries), all these causes, completely beyond the control of the underdeveloped country, might profoundly affect its foreign trade, its balance of payments, and eventually the condition of its domestic economy.

Two examples illustrate this vulnerability. Well over 90 per cent of Venezuela's exports is made up of petroleum, and 60 per cent of all its budgetary revenue comes from the same source. Another 18 per cent of the same revenue is provided by customs duties levied on imports by the oil corporations. Thus, about 78 per cent of its budgetary income derives directly or indirectly from the extraction and export of oil. It is easy to imagine the plight of Venezuela if the international market were to be saturated by an overproduction of oil and if its own output were to be reduced. The copper exports of Chile provide approximately one-third of its public revenue. If the price of one pound of this metal were to fall by one cent, the budgetary revenue would suddenly drop by 4 million dollars.

Foreign exports amount on the average to about 20 per cent of the total national income of the underdeveloped countries and are the source of foreign currencies which buy imported goods, including the equipment necessary for economic development. Yet the value of these exports can vary as much as 30 per cent from one year to the next. Annual variations in the international prices for primary commodities are one source of the trouble. The other is the progressive fall in these prices in comparison to the prices for manufactured goods over a period of many decades. The annual variations for eighteen important primary commodities, which represent the major articles of export from the underdeveloped countries, can be measured by the following data: over the period from 1901 to 1950 the prices of these items fluctuated on the average by 14 per cent each year, the volume of exports by 19 per cent, the export earnings by 23 per cent.

The loss of expected earnings of foreign currencies might cancel in an unlucky year the benefits of foreign economic assistance.

In the last analysis, those who pay for these fluctuations are the workers who might lose their jobs in the extracting industry or face a cut in already meager wages and the peasants who might be forced to sell their produce at a lower price or be left with an unsold surplus.

It is understandable that the underdeveloped countries consider the stabilization of prices for primary commodities a matter of great international urgency and importance. So far, the advanced countries have not been inclined to tackle the matter. Moreover, the underdeveloped countries producing the same staple article would find it difficult to agree on quotas of output; yet without such quotas no agreement on the stabilization of prices could be contemplated. It is no less understandable that the underdeveloped countries see their ultimate salvation in economic development and the achievement of a diversified economy.

THE ERA OF EQUAL OPPORTUNITY

It would be naive to seek the remote reasons for underdevelopment in considerations of race or climate. At the time of the great geographical discoveries the cultural level of development in Asia was comparable to that of Europe. Prior to that time there were long periods when present-day Western Europe lived in a condition that was culturally inferior to that of many non-European areas which we now call underdeveloped. Britain, the first country to industrialize, was a barbarian land at the time of the Roman conquest, as was Germany in the same epoch. But several Asian countries, notably India and China, and one African, Egypt, had by that time built rich civilizations. For a period in the Middle Ages the Arabs were culturally superior to the Western Europeans who were only slowly emerging from their Dark Ages. Such examples could be multiplied to prove that cultural achievements are due neither to race nor to climate. Brilliant civilizations have existed in all sorts of climates, and the very cradle of the European civilization was located not in western or northern Europe but in the Mediterranean Basin. The gradual shift of economic centers from Mediterranean Europe, in particular Italy, toward northwestern Europe was mainly due to the discovery of new maritime routes which made it possible to bypass the Mediterranean Sea and the Near Eastern land route controlled by the Moslems; this discovery, not the "Nordic" race or the climate, offered a historical opportunity to the countries bordering on the Atlantic.

The religious explanation is no more satisfying. It is tempting to see in the chronological sequence of the Reformation and the opening of the era of scientific progress a relation of cause and effect. However, science owes its progress in Europe to Protestants, Catholics, Greek-Orthodox Christians, Jews, agnostics, and atheists. Catholic Belgium was the first continental country to industrialize and remains ahead of predominantly Protestant Holland. The Catholic Rhineland was industrialized earlier and on a larger scale than either predominantly Protestant Eastern Germany or Catholic Bavaria. Japan, neither Catholic nor Protestant, was the first Asian country to undertake its modernization, but other Asian lands, also affected by the Buddhist religion, remained stagnant.

The particular political regime does not seem to be an important factor. It is true that the Western countries were industrialized under a constitutional form of government which was founded on respect for individual rights and on the limitation of the power of the executive. Yet these countries were not democratic at that time in our sense of the word. During the period of its industrialization Germany had an autocratic form of government in which the executive was independent of parliament. Russia began its industrialization under the Tsarist regime and has reached the rank of the second industrial nation under the totalitarian Communist regime. Eastern Europe and China are being industrialized under the same type of government. There is no necessary connection between the form of government and the level of economic development.

Colonial policy prevented a balanced economic growth, especially after the completion of the European industrial revolution (see Chapter 4). The colonial powers deliberately kept their dependencies in the condition of suppliers of raw materials and foodstuffs and consumers of European industrial goods. It is in the nature of things that only a national leadership can truly serve the interests of its own people. The Indian Five Year Plans, for instance, were not and perhaps could not have been conceived by the British colonial administration. It is also true that the colonial powers became interested in the balanced development of their possessions only after the Second World War and under the pressure of events which that war had set in motion.

But the influence of colonial policy cannot explain the slow reaction to modern European concepts on the part of those countries which never fell under colonial rule. China faced the same aggressive Western challenge as did Japan; yet its response was slow and truly gathered momentum only after the Communist Revolution. The Latin American countries had the same initial chance as the United States, and their independence is not so much more recent than that of their northern neighbor. Neither China nor Latin America lacked in natural resources; as a matter of fact, certain European countries carried out their industrialization without sufficient or varied natural resources and without preferential access to raw materials in colonial dependencies, which they did not possess and which other European countries controlled. Sweden and Switzerland are the striking examples.

Colonialism cannot explain the fact that it was Europe which took the lead in modern scientific and technological progress. There is no satisfactory explanation of the scientific and technological progress of Europe which during the last few centuries has left other peoples in the condition of underdevelopment, just as there is no satisfactory explanation of the Greek "miracle" which only in retrospect seems almost a matter of predestination.

The exploitation of nature to meet human needs is common to *homo sapiens*, as the discovery of fire and of agriculture demonstrates. But during the last four centuries, only Europe has made a systematic use of this universal human capacity. The essence of the scientific age consists in the refusal to take nature as a basically unchangeable factor and in a systematic attempt to adjust nature to human needs. This attitude is at the root of modern culture. The problem of modernizing the underdeveloped countries consists in transferring this European attitude, with all its economic and social implications, to the other continents.

It was not a doctrinaire bias on the part of Karl Marx and other socialists of the nineteenth century to consider the relations between the working class and the upper and middle classes the dominant social problem in the industrialized West of their time. The rapid progress in per capita productivity, the constant rise in living standards, and the political pressure of the organized working class have since brought a gradual but decisive change which the socialists of the nineteenth century did not foresee. The worker and the peasant have been or are being integrated within their Western societies. The process is visible everywhere but is not advanced equally in all Western countries; it is practically completed in the United States, while it is in an early stage in France or in Italy. In the advanced countries this process is resulting in the social integration of the so-called common man. His share in the national income is assured in the form of decent living standards and an expanding network of social insurance; his bargaining power is guaranteed by political and professional organizations; his voice is heeded by politicians because of universal suffrage; his leisure time is being taken care of by various means, including mass media of information and entertainment. Formerly forgotten, the common man has acquired a material and cultural stake in his own country and has come to feel that a debacle of his nation would entail his own personal catastrophe.

The remedy for the social ills of the nineteenth century, which Marx and other socialists saw in the achievement of social equality in the future socialist society, has been discredited by the country which claims to have carried out the first Marxist revolution. The existence of a highly stratified society in the Soviet Union several decades after the October Revolution has proved that social equality cannot be reconciled with the division of labor, i.e., the great diversification of social functions which individuals perform in a modern country. The performance of these functions requires diversification in professional training, which, in turn, results in unequal education among the members of the society. The same diversification of functions means that certain individuals command or supervise other individuals; they are, in Orwell's words, "more equal." Finally, the Soviet experience has demonstrated that a variety of social functions of unequal importance to the state brings about very unequal material compensation for work. This century has replaced the dream of social equality with another ideal, the ideal of equal opportunity. The socialist dream envisioned the advent of a society in which all individuals would have equal incomes and presumably equal education. The ideal of equal opportunity is more realistic because it can be realized. It means that each child should be offered the same initial chance of acquiring education at all levels regardless of the financial means of his parents. This ideal proposes that all should be given an equal chance at the start of life but takes into account the diversity of social functions and the fact that human beings are unequally endowed with ability and perseverance; it does not presume that an equality of social status can be realized among those who have reached maturity.

The Western and Communist societies are engaged in the process of realizing this equality of opportunity. The means are different and determined by the nature of each regime, but the goal is the same of providing every child, insofar as possible, with an equal chance for education and hence for social ascension. Free public education and scholarships at the more advanced levels open membership in the national elite to all children on the sole condition of talent and industry. The parents, who know that they have to live in an unequal society, whether Western or Communist, are offered moral compensation in the knowledge that their children, if they merit it, may move upward on the social ladder. When access to the national elite is thrown open to all talent, the quality of national leadership improves. Social inequality is tolerable if it is founded on the natural inequalities of men and if potential aptitudes have been tested at an early age through processes of education equally accessible to all.

This ideal of equal opportunity at the start of life and hence of full social mobility is becoming a part of modern society and thereby also a part of the program of modernization which holds an irresistible attraction for the underdeveloped countries. The term equal opportunity has acquired an additional meaning in our time. For the underdeveloped countries, it means an equal opportunity among nations to enjoy the benefits of modern progress. They feel that this century should be the era of their chance to become modern. Their awareness of their backward and miserable plight makes them conscious of the contrast between them and the advanced nations. The West is confronted with a new social problem which has international dimensions. The conflict between its own social classes has lost the bitterness which it had in the past century and has been eclipsed by the new contrast between the rich and poor nations. The Western laboring classes have acquired or are acquiring a peaceful "bourgeois mentality"; the revolutionary mood, the ardent desire to alter the existing situation completely, is now to be found in the underdeveloped countries. The West no longer faces the belligerent pressure of its own masses, which have ceased to be proletarian; it is now confronted with the mounting and impatient clamor of the proletarian nations. These nations have achieved their political emancipation; they have acquired, as Western individuals did by the end of the eighteenth century, equality before the law, i.e., a legal status of equality with the advanced nations. Again like Western individuals in the last century, they now aspire to progress from a legal status of equality, the consequence of their political emancipation, toward an approximation of equal economic and social opportunity.

The pressure of the aspirations of the underdeveloped countries and the competition for their political sympathies between the Western and Communist blocs have produced a deep alteration in the Western outlook. Nineteenth-century liberals and socialists did not look beyond the frontiers of the Western community. They were preoccupied with the social conflicts within their own national societies and paid little if any attention to the non-European peoples. The liberal concept of human solidarity was in fact mainly applied to white men. It was generally felt that a mysterious predestination sanctified the international division of labor into the advanced manufacturing nations and the countries producing raw materials and foodstuffs which the more fortunate nations needed. Nowadays the aspirations of underdeveloped populations are recognized as legitimate. The Communist competition does not allow for continued indifference. The Western nations have acknowledged that their own future is tied up with that of the underdeveloped areas. The main problem of the second half of this century is whether the revolution of modernization will be made against the West or in co-operation with it, not whether it will take place at all.

Once the underdeveloped countries realize that their backwardness and poverty are not preordained and can be overcome, they begin to feel their inferior status acutely. Dr. Ambdekar, the late leader of the Indian Untouchables, said: "What is new is not the Indian poverty; it is as old as the world. It is that the Indian people begin to get impatient with their poverty."

The peoples to whom modern history seemed to assign the place of pariahs of the world know from the record of international relations that the world is seldom charitable to weak nations. The colonial subjugation by the stronger Western nations has taught this lesson to many of them; others, who were lucky enough to preserve their independence during the colonialist era, know that a country which is economically weak cannot win arguments with a more powerful state. They have also learned from the rapidly enhanced international position of the Soviet Union that economic and technological development provides the key to advancement in international status. They seek greater power founded on a solid economic base as a means for preserving their independence and for being treated with respect.

The underdeveloped countries have two assets. First, they are favored by their numbers and their demographic trends. Not only do they form about 60 per cent of mankind, but their natural growth is bound to be much more rapid than that of the populations of advanced countries. Their numerical preponderance will increase each year. This rapid growth in population slows down their economic development, but if they overcome the difficulties and eventually acquire economic power roughly proportionate to their numbers, they will take a very important place on the international stage. Secondly, they already possess a marginal and vicarious power conferred by the competition between the two rival blocs. As the West and the Communist bloc vie politically, economically, and ideologically for their present and future sympathies, they can tap both sources of economic and technical assistance. They can maneuver politically between the two blocs and can afford a foreign policy much more independent of the great powers than would have been possible if the same powers were in basic agreement.

However, it is not easy to catch up with the advanced countries. As we have seen, the secular trend in international trade does not favor the exporters of primary commodities. It will be shown later that the problems of the revolution of modernization are by far more difficult and more complex than were the economic and social problems of the Western Industrial Revolution. The rapid and constant increase in the per capita labor productivity and the no less rapid scientific and technological progress in the advanced countries constantly widen the gap between the two categories of peoples. The rise in the living standards of the advanced countries is constant; the living standards are improving only slightly, if at all, in the underdeveloped countries, which must first save in order to invest in their own development and which, if faced with overpopulation, run the risk that every increase in their national income might be eaten up by the natural increase of the population.

Once an underdeveloped country begins to develop its own industries, it will find it difficult to sell its manufactured goods on the international market where it will meet stiff competition from the advanced countries whose more efficient industries can produce at a lower cost. It could compete by keeping wages low and thus compensate for its inferior techniques of production and management. The advantage of low wages will in due time be offset by the progress of automation in the advanced countries. In any event, the new industries will for many years demand custom protection for the domestic market against foreign competition in order to survive their vulnerable period of childhood.

There is however a brighter side to the question of economic development. A latecomer has at its disposal the vast store of technological knowledge and experience which the advanced countries have accumulated. The industrialization of Great Britain was more difficult and much slower than that of the other Western nations. Later on Japan and still later Russia did not need to work out for themselves the necessary knowledge; it was already available. Moreover, a country which founds new industries is not slowed down by the vested interest in existing though outmoded equipment and can adopt from the start the latest known techniques if only it has the skilled personnel to apply them. The rapid economic growth of the Soviet Union has familiarized the world with the advantages of a planned development in which the government directs investments toward the most crucial or needed branches of the national economy. The Indian and French experiences have proved that the planning of national development is possible without the total nationalization of the means of production and can co-exist with private enterprise. This planned and balanced growth allows for a quicker pace than the spontaneous and possibly chaotic development which occurs when central guidance is lacking.

Our epoch promises to offer an equal opportunity to individuals and to peoples. A society which is sufficiently advanced and prosperous can easily afford to guarantee this equal opportunity in education to all its children. Once offered this opportunity, the children and young people must prove their mettle and succeed or fail in school competition. Will the advanced nations be willing to offer an equal opportunity to the underdeveloped countries by providing them with economic aid of sizable proportions? If they do, the main burden of toil and sacrifice will still rest on the shoulders of the peoples who have undertaken the heavy task of their own modernization.

The disparity among nations is infinitely greater than among individuals. Nations differ in the size of their populations and in the wealth of their natural resources. A small country with few natural resources can never hope to achieve the same results as the United States and the Soviet Union. Moreover, some countries, exactly like some individuals, will make less effort than others. It is inevitable that by the end of the era of modernization certain of the present underdeveloped countries will become more prosperous and more powerful than others. The ideal of equality among nations is as visionary as the ideal of social equality among individuals.

Assuming that our transitional era will eventually produce, after the lapse of several decades, an international environment in which the conditions of existence will be comparable if not equal in most of the countries of all continents and in which all children, white and colored, will enjoy equal opportunity in education and equal access to the national elite, then the proportion of mankind that is actively participating in the intellectual progress of the race will be much greater than at present. The result may be a brilliant efflorescence of human civilization without precedent in history.

MODERN PROGRESS AND THE EUROPEAN CIVILIZATION

If the citizen of an underdeveloped country who is interested in its modernization were to look dispassionately at the Western-Soviet struggle, he would perceive a large area of basic agreement between the parties but would also discover the exact nature of the issues which separate them. He would see that both parties agree on the meaning of modern progress. This concept of progress, as defined both in the West and in the Soviet Union, includes the following elements:

1. An infinite development of science and of man's control over nature.

2. The technological use of scientific progress for various practical ends, peaceful and military.

3. One of these ends is a growth in production and per capita productivity that results in a constant increase in the quantity and quality of consumer goods. In other words, one of the goals of modern society, in both the Western and the Soviet interpretation, seems to be a constant rise in the living standards of all social classes. This goal is dynamic, because scientific and technological progress constantly creates new needs and in turn supplies the means for their satisfaction. New inventions occasion new needs and prevent modern man from having a feeling of saturation.

Mr. Khrushchev made this element of modern progress his own on the occasion of the Twenty-first and Twenty-second Congresses of his party (January, 1959, and October, 1961). He said that the future Communist society, which his party claimed to be the next and not too distant stage of the Soviet evolution, would be distinguished by a great abundance of consumer goods, at least those goods which he called necessities (he was prudent enough to stress that luxurious consumer goods would never be produced in abundance). His words, if translated into nonideological language, meant that his party was guided by the ambition to provide the Soviet citizen, at some unspecified date, with American living standards.

4. The other result of technological progress is the constant improvement in working conditions: a shorter work day, a longer period of leisure, and eventually automation that should allow for a very short work day and would transform industrial workers into machine supervisors.

5. The welfare state, i.e., a state in which the problems of disease, unemployment, disability, and old age are taken care of by public social insurance and in which the state feels obliged to protect the interests of wage-earners.

6. Equal educational opportunity as a counterweight to the social stratification founded on the diversity of social functions and consequently on the degree of education and of personal efficiency.

7. The cult of organization and efficiency, which is characteristic of all economically advanced countries, including the Soviet Union. The Western organizations are basically spontaneous, while the Soviet are Party-manipulated, but there is no disagreement on the need for a tight and efficient organization of modern society.

8. Entertainment and/or culture are channeled to the masses through

various devices, including the mass media of information. As a result, a wide-open debate is going forward in all the advanced countries about what the masses need or want and about what they should get as their share of national culture or of mere entertainment.

The areas of disagreement between the Soviet Union and the West are two, aside from the conflicts of national interests which are real but would have existed even in the absence of the ideological struggle:

1. Private versus public ownership of the means of production. The Communists advocate the total socialization of all the means of production, including the collectivization of agriculture. The West offers a more complex solution. Basically, private ownership of the means of production is upheld. But if the private operation of these means is inefficient or otherwise harmful to the general welfare, nationalization is not rejected offhand, as the postwar record of Western Europe proves. The Western state restricts the freedom of private enterprise to protect the general interests of the community, especially those of the workers and the consumers. Public control of privately owned means of production is being extended. Moreover, management and majority-ownership of the big corporations are being separated. From the point of view of the worker the Western system might be better than the Communist, because the labor unions are independent of both the employer and the government and can freely promote the interests of their members. The Communist experience has proved that, if the state becomes the sole employer following total nationalization, the employee is helpless and his labor union is nothing but another tool of the government-employer.

2. The other and all-important issue is the problem of the condition of the individual within modern society. Is he to retain his freedom or is he to be totally integrated and thus reduced to the position of a pawn manipulated at will by the ruling oligarchy?

The regime of modern political democracy (this regime should not be confused with the direct democracy of the ancient Greeks, economically founded on slave labor, or with the constitutional system based on a restricted franchise) gives the following answers to this question:

1. Universal suffrage is extended to all adult citizens irrespective of sex, race, and religious or other beliefs.

2. Citizens delegate their powers (indirect democracy) to elected representatives who form the legislative and executive branches of government. The elections take the form of a free and secret choice between two or more parties and candidates. Citizens do not formulate policies but decide in whom this power should be vested for a limited period of time.

3. This choice postulates the existence of two or more political parties and of a time-limit on the duration of elective mandates. The right of the electorate to choose policy-makers every few years from among the competing parties and candidates has the important consequence of making the elective officers responsible to the electors. The government (the chief

executive or the cabinet, and the legislators) is restrained by the fear of losing the next election.

4. Citizens may truly exercise the right of choosing their representatives only if they enjoy the individual freedoms of expression, of access to information, of assembly, and of association. They are free to have any beliefs, to voice any opinions, to convert other citizens to their views, to have access to any information, and to combine in organizations founded for the defense of their sectional interests or for the propagation of their particular beliefs. The democratic state is ideologically agnostic and founded on the toleration of conflicting views among its citizens. It expects from its citizens only respect for the substance of the regime and, like any other state, an undivided loyalty.

The existence of individual freedoms implies that citizens have non-identical interests and views. The society is avowedly pluralistic. Minorities have the right to profess their views, to organize, and to attract the support of other citizens. The underlying assumption is that a minority can and may become a majority.

The individual usually cannot influence the politics of a democratic mass society, but he becomes a force if he combines with other individuals of similar beliefs or interests. Freedom of association opens the way to the formation of organized social groups of all sorts (ideological, economic, charitable, professional) which constantly exercise an influence over the ebb and flow of national and local politics.

5. In fact the politically active citizens, who always constitute a minority of the adult population, influence the views of the more or less passive majority. However, this majority make up their minds at the time of elections or when they support the activities of their organized social groups. The numerical majority decides the elections. This delegation of powers of the people by a majority vote to the elected representatives is founded on the rejection of the elitist principle, i.e., of government by a minority of the politically wisest citizens (the elite). Political democracy rejects this principle, not because it believes that the numerical majority must always be wiser than a minority, but because it considers that it is impossible to ascertain any fair and reliable criterion for the selection of the political elite. If any proposed criterion is arbitrary and would perpetuate power in the hands of a self-appointed clique, if there is no scientific procedure for evaluating the political wisdom of individuals (a highly relative notion), then there is no justification for transferring power from the majority to an elitist minority. Political democracy assumes, therefore, that all adults are equally wise or unwise in politics, provides all of them with the ballot and the right to be elected, and confers the power of ultimate decision on numerical majorities.

The minorities must accept the decisions of the majority but must also retain the right to criticize and to aspire to become a majority.

The image of modern progress, which is the goal of the process of modernization in the underdeveloped countries, is not without reason similar in the West and in the Soviet Union. It is the product of one and the same civilization to which both the West and the Soviet Union belong.

This civilization, usually called, with characteristic ethnocentrism, *Western*, extends farther than the West or Europe. Its present geographical realm embraces every country where the educated people have the same cultural background and acknowledge the ancient Greeks as the original founders of their intellectual heritage. Thus defined, this civilization includes not only the West but also Latin America, Eastern Europe, Russia, and Oceania. It extends from the Pacific coast of the Western Hemisphere to the Pacific coast of the Soviet Union. Its original motherland is Europe, but it has its younger branches in the Western Hemisphere, in Russia, and in Oceania. This civilization may be appropriately called *European* since its birth place was in Europe and since this adjective, unlike *Western*, has no political coloration.

If civilization is understood, as it should be, as something much wider and deeper than a set of political ideals, if it is a complex of all ideas, if it includes social institutions and ways of life, literature, arts, music, and science, then it is absurd to equate the present political West with the extension of our civilization. To excommunicate Russia and Eastern Europe because they profess a different ideology would amount to a singular impoverishment of the contents of civilization by reducing it to politics only.

Logically, the claim that a civilization can embrace only one ideology leads to extravagant consequences. The West is now a group of political democracies. If one were to use political democracy as the criterion of our civilization, he would have to conclude that the origin of this civilization does not go further back than the nineteenth century. If one attempted to weave a history of this civilization out of those events and those individual lives which, in retrospect, seem to endorse Western democracy in its present form, he would discover that he picks out and binds together various fragments of European history often unconnected in time and that he singles out as our spiritual ancestors certain thinkers who were isolated in their own lifetime and were considered heretics by their contemporaries. This naive history of the Western heritage is hardly digestible to anyone who is endowed with a critical mind. We are, whether we like it or not, the descendants not only of Athens (which was half-slave) but of the whole of ancient Greece, which neither always nor everywhere was democratic, of ancient Rome and of the Middle Ages, where political freedom was not the most fashionable merchandise, and of absolutist Europe. We cannot renounce our whole past nor any particular part of it only because political democracy in the modern sense was unknown to our ancestors, who often preferred forms of government disrespectful of individual freedom. The history of our civilization is not composed only of the Athens of Pericles, of the English revolutions of the seventeenth century, of the American and French revolutions of the eighteenth century, and of the recent period of emancipation of the common man and of democracy founded on universal suffrage. Every period within a duration of some 2,500 years has contributed to what we are culturally and has provided us with some of the standards which determine what we like and dislike.

We should not write off Virgil and Ovid because they lived after the overthrow of the Roman Republic or should not jettison the legacy of Roman law because this law was developed and codified under the absolutist emperors. The feudal period of medieval Europe coincided with the cultural restoration after the collapse of the Dark Ages and with the extension of the European civilization to those parts of Europe which had never belonged to the Hellenistic civilization or had lived on its fringes. The Renaissance, of which we are so proud, was born in Italy where neither political democracy nor individual freedoms flourished. We cannot deny our debt to Bach, Mozart, and Beethoven, to Kant or Hegel, to Descartes or Watteau, simply because they lived under absolutist governments and because some of them did not feel particularly unhappy about it.

Nazi Germany and Fascist Italy were not excommunicated from the common civilization in spite of their ideological aberrations. Yet there are now people who would gladly excommunicate Russia because it challenges the West on ideological grounds.

It cannot be helped that a civilization 2,500 years old has had a checkered political history. Respect for the individual freedoms has been characteristic of relatively short periods of this history and even then it has not been geographically universal. The concept of a civilization is much richer than the history of a political ideology.

Russia began its cultural career at the time of its conversion to Christianity, as did many other European nations which had not belonged to the Roman Empire. Christianity brought with it the legacy of the Hellenistic civilization. Russia was converted by Byzantium, not by Rome, but Byzantium was at that time culturally much superior to the European West. After its conversion, Russia developed culturally as a branch of the Byzantine civilization, which was a twin sister of the Western, both of them daughters of the Hellenistic civilization. After the Mongol conquest in the thirteenth century Russia became a cultural desert. After it had begun to restore its cultural life in the second half of the seventeenth century, Russia could no longer look toward Byzantium, conquered in the fifteenth century by the Turks; it could only turn toward the West. The gate which Peter the Great threw wide open to Western influence has not been closed since.

No cultural manifestation in Russia during the last two and a half or three centuries can be understood without constant reference to Western influence. The same is true of the other younger branch of the European civilization, the American. Of course, each nation, having its own history, brings forth its own interpretation of the common cultural heritage. This is as true of England if compared with Italy, of France if compared with Germany, as it is of Russia or the United States. Nevertheless, whether a nation belongs to a particular civilization depends on whether its culture can be fully understood in terms of that civilization. The Chinese, Indian, or African culture cannot be understood only by reference to the European civilization; the Russian culture of the last three centuries can.

Russia has contributed brilliantly to our common civilization in literature, music, and science. Our common heritage would be painfully diminished if we relegated Tolstoy, Dostoyevsky, Turgenev, Tchaikovsky, Lobachevsky, Mendeleyev, and scores of others to a separate civilization.

It would be equally ludicrous to exclude Eastern Europeans from the realm of the European civilization only because they have Communist regimes and in spite of their former long cultural association with the West (a millennium in the case of Poland, Czechoslovakia, Hungary, and parts of Yugoslavia; and one or one-and-a-half centuries in the case of Rumania, Bulgaria, and other parts of Yugoslavia).

It is not unusual in the history of our civilization for its realm to be rent apart by the opposition between two different concepts of the good society. A fierce ideological struggle divided ancient Greece at the time of the Peloponnesian War, as it did Europe during the Religious Wars. Europe was again ideologically divided at the time of the French Revolutionary and Napoleonic Wars. Yet we, who can now afford to look at these periods with detachment, never assert that two civilizations were facing each other on the battlefields. Actually, these ideological wars were civil in nature, and cultural brethren fought each other. Their bitterness stemmed from their being fratricidal wars. The same was true of the hostile confrontation of the West with Fascist Italy and Nazi Germany, and the same is true of the present conflict with Russia. We are ideological enemies, and yet neither side can renounce the cultural bonds which tie it to the other. Marxism itself is a Western doctrine, and Lenin, the prophet of the opposite camp, cannot be read intelligently by anyone who does not know of the existence of Hegel and of the Western (French, English, and German) socialists. Yet this ideological struggle is very real: it is waged on a global scale, for high stakes, and in the name of fervently held, truly antagonistic concepts of the best society.

The revolution of modernization is nothing but the borrowing of the ideas of this European civilization by peoples who have been reared in other civilizations. When they adopt our science and technology, our concepts of a modern state and modern armed forces, our ideologies, whether democratic or totalitarian, and our notion of modern progress, they are borrowing from the European civilization. The triumphant march of our civilization is profoundly altering the cultural environment of other peoples. This is not a new phenomenon in cultural history, but its geographical dimensions have always been much more limited. The culture of ancient Greece conquered the Mediterranean lands and parts of Europe north of the Alps. Christianity later extended this cultural influence to Northern, Central, and Eastern Europe. The Arabs, the Chinese, the Indians radiated their culture beyond the borders of their countries over long periods of time. But never before in history has the influence of a civilization extended to all four corners of the world.

Politically, there are two channels of this influence: the Western and the Soviet. The modernization of China, North Korea, North Vietnam, and Outer Mongolia includes more than the transplantation of the Russian political ideology and form of government; it also involves the geographical extension of many European concepts which are not at issue in the ideological conflict between Russia and the West. The European civilization has penetrated other underdeveloped countries but under the Western flag or under both flags. Of course, it is not an indifferent question under which ideological flag our civilization makes its cultural conquests. This question relates to the whole problem of the present and future distribution of Western and Soviet influence throughout the world.

The underdeveloped countries that want to become modern aspire to be like the nations which participate in the European civilization. Regardless of who the standard-bearer is in each particular country, the ultimate winner is the civilization which we share with the Russians. This conquering march of our civilization involves much more than the mere reception of science and technology, for the assimilation of these two aspects of European civilization would be useless without the simultaneous acceptance of other elements of modern progress as defined by the same civilization.

It is interesting to note a historical analogy. The maximum geographical extension of the Greek cultural influence took place only after the Greek political decline which followed the Peloponnesian War and the Macedonian conquest. The cradle of our civilization, Europe, has lost its former dominant international position, but the civilization itself is extending its influence universally.

The two rival standard-bearers, the West and the Soviet Union, offer the concept of modern progress to the underdeveloped countries, but they themselves have not yet found the answer to the question whether this modern progress is a self-sufficient goal or should be a means for the attainment of some higher objective. They both act as though modern progress were an end in itself.

The cultural superiority complex that characterized Asia, notably China, Japan, and India, the feeling that they did not need the outside world which was inhabited by troublesome barbarians, proved impractical and collapsed on contact with the superior power of European nations. The opposite attitude, the desire to learn from the Europeans, has created an issue which is not yet settled: what elements of European knowledge should be absorbed and what traditional native values should be preserved? The simplest solution, actually adopted by the Japanese during the Meiji period, is to limit the process to the absorption of European science and technology and European methods of administrative and military organization. The Japanese have learned that they could not be more successful than Peter the Great was in separating these aspects of the European culture from the others. All European ideas penetrate through the door opened for science and technology. However, not all of them will take root on foreign soil. Each underdeveloped country will have to find out for itself the desirable synthesis of European and native values, the future foundation of its modern existence.

The process of modernization will not bring forth a culturally uniform world composed of many replicas of the nations which now form the European civilization. The Asians have their own splendid legacy of great civilizations. The Africans are justified in wanting to rescue as much as possible of what they call their own personality. The culture of the Indians of Latin America will probably reassert itself after their full integration within Latin American societies. The past can never be wholly exorcised. National pride will not permit a slavish copying of everything European. Yet by the end of the process of modernization the element of European civilization will remain as an integral part of the native cultures.

The world of the twenty-first century will be culturally diversified but will have a common denominator in this European component. The price which our civilization will have to pay for its unprecedented success will be a relative decline in the power of its member nations and a relative rise in the power of other peoples made stronger by their modernization. The law of numbers has been violated during the four centuries of the political expansion of the white man, but it will have its revenge. The present situation, in which a developed minority of mankind (the United States with its Western allies, and Russia) exercises a crucial influence in international politics, cannot last forever precisely because the revolution of modernization will wrest from this minority the monopoly of its scientific, technological, and organizational knowledge. The underdeveloped countries will eventually meet the present privileged nations on terms of equality, for the first time since the voyage of Vasco da Gama.

THE DIFFERENCE BETWEEN THE REVOLUTION OF MODERNIZATION AND THE INDUSTRIAL REVOLUTION. THE DEMOCRATIC ILLUSION.

A great many Westerners, like the Russian Marxists, are inclined to adopt an ethnocentric interpretation of history and to visualize the future of the world as a universal triumph of their own ideals and values. This ethnocentric view of the future is characteristic of the peoples who have been successful in their social and economic achievements. Since political democracy is the outcome of the Western historical evolution, the Westerner is prompted to forget that other countries have a different historical background and is inclined to believe that universal history unfolds, for some mysterious reason, toward the eventual triumph of democracy in all countries, Communist and underdeveloped alike. This interpretation of history bears a striking resemblance to the Marxist philosophy of history. Both overlook the wealth of alternatives among which human beings may choose the direction of their future development. Both hold that all the roads of history lead to Rome except that a Westerner is sure that political democracy is this Rome and a Russian or other Communist no less firmly asserts that it is the universal Communist society. Both views are deterministic. It is ironic that a non-Marxist Westerner adopts, usually without realizing it, two arguments from the Marxist philosophy: historical determinism, and the determining influence of economics on human ideals and values. The West is prosperous and its population is literate; it has a democratic form of government. The further argument runs as follows: every country, after becoming economically developed, prosperous, and literate, will necessarily crown its success with a democratic superstructure. The Soviet Union, which is literate, industrialized, and entering the stage of rising living standards, will inevitably evolve into a political democracy. The same argument is applied to the underdeveloped countries, but the dose of optimism in their case is much greater. They are expected to better the West and have a working democracy while undergoing the painful process of modernization, i.e., even before attaining the level of prosperity and literacy. A Communist replies with equal conviction that a modern economy requires the nationalization of the means of production and centralized planning which cannot properly function unless directed by a single party protected against errors by the "infallible" doctrine of Marxism-Leninism.

People who believe in the inevitable universal extension of political democracy forget that this system of government, the finest but also the most difficult to operate, has never been predominant in any period of history. Moreover, modern democracy, founded on the political emancipation of the common man, is a very recent phenomenon. In our own time it is restricted to a minority of mankind. Several countries which are members of the European civilization have chosen other paths in this century and have lived under different regimes, Communist, Fascist, or authoritarian.

This sanguine view of the prospects of democracy in the countries undergoing modernization is grafted on another optimistic assumption. There is an inclination to simplify the nature of the latter process and almost to reduce it to a question of sufficient foreign aid. However, the problem of economic development can be greatly alleviated by foreign assistance but cannot be solved otherwise than by the effort of the underdeveloped country itself. Moreover, modernization is a social upheaval, because it demands a thorough reconstruction of social institutions. The revolution of modernization is by far a much more complex and painful process than the Industrial Revolution was in the West.

The West was economically and socially "prepared" for the Industrial Revolution by its own prior history. It had at its disposal accumulated capital and could supplement it either by draining capital from its colonies, as in the case of Britain, or by borrowing from other Western countries, as in the case of those nations which industrialized later than Britain (the United States, for example). The international financial market was willing to invest in the building of foreign railroads and in the founding of new industries; there was no discouraging fear at that time of social upheavals and of the confiscation of foreign assets. The Western economic and social institutions were adequate to deal with the problems involved in industrialization, and qualified personnel, including managerial personnel, was disponible.

The West carried out its process of industrialization at a time when social concepts were very different. The image of the welfare state was unknown. The labor movement was in its infancy and had little if any bargaining power. The process could be mostly financed by what we now call the exploitation of workers. In Britain the sixty-hour work week, children of five or six sitting at the looms, women gaining their livelihood in the mines, miserable wages, and slum housing—these were the conditions of the working class at the time of the Industrial Revolution. The workers forcibly saved in the negative sense of being given only bare subsistence wages. This was the main source of capital for further investment and industrial expansion. Only after the completion of the Industrial Revolution, around 1860, did the rising national income begin to yield its first benefits for the working class; their real wages slowly started to rise.

The Western countries were the first in the world to industrialize and had before their eyes no image of already industrialized societies by which they would have been compelled to measure the speed of their own progress and its cost for their people. They did not have to hurry to catch up with some other country nor could their working classes point to the existence of high living standards in some foreign land. Yet the Industrial Revolution was far from a peaceful process. The workers rioted and revolted. They destroyed the machinery which for them symbolized their misery. The British Chartist movement of the 1840's clamored ineffectively for improvement in the workers' lot. The French workers rose in 1848 in a spontaneous and unsuccessful revolt. Finally, in 1871 came the desperate revolt of the Paris Commune. We are apt to forget that the common man won full political capacity for defending his interests only after the completion of the Industrial Revolution. The twin features of contemporary Western societies—political democracy founded on universal suffrage, and the welfare state—are later in date than the Industrial Revolution.

Western industrialization took place under all sorts of constitutional regimes which could not be called political democracies in the modern sense. The common man had no ballot or, if he had, he was unable to cast it meaningfully in the absence of his own pressure groups and of political parties willing to defend his interests or important enough to influence governmental decisions. He was hampered in various ways in his efforts to form labor unions. The governments were in the hands of the upper and middle classes.

The British industrial revolution was carried out under a government which was not responsible to the common man, who was not an elector, had no representation in parliament, and could not fight back owing to the lack of an effective professional organization. The first Reform Act was passed in 1832, but the working class obtained their suffrage only in the last decades of the nineteenth century. In 1791 the French Revolution forbade the formation of professional organizations. The strike became legal in 1864, and labor unions were not legalized until 1884. Universal suffrage came to France in 1848. In 1905 the ten-hour workday was not yet generally accepted in the United States, and the process of economic expansion was greatly accelerated by the mass immigration of helpless European labor whom no organization effectively protected.

Examples from other countries could be multiplied, but the fact remains the same. Modern democracy, based on universal suffrage and on the effective mass organizations of common men, came to the West only in this century, long after the completion of the process of industrialization.

The process of industrialization or modernization was not always carried out by a constitutional regime at least responsible to criticism from its own social class. Tsarist or Soviet Russia and Germany had no parliamentary government at the time of their industrialization. The non-European countries are even more interesting in this respect because they faced the full-scale problem of modernization, including the reception of several European social institutions. Japan carried out its modernization within a few decades (called Westernization at that time) under the authoritarian government of the Meiji period. It neither copied the Western form of government, except for external paraphernalia, nor did it rely, as the West had done, exclusively on private initiative. The tools which the ruling group used were several, and all proved effective. Nationalism was inculcated in the Japanese people through the medium of the elementary school. This nationalism, centered around the worship of the emperor as the symbol of the Japanese race, morally alleviated the hardships which the economic change imposed on the Japanese worker and peasant who accepted this added burden as a part of their patriotic duty. It was the state much more than genuine private initiative which presided over the process of modernization. The state founded factories, sent young Japanese to Western schools, and invited numerous Western technical advisers (at one time their number surpassed 5,000).

Kemal Atatürk modernized Turkey under an authoritarian government which brooked no opposition and which broke down archaic social institutions by ruthless means. The modernization of China was first attempted by the Kuomintang and is now carried out by the Communist party, neither of which has practised the democratic form of government. The same process in India is directed by the Congress Party which observes the rules of the parliamentary system of government but is in fact the dominant party not yet hampered in its policies by any effective opposition party. The new African states such as Ghana or Guinea are moving toward a modern future under the guidance of one-party governments.

The successful industrialization and social modernization of Japan and Russia clearly demonstrate that retarded societies can modernize without borrowing from the West the form of government by popular consent. The Industrial Revolution was carried out in the West and in Russia without asking the common man whether he wanted to pay the price; the revolution of modernization also took place in Japan without seeking popular approval in due form. It is, therefore, at least uncertain whether the present underdeveloped countries can do better. Popular consent would mean in their case that the common man would freely agree to postpone the realization of his dream of better living conditions, would sacrifice this dream for the sake of his children or rather grandchildren, who would be the first to taste the fruits of his labor and privations, would willingly support the destruction of age-old social institutions, and would tolerate a freely elected government which could modernize his nation without the constant fear of being overturned at the next elections.

The underdeveloped countries are confronted with an altogether different situation from that of the West at the time of its industrialization. They cannot draw investment capital from colonies, which they do not possess. The private financial market is unwilling to invest in their development while it has much safer and more remunerative prospects in the developed countries. They have not the readily available institutions and personnel which the pre-industrial West possessed. The social concepts of today do not allow any government to ignore the masses with impunity. Above all, the underdeveloped countries are haunted by the image of the industrial West with its high living standards for every social class. The paradox consists in the fact that this exhilarating image is contemplated in abstraction from its historical background. The long and painful road which the advanced countries had to tread before they reached their present stage of development is seldom remembered.

The underdeveloped countries want three things at the same time: to become modern and endowed with a balanced and well-developed economy; to achieve this objective within a span of time much shorter than the advanced countries needed; and to enjoy the fruits of modernization (decent living standards) while still engaged in the process of development. They seem to forget the Western and Soviet experiences which teach that economic development takes time and is bought at the price of saving from popular consumption. Yet they are all starting their process of development from a level much inferior to that of the West or Russia of the pre-industrial age.

Karl Marx observed the process of industrialization in a capitalist society, in particular in Britain. He had no way to compare its social cost with that of industrialization carried on under a different economic regime which did not exist in his time. Quite understandably he ascribed all the social ills of that process to capitalism itself. Soviet industrialization has made a comparison possible. It also was carried out at the expense of the popular masses, the workers and the peasants. We know what Marx could not know, namely that any regime, capitalist or Communist, cannot invest in industrialization except by saving from popular consumption.

This sad truth places the elites in the underdeveloped countries before two dilemmas which the West of the Industrial Revolution did not know. They are subjected to growing pressure from their populations, which want modernization to progress rapidly. They are also expected to combine this quick process with a constant and visible rise in living standards. Plautus said that it was difficult to blow and swallow at the same time. The government of an underdeveloped country cannot afford a sizable increase in living standards, a full-fledged and costly system of social insurance, and a no less costly progressive labor legislation, for fear of squandering the national savings and failing in the task of economic development. It has, however, to face the labor unions and the peasant organizations as well as possibly demagogic claims on the part of an opposition which is by no means necessarily Communist. It is confronted with the prospect of vast popular discontent. The masses are becoming, as a result of the process of development, gradually more urbanized (at this stage urbanization usually means the trading of rural misery for urban misery), and are more accessible to subversive propaganda and organization. The Russian and Chinese Communists proved that even rural masses can nowadays be reached and organized for revolt through modern means of communication. The spread of literacy will make the masses more difficult to manage. In any event, the average man might not be inclined to find solace in the prospect that his toil and low living standards will pave the way toward a brighter future for his grandchildren. Modernization for very backward countries will be a leap from the Middle Ages into the second half of this century. It implies a long period of instability, of drastic social adjustments, of low living standards. It fully deserves the name which was given to the Western process of industrialization; it is a great revolution. For this reason the underdeveloped countries might find it at least as difficult as the West and Russia to carry out the deep social transformation under a democratic government.

Moreover, a country's system of government must be made to the measure of the conditions existing in that country and cannot be bought off the rack. De Tocqueville said it in 1831: "The more I see this country [the United States] the more I admit myself penetrated with this truth: that there is nothing absolute in the theoretical value of political institutions, and that their efficiency depends almost always on the original circumstances and the social conditions of people to whom they are applied." The operation of any system of government depends less on its written constitution than on those unwritten conventions—political habits. Political democracy requires the existence of its own habits, which are in themselves the restraints without which it cannot survive: the toleration of co-existent and widely different opinions and beliefs, and the acceptance of the rules of the game, namely that the majority should be able to govern as long as it remains a majority and should relinquish power if it becomes a minority. Judged by the experience of the Western countries, modern democracy presupposes the existence of the following prerequisites: the mass literacy of its citizens, their broad access to media of information (newspapers, radio, television), complete freedom of information on public affairs, adequate living standards acting as shock-absorbers of political passions, social mobility and an ever-greater equality of opportunity as the means of preventing widespread social frustration, the individual sense of self-reliance and of personal dignity, strong associations through which citizens can effectively express their preferences and protect their beliefs and interests, a tradition of tolerance, the existence of a legally organized opposition which is free in its striving to win over the support of the majority of citizens, free and honest elections as a device for transferring power from one part to another, civilian supremacy over the armed forces, and the absence of foreign control and domination. Of all these prerequisites the underdeveloped countries usually have only the last one.

One can legitimately wonder why the homeless of Asian cities who spend the nights in the streets, the slum-dwellers of Asia, Africa, and Latin

America, the landless peasants and the miserable workers of the three continents, those hundreds of millions who live on the margin of their societies, should feel an attachment to any form of government. Illiteracy is an almost impassable obstacle to government by the people. This does not mean that a literate society is in no danger of succumbing to the totalitarian or authoritarian form of government. A highly literate Germany had the Nazi regime which only total military defeat and foreign action eventually eliminated. Soviet society is also literate with a high proportion of university-educated people, but it is governed by the party oligarchy. Literacy is only one of the many conditions of a modern working democracy.

One should not confuse elections in general with the considered expression of preferences by the electorate. An illiterate voter can be provided with an electoral bulletin on which a pictorial symbol is printed and thus be enabled to make a choice between competing candidates. But is he able to make a judgment on the issues which divide the candidates? The printed word cannot reach him directly. It is true that the impact of the press or of a pamphlet might extend further than the persons who are literate. The illiterates listen to others who repeat what they have read. Broadcasting seems to overcome the obstacle of illiteracy, but in fact there are certain limitations. In multilingual countries broadcasts which do not cover all the spoken languages may miss a good portion of the potential audience. The lack of electricity might deprive a region of all access to radio. Elsewhere the population is too poor to buy individual receivers. The village loudspeaker seems to solve the problem, but it chains the audience to the program which the government channels to its population. The motion picture provides a distorted image of the outside world to the literate and illiterate alike, but the moviegoer is mostly the city-dweller, not the peasant who represents the great majority of the population.

The illiterate peasant is not unintelligent, but his personal experience is limited by the horizon of his own village and its immediate neighborhood. His ballot can be bought, or he may be fraudulently persuaded to cast it for a candidate who does not care about his interests. He is helpless if the electoral commissions, staffed by the stooges of the government or of the upper classes, falsify the lists of voters or the electoral results.

The democratic principle of a numerical majority can become a threat to the minorities in many underdeveloped countries where there exists no tradition of benevolent toleration of minorities and where those minorities of religion, race, language, nationality, caste, or tribe might fear, not without reason, that they will be discriminated against or persecuted by a government elected by the majority of the population. The working democracy does not consist only of periodical elections and of returning a majority government.

The underdeveloped countries have had a historical tradition very different from that of the Western countries. This tradition is that of authoritarian governments, either native or colonial. As a British author puts it, the colonial populations were told like children that spinach was good for them but were not asked whether they liked spinach. The belated effort by Britain and France to train their dependencies in self-government under the benevolent supervision of the colonial administration might not have lasted long enough to sink the deep foundations needed for the democratic system of government.

The idea of a legal and strong opposition is not a part of the tradition. In the past, opposition has usually meant an attempt to subvert the native or colonial government. The letters *P.G.* which the prime minister of the self-governing Gold Coast proudly displayed on his cap stood for *Prison Graduate*. It can be doubted whether imprisonment for anticolonial activities is the best training for the practice of political democracy. The native opposition does not necessarily feel that it should wait patiently for a legal opportunity to replace the existing government and is often tempted to seize power by intrigue or violence.

Parliaments, if copied from the West, either have large majorities which support the governing party and are docile instruments in the hands of this party, or are the refuge of vested interests which manipulate the elections to ensure a parliamentary majority ready to protect the upper classes, or are meaningless paraphernalia which conceal a one-party system of government.

Discussions about democracy are often confused by the dual meaning of this word. It may refer to political democracy, i.e, government by the people, or it may refer to what is now called social democracy, i.e., a social system in which shocking disparities in income are eradicated by various means (from progressive direct taxation to nationalization of the means of production), in which gradually increasing equality of opportunity at the start of life is being provided by broad access to education, in which social mobility is a pervasive characteristic of the community, and in which society feels responsible for the welfare of its sick, old, and unemployed members. Social democracy can be achieved under the regime of political democracy, as it has been in the West, or under an authoritarian government, as demonstrated by the U.S.S.R. Nowadays, political democracy is government by the people and for the people. An authoritarian government, sincerely committed to the goals of social democracy, may be called government *for* the people but certainly not *by* the people. (However, this government is preferable to one which is neither of the people nor for the people, a phenomenon not so rare among the underdeveloped countries.) It is illegitimate to claim that a guided democracy is a political democracy or that the best-intentioned dictator or *caudillo* practices government by the people, although his objectives may be those of social democracy. The two types of democracy should not be confused.

The lack of historical and other preconditions for political democracy favors the appearance of the concept of political tutelage. The masses, who cannot possibly understand the issues involved in the economic and social modernization of their country, must be guided toward their better future by an elite who knows better what their true interests are. The early exponents of this concept were the contemporaries Dr. Sun Yat-sen and Lenin. The father of the first Chinese Revolution felt that his party, the Kuomintang, should for a period of time act as the guide and tutor of its people. Lenin entrusted the mission of tutelage of the laboring masses to the Communist party, the enlightened guide enabled by Marxist doctrine to foresee the predestined course of history and thus to determine what the permanent interests of the proletariat are. The concept of political tutelage is not necessarily Communist; the idea of the enlightened despot is very old. Its popularity in the underdeveloped countries is due not only to the political immaturity of the masses but also to the wide gap which divides these masses from their educated elites. These elites are Western-educated and intellectually unable to communicate with the illiterate masses. It is not surprising that they are often inclined to distrust the masses with great decisions and to feel that they are themselves obliged to act in their behalf as the custodians of national interests.

The government of political tutelage should not be confused with a socially reactionary government. The ruling group in a government of tutelage may well be composed of people of modest origin who are not impelled by any vested interest to resist economic and social reforms. They may, on the contrary, be strongly motivated by the desire to modernize their country and eventually to improve the lot of the common man. The concept of political tutelage raises two questions: is it probable that a people kept in tutelage will learn how to operate a democratic form of government, and will the holders of power succumb to the temptation to perpetuate their tutelage instead of gradually terminating it? In any event, this arrangement leaves to the masses the modest role of the Greek chorus which is asked in this drama to work and to applaud the policies of their tutors. The immediate future of the underdeveloped countries may depend mainly on whether the chorus will, with conviction, sing in unison with the leading actors.

The authoritarian regimes in the underdeveloped countries can be of various types: a dictator usually supported by his own political organization, a one-party system, a junta of professional military officers, or a combination of all three. The leader, who is either a dictator or a man able to impose his decisions by the sheer prestige of his name, is usually the former leader in the struggle for national independence (there are several examples in Asia and Africa, such as Nehru, Sukarno, or Nkrumah) or in the revolution which founded the present regime (Atatürk, Nasser, Fidel Castro, and a few others). He enjoys the popularity and prestige due to his role in the crucial events of the past. His personality helps to bring within the reach of the politically unsophisticated masses such abstract notions as the state, the government, and the nation. These abstract concepts are almost identified with him, and the confused aspirations of the masses are personalized in him. This attitude toward the leader, which Latin Americans call *personalismo,* is a reversal of the democratic practice; people follow a policy because of the leader, not the leader because of his policy. It is only fair, however, to observe that the revolution of modernization creates a condition of great and protracted emergency and that in a national emergency even old democracies look toward a leader who is able to give a sense of direction and who becomes a visible rallying point. The names of Churchill, Roosevelt, and De Gaulle come to mind.

A group of military officers might step into national politics and either exert an indirect influence from behind the scenes or seize power overtly. They may be the allies of conservative forces, as they often are in Latin America. They may, on the contrary, be the advocates of modernization, as they are in Turkey and Egypt. They may step in in despair at seeing a succession of unstable, weak, inept, and corrupt governments, as they did in Pakistan, Burma, and Egypt.

The one-party system can be of two types. The first type frankly suppresses all other parties or denies them any freedom of activity; Ghana, Guinea, and several other African states provide the illustrations. The other type is more subtle and can legitimately claim to be democratic. The opposition parties are not restricted in their activities and operate as in a Western multiparty system; free elections are periodically held. But the dominant party holds in fact a monopoly of power because of its constant electoral victories. The two examples of this type of one-party system are the Congress Party in India (in national but not always in provincial politics) and the Mexican Party of Revolutionary Institutions. The process of alternation in power by two or more parties, a regular feature of Western democracies, is in fact suspended, exposing the ruling party to the risk of corruption and political mummification. India has undertaken the heavy task of modernization under a parliamentary regime in spite of difficulties which are in certain respects greater than in a number of other countries (archaic institutions such as the caste system or the cult of the cow, linguistic diversity of the population, etc.). The operation of this system has been successful so far owing to the unrivaled prestige of the Congress Party and to the Western training of the present generation of Indian leaders who are familiar with European ideas and with British parliamentary institutions. The question which remains to be answered is whether the parliamentary regime will survive the disappearance of the present political leaders or a decline in the prestige of the Congress Party.

The belief that political democracy is going to preside over the process of modernization or to become its necessary and final outcome (the latter prospect is more credible than the former) is like the nineteenth-century Western conviction that the whole world was bound to become Christian. The record of parliaments in certain underdeveloped countries is not very encouraging; elected in fraudulent elections by illiterate voters, they have been devoting their time and energy to the defense of vested interests. These parliamentary debates offer a no more edifying spectacle of democracy than Runnymede did when lay and church magnates wrested the charter of their own privileges from the king without suspecting that this Magna Charta would be reinterpreted in the seventeenth century as the foundation of English freedoms. It is no more encouraging to realize that governments have been changed during the last three decades forty times in the fifteen Latin American republics as the result of military coups, mob violence, or revolutions. It is true that the old-fashioned reactionary military dictatorships are disappearing, but it is also true that their successors, the democratic regimes, are often shaky, that the armed forces interfere in Argentinian national policies, that in 1961 the Brazilian army imposed a fundamental change in the constitution, and that the Fidelist regime, which does not lack sympathizers elsewhere, frankly refuses to hold elections and is a one-party system and "a people's democracy" like its sister regimes in Eastern Europe.

All this does not imply that political democracy is the providential privilege of the West, which lived for many centuries under different forms of government. Once the process of modernization is completed, it is possible that the present underdeveloped countries, or some of them, will evolve their own systems founded on respect for the individual freedoms. The native of an underdeveloped country is perfectly able to understand the essence of political democracy and may even, in theory, favor this form of government; yet he may feel at the present time that this particular form of government could not function in his own country during the period of revolutionary transition.

Another fallacy, which was current in the West until the appearance of Soviet sputniks, claimed that original thought in science and technology could be produced only in the atmosphere of political freedom. The Soviet Union proved that it was feasible to compartmentalize free thought, to encourage free research in mathematics, science, and technology while denying freedom of thought in literature, the arts, and the social sciences. It demonstrated that scientific progress was possible at the same time that literature, the arts, and the social sciences were condemned by party censorship to an anemic existence. This is a lesson which cannot escape the attention of the underdeveloped countries. Moreover, an authoritarian government of an underdeveloped country does not need at the present stage of development to generate original scientific thought; it suffices to borrow the ideas already known in the advanced countries.

Another cliché is that an economically developed country with decent living standards is necessarily less aggressive in its foreign policy than a country whose population suffers from undernourishment. History proves, however, that there is no necessary relation between economic prosperity and peaceful policy. Britain, France, Germany, and Austria-Hungary were not on the brink of starvation when they plunged into the First World War. Nazi Germany was not a land of illiteracy and misery when it unleashed the Second World War. The successful industrialization of Britain gave it a national power which made possible the consolidation and extension of its empire. A developed and democratic French Third Republic founded another extensive colonial empire. Prosperous and democratic Netherlands and Belgium were not reluctant to hold on to their colonial possessions. Germany, Japan, and the Soviet Union became a threat to the international status quo only after they acquired great power as a result of their industrialization. The theory that a prosperous Soviet Union will necessarily renounce the ambition of extending its ideological and political influence cannot be substantiated any more than the opposite theory. Similarly, large and populous countries such as China and India, once modernized and powerful, may feel happy within their national frontiers or may, on the contrary, seek external expansion.

Looking at the problem of the present and future regimes of the underdeveloped countries from the point of view of the external interests of the advanced nations, it is not the nature of a regime that is important but the kind of foreign policy it follows. Two regimes professing the same ideology can be at loggerheads, as history has proved more than once. Two regimes, devotees of opposite ideologies, can work closely together in foreign affairs. Unless he is a fanatic unable to tolerate the ideological diversity of the world, the analyst of the relations between two countries will always ask the most practical question first: is there a conflict or a coincidence of interests and foreign objectives between the two regimes, regardless of what their form of government or social system may be?

THE ECONOMIC AND SOCIAL SUBSTRUCTURE

Modernization entails two inseparable processes: development of the economy and transformation of the social structure. Economic development brings in its wake social readjustment to a new type of economy, and the transformation of social habits and attitudes conditions the success of economic expansion. Those social institutions which hinder social mobility or which reduce the material incentives to higher labor productivity or to greater individual initiative must be deliberately if gradually eliminated.

One of these retarding institutions is the caste system in India. Another is the concept of the joint family, which is widespread in Asia and Africa. This concept affirms the solidarity of the family, understood as a clan, and binds its members together, including distant relatives. The joint family is a sort of primitive substitute for state social insurance; a relative, close or distant, who is in need has the moral right to be assisted by those members of the joint family who fare better. This family insurance against starvation and other economic risks discourages the enterprising individual whose hard work and ingenuity could significantly raise the living standards of his immediate family if his surplus income were not absorbed by multiple moral obligations to distant relatives. The simplest solution would seem to consist in substituting state social insurance for this type of archaic clan insurance. However, an underdeveloped state, which must divert a large share of the national income to capital investment, cannot afford a satisfactory system of social insurance for its needy citizens. Moreover, these needy citizens usually suffer, first of all, from unemployment or underemployment; they need jobs which only economic development can provide. The welfare state is a very recent concept and the end-product of economic development in the advanced countries. An underdeveloped country cannot hope in the near future to provide sufficient assistance for its sick, disabled, or old citizens. The joint family cannot be expected to disappear overnight, because there is no satisfactory substitute for the time being. The process of urbanization and industrialization might, however, gradually loosen the traditional ties between those members of the joint family who have settled in the cities and the other relatives who have stayed behind in their native village.

Another widespread and retarding institution is the inferior status of women. This tradition hampers the social mobility of half the population and deprives the country of the full use of the working capacity and talents of that half. It is interesting to note that the Communist governments never delay their attack on this institution, as can be seen in Soviet Central Asia and in China; the emancipation of women is a part of the Communist program of modernization.

Another obsolete custom is the religious significance or social prestige which is attached to cattle in India and in Tropical Africa. This tradition results in an unproductive accumulation of cattle, which becomes a drain on the resources of the country. The problem is more easily solved in Africa where social rank is often measured by the number of heads of cattle a man possesses. The development of the economy will substitute other symbols of social status. The same problem is much more difficult in India where the prohibition against the slaughter of supernumerary cattle is sanctioned by the Hindu religion. The slaughter of cows is forbidden by law in six provinces of India. The surplus cattle is estimated at one-third of the total, which amounts to 200 million head, i.e., one cow per two inhabitants of India. This surplus competes with the fast-increasing population for its share of food. Yet the strong resistance to the slaughter of cows proves that the problem of modernization is not simply a question of rational choices or a problem which outsiders can solve. It is up to each underdeveloped country, and to it only, to make the dramatic choice between economic growth and the disruption of age-old customs, on the one hand, and the preservation of existing social institutions and economic stagnation, on the other.

The main problem consists in the collective ability or disability of a country to break down the crust of obsolete institutions which stand in the way of modern life. The capacity of individuals to adjust to new conditions has been abundantly proved in the migratory movements of the last and present centuries. A peasant from Eastern or Southern Europe, often illiterate, who emigrated to the United States or Canada, and a Chinese or Indian peasant who settled in either of the two hemispheres, made two formidable adjustments: he changed his occupation, for instance by becoming an industrial worker or a small retail trader, and he adapted himself to a totally foreign environment. The individual in the underdeveloped country is today confronted, as an individual, with the much easier problem of changing his habits at the same time that his own country, where he remains, is changing its own institutions. His personal adjustment is less painful than that which was expected of an emigrant who settled in a foreign land, and is a part of the national evolution.

The emigrant of the former era was ready to make the necessary adjustment for the sake of the higher income which he expected to earn in a foreign country. Today, material incentives should help in the adjustment of individuals to their economic development. We have proof that material incentives stimulate individual initiative. The African and Malayan peasants demonstrated, in developing new cultures which promised high returns, that they were sensitive to the expectation of profit.

It has been said, apropos of the process of modernization, that the only way to learn how to play the flute is to play it. Unfortunately, this is only part of the truth. One must desire to play it and patiently bear the frustration of long training before playing it well. Nor is this all: one must also have the means for buying the flute. In other words, the population concerned must be ready to reform or abolish time-hallowed habits and pay the price of necessary material and moral sacrifices. Not only must the old way of life make room for the new, but also modern attitudes should be adopted, such as efficiency and social discipline, punctuality, taking initiative as opposed to following routine, honesty, perseverance in the face of great difficulties, and the conviction that nature can be adjusted to human needs and the environment improved by human action. This psychological readiness to play the modern flute does not solve the other problem of being able to buy it. The cost of the flute, i.e., modern equipment, will have to be borne by the population out of savings diverted from consumption. But it is here that the outsiders, the advanced countries, can be of great help by bearing a part of the cost through economic assistance.

Economic development makes sense if it aims at producing a balanced economy which will no longer depend on the exports of a few commodities and which will encompass the whole country. Most of the underdeveloped countries have a few or several centers which pulsate with economic activity; these islands are surrounded by a sea of underdeveloped areas. The island might be a modern Latin American capital city where prosperous districts are encircled by a ring of slum areas and by an outer and vast ring of Indian villages where life goes on as in the pre-Columbian age, or another no less modern capital where the government keeps the urban population satisfied at the cost of neglecting the needs of poor rural areas. It might be an oil or mining center run by an efficient foreign corporation or a harbor city where easy access to foreign markets provides an economic stimulus. It might also be a modern factory built by the government as a showpiece against a background of backward and miserable villages.

Balanced development must give priority to the construction of the social and economic substructure. This substructure should include a national network of roads, railroads, and telecommunications in order to provide all the areas of the country with a fair chance of participation in economic development; harbor facilities for foreign trade; expansion of the supply of energy; the reclamation of land and agricultural extension services to ensure an increase in the volume and quality of agricultural production; the building of schools, hospitals, and other public health services.

To take one example, there is usually a staggering contrast between the untapped resources and the actual use of energy. This aspect of underdevelopment can be seen from the following figures for 1952: the developed countries of North America, Europe (including the Soviet Union), Japan, and Oceania produced 1,061,523 million kilowatts; the underdeveloped countries of Asia, the Near East, Africa, and Latin America, only 77,490 million. Yet energy resources usually exist either in the form of coal or oil deposits or in the form of potential hydraulic energy which could be tapped by the harnessing of rivers. Eventually the underdeveloped countries, like the advanced countries, will be able to use atomic energy.

The problem of the substructure includes the urgent need for efficient statistical and geological services without which a developing country can only move forward blindly, in ignorance of its true needs and of the available natural resources.

One of the foremost tasks in building the social substructure is the expansion of education at all levels and of all sorts. This is a precondition of economic development and of modernization in general. For instance, capital goods imported from abroad will rust without skilled personnel who know what to do with them and how to use them for productive purposes. The lack of proper skill among the native personnel limits, more than any other factor, the capacity of an underdeveloped country to absorb foreign economic assistance, which amounts to the importation of capital goods at the expense of a foreign government.

The proportion of illiterates in the populations (ten years of age or older) of various parts of the world is shown in Table 4.

TABLE 4

PROPORTION OF ILLITERATES IN POPULATION (10 YEARS OF AGE OR OLDER)

Area	Per Cent
United States and Canada	2
Europe	8
South America	42
Central America	48
Asia	70
Africa	90

In South Asia (Afghanistan, Ceylon, India, Nepal, and Pakistan) with a total population of 585 million (18 per cent of the total population of the world and 28 per cent of that of the non-Communist world) the average illiteracy rate is about 80 per cent. In Thailand, Vietnam, Cambodia, and Laos the rate is the same. The situation is worse in the sub-Saharan Africa where the rate attains 90 to 95 per cent in several countries and seldom falls below 80 per cent. In the Near East the best situation prevails in Lebanon with its 55 per cent rate and the worst in the most backward countries, Saudi Arabia and Yemen having rates of over 95 per cent. Except for the few semi- or unevenly developed countries, such as Argentina, the illiteracy rates for most of Latin America are high and vary between 40 and 80 per cent.

The progressive elimination of illiteracy is a precondition of successful modernization, including economic development. A steel mill or a hydroelectric plant built in a corner of an illiterate country may create an image of progress, but the population will remain as unprepared for modern life as before. The problem of creating interest in education is not as formidable as it might seem; an illiterate person of today, if he has, even intermittently and from afar, observed the economic and social superiority of the literate person, does not need to hear long arguments to be convinced that education is the key to his or his children's advancement. In Africa racial discrimination provides another argument for education, which is the main asset of the white man.

It is impossible to assign an order of priority to the three levels of education. A university-trained elite could accomplish little in the midst of an illiterate population ignorant of modern skills. A literate population can be organized for modern production only by university graduates and by technicians and foremen with a secondary education who can serve as intermediate links between the university graduates and the laboring population. The three levels of education are clearly interdependent. Students at the universities come from the ranks of those who have completed their secondary studies; high schools recruit their students among those who have graduated from the elementary schools. The elementary school teachers must have a secondary education, and the high school teachers are trained at the colleges and universities. The same interdependence is later reflected in the social division of labor. The elementary schools meet the demand for the workers and other employees of the lowest category; the high schools and secondary technical schools supply clerical employees, typists, stenographers, highly skilled workers, and mechanics; the agricultural and technical colleges provide instructors and technicians. The universities train the administrators, managers, scientists, and other experts. This balanced educational system cannot be built in one generation precisely because of the interdependence between the three levels. The most effective progress is a gradual but well-balanced advance on the whole educational front.

The problem of primary education is not just to make sure that all children are enrolled at the age of six or seven but to prevent their dropping out after one or two or three years of schooling, as they often do in the underdeveloped countries, and regressing to their former illiteracy.

The size and quality of the university-educated intelligentsia must be constantly increased. However, an uncontrolled and spontaneous growth could produce an explosive social situation. The outline of this situation can already be detected. Certain professions (for instance, law and the social sciences) are traditionally surrounded with a halo of social prestige; moreover, the facilities for this type of higher education can be provided at a relatively low cost to a great number of students. If young people flock to those studies, disregarding the need of the country for different professions and the future prospects of their own employment, and if they can be accommodated in the classrooms, the consequences are self-evident. Young people cannot find employment in the field of their specialization which is already overcrowded. The same risk is run by the students who are sent abroad and left free to choose their own specialty. They might select the field to which their own society attaches traditional prestige but which does not promise adequate employment or they might select a very advanced branch of science or technology for which there is no immediate need in their own country. In both cases they might be unable to find adequate employment after returning home. Whether trained abroad or in their own country, those "supernumerary" young people will have to accept any job to earn their living, usually a job poorly paid and unrelated to their academic background. They will not blame themselves for having chosen the wrong specialty. Their personal frustration will quickly be linked in their minds with the general social and economic ills of their underdeveloped country. They will become the potential recruits for revolutionary organizations, which find in them the necessary enthusiasm and capacity for mobilizing the popular masses for a revolution.

Progress in education, as in other fields, must be planned by the government to conform with the immediate needs of the country. These plans should include agreements with the countries which play host to native students sent abroad, agreements which would channel these students toward the professional training required for the modernization of their country. In other words, the student should be sure in advance that his academic studies offer him a fair chance of adequate employment and that he will be truly useful to his own people. Generally speaking, the underdeveloped countries need fewer lawyers and no great increase in the number of social scientists, but medical doctors, pharmacists, trained nurses, teachers on whose numbers and quality the whole future of their country depends, geologists, statisticians, economists, agricultural experts, veterinaries, business managers, engineers, scientists, and public administrators. The unavoidably great role which the government must play in the process of modernization creates an urgent need for well-trained public administrators, who are called upon in an underdeveloped country to perform functions which are usually left to private initiative in an advanced country.

Foreign corporations which operate in an underdeveloped country can be of assistance if they consistently follow the policy of increasing their native managerial and engineering staff by training and promoting local people. This policy commends itself even from the point of view of the interests of the foreign corporation, because the association of native business executives with the management of foreign enterprises helps to deflect the everpresent danger of nationalization.

AGRICULTURE AND THE PEASANTS

An underdeveloped country is essentially agricultural although it might have a small industrial base (usually light industries working for the domestic market) and derive a part of its national income from the production of raw materials for export. In most of those countries agriculture accounts for at least 50 per cent of the national income; extracting industries are frequently another important source of revenue.

Comparison between the advanced and underdeveloped countries proves that the smaller the relative weight of agriculture as a source of national income and the smaller the proportion of the active population engaged in agriculture, the higher the living standards.

The bulk of the population in the underdeveloped countries are peasants. Approximately 50 to 85 per cent of the total population depend on land for their livelihood. By contrast, 84 per cent of the total population in the United Kingdom, 72 per cent in Germany, 60 per cent in Belgium,

55 per cent in France, 52 per cent in the Soviet Union, are urban residents. Economic development results in the shift of manpower from agriculture to other occupations (secondary and tertiary industries). For instance, between 1870 and 1930 the percentage of the active population engaged in agriculture decreased in the United States from 54 per cent to 23 per cent, in France from 42 per cent to 25 per cent, in Japan from 85 per cent to 51 per cent, in Germany from 39 per cent to 22 per cent, in England from 15 per cent to 7 per cent.

Progress in agricultural techniques not only causes a considerable reduction in the number of people engaged in agriculture but also produces much higher yields per person. In the advanced agricultural areas the percentage of the total population engaged in agriculture is strikingly low; in 1948-50 it was as low as 29 per cent in Denmark, 21 per cent in New Zealand, and 28.5 per cent in the state of Iowa. In 1950 India had 306 million acres under cultivation, and the United States 360 million. In India 73 million people were working in agriculture, in the United States only 8 million. But the American yield of wheat per acre was over 1,000 lbs.; in India the yield per acre was less than 600 lbs. The American yield of cotton per acre was 313 lbs. against only 66 lbs. in India. Superior techniques account for this amazing contrast between the yields and the number of persons working per acre.

Table 5 indicates that the underdeveloped countries produce much less per acre and per person than the advanced countries.

TABLE 5

YIELDS PER HECTARE AND PER PERSON FOR VARIOUS REGIONS OF THE WORLD (1950-51)

Region	Yield Per Hectare (in Metric Tons)	Yield Per Person
Africa	0.83	0.14
Asia	1.19	0.23
Europe	1.60	1.02
North America	1.53	2.46
South America	1.31	0.45
Oceania	1.47	2.28

The contrast between the advanced and underdeveloped countries is less regarding the yield per acre than regarding the yield per person, because primitive agricultural techniques can be partly compensated for by the use of greater manpower on each acre.

Two-thirds of the population of the world, who live in Latin America, Asia, and Africa, account for only about one-third of the agricultural production of the world despite the fact that these areas are essentially agricultural. But the first industrial nation, the United States, accumulates agricultural surpluses each year.

The introduction of improved agricultural methods would result, as it did in the advanced nations, not only in much higher yields per acre but also in a considerable reduction of manpower required for work in agriculture. The surplus manpower released by modern techniques would have to look for nonagricultural jobs which only economic development could provide. Only a portion of them could be resettled on the land reclaimed by irrigation, drainage, deforestation, or other methods. Unfortunately, in many underdeveloped countries, notably in Asia, there is not much land which could be reclaimed. However, some improvement in the amount of cultivated land could be achieved. To take as an example, not sub-Saharan Africa or Latin America where prospects in this regard are much brighter, but the Near East, an area of agricultural settlement going back to time immemorial and mostly composed of desert, the present 5 to 6 per cent of land which is cultivated could be considerably increased by irrigation. However, the problem of irrigation often involves more than obtaining a sufficient supply of water. The state concerned must have the financial capacity for the required outlay or the assurance of foreign aid. Moreover, the same river might flow through the territories of more than one state. The irrigation project must then be co-ordinated between the riparian states. This co-ordination might be rendered difficult or almost impossible by unfriendly relations between the states concerned or by their inability to agree on a distribution of the water supply that seems fair to all of them. Israel is deadlocked with the Arab states over the use of waters from the rivers Jordan and Yarmuk. India and Pakistan only recently, and after much friction, arrived at an agreement concerning the distribution of waters derived from the system of the Indus River, a problem of vital concern to northwestern India and to West Pakistan. The use of waters of the River Nile vitally interests Egypt and Sudan, not to mention other countries such as Ethiopia, Uganda, and Kenya.

Rural unemployment caused by improved agricultural techniques would increase the concealed underemployment of the peasant population. Even with the primitive methods of cultivation now in use, the villages are overcrowded, and their population is growing steadily as a result of natural increase. In other words, the peasants do not work as much as they could because there is not enough land for each of them. The Vietnamese peasant works on the average 125 days per year, the Egyptian 160 days, the Indian from 100 to 200 days depending on the irrigation facilities and on the opportunity for two or only one annual harvest. Low productivity per person, concealed underemployment, and miserable living standards are all different facets of the same problem of economic underdevelopment and rural overpopulation. This overpopulation is a relative notion, because the surplus of rural population could be absorbed if the country were economically developed and could offer jobs in the secondary and tertiary industries.

Of course, overpopulated villages with very low living standards are a small market for manufactured goods. There is an interdependence between industrial and agricultural development. Industries could supply agricultural machinery, fertilizers, and other products needed by an advanced agriculture, while the rural population, using modern techniques and enjoying better living standards, would provide the industries with a market for manufactured consumer goods.

In any event, an underdeveloped country which wants to move forward must steadily increase its agricultural output, because agriculture is the main source of its national income and also the principal potential source of capital for industrialization and other capital investment. A constant increase in agricultural production is also urgently needed to meet the rising demand for foodstuffs caused by the rapid natural increase. For all these reasons agriculture is the crucial problem for an underdeveloped country.

But the problem of agriculture cannot be reduced only to its economic terms. Since the peasants form the bulk of the population, agriculture also has political and social aspects of the first magnitude. The peasants, mostly illiterate, dispersed in thousands of villages, mainly or exclusively interested in the immediate problems of their narrow environment, seem to be a passive multitude whom the government can ignore with much greater impunity than they can ignore the urban population, which is intellectually more alert and concentrated in the large cities. However, the peasantry proved during the Russian Civil War and, above all, in the Chinese Civil War that they could be aroused and organized for revolutionary action. The techniques are now known and could be used elsewhere. The revolutionary party must only have the ability to couch its immediate objectives, true or alleged, in simple terms which would make these objectives attractive within the framework of rural issues. If the educated revolutionary elite are able to communicate with an illiterate or semiliterate peasant and talk to him in terms whose meaning he can grasp with the help of his own daily experience, he can become an effective weapon in a revolutionary struggle and make up for the nonexistence of large urban masses. Neither his misery nor the overcrowding of villages can be dismissed as unavoidable evils, because sooner or later a new elite would emerge to proclaim that these evils can be eradicated.

It has been calculated that about half of the rural manpower in Egypt and about a quarter in South and Southeast Asia could be shifted to other occupations if this opportunity existed and without any improvement in the present agricultural techniques. These are the unemployed of the underdeveloped countries. If a country of this type is also made up of large estates whose ownership is heavily concentrated among a minority of the population, and if the peasant majority are agricultural laborers, tenant farmers, or owners of dwarf holdings, the foremost political reform is the splitting up of the large estates.

Economically it is a moot question whether land reform would result in a rise or fall of agricultural output. On the one hand, a tenant farmer or a landless agricultural laborer would find it in his own interest to make the best use of his newly acquired plot of land. On the other hand, a large estate is better suited for mechanized agriculture and has larger means for investment than a small holder. The economic value of land reform depends on local conditions, among others on the type of large estates to be split up (they can be technically progressive or exploited by methods which are no better than those of the peasants) and on the nature of the crops, some of which might allow for high yields on small holdings and others require a large acreage for rational exploitation. But the problem of large estates in a country with rural overpopulation is essentially political. The land-hungry peasant will not be swayed by the best economic arguments.

Land reform will of course be opposed by large landowners defending vested interests. The splitting up of large estates would not only reduce their wealth but also break down their political power. However, the choice is not between the status quo and land reform but between reform peacefully carried out and a revolutionary upheaval. This much can be learned from the experience of the Russian and Chinese revolutions.

The postwar years offer an interesting contrast. A thorough land reform was carried out in Japan under heavy pressure from American occupation authorities who could disregard local vested interests. This reform greatly contributed to political stability in the rural districts of Japan. By contrast, the government of independent India has not been able to carry out a significant land reform. Yet 15 per cent of Indian peasants are landless and another 15 per cent own so little that both groups earn their living by working for larger landowners. Their income is less than a half of the national low average of $70 per capita. The lack of action is due to the fact that land reform lies within the reserved jurisdiction of provincial legislatures which do not dare to challenge the landowners.

The problem of land reform can be greatly complicated if foreigners or alien corporations are among the large landowners. The anger of peasants, hostile to the existence of large estates, is then coupled with xenophobia. The foreign government is placed in an awkward position. It can press for a full and fair compensation but will be blamed for indirectly opposing a social reform generally considered necessary. It can accept the losses by its citizens as an inevitable part of social change but then will be criticized at home for its failure to protect the interests of its nationals abroad. The absence of a strong reaction might be understood by other states as an unintentional encouragement to expropriate the assets of its citizens without compensation or against a very inadequate one. As often happens in international politics, the choice lies between two evils.

If the nature of the crops is such that large-scale cultivation is preferable, for instance because it allows for full mechanization, or if the peasants should be organized for the purpose of credit or marketing, agrarian reform raises the question whether it is not necessary to encourage peasant co-operatives for joint production or for other purposes. The Communist collective farm is prompted, not only by doctrinaire bias, but also by the consideration that a large estate should be, at least in theory, more productive than a small peasant holding. The Communist cycle proceeds through the following stages: (1) They win the peasants over by promising to abolish the large private estates; (2) If, with the help of peasant support, they seize power, they carry out their promise; (3) After the lapse of time required for the consolidation of their control over the country, they take back the small holdings, formerly distributed to the peasants, and pool them in collective farms which are the Communist form of large estates. In addition to the deceit involved, the objectionable part of this operation is the ruthless compulsion applied to the peasants in the third stage to force them to join the collective farms. However, voluntary producer co-operatives could offer a solution, if the peasants were persuaded that they would be better off by pooling their resources.

Agrarian reform does not necessarily reduce output. For instance, rice culture returns high yields on small holdings. The average Japanese rice yield is 4,000 to 4,500 lbs. per acre, which is higher than the average yield obtained on American mechanized farms and four times the Indian or Pakistani yield. This extraordinary result is being obtained on very small holdings by virtue of the garden-like cultivation of rice paddies, the use of tested seeds, irrigation, natural and artificial fertilizers, and other means of intensive cultivation.

Agrarian reform involves more than the distribution of large estates. Peasant holdings are often fragmented into several separate strips interlocked with other peasants' strips. This checkerboard of noncontiguous strips hinders the use even of draught animals. Agrarian reform would require a consolidation into one holding of all the strips of land separated from each other but owned by the same peasant. Another problem is the growing fragmentation of small holdings through the process of inheritance, a fragmentation that constantly diminishes the average peasant acreage. Yet the state cannot introduce laws limiting land inheritance to one son if the other children cannot be offered either plots of land in a different province or nonagricultural jobs.

Agrarian reform is not the final solution to the problem of rural overpopulation. First, there might not be enough land in the large estates to endow every peasant family with a sufficient holding. Secondly, the land that can be reclaimed might also be inadequate to provide the additional holdings needed. Thirdly, rural overpopulation is each year aggravated by the rapid natural increase. Finally, improved techniques of production will have the same consequences that they had in the advanced countries: a large part of the rural manpower in the villages will be rendered economically useless. Mass emigration, one of the remedies that helped Europe during its period of rapid natural increase, is out of the question for the underdeveloped countries since the countries of immigration are now practically closed, especially to colored people. Only one solution remains —the development of secondary and tertiary industries, in other words the creation of nonagricultural jobs for the "supernumerary" population.

More than land reform is needed to improve the condition of the peasant. A state-controlled rate of interest could deliver him from the clutches of the moneylender, who is often his own landlord. The government could encourage better agricultural methods, the planting of new crops for which there is a demand at home or abroad, and peasant self-help. Since the peasants are usually underemployed, they represent a formidable potential labor force which could be used with profit for themselves. The Indian Community Development project, which was inaugurated in 1952, merits in this respect the attention of other underdeveloped countries. The project consists in the training of development workers who are later assigned to various villages, where they familiarize themselves with the local problems and needs, gain the confidence of the peasants, and eventually try to persuade them to improve their own lot by concerted action. The state helps with technical advice and a modest financial contribution. The main investment, however, is the peasant labor. The peasants build schools and local roads, dig village wells, construct local irrigation canals, spray DDT to counteract malaria, and engage in other projects of immediate value to their own village.

The state can also help the peasant by providing cheap credit, supplying rural extension services, and building roads and railroads to connect rural areas with domestic or foreign markets. Foreign economic and technical assistance can be of great help in all these attempts to improve the lot of the peasant. But the main social measure, the splitting up of large estates, remains within the exclusive jurisdiction of the local government; foreign governments can offer only encouragement and even this may be denounced by the vested interests as undue interference in domestic affairs. Foreign governments could do much to alleviate the lot of the peasant if they acted in concert to stabilize international prices for primary commodities. The fluctuation of these prices on such products as coffee, sugar, tobacco, and cotton can be disastrous for the peasant producer, but the remedy is beyond the reach of his own government.

Despite the uncertainties of the international market, an underdeveloped country has a vital interest in the production of raw materials for export, another important source of national income. The export of primary commodities (foodstuffs and raw materials) supplies foreign exchange for buying the capital equipment which economic development requires. An underdeveloped country is well-advised if it tightly controls its own imports and prevents the squandering of foreign exchange on luxury consumer goods; insofar as possible, it should spend every penny of foreign exchange on the capital goods which are an investment in its future.

The extraction of raw materials stimulates at least a local economic development. It cannot proceed without the building of such facilities as ports, railroads, and power stations. These facilities can be used for the development of secondary industries working for the domestic market. Moreover, it may be possible to found processing industries for the local transformation of raw materials; mineral deposits or oil fields can be the foundation for an ore smelter or an oil refinery which in turn will supply more jobs for the local manpower and a greater amount of foreign exchange.

The extraction of raw materials is usually in the hands of foreign corporations. If they are willing or compelled by the local government, they can form a nucleus of managerial and industrial skills by training a growing number of native employees of all ranks. In its own long-term interest, the foreign corporation often follows the policy of investing a part of its profits in the welfare of its native employees (schools, housing, public health services); in this way it contributes to the growth of a more vigorous and enterprising native element who may become a human factor of importance in the general economic development of the country. The wages paid by the corporation, its local purchases of supplies, the royalties and taxes it pays, provide additional purchasing power and budgetary resources. These budgetary resources could be ploughed back into economic development by the local government; the additional purchasing power supplied to the population could stimulate the growth of domestic light industries.

URBANIZATION AND INDUSTRIALIZATION

The growing and often rapid urbanization of underdeveloped countries is misleading if used as an index of general economic progress. It can reflect only a marginal development of one or a few areas within a country which otherwise remains stagnant. If urbanization is more general but is not accompanied by a parallel economic development, it is due to demographic pressure. Rural overpopulation drives the peasants toward the cities in the hope, frequently vain, of finding a better livelihood. The cities become an agglomeration of slum districts without water, light, drainage, paved streets, transportation, or public health services. In effect, the immigrant peasant trades his rural misery for an urban poverty which is no less hopeless but even less healthy. The impressive statistics on the rapid growth of large cities with a million or several million inhabitants reflect, not a sound economic development, but rural despair and overpopulation. The conditions in which these modern urban proletarians live in the fast-expanding cities of Asia, the Near East, and Latin America are often worse than those which appalled Karl Marx in England more than a century ago.

Urbanization, when unrelated to general economic growth, carries with it the germs of political instability. The urban proletariat has ample reason for discontent. It is not restrained, unlike the rural population, by traditional ways of life and is prone to support any movement which promises a change in existing conditions because any change is welcome as a promise of a better tomorrow. The governments are compelled to attend to the urban proletariat who might turn against them in a blind fury of despair. Yet the poverty of the country makes it difficult to keep promises of better wages, social security, and improved living conditions. The rising expectations, which are more lively in the cities than in the villages, can easily end in bitter frustration. The Westerner can measure the gravity of the problem by consulting the history of industrialization in the West and adding to it a new factor, unknown at that time, the existence of modern techniques of mass propaganda and mass organization.

In a few Latin American countries the problem is "solved" by concentrating the national welfare effort on the cities and completely neglecting the rural areas. The urban population enjoys a higher per capita income than the rural population and has incomparably better educational and public health services as well as a monopoly on social security, but the rural areas are left more or less to themselves. This sort of social disequilibrium is aggravated by the concentration of a large portion of the population in the capital city or a few other large cities. The most striking examples of this top-heavy urban concentration are Havana, Montevideo, Buenos Aires, and Caracas, which harbor from one-third to one-fifth of the total population of countries in which they are located. One-third of the Uruguayan population, who reside in Montevideo, have practically a monopoly on the state educational, medical, public welfare, and social security services; one-third of the adults have state jobs which eat up most of the national budget. This welfare city is mostly supported by the ill-fed, ill-clothed, and ill-housed agricultural workers who produce wool, meat, and hides which form the bulk of the export trade.

The rapid if socially unhealthy growth of large cities can be seen from the following data chosen at random. More than one-third of the urban population of India and Pakistan were born in rural areas; three-fourths of the population of Bombay immigrated from the villages. The overcrowded conditions are reflected in a very high average density of the urban population. Calcutta, for instance, has 80,000 people per square mile while New York has only 25,000; but there are no skyscrapers in Calcutta and the population live in one- or two-story tenements.

The fact that a large part of the urban population is composed of recent rural immigrants indicates that communications between the city and the village are not severed. The city dweller usually maintains close ties with relatives and friends left behind in the village. Political ideas can travel swiftly from the city to the rural areas.

The slogan of industrialization lights up eyes in the underdeveloped countries. This is understandable for several reasons. First, all the advanced countries are industrial. They enjoy infinitely higher living standards; the Soviet Union, if compared to Asia, Africa, and Latin America, is no exception although its living standards are lower than those of the West. Their labor productivity, due to the modern structure of their economies, produces an impressive per capita national income; in other words, they are prosperous. They are also powerful. China or India are much more populous than the United States or Russia, but they remain second-class powers because their economies are less developed. The benefits of the welfare state are the privilege of industrial nations which can afford it.

Secondly, the underdeveloped countries, subjected to the heavy social pressure of rural overpopulation, cannot hope to solve their problems merely by distributing the large estates, improving agricultural techniques, and reclaiming land. They have to provide nonagricultural jobs for their surplus population. Progress in agriculture requires an industry capable of supplying machinery, fertilizers, insecticides, and other products. If this progress results in a higher income for the peasants, they will ask for a greater supply of manufactured consumer goods, which the domestic factories could provide. Finally, a country which wants to free its economy from the bondage of dependence on a few staple exports is tempted not only to diversify its agricultural production but also to build up industries for the domestic market and to become more independent of foreign imports.

There is a lingering suspicion in the underdeveloped countries that their desire to industrialize is being greeted with mixed feelings in the advanced countries. The development of light industries will temporarily cut down the market for imported manufactured consumer goods. A country bent on industrialization will take measures to restrict these imports in order to save its purchasing power for buying foreign equipment rather than consumer goods. If it develops processing industries, these will cut down the profits of the developed countries. An oil refinery or an ore smelter built close to the sources of raw materials will deprive a developed country of profits derived from the refining process which formerly took place on its national territory. It might have to pay more for foreign-produced aluminum, flour, or refined oil than it formerly paid for bauxite, grain, or crude oil, unless the lower cost of transporting these less bulky processed goods kept their price down. The foreign corporation which operates an extractive industry will be asked to share its profits with the local government on the basis of prices which are much higher for the semiprocessed commodities, while now it pays its royalties on the basis of low prices for crude raw materials. Eventually, full industrial development in the present underdeveloped countries and the resulting increase in their demand for raw materials may cause a rise in the international prices for these materials, a prospect which holds little appeal for the industrial nations of today. However, the Western nations should not forget that the Communist countries provide an alternative source of economic and technical assistance and should not underestimate the impact of the Communist propaganda for industrialization. A concealed coolness on the part of the West toward the industrialization of the underdeveloped countries would be futile, because it could not stop but only delay the process, and politically unwise at a time when the West is competing for the sympathy of the underdeveloped countries.

Industrialization involves several prospects and risks:

1. The resources of the country, including its sources of energy, should be sufficiently known to avoid the building of industries which would not find raw materials at home and would have to buy them abroad at exorbitant prices. This problem is less important for a very large country with a diversified wealth of natural resources, such as India, which can take courage from the successful development of the United States or the Soviet Union. But a small country must weigh in advance the cost of competing for foreign raw materials with other developing countries, with the West, and with Communist Eastern Europe.

The domestic market is usually small and inelastic. Two-thirds of the population are peasants who have little or no means for buying more manufactured goods than they buy at the present time. The native light industries can eliminate the need for foreign imports of manufactured consumer goods but have rather dismal prospects for a further expansion of the local demand. Their hope lies, first of all, in the improvement of agricultural production and in the increase of peasant purchasing power.

Foreign markets might elude the grasp of new industries not only because our world is protectionist but also because of stiff competition from the advanced countries with their more efficient production and marketing methods. Domestic tariffs will protect the national market of the developing country but will have their counterpart in foreign tariffs.

2. The processing industries, which increase the value of exports, and the light industries, which produce for the domestic market and allow for the reduction of imports of consumer goods, should have a high priority. High priority should also be given to industries which produce for agriculture (machinery and chemical products), because it is agriculture which will supply the initial investment capital for further industrial development.

3. Industrialization is inconceivable without the expansion of agricultural output. One reason is that agriculture is the main source of national income. The other reason is also self-evident. The men who have left their villages to work in the new industries must buy the food which they used to produce. The peasant can no longer produce for his own family alone; he must also supply the new industrial worker.

4. Industrial development is accompanied by the foundation or growth of cities. As a result, the government must support a huge overhead expenditure for urban housing, sanitation, and other facilities even if these facili-

ties remain primitive by modern standards. The urban proletariat will seldom be content in a developing country which cannot afford high wages or adequate social insurance. No country can efface the alluring image of the advanced countries or escape the agitation of organized labor for improved living conditions. Industrialization will create an unstable situation in the cities.

5. It will provide an opening for the overpopulated villages, but its other aspects will have little appeal for the peasantry. It will demand the pre-emption of a large share of agricultural income for industrial and other capital investment. This will preclude any notable rise in rural living standards. The means used can be heavy rural taxation or Communist collectivization of agriculture, but the result will not please the peasants.

6. The developed countries have a tremendous lead in technology which the underdeveloped countries will not be able to overcome in the near future; hence, the prospect of successful competition on the international market will be dimmed for a long time to come. They could compete by virtue of lower wages, but tariffs and eventually automation will be the answer of the advanced countries. The developing country will be hampered in the initial stage of industrialization by the lower efficiency of its managerial and engineering staffs, the lower productivity of machinery due to the lack of industrial discipline, less skill and greater carelessness on the part of its workers, more frequent breakdowns and longer delays for repairs, and a lower output per capita due to the poor health and inadequate nutrition of the workers and the absenteeism and fluidity of labor. Workers who only recently were peasants and have family ties with the villages may migrate to the cities to earn industrial wages but remain on the job only long enough to pay the taxes due from their rural homesteads, to pay their debts, or to save a little money, and then return to familiar rural surroundings. Inadequate urban living conditions and low wages, inseparable from the initial stage of industrialization, will cause a large turnover in industrial manpower, as they did in England during the first stage of the Industrial Revolution. The fluidity of labor also plagued Soviet industries at the same stage of development. The poor laborer flees the misery of his village by going to the city, but urban misery may drive him back to his village. Despair and hope may keep the migrant laborers shuttling helplessly between village and city.

7. The present prospects for attracting private capital toward investment in new industries of an underdeveloped country are rather dim.

8. Since the available means for economic development are very limited, the government of a developing country will have to husband them very cautiously. It will have to plan and control its development to ensure balanced growth. The not unusual practice of engaging in costly prestige projects which are not necessary in the present stage of development, such as embellishing the capital city, building a modern highway instead of the

badly needed network of rural roads, or founding a factory which is unrelated to the present needs of the national economy, amounts to squandering already meager resources. The penalty for imprudence, however, is often swift and sure; the government will be replaced by a new ruling elite who will not wait for a ballot verdict.

ECONOMIC UNIONS

The economic development of small and medium-sized countries would be facilitated by the formation of regional unions in which the member-countries could pool their resources. An economic union would offer definite advantages:

1. A large market reduces the overhead cost of production and allows for lower prices which in turn stimulate demand. The free competition promotes the efficiency of industrial enterprises. Industries which produce for a large market have the necessary means for research, which is essential for technological progress. Only a large market permits the creation of a fully developed industrial complex, because a vigorous industry creates a demand for the products of a related industry.

2. The excess of production in the territory of one state can be absorbed in the territories of other participating states.

3. Their natural resources are combined, their deficiencies are mutually offset, and they can establish a broad base for a modern economy.

4. Their exports are also combined. Assuming that each participating country relies on one or a few staple products for the earning of foreign currencies, they achieve together a much more diversified export of several raw materials and foodstuffs. Since the fluctuation of prices on the international market does not evenly affect all the primary commodities, the losses on certain items can be compensated by gains on other articles or, at least, the amount of losses can be reduced for the whole union by the unequal fall in the demand for each particular product. The result would be less disastrous than it would be for each participating state if it remained isolated and had to bear the full brunt of the fall in prices for its staple product.

5. An economic union, representing a developing market and a large population, would be better able to negotiate with its usual customers among other states and would represent a potentially significant international force.

The formation of common markets between the underdeveloped nations requires the expansion of interconnecting transportation facilities in order to stimulate mutual trade. For instance, the small volume of trade in the Latin American countries is due not only to their tariff walls and their inadequate purchasing power but also to the lack of a developed continental system of transportation. The deficiency of this system gives precedence to maritime trade with North America and Europe.

An effective economic union calls for much more than the abolition of all restrictions on trade between the participating states and the erection of a common wall of tariffs against outsiders. In order to provide all the partners with an equal chance to benefit from the common market, the participants must evolve common financial and fiscal policies, joint control over an equitable distribution of capital investment, the elimination of barriers against the free migration of labor, and a co-ordinated policy regarding labor and social insurance legislation. A common market, in which the manpower could not be distributed according to the actual demand because of national restrictions on immigration, in which no measures were taken to encourage investment in the countries or areas so far less developed, in which one participating state would be favored over another because its manufacturers pay lower taxes or spend less for social insurance and can therefore compete on better terms, would be a profitable venture only for the economically strongest partner with the least developed social legislation but would perpetuate the stagnation of other participating states. The need for a general co-ordination of economic, social, and fiscal policies of the member-states makes it not improbable that a truly effective economic union might lead step by step toward a political union.

Logically, the economic union is the best solution for small and medium-sized countries, developed or underdeveloped, if they want to win or retain a place in the international life of this century, which seems to favor the economic giants. But logic is seldom the winner in international relations. In any case the history of the postwar period records so far only one successful economic union, the Western European Community of Six, but this is a union of fully developed nations.

To succeed, an economic union must overcome many difficulties: traditional animosities between neighboring peoples; fear that the union would result in the dominance of one partner over the others; resistance by vested interests which fear their eclipse under the free competition across national frontiers (these vested interests might be those of a backward agriculture or those of less efficient industries); and opposition, usually concealed, by other states which may be hostile to the creation of the union for economic or political reasons and may prefer to deal as before with each member of the union separately.

The underdeveloped countries have even more urgent reasons than the six Western European nations had to look toward regional economic unions as their plank of salvation. They can learn from the experience of the Six, in particular that the formation of a regional union does not require the elimination of national loyalties of the member-states. The larger allegiance to the Community should grow from the existing roots of national loyalties (see Chapter 9).

PLANNED GROWTH

The difficulties of economic development are so many and the need for a balanced growth so great that the government confronted with this immense task is compelled to have a long-term plan. It must know what the probable national income will be during the next several years, including the income from such sources as agriculture, the extractive industries, and foreign aid. There will be several uncertainties in this forecast of the future. The expected increase in agricultural output might fail to materialize foı various reasons, including natural disasters such as drought. The international demand for exported primary commodities might fall short of expectations, and the fund of foreign currencies, which the government planned to use for purchasing foreign equipment, might be much smaller than anticipated. Foreign aid commitments might be pledged for one year only, and their renewal might hinge on domestic events in the assisting state.

Nevertheless, how the national income will be earned and how it will be invested must be defined to avoid chaotic zigzags and to give a sense of direction to national life. An unplanned and unco-ordinated development will not only be more costly for a country which cannot afford waste but may also end in failure.

The concept of planning has been popularized by the practice of the Soviet Union and other Communist countries which have tried to solve their problems of economic growth systematically. Of course, they have no choice in the matter because of their total nationalization of the means of production. However, the Western countries, when faced with the emergencies of the two world wars, did not hesitate to plan their production and distribution of goods. The underdeveloped countries are all placed in a situation of prolonged emergency because they want to transform their economies radically, rapidly, and in spite of serious handicaps.

One must expect that the government will play a crucial role in the process of development and will control the national economy. State-owned and privately owned enterprises will probably co-exist in the non-Communist countries as they did in Japan during the Meiji period. The government will be expected to formulate tariff policies attuned to economic development. Free trade, as proved by the experience of the Common Market, is a healthy stimulus if it takes place among equals, i.e., among the developed nations. It would kill nascent industries in the bud, as the Western countries knew only too well at the time of their industrialization, which was protected by high tariffs. But the need to protect the domestic market by tariffs and other restrictions against competitive foreign imports can be illustrated also by the experience of underdeveloped countries. The Egyptian textile output amounted in 1930 to only 3 per cent of domestic consumption. After the introduction of a protective tariff in 1930, domestic production rose dramatically and in 1950 reached a level equal to 90 per cent of domestic consumption. India had imported British textiles until the tariff was enacted at the close of the First World War. By 1950 it was able not only to satisfy its domestic demand but to become the leading textile exporter in the world. Protective tariffs might have another beneficial effect. If the prospects are good for the expansion of the domestic market and if the foreign investor is not frightened away by the threat of nationalization or arbitrary treatment, foreign capital might bypass the import restrictions and found factories within the protected area. Several industries were built by foreign investors in Canada, Australia, and South Africa to circumvent protective tariffs. The same reason has prompted American capital to build factories in Britain and in the countries of the Common Market.

Unnecessary imports will have to be curtailed by tariffs, quotas, and outright prohibitions. The precious fund of foreign currencies, indispensable for the purchase of capital equipment, will have to be protected also against the flight abroad of domestic capital.

The government will have to shoulder the heavy burden of erecting the social-economic substructure—building roads, railroads, and harbors, establishing telecommunications, reclaiming land, developing sources of energy, and building hospitals and schools. It will also have to define the terms of co-operation with foreign private capital and to negotiate with advanced countries the conditions of their economic and technical aid. It will have to step in wherever private initiative proves inadequate and otherwise participate in economic activities such as public utilities or even industrial enterprises.

This need for planning and for constant state intervention indicates a difficulty that will for a time plague the governments of many underdeveloped countries. Planning and implementing a plan requires more than a government composed of well-intentioned and sensible men. The government cannot plan and act in the void; it must be competently advised and its plans competently executed. This calls for a corps of well-trained public administrators who will have to perform some of the functions left to private organizations in the advanced nations. It also requires a large number of specialists beginning with economists and statisticians and ending with veterinaries and land surveyors. But the underdeveloped countries are short of this personnel precisely because they are underdeveloped. Hence the urgent need for foreign technical assistance.

A plan for balanced economic development is the precondition of rational economic aid. To finance a project which has little relation to the growth of the total economy or which could not be operated effectively for want of qualified native personnel is to waste the money which the taxpayer of the advanced country earns with the sweat of his brow. The great expectations raised in the underdeveloped countries by these unco-ordinated projects turn into equally great frustrations when these projects fail, frustrations that can threaten an already precarious political stability. It is in the interest of both the recipient and the assisting government to relate economic aid to a long-term program of development which is founded on a careful calculation of native human and material resources.

The manifest preference of the underdeveloped countries for some sort of mixed economy, for state regulation of economic life combined with the survival of private enterprise, for what they call socialism in their loose terminology, is also due to another cause. Private enterprise usually enjoys a very poor reputation. If it is native, its outlook is that of Western capitalism of a bygone age and its policies aim at a quick profit derived from small sales, high prices, and low wages. This antiquated capitalism contrasts with modern American capitalism, which has long espoused large sales, relatively low prices, and high wages, the worker being considered a prospective consumer.

Foreign corporations suffer from the bad reputation they often earned before the present awakening of the underdeveloped countries. They were protected in the colonial possessions by their own countrymen, the colonial administration; reciprocally, they were one of the pillars of the colonial regime. They often sought a quick profit, paid low wages to the native employees, were reluctant to train the natives for the managerial and engineering jobs, were unwilling to give the local government, if the country were independent, a fair share of profits, and were inclined to support any local government, even if tyrannical, corrupt, and hated by the population, if it were pliable to their wishes. It was not unusual for these corporations to elicit from their own government political and military support for this type of native government. Some of the corporations followed a more enlightened policy, but as usual in human affairs, the bad examples are better remembered than the good ones.

It should be added that the official foreign policy of an advanced country may be incompatible with the activities of some of the corporations of its nationality. Foreign policy can be distorted to the prejudice of the long-term interests of the developed country, not only by the connivance of the government in the illegitimate policies of its corporations operating abroad, but also by private malpractices which the government disapproves of but is unable to stop. The foreign population who witness these malpractices at close range may become incensed against the government concerned regardless of the best intentions of its official policy. The poor foreign record of a corporation which operates both at home and abroad may easily escape the attention of its countrymen. The corporation may, like Janus, have two faces. Its domestic policies may be enlightened because it operates at home under many restraints, including public opinion; but its policies in the underdeveloped country may be ruthless and exploitative because the same restraints are absent if the foreign government is pliable and corrupt.

In a number of countries of Southeast Asia private enterprises are largely in foreign hands, not only Western corporations but also alien small businesses, whether Chinese or Indian. This circumstance does not make private enterprise more attractive to the local population.

INVESTMENT CAPITAL FORMATION AND ITS DOMESTIC SOURCES

Judging from the history of the present advanced countries, the successive stages of economic development should follow the following sequence:

1. The stage of initial economic stagnation. National income is principally derived from agriculture and the extractive industries. The rate of annual investment is 5 per cent or less of national income and is patently insufficient for economic progress. Social institutions are obsolete by modern standards. There is a painful shortage of manpower skilled in modern methods of production. Most of the underdeveloped countries are still in this first stage.

2. The stage of gradual development. Agriculture and the extractive industries increase their output; 10 or more per cent of national income is being invested in the building of the social-economic substructure and in the founding of new industries; skilled manpower is being trained. Necessarily, this stage will be of long duration.

3. The stage of full economic growth. The society is using its human and natural resources to the extent permitted by modern technology. This stage presupposes that the country is already endowed with social institutions which fit into the new economic framework, has a skilled manpower, and is able to reinvest between 10 and 20 per cent of its national income to maintain an uninterrupted growth. The nation has become modern; its production is diversified; and industries and services make the greatest contribution to the national income.

4. The last stage, that of the welfare state. The society feels rich enough to distribute bonuses (mostly earned by the toil and sacrifice of former generations who paid for the economic development) in the form of high living standards, social insurance, and universally accessible education. The Western countries have achieved this stage and the Soviet Union is entering it, but the underdeveloped countries, Communist and non-Communist, will probably have to wait for the advent of the twenty-first century before they enjoy the benefits of the welfare state.

At some time toward the end of the second stage, the developing country begins to accumulate enough savings from its expanding national income to be able to dispense with foreign aid. It stands on its own feet.

The present underdeveloped countries face a problem which never complicated the economic development of the West, namely a very high rate of natural increase of the population (see Chapter 6). The Western birth rate was high at the time of industrialization but was kept in check by a relatively high mortality rate, which was only slowly declining, and by mass emigration overseas. Progress in medicine and public sanitation had not preceded their industrialization but was making headway during the process of economic development. Its full effect, a rapid fall in the mortality rate, was felt only after the completion of that process.

The impact of modern medicine has affected the underdeveloped countries at a much earlier stage, at a time when they are still underdeveloped and poor. The mortality rate is declining rapidly as a result of the battle against epidemic and endemic diseases, a battle which yields visible results at a small financial cost. But the birth rate remains very high; hence, the population increases very rapidly.

The problem is not equally serious for all countries. Those areas which are not overpopulated in relation to their untapped resources, such as Latin America and Tropical Africa, can absorb large increases in population if they are able to move forward rapidly enough in their economic development. Others, like China, India, and Pakistan, face a very serious problem not only of fast-increasing overpopulation but also of a possible shortage of food.

The underdeveloped countries are facing a dramatic dilemma. Will their natural increase outstrip the growth of their national income per capita? If so, the growth of national income would be absorbed by the fast-increasing population, and the country would remain in the same poverty as before.

It is usually estimated that the annual natural increase of from 1.5 to 3 per cent (the present rates for the underdeveloped countries) would require the investment of from 10 to 20 per cent of the national income in order to ensure the annual growth of the national income per capita by 2 per cent, i.e., to keep the increase of national income ahead of natural increase. At the present time these countries usually invest only 5 per cent of their national income. But if they made a heroic effort to invest from 10 to 20 per cent and were aided in this effort by significant and constant foreign economic assistance, this high percentage of investment would still conceal the bitter truth that little room remained for improvement in the living conditions.

Natural increase also calls for a fast-growing agricultural output to feed an ever larger population. A developing country, which needs to meet the foreign exchange bill for imported capital equipment, will have few resources left for importing large quantities of food for domestic consumption. It is actually expected to pay for imported capital equipment and indispensable manufactured consumer goods by increased exports of its primary commodities, including foodstuffs. The United States, Canada, and Russia partly financed their industrialization by exports of grain and timber, Sweden did it with timber and iron ore, Japan with silk.

The Asian race between national income and natural increase can be illustrated by the following data established by the United Nations Economic Commission for Asia and the Far East. The rate of annual investment in non-Communist Asia is around 5 per cent of national income; the corresponding figure for the advanced nations is 15 per cent or more. In Asia the annual natural increase averages 2 per cent or more (in some countries it reaches 2.5 or 3 per cent) and makes this 5 per cent increase in the national income hardly sufficient to accommodate population growth, while the per capita income remains stationary or is in danger of declining. If this situation were to continue and if every increase in national income were to be absorbed by natural increase, the future of these underdeveloped countries would be bleak indeed. The developed societies continue to expand their economies rapidly and their prosperity grows steadily; the gap between the two types of countries, the haves and the have-nots, will at the present rate become progressively wider instead of being gradually closed.

The economic implications of rapid natural growth extend beyond the direct relation of this growth to the national income. The proportion of dependents (mainly children) is expanding, while the proportion of the active population is declining. United Nations data indicate that the producing segment of the population represents 55 per cent of the total in the underdeveloped countries and 65 per cent in the developed nations. Moreover, the per capita labor productivity of the active population is notoriously lower in the underdeveloped countries than it is in the advanced countries; yet this less productive active portion of the population must bear the heavy burden of many more dependents.

These data suffice to demonstrate the vital role of foreign economic aid. An underdeveloped country, left to its own resources only, could, of course, further compress its low domestic consumption and extract for investment the required 10 or more per cent from its national income and thus try to keep ahead of natural increase. This is being attempted in China. But it is questionable whether a nontotalitarian government could survive such a harsh operation over several decades. Foreign aid relieves the situation by the transfer of capital from the advanced to the underdeveloped countries.

The issue of economic development, including industrialization, is largely the choice between investment and consumption. This is true of the developed and underdeveloped countries alike, but the choice is harsh for the latter countries where the level of consumption is already very low. Excluding foreign aid, economic development can be financed from the following sources:

1. Since agriculture is the main source of national income, it must make the principal contribution to capital investment, as currently proved by the experience of the Communist countries. The low living standards of the peasants will make this contribution both difficult and unpopular; the

Communist regimes have overcome peasant resistance by collectivizing agriculture and by seizing control over agricultural income. If agricultural output is increased owing, for instance, to improved techniques and if the peasant has a larger income than before, it is far from certain that he will make this surplus available in one form or another for investment in the economic development of the country. He might be reluctant to entrust his savings to state or private banks; he might simply hoard them or use them for other purposes such as increasing family consumption (a great temptation for poor people who have never eaten to their satisfaction), paying off his mortgage, or taking better care of his joint family.

One way to force the peasant to convert his additional income into savings to be used for capital investment would be to step up rural taxation, a measure which cannot be popular with the peasants. They will question the purpose of those policies which had alleviated their lot and had brought about an increase in their income, if this additional income is largely taken away by higher taxes.

2. The upper classes in the underdeveloped countries are usually reluctant to invest in the economic development of their own nation, for instance in industrialization. Their income is partly spent on luxurious living at home or abroad, including the importation of expensive consumer goods. If they save, their savings are invested in real property which traditionally is the favorite form of investment for reasons of prestige and security, in gold and foreign currencies, in short-term commercial speculations, in accounts at foreign banks, or in the stocks of the advanced nations.

However, these classes could frequently make large contributions. The mission of the International Bank for Reconstruction and Development has calculated that, if only 10 per cent of the income of the upper one per cent of income-receivers in Nicaragua were productively invested, the rate of investment would be increased by 50 per cent over the present level. This problem has its political aspect. If the whole population, in particular the peasants, are asked to pay for economic development, as they should be, public discontent can more easily be kept under control by demonstrating that the government seriously taxes the upper classes and thus ensures a more equitable distribution of incomes and hence a more equal exaction of sacrifices.

The government could siphon off a part of the income of the upper classes by taking serious measures against tax evasion, which commonly plagues the underdeveloped countries, and by introducing progressive income and real property taxes; it could promote domestic investment by taking measures against the hoarding of gold and foreign currencies, against investment in foreign countries, and against the purchase of luxurious foreign consumer goods by enacting either high tariffs or outright prohibitions. Land reform, with a low ceiling on the maximum acreage which one family can own, would preclude the traditional investment in land.

These measures cannot be enacted by a government which is the prisoner and spokesman of the upper classes. Yet how often the diplomatic representatives of this type of government eloquently press the advanced countries in the United Nations and elsewhere for an increase in foreign aid while their own social class has not the slightest intention of making their contribution toward a brighter future for their own countrymen.

3. The general population, both urban and rural, could be made to contribute by indirect taxation which reduces consumption and thus increases the available national savings. The sales tax has been the principal means of financing Soviet industrialization; its rates remain very high, often amounting to more than 50 per cent of the retail price of consumer goods. This form of taxation is socially inequitable but is easy to enforce.

4. High interest rates are another way of enticing savings which the state or private banks could use for investment.

5. If prices on the international market permitted it, the production and exportation of primary commodities could be stepped up. Under very favorable circumstances the government could apply pressure to foreign corporations operating extractive industries and ask them to pay higher taxes or to give it a greater share in profits or compel them by currency regulations to reinvest a larger share of their profits in the country. However, measures of this kind have an obvious disadvantage; they have an adverse effect on the future investment of foreign private capital.

This summary survey indicates that the financing of economic development will never be a popular policy with the upper classes, foreign corporations, and the general public, including the peasants. An effective program will always entail a regime of austerity for the simple reason that economic development must be paid for and that its results become clearly profitable only to the third generation at best.

There is another source of investment, the surplus population. The very concept of overpopulation implies that a country does not have enough jobs for its active population and suffers from chronic but concealed unemployment. This unhappy situation can be turned to the advantage of the underdeveloped country if it uses its unemployed as a sort of investment capital for the construction of the economic and social substructure. Unskilled labor can be employed for certain public works such as building canals, dams, roads, schools, planting trees to conserve rainfall, building embankments to prevent soil erosion, digging village wells, and so on. The peasants are available either during the period of forced seasonal idleness or, if they are too numerous for the land at their disposal, even during the seasons of intense agricultural activity.

The advanced countries were compelled to use this method to provide work for their unemployed during the Great Depression. The Soviet Union herded millions of people, usually innocent even by its own standards, into the so-called correctional labor camps in order to have an immense pool of cheap labor for the construction of canals and roads, for felling trees and mining in the unhealthy climate of its far north, and for similar purposes. After it had entered the stage of full economic development, it no longer needed this type of slave labor; the post-Stalinist amnesties released the camp inmates except for the true political or common criminals. The former method became obsolete. A country like the Soviet Union of today, which is developed and suffers from a shortage of manpower, cannot afford to waste its labor force in the camps. The camp inmate never works as efficiently as the free worker who bears the responsibility for the well-being of his family and is spurred to greater productivity by the material incentive of wages.

China, which has only begun to develop, is in a different historical stage. It has mobilized its vast manpower, men and women, and tries to use it to its full working capacity for low compensation, usually amounting to the cost of shelter and subsistence food. The ruthless nature of the totalitarian state enables it to employ its vast manpower under public management and for any work deemed necessary. Very often manpower replaces machinery which is not yet sufficiently available.

A nontotalitarian state would have to use different methods, from a quasimilitary draft to sheer persuasion, but would be well advised to enlist its "superfluous" manpower for constructive purposes. The existence of this manpower carries with it a rather obvious implication that the Western equipment and methods which have been invented as labor-saving devices are economically and socially undesirable in the overpopulated countries.

FOREIGN PRIVATE CAPITAL

Private capital from foreign countries played a great role in the history of Western industrialization. Unfortunately, the prospects for foreign private investment in the development of underdeveloped countries are much less bright today than they were in the nineteenth century. The economic and social substructure cannot be built with the assistance of foreign private investors. Public utilities, such as power stations, transportation, and communications, do not entice private capital, because nowadays the local government is under domestic pressure to control the price of services in which the average consumer is interested. Because they cater to the public at large, public utilities are a tempting target for nationalization. In any event, private corporations cannot undertake on their own huge projects such as multi-purpose river-valley schemes. Finally, private enterprise is not a charitable venture and cannot be expected to build schools and hospitals. The burden of erecting the economic and social substructure falls on the shoulders of the developing state whose Herculean task can be eased only by foreign assistance, i.e., by intergovernmental transfers of public funds.

There are several reasons why both secondary and tertiary industries in the underdeveloped countries may have a very limited appeal for foreign capital. First, the prospective demand is not impressive in an underdeveloped country. Secondly, the process of modernization carries with it the risk of political upheavals and the everpresent threat of nationalization. If an underdeveloped country is not Communist and does not believe in the total nationalization of all the means of production, it may still be tempted to seize foreign assets as a measure of reprisal (the Indonesian seizure of Dutch assets in response to the Dutch refusal to transfer the jurisdiction over West Irian is an example), or as a move toward greater economic independence (the Mexican nationalizations after the revolution of 1910 provide an illustration), or as a part of the general program of economic and social transformation (for instance, the nationalizations in Egypt, which were a part of the "socialist" program, or the nationalization of tin mines in Bolivia). People who are inclined to associate every nationalization with Communism should recall that the Mexican revolutionary government nationalized American assets prior to the Russian October Revolution. It was not the example of a Communist government but the drive to win greater economic independence that inspired the Mexicans to expropriate American assets vested in the important branches of the Mexican economy, notably oil. Nationalization affected foreign holdings in oil, land, and transportation, and legislative restrictions were placed on the ability of foreigners to acquire property of this type.

National self-assertion in the underdeveloped countries has made the atmosphere more propitious for the state seizure of foreign assets than it was prior to 1914. Foreign capital which operates extractive industries or plantations, both oriented toward the export market, may appear to the nationalist natives to be engaged in shipping abroad the natural wealth of the country and may become the target of xenophobic propaganda. The foreigners employed by that capital in managerial and engineering capacities receive much higher salaries than those of the native middle class, arouse envy, and intensify nationalist resentment. In many underdeveloped countries the modern middle class is practically nonexistent, but the foreign exploitation of extractive industries and plantations is managed by people who belong to the foreign middle class. These people either reside near the site of the industrial or agricultural operations or control these operations from their own country. The rank-and-file workers are natives. Xenophobia is then grafted onto class conflict between the foreign middle class ("bourgeoisie") and the native working class. Also, the fear is always present that foreign capital might succumb to the temptation to interfere in the domestic politics and influence the foreign policy of the country. Whatever might be the reasons for the nationalization of foreign assets in each particular case, compensation might be refused altogether or paid in inconvertible local currency or in governmental bonds of uncertain future value or estimated at a fraction of the real value of the property. Foreign assets might not be threatened by outright expropriation but be seriously affected by other measures such as unexpected legislative enactments which modify the conditions of exploitation. Local taxation might be made to discriminate against foreign enterprises; foreign corporations might be compelled to employ a certain number of natives, even if they are not properly qualified, in responsible positions; they might be asked to accept the participation of local capital and to give it a controlling vote regardless of its actual share in the total assets of the corporation; they may not be allowed to repatriate their profits or a major part of them.

Thirdly, the investment of private capital in many underdeveloped countries may be unprofitable for reasons other than the size of the market. The sources of necessary supplies and equipment are located at a great distance, usually in the undeveloped countries; this increases the cost of production. The local workers are paid much lower wages than Western workers, but they are less skilled and less productive at least during a long initial period; in consequence, they might be on balance more costly than Western workers. Managerial and engineering personnel and frequently certain categories of highly skilled workers cannot be recruited locally for lack of suitable candidates; if imported from the West, these employees expect higher salaries and wages than they receive in their own countries as a compensation for life in a foreign and much less comfortable environment. The shortcomings of the local economic-social substructure demand certain investments which are not necessary in a developed country. A private enterprise is expected to provide its personnel with housing, medical assistance, schools, and other welfare facilities; it might be forced by circumstances to build its own means of transportation and its own power station. All these problems, unknown in the advanced countries, increase the cost of production and may frighten away a prospective investor unless they are counterbalanced by the prospect of unusually high profits which only exports to the international market can offer. This is the reason why private investment is attracted to the plantations, mines, and oil fields which produce for export.

Finally, the developed countries of North America and Western Europe offer excellent prospects for private investment without the risks current in the underdeveloped countries.

American investments in 1961 were distributed as follows: Western Europe, 1.5 billion dollars; Latin America, 500 million; other underdeveloped countries, one billion. These figures include reinvested profits and must be compared with the income realized in the same year from former investments. This income was 520 million for Western Europe, 770 million for Latin America, and 1.5 billion for other underdeveloped countries. In other words, the net transfer of new capital took place only for the benefit of Western Europe. Canada was another beneficiary, with a billion investment in 1961.

Foreign capital comes to the underdeveloped countries only if the prospect of large profits, which can be extracted within a reasonably limited period of time, counterbalances all the risks. Profits made by American private business at home and abroad, according to a study made in 1951 for the United States Senate, are shown in Table 6.

TABLE 6

PROFITS FOR U. S. PRIVATE BUSINESS AT HOME AND ABROAD (1951)

Industry	Foreign Investment	Domestic Investment
Agriculture	21.8%	9.1%
Mining and smelting	16.7%	6.4%
Petroleum	24.2%	11.5%
Manufacturing	16.0%	10.4%
Public Utilities	3.0%	5.4%
Trade	16.2%	8.3%
Other	12.9%	9.6%

The margin of profit for the plantations, mines, and oil fields is so wide that it entices private investment by promising that a rather short period of operation will return the invested capital and supply large profits. Other investments are much less attractive, and public utilities offer no inducement.

The underdeveloped countries have an obvious interest in foreign private investment. Every penny which comes from abroad alleviates the problem of financing domestic development. Foreign investment enlarges the fund of disponible foreign currencies, increases the royalties and taxes paid to the local government, gives employment to local manpower, and brings with it technological know-how. The flow of foreign capital should be stimulated by the underdeveloped countries, which cannot eat their cake and have it, cannot clamor for foreign capital and threaten it with nationalization and arbitrary measures. The advanced nations could also help by enacting legislation which would protect their corporations operating abroad against double taxation and against certain extraordinary risks such as nationalization.

WESTERN INTEREST IN THE UNDERDEVELOPED COUNTRIES

It would be dishonest to pretend that the intense and growing Western interest in the economic development of the poor countries is due only or mainly to humanitarian considerations. This interest did not exist as recently as prior to the Second World War. Yet the underdeveloped countries were as poor as they are now, and their populations suffered from the same ills of economic backwardness. The last war and subsequent events brought about a basic change in the Western attitude. Indifference gave way to a great debate and to programs of assistance. The national self-assertion of the underdeveloped countries did not emerge fully until after the Second World War. The Western colonial retreat deprived the West of its decisive influence on the political life of former colonial territories. The economic dependence of the West on imported primary commodities is as great as ever, but access to the sources of these commodities can no longer be taken for granted. The surprisingly rapid rise in Soviet strength and the postwar appearance of a whole Communist bloc, whose realm extends to one-third of mankind, have faced the West with a powerful competitor. This rival bloc made it clear in the fifties that it intended to wage its main battles in the underdeveloped areas in order, as Soviet commentators never tire of saying, to "isolate" the West and to cut it off from the sources of primary commodities.

Placed under twofold pressure from the Communist rival and from the underdeveloped countries themselves, the West is forced by the international constellation to take a stand on the problem of modernization or suffer a major if not decisive defeat. The choice is not between indifference or action but between the various forms of action.

The Western countries possess no magic formula for modernizing the underdeveloped majority of mankind. Many developments escape Western control. The main burden cannot be shifted from the shoulders of the underdeveloped countries themselves. They must define their goals and set the pace of change; they must do the work and save; they must be willing to adopt the modern outlook. It is their perseverance that will decide the issue. Their failure would nullify the effects of the wisest and most generous Western assistance.

It is only sensible to assume that the process of modernization will take several decades. The most misleading analogy for the problem of Western aid is the Marshall Plan, which helped Europe in its postwar rehabilitation. The underdeveloped countries cannot be rehabilitated since they have never been prosperous and modern. The problem is not that of rebuilding a war-damaged modern economy but the much more difficult problem of creating a modern economy and society. This is a time-consuming task. It cannot be safely assumed that each population will patiently toil and be willing to give their government as much time as it needs. The local governing elites may be living on time that is borrowed from popular impatience, an impatience which originates in rising expectations. The truly dangerous time is less that of stagnation than that of modernization, which brings in its wake not only economic development but also exorbitant hopes and the breaking down of old patterns of life.

Western public opinion should be prepared in advance for, and not discouraged by, the battles which might be lost here and there in spite of a helpful Western policy. The issue in this protracted struggle for the future of the underdeveloped two-thirds of mankind is whether the West should fight it out in spite of disappointments and failures or capitulate in advance and accept by implication that a vast majority of mankind may one day be united against it.

Generally speaking, the West must be psychologically ready to live for an unforeseeably long period in an environment that is both unstable and full of risks. Neither nuclear danger nor nationalist unrest will suddenly disappear; the stiff political competition with the Communist bloc will not be suddenly terminated by a summit conference, and the revolution of modernization will not proceed smoothly and without unpleasant surprises. "Normalcy," as understood in the nineteenth century, does not belong to our time.

The surprises may come for various reasons, all of them beyond Western control. The government in one underdeveloped country may be the prisoner or spokesman of conservative vested interests and may do nothing for the future of its poor masses. In another underdeveloped country the government may be well-intentioned but inefficient or understaffed. Even if efficient and showing actual progress, it may be overturned by the irresponsible intrigues of rival politicians or by a popular upheaval due to frustrated hopes for a quick improvement in living conditions. The program of development may be jeopardized or slowed down by an insufficient accumulation of investment capital from domestic sources, by a sudden fall in the prices or the volume of exports, by errors in planning, by the political need to allocate for consumption more than was originally planned, or by an unexpected delay in producing trained manpower. The local governments have the ungrateful task of convincing their countrymen that social transformation is the necessary condition of economic progress, that economic development must be bought at the price of savings diverted from consumption, and that the benefits will be fully enjoyed only by future generations. This is not a mission that makes any government very popular.

The local Communists will never relax. They will complicate the task of the government because they think of themselves as the next or the next-but-one government. Their true responsibilities will begin on the day they seize power. In the meantime, they can outbid all political opponents in the use of irresponsible propaganda. Their arsenal is full of arguments always related to existing issues: they can promote the cause of one national group against another within the same state; they always incite their countrymen against Western private capital and call for its nationalization irrespective of the consequences; they clamor against Western governmental assistance as a disguised imperialist venture; they masquerade as the most vociferous nationalists, but their scapegoat is always the same, the West; they promote discontent among the peasants, the workers, and the underemployed intelligentsia, and organize them for future action; they support industrial strikes and ask for modern social insurance and labor legislation which a developing but poor country cannot afford. They never clamor in the void, because an underdeveloped country is the breeding ground of social grievances. Their opponents might be unable to form a common front in self-defense because of their own quarrels. The Communists usually capitalize on public impatience by pointing to the Soviet record of economic successes, which they unduly inflate by never mentioning two facts: that in 1917 Soviet Russia was a semideveloped country with an industrial base and a skilled urban manpower, and that it was favored by a great wealth of natural resources. They also fail to mention the cost of Soviet industrialization in human toil, tears, and lives.

The underdeveloped areas of Asia, the Near East, Africa, and Latin America are vitally important to the West for several reasons. They represent crucial strategic positions, prospectively a huge market for the Western industrial output, a storehouse of primary commodities, and potentially, if economically developed, a tremendous international power. Their wealth of natural resources is much greater than their known deposits; none of them have been geologically surveyed as carefully as the advanced countries, and some have never been surveyed. The Western countries import from the underdeveloped countries twenty times as much as the Communist bloc. This is a Western weakness and also its strength; weakness because it reflects the dependence of Western economies on external supplies, but also a great strength because it makes the West important to the economies of the underdeveloped countries. The other strength of the West is its production, which is more than twice the output of the Communist bloc; hence the Western capacity for economic assistance. Economically the West and the underdeveloped countries need each other.

The advanced countries could adjust their economies to the loss of a part of the vast underdeveloped area, as they did during the Second World War, but could hardly survive if access to the whole area were barred by unfavorable political developments. It is true that a limited shortage of raw materials can be met with perfected technological processes and a greater expenditure of energy, that substitutes can be produced (plastics, for instance, can partly replace metals), and that new sources of energy can be provided. Existing low-grade ores could be mined again with a higher use of energy per unit of output. It is, however, cheaper to import high-grade ores. In due time, atomic and solar energy will be largely substituted for coal and petroleum but not until the commercial cost of the new energy has been lowered. If the cost were of no consequence, the West could shift from crude petroleum to oil shales and to the liquid fuel obtained by hydrogenation from coal. If faced with the eventual depletion of international resources, mankind might turn in the remote future to the extraction of primary commodities from ordinary granite rock and sea water. For the time being, cost considerations make it necessary to rely on the available raw materials, including those which are imported from the underdeveloped countries.

The United States, the first industrial power, annually uses per capita eight tons of steel, eight tons of energy measured in coal, and over twenty tons of raw materials. The industrial growth of this or other countries entails an annual increase in the per capita consumption of these commodities. The United States consumes almost half the output of raw materials in the non-Communist world. The growth of the American economy and the depletion of domestic resources call for an increasing importation of foreign raw materials, such as iron ore from Venezuela, Labrador, and Liberia, petroleum from Latin America, copper from Chile and Peru, and bauxite from Jamaica. Seventy-five per cent of stockpiled strategic raw materials has come from the various underdeveloped countries.

Except for natural rubber, tin, and manganese, the United States does not depend much on Asian supplies. Asian supplies could be replaced by imports from Latin America and Africa and by substitutes such as synthetic rubber. Also, American private investments are small in Asia except for Near Eastern oil. But Asia in full economic development could become an export market for American capital goods. Africa looms larger on the American horizon because of its deposits of uranium and nonferrous metals.

The economic dependence of Western Europe on raw materials imported from the underdeveloped countries is incomparably greater. The European Community of Six is the largest importer of primary commodities in the world. Near Eastern and North African (the Algerian Sahara and Libya) oil is indispensable for Western Europe. The expected growth in the oil requirements of the Western Hemisphere makes it improbable that Latin American oil could significantly relieve this Western European dependence on Near Eastern and North African oil. Western Europe imports tin, rubber, iron ore, manganese, copper, and other metals, coffee, cacao, vegetable oil, and other items from Asia and Africa. This Western European dependence on imports from other continents is indirectly of concern to the United States as long as the fate of Europe is considered vital for American survival.

The two cases of Britain and Japan, both allies of the United States, dramatically illustrate the problem. Well over half of Britain's food is imported, and paid for mainly by industrial exports. It exports from 22 to 23 per cent of its output. Isolated from its present overseas markets and sources of primary commodities, it would collapse economically. Its prosperity is also due to the income derived from the services, such as shipping, insurance, and banking, which it renders to the large sterling area and several other countries; the underdeveloped areas, for instance those producing oil, are also a source of revenue in this respect.

The Japanese situation is even more precarious. The overpopulated islands of Japan are short of both raw materials and foodstuffs. Over 90 million people live in a territory the size of California, and only 16 per cent of this territory is arable land. Japan produces only 20 per cent of its requirements in iron ore, lacks in high-grade coking coal, imports 95 per cent of its requirements in oil, must buy all its wool and cotton abroad, imports 10 per cent of rice consumption, and imports other cereals and foodstuffs. It must rely on its expanding industries to take care of its annual natural increase of 900,000. The future of Japan is tied to its trade with Asia principally, but also with the Near East, Africa, Latin America, and, of course, the United States and Western Europe.

A quick glance at various underdeveloped areas will illustrate their value as storehouses of primary commodities. From the Western European point of view the Near East is an area second in importance to Europe itself. The British Royal Institute of International Affairs maintained in a study published a few years ago that: "Indeed, the crucial role of oil in all modern industry may well be argued to have now made the Middle East an area almost as vital to Western survival as Western Europe itself." Western Europe, including Britain, derives 75 per cent of its oil supplies from the Near East where the estimated oil reserves amount to 70 per cent of the known reserves of the world. Near Eastern oil is shipped also to Asia, Oceania, and East Africa, while exports from the Caribbean area tend to be absorbed by the Western Hemisphere, in particular by the United States, and by West Africa. Western European dependence on Near Eastern oil could be somewhat reduced by the output of the newly discovered oil fields in the Sahara and in Libya and in a more remote future by the full exploitation of atomic energy. However, this dependence is so great at the present time that a sudden denial of Near Eastern oil would throw the Western European economy out of gear; actually the crisis in the fall of 1956 gave Western Europe a foretaste of a shortage of this type.

Western Europe derives more than petroleum from its exploitation of Near Eastern oil. The extraction and marketing are in the hands of American, British, Dutch, and French companies; it is mainly an American-British business. The profits which these companies share according to a 50-50 formula with the producing countries are calculated on the prices for crude oil, but the profits made on refined oil, which companies sell at a much higher price, are not shared with the local governments. Only 25 per cent of Near Eastern oil is locally refined; the rest is mostly shipped to European refineries. Profits from refining, shipping, and marketing oil remain in Europe or in the United States. The royalties which the British-protected sheikdoms of the Persian Gulf, such as Kuwait ("independent" since 1961), Bahrein, and Qatar, derive from oil are invested in Britain. All these additional benefits, especially important for Britain, would be lost if the West were deprived of its present economic control over Near Eastern oil.

Western Europe depends also on those Near Eastern countries which provide transit for the shipments of oil. Pipelines owned by the oil companies lower the cost of shipping by bringing oil to the Mediterranean ports; they cross Jordan, Syria, and Lebanon. The Suez Canal is an important waterway for oil shipments, but it lies within Egyptian territory. It would be possible to avoid both the pipelines and the Suez Canal by using very large tankers, which would circumnavigate the Cape of Good Hope, but this would increase the cost by adding 5,000 miles of sea route.

One of the paradoxes of the Arab Near East is that this area, so richly provided with oil which it hardly needs for itself, is deprived of any other mineral resources of importance. The other paradox is the uneven distribution of oil resources. The contrast is glaring between Saudi Arabia, Iraq, Kuwait, Bahrein, and Qatar, which receive more than 500 million dollars in oil royalties every year and which have, with the exception of Iraq, hardly any domestic opportunity for investing these royalties, and Egypt, Syria, and Lebanon, which have sizable numbers of trained people and urgently need investment capital for economic development.

The relations between the Near East and Western Europe are characteristic of relations in general between the West and the underdeveloped countries. Western Europe is the main customer, and no other country could replace it which has an equally great need for Near Eastern oil. The West supplies the marketing and other services, equipment, and the managerial and engineering personnel, all indispensable for oil exploitation. It provides the oil-producing countries with a large share of their national budget: 25 per cent for Iraq, 50 per cent for Saudi Arabia, and 75 per cent for the Persian Gulf sheikdoms. Co-operation between the two parties seems to be mutually imperative.

However, in addition to historical and political reasons for anti-Western resentment (see Chapter 4), the oil exploitation itself might be the source of disputes. The oil-producing countries might raise the question of a revision of the 50-50 formula and ask for a share in the profits which would take into account the international price for refined oil. The countries which provide transit for the pipelines might also claim higher royalties. After the nationalization of the Suez Canal, one cannot exclude as impossible the nationalization of oil resources. This would call for a new arrangement similar to that which followed Iranian nationalization; the Western companies would limit themselves to the management of nationalized oil fields. The Near Eastern countries might press for their participation not only in the local managerial-engineering personnel but also on the governing boards of foreign companies, to gain insight into profits made after the shipment of oil abroad.

The West has vital interests other than oil. The Suez Canal is an all-important waterway through which Western Europe trades with Asia and Oceania. Britain alone ships 25 per cent of its exports and imports through the Canal. India, Pakistan, Ceylon, Burma, Indonesia, Malaya, and East Africa use the Canal for their exports to Europe of tea, coffee, rice, rubber, tin, and other products. To take one example, 70 per cent of Indian trade traverses the Canal.

The Near East is also strategically important. Even in our nuclear age, which seems to have made many strategic considerations obsolete, it should not be forgotten that air and missile bases located in the Near East are closer to most Soviet industrial and oil-producing centers (Baku, Donets, the Urals, southern Siberia, and Central Asia) than bases situated in Western Europe. The Near East is a land bridge between the three continents of Europe, Asia, and Africa, a vital hub of world sea and air transportation, and a gateway to Africa and Asia. A hostile power, installed there politically, could deny oil to Western Europe or make it very expensive and would be in an excellent position to extend its influence to Africa and Asia.

The crucial importance of the Near East is best proved by the constant struggle between the great powers for its control. Today, it is not only the arena of competition between the Western powers and the Soviet Union but also the theater of traditional divergencies of views among the Western powers themselves. American direct interests are related to the American share in the oil industry and the American bases. Indirect interests are tied to the global distribution of power between the two rival blocs and to the interests of the NATO allies, particularly Britain. This combination of direct and indirect interests made the United States the principal Near Eastern great power. Its appearance in strength during the last war was followed by the Truman Doctrine, which proclaimed the American interest in Turkey and Greece and resulted in the intervention in Lebanon after the 1958 Iraqi revolution, the presence of the Sixth Fleet in Mediterranean waters, and the building of a ring of bases. The American interest has never declined although the United States is independent of Near Eastern oil supplies.

The Soviet Union is the main competitor of the West and has been very active in the Near East since 1955. At the time of its entry into the Near-Eastern area, which had been the main cockpit of Russian-British rivalries prior to the First World War, it was favored with several advantages. Except for Turkey and Iran, no other country of the area had ever faced Russian imperialism. The Arab grievances were all anti-Western. The Arab nations have territorial quarrels with Britain (the formally independent Kuwait is coveted by Iraq and possibly also by Egypt and Saudi Arabia, which is quarreling with Britain over the oil-bearing Buraimi oasis; Yemen disputes frontiers with the British Aden protectorate; Bahrein is claimed by Iran) and resent the British protectorates over Arab-speaking lands, such as the Aden protectorate, Bahrein, Qatar, Muscat, Oman, and the Trucial Coast. They have not forgiven the West for its sympathy with Israel. The West is the whipping boy of Arab nationalism, but the Soviet Union is the enemy of the West. A coincidence of interests seems to follow logically. The Soviet Union has capitalized on this situation with great adroitness. It did not need to fire a shot to force the gates of the Near East. Political support, military supplies, economic assistance, and its anti-Israeli stand endeared the Soviet Union to Egypt and Iraq. It won political friends on both sides of the Suez Canal. However, the Soviet Union has also discovered since 1955 that any great power is faced in the Arab Near East with two difficulties: sensitive Arab nationalism suspicious of any foreign interference, and the constant need to maneuver between the shoals of inter-Arab rivalries. Both Iraq and Egypt look with suspicion upon Soviet sympathy with local Communists, and these two countries are not friendly with each other.

The loss of its Asian empires has forced Western Europe since the last war to take a lively interest in African resources. The interests of the two parties are not mutually exclusive. Europe needs African primary commodities, but it can offer Africa economic and technical assistance for its balanced economic growth. The true problem is not whether they should co-operate but on what terms. These terms depend not only on developments in Africa but also on the future of the Common Market and its extension to other countries, Britain in the first place. It is possible that the two continents will engage in an organic economic co-operation for their mutual benefit. The resources of Africa in raw materials are not yet sufficiently surveyed; but pessimistic views were rebuked by the unexpected French discovery of oil, natural gas, and mineral deposits in the Sahara. The known reserves in Africa are large and include iron ore, copper (Northern Rhodesia and the Congo), bauxite, molybdenum, tin, manganese, phosphates, industrial diamonds, columbite, berillium, chromium, gold, uranium, asbestos, graphite, lead, zinc, vanadium, nickel, lithium, platinum, and oil. As an actual producer, Africa accounts for practically the whole world supply of industrial diamonds, 94 per cent of columbite, 84 per cent of cobalt (both indispensable for making heat-resistant steel), 70 per cent of vanadium, 41 per cent of berillium, 33 per cent of manganese, 29 per cent of chromium, 21 per cent of copper, 13 per cent of tin, and 50 per cent of gold. It also exports palm oil, sisal, cocoa, peanuts, cotton, and coffee.

Southeast Asia is another important area although its loss in the Second World War did not prevent the Allied victory. It lies across the main sea and air routes between the Pacific and Indian oceans with communication centers such as Singapore, Bangkok, Saigon, and Manila. The loss of the area would seriously complicate the Western defense of Japan, the Indian subcontinent, Australia, and New Zealand. The bipolar image of the world causes many people to view international problems exclusively in terms of the Western-Soviet competition. A look at Southeast Asia reveals that not all international issues can be confined to this bipolar framework. A conflict of vital interests between China, Japan, and India would come into the open if the West were to withdraw from that part of Asia. The stakes are high for these three Asian great powers. China, India, and Japan are rice importers and will have to increase their imports to take care of the needs of their fast-increasing populations. Burma, Thailand, and Indochina are the rice basket of Asia. Ninety per cent of natural rubber enters the international trade from this area; Malaya, North Borneo, and Indonesia are the main producers. Malaya, Indonesia, and Thailand are among the principal world exporters of tin. These three countries and Burma export tungsten. The oil production of Brunei, Borneo, and Indonesia is not without significance for the Asian countries. All three Asian great powers are interested in these and other primary commodities produced in Southeast Asia. Each would greatly strengthen its power by gaining political control of the area, and no local state could offer effective resistance. The two remaining powers would be threatened if one of the three succeeded in conquering Southeast Asia. While India has a vital interest in preventing this area from falling into unfriendly hands (for the time being it is the West that takes care of this interest), no one could stop the combined drive of China and a Communist India. Only Indonesia and other island territories of Southeast Asia could benefit from the protection of Western naval and air forces. A Communist India would probably also determine the nature of the regime in Pakistan, Afghanistan, and Ceylon.

Latin America is another area vital to the future of the Western advanced countries, particularly the United States. Militarily it is less accessible to the Communist bloc than Asia and the Near East, but politically it may be equally vulnerable, as evidenced by developments in Cuba. The close economic links between the Latin part of the Western Hemisphere and the West are reflected in their mutual trade. Trade with the United States, Canada, Western Europe, and the sterling area amount to approximately 90 per cent of the total Latin American trade. Latin America supplies 70 per cent of the world's exports of coffee, two-thirds of bananas, one-third of cane sugar, one-third of cacao, one half of meat, large quantities of wool, cotton, skins and hides, timber, and tobacco. However, its main economic significance for the developed economies lies in its output and exports of oil and such raw materials as iron ore and nonferrous metals. Its reserves, larger than those of the United States, are estimated in the following fractions of the world's reserves: one-third of copper and iron ore deposits, one-tenth of oil, tin, zinc, and lead, more than one-sixth of nickel and manganese, and two-fifths of bauxite. The Latin American share in the output of raw materials of the non-Communist world is impressive; in 1957, 22.5 per cent of oil, 11.2 per cent of iron ore, 55.6 per cent of bauxite, 20 per cent of lead, 20.3 per cent of copper, 16.4 per cent of zinc, 17.9 of manganese, 20 per cent of tin, 25 per cent of antimony, 42 per cent of silver, and 33 per cent of vanadium. The Latin American share in the foreign imports of raw materials into the United States is no less impressive: 97 per cent of all imported antimony, 70 per cent of copper, 52 per cent of tin, 62 per cent of zinc, 47 per cent of iron ore, and 83 per cent of oil. These imports give the United States a greater economic independence from the Eastern Hemisphere. Another advantage of the Latin American sources of raw materials is that the extraction is mostly controlled by United States corporations, which partly reinvest their profits but partly repatriate them. The American corporations control the following percentages of output: 81.8 per cent of iron ore, 94.4 per cent of manganese, 100 per cent of chromium, 58.7 per cent of wolfram, 100 per cent of nickel, 100 per cent of molybdenum, 91.2 per cent of copper, 92.9 per cent of lead, 90.8 per cent of zinc, 92.1 per cent of vanadium, 31.5 per cent of antinomy, and 98 per cent of mercury. In 1958 United States private investment in Latin America was over 11 billion dollars, half of it in the extractive industries.

Latin American underdevelopment can be measured by contrasting its impressive output of raw materials with only 3.5 million tons of steel produced in 1957 for a population of 170 million people.

The significance of Latin America for the United States is also related to the Panama Canal and generally the Caribbean area. The Panama Canal has an importance for the United States comparable to that of the Suez Canal for Europe. The Caribbean Sea is the nerve center for vital transportation of oil, iron ore, and nonferrous metals. The same area is covered with a network of United States naval and air bases which extend from Puerto Rico and Guantanamo (Cuba) to Trinidad, Jamaica, Bahamas, Bermuda, British Guiana, and the Panama Canal Zone. Militarily, northeastern Brazil, the part of the Western Hemisphere which is closest to Africa and Europe, has an obvious strategic significance.

WESTERN POLICIES AND NONCOMMITMENT

The Western nations have the power to influence developments in the underdeveloped countries, and they can use this power in the following ways:

1. In their foreign policy they should never tire of seeking a reconciliation of national interests. The process is not always easy but should be facilitated by the coincidence of long-term interests. Both the West and the non-Communist elites in the underdeveloped countries share the objective of carrying out modernization without the replacement of these elites by the local Communists. This overriding consideration should encourage both sides to search for compromise solutions of current disputes.

2. The lowering of barriers against imports from the underdeveloped countries—against their textiles, for example—and a serious attempt to stabilize the prices for primary commodities would be as important as economic assistance as a means of enabling the underdeveloped countries to earn foreign exchange and buy capital equipment.

3. Economic aid, i.e., the periodic transfer of public capital from the developed to the underdeveloped countries, aims at making the period of development shorter and less painful. This aid should be accepted by the West as a long-term partnership in a carefully planned venture of importance to both parties.

4. Technical aid, which is relatively inexpensive, consists in offering expert advice on matters of modernization and in training native skilled manpower. This training can be effected either by Western missions sent to the underdeveloped countries or by Western universities and other schools at which students from these countries are enrolled. This assistance should never aim at a wholesale transfer of Western institutions, which have developed under entirely different historical conditions, but at a selection of those institutions which are indispensable to the functioning of a modern society and at their adaptation to local circumstances.

5. Military aid might also be necessary if a non-Communist government is threatened with Communist external aggression or with a Communist (not just leftist) domestic coup.

What is needed in the first place is a psychological adjustment to the post-colonial era. Paternalism, notions of racial superiority, national ethnocentrism, and the "white man's burden" are out of place. The fact that the underdeveloped countries intend to remain politically independent in the full sense, that they aspire to becoming more independent economically, and that they dislike being treated as mere pawns on an international chessboard, must be accepted with good grace. One should also try to understand their view of the global distribution of power. For them, the mutual neutralization of the two rival blocs is a welcome phenomenon; it is the foundation of their power, a vicarious power which would be threatened by a sudden and serious weakening of either bloc.

Because the two blocs neutralize each other, the underdeveloped countries have a choice of policies. They can commit themselves to either bloc or remain uncommitted. If one were to commit itself to the opposite bloc, the West would have no choice but to include it among its enemies. However, a torrent of anti-Western verbiage should not be confused with an actual commitment to the Communist bloc. It is only prudent never to consider that any commitment is irrevocable and that an enemy must remain an enemy forever.

If a country wants to commit itself to the West, the Western power or powers should carefully weigh three considerations:

1. What particular asset (a strategic location, a place for advanced military bases, a reliable army though deficient in modern equipment, a source of vital raw materials) the underdeveloped country is able to offer in compensation for the Western commitment to defend it against external aggression. This consideration is important because a local commitment always carries with it the risk of a general war, and this risk should not be assumed without good reason.

2. Whether a military alliance concluded with one country in an area will upset the local distribution of power and cause bitter resentment on the part of other nations located in the same region. If this is the case, the West should consider whether the acquisition of a new ally is worth the deterioration of relations with these other countries. The inclusion of Iraq and Pakistan in the Baghdad Pact and of Pakistan in SEATO was paid for by the deterioration of Western relations with Egypt, Afghanistan, and India. From the point of view of other countries in the area the Western military commitment to their neighbor and possible rival entails arming that neighbor and giving him diplomatic support. This either weakens the position of these other states within the context of the local distribution of power or compels them to spend more money on armaments, money which they badly need for other purposes.

3. Whether the West will be able and willing to honor its military commitment in a distant area in spite of the nuclear risks of our time. It would be equally unwise to fail in the hour of danger to honor the promise of defending a country and thus to undercut Western prestige in the world as it would be to enter into commitments which could be carried out only at the risk of a general nuclear war. This aspect of the problem is important in view of the difficult logistic problems which are involved in a peripheral war, necessarily an overseas operation for the Western nations.

The same argument applies even more to the overseas commitments of the Soviet Union. The Soviet naval forces are much weaker than those of the West. However, the Soviet government rather imprudently entered on May 23, 1963, into its first overseas commitment. The Soviet and Cuban governments agreed in their joint communiqué of that date that in case of an invasion of Cuba by the United States the Soviet Union "shall provide it [the Cuban people] the assistance necessary for the defense of liberty and independence of the Cuban Republic by all the means in the possession of the Soviet Union." If this guarantee is seriously offered, if it is more than "nuclear blackmail," an American invasion of Cuba would place the Soviet Union before a terrible dilemma: either to use strategic nuclear weapons on the United States with the certain expectation of becoming the object of American nuclear retaliation (probably the last thing that the Soviet government wants), or to face a naval defeat, or to renege on its solemn promise and do nothing effective to protect the Cuban regime.

Judging from the present trend of events, noncommitment is the most probable choice of an underdeveloped country. It has been proved that the West cannot prevent this choice. Moreover, it rarely would have an interest in doing so. Noncommitment would not prevent the West from aiding an uncommitted country if the latter were attacked by a Communist power directly or by proxy. In time of peace the West is likely to lose a few advantages, such as the location of a military base, but the loss is rarely of crucial importance. Moreover, noncommitment has two facets; the uncommitted nation reserves its freedom to make future decisions, but so does the West which is then under no obligation to assume the risks of defending an uncommited nation in an emergency. The Soviet Union accepts noncommitment as a legitimate policy (it rejects it for the members of its own bloc, as demonstrated by its reaction to the Hungarian proclamation of neutrality in 1956). Therefore the West has little choice in the matter.

The policy of noncommitment (also called political neutralism or nonalignment) is not new, but our age has given it a new lustre. Whenever any two states are not bound together by a treaty of alliance, they remain uncommitted, i.e., they are free to formulate their policies regarding the issues to which either of them and a third state are parties, in any way which seems most prudent from the point of view of their national interests. The European great powers were mutually uncommitted for the better part of the nineteenth century. The United States remained formally uncommitted from the denunciation of the French alliance (1798)[1] to the conclusion of the North Atlantic Treaty (1949). Three small countries (Switzerland, Belgium, and Luxemburg) were not only uncommitted but were actually obligated by international treaties to observe permanent neutrality in peace and war. Nonalignment was the normal foreign policy between 1815 and the rise of alliances in the last decades of the nineteenth century. The present attention paid to nonalignment is due not to its novelty but to the commitment of the great powers to either of the two rival blocs. Hence, the choice of a smaller nation in favor of noncommitment makes the news.

The reasons for adopting a policy of nonalignment vary from country to country but can be generally stated as follows:

1. The nuclear age has increased beyond measure the risks of a military alliance, especially for countries with a small territory and a small population. The minor ally of a nuclear power can never be completely sure that the massive deterrent will be used in his defense at the risk of exposing the territory of the major ally to nuclear retaliation. It is also uncertain whether the major ally would be able to rescue his minor and perhaps distant ally by using only non-nuclear means.

2. All the underdeveloped countries face the major problem of modernization, which requires the utmost concentration of national energy. Most of them are also confronted with the difficult question of national integration. These two problems loom so large that they usually prefer to be left alone by the great powers and not to multiply their difficulties by being dragged into the vortex of competition between the two hostile blocs.

3. They know that the same competition provides them with a vicarious national power which allows them to charter an independent course of policy. In a dispute with the West, they can count on Soviet

[1] The French alliance, formally denounced in 1798, was in fact terminated in 1793 by the American proclamation of neutrality.

political and sometimes economic support; in a dispute with the Communist powers, they can expect Western support.

4. They need economic assistance from all quarters, and they welcome every new avenue for the export of their primary commodities. Noncommitment opens the door to Communist aid without closing the door to Western aid. It may, in fact, promote competition between the two blocs, the uncommited country being the beneficiary.

5. Their main preoccupation is the regional distribution of power, while commitment to either of the two blocs is a matter of the global distribution of power. This global distribution of power between the two blocs does not concern them so long as they feel that some balance is maintained. Moreover, the underdeveloped countries, with very few exceptions, have never had any bitter experience with the Communist bloc and are unable to understand Western anxieties in this respect.

Of course, the motivations are not the same in every case. If the developed but uncommitted nations are included in this survey, the variety of motivations can be seen even more clearly. Sweden pursues a neutralist policy because its neutrality has preserved it since 1815 from the risks of war and because it is one of the conditions of Soviet respect for Finnish independence. In 1955 Austria chose the status of permanent neutrality in order to get rid of foreign troops and to recover full independence. Switzerland acquired the status of permanent neutrality in 1814-15 and twice escaped the danger of being involved in world wars. Yugoslavia, dangerously located on the borders of the Soviet bloc and at odds with the Western ideology, has different reasons from the other European countries for remaining politically uncommitted; its motivations are also different from those of Ceylon, geographically remote from the stage of great-power politics.

Because the national interests of uncommitted countries are not identical, policies of noncommitment differ. These policies shade from the United Arab Republic's tendency to favor the Soviet Union, through the unimpeachable neutrality of Switzerland, which officially avoids expressing opinions on controversial international issues, to Sweden's traditional orientation toward the West.

The Indian policy has demonstrated the advantages of nonalignment. India, unlike Pakistan, firmly refused to participate in the Western system of alliances. Nevertheless, it received a big share of Western economic assistance, notably from the United States. It also received military supplies from both Great Britain and the United States. Yet its nonalignment allowed India to establish friendly relations with the Soviet Union and the East European Communist states and to benefit from their economic assistance. India was winning on both cards. Moreover, it enjoyed high prestige among the other uncommitted nations.

Two aspects of its foreign policy, which were not necessary ingredients of noncommitment, were unwise. One was an almost unlimited trust in verbal assurances of friendship from the Communist Chinese; verbal promises by any nation should not be taken for a final statement of future policies. The other was a propensity to moralize and to criticize the West, especially the United States, in a show of independence of the main source of economic assistance. It was fortunate for India that these verbal aspersions were never taken very seriously by the United States.

After the Chinese attack, India did not need to beg for military support from the United States and Britain. Their self-interest advised the Western powers not to delay the shipment of military supplies. If India had had an alliance with the West, the result would not have been different. The benefits of nonalignment in peacetime and in the hour of danger were clearly demonstrated.

The fact that uncommitted governments often play one bloc against the other is part of the game and should be accepted philosophically. The economic and technical assistance which the Communist bloc extends to an uncommitted nation is also a part of the game. If it does not create an imbalanced dependence on the rival bloc, this aid should be welcomed rather than resented. Every bit of assistance given to a non-Communist regime, whatever its source, fortifies it and helps it to solve its domestic problems.

Also, the torrents of anti-Western eloquence which are fashionable in the domestic politics of the underdeveloped countries should be calmly withstood. These countries cannot be expected to forget the colonialist era in a few years or to shed easily suspicions which are the product of many years of exploitation by the West. Most of them need the image of "Western imperialism" for domestic reasons, namely to divert popular attention from the great difficulties inherent in the process of modernization and to mobilize national energy for the tasks ahead. This verbal abuse, which is not accompanied by a definitely hostile policy, does not affect the distribution of power between the two blocs.

FOREIGN AID

Economic assistance consists in the transfer of capital through public channels (intergovernmental arrangements or international agencies) from the developed to the underdeveloped countries. The Western capacity for aid and the needs of the non-Communist underdeveloped countries can best be measured by the fact that the Western nations produce a national income more than five times greater than that of underdeveloped countries.

The political question of whether it is necessary to transfer a portion of the national income of the developed nations to the underdeveloped nations is somewhat rhetorical; anti-Western policies of the Communist bloc leave practically no alternative. The next question is whether the Western governments should concentrate their assistance on certain areas which are deemed most important from the Western point of view rather than run the risk of doing too little for all the underdeveloped countries. The difficulty consists in selecting the areas which are considered most crucial to the West. If the Indian process of development were to end in failure (Indian success or failure will be mostly measured by the Chinese achievements) and if the next government of this second largest country in the world were Communist, not only would the global distribution of power be markedly tilted against the West but the other Asian countries would probably follow suit and adopt the Communist method of modernization. The loss of Southeast Asia would strategically endanger the positions of Japan, India, Australia, and New Zealand. The Near East is vital to the Western European economies. Africa and Latin America are the source of raw materials of increasing importance for the West. There is no choice but to wage the battle for economic development on the whole front.

However, in determining which countries should be assisted and how the assistance should be given, three questions should be answered. First, has the assisting state any political interest, immediate or long-term, in providing aid to a particular country? Second, if it has, what are the chances that the assisted regime will survive and not be replaced by another regime which would be hostile to the assisting state? Third, what is the absorptive capacity of the recipient country? This capacity is conditioned on the present level of development, not only economic but also social, including the quantity and quality of skilled personnel. If the absorptive capacity is low, technical assistance should have priority, since it helps the assisted country to raise its absorptive capacity.

The concept of economic and technical aid would have eventually emerged after the last war because of the political emancipation of the underdeveloped countries and the fierce competition between the two blocs. Nevertheless, the honor of the initiative belongs to the United States. It was President Truman who formulated the famous Point Four in his inaugural address of January 20, 1949. The ideas he expressed there have since become the landmarks of international life:

> We must embark on a bold new program for making the benefits of our scientific advances and industrial progress available for the improvement and growth of underdeveloped areas. . . . I believe that we should make available to peace-loving peoples the benefits of our store of technical knowledge in order to help them realize their aspirations for a better life. And, in co-operation with other nations, we should foster capital investment in areas needing development. . . . We invite other countries to pool their technological resources in this undertaking. Their contributions will be warmly welcomed. This

should be a co-operative enterprise in which all nations work together through the United Nations and its specialized agencies whenever practicable. It must be a worldwide effort for the achievement of peace, plenty and freedom.

Economists differ widely on the question of how much should be spent on economic aid. This aid is usually measured in a percentage of the incomes of the developed nations and in the relation of this percentage to the expected increase in the national income of the underdeveloped countries. A reliable long-term calculation cannot be computed for several reasons. First, the absorptive capacity of the recipients will grow in proportion to the increase in their skilled manpower and the development of their economic and social substructure; but these factors, decisive for absorptive capacity, might grow rapidly in one country and at a disappointingly slow pace in another. Human beings do not react equally to the same challenge in every country and at all times, and their reactions cannot be predicted with mathematical precision. Secondly, economic development might not progress in a straight line, as confidently planned, and the achievement of a self-sustaining economy, which would mark the end of the need for external assistance, might be delayed by unforeseen reasons such as political or social disturbances. Thirdly, a country which has reached the level of self-sufficiency, is able to reinvest from 10 to 20 per cent of its steadily growing national income, and seems at last to be independent of foreign aid might be confronted with rising popular pressure for higher living standards. The continuation of foreign aid might then be the price for avoiding a revolution. Finally, the race between the growth of per capita national income and natural increase might upset optimistic projections concerning the amount of foreign aid needed and compel the assisting nations to increase this amount. Neither an optimistic nor a pessimistic forecast is foolproof, because the most rigorous calculus of probabilities cannot foresee all the courses of action, rational and irrational, which men may choose to follow and cannot provide certain conclusions in an equation where there are too many *x*'s.

The United Nations experts calculated in 1949 that the advanced nations should provide annually 14 billion dollars (this amounted at the time to 4 per cent of their national income) in order to assure to the underdeveloped countries a growth of 2 per cent in their per capita national income. This calculation included China among the recipient countries but did not take into account the cost of building the economic substructure and was limited to the cost of industrialization and of improvement in agriculture; moreover, it was founded on an unrealistic figure of 1.25 per cent for the natural increase while the actual rate is much higher. Finally, it overlooked the cost of maintaining and replacing the equipment.

Some of the American estimates are even more optimistic, because they assume that the absorptive capacity of recipient countries will be greatly restricted and will, by implication, limit the amount of foreign aid that can usefully be accepted. They suggest that the annual amount of 2.5 to 3.5 billion dollars will be all that the underdeveloped countries can absorb. This calculation may be accurate for today but overlooks the fact that effective aid will stimulate the growth of absorptive capacity and that the annual amounts of assistance will have to grow steadily. Only after many years will these amounts begin to decline, a number of recipient countries having reached the stage of self-sufficient accumulation of capital and having in consequence disappeared from the roll.

Some of the French experts make very pessimistic forecasts. They think that foreign aid, to be efficacious, must cost the developed countries in the beginning years from 4.4 to 7.5 per cent of their national income and will later become more expensive owing to the rapid natural increase in the underdeveloped countries and to their growing absorptive capacity. They say that it would amount in thirty-five years to between 8.8 per cent and 13.2 per cent of the national income of the advanced nations. This massive aid, they consider, would be capable of sustaining for 35 years an annual increase of 2 per cent in the per capita national income. This calculation might be too pessimistic, because it does not take into account the capacity of underdeveloped countries for stepping up their own accumulation of investment capital by keeping the lid on rising consumption, by stimulating domestic savings, and by using underemployed manpower for constructive purposes. It might also have overstated the initial absorptive capacity of most of the underdeveloped countries.

The inherent uncertainty of all these estimates can be illustrated by the following example. The United Nations experts thought that foreign aid to Latin America should amount to 550 million dollars annually. A later study, made by the International Bank for Reconstruction and Development, raised this sum to 2 billion dollars.

All the calculations, optimistic or pessimistic, point to the need for massive assistance, but they vary in amount and may prove to have underestimated or overestimated the amounts actually needed throughout the coming years. These global calculations assume that the same amount of capital invested in one country would generate the same per capita increase of national income as it would in another country if only both are in the same stage of economic development. However, the social and political conditions might be very different. To take an extreme example, the same capital will probably produce a higher increase in a Communist country where the government is not reluctant to use ruthless means in compressing domestic consumption and in mobilizing the whole available manpower, than in another where the government pays greater attention to the wishes and needs of the population. The forecasts usually make the mistake of treating all the underdeveloped countries in the same stage of development as interchangeable units. Yet they differ widely in their social institutions and political regimes. These differences escape any exact computation and make mathematical equations or logical constructs of uncertain value.

The amounts of economic aid should vary according to the absorptive capacity of the recipient countries. This capacity is the ability to use the transferred capital productively. It is limited by the number of skilled workers, competent managers, engineers, foremen, public administrators, and other specialists, by the available means of transportation for bringing raw materials to the production centers and for shipping goods for domestic consumption and for export, by the existing supply of energy, by the repair and maintenance facilities, by the availability of raw materials for industries and of machinery or fertilizers for agriculture, and by several similar factors.

A very backward country will require, in the first place, technical assistance, which is relatively inexpensive, for training its manpower, and such economic aid as is needed for laying the foundations of its economic and social substructure (education, public health, roads, sources of energy, etc.). If it is already developing, it will need a much greater amount of aid. India is a good example; its substructure is fairly adequately developed and its skilled manpower large enough to warrant very considerable economic aid for its further economic development, including industrialization.

The assisting nations should be aware of the risk that the day of self-sufficiency, which the experts and planners forecast, may be postponed by the immoderately rising rate of natural increase or by the popular clamor for higher living standards. Statistics are not reliable in the underdeveloped countries. India discovered in 1961 that its actual rate of natural increase was much higher than had been reflected in the statistics. This unpleasant discovery made it necessary to modify some of the forecasts of future developments. Even a Communist regime cannot wholly disregard the popular pressure for improved living conditions. The laboring masses hold a sanction in the form of lower productivity. There is no lack of illustrations. In 1956, the Polish regime was compelled by riots to make concessions to the popular demand for a larger consumption. Since 1953, the Soviet regime has been under similar pressure and has been constrained to pay greater attention than before to the output of consumer goods and to housing. In the face of declining productivity, the ruthless Chinese regime was unable to maintain the austere regime of the communes. A non-Communist regime will be more sensitive to this popular pressure and may therefore be unable to reinvest as much as planned from the national income.

To make sense, foreign aid must be integrated with the long-term program of development of the recipient country. It must also be adjusted to the local possibilities of development. It makes sense to help India develop its heavy industries, because it has ample deposits of rich iron ore and sufficient sources of energy (coal deposits and the hydroelectric potential) and its skilled manpower is rapidly increasing. The same policy would be unwise toward an economically backward country where modern industrial equipment would rust and be wasted and where effort should be concentrated on building the substructure, improving agriculture, and developing light industries.

Economic aid can be extended in various forms: grants; loans reimbursable in the local currency, i.e., which will be repaid in the available goods of the recipient country (this is the usual mode of repayment of Soviet loans); and loans repayable in the hard currency of the creditor nation. The soft-currency loans might conceal grants and not be expected to be repaid. The hard-currency loans are practical only when the developing country is close to self-sufficiency and is expected to be able to repay them. In any case, the loans granted to the developing countries should be long-term and with a low rate of interest (the Soviet rate of 2.5 per cent seems reasonable) in order not to endanger the solvency of the recipient country. Economic aid is not a profitable commercial transaction or a good financial investment and is not meant to be. It is a political operation calculated to forward the process of modernization and to prevent that process from culminating in a world that is hostile to the donor state.

A part of foreign assistance can come from the agricultural surpluses which accumulate in some of the developed countries, particularly the United States. Economic development will involve the mobilization of underemployed manpower for building canals, roads, schools, and dams, for reclaiming land, for work at the state-founded plants, and for other purposes. The wages paid by the government will be spent mainly on food and clothing. The demand for foodstuffs and fiber will grow. The shipment of food and fiber surpluses as grants or soft-currency loans would help the recipient country meet this rising demand without depleting its precious fund of foreign currencies through the purchase of the same goods on the international market. This use of unsold surpluses from the developed countries would parry a classic argument against the capitalist system: it would attenuate the glaring contrast between the underfed and poorly clothed masses in the underdeveloped countries and the unused surpluses in the other countries.

The problem is not just that of shipping the surpluses to the countries short of these commodities. The distribution of unsold surpluses would undermine the market for those underdeveloped countries which produce the same commodities and already have surpluses on hand. Assistance to one category of underdeveloped countries would thus increase the misery in others. The solution would consist in the creation of an international pool of agricultural surpluses to which both the developed and the underdeveloped producing countries would contribute. However, the contribution of the advanced nations would be twofold: they would supply their surpluses, and they would provide payment for the surpluses supplied by the underdeveloped nations. This operation would be feasible on the condition that the recipient countries could have recourse to the pool only to meet an increased domestic demand and that the producing countries were mutually bound by the obligation not to increase their production and the accumulation of surpluses.

Whatever the nature of assistance, it should be pledged for reasonably long periods, for instance for five years each time. The recipient country cannot otherwise safely charter the course of its development.

The success of foreign aid should be measured differently in each stage of development. In the first stage it should be evaluated by the growth of the economic and social substructure and of the income derived from agriculture and extractive industries as well as by the development of light and raw-material processing industries. The increase in the per capita national income will be slow, because the returns from the investment in the substructure will become visible only after the lapse of time and only indirectly in the form of an invigorated economic life that is finally placed on a sounder base. Later on, progress should be measured by the annual increase in the per capita national income but not by the rise in the living standards, which will be disappointingly low if investment is to be maintained at the required level. At all times, the success of foreign aid should also be measured by the adjustment of social institutions to the requirements of a modern society.

Economic aid can be channeled in various ways: bilaterally, regionally, or through the United Nations. Each channel offers certain advantages and has its defects. Bilateral assistance gives the donor country direct control over the use of its money; the national origin of aid is known to the population of the recipient country; bilateral assistance can be used by the donor country as a bargaining point in negotiations with the recipient country on other subjects and can possibly influence the foreign policy of the latter country. However, the recipient country can blackmail the donor country by all sorts of arguments into financing unreasonable projects or offering greater aid than intended: the Communists, they could argue, would overthrow the present government if ample aid were refused; a military base would have to be liquidated unless aid is stepped up; the recipient country would turn to the Communist bloc for assistance and its foreign policy would become less favorable to the West. Bilateral bargaining over projects to be financed and, later on, bilateral control over their implementation might raise in the recipient country an outcry of foreign interference in domestic affairs.

The United Nations would offer the great advantage of associating all donor and recipient countries in a partnership. Each application for aid would be scrutinized first by the neutral staff of the United Nations and secondly by the governments of both developed and underdeveloped countries. The latter countries, which are competitors for the same funds, could be expected to act as mutually severe judges of the rationality of the projects submitted. Complaints concerning foreign interference in the domestic affairs of the recipient countries could not be addressed to an international agency of which they are co-masters. Their national sensitivity would be fully respected. The underdeveloped nations have often expressed their preference for this form of assistance.

The trouble with the United Nations is that it often becomes an arena for conflict between the hostile blocs. It remains uncertain whether one of the developed nations, the Soviet Union, would be willing to pool its resources with those of the Western countries in this universal scheme of international aid. The Soviet government has several times declared that it prefers its bilateral assistance to association with a larger program of aid. Judged by debates in the United Nations, the Western governments are no more enthusiastic about the idea. If the Soviet Union were to refuse to contribute to a United Nations economic aid fund, the very structure of the organization would nevertheless provide that nation with many opportunities for interfering. A situation would be created in which the Soviet Union could continue to channel its aid through bilateral agreements but would retain the right to supervise Western assistance given through the intermediary of the United Nations. It is possible that Communist China will eventually be represented in the United Nations; in that case, a large part of the United Nations aid would have to be given to that country on the ground of its enormous population; this prospect has little appeal for the Western nations. The voting system in the General Assembly is another obstacle. It is unreasonable to expect the Western nations, which would be the most important contributors to the United Nations fund but which would represent a minority of votes, to underwrite expenditures which the majority of the General Assembly, composed of the underdeveloped countries and the Communist states, could impose.

The battles which the underdeveloped nations have fought year after year in the General Assembly for the creation of the Special United Nations Fund for Economic Development (SUNFED) have not prevailed over opposition from the prospective contributors, the developed countries. The United Nations has been given means for carrying on an extensive program of technical assistance and for implementing pilot projects but not for massive economic aid.

One of the Specialized Agencies of the United Nations, the International Bank for Reconstruction and Development, grants loans for the development of the economic substructure (electrical power in the first place, transportation, communication, etc.), but its loans, although granted for from ten to twenty years, carry an interest rate which is higher than the national rates in the advanced countries from which it borrows money.

Its rates vary from 4 to 6 per cent, while the Soviet rate for loans to the underdeveloped countries is 2.5 per cent.

The third form of assistance is regional. This is also a partnership but limited to the assisting Western powers and the recipient countries located in a given region. This form of aid has much to commend itself. It is dissociated from the political battles within the United Nations. The recipient countries acquire the habit of thinking of their needs and programs within a regional framework and can learn from this experience about the potential usefulness of regional economic unions. The regional co-operation of the assisting and recipient states offers the same advantages as the channeling of aid through the United Nations: complaints of undue interference in the domestic affairs of the recipient country are avoided, complaints that are likely to be voiced when assistance is bilateral; the rationality of requests for aid can be examined by a regional body in which both the assisting and the recipient states are represented, and the implementation of projects can be jointly controlled. The regional scheme has none of the political disadvantages of aid channeled through the United Nations.

There are already two examples of regional assistance. The older one is the so-called Colombo Plan established in 1950. The purpose of this Plan is to help the Asian countries which represent together a quarter of the population of the world. The members of this regional organization are the United States, Great Britain, Australia, New Zealand, and Canada (the contributing states), and India, Ceylon, Pakistan, Nepal, the Federation of Malaya, Singapore, Burma, Indonesia, Cambodia, Laos, and South Vietnam (the recipient countries). The purpose of the Colombo Plan is to help in building the economic and social substructure (electrical power, communication, transportation, education, housing) and in improving agriculture.

The other example is the regional assistance which the United States has been extending to Latin America since 1959-60. The well-known dictum that to rule is to foresee, is wise, but hindsight is always more enlightened than foresight. The present moment singles out certain problems as the most urgent while it counsels the postponement of other problems; several years later it becomes obvious that the solution to a problem which did not seem urgent at the time would have prevented many subsequent difficulties. This principle is illustrated by the postwar policy of the United States toward Latin America. The events of the postwar years assigned priority to the rehabilitation of Europe, to which the United States offered the Marshall Plan. The European colonial retreat and the Soviet offensive in the fifties shifted attention to Asia and later to Africa. The visibility of a geographical area in Washington is due to the stress of contemporary events which make one area more fashionable for a time than others. It becomes fashionable to talk mostly about this area, to demand a huge battery of experts on this area, and to press for an active policy toward this area, including economic aid. Yesterday Europe, today Asia, tomorrow Africa, and after tomorrow Latin America—each tends to monopolize attention for a time, in relation to the amount of front-page news about it and the extent of Communist activities. At the same time other areas may remain neglected or arouse only a slight interest. This was the case with Latin America, which seemed to remain dormant by comparison to other continents and was taken for granted. It was neglected in the United States schemes of foreign aid. The rumblings of the fifties (the revolutions against the old-fashioned military dictators and the formation of moderately leftist governments) passed somehow unnoticed until the rude awakening of the Cuban revolution with its anti-United States orientation. The Fidelist movement, which is now frankly a Communist movement, posed a most important problem for the United States and the ruling political groups in Latin America. The problem may be stated as follows: Is it possible to carry out the economic and social transformation of Latin America peacefully, through the generous help of the United States and the farsighted policy of Latin American governments, or can that transformation be effected only by revolutions of the Cuban type, which break down all opposition by totalitarian means?

The Cuban challenge compelled the United States to act and to assign a high priority to economic assistance to Latin America. The era of complacent belief that private capital would suffice for the necessary transfusion of funds was ended. The oft-repeated appeals of the Latin American governments were at last heard, and the Cinderella of the United States aid programs became a favorite child.

The new attitude of the United States was reflected first in April, 1959, at an American Conference held in Buenos Aires where the governments of the Western Hemisphere signed the Charter of a one-billion Inter-American Bank for Development, to be financed mainly by the United States, and later in August, 1961, at the conference held in Punta del Este. It was at this conference that the United States and the Latin American governments signed the Charter of the Alliance for Progress, a concept born in Washington but corresponding to the wishes of Latin America. The basic ideas of this Charter, signed on August 17, 1961, are as follows:

1. The economic development of Latin America should aim at a steady increase in the average income and at the narrowing, as quickly as possible, of the gap between Latin American living standards and those of advanced countries.

2. This requires not only the effort of Latin Americans themselves but also substantial external assistance. The signatories agreed that Latin America would need over the next ten years a minimum of $20 billion. However, the United States avoided a strict commitment except for one billion dollars to be supplied in public funds during the twelve months be-

ginning with March, 1961. The United States promised only that it would supply a major part of this 20 billion and would do it principally by the transfer of public funds. It remained understood that an undetermined part of the same 20 billion would be supplied by private North American capital and by the Western European countries and Japan. The signatories could not state what proportion of these funds would be supplied by European and Japanese private capital and what portion would consist of governmental aid.

It remains to be seen whether the United States Congress will be willing over the next ten years to assign large sums for economic assistance to Latin America, whether the European and the Japanese governments will follow suit, and whether North American, European, and Japanese private capital will come in with investments. In other words, one cannot be sure that this sum of $20 billion, estimated to be the minimum, will be made available during the next ten years. This only partly depends on the policy of the United States. Assistance by the United States will take the form of development loans to be granted on a long-term basis (up to fifty years if necessary) and at a very low or zero interest rate.

3. It hardly depends on the United States whether the other obligations of the Charter are carried out. It can exert some pressure by conditioning its assistance on social reforms to be undertaken by the recipient countries; it can help in certain respects by providing technical assistance. But the main burden lies on the shoulders of the Latin American governments. The Charter of Punta del Este suggests several reforms which obviously are urgently needed; the Latin Americans have been the first to point out their urgency, but this has not so far spurred their ruling groups to action. The reforms advocated by the Charter are as follows: agrarian reform, including the distribution of the latifundia among the peasants; the wiping out of illiteracy and the extension of primary, secondary, technical, and higher education; improvement in urban and rural housing, public health, and sanitation; fair wages and satisfactory working conditions for the industrial workers; fiscal reforms to prevent tax evasion and to redistribute national income by taxing the wealthy classes more heavily; inter-state integration through free-trade associations, customs unions, and similar arrangements.

The program is sound, but the question remains whether the Latin American upper classes have understood the warning of the Cuban revolution and have realized that their time will be running out if they refuse to carry out the social reforms solemnly announced by the Charter. It is only fair to add that not all of these reforms can be realized easily in spite of the best will of the governments. It will not be a quick or simple operation to wipe out illiteracy in those countries where large Indian populations are not yet integrated culturally and often do not know the Spanish language. Fair wages, satisfactory working conditions, decent urban and rural housing, high levels of public health and sanitation, all this is extremely desirable but is an integral part of developed societies; it will take a long time in Latin America to acquire these features of the welfare state, which is the product but not the condition of economic development.

4. The Charter stresses two points of importance from the North American point of view: the strengthening of democratic institutions, and the role of private enterprise. The implementation of these two principles depends on the Latin American countries but not on the United States. The future will tell whether they have preferred the democratic way of life or the authoritarian one, private enterprise or state-owned industries or a mixed system.

5. By contrast, it will be mainly within the power of the United States to make a reality of another important pledge of the Charter which promises a lasting solution to the grave problem of price fluctuations for Latin American primary commodities. The United States is the principal importer, but it will need the co-operation of other importers (the Western European countries) and of the Latin American and other producing countries. An international agreement must have the signatures of all the principal importing states and of all the main producing states to have practical meaning. It will not be easy to convince the importing countries that they should agree to a stabilization of prices, and the producing countries that they should accept quotas on output. However, the effects of foreign economic assistance might otherwise be cancelled periodically by losses caused by sudden fluctuations in the prices and the volume of exports of Latin American commodities.

If the regional method were generally adopted, the non-Communist world could be subdivided into the following regions: the Far East, South and Southeast Asia (the area now covered by the Colombo Plan), the Near East, North Africa, Tropical Africa, and Latin America.

The problem of the balance of payments raises the question whether economic aid should be granted in convertible currency or should be provided in a currency which must necessarily be spent in the donor country. The Soviet rubles are always unconvertible and must be spent in the Soviet Union. The answer cannot be as simple for the United States. If the currency is convertible, the recipient country can make the best use of it by buying equipment where it is cheapest and by calling on the services of those experts whose salaries are lowest in spite of equal qualifications. The donor country might also want to strengthen the economy of another developed country, its friend, by giving permission to spend its currency granted in aid on purchases effected in that country. Japan is a case in point. Otherwise, dollars could be tied to the American market for two important reasons: to protect the United States balance of payments and reduce the outflow of dollars, and to offer a larger demand to American industries. The unconvertibility of dollars would add a domestic argument in favor of foreign aid. The American taxpayer, who pays for the United States foreign assistance programs, will know that he thereby stimulates the growth of the national economy.

Technical assistance consists in introducing new or improved techniques, providing experts, and training the personnel of the recipient country. It is relatively inexpensive and, like economic aid, can be channeled through the United Nations and its Specialized Agencies, through regional agencies, or bilaterally. The new techniques can be related to agriculture or industry, public health or education, or any other economic or social aspects of modernization. They might, for example, involve better methods of cultivating rice and raising the output per acre or the use of better seeds or of pest controls. They might entail the eradication of epidemic and endemic diseases. The World Health Organization has cured millions of people of tropical diseases by injections of penicillin; assistance in the fight against malaria (the average cost per head amounting to twenty-five cents) has been making other millions fit for productive work. The result is not only greater human happiness but also higher labor productivity.

Technical assistance has three aspects:

1. Certain countries (in particular those African countries which recently acquired their independence) are so short of administrative and managerial personnel and other specialists with a university education that they need to hire foreign experts in the capacity of temporary civil servants. These experts are expected not only to head various branches of public administration but also to train their local successors.

2. Experts are also sent on shorter missions with the objective of teaching new techniques or training the local personnel or both. This job, like the former, requires from the foreign specialist not only professional knowledge but also the ability to adjust to conditions altogether different from his national environment. This ability cannot co-exist with national ethnocentrism, i.e., the stubborn refusal to concede that foreign peoples have evolved in different circumstances and have the right to possess different "self-evident truths" and ways of life. It includes the capacity to adjust the techniques of one's own country to the conditions existing in the recipient country, which are, by definition, more backward. These techniques should be modified or simplified or economically calculated in a different manner. For instance, the existence of underemployed manpower might compel the foreign expert to substitute human force for the machinery which would have done the job in his country. An extremely capable expert who performs his functions to the best of his knowledge would nevertheless be a failure if he did not make these adjustments. He would also fail in his task if he did a splendid technical job and in the process acquired many friends among the native people but neglected to train his local successors.

3. The training of students and older people at the universities of

the advanced countries makes sense only if they can be immediately employed on returning to their native land in the capacity for which they have been educated abroad. The returns for the assisting country are threefold: first, it helps in the modernization process; secondly, it gains the personal gratitude of the foreign student who later acts as a channel of intellectual understanding between the two countries; thirdly, there is a chance that the student may be "converted" to the political ideology of the host country.

The United Nations and its Specialized Agencies have been very active in all the fields of technical assistance. They protect the recipient country against the risk of being flooded by experts of one nationality only. They can hire specialists in all countries, developed and only developing. An agricultural specialist, for instance, who is a native of a developing country is able to teach in another less developed country successful techniques used in his homeland. Another specialist, familiarized with the problem through the experience of his country, can help to train foremen and skilled workers. A specialist recruited in a developing country, if he has the know-how, is better equipped to understand the problems of another developing country, because his own nation has been undergoing the same process. His remuneration is usually lower than that which his colleague from an advanced country would expect.

The difficulty of technical assistance consists in the limited number of specialists who are available at any time. Usually they are employed at home and, in the case of prosperous nations, might be unwilling to trade their home security, career prospects and comfort, familiar surroundings and high income, for a much less attractive venture abroad. The Communist states solve this problem by compulsory assignment of their nationals to jobs of technical assistance abroad. The United Nations have solved the same problem by creating a multinational pool of experts.

The multinational character of United Nations technical assistance does not mean that the nationality of a specialist is of no consequence. He is sent by the international organization but he cannot help being familiar with the products of his native country. An American doctor cannot be expected to be familiar with European pharmaceutical products, a French engineer with British equipment, or a British teacher with Canadian textbooks. Each specialist, though employed by the United Nations, inevitably promotes imports from his own country.

The United Nations technical assistance program has the general support of the member-states, who provide the financial means. Over a hundred countries are the recipients and benefit from the services of thousands of experts and from many fellowships for studies abroad. The major fields of assistance are agriculture, health, economic planning, surveys of resources, training of public administrators and other specialists, education, public utilities, transport, and communications. In 1958 the cost of this assistance was less than 9 million dollars. The United Nations recently began to supply on request experts for executive and managerial posts; these experts become for the duration of their assignment the civil servants of the recipient country; the required supplement to their salaries is paid by the United Nations.

Military assistance, like economic and technical aid, is politically motivated but its purpose is different. Its objective is to increase the security of the assisting country indirectly or to extend the sphere of its external influence. This objective is so directly associated with the national interests of the assisting state that military aid easily attracts popular support. The taxpayer of the advanced country often cannot grasp his own long-term interest in supplying economic and technical assistance to the underdeveloped countries, but he is quick to see the advantage of enlisting additional manpower for the defense of his nation. The same legislator who is inclined to be miserly when it comes to economic assistance can be very generous, even wasteful of public money, with respect to military aid.

There are several reasons for granting military assistance:

1. It may be the price for a base located on foreign territory. This base can serve to disperse retaliatory power, to shorten the distance between the planes and intermediate-range ballistic missiles of the assisting state and their prospective targets, or to provide electronic listening posts located close to the territory of the potential enemy.

2. It may be the price for winning the political friendship of the assisted state. In 1955, for example, the Communist bloc began to supply military equipment to Egypt and Syria after the Western powers had declined to do so for fear of disturbing the balance of armaments between Israel and the Arab states. This move, followed by massive economic assistance, bought the friendship of the United Arab Republic and made the Soviet Union a Near Eastern power. A similar policy toward Iraq, after the revolution of 1958, further strengthened the Soviet position on both sides of the Suez Canal and in the Persian Gulf. However, after the second Iraqi revolution, the Soviet government learned a lesson familiar to the Western powers. Political instability in the underdeveloped countries and their desire to balance one foreign influence with another are likely to produce unpleasant surprises for the great powers. The new Iraqi regime proved to be much less friendly to the Soviet Union than its predecessor. The former heavy Soviet investment in Iraq in the form of economic and military aid did not pay the expected political dividends. The Soviet experience in Guinea has also been disappointing. Massive assistance has not assuaged Guinean suspicions of Soviet intentions nor has it prevented Guinean co-operation with the Western powers. Western and Soviet relations with the Third World have demonstrated that competition between the West and the Soviet Union is a continuous battle with varying fortunes but a battle which a third party, the uncommitted nations, greatly influences.

3. Military aid may be calculated to strengthen the armed forces of a friendly country against foreign aggression or a domestic coup.

4. It may be justified when the requesting state might be forced by its denial to turn to a rival great power for help and in consequence might alter the course of its foreign policy.

Military assistance can also be extended to developed countries, as evidenced by the scope of United States assistance to its allies in Europe. Aid to a developed country can be justified only if that country spends on military expenses a higher proportion of its national income than the assisting country.

Military aid may take several forms, such as the sale of weapons, the extension of credits for the purchase of military equipment, the supply of arms as a grant, or the training of armed forces in the modern techniques of warfare.

As a rule, military assistance comes mainly or exclusively from one advanced country, unlike economic and technical assistance, which can flow concurrently from several sources. The armed forces need to have uniform equipment. This need creates a dependence on the military instructors and spare parts of one nation. The supplying state gains another advantage in that it usually exports obsolescent military equipment, the up-to-date weapons being used by its own armed forces and being supplied to economically and technologically advanced allies.

Military officers who have been trained by personnel from the advanced countries may acquire a familiarity with modern technology and its social implications which can prove useful to their underdeveloped country.

Economic aid may be tied to military assistance if the country receiving military aid needs funds to buttress its shaky economy or if the building of the means of transportation and communication is required for military purposes. The same harbor, railroad, or telephone line can serve both for military and civilian purposes.

Foreign assistance cannot produce the desired results unless it is preceded by a careful examination in each case of the transferability of techniques and institutions. Seeds which produce excellent harvests in one climate and soil may prove disappointing in a different climate and soil. The tractor, indispensable for an advanced economy with a small agricultural manpower, will only increase the underemployment of overpopulated villages or be simply unusable if peasant plots are very small and divided into many interlocking strips. Methods of public administration or of business management, which are the products of a developed society, may not work in a backward society without very significant modifications. There are no general principles of transferability which hold true for all underdeveloped countries, because their historical backgrounds are so different and because their cultural and economic levels are far from identical. Each technique and each institution produced in an advanced society should be examined carefully in the light of the conditions and needs of each underdeveloped country. This preliminary examination indicates which institutions and techniques are transferable and how they should be adapted to conditions in the recipient country. After a time, the latter country will be able to see what further adjustments should be made and which techniques and institutions have proved in actual experience to be unsuitable. Trial and error cannot be altogether avoided, but a careful preliminary study should make this process less costly.

The lessons of our own civilization are very instructive in this respect. The parliamentary regime, which is the fruit of English historical development, was eagerly copied by continental Europe. After adjustments to different historical backgrounds and national mentalities, the English model evolved into the continental parliamentary system, which is very different from the original. Continental Europeans would be the first to pay tribute to the London metropolitan police but they have been unable to imitate them. The continental policeman is an agent of the state repressive power and is looked upon as an evil made necessary by the imperfections of human nature. His counterpart in London is regarded by the population as a friend who has the moral right to expect their co-operation. The former is armed, the latter performs his functions without carrying any arms.

If institutions are not easily transferable within the same civilization, it follows that they cannot be transferred from one civilization to another without careful planning.

CHAPTER VI

The Third World—the Demographic Explosion

TOTAL NUMBERS, AGE COMPOSITION, DEMOGRAPHIC FORECASTS

Population is the central element in national power; natural resources, economic equipment, and military weapons become meaningful only if related to the human beings who use them. The total size of the population is important in itself, for it is the manpower actually or potentially available for productive and military purposes. A modern great power must have a large population, not only because its economic and military strength is conditioned by the number of people available, but also because a large population has a better chance of producing the many scientists, technologists, and other specialists who are required for participation in the race for scientific and technological superiority; this superiority is a prerequisite for becoming or remaining a great power. A very large population might be able to immobilize sizable armies of a technologically superior enemy, at least in a war waged with conventional weapons. China has proved this twice: by preventing Japan from conquering the whole country and from extinguishing its resistance, and by fighting the Korean War to a standstill. A very large population, living on a vast territory, is less vulnerable to the effects of nuclear war, its human losses being proportionately less crippling. A comparison of China with the United Kingdom illustrates the difference. This is not to say that even the largest population would escape the effects of stratospheric fallout. Moreover, the political and social centers of the largest country could be wiped out by the nuclear weapons; this devastation would disorganize its social life, undermine its regime, and force the survivors to remake their existence on a level which would appear very primitive by comparison to conditions before the war. In other words, the nuclear war would be devastating for all countries, large and small, but the chances of a biological survival of the crippled society would probably be greater for a numerous population.

People who are appalled by the sheer number of the total Chinese population could be reassured by the fact that the 680 million Chinese are almost counterbalanced by the combined populations of Japan, India, and Pakistan, which together amount to 630 million. These three countries are not particularly friendly to China and may become less so in the future. Moreover, Japan is already an industrial country, while China is still undergoing economic development, so far with varying fortunes.

The estimated total population of the world in 1960 was 2,995 million. This represented an increase of 500 million from 2,495 million in 1950. In other words, the average annual increase was 50 million during the decade between 1950 and 1960. The geographical distribution in 1960 was as follows: Asia (excluding the U.S.S.R.), 1,679 million; Europe (excluding the U.S.S.R.), 427 million; the Western Hemisphere, 405 million of whom 199 million lived in North America (the U.S.A. and Canada) and 206 million in Latin America; Africa, 254 million; and Oceania, 16.5 million. The percentages by hemisphere were as follows: the Western Hemisphere, 14 per cent; the Eastern, 86 per cent; the Northern, almost 92 per cent; and the Southern, scarcely over 8 per cent.

The hundreds of millions living in the underdeveloped countries do not make up in size of population for their economic and technological backwardness. Their true strength is only potential and will acquire full meaning only after a long period of development which would make them comparable to other millions in the present developed countries.

Sheer numbers of the total populations cannot be mechanically compared for other reasons. The true value of a population depends on its intellectual and moral qualities, including the characteristics of its political leaders and of its educated elites. The fear of risks, a reluctance to sacrifice personal comfort, a lack of patriotic spirit, an inept leadership can sharply reduce national power which would look very imposing if calculated in the millions of inhabitants, in the number of modern factories and research centers, and in the number of scientific and technological specialists. An imposing façade of material strength, hiding a moral vacuum, will crumble in a conflict with a nation that is morally and intellectually superior unless the latter nation is hopelessly outmatched in material power.

Another important aspect of the demographic problem is the age composition of the population. In considering the age-group of persons between fifteen and sixty-five (the active population), the question arises as to how many dependents they must support. These dependents can be divided into two groups: those below the age of fifteen, and those above the age of sixty-five. Both groups do not produce or produce relatively little; their survival is ensured by the work of the active population. Assuming that all other conditions are equal, a country with a larger active population and a smaller proportion of dependents has a per capita national income which is higher than another country with a larger proportion of dependents.

The relation of women to the active population is also important. Do they contribute fully to the productive work, are they socially emancipated, and do they form a part of the active population, or are they confined to their domestic chores by custom or by the care of numerous children? The total number of the population does not reveal either the women's participation in productive work or the proportion of dependents.

The demographic trends are reflected in birth and mortality rates and in the resulting rate of natural increase. If the birth rate is much higher than the mortality rate, the proportion of dependents less than fifteen years old will tend to increase. If the birth rate declines and is close to the mortality rate, there will be a constant increase in the proportion of dependents over the age of sixty-five.

The forecasts of demographic trends are founded on statistics of the same trends in the past. They provide some guidance, but two reservations should be made concerning their "infallibility." First, these forecasts deal with expected human behavior and can be refuted by unexpected behavior. The predictions of the thirties, based on the previous vital statistics, foretold the continuation of the fall in the Western birth rate. The sudden rise in this rate in the late thirties and in the forties came as a complete surprise.

Secondly, the forecasts are mainly founded on Western demographic history, and it is not certain that non-Western societies will behave exactly like Western societies in similar stages of economic development. For instance, the small-family pattern appeared in the West in the wake of rising living standards. It is not certain that another society would continue to have a very high birth rate until it reaches its period of prosperity. As a matter of fact, one Western country, France, experienced a steady fall in its birth rate long before its popular masses reached the stage of decent living standards. This trend began in France as early as 1760. It is possible that the underdeveloped societies of today, which face a frustrating race between natural increase and the rise of per capita national income, might follow the footsteps of France rather than of the other Western countries and reduce their birth rate while still living on a subsistence level. It is equally possible, perhaps more probable, that they will continue to have a very high birth rate until they improve their living conditions decisively.

THE FIRST STAGE OF THE DEMOGRAPHIC CYCLE

Keeping in mind the two reservations noted above, it can be said that the demographic evolution of human societies falls into three stages. The first is characterized by high birth and mortality rates; it is the pattern of all pre-industrial societies, including Western societies prior to the Industrial Revolution and the present underdeveloped societies as late as the 1930's.

The birth rate ranges between 35 and 50 per thousand and the death rate is 30 or more per thousand. The natural increase is steady but rather slow. The large number of children born is greatly reduced by the high infant mortality. Life expectancy is very low and fluctuates between twenty-two and thirty-five years.

The country which shows this demographic pattern is not only economically undeveloped but still unaffected by the progress in medicine and public sanitation which has taken place in the developed countries. The living standards are very low, and inadequate nutrition reduces resistance to disease. The parents, who live in poverty and squalor, procreate without thinking of the family budget. They are usually peasants, and the child is a prospective helper at an early age who is not expected to attend school, at least not for long periods of time. They are illiterate or semiliterate and either do not know of preventive means or cannot afford to buy them or do not care to use them. The children, the parents know, will be reduced in number by the high mortality rate. The survivors will take care of the parents in their old age, the state providing no social insurance for the aged. The parents have several incentives for procreating a large family but hardly any for avoiding it.

In several underdeveloped countries there are also other factors which bring about a high birth rate. The customary nuptial age might be very low; unmarried people are socially censured; the women have a subordinate social status which confines them to the role of mother and housewife; in the Moslem countries the child provides the mother with some protection against an easy divorce by creating an emotional tie with the father.

In most of the underdeveloped countries the birth rate is higher than it was in pre-industrial Europe, because the rate of marriage is higher and also because the marrying age is younger. The natural fecundity seems to be approximately the same. At the beginning of the nineteenth century pre-industrial Europe had a birth rate ranging from 35 to 40 per thousand. In Africa the same rate is from 40 to 56.8 per thousand, in Latin America from 22.3 in semideveloped Argentina to 55.4 in Costa Rica, in Asia (excluding industrial Japan) from 34 in China to 50 in Burma.

The high mortality rate of the first demographic stage is due to the epidemic and endemic diseases which take a heavy toll of children, to poor nutrition, to unhealthful housing conditions, to a frequent lack of pure potable water, and to a shortage of medical help. Slum urbanization does not improve and often worsens these conditions of existence. Until the late thirties (at that time the death rate began, for reasons to be explained later, to decline) the underdeveloped countries had a mortality rate comparable to the high rate of pre-industrial Europe. These rates were, before 1800, 33 per thousand in France and 28 in Sweden, figures which are not much different from the rates in the underdeveloped countries in the thirties: India 24, Egypt 27, China 33, Northern Africa 35 to 40, Mexico 25.

Assuming that the average birth rate in this stage is around 40 per thousand and the death rate stands at 30 per thousand, the population increases at the moderate rate of 10 per thousand. Life expectancy is low and oscillates around the figure of thirty years, as it did in Europe in 1800.

THE SECOND STAGE: THE POPULATION EXPLOSION

The second stage, now called the population explosion, is characterized by the continuation of a high birth rate and by a death rate which is rapidly declining. Therefore, the population increases at a rapid rate, the young-age groups dominate the stage and in turn cause an accelerated rate of natural increase. The nation is biologically young. Its active population has to support a growing proportion of children under fifteen years of age. The mortality rate is declining but not rapidly enough to increase significantly the proportion of dependents over sixty-five.

Western Europe entered this stage around 1800. This change in the demographic pattern was only indirectly due to the Industrial Revolution. The true reason for both was the scientific progress which made the Industrial Revolution possible but which also brought about a rapid advance in medicine and later a steady improvement in public sanitation. Since the living conditions of the masses, rural and urban, remained very low for a few generations, the birth rate stayed high. England provides a good illustration of this process. The death rate, which in the 1740's remained between 30 and 35 per thousand, declined by 1800 to 27 and by 1860 to 22. But until 1880 the birth rate remained almost as high as in the eighteenth century, around 35 per thousand. The time-lag between the downward trends of the two rates lasted for more than a century. In the other Western European countries this time-lag was at least fifty years long; this was the interval between the beginning of the fall in the mortality rate and the beginning of the fall in the birth rate. It is this time-lag that produced in Western Europe the surge of population growth and is now causing a similar demographic phenomenon in the underdeveloped countries. These countries have entered the second stage, however, under economic circumstances which are very different from those of Western Europe in the nineteenth century.

The "white" peoples of the present developed countries experienced the population explosion much earlier than the predominantly "colored" peoples of the underdeveloped countries. During the period between 1870 and 1914, for which we have reliable data, the European population rose from 300 million to 452 million in spite of the mass overseas emigration. France was the first European country to undergo a progressive decline in the birth rate (earlier than a decline in the mortality rate); therefore, its natural increase was not so spectacular as that of other European nations. Yet its total population increased during the last century from 28 million to 40 million. The British and the German populations jumped during the same period from 10 to 40 million and from 25 to 60 million respectively. This uneven increase in the total populations of France and its main European rivals was one of the causes for the decline in French political stature. The uneven rate of increase between 1800 and 1940 of the populations of various continents is evidenced by these figures: Europe increased from 185 to 534 million, Asia and Africa from 661 to 1,406 million, and the Americas from 25 to 276 million (mass immigration was one of the principal reasons of this spectacular growth).

The present population explosion in the underdeveloped countries proceeds at a rate of natural increase which is as high as that of Europe in the nineteenth century and frequently higher. The Indian population increased during the decade between 1941 and 1951 by 42 million at an annual rate of 1.35 per cent. The quickening tempo of Indian natural increase can be measured by the fact that the annual rate for the first half of this century was 1.25 per cent but in 1958 reached 1.99 per cent; this is still a rather low rate if compared to the rates in several other underdeveloped countries and can, therefore, be expected to rise in the future. Egypt increased its population from just over 9 million in 1897 to over 26 million in 1960. The population of Venezuela increases twofold every twenty years, that of Ceylon every twenty-five years, and that of Puerto Rico every twenty-six years. The population increase is proceeding inexorably in all underdeveloped countries but at an uneven pace. The Latin American countries and a few Asian and African countries lead the way owing to a more speedy reduction in their mortality rates. Other Asian and African nations follow suit at a slower pace; the most dramatic reductions in their death rates and no less dramatic increases in the rates of their population growth still lie ahead of them and will probably take place in the near future. The speed of population growth can be appreciated when it is realized that the Latin American population increases by almost one-third every ten years, the average annual rate being 2.3 for South America and 2.7 for Central America. This percentage of growth produces each year progressively higher absolute figures of natural increase, because the 2.3 or 2.7 per cent applies each year to a population larger in total numbers.

The European population increases at a rate much slower than that of the underdeveloped countries. The disequilibrium which favored Europe in the nineteenth century has been reversed to its disadvantage. Between 1920 and 1952 the European population grew by 22 per cent as compared with 28 per cent for Asia, 46 per cent for Africa, and 76 per cent for Latin America.

The annual rates for the main geographical areas, according to the United Nations Yearbook for 1961, are shown in Table 7.

TABLE 7

Area	Total Population (in Millions)	Birth Rate	Death Rate	Natural Increase Rate
World	2.995	3.6%	1.8%	1.8%
Africa	254	4.7	2.5	2.2
Northern Africa	88	4.5	2.3	2.2
Tropical and Southern Africa	166	4.8	2.7	2.1
America	405	3.4	1.3	2.1
North America	199	2.5	0.9	1.8 (including immigration)
Central America	66	4.2	1.5	2.7
South America	140	4.2	1.9	2.3
Asia	1.679	4.1	2.2	1.9
Southwest Asia	77	4.8	2.2	2.6
South-Central Asia	559	4.1	2.4	1.7
Southeast Asia	214	4.1	2.1	2.0
East Asia	829	4.0	2.0	2.0
Europe (excluding U.S.S.R.)	427	1.9	1.1	0.8
Northwestern Europe	142	1.8	1.1	0.7
Central Europe	139	1.9	1.1	0.8
Southern Europe	146	2.1	1.0	0.9 (including emigration)
Oceania	16.5	2.4	0.9	2.4 (including immigration)
U.S.S.R.	214	2.5	0.8	1.7

A glance at this table reveals very interesting data. The rate of natural increase is lowest in Europe. The high natural increase in Oceania is due to a fairly high birth rate and a large immigration. Latin America and Southwest Asia have reached the highest level of natural increase. The comparatively lower rates for other underdeveloped areas were mainly due to rather high death rates which are bound to be reduced. These areas have not yet reached the peak of their population growth. Several countries, not all of them located in Latin America or Southwest Asia, have attained very high levels of natural increase: Egypt 2.4 per cent, Ghana 3.02 per cent, Southern Rhodesia (Africans) 3.04 per cent, Malaya 3.14, Taiwan 3.16, Guatemala 3.2, Sudan 3.32, Mexico 3.36, Jamaica 3.38, El Salvador 3.82, Costa Rica 4.75. These rates foreshadow the future pace of growth in all the other underdeveloped countries, which are, for the time being, slowed down in their population increases by their still high mortality rates.

The rates of natural increase quoted above are higher than those of Europe at the time of its demographic revolution for two reasons: death rates are now reduced much more quickly than in the nineteenth century, and most of the underdeveloped countries have birth rates higher than the European birth rate of the time. European birth rates were not higher in the past century than 40 per thousand. The same rates are: 43 per thousand in the Congo (Leopoldville), 43 in Brazil, 44 in Tanganyika, 44.8 in Southern Rhodesia (Africans), 44.9 in Tunisia, 45 in Mexico, 45 in Iran, 49.5 in Guatemala, 49.6 in El Salvador, 50 in Burma, 51.7 in Sudan, 55 in Ghana, 55.4 in Costa Rica, 56.1 in Ivory Coast, and 56.8 in Northern Rhodesia (Africans). By contrast the present European birth rates are low, varying from 13.9 per thousand in Sweden to 24.9 in the U.S.S.R.. The industrial countries have generally low rates: Belgium 16.9, France 18.4, West Germany 18.2, Italy 18.8, Switzerland 18.1, and Britain 17.8.

Another way of looking at the problem of natural increase is to point out that the annual rate of 30 per thousand results in a twofold increase of the population within twenty-three years and that the rate of 20 per thousand brings about the same increase within thirty-five years. The acceleration of the trend can be best observed in Latin America where the rate of natural increase was only 18 per thousand between 1928 and 1938, rose to 21 per thousand between 1938 and 1948, and has now reached an average of between 23 and 27 per thousand.

The demographic revolution in the underdeveloped countries is due to the same cause as the spectacular European growth was in the nineteenth century. Both were set in motion by a sharp reduction in the mortality rate. The process is unequally advanced. In 1961 the annual death rates for the various areas of the world were: Africa, 18 per thousand in Senegal and 33.3 in Ivory Coast; Latin America, 6.7 per thousand in Puerto Rico, 7.9 in Costa Rica, but a high 20.6 in Brazil; Asia, 35 pro mille in Burma, 25 in Iran, 20 in Indonesia, 19.2 in India, but only 9.5 in Malaya and 6.7 in Taiwan. In 1961 European mortality rates ranged between 12.9 per thousand for Belgium and 12 for Britain, on the one hand, and 7.6 per thousand for both the Netherlands and Poland, on the other. The Soviet rate was 7.1 per thousand. The other advanced countries had comparably low rates: Canada 7.7, U.S.A. 9.3, Australia 8.5, New Zealand 9. Whenever the mortality rate in the poorer countries is lower than that in the prosperous nations (7.9 per thousand in Costa Rica versus 12 per thousand in

Britain, or 8.9 in Jamaica versus 11 in France), this situation, which looks bizarre and incomprehensible at first glance, is due to a much younger age composition in the poorer countries.

The dramatic decline in the death rate, the cause of the population explosion, has its precedent in Western history. For various reasons, however, the decline is now more rapid. Relatively cheap but effective techniques for preventing and curing epidemic and endemic diseases were unknown in the nineteenth century. The European lower social classes could not afford medical help, which was still very expensive; the modern concept that society has a moral obligation to save human lives and preserve human health regardless of the means of the sick person was alien to the European outlook of the past century. Only in this century has the problem of social welfare been transferred from the realm of Christian charity to that of state social insurance. Today the advanced countries come to the aid of the underdeveloped areas either directly or through contributions to international agencies such as the World Health Organization. They provide this help with greater zeal than they offer economic aid. The saving of human lives appeals to the moral imagination and is incomparably cheaper than helping to provide new opportunities for employment and better living in an expanding economy.

The decline in the mortality rate is not due to improved living conditions but to modern and relatively cheap medicines and public health techniques such as antibiotics, sulfa drugs, spraying D.D.T. against malaria, and vaccination. The use of D.D.T. alone reduced the death rate in Ceylon in ten years by a percentage which Europe of the nineteenth century attained only in six decades.

During the last three decades mortality rates declined by 40 per cent in twenty-three underdeveloped countries scattered all over the world. Of the seventy-six countries for which the United Nations had available data, seventy showed throughout the fifties a clear trend toward a declining death rate. This decline is due in part to a markedly lower infant mortality (children under the age of one year), a phenomenon that began in the underdeveloped countries in the 1930's. The potential for a further decline in the general death rate and hence for an increase in natural growth can be imagined if one considers the wide gap in the rates of infantile mortality between the underdeveloped and the advanced countries. In the underdeveloped countries in 1960 these rates were: 70 per thousand in Brazil, 71.8 in Madagascar, 75.1 in Mexico, 99.8 in Colombia, 103.4 in Peru, 113.1 in Ghana, 117.9 in Algeria, 144.3 in the Congo (Leopoldville), 145.9 in India, 150 in Indonesia. These cold figures reveal that 150 out of every thousand Indonesian children die before reaching the age of one year. The statistics for the advanced countries tell a different story: 35 per thousand in the U.S.S.R., 30.7 in Japan, 25.2 in the U.S.A., 22.8 in New Zealand, 22.5 in Britain, 21.1 in Switzerland, 20.2 in Australia.

The death rate among children between the ages of one and four years has also been subject to an impressive decline. The average reduction in this rate for the period between 1945 and 1960 was as high as 40 per cent. But again this does not mean that the gap, which in this respect also divides the underdeveloped from the advanced countries, has been closed. For the advanced nations the rate was: 1.3 per thousand for Belgium, 1.2 for France and the Netherlands, 1 per thousand for Norway and New Zealand, 1.1 for the U.S.A., 0.9 for Britain, and 0.8 for Sweden. This rate was drastically different for India (44 per thousand) and for Guinea (52 per thousand), two typical underdeveloped countries. However, this mortality rate for small children has also been declining due to the more effective struggle against infectious diseases of childhood and against smallpox, typhoid fever, tuberculosis, malaria, venereal and other illnesses.

Generally speaking, the decline in the death rate for children and adults alike had begun in the underdeveloped countries during the period between 1920 and 1945, but the impressive results have become evident since 1945. Beginning with that date the declining trend was accelerated by foreign assistance, bilateral and multilateral. The general mortality rate declined between 1937 and 1960 in India from 22.8 to 19.2, in Mexico from 23.7 to 11.4, in Puerto Rico from 19.7 to 6.7. Yet the birth rates remained high in these and other underdeveloped countries. They were in 1937 and 1960 respectively: 33.2 and 39.1 per thousand for India, 44.1 and 45 for Mexico, and 38.8 and 31 for Puerto Rico. This contrast between the trends in the birth and death rates reveals the secret of the population explosion.

The maximum average rate of natural increase will probably oscillate around 35 per thousand (the birth rate being 45 per thousand and the death rate 10 per thousand). But there are certain countries which have already passed this mark: Costa Rica with 47.5 per thousand natural increase, El Salvador with 38.2, or Brunei with 45 per thousand.

The death rate has so far been reduced by inexpensive means. A marked advance below the rate of 10 per thousand, which is being made by the developed countries, is probably beyond the reach of the underdeveloped countries. This advance can be bought only at the high price of a large medical establishment, a modern level of public sanitation, adequate nutrition, in short, at the price of thorough modernization. In other words, a further compression of the mortality rate below 10 per thousand will be one of the fruits of modernization but cannot precede it.

The drama of the population explosion of this century consists in the fact that it hits the economically backward and poor countries. There exists no analogy with the statistically similar demographic phenomenon in Europe of the nineteenth century. In Europe economic development (the Industrial Revolution) paralleled the rapid growth of the population, but the quickening pace of natural increase in the underdeveloped countries threatens to outrun expected increases in the per capita national income.

The density of population in some of the underdeveloped countries is already higher than that of Europe in the past century. Of course, a comparison of the number of people per square mile can be misleading. A square mile can be an industrial or an agricultural area, the soil can be fertile or barren, the climate can be favorable or unfavorable. However, Table 8 provides a rough comparison.

TABLE 8

WORLD POPULATION DENSITIES

Area	Density of Population per Square Kilometer
World average	22
Africa	8
Northern Africa	9
Tropical and Southern Africa	8
America	10
North America	9
Central America	24
South America	8
Asia	62
Southwest Asia	14
South-Central Asia	109
Southeast Asia	48
East Asia	71
Europe (excluding the U.S.S.R.)	86
Northwestern Europe	63
Central Europe	137
Southern Europe	86
U.S.S.R.	10
Oceania	2

The density of developed Europe is lower than that of South-Central Asia, which includes India and Pakistan, and the figures for East and Southeast Asia are still impressive if compared with the European. Yet all those countries, except for Japan, are economically underdeveloped and rapidly increasing in population. Poverty goes there hand in hand with a high density of population, and the density increases every year. The low figures for Tropical and Southern Africa as well as for South America indicate that those areas have vast space to accommodate much larger populations if their economies are developed in proportion to their available land and other natural resources. However, four countries in the Caribbean and Central American region: Haiti, El Salvador, Cuba, and the Dominican Republic have reached a density of population which is from three to six and a half times greater than that of the United States.

Some of the underdeveloped countries are clearly overpopulated by any standard. Puerto Rico with 264 persons per square kilometer, Egypt with 538 (counting only the settled area and excluding the desert), and Java with 400 persons are the most dramatic cases. Central Europe, which is economically developed, has only 137 people per square kilometer. If the United States had the Indian density of population (136 persons per square kilometer instead of the present 19), its population would amount to 1,300 million; at the Puerto Rican density the same population would reach 2 billion.

In certain cases the high density could be relieved. Indonesia could resettle the teeming millions of Java on its other, less populous islands. Egypt is reclaiming a large area for settlement by building the Aswan Dam. Southeast Asia is in this respect in a more favorable position than India and Pakistan, having an average density that is almost 60 per cent lower.

The rapid population increase of Europe in the last century was absorbed not only by industrialization but also by overseas emigration at a time when the new countries of the Western Hemisphere and of Oceania welcomed cheap white labor. Between 1800 and 1924 this emigration to the Americas transplanted approximately 60 million people of whom 36 million went to the United States. Ten million later returned to Europe, but the balance of 50 million helped to relieve the older continent's demographic pressure. There are no outlets today for a mass emigration of "colored" people. Moreover, the emigration of today would have to be of gigantic dimensions, far greater than the European emigration of the last century, to relieve the situation in Asia significantly. The total European emigration of 125 years was approximately equal to the population increase of India and Pakistan within only one decade.

Assuming that the opportunity for emigration existed, there would still remain the problem of costly overseas transportation and equally costly resettlement in a new country. Neither the poor emigrant nor his underdeveloped native country could afford this expenditure. Moreover, emigration is a solution of despair. The country of the emigrant finds relief from demographic pressure but at the price of wasting the investment which has been made to raise an able-bodied person and of losing millions or hundreds of thousands of young men or women of vigorous and adventurous type who would have been an asset to their native land.

There is another difference, already noted, between Europe of the nineteenth century and the present underdeveloped countries. The fall in their mortality rate is much more rapid and their birth rate tends to be higher. These countries live in a pre-industrial age, are poorer than the Europe of 1750, and yet have mortality rates that are frequently lower than those of Europe in 1900 (18 per thousand) and birth rates that are higher. These conditions create a demographic disequilibrium which Europe did not know.

Their life expectancy is still low by the standards of advanced countries where it exceeds sixy-five years. According to the latest available data of the United Nations, life expectancy in the developed nations is as follows:

Country	Males	Females
Canada	67.61	72.92
U.S.A.	66.50	73
Austria	61.91	66.97
Belgium	62.04	67.26
Denmark	69.19	72.60
France	67.20	73.80
Germany (West)	66.69	71.94
Italy	65.75	70.02
Netherlands	71	73.90
Norway	71.11	74.70
Sweden	71.69	75.24
Switzerland	66.36	70.85
U.S.S.R.	64	72

The statistics for the underdeveloped countries show a very different picture:

Country	Males	Females
Congo (Leopoldville)	37.64	40
Ghana	38	38
Ivory Coast	35	35
Northern Rhodesia (Africans)	37	37
Southern Rhodesia (Africans)	48	49
Senegal	37	37
El Salvador	49	52.50
Guatemala	48.82	43.50
Mexico	37.92	39.79
Brazil	39.30	45.50
Chile	49.84	53.89
Cambodia	44.20	43.30
India	32.45	31.66

To take two extreme examples, there is a dramatic contrast between the Swedish life expectancy of over seventy-one years for males and the Indian of only thirty-two and a half years, although the latter figure is an improvement on 1901 when it stood at twenty-two years. The average European life expectancy before the Industrial Revolution was around thirty years. The generally better situation in the present underdeveloped countries is due to their lower mortality rate.

There are people who say that it is a mistake to assist the underdeveloped countries in reducing their death rates and thus to compound their difficulties by intensifying the population explosion. They overlook not only the humanitarian aspect of the question but also the demonstrable fact that the same measures which reduce the mortality rate also stimulate labor productivity by eliminating debilitating diseases.

A rapid natural increase results in a growing proportion of dependents under the age of fifteen. The population is predominantly young. The usual distribution of age groups is as follows:

Age Group	Per cent of the Total Population
0-15	36-46
15-65	52-59
65-	2- 5

The contrasting age composition in the Western European countries is as follows:

Age Group	Per cent of the Total Population
0-15	21 -26
15-65	62.50-68
65-	10.50-12

The active population in the underdeveloped countries (people between the ages of fifteen and sixty-five), who represent only 52 to 59 per cent of the total population, have to carry the heavy burden of supporting a large proportion of young dependents to whom the smaller proportion of old dependents must be added. This burden of dependents is lighter in the advanced countries, where the active population amounts on the average to 65 per cent.

Of course, the cost of sustaining dependents below the age of fifteen is in most of the underdeveloped countries less than it seems at first glance. The children begin to work at an early age. Those countries, however, which, like India, still suffer from a high mortality among children, spend a large share of the national income on rearing children who later die before reaching the age of fifteen and never join the active population.

The problem of young dependents will be aggravated by the gradual spread of compulsory education, since school attendance will postpone the time when young people earn their own living. Here lies another contradiction between the problems which assail the underdeveloped countries. On the one hand, they must introduce universal education to become modern and economically advanced. On the other, dependents under the age of fifteen will be prevented from performing the work which a great many of them now perform.

If the advanced countries had kept their pre-industrial birth rates and had nevertheless experienced a progressive reduction in their mortality rates, their present populations would have attained a gigantic size. It has been calculated that, if France had maintained its eighteenth-century birth rate and if its death rate had decreased at its actual pace, the present French population would have reached about 500 million. It is highly doubtful whether these 500 million would now have the living standards of the present 48 million Frenchmen. Increases in the national income would probably have been eaten up by a natural increase of these dimensions.

The problem of the underdeveloped countries can be reduced to the following two questions:

1. Will the decreasing proportion of the active population (ages fifteen to sixty-five) be able to raise their labor productivity and hence the annual national income sufficiently to sustain the growing proportion of dependents under the age of fifteen and at the same time to prevent a deterioration in the present low living standards?

2. Will they be capable of doing even more? Specifically, will they be able to work so hard and so efficiently and to live so frugally that the country can progress well ahead of its natural increase? Will they be able to increase the per capita national income steadily in spite of the growth in population and thus produce the national savings which are indispensable for capital investment in economic development?

The task, measured by the natural increase of 2.5 to 4 per cent annually, will be extremely difficult, especially for those countries which already have a high population density or inadequate natural resources.

The rapid natural increase calls urgently for the expansion of food output. Economic development requires much more than maintaining the present low intake of calories and the present diet deficient in proteins. It is conditioned on a rising labor productivity which cannot be reasonably expected from an undernourished population who live on a daily intake of less than 2,000 calories and on a diet poor in proteins. The expansion of food production should not only prevent the per capita consumption from being reduced by the natural increase but also allow for a notably better nutrition.

Certain Western demographers, who extend the present demographic trends into a very distant future, express their alarm at the prospect of mankind being unable to produce enough food for its sustenance and eventually crowding itself off the earth. These alarmist views, sometimes influenced by the fear that the "colored" flood will engulf the West, do not take into account two factors. First, the population explosion in the underdeveloped countries will not last forever; eventually it will be checked as it was in Europe, by economic development and a rise in the living standards. Secondly, scientific and technological progress will in due time allow for the extraction of food and raw materials from sources now untapped, such as ocean water or ordinary rocks. For the time being, the agricultural surpluses which are chronic headaches for quite a few advanced countries could, if intelligently used, bring some relief to the underdeveloped areas having a deficient food output. Moreover, there are no physical obstacles to expanding food production and keeping abreast of the population growth during, say, the next fifty years. The cultivated land can be substantially increased and the general use of progressive agricultural techniques, practised in the advanced countries, could greatly improve the yield per acre. The practical problem is not that of what may be done but what will be done to take care of the fast-expanding population.

The demographic revolution could be slowed down by birth control.

However, Western demographic history offers no encouragement in this respect. The exceptional case of France does not provide any clues, because it is unknown why the French peasant of the second half of the eighteenth century and the first half of the nineteenth century, who still lived in poverty, decided to limit the size of his family. The West went through a long time-lag (at least fifty years) between the beginning of the fall in the mortality rate and the first symptoms of a downward trend in the birth rate. The reasons for the falling birth rate were numerous and can be listed as follows: (1) the prohibition of child labor and the introduction of universal education, both of which increased the cost of raising children; (2) a better knowledge of the child's needs; (3) a decline in infant mortality and the realization by the parents that all their children would probably reach adult age; (4) old-age social insurance which made the parents more independent of their offspring; (5) a decrease in parental authority; (6) the emancipation of women; (7) greater social mobility and hence greater economic independence for young people, who were able to find jobs far away from their parents' place of residence; (8) a higher level of general education and a greater sophistication of prospective parents; (9) higher living standards and the growing needs of both parents and children, resulting in a careful computation of the family budget; (10) urbanization insofar as it was integral with a developing society; slum urbanization in an underdeveloped country cannot have the same effect.

These reasons for birth control in the West should not be regarded as deterministic. The unexpected rise in the American birth rate serves as a warning that human choices are less foreseeable than often supposed. People do not live by material comfort alone and sometimes refuse to abide by statistical forecasts. Even if these reasons were deterministic, they would be inoperative in the underdeveloped countries simply because these countries are underdeveloped. Moreover, the young age composition of their populations is in itself a powerful factor in speeding up the natural increase.

The only advanced Asian country, Japan, has had a demographic history which recalls the Western pattern. For a long time, a reduction in the mortality rate was unaccompanied by any fall in the birth rate. The total population of developing Japan jumped from 30 to 90 million. Only recently, under the delayed impact of modernization, has the birth rate begun to fall. The rate of natural increase, which in 1947 was still as high as 20 per thousand, declined in 1961 to 9.4 per thousand. The birth rate was reduced between 1920 and 1961 from 39.8 per thousand to 16.8 per thousand (the American birth rate in the same year was 23.4 per thousand). In 1961 the Japanese mortality rate was as low as 7.4 per thousand; the life expectancy for males was 65.37 years and for females 70.26.

Governments and private organizations can promote the concept of birth control and provide the means of contraception. This is being done in India but so far with insignificant results. Can the underdeveloped countries escape the Western cycle and have an effective birth control in economic conditions entirely different from the Western? Will a population, poor and mostly illiterate, respond to propaganda favoring birth control? In any case, the decision to promote birth control is a matter to be examined by the countries concerned and cannot be imposed from abroad. Western demographic history indicates that religious beliefs, if they are contrary to contraception, prove to be ineffective; social and economic factors have brought about birth control in all Western countries regardless of their religious denominations.

Western bystanders should be cautious about giving advice. Western propaganda for birth control in the underdeveloped countries might boomerang politically. It might arouse the suspicion that the Western well-wishers are motivated, not by humanitarian reasons, as most of them are, but by a fear that the Western world will be swamped by the teeming billions of "colored" people. This suspicion could be deepened by a reminder that the nineteenth-century Western enthusiasts of birth control were motivated by a similar fear that the upper and middle classes would be submerged by the numerical growth of the lower social classes. Moreover, the nationals of underdeveloped countries who read Western publications on demography could quote a number of Western authors who favor an increase in the birth rate of their own countries but vigorously advocate birth control in the non-Western lands. These authors can plead in their defense the different economic conditions in the West, but the argument may sound unconvincing to those who are deeply suspicious of Western motives.

The stand taken by the American government in 1963 seems the best that could be adopted. The United States will refrain as before from any propaganda on birth control which would aim at "converting" foreign peoples to the concept of the small family, but it will provide advice and assistance to those governments which ask for help. The initiative is left with foreign governments, and the motive for American assistance cannot be impugned.

The Communist parties usually deny the gravity of the demographic problem; they glibly insist that all the social and economic problems related to a rapid natural increase could be effectively solved by the adoption of the Communist system. They are opposed, as a matter of principle, to any birth control. It is interesting to note that the one Communist party which has had to face the demographic dilemma in all its gravity, the Chinese, has not clung to this general Communist line. The Chinese situation is not different from that of India or Pakistan. A population of 680 million (almost a quarter of the total population of the world) is increasing at an annual rate of 2.3 per cent or by about 16 million. China's agricultural output does not grow at the same rapid rate, as evidenced by food shortages during the last few years and purchases of grain abroad. So far, the Chinese party has followed a hesitant policy. For a time they sponsored birth control by distributing pertinent information; later, they abandoned this policy without, however, condemning birth control or denouncing it as antisocial; recently, they have resumed public support of birth control. The only European party to promote birth control is the Polish party, which launched a campaign in its support a few years ago to alleviate economic problems caused by a high postwar birth rate.

THE THIRD STAGE: DECLINING RATE OF NATURAL INCREASE

An advanced country, endowed with a modern economic and social structure, enters the third stage of demographic evolution. This stage is marked by a continuation of the gradual fall in the mortality rate and by a rapid fall in the birth rate. The natural increase, which was at its peak in the second stage, now begins to level off. This is the stage when birth control becomes a general practice and the small family appears. We have already noted the several economic and social reasons for the emergence of this new social attitude. Generally speaking, the whole of Europe, the Soviet Union, and Japan have in common a declining natural increase, although their rates are not identical. These rates are higher for Eastern and Southern Europe, and the Soviet Union, because these areas entered the third stage much later than the West.

Before 1937 it was taken for granted that the downward trend of the birth rate could not be reversed. Quite unexpectedly, between 1934 and 1942, the Western nations began to show a sudden increase in their birth rate. France, whose birth rate had fallen uninterruptedly since 1760 and reached a very low level of 17.3 per thousand in 1932, witnessed a reversal of the trend in 1942. In 1947 its birth rate climbed to 23.8 per thousand. A similar reversal took place in all the Western countries during the years between 1934 and 1942. The period of a relatively high birth rate did not last very long. The birth rates began to level off in the late forties. In 1961 the rates in Western Europe were as follows: Austria 18.5 per thousand, Belgium 16.9, Denmark 16.6, France 18.4, West Germany 18.2, Italy 18.8, the Netherlands 21.2, Norway 17.5, Sweden 13.9, Switzerland 18.1, Britain 17.8. Consequently, the rate of natural increase was well below 10 per thousand (enclosed between the rate of 9.4 per thousand for Italy and 4 per thousand for Belgium).

Higher natural increase rates still prevailed in 1961 in Eastern and Southern Europe where they were, for instance, 13.6 per thousand for Yugoslavia, 13.1 for Poland, 12.9 for Portugal, 12.7 for Spain, and 17.8 for the U.S.S.R. The only Western European country to have a similar rate was the Netherlands with 13.6 per thousand as its rate of natural increase.

The return of Europe to a low birth rate after a short interval might suggest the conclusion that a decline in the natural increase cannot be halted for long once it has started. This conclusion seems to be supported by what we know of the demographic history of ancient Greece and Rome. However, the recent American record should make one cautious in adopting this deterministic attitude. The United States had followed the usual pattern of advanced countries until the middle thirties. The birth rate declined in 1933 to its lowest level of 16.6 per thousand. This downward trend was reversed in 1937 as unexpectedly as in Western Europe. In 1947 the birth rate reached the high figure of 25.7 per thousand and has since remained well above 20 per thousand. The rate of natural increase, which in 1940 had been only 7 per thousand, rose in 1961 to 14.1 per thousand. Since the American birth rate is higher than the Western European, the age composition of the population is also different. The proportion of children under fifteen is higher (31 per cent), and the proportion of the active population and of people over sixty-five is smaller (60 per cent and 9 per cent respectively).

Why is it that a highly developed nation such as the United States, which enjoys the best living standards ever attained, has suddenly refuted the demographic predictions and reversed the trend in the vital statistics? The question is interesting because it has become a cliché to accuse Americans of being materialistic, of desiring nothing from life but more and more comfort. Yet American parents have sacrificed a part of their material comfort for the sake of having larger families. They have done so in the absence of the motives for having a large family that exist in the underdeveloped countries. They are literate, calculate their family budget, and want to continue purchasing durable consumer goods; yet in spite of the growing cost of raising and educating their children, they choose to have families which are not small by the standards of the 1930's. The phenomenon cannot be explained mathematically; apparently Americans have begun to feel that man cannot live by durable consumer goods alone. However, it is not certain that this new social behavior will last forever and that a downward trend in the birth rate will not return.

What are the problems of a country with a declining rate of natural increase? Its proportion of dependents under fifteen is steadily decreasing because of the fall in the birth rate; this trend is compounded by the general ageing of the population. The proportion of young dependents in North-West-Central Europe (economically the most developed parts of Europe) accounts for approximately 24 per cent of the total population. It should be recalled that the average for the underdeveloped countries is 40 per cent. In other words, the advanced country is biologically older than the underdeveloped country with a fast-expanding population. The shrinking proportion of young dependents does not notably reduce the cost of their upbringing. Their needs are incomparably greater than those of their poor contemporaries in the underdeveloped countries. They expect in particular to acquire a high school education; a growing number hope to obtain a higher education. Whether the cost of education is borne by the parents or by the state, the resources are provided by the work of the active population.

The falling mortality rate and the extended life expectancy are reflected in the increasing proportion of people over sixty-five. The average proportion in North-West-Central Europe is 11 per cent. This proportion is bound to grow with the expected further decline of the death rate. The burden of supporting the aged is increasing. The concept of the welfare state entails old-age pensions and a variety of other forms of assistance for the aged, including medical assistance. This burden is not lightened, as it is in the case of young dependents, by the hope that the beneficiaries will later join the active population. The expense is not an investment in the future but a social debt paid to those who have contributed to the prosperity of the country.

The active population reaches its optimum figure at this stage, from 62.50 to 68 per cent. Never before in history has the active population attained to this proportion of the total. The economic consequence is obvious. The large proportion of people engaged in useful work produces a very high national income per capita for the total population, including the young and old dependents. This is one factor in the great prosperity of the advanced countries, another being high per capita labor productivity due to economic and technological development. It is one of the ironies of our time that an increase in automation, with a consequent reduction in the manpower requirement, coincides with an increase in the proportion of the active population. Unless output is greatly increased or working hours are drastically reduced, automation will result in large-scale unemployment at a time when the advanced countries are favored by the highest proportion of working people.

The manifest contrast between the demographic trends in the advanced (mostly Western) nations and those in the underdeveloped countries (mostly of non-European origin) may partly explain why the populations of European stock have ended their period of political expansion, a period that began with the circumnavigation of the globe and the conquests of the sixteenth century and came to an end in this century. The West is demographically in retreat and politically on the defensive.

If a demographer of 1900 had extrapolated the trends then evident in the statistics of prior decades, he would have predicted for 1950 a total European population which would have been much larger than it actually was. His error would have been due not only to the later rapid decline in the birth rate but also to the tremendous human losses which Europe suffered in the two world wars. These losses, made up of military and civilian casualties, were compounded by birth "deficits" due to the wartime separation of the two sexes (military service, conscripted labor, internment in the concentration camps) and to proportionately great losses in the young-age groups with the highest fertility rate.

Except for France, Western Europe entered the stage of a declining birth rate after 1870. France, whose record in this respect was a century older, faced for a time the last and most agonizing problem of an ageing society, the specter of depopulation. Its death rate, although declining, exceeded in 1936-39 the faster-decreasing birth rate. The actual decline in the size of the total population was concealed by a large foreign emigration, chiefly Southern and Eastern European, which took place during the period between 1921 and 1933. Almost two million people settled in France and made up for the numerical decline of the population of French extraction. If the trend toward a constantly decreasing birth rate were to continue indefinitely in North-West-Central Europe, the same specter of depopulation would haunt these most advanced European areas, while the populations of the underdeveloped countries will certainly grow at a fast rate and in several cases at a rate faster than at present.

The risk of relying too much on demographic forecasts is demonstrated by recent population trends in France. Before the war, the declining curve of the French birth rate seemed to be irreversible. This rate was 32.8 per thousand in 1801, 22 in 1901, 14.6 in 1938. Then it suddenly jumped in 1943 to 15.7, in 1947 to 21.4, and then dropped in 1958 to 18.1, a figure that is still much higher than the rate in 1938. The present annual total is 800,000 births. During the last twenty years the French population has increased from the prewar 40 million to the present 47.5 million. France, which seemed before the war to be condemned to a slow depopulation, now expects with confidence to have one of the youngest age compositions among the Western European nations.

Demographic pressure, whether actually existing or only invented for propaganda purposes, has sometimes been exploited to justify an expansionist foreign policy. It was invoked by the Nazis in their theory of "people without living space" at a time when Germany was in fact increasing its population at a very slow rate. The emptiness of this slogan was exposed after the war by the influx into West Germany of millions of Germans from Eastern Europe and East Germany. Today, more than one in every five West Germans lived elsewhere before the war or had parents living elsewhere. They have all resettled and found jobs in the booming West German economy. The per capita income of West Germany is now higher than before the war when the population was smaller, and there is a certain shortage of manpower which calls for the immigration of workers from other European countries, notably from Italy. Postwar Japan does not seem to be worse off than before the war in spite of its increased population and the loss of its prewar control over access to Chinese raw materials and markets. These two cases prove that a rapid development of the domestic economy can alleviate the problems of overpopulation when these problems are real, as they were in Japan, or enable people to disregard demagogic slogans that exaggerate such problems when they are more imaginary than real, as they were in Germany. Demographic pressure can, however, become the source of an aggressive foreign policy if economic development lags behind the natural increase and no effective remedy is in sight.

CHAPTER VII

The Ideological Conflict

PRELIMINARY REMARKS

Even if the countries which belong to the European civilization were not rent by ideological conflict, the vast and complex problems of national self-assertion and modernization among the underdeveloped two-thirds of mankind would suffice to unsettle international conditions for several decades to come. If the statesmen of the nineteenth century had commanded the present nuclear arsenal, they would probably have been relieved that, unlike their ancestors of the sixteenth and seventeenth centuries, they were under no compulsion to multiply the risks of international politics by engaging in ideological crusades. Is it a characteristic of our age that we seem to take a perverse pleasure in compounding the unprecedented difficulties and dangers of our time? The revolutionary trends that pulsate in the underdeveloped continents and the existence of the ultimate nuclear sanction for mistakes in foreign policy do not seem to suffice. An ideological conflict over rival concepts of the best society is superimposed at a time when Asians, Africans, and Latin Americans are engaged in an arduous effort to achieve, not the best, but only a better society and when mankind daily runs the risk of the disappearance of all societies in a collective nuclear suicide.

It has been said that men differ from animals in their unique capacity to persecute and exterminate one another for the sake of general ideas which they hardly understand. Certainly it is true that the fiercest human struggles have been fought over conflicting ideologies. These concepts have paved the way to power for those men who have known how to manipulate both abstract ideas and their fellow-believers. If the leaders themselves firmly believe in their ideas, they become ruthless fanatics.

It was Voltaire who remarked that fanatics are more dangerous than rascals because rascals understand reason but it is impossible to make a fanatic listen to reason. Fanatical leaders who arrogate to themselves the exclusive right to interpret the ideology lead their credulous followers into battles against multitudes of believers in other ideologies. Skeptics and agnostics are resented by both camps. In the past these ideological battles were called religious wars; they are now called ideological conflicts. Like our forebears of the sixteenth century we live in a time when fanatics divide human beings into the two rigid categories of the pro's and the con's and when the independent-minded run the risk of being denounced as heretics or traitors.

At the same time that the European civilization is being torn asunder by ideological conflict its culture is conquering the realms of other civilizations. Its hour of greatest cultural triumph is also the hour of its "religious war."

The cliché is true, though rather meaningless, that the problems of our epoch would have existed without Communism or the Communist bloc. The nuclear revolution in military technology was due to science, not to Communist ideology. As a matter of fact, the first and only use of nuclear weapons cannot be blamed on a Communist power. The national awakening of the non-European countries began before the October Revolution, as shown by the early nationalist movements in India, Indonesia, China, and the Arab Near East. The crisis of the colonial system and the movement for the modernization of retarded societies would have occurred, quite independent of Communism and the Communist movement, as a result of the irresistible impact of the European ideas of equality and national self-determination.

The Communists have not created the fundamental problems of contemporary mankind; they have never had this ambition. Their appearance as a powerful movement on the stage of international politics has a different significance. What would have been a slow waltz has become a rock-and-roll. They have proved their ability to seize historical opportunities which they did not create. They have a sense of direction and do their best to lead the dancers toward a destination which they call the universal triumph of socialism.

They have repeatedly demonstrated their sense of historical opportunity. Lenin did not create the Russian peasant problem or the social pains of the initial stage of industrialization, nor was he the cause of the inefficiency of the Tsarist regime or of the Russian debacle in the First World War. But he had the political genius to discover that the situation in 1917 offered his party an opportunity to seize power in Russia. Stalin did not make Hitler the chancellor of Germany, but he knew how to exploit the consequences of the war between the Western democracies and Nazi Germany for an extension of the Communist realm to Eastern Central

Europe. Mao Tse-tung bore no responsibility for the Chinese peasant problem or for Japanese aggression; it was not his fault that the Kuomintang was unable to cope with the problems of China. He only capitalized on these circumstances and thus won power for his party.

The relationship between ideology and power is very complex. Ideological considerations can become one of the main reasons for the use of power. The Moslem conquests, the Crusades, the Religious Wars, the wars of Revolutionary France, the Allied intervention in the Russian Civil War, the Soviet intervention in Hungary are several examples which can be added to the illustrations supplied by civil wars. Ideas can conquer human minds without the initial support of organized power and even in a struggle against it. This has been proved by the history of several religious movements, including Christianity of the first centuries of our era, and by the successes of the Marxist ideology prior to the October Revolution. But ideas can spread faster and farther if supported by organized power; the outer limits of their expansion are often determined by the outcome of a contest of power. The conversion of Constantine the Great certainly contributed to the Christian triumph within the Roman Empire. The later conversions of various pagan European populations were to some extent due to the actual use of force either by a Christian foreign ruler (for instance, by Charlemagne in his conversion of the Saxons) or by a converted native prince who did not hesitate to use coercion in order to make Christians of his subjects (examples abound in the medieval history of Central and Eastern Europe). Among other causes, the conversions to Christianity were due to the prestige enjoyed by Christian kingdoms which were more powerful than their pagan neighbors. Conversion was required for admission to the medieval society of civilized peoples. Similarly, Soviet power played a major role in extending the Communist regime to Eastern Europe, as did Chinese power in ensuring the survival of Communist governments in North Korea and North Vietnam.

The delimitation of the zones of influence between two rival ideologies was frequently the outcome of a contest of power. The battle of Poitiers decided the question whether Europe would be Moslem. The failure of the Western crusades settled another issue, whether the Near East and North Africa would remain Moslem. The Religious Wars ended in a compromise which was founded on a frank recognition of power as the final arbiter between the Catholics and the Protestants. *Cuius regio, eius religio* was an admission that each prince could impose his religion on his subjects, presumably by virtue of his being the holder of power. The ideological frontier which cuts Europe into two parts divided by the Berlin wall is due to a stalemate between the two contending powers. Although it is true that every ideological struggle is a battle for human minds and that ideas know no frontier, it should not be forgotten that power plays an extremely important role in this struggle.

Success, which may be partly due to power, certainly enhances the attractiveness of an ideology. Most of the major religious movements gathered their greatest number of converts after the first impressive triumphs demonstrated that they were an irresistible tide of history. The victory of the Western nations in 1918 convinced many people, particularly in Eastern Europe, that democracy was the best form of government. Many of these converts owed their conversion less to a deep faith in democratic values than to their having been impressed by the military prowess of the Western democracies; their "democratic" convictions usually did not last long. The views of a large part of mankind on the merits of Nazism and Fascism fluctuated in the late thirties and early forties *pari passu* with the political and military fortunes of Germany and Italy. Today many people are inclined to evaluate the soundness of Leninism, and, by implication, of democracy, by the scientific, technological, economic, and political successes of the Communist states, notably Russia and China.

COMMUNISM AND THE WEST

If one asked the question what Communism practically offers as a social-economic regime, the answer would differ for the Western and the underdeveloped societies. The original Marxism, which was conceived as a doctrine of social change in the Western industrial societies, is dead. Leninism, an offspring of Marxism, is very much alive but represents a doctrine of modernization for the non-Western underdeveloped societies.

Socialism, including Marxism, was originally a protest against the social inequities which accompanied the Industrial Revolution. It was born at a time when the manufacturer ruthlessly exploited the industrial worker and extracted from his sweat the greatest possible profit, which was reinvested in Western economic development. The social evils which later accompanied Soviet industrialization revealed the truth that no regime could avoid extorting from its masses the means for economic development. What Karl Marx wrote about the conditions in Britain during the Industrial Revolution could have been applied to the Soviet society in the same stage of economic development. Low wages, slums, high prices due to the state sales tax which was calculated to reduce popular consumption, Draconian labor discipline, were the regular features of the industrialization of the Soviet Union as they were of the industrialization of Britain. The Communist state did what private manufacturers had done before; the underlying reasons for their behavior were the same. If the Soviet society now witnesses a slow and gradual rise in living standards, this is due to the same cause which earlier produced the same improvement in the West, namely the completion of the foundations for an industrial society.

The socialists of the nineteenth century, including Marx, could observe only capitalist industrialization and quite naturally detected in capitalism itself rather than in the process of industrialization the cause of the social evils they witnessed. Hence, private ownership of the means of production was proclaimed to be the cause of social inequities. Socialism proposed to replace this ownership with public ownership of all the means of production and thus to usher in a new society founded on social equality. Marx simplified the problem in thinking that all social evils could be traced to private ownership; he expected that total socialization would change human nature, make coercion unnecessary, and finally result in a gradual withering away of the state, which he held to be a capitalist tool of oppression. He could not check the veracity of his propositions against the Soviet experience, which has proved that human nature cannot be changed by any new mode of production and that in a nationalized economy the state becomes a much more ruthless tool of coercion than in the capitalist economy.

He did not believe that the capitalist society could change through evolution. Projecting contemporary trends far into the future, he was sure that the concentration of capital would constantly reduce the number of capitalists and increase the numerical proportion of impoverished proletarians. Inevitably, the mass of proletarians would revolt, overthrow the tiny class of capitalists, and socialize the means of production in order to usher in a new historical era in which man would no longer have the opportunity to exploit man. How could he foresee that the Western industrial workers would acquire a middle-class mentality in an increasingly prosperous society or that public ownership of the means of production would bring about a new form of exploitation by a social class which did not exist in his time?

His predictions were refuted by later developments in the West. The process of industrialization was completed, and its repulsive symptoms began to disappear. Technological progress made productivity much more dependent on machines than on human labor. Mass production demanded that the producer also be a mass consumer. The Western societies were enabled by the toil and privations of former generations to gather the harvest which we call the welfare state. The social conflicts lost their bitterness. It is true that this general picture of contemporary Western conditions calls for certain qualifications in the case of those Western nations which have not yet fully achieved a fair distribution of national income and a broad social access to higher education; France is a case in point.

The transformation of social conditions in the West has taken place without the revolution which Marx predicted, and Marxism has lost its appeal for the Western worker. The Western socialist parties, formerly Marxist, have openly or implicitly renounced Marxism and have shifted to the position of reformist parties organized to defend the interests of all people who earn their living, whether "workers" or not. The Western Communists have been unable for the same reason to muster a large following in any Western country except France and Italy, where their partisans have, however, remained in the condition of a numerically frozen minority vegetating on the margin of national life.

The main tangible fruit of a Communist revolution is the modernization of a semideveloped or underdeveloped society. Leninism cannot offer anything in this respect to the economically developed nations, which are actually more advanced than the Soviet Union. However, Soviet practice harbors two challenges to the West. First, it raises the question which society, the capitalist or the socialist, can produce more abundantly and more efficiently. Perhaps a very distant future will supply the unexpected answer that both types of economy are able to advance at an equal pace. Secondly, the Soviet school system, as adopted in the post-Stalinist era, offers equal opportunity of access to education at all levels. This compels the West to accelerate its process of equalizing educational opportunities for all children and youth, regardless of their financial means.

The Western challenge to the Communist societies of Russia and Eastern Europe is of a different nature. The spectacle of modern and yet free societies will always exert a disconcerting influence by providing a yardstick by which the Communist society can be judged by its own independent-minded members.

LENINISM AND THE UNDERDEVELOPED COUNTRIES

Karl Marx proved to his satisfaction that the socialist revolution would be an inevitable consequence of the development of capitalist society. A socialist revolution in a precapitalist society would have been for him a contradiction in terms. Yet the first "Marxist" revolution took place in semideveloped Russia where both capitalism and industrialization were still in their infancy. The "Marxist" regime was installed in Eastern Europe in the wake, not of a spontaneous revolt by industrial workers, but of military occupation by Soviet troops. Moreover, most of Eastern Europe at the time was semideveloped. Another "Marxist" revolution took hold of an entirely underdeveloped China. "Marxist" regimes were established in other underdeveloped countries, such as North Korea, North Vietnam, Cuba, and even nomadic Mongolia.

The failure of Marxism in the highly developed societies and the triumphant progress of Communism in the semi- or underdeveloped countries are reflected in the new doctrine called Leninism. The Communists continue to claim that they have remained orthodox Marxists and append the word *Leninism* to *Marxism*. Actually, they carry over from the original Marxism only two elements: hostility to private ownership of the means of production, and the Marxist philosophy of the universe and of history. They have otherwise rejected Marxism in fact by upholding the un-Marxist view that the socialist revolution can take place in any society, however primitive economically. This doctrinal weakness is also the source of their political strength, because it enables them to advocate revolution in the very countries where revolutionary opportunities exist; these opportunities do not exist in the West, but they abound in the semideveloped and underdeveloped areas.

Lenin revitalized the radical wing of the Marxist movement by his two doctrinal contributions. First, he looked at the capitalist society from a point of view much broader than that of Marx. The founder of the so-called scientific socialism concentrated his whole attention on social conflicts within a fully developed capitalist society; for him the socialist revolution was to be the consequence of national developments within each separate industrial society. Lenin looked at the whole world and discovered the economic dependence of the advanced societies on the raw materials and markets of the non-Western underdeveloped countries. He widened the scope of the revolutionary problem and proclaimed that the capitalist system in the advanced countries could be attacked, not only by the frontal assault of domestic revolutionary forces, but also by an enveloping movement that would undermine the capitalist economy by cutting it off from its sources of primary commodities and from markets for its industrial goods. He discovered the revolutionary potentialities of the Third World at a time when few people paid any attention to this aspect of the international situation. The whole world, including the underdeveloped areas, became in his interpretation the future stage of the revolutionary movement. Western capitalism was to be assaulted and undermined, not only by socialist revolutions in the Western countries, but also by anticolonialist movements in the underdeveloped continents. The practical problem for Lenin was to disrupt the capitalist chain anywhere; he thought that this chain could always be broken at the weakest link, but not necessarily where the economy was most developed. Later Communist experience has proved that the weakest links were the underdeveloped countries or those nations whose territories were occupied by Communist troops.

Secondly, Lenin redefined revolutionary opportunity. Unlike Marx, he did not see this opportunity confined only to the highest stage of capitalist development. He deduced his own definition, not from an aprioristic forecast of future developments, but from an analysis of actual historical experience. He listed four conditions for a successful revolution: (1) a calamity overtaking the country; (2) a general discontent with existing conditions brought to the surface by the national disaster; (3) the loss of faith by the ruling class in its own capacity to solve the problems arising out of the national crisis; (4) the existence of a revolutionary group ready to channel popular discontent into a movement against the existing regime. These four conditions can exist at any historical time and in any society; they are divorced from Marxist economic premises. They aptly sum up the historical record of all revolutions. Lenin himself tested the correctness of his thesis in his own country. Russia was ready for a revolutionary upheaval according to his theoretical premises, even if it were unready for a truly Marxist revolution according to the original doctrine of his spiritual master. In 1917 the cumulative effect of several causes created a situation which could be called a national calamity. Discontent was widespread. The ruling class lost faith in its capacity to cope with the situation. A well-organized group of revolutionaries, Lenin's Bolsheviks, was ready to channel the discontent in the direction which they determined. The Chinese Communists again proved the correctness of Lenin's analysis.

Stalin added a new element by demonstrating in Eastern Europe what had been proved many times before—by revolutionary France for example—that the superior military power of a foreign state could install any regime in any country. In 1944-45 his troops completed the "ideological" conquest of Eastern-Central Europe. The Communists now know that their revolutionary victory can materialize (1) as the result of a spontaneous domestic development properly directed by the Communist party (Lenin's thesis), or (2) as the result of external military intervention by a Communist great power, if international circumstances permit (Stalin's practice).

Lenin was one of the few Europeans who detected before the First World War the potentialities of the national awakening of non-European populations. He foresaw that this awakening, the shaking off of colonial chains, would of necessity be anti-Western. He deduced the practical conclusion that the West could be simultaneously attacked on two fronts: the Communist front directed against the Western capitalistic system itself, and the nationalist front of colonial and semicolonial non-European populations directed against Western political and economic dominance. He taught his disciples that warfare on the two fronts should be coordinated to make it more effective and that non-Communist nationalists engaged in the struggle against Western imperialism should be looked upon as valuable though temporary allies.

Leninism, as a doctrine tailored to fit the underdeveloped countries, leads logically to the contemporary claim that the socialist system of economy is a short cut toward rapid economic development and social modernization. One link in the original Marxist historical sequence (the primitive collectivist society, the slave-owning society, the feudal society, the capitalist society, and finally the socialist society) is conjured away. The most backward societies (Mongolia is an example) are told that they do not need to pass through the capitalist stage of development, which is allegedly outmoded, and should jump directly from the "feudal" stage into the socialist. In other words, all countries, advanced and retarded alike, are offered the same recipe: the total socialization of all the means of production, even if these means are the camels and horses of nomadic tribesmen. The argument which is used refers mainly to the Russian experience. Russia of 1914 is inexactly presented as a completely underdeveloped country similar to the non-European underdeveloped areas of today. The Communists say in effect: "Look at Russia. It was in your condition as late as 1917 but has become the second industrial power in the world and is competing for the conquest of outer space. The socialist system is the key to its astounding success." Without underestimating the tremendous effort made under the Soviet regime, one cannot overlook the rapid rate of Russian industrialization during the several decades prior to the October Revolution, the existence of a sizable industrial base and of a large skilled manpower in the cities, a long scientific and technological tradition, and the fairly modern structure of the Russian state. The Communist party began its own industrial drive with all these assets. It did not start from scratch as most underdeveloped countries must now do; it also was favored by an unusual wealth of natural resources. Oversimplified Soviet propaganda obscures these facts. Indeed, the thesis that all countries, advanced or backward, are ready for socialism would be better buttressed by the economic and technological success of China. It was a genuine underdeveloped country in 1949 at the time of the Communist victory. If China succeeds in becoming modernized within a reasonable period of time, its example will be more convincing than that of Russia.

The Communists discovered much earlier than the West that contemporary international politics are triangular in nature. Glancing at the international stage from the Western point of view, it must be conceded that the struggle with the Communist bloc would have been greatly simplified if the underdeveloped countries did not exist or had no economic and strategic significance. The problem could then be reduced almost to the military terms of mutual deterrence. In the same way, the West would not have been greatly troubled by the new trends in these countries and could cope with these trends almost on its own terms, if the Communist competitor were not everpresent.

Why is it that the Communists have selected the underdeveloped countries as the main battlefield against the West? The Leninist doctrine supplies a twofold answer. There is the immediate opportunity of co-operation with the non-Communist ruling groups in those countries if they have some accounts to settle with the West. There is the other, more distant opportunity for the local Communists to seize power. The underdeveloped countries are cast in two roles: as temporary allies against the West, but also as the stage of future Communist revolutions.

Whenever and wherever the colonial past or a current dispute shadows the relations between an underdeveloped country and a Western nation, the opportunity arises for the Communist states to become a third factor in the equation. The irruption of the Communist, mostly Soviet, influence is felt by the West almost as a sacrilege; the memory of the time when the Third World was its exclusive game preserve dies hard in the West, and outsiders look like poachers. The same hostile reaction cannot be expected from the Third World. Its nationalism is anti-Western in origin; the colonial powers were all Western. Dissatisfaction with the present international division of labor, which assigns to the underdeveloped countries the subordinate role of sources of primary commodities and markets for industrial goods, has of necessity an anti-Western undertone, because most of the trade continues to be with the industrial West. If an underdeveloped country nationalizes foreign assets or tightens its control over foreign corporations, the assets and corporations are invariably Western. Disputes over the elimination of the remnants of colonialism or over other subjects usually involve a former colonial power, again a Western nation.

In these circumstances, the Communist states, the enemies of the West, seem to be useful friends or at least a handy counterbalancing factor. The existence of the Communist bloc appears in Western eyes as an unmitigated evil; but the same competitive center of power means for the Third World an opportunity for political maneuvering which was denied it during the four centuries of undisturbed Western dominance. The very conflict between the two blocs has placed the Third World in the advantageous position of being the prize for which the two parties contend. Both adversaries are compelled by their competition to court the underdeveloped peoples and to shower favors on them. It is not impossible that both competitors may ultimately be "cheated," if the Third World develops successfully, as a result of their assistance, but does not become a vassal of either bloc.

The main objective of the Communist bloc in cultivating friendly relations with the non-Communist governments of underdeveloped countries is to make them more independent of, if not more unfriendly to, the West. This objective is pursued by the following means:

1. The simplest and the least expensive consists in backing up every underdeveloped country which is engaged in a dispute with a Western power. The occasions are frequent, because the relations between those countries and the West will continue for some time to be plagued by disputes which arise out of the colonial era and over the nature of future relations. The Communist bloc never hesitates to support the non-Western party to the disputes. This has been proved many times: in the Indian-Portuguese quarrel over Goa; in the Indonesian-Dutch dispute over West Irian and the nationalization of Dutch assets; in the 1956 conflict between

Britain and France, on the one hand, and Egypt, on the other, over the nationalization of the Suez Canal; in the United States dispute with Cuba; and in several other instances. There is no good reason why Russia or China should modify this policy, which makes sense from their point of view.

The Communist bloc invariably sides with every colonial movement for self-determination or against racial discrimination; all these movements, now located in Africa, are directed against a Western colonial power. In the United Nations, the bloc supports the most extreme anti-colonialist positions and does its best to earn the reputation of being a friend of oppressed peoples.

If an underdeveloped country is committed to the West, the Communist diplomatic effort aims at persuading it to adopt a neutralist policy. Two arguments are used. One brutally points out the risk of nuclear annihilation of all Western allies by Soviet rockets. The other lures with the prospect of economic assistance; this argument may be more potent since it offers the prospect of receiving aid from both blocs.

2. Economic and technical assistance, including credits, is usually reserved for the uncommitted nations. Yet this aid places the Communist governments before a dilemma. Their credits and supplies of capital equipment, when added to Western economic assistance, provide the non-Communist governments with a better chance of carrying out their program of economic development. The greater this chance, the less likely it is that the local Communists will be able to capitalize on the mistakes of the non-Communist elites and seize power.

Moreover, economic assistance is a sacrifice. The Communist programs of rapid industrialization, of maintaining a high rate of economic growth, and of surpassing the West in total industrial output, would demand that every piece of capital equipment should remain at home or be exported only to another Communist state. Exports of capital goods to the non-Communist countries amount to the subordination of a long-term perspective to the need of exploiting an immediate opportunity.

However, the Western programs of assistance leave no choice. The underdeveloped countries are now used to considering foreign aid as the most tangible proof of friendship. The Communist governments perhaps find some comfort in the thought that no amount of foreign assistance can eliminate the political and social stresses of the long transitional period of modernization and that the local Communist parties will always have their chance.

Communist long-term loans are granted at a very low interest rate, usually 2 or 2.5 per cent, but they can be used for buying goods only from the lender country. The nominally low interest rate might prove in fact to be higher if the prices charged for the goods purchased in the Communist country are higher than the prices on the international market. These loans are repayable in goods which the debtor country produces; this arrangement is helpful, because the underdeveloped countries always find it difficult to secure large amounts of hard currencies.

The trade between the Communist bloc and the underdeveloped countries consists in barter arrangements. The underdeveloped country sells its surpluses and the Communist country imports those primary commodities which it needs. But if the latter country does not need the primary commodities with which it is paid for its capital goods, it frequently resells them on the international market and thus undercuts the price to the prejudice of the producing countries. The appearance of the Communist bloc on the market of the underdeveloped countries provides these countries with greater bargaining power in their negotiations with their main commercial partner, the West, but it does not significantly reduce the importance of this partner. The West continues to import twenty times more than the Communist bloc from the non-Communist underdeveloped areas.

Economic and technical assistance from the Communist bloc does not make the recipient politically dependent unless this aid is not sufficiently counterbalanced by Western aid.

3. The third means used is military assistance. Unlike economic aid, military assistance exacts no sacrifice from the Communist power. Military weapons, like durable consumer goods but unlike capital equipment, do not affect the capacity for production of the country which exports them. Moreover, the weapons which a developed country sells or offers to an underdeveloped friend are usually obsolescent or obsolete. An underdeveloped country turns to the Communist states for military supplies when it has no other choice, the West having refused to be the source of supplies. The Western refusal to sell weapons to Egypt for fear of upsetting the regional balance of armaments offered the Communist bloc a chance to enter the Near Eastern stage. Communist military supplies are meant to buy the gratitude of the recipient country and to increase Western difficulties in relation to that country.

4. The least expensive way to make friends is through the use of political propaganda. Communist political warfare harps on all the anti-Western themes. One of the topics is racialism in the United States, South Africa, and the European colonies in Africa. Another is anticolonialism, which finds a responsive cord among Asians and Africans, who usually know nothing of the Communist doctrine of self-determination. Lenin, who formulated this doctrine, made it crystal clear that Communists should support all movements for national self-determination in the Western colonial possessions and the semicolonial countries. His reason was practical. Each movement of this type was directed against the Western "imperialist" countries and on this score should be welcome. But he made a major reservation. He said that the right to national self-

determination must always be subordinated to the higher cause of socialism. He thus condemned any secessionist movement within a Communist state, because this movement would weaken the cause of socialism by the territorial amputation of the Communist state. This reservation helps Russia and China to maintain their dominance over non-Russian or non-Chinese nationalities. Asians and Africans, who find the Soviet federal system of government a very attractive solution to the problem of nationalities, forget that the centralization of all power in the hands of the Communist party rules out any true autonomy for the same nationalities. But an Asian, an African, or a Latin American, if engaged in a struggle against a Western power, cannot be expected to be interested in these considerations.

The attack on political colonialism still pays dividends because of the survival of European dependencies in Africa. But the gradual Western retreat even from Africa makes this topic increasingly less profitable as Communist propaganda. For this reason anticolonialism has received a new interpretation. The politically emancipated peoples are being told of the dangers of "neocolonialism"—i.e., *economic* subordination to the West. The way of salvation is openly suggested—the nationalization of Western assets, the intensification of trade with the Communist bloc, and a rapid industrialization. The attack on neocolonialism feeds on the unavoidable friction between foreign corporations and native governments or local populations, and on no less unavoidable difficulties in the trade relations between the West and the underdeveloped countries.

The slogan of industrialization (Communists understand by it mainly the building up of heavy industries) cannot but evoke a sympathetic response. Industries are the symbol of advanced and powerful nations. This slogan carries with it not only an indictment of the present international division of labor but also the promise of a better future for the have-not nations. However, it is double-edged. It might prove embarrassing for the non-Communist elites in the underdeveloped countries for two reasons. First, the pressure exerted by external and domestic Communist propaganda might force them to spend the meager resources of their country on building a steel mill in the midst of economic stagnation instead of carefully implementing a program of balanced development. Secondly, both the Soviet leaders and the local Communists never miss an occasion for stressing that the "Soviet miracle" of becoming a developed country within the span of a few decades is due to "the correct leadership." The populations of the underdeveloped countries are given to understand that they can expect a better future only if they follow the correct—i.e., the Communist—leadership.

The Communist states do their best to place themselves at the head of the anticolonialist movement and to raise the banner of the have-not nations against the prosperous West. Judged by the history of the fifties and sixties, their diplomatic and propaganda efforts have not been unfruitful. But their doctrine tells them that there cannot be a lasting friendship with any "bourgeois" government, whether that government controls an advanced or an underdeveloped country. Actual experience in the Arab Near East and in Africa cannot but confirm this doctrinal view. It is understandable that the Communist governments cannot lose sight of the second opportunity in the underdeveloped countries, the opportunity for a Communist revolution.

The Communists hope that the revolution of rising expectations will turn into a revolution of rising frustrations; the higher the expectations, the greater the frustrations. A conspicuous failure of the non-Communist government in carrying out the process of modernization might acquire the significance of what Lenin called a national calamity. But an honest effort at modernization would also be beset with risks and difficulties. The population explosion can every year threaten to annul the effects of all efforts to increase the per capita national income and to accumulate investment capital. Wealthy and politically dominant classes might deliberately slow down the pace of progress by sabotaging the attempts to terminate large-scale tax evasion or to increase direct taxation, by resisting measures which would stop the flight of capital abroad or the importation of luxury goods, by opposing the governmental policies which aim at the distribution of large estates or at the promotion of social mobility. The high hopes of the laboring masses, stimulated by the image of Western living standards, for a quick and visible improvement in their present miserable conditions will be frustrated by the urgent national need for saving from consumption for the sake of capital investment. The extension of literacy and increasing urbanization will make the popular discontent more articulate and potentially more explosive. Social reforms and the elimination of obsolete but age-old institutions can arouse a widespread resistance. The problem of national integration might prove very difficult in many countries where the linguistic, racial, or tribal groups might prefer to retain their sectional loyalties rather than to see them diluted in an over-all national consciousness.

Not only stagnation but also the very process of modernization could create, though for different reasons, the revolutionary opportunity which Lenin had in mind. However, the new power elites could be Communist or non-Communist; there lies the crux of the international future.

The Communist advantage lies in their appeal to those who are hungry or never eat to their satisfaction, to those whose children have little, if any, opportunity to acquire an education and better their lot, to those for whom any change seems to announce an improvement in their condition. The Communists do not promise individual freedoms, but this is a minor consideration for people who have never had a solid democratic tradition but who want economic progress and social mobility.

The Communist slogans are always adjusted to popular aspirations. They promise the landless peasants and agricultural laborers the distribution of large estates into privately owned small holdings. The peasant does not suspect that the same party which champions land reform and offers him a private plot of land intends, if victorious, to take this plot away and to restore large estates in the form of collective farms. The urban proletariat, who are in a worse condition than the British workers at the time of the Industrial Revolution, are promised everything they want, from higher wages and better housing to social legislation. The Communists will not tell the industrial workers that the Soviet Union forbids strikes and free bargaining for labor conditions, that Soviet workers are subject to a harsh labor discipline, and that Soviet labor unions are controlled by the government. The worker or peasant, preoccupied with his immediate misery, would in any event probably be uninterested in stories about real conditions in Russia or China. He thinks that his situation cannot possibly become worse and that any change would of necessity be for the better.

However, the rural and urban populations can be only the tool of political action. The Communist party, the hand that would manipulate this tool, is mostly recruited from the educated classes. It is of crucial importance for the party to conquer the minds of a large section of the intelligentsia, especially of the young who are less afraid of risks and new ideas. There are several reasons why a young man, an educated native of an underdeveloped country, would be attracted to Communism and would enroll in the Communist party:

1. He might hold that only an authoritarian system of government could work in his country, where the revolution of modernization could not be speedily carried out with the assent of the majority.

2. The democratic society, which is avowedly pluralistic, cannot have a single officially sponsored ideology. It is distinguished from other societies by its toleration of all possible and conflicting outlooks. The young citizen of an underdeveloped country whose traditional values have been undermined by his intellectual contacts with modern ideas might be disconcerted by the welter of conflicting Western outlooks and discouraged by Western skepticism, relativism, and agnosticism. He may desperately crave a new faith which would restore his self-confidence and give him a sense of direction. Communism offers a rock of dogmatic faith on which he can stand freed of his former doubts. Marxism appeals precisely because the Communists equate it with absolute truth.

3. If the young man aspires to see his country modernized at a rapid pace whatever the social cost, he will discover in Leninism the short cut for which he has been looking. Of course, he must accept a key condition, a system of government by a noncompetitive elite which ruthlessly casts aside obsolete institutions and pushes economic development forward

at the cost of hard work and great sacrifices exacted from the population. He may not be repelled by the prospect of this "enlightened" tyranny since his present government is probably not democratic and may be, on top of everything else, inefficient.

4. The Communist revolution promises a sudden and complete change of power elites. The young man who cannot find employment commensurate with his education may well be tempted by the prospect of becoming a member of the new power elite. The spectacle of Soviet social inequities and social stratification need not repel him. He has seen enough of social injustice in his own country. Social stratification exists everywhere. In any case, if he is to belong to the post-revolutionary Communist upper class, he knows that he will have a high income, social prestige, and a share in power, all things he might despair of obtaining under the present regime.

5. The contradiction between the ideological tenets of the original Marxism and actual Communist practice might not arouse his indignation. He may think that this disparity between the ideal and the actual, between theory and practice, is an inevitable aspect of social life and point to the contrast between Christian morality and actual practice or between the tenets of democracy and its shortcomings such as racial discrimination or colonialism. Given the imperfections of human nature, he may feel that a certain amount of ideological hypocrisy is a normal phenomenon. He will not be inclined to single out the Communists for blame.

6. If he has inherited from his native environment strong anti-Western feelings, Communism will offer him an ideal opportunity to express them.

7. The growing power and the economic and technological progress of the Communist bloc may convince him that Communism is the wave of the future. He may feel that this is the time to declare himself in order to share later in the spoils of victory.

8. The nationalization of the means of production does not alarm him. The assets of his nation belong either to his upper-class countrymen, whom he scorns as reactionaries, or to Western corporations whose welfare is of no concern to him.

9. The fashionable semantics may lure him to the Communist party. *Socialism* is a popular word. It means, it is true, many things to many people, but it is fashionable in the underdeveloped countries to call oneself a socialist. The word *socialism* may simply imply an intention to modernize the country or belief in a planned program of economic development, or an inclination to pay some attention to the needs of the laboring masses, or the desire to expropriate the large latifundia and distribute the land among the peasants, or the wish to nationalize foreign assets, or the word may simply be synonymous with *progressive* in the vaguest sense. But this same word can also be used as a synonym for *Communism*. Western confusion regarding the meaning of the word does not help to

solve this semantic puzzle which abets the Communists in their campaign for what they call a "socialist" regime.

This analysis is not intended to prove that most young men will be attracted by Communism or that most of the workers and peasants will support the Communist parties. It merely explains why the Communists consider the underdeveloped countries the weak links in the capitalist chain and why they see there their best revolutionary opportunity for many decades to come.

The National Front is one of the devices which the Communist parties use in their attempt to undermine the Western position in the underdeveloped countries and to consolidate their own influence. The National Front is a rally of Communist and non-Communist forces on a common platform of limited co-operation. This platform is acceptable to the Communist parties if it combines two elements: an anti-Western attitude, and a moderate program of domestic reforms required by local conditions.

The Statement which all the Communist parties of the world adopted in 1960 at an international congress in Moscow and which constitutes an approximate codification of the doctrines and tactical precepts of modern Communism strongly recommends the formation in all the underdeveloped countries of "the united national-democratic front of all national patriotic forces." These National Fronts should fight for land reform, for "the uprooting of the imperialist economic domination," for "the foundation and expansion . . . of the state sector of national economy, in particular of state industries independent of foreign monopolies," for "the expansion of economic and cultural co-operation with the socialist countries." If one examines the publicly advertised programs of the Communist parties in the underdeveloped countries, he is amazed by their moderation. These are the minimum programs which have little in common with the maximum programs to be carried out after the Communist seizure of power but which are calculated to serve as a platform for co-operation with non-Communist parties and organizations. These minimum programs call for the redistribution of land among the peasants, for the expropriation of Western assets but certainly not for the nationalization of native enterprises, for high protective tariffs, for advanced social legislation, for rapid industrial expansion, for close trade and other relations with the Communist states, for a foreign policy of noncommitment, and for a strong nationalist self-assertion of which the West is the scapegoat. These programs are not of a nature to repel the non-Communist but progressive organizations. The National Front is expected to enhance the respectability of the Communist party by enlisting the trust and co-operation of the non-Communist parties, to create conditions favorable to the infiltration of various strata of the population, and to introduce Communist influence into the government and public administration if the National

Front succeeds in forming a coalition government. In the meantime the anti-Western attitude of the Front, the *sine qua* condition of Communist participation, furthers the foreign policy of the bloc of Communist states. The 1960 Statement adds that, if for local reasons the National Front cannot be formed, the Communist parties should "support the actions of national governments . . . which undermine the positions of imperialism," the last word being a synonym of the West. The same Statement absolves the "national bourgeoisie" (non-Communists) that assents to co-operate with the Communists by calling it "progressive."

THE PROTOTYPE OF THE COMMUNIST BEST SOCIETY

Unlike the Religious Wars, which were fought over the best method of achieving eternal salvation, the contemporary ideological conflict is over the best form of temporal society. Since the Soviet regime is the oldest of the Communist states, having lasted forty-six years, it is only fair to seek an example of the Communist "best" society in that country, a country which proudly claims the title of the most developed socialist state. The defenders of that regime can no longer plead that its defects are due to its infancy; moreover, its actual experience of several decades yields insight into the process of economic development and social modernization under a one-party regime and in a fully nationalized economy.

After the October Revolution, the Soviet leaders had to define the most urgent task of the new government. They chose the industrialization of semideveloped Russia. Step by step this goal overshadowed the nineteenth-century socialist dream of a society of equals. Russia became a great modern power, but the Marxists of the past century would have found it difficult to recognize in the Soviet Union the realization of their vision of the future.

The Soviet society, like any other, is pluralistic in fact, although party propaganda claims that Soviet citizens are one-minded. To take but one example, even the party does not deny that many Soviet citizens are religious although the regime is officially committed to atheism. Moreover, even the most authoritarian regime cannot penetrate into the recesses of human minds. It can know what its citizens say but not what they really think. It can compel them to say what it wants but cannot prevent them from thinking what they want. However, the party consistently fights against the expression of pluralism and insists on a single pattern of social relations and on one set of dogmas. The party has no choice in the matter. Since it claims exclusive validity for the Marxist philosophy, it cannot tolerate other outlooks, which from its point of view are necessarily harmful errors. It considers itself the repository and guardian of this only and absolute truth about the universe and the meaning of human history and therefore does not permit any rival party or organization, which in its view would propagate ideas that are erroneous by definition and hence harmful to human progress.

This monistic outlook of the party results in wholesale control of all the activities of Soviet citizens. Such control is further justified by the claim that Soviet citizens are unanimous on all matters of social concern, a claim which is buttressed by the results of all Soviet elections. Almost all registered voters cast their ballots; almost all ballots (well over 99 per cent) are invariably cast for the party-sponsored candidates. It is true that there is only one candidate for each elective office and that no competitive candidates are allowed.

Soviet society is highly stratified, the socialist dream of social equality having been in fact consigned to the limbo of other human dreams. Both Marx and Lenin expected that the nationalization of the means of production would bring about a society of social equals in which, as both of them said, the salaries of the highest dignitaries would be the same as the wages of the industrial workers. This expectation has been disappointed. The drive for rapid industrialization and for equally rapid progress in science and technology made the party aware of the vital importance of a well-trained, university-educated intelligentsia and made it worship at the modern altars of managerial and technological efficiency. This preoccupation with efficiency (rapid increase in output, better quality of goods, lower cost of production, increasing labor productivity, constant technological progress) is clearly reflected in the deliberations of party congresses. Were the reader of the verbatim records to forget the Marxist-Leninist references and their political implications, these discussions would strike him as the records of a matter-of-fact convention of any country's business executives. The party fully realizes that technological and economic efficiency depends on skilled manpower, particularly on that section which is university-educated. It knows that this intelligentsia runs its own party machine and the state administration and that it makes the national economy work. Further, the party is not unmindful of the high social cost of producing a well-trained intelligentsia, the nerve center of the whole society, and is well aware of the fact that to fulfill its crucial role the intelligentsia must be kept satisfied, for it will expect a reward for its work. Thus, a highly stratified society has been formed.

Officially, the party acknowledges the existence of "two and a half" social classes: the industrial workers, the peasants, and the intelligentsia, which is modestly called a "social stratum." The industrial proletariat was the historical hero in the Marxist social drama. It was expected not only to make the socialist revolution but to become the ruling class in the socialist society. The cult of efficiency, probably unavoidable in any modern society, produced a different ruling class—the intelligentsia.

The socialist regime has not changed human nature. This fact is implicitly conceded by the party, which never tires of denouncing the social offenses committed daily by Soviet citizens, including party members, and which long ago recognized that men worked more efficiently if given the material incentive of a higher income. Its wage policy for all social classes promotes a wide range of incomes. A highly skilled worker is paid much more than an unskilled worker; the manager of a factory gets a salary and bonuses which make for an income several times higher than that of his average employee; a mechanic on a collective farm is paid much more than a rank-and-file collective farmer. The same is true of the intelligentsia; though in general they represent the new upper and middle classes, their incomes are also highly differentiated.

Their higher income and better education provide the intelligentsia with social prestige. Moreover, the advisory and main executive functions in the Soviet society are exercised by the same social stratum, which thus has a share in power.

The Soviet experience, no less than earlier lessons of history, proves that one of the main results of a revolution is to replace one elite with another and institute new criteria for the recruitment of elites. There are two basic criteria for the recruitment of Soviet social elites—political conformity, and higher education. The October Revolution resulted in the triumph, not of the Marxist hero-class, the industrial proletariat, but of the intelligentsia.

This social class has accumulated a number of vested interests both intangible (social prestige) and tangible (high income). Its loyalty to the regime is the condition on which the Communist system functions. If the intelligentsia as a class were to refuse its services, the Soviet Union would come to a standstill. The party cannot be run without the daily work of its secretaries and other paid functionaries; the armed forces and the security system cannot operate without their military and police officers; and the same is true of all social organizations and all branches of government in which university-educated people provide the leadership, know-how, and organizational skill. There seems to exist a tacit understanding between the ruling professional politicians (the party leadership) and the intelligentsia. Individual members of the intelligentsia can be punished for lack of political loyalty or inefficient performance, but the exalted status of the class cannot be challenged. This is why it seems improbable that Soviet society will ever return to the early socialist dream of social equality. But the party will always be vulnerable to revivalist egalitarian movements which could accuse it of having abandoned the main goal of Marxism. This revivalist sentiment might prove strong among young people who are not yet preoccupied with acquired personal interests.

The college diploma or its equivalent opens the door to all better paid and more highly respected careers. If a man armed with such a diploma proves his efficiency, he is sure of three rewards. First, his income will eventually be incomparably higher than that of a skilled industrial worker. This affords him several advantages: a relatively high living standard for himself and his family; a better apartment or his own privately owned dwelling house—in the case of the most successful, a *dacha* (a summer or countryside house)—and his own or official car (the latter provided with a chauffeur), bank savings for his old age, and the right to leave his accumulated earthly belongings to relatives (the right of inheritance includes not only spouse and children but also grandparents, grandchildren, brothers, and sisters). Secondly, his social function, his high income, and his education give him social prestige. And thirdly, since he acts as adviser or executive agent to those who formulate party policies he has power over his fellow citizens.

The Party Central Committee, which is the highest Soviet advisory body and also the occasional battlefield for political supremacy in the party, is itself composed of the highest members of the intelligentsia (the dignitaries in the state, party, and other organizational hierarchies, and the most trusted intellectuals).

"Rotten egalitarianism," as it is called in the Soviet Union, has been rejected. Soviet citizens are meant to be unequal.

However, Soviet children are given equality of opportunity at the start of life. Access to education at all levels is free. The poverty of parents does not prevent their child from acquiring an education; but compulsory education is limited to the eight-year junior high school. Since there are no school fees at any level, the completion of secondary and higher studies depends on merit, which in the Soviet Union entails not only talent and working capacity but also a great deal of perseverance.

This system is not calculated to produce an egalitarian society in which all citizens have a roughly comparable amount of education. If it had ever thought to approximate this ideal, the party abandoned it in 1958 when it officially repudiated its plan for compulsory universal secondary education. But the same system alleviates the hardships of social inequality by providing children of all social classes with an equal opportunity at the beginning of life. By giving all young people an equal chance to develop their abilities through education, the system is also able to exploit the human resources of the nation more fully than would otherwise be possible. No talents are wasted, and no gifted and hard-working young people are refused access to the intelligentsia merely because they have no means to bear the cost of higher education. The Soviet society, like Western societies, is founded on the principle of social mobility.

Social inequality is probably an inevitable consequence of the division of labor. Some of the functions into which labor is divided require considerable education, others do not; some involve directing the work of other individuals; others involve being directed. Necessarily, society considers certain of its members less replaceable than others. Social prestige is unevenly distributed in any society, including those which claim to be Marxist. Inequality of social prestige is as important as inequality of income.

The party promises that the next stage of development, called Communism, will introduce a great abundance of consumer goods. The slogan of this next stage in the Soviet development is "From everyone according to his ability; to everyone according to his needs." The slogan carries the promise of material equality for all citizens. If all of them could satisfy their material needs, they would enjoy equal living standards although they would remain unequal in their education and in the importance of their social functions. It seems at first sight that an almost unlimited abundance of consumer goods would allow for their distribution irrespective of the quality and quantity of work performed by the citizens.

This simple proposition is, however, too simple. Soviet living standards are still much lower than Western living standards because, among other reasons, the foundations of a fully developed industrial society were laid in Russia later than in the West. It will take the Soviet Union a few decades to achieve living standards comparable to those of the West. At that time, however, material equality will still be unattainable because human needs are as dynamic as the technology of production. Every new invention creates new needs. The output of new durable consumer goods cannot in the first stage following invention satisfy the needs of all prospective consumers. The progress of technology carries with it the corollary of initial shortages of new products. Moreover, Western and Soviet production is not limited to one single type of durable consumer goods. The Soviet Union, for instance, produces several types of cars, television sets, and other durable goods; the qualities and prices have a wide range. The question necessarily arises of who should receive the goods of better quality.

This problem was implicitly acknowledged in 1959 at the Twenty-first Party Congress. Khrushchev carefully made the distinction between needs and luxuries and explained that Soviet society, in its next stage, will interpret the slogan "To each according to his needs" in the restricted sense that all essential needs should be satisfied but not all luxurious needs. This means, in effect, that all Soviet citizens will have sufficient food, clothing, and shelter, and a minimum of durable consumer goods. This is the situation of an average American citizen. The promise amounts to saying that Soviet citizens will in due time enjoy American living standards. Khrushchev's interpretation presupposes that the Soviet state will determine at each stage of technological development which needs are essential and which luxurious, and which category of citizens will receive incomes that will enable them to satisfy the luxurious needs, i.e., to purchase new goods as yet produced in a restricted quantity and goods of better quality. Judging from the history of the Soviet Union, the highly educated citizens, occupying the most important social positions, will be deemed worthy of having their luxurious needs satisfied. Material equality is no more probable than equality of social prestige. Social stratification is bound to remain a part of the Communist society as it has been of every other society.

The dissident Yugoslav Communist Milovan Djilas made a penetrating observation when he defined property as the right to control the use of things owned and to distribute the income derived from such use. The naked title of ownership is meaningless without these two attributes. Nationalization of the means of production changes the title of legal ownership by substituting the state for private individuals or corporations. However, it also transfers control over the use of property and over the distribution of income from private owners to those people who control the state, the new corporate owner. The Soviet experience has proved that those who control the state are also members of the new upper and middle classes. They determine how the national wealth should be used, what should be produced (for instance, they fix the respective outputs of capital and consumer goods), and finally how the national income should be distributed. They decide how much should be reserved for military expenditure, capital investment, education, and public welfare, and how much should be distributed among individual citizens as salaries and wages. The actual scale of Soviet incomes proves that these middle and upper classes do not fail to reserve for themselves a lion's share of the national income. This is why the citizens of Poland, another Communist state, joke that capitalism is the exploitation of man by man, while socialism is a regime which reverses the order of the last three words.

The nationalization of the means of production has not brought about social equality but certainly has provided the ruling party with a powerful tool of coercion. The state is the only employer. The state fixes the salaries and wages of all citizens. The party, which rules the state, can refuse employment, punish with a lower income, or reward with a higher paid job. Every citizen is dependent on the party for his daily bread; if the party wants, the bread is thickly buttered.

The life of Soviet society is centered around the Communist party. The society itself is stratified, and the party is founded on the elitist principle. Lenin believed that a socialist revolution could be successfully carried out only by a tightly knit group of Marxists who would be able to understand the laws of social development and hence to detect the permanent interests of the proletariat and of all the other toilers. Unlike Marx, Lenin considered that the true hero of the contemporary social drama was not so much the proletariat as its "vanguard," the revolutionary party armed with the Marxist doctrine that would enable it to follow the laws of history toward a future Communist society. According to Lenin, the proletariat as a class could detect only its temporary interests (for example, its interest in a rise in wages obtained through a strike or through negotiation with the employer), while the same temporary interests could relegate the permanent interests (the total transformation of productive processes and the abolition of private ownership of the means of production) to a secondary place. Only a Marxist party was capable of protecting the proletariat against its shortsightedness; the party alone had the doctrinal knowledge and also the will to identify the permanent interests, to subordinate to them all temporary proletarian interests, and hence to lead the proletariat toward a secure and bright future through the door of socialist revolution and into a period of social reconstruction. This party was "the vanguard of the proletariat" because it identified itself with the permanent interests of the working class; neither all its members nor its leaders needed to be of proletarian descent. Lenin and most of the early Bolshevik leaders were in fact the descendants of middle-class families.

This leading role of the elitist party continues to be one of the dogmas of the Communist parties. The party is composed by definition of the best men, those who know the Marxist laws of history and are primarily committed to the protection of the permanent interests of the toilers. The party is thus placed above the proletariat and cast in the role of its undisputed leader. This elitist concept denies that men could ever be politically equal.

The same concept makes admission to the party very difficult. Only the best citizens can be admitted. The total membership is deliberately kept low, because the party does not wish to become a mass organization but reserves for itself the role of the political and intellectual leader of the masses. The actual membership falls short of 5 per cent of the total Soviet population. The remaining 95 per cent are non-party people, not because they do not want to join the party, but because the party will not admit them.

The same elitist principle operates within the party. A clear distinction is made between the functions of the party leadership, on the one hand, and those of the rank-and-file members, on the other. The leaders monopolize the formulation of policies by virtue of their being deemed the wisest among the politically best, while the members implement the policies and act as channels of communication with the non-party population. The party machinery serves as a link between the top leadership and the ordinary members. This hierarchy is a necessary consequence of the elitist principle which postulates a gradation in political wisdom and the existence of an elite within the elite. It is perhaps no less necessary that the top party leadership determine for themselves the actual composition of the supreme elite.

This party holds total power within the Communist society. Its power monopoly is justified by the elitist principle of government of the many by the gifted few and by the claim that the party is the only repository of the Marxist absolute truth. The party forms a single and noncompetitive power elite.

There is only one political party and one association for each field of human activity, and all such associations are controlled from within by a nucleus of party members who are also members of the association. There is only one labor union for a given type of industrial work, one professional organization, one youth organization for a given age group (Little Octobrists, Pioneers, and the Communist Youth Union). All associations are licensed by the state, which may dissolve them at its pleasure. To form an unlicensed association is a crime. These associations perform an important role, because they are the channels through which the party conveys its instructions to the 95 per cent of the non-party population. At each level of all organizations the nucleus of party members provides the stimulus and direction for social activities and makes sure that these activities are carried out in consonance with party expectations.

The party also controls all state activities. However, the party has total power not only because it controls the state machinery, with its various means of coercion, and all social associations, but also because it controls the distribution of income derived from the nationalized means of production. This merger of political with economic power gives the party highly effective sanctions for enforcing conformity among the citizens. In the last analysis, the Soviet composer, painter, or poet is just as much a state employee as a scientist, an engineer, a post office employee, or an industrial worker. They can all sell their labor only to the state. Daily police terror is not a necessary tool of coercion, a fact clearly realized by the Stalinist heirs; the economic sanction for "good" behavior is a less drastic but equally effective means of pressure. Not only politically but also economically it is more difficult to be a nonconformist in the Soviet society than in any society known in history.

The combination of total power with the claim of infallibility of party doctrine has produced a conformist society, monistic in its external appearance. Marxism is supposed to have the answers for all crucial questions: what is the origin and meaning of the universe and life, what are the laws of historical development, what is the best society and how should it be organized, and what is the place of the individual in this society? The Communists claim that this doctrine is valid for all time and is an absolute truth. The party, or rather its leadership, professes to be the only legitimate guardian of the purity of this absolute truth. Only the party interpretation is deemed correct; any other is stigmatized as dogmatism, sectarianism, or revisionism.

This fundamental assumption that a philosophy is absolutely true and beyond all criticism is religious in nature and requires from the ideological adherents an act of faith in the infallibility of the doctrinal founders, Marx, Engels, and Lenin. Only an infidel could question this infallibility, and only a heretic could disagree with the current party interpretation of this infallible doctrine.

This quasi-religious approach to Marxism-Leninism has certain important consequences. It gives the party the moral right to formulate the binding party line in all fields of human activity. The monopoly of political and economic power makes this party line effective. The party claims to know best not only in politics, economics, and social organization, but also in music, the plastic arts, and literature. It imposes its own standards of the true and the beautiful in all fields of creative thought. The party line in esthetics is called "socialist realism." The party can and does change its interpretation of Marxism-Leninism, but it has a monopoly on the privilege of doing so.

If Marxism-Leninism is held to be absolutely true, there is no room either for believers in other ideologies or for agnostics. To tolerate other views is either to be lax in defending the truth or to concede that the doctrine is fallible. A sincere Communist is immune to all rational arguments which could be advanced against the validity of various Marxist propositions. As with other true believers, his faith is his shield. A believer and an unbeliever can never meet intellectually, because they move on different planes. The one accepts his doctrinal assumptions on faith as an absolute truth which leaves no room for other assumptions. The other lacks this faith and can never admit that the believer's creed is an absolute truth impervious to all rational criticism. An abyss of incomprehension will always divide a believer from an unbeliever. Moreover, the believer finds it much more difficult than the agnostic to tolerate the beliefs of others, whose "self-evident truths" must be for him self-evident errors.

Marxism-Leninism offers its followers a comprehensive and coherent interpretation of the universe, determines their hierarchy of values, defines the norms of good conduct for them, and imbues them with an enthusiasm akin to that which filled the hearts of religious crusaders. It fulfills the function which was once peculiar to organized religion. It is a secular religion. This aspect of Communism makes it particularly attractive to those who have lost another religious or secular faith but do not want to remain agnostics. The quasi-religious attraction of Communism is strengthened by its mythology, which has been influenced by Christianity: the happy primitive society with its communal property replaces the lost Paradise; the proletariat or the party is cast in the role of the Messiah; private ownership of the means of production is conceived as the original sin; and the promise of final salvation becomes the millennium of the Communist era. Marxism-Leninism combines the Christian theme of eventual justice for the poor, humiliated, and oppressed, the Promethean theme of man's triumph over nature, and the rationalist theme of the perfectibility of human nature and human society. The convert, like converts to other religions, finds a new meaning in life.

There is one field of human thought in which the party tolerates free research, namely science and technology. The party seems to be resigned to the fact that a strict regimentation of literature, arts, music, and the social sciences will result in a deterioration in the quality of these creative activities. But such activities are all but expendable for a regime which is bent on the one major goal of economic expansion. Scientists and technologists are not expendable, because their free research is a necessary condition to economic progress. Otherwise, the party leaders act as philosopher-kings who know best what is true and beautiful.

The party line is buttressed not only by state coercion and control over jobs and incomes. The party also controls education, all schools being public and all youth organizations being supervised by party members. Also, all sources of information are directed by the party. Soviet libraries have an index of prohibited books which can be read only with special permission. Soviet teachers and youth organizations are expected to promote the party line. All printing presses, all publishing houses, all newspapers and periodicals, radio and television, the theater, motion pictures, and all the assembly halls are owned directly or indirectly by the party. The Soviet citizen is bombarded daily with information inspired by the party. Soviet citizens cannot legally hear views contrary to the party line.

The nonconformist who dares to express disagreement either publicly or privately is guilty of the uniquely Soviet criminal offense of "anti-Soviet propaganda." Other nonconformist activities, such as founding an association without state approval, are punished as crimes against the state.

All loyalties must be subordinated to supreme allegiance to the Soviet state and regime. Thus, strictly speaking, there is no private domain in Soviet society. This total control by a monopolistic party is appropriately termed a totalitarian regime.

The Communists believe and do their best to convince other people that their ideology and system of government are the wave of the future. This theme of the historically predetermined, universal triumph of Communism reflects the conviction of Communists and constitutes a handy propaganda device for undermining the self-assurance of those who would presume to resist what seems to be a tide of history. This apocalyptic propaganda is meant to weaken the moral fiber of opponents, to attract the wavering and hesitant, and to inspirit the Communists themselves. It conveys the image of a Communist world that is marching inexorably against all possible resistance toward an ultimate and universal triumph which history itself has predestined, and the reverse image of a capitalist world that is decrepit, unsure of its own destiny, and aimlessly drifting on the waves of history toward its final destruction.

The Communist conviction that Marxism-Leninism is an absolute truth which must triumph because it is self-evident is not a new phenomenon in the history of major ideological movements. This was the conviction of Christians and Moslems, of Catholics and Protestants, at the height of their spiritual expansion. Such a conviction has always served to exhilarate the faithful and to intimidate their enemies.

Soviet society lives by two moralities: traditional morality divorced from its religious context, and the Leninist morality. Traditional morality regulates the relationships between loyal citizens, who are expected to be selfless, imbued with a high sense of social responsibility, efficient state employees, good parents and children aware of their family obligations, and honest and virtuous in accordance with the criteria known to other societies. But the same citizens are told to be guided by a different morality in their relations with domestic or foreign "enemies of the people," i.e., persons who intentionally or unintentionally hinder the progress of socialism.

Lenin formulated this morality in the following words: "We say: morality is what serves to disrupt the old exploiting society and to rally together all the toilers around the proletariat which is building up a new society of the Communists." A contemporary Soviet commentator writes: "Marxism-Leninism sees the highest criterion of Communist morality in the struggle for Communism." Thus, the morality of means and actions must be evaluated from the point of view of their relation to the ultimate goal, the victory of Communism. The same means can be moral or immoral depending on its effect on the attainment of that ultimate end. One out of several illustrations which Lenin gave will make this point clear. Lenin did not consider violence and war as immoral per se, as do certain Christian sects. He distinguished between just and unjust wars. Just wars were those waged against the capitalist enemies of socialism: wars conducted by socialist states, civil wars directed against the existing capitalist regime, and colonial uprisings against an "imperialist" Western power. Unjust wars were all wars waged by capitalist states. Dishonesty of means did not exist for him as an absolute proposition; he recommended to his disciples that they use, if necessary, means which we should call dishonest, if these means could be justified by the ultimate objective—the triumph of the socialist cause. This Leninist morality gives Communist politicians considerable latitude in formulating their foreign and domestic policies and in choosing the most practical means for carrying them out.

It is not difficult to demonstrate that there is a discordance between the original egalitarian Marxist doctrine and actual Communist practice. But it does not follow that the Communists are cynical power-seekers who do not believe in their own doctrine. They have only succumbed to the general law which governs the relations between an ideology and the organization founded to propagate it. The organization (in this case the

Communist state and the Communist movement) acquires its own needs, and its survival requires certain accommodations with the original tenets of the doctrine. But those who have made these accommodations could argue that they were necessary to preserve the substance of the doctrine, which would have withered away without a strong organization to defend and propagate it. They will never agree with their critics that in the process of accommodation they have sacrificed the very substance of the original doctrine. They may be wrong in their contention, but they are sincere insofar as they retain a residual faith adjusted to the exigencies of practical life. It is because of the sincerity of this residual faith that the foreign relations of Communist states are immensely complicated by the ideological factor.

PROLETARIAN INTERNATIONALISM

The Communist political orbit is made up of two circles: the bloc of Communist states, of which there are thirteen, excluding "revisionist" Yugoslavia (Albania, Bulgaria, Rumania, Hungary, Czechoslovakia, Poland, the Democratic German Republic, the Soviet Union, China, Mongolia, North Korea, North Vietnam, and Cuba); and the international Communist movement, which unites ninety parties, those which rule their own countries and those which hope one day to seize power. The Communist party is the common denominator of the two circles. Practically every country has its own Communist party, legal or illegal. The total membership of this vast missionary army has reached the imposing figure of 42 million, of whom probably 5 million operate in the non-Communist countries.

It would be a mistake to measure the influence of the party by the number of its regular members. The party is elitist and does not want to expand its ranks. It prefers to limit admission to those who prove beyond doubt their ideological conviction, devotion, and political ability. This consideration is even more important for a party which operates in a non-Communist environment where defection by a party member could prove extremely harmful to its interests. The influence of the party should be measured by the extent of its infiltration of the non-Communist society through party members and sympathizers. The Communists themselves stress in their literature the crucial importance of infiltrating the state bureaucracy and armed forces as well as various associations, in particular the labor unions and the peasant organizations. Their purpose is served by various front organizations in which the Communists might be a small fraction of the total membership but in which they exercise a determining influence on the orientation of the association's activities. The best-known international front organizations are the World Peace Council, the International Federation of Trade Unions, the International Federation of Democratic Youth, and the International Democratic Women's Federation.

The distinction which the Communists make between the party and the state is politically rather irrelevant, because the party is the kernel of the Communist state's administration on all territorial levels. The party leaders are in fact the government of the state though they may not all hold ministerial portfolios. With the same persons governing both the state and the party, the Communist states enjoy an advantage denied to other states. They have at their disposal not only the usual inter-state channels of communication but also the less formal and more confidential inter-party channels. The co-ordination of general state policies is ensured through inter-party channels. The great issues are discussed and if possible settled at the summit meetings frequently held by the top party leaders. The practice of personal or summit diplomacy, popular in all states, is common in the relations between the Communist states. These summit meetings are of various types: bilateral exchanges of visits; regional meetings, a device often used in the relations between the Soviet Union and its Eastern European allies; the participation of foreign guest-delegates in the national congresses of various Communist parties; and the general gatherings which have been held twice since the last war, assemblies of representatives of all Communist parties who met in Moscow in 1957 and 1960. All these summit meetings provide the party leaders, who are also the heads or important members of their national governments, with ample opportunity for consultation and for the co-ordination of their domestic and foreign policies.

Although the distinction between the state and the party is politically meaningless, it enables the government of a Communist state to disclaim responsibility for the actions of Communist parties operating in non-Communist countries with the avowed aim of subverting the existing regime. The Communist politicians, in spite of the fact that they combine the functions of ministers of state with those of party leaders, insist that their government cannot be held accountable for their own activities within the Communist movement. The non-Communist states have accepted this fiction, because they could not entertain diplomatic relations with the Communist states if they officially charged them with responsibility for the support of actions and policies of foreign Communist parties.

The same fiction is useful in the relations between two Communist states if their respective party leaders strongly disagree on the interpretation of Marxism-Leninism or on the orientation of their respective policies. If these leaders have, however, compelling reasons for maintaining a certain amount of co-operation, they can have recourse to the legal fiction that the state is an entity completely separate from the party. They can claim that the two parties continue to disagree but that this need not prevent the two states from collaborating on various specific matters.

This technique has been used since 1955, with varying degrees of success, in the relations between Yugoslavia and the Soviet Union, and could in the future prevent a diplomatic rupture between any two Communist states in spite of a rift between the respective parties.

The two circles of the Communist orbit are supposed to be bound together by proletarian or socialist internationalism, which rests on the assumption that the national and personal interests of party leaders should always be subordinated to the superior interest of the whole movement. This all too simple assumption invites the practical question of who is entitled to define this superior interest if any two parties happen to disagree on ideology or on practical policies. Since the dissolution of the Comintern in 1943 the movement has no international body to whom parties can submit their disputes. This practical problem has acquired great importance in the last several years.

The socialist system of states and the Communist movement have, since the 20th Congress of the C.P.S.U. (Communist Party of the Soviet Union), entered a new stage of their history. The era of a highly centralized movement is ended. The position of the Soviet party, as the undisputed leader of the Communist bloc of states and of the movement, is no longer generally accepted. The present stage is that of a less centralized movement in which policies must be co-ordinated through consultation and negotiation rather than through sheer compliance with Soviet instructions. There is no longer any certainty that every inter-party dispute will be resolved according to Soviet wishes. The crucial issue is whether the Communist parties, accustomed by their histories to highly centralized party discipline and intolerant of factionalism within their own national organizations, will be able to tolerate divergent views among themselves and will accept co-operation founded on give-and-take compromises.

As paradoxical as it might seem, the "ideal" situation existed before the last war. The Communist movement was at that time much weaker, and only one party had conquered a state of its own. The paramount influence of the Soviet party could not be disputed by other parties, which were feeble and unable to think seriously of an independent line of action. Proletarian internationalism was an undisputed reality. The divergencies of view between the leaders of various parties were effectively settled by arbitration which the Soviet party imposed. Soviet leadership was the universally recognized center of the movement, because it had at its disposal all the power which control over the Soviet state had given it. It had its own state treasury and enjoyed the undivided prestige of being the only successful party. The October Revolution was at that time the only socialist revolution. The Soviet regime supplied the other parties with an eschatological image of the future condition of mankind.

The Soviet party experienced no insuperable difficulties in eliminating insubordinate leaders of foreign parties and in selecting new leaders at its own pleasure. The histories of Communist parties provide many examples of docility toward Moscow during the inter-war period. The Comintern itself was in effect a channel of communication for the Soviet party, which manipulated it at will. The record of foreign parties faithfully reflected every change within the Soviet party. One had to be a Stalinist to remain in the ranks of any Communist party. Stalin's orders were equally binding on his own and foreign parties. This was so true that the congresses of the Comintern were eventually discontinued as a cumbersome and superfluous formality. It was more practical to send the instructions of the C.P.S.U. to the leaders of other parties. Discipline was so great that the mass purges, which affected so many foreign Communists as well as internationally known leaders of the Soviet party, did not shake the unreserved loyalty to, and the blind faith in, Stalin and the C.P.S.U.

This foreign attitude toward Moscow amounted to an almost mystical attachment to the Soviet party, which was the only party to have built a socialist system and which held the promise of a great future for all believing Communists. Such unreserved devotion was due not only to the power and prestige of the Soviet party but also to a psychological weakness of the foreign Communists. They were cut off from the mass of their own countrymen by their self-proclaimed intention to overturn the domestic status quo. This political attitude confined them to the position of a permanent and uncompromising opposition. They lived on the margin of national life. Their moral isolation was made endurable by the conviction that they were the vanguard of mankind and would sooner or later become the masters of their own countries. This uplifting faith in ultimate victory rested on two foundations: Marxism, with its deterministic interpretation of history, and the tangible existence of the Soviet Union. Every political and economic achievement of the Soviet regime had to be magnified beyond its merits and every shortcoming had to be overlooked in order to maintain an enthusiastic faith in the Communist cause.

This situation began to change in 1944-45 with the appearance of Communist-controlled states in Eastern Europe. A Communist party which forms its own national government is no longer a group of isolated nonconformists. The party members have become rulers who impose their will on their countrymen. Their following is rapidly increased for several reasons: success attracts people and makes them believe that Marxism is truly the wave of the future; others want to make careers and must remain on good terms with the ruling party which makes and breaks all careers; still others wish only to earn their daily bread and must accept a *modus vivendi* with the new regime; finally, the party wields an undivided political power and is, in the last analysis, the sole employer in a society where all the means of production are being gradually socialized. Delivered from the risk of isolation, the party now faces the opposite risk:

its ranks may be swollen by the mass accession of opportunist elements. The party leaders, who at the same time are the government of their nation, feel less need than before for a vicarious sense of power derived from the might of the Soviet Union. Their power is now founded directly on the existence of the state which they control. They stand on their own feet.

The national state, the mainstay of their power, becomes a factor of great importance. Prior to their seizure of power they were the political enemies of their own state and devoted friends of a foreign state which was for them the bastion of the Communist movement. Now they bear the responsibility for their nation and are compelled to look at the world from the standpoint of their own capital. They are apt to discover the existence of national interests which may no longer be equated with Soviet interests. They begin to learn that these national interests might not always coincide with those of other Communist states. Their trade with other Communist states teaches them this simple lesson. Marxism-Leninism has no ready answer concerning the prices to be charged for goods exchanged between the socialist states. It does not supply any clear-cut formula for the specialization which the co-ordination of plans requires from those states; each of them might feel that its prospects are dimmed by the restrictions which the socialist division of labor imposes on its own full-scale industrialization.

The first crack in the monolithic pyramid of the Communist movement appeared in 1948. One brick fell loose to become the foundation stone of an independent Communist state which refused to carry out Soviet orders. Inevitably, this refractory brick was engraved with its own national coat of arms. Yugoslavia was expelled from the Cominform.

The Soviet top of the pyramid was confronted for the first time with a serious case of disobedience. In vain Stalin used the prewar technique of appealing to the Yugoslav party and asking it to replace the rebel leaders with new ones who would be acceptable to Moscow. This time he was disobeyed. The great success of the postwar years, the extension of the Communist realm to a large part of Europe, was paid for with the first successful revolt.

It is interesting that the Yugoslavs did not begin their dispute with the Russians by formulating their own heretical creed. In 1948 they were orthodox. Their many complaints were all related to the interests of their state and to the autonomy of their party. The long list of topics about which the two parties quarreled included the following: Soviet intelligence activities and attempted infiltration by Soviet agents of the Yugoslav public administration, party machinery, and army; Soviet economic exploitation through mixed Soviet-Yugoslav corporations; half-hearted Soviet support for the Yugoslav claims to a part of Austrian territory and to Trieste; and the Soviet veto cast against Tito's plans for building around Yugoslavia a Balkan federation which would include his own country, Bulgaria, Albania, and later a Communist Greece. The prewar thesis that the interests of the Communist movement, as defined by the Soviet Union, were superior to those of the various foreign parties was no longer unquestionable for the Yugoslav Communists. Their assumption of the responsibility for the government of their country altered their political perspective; Belgrade became as important as Moscow.

The Soviet and all other Communist parties denounced the Yugoslav rebels as traitors and hirelings of the West, but the Russian wrath proved to be powerless to reverse the course of events in Yugoslavia. The unity of the movement was preserved, but the precedent for a successful revolt against the Soviet leadership was nevertheless established.

The years 1948-53 witnessed certain developments which portended new challenges to the unity of the movement. The Yugoslavs proved during these years that Moscow might be unable under certain adverse circumstances to reduce a foreign party to obedience. The year 1949 brought the final victory of the Chinese party, the only party outside the Soviet Union to seize control over the government of a great power, at least a potential great power. The magnitude of the Chinese state vouched for the independence of the Chinese party. Moreover, unlike the Communist parties of Eastern Europe, North Korea, and Mongolia, the Chinese party had risen to power without exclusive dependence on the Soviet Union. It was obvious that if the Chinese party were to disagree with the Soviet it would be in a much stronger position than the Yugoslav party to defy Moscow and yet retain control over its own country.

The post-Stalinist period brought the inner problems of the Communist movement into the open. This was due not only to the Communist seizure of power in several countries, but also to events which were taking place within the Soviet Union. The process of de-Stalinization, which began quietly after the death of Stalin in 1953 and was officially announced in 1956, could not but produce staggering effects in other parties. The removal of Stalin from the Communist pantheon, where he had in his lifetime been venerated equally with the three founding fathers of the movement, was an upheaval for Russian and foreign Communists alike. The Soviet decision was arrived at without consultation with foreign party leaders, who were taken aback by the anti-Stalin drive launched by the Soviet party at its Twentieth Congress in 1956 and never relaxed since. It is easy to imagine the embarrassment of these foreign leaders who, having established their authority on the claim of being Stalin's faithful disciples, were now suddenly informed by Moscow that their great Marxist-Leninist leader was really a monster. They had to explain to their own parties not only why they had invariably obeyed Stalin and had forbidden any questioning of his decisions, but also whether the eschatological image of the Soviet Union, the Promised Land, was still true or should be revised. It was far from easy to circumvent this dilemma:

either Stalin was truly a tyrannical dictator, as Khrushchev depicted him, and his will was all that mattered for a period of almost thirty years, so that all the crimes but also all the achievements of the Soviet regime must be traced back to him, or else his colleagues on the Soviet Political Bureau, including all the top Soviet leaders in 1956, had to share with him the responsibility for both the crimes and the achievements. An intelligent Communist could hardly swallow the version adopted by the Twentieth Congress that the crimes were Stalin's personal misdeeds and engaged only his responsibility while the achievements were due to the collective wisdom of the Central Committee. Only much later, in 1961, was the Twenty-second Congress able to offer an improved version which absolved only one close collaborator of Stalin, Khrushchev, of any responsibility for the mass purges, but widened this responsibility from Stalin and Beria to the whole "anti-party group," to all Stalin's other colleagues who were also Khrushchev's rivals to Stalin's succession.

The struggle against the cult of personality, as the process of de-Stalinization was called, was meant to be accompanied by a certain relaxation within the Soviet regime and in the relations between Moscow and other Communist capitals. The forthcoming shape of inter-state relations within the Soviet bloc was implicitly heralded as early as 1955 by Khrushchev's visit to Belgrade. He went there to ask forgiveness for the sins committed by Stalin. He probably hoped to convince Tito of the best intentions of the post-Stalinist leadership and gradually to persuade him that he should come back to the common fold from which Stalin had expelled him. But Yugoslavia had in the meantime evolved its own form of the socialist regime. It was compelled by isolation to trace its own road to socialism, which eventually became very different from the Soviet route. Soviet tolerance of this divergent road to socialism caused many Eastern European Communists, until now unconditionally obedient to Russia, to wonder whether they too had the right to their own national roads, i.e., to greater autonomy for their parties.

The official Soviet thesis that Stalin had often been wrong in his decisions and had sometimes been guided by whim rather than reason undermined that article of Communist doctrine which had justified a highly centralized movement, namely the infallibility of Soviet leadership. If Stalin had exterminated loyal Communists because of his mania for persecution and if the Soviet party had been helpless to prevent these crimes, had his successors any valid title to the supreme leadership of the Communist movement? Stalin had been considered infallible. His successors were all his close companions and assistants. Their revelations of his former crimes proved by implication that they were either weak cowards or his willing accomplices. In either case, they could not pass for having steel-like characters and infallible wisdom. Doubt was raised regarding the right of the C.P.S.U. to govern the movement.

The execution of Beria and the purge of his Soviet and Eastern European associates reduced the prestige and power of the political police. The Soviet party line toward the intellectuals was becoming milder, and this could not but influence the other Communist countries. The thaw was a fact, although the parties did not intend to bring in an uncontrolled spring. The intellectuals in several Eastern European countries began to stir. A certain amount of criticism of the Soviet Union and of the domestic regime could be expressed in the Eastern European press.

The ruthless Soviet suppression of the Berlin uprising in 1953 did not seem to have discouraged the Eastern Europeans. The workers' revolt in the Polish city of Poznan in the early summer of 1956 was the first ominous rumbling. The growing frustration within the Polish party was paralleled by mounting discontent in the country. Both the party members and the population resented the tight Soviet protectorate, including the infiltration of the security police by Soviet agents, the tenure of high military posts by Soviet citizens in Polish uniforms, the unregulated status of Soviet troops stationed in Poland, the high prices for Soviet imported goods and the low prices for Polish exported products, notably coal, and so on. The population desired not only a greater independence for Poland but also a relaxation of the domestic regime, i.e., a concession from the party itself. The wishes of the party and of the population were not wholly identical but largely coincided, and both aspirations could be satisfied only by wresting concessions from the protecting power.

Polish discontent was not essentially directed against the party as long as the party leaders were prepared to tolerate the disbanding of collective farms, to grant a greater freedom of expression, to make an effort to improve living standards, to conclude a truce with the Catholic Church, an important issue for a country predominantly Catholic, and to stand for national dignity in relations with the Soviet Union. The party felt that it should quickly cement this tacit understanding with the people by making changes in the party leadership which would give the Poles conspicuous proof that something new was truly forthcoming. The rehabilitation of Gomulka and his eventual election to the post of the Party First Secretary were steps leading toward this tacit covenant between the party and the people. The party remained Communist, and the great majority of the people were not converted to Communism, but both found common ground in the aspiration for greater national independence. The party which Gomulka headed in the crucial month of October, 1956, was not threatened with a domestic uprising; it could rely on popular support in any showdown with Russia.

The Soviet party was not confronted in Poland, as it was later confronted in Hungary, with an emerging non-Communist regime but merely with a demand for greater domestic autonomy for a Communist party. The Polish alignment with the Soviet Union in international affairs was not at stake in October, 1956. Yet the first Soviet reaction was as sharp as one would have expected from Stalin. The Soviet leaders came uninvited to Warsaw to bring last-minute pressure on the Polish Central Committee and to cow it into obedience. The Soviet troops on the Polish borders were alerted, and those regiments which were stationed in Poland were ordered to march on Warsaw. It seemed for a short time that an armed clash between Russia and Poland, between the Soviet and Polish parties, was unavoidable. Suddenly, the Soviet leaders, angry as they were, agreed to negotiate with the Polish leaders about the shape of their future relations, and Soviet troops received the order to march back to their bases. A compromise was reached between Warsaw and Moscow. It is most interesting that the short but sharp clash between the two parties did not result in the unconditional surrender of the junior party. This clash amounted to a conflict between the national interests of the two countries. The outcome was the Soviet concession of greater autonomy to the Polish party in domestic matters.

There are two reasons which may account for the retreat of the Soviet leaders: the moderate nature of the Polish demands, which did not threaten to upset the ideological and political status quo in Eastern Europe, and the proximity of Germany. The Soviet government could not be sure that an armed conflict between Russia and Poland would not spark an uprising in East Germany. Could they be certain that Central Europe, aflame for several days, would not eventually involve Western Germany in an intervention and that this would not lead to a general war with the West?

The Hungarian revolt of the same fall was different. The people rose up against the party, which proved itself unable to give direction to the popular discontent. Nagy was brought to power too late, at a time when the party had already lost control over the rapid course of events and was fast disintegrating. Its membership, unduly inflated in the postwar years, did not care about the party and deserted it as soon as they realized that the wind was blowing the other way. Nagy could not save the party from disaster and formed a multi-party government, thus putting an end to the Communist regime. Eventually he requested the Soviet Union to release Hungary from the military bonds of the Warsaw Treaty and to recognize it as a permanently neutral state. Russia was faced with the prospect of a twofold defeat: first, as a great power, Russia would have lost an ally; secondly, as the center of the Communist movement, it would have allowed the restoration of a non-Communist regime in Hungary. This defeat, which would have started a process of general retreat from Eastern Europe, Russia could not possibly accept. Its answer was military intervention.

The fifth revolt against Soviet supremacy in Eastern Europe, after the Yugoslav rebellion in 1948, the Berlin riots in 1953, and the Polish and

Hungarian revolts in 1956, was the defiant challenge launched in 1960-61 by the Albanian party. One of the main reasons for the Albanian-Soviet dispute is that the two countries have widely different attitudes toward Yugoslavia. Prior to 1948 Albania was subjected, unlike the other Eastern European countries, to a dual protectorate, the Soviet and the Yugoslav. The Albanian hostility to Tito and to the Yugoslav party may be due to recollections of the period between 1944 and 1948, but it may also be due to considerations of national interests. A large part of Yugoslavia around Kossovo, mostly populated by Albanians, is an Albanian *terra irredenta.* The present Albanian leaders firmly sided with Stalin in 1948 and during the following years and liquidated those colleagues who were suspected of having pro-Titoist sympathies. They thus have their own reasons for distrusting Tito and disliking any Soviet move which amounts to a friendly gesture toward their enemy. They might also have been disturbed, as the Yugoslavs were in 1948, by the infiltration of their party by Soviet sympathizers; the purge which they carried out in 1960-61 and which was strongly resented in Moscow seems to confirm this hypothesis.

There were signs in 1962-63 that the Rumanian party strongly resented the Soviet plan for the "socialist" division of labor, a plan which would relegate Rumania to the position of producer of oil and oil equipment, petro-chemical products, and foodstuffs but would discourage the development of other industries. This was the first time that the Rumanian party made a show of disobedience.

These various developments in Eastern Europe can be summed up in several conclusions:

1. It is important to note that several parties have remained quietly obedient: the Czechoslovak, the Bulgarian, and the East German. They faithfully stood by Stalin and have since followed every zigzag of post-Stalinist policy. They may sometimes have complied reluctantly, but they have complied. The East German party has the least choice in the matter. The presence of several hundred thousands of Soviet troops guarantees the obedience of the German party to the U.S.S.R., but the withdrawal of these troops would probably spell the end of the Communist regime in East Germany.

2. The geographical location of the several Eastern European countries plays an important role. Yugoslavia had broad and direct access to the West at the time of its open breach with the Soviet Union. Albania is cut off from direct contact by land with the Soviet bloc. Its neighbors do not sympathize with it but have no interest in helping to restore Soviet influence. The critical question for the Albanian party is whether little Albania can continue in hostile isolation from both European blocs, the Soviet and the Western. The Polish proximity to Germany probably had a bearing on the course of events in Poland in October, 1956. Hungary had a common frontier with non-Communist Austria, but the latter coun-

try, permanently neutral since 1955, could not actively support the Hungarian insurrection. Czechoslovakia and Rumania, traditionally inimical to Hungary, had ideological as well as national reasons for being unfriendly toward the insurgents. Soviet troops were at that time stationed in both Rumania and Hungary. The Hungarian revolt had at first evoked a sympathetic reaction in the remaining neighbor, Yugoslavia, but this sympathy did not last long. It ended when a multi-party government emerged in Budapest and before the second Soviet intervention. Geographically and even more politically, Hungary was isolated in November, 1956.

3. The events of 1956 proved that the Soviet Union might make limited concessions to another Communist state but that it would not capitulate before the threat of an ideological or political disintegration of its Eastern European zone of influence. Since Stalin's death Moscow has been ready to tolerate national variations on the main Soviet theme as long as the Eastern European parties retain control over their respective countries, acknowledge the over-all ideological authority of the Soviet party, and support Russian foreign policy. This flexibility is due, among other reasons, to changes which have taken place within the Communist movement. It suffices to compare two developments. The Russian excommunication of Yugoslavia in 1948 was backed up by all parties without exception; thirteen years later, the anathema cast against Albania met with an open Chinese protest and with an embarrassing lack of support or a halfhearted support on the part of several other Asian parties. Obviously, the Communist movement is no longer exclusively centered in Moscow.

4. The quick disintegration of the Hungarian party in 1956 serves as a reminder to other parties that they too may one day be faced with a domestic revolt that cannot be suppressed without outside help. The ultimate remedy will be to appeal to the Soviet Union for military assistance. Soviet military intervention has twice proved effective, in East Berlin and in Hungary. Friendship with the Soviet party represents a guarantee against domestic uprisings as well as external threats.

5. The year 1956 demonstrated that the Western powers would not support an insurrection in Eastern Europe for fear of a nuclear conflict with the U.S.S.R. In this regard, the collapse of the Hungarian uprising strengthened Soviet supremacy in Eastern Europe by making it clear that armed revolt would be futile.

6. The inability of the East German and Hungarian parties to deal effectively with domestic revolts should not blind us to other facts. The Polish party successfully challenged the Soviet party only because it had not lost control over its own country and could rely on popular support. Both the Yugoslav and the Albanian parties have remained in power, not only without Soviet assistance, but in spite of open Soviet enmity. Both

parties have demonstrated their ability to survive while isolated from other parties.

7. The co-operation of Eastern Europe with the Soviet Union is motivated, not only by ideological affinities and the proximity of Soviet military might, but also by economic considerations. Eastern Europe greatly needs Soviet raw materials such as iron ore and oil. The slowly emerging "socialist division of labor" increases the mutual economic dependence. The Council for Mutual Economic Aid, founded in 1949, is a body for the promotion of close economic co-operation. It is a European organization composed of the U.S.S.R., Poland, Czechoslovakia, East Germany, Rumania, Hungary, Bulgaria, and Mongolia. Albania, formerly a member, seems to have been expelled in 1961 or 1962. Mongolia, a Soviet protectorate in Asia, is the only non-European member. China, North Korea, and North Vietnam have only the status of observers. Cuba is not officially represented. The main business before the Council in the late fifties and early sixties has been to co-ordinate plans for development on the basis of a rational division of labor among its European members and to outline joint policies toward the nonsocialist states. Only the Soviet Union is to remain a fully diversified economy. The Eastern European countries must gradually specialize according to the types of raw materials and the kinds of human skills they possess. The jointly planned exchange of raw materials and finished products is meant to ensure co-ordinated growth and further specialization. Joint projects, such as laying pipelines for the transit of Russian oil to Eastern Europe and developing a combined power system, are also forms of economic co-operation between Eastern Europe and the Soviet Union. With each advance toward economic integration it will become more evident that an Eastern European country which drifts apart from the Soviet Union will have to face, in addition to other risks, the problem of a disrupted economy.

The European character of the Council for Mutual Economic Aid reveals the uneven solidarity of the Communist states. The exclusion of China, North Korea and North Vietnam indicates that the European Communist states are unwilling to undertake the heavy cost of economic development of the retarded Asian countries. It is also interesting that the Warsaw Treaty military integration, under the Soviet Supreme Command, is limited to Europe, although the U.S.S.R. has bilateral military assistance treaties with China, Mongolia, and North Korea. Cuba received in 1963 a unilateral Soviet guarantee against invasion by the United Staes.

In two Eastern European countries the Soviet alliance rests on a coincidence of national interests. Poland and Czechoslovakia realize that the Soviet protectorate shelters them against German claims for a revision of frontiers and for the readmission of millions of Germans expelled from Polish and Czechoslovak territories in the post-war period. The other Eastern European countries have no national disputes with Germany.

The Soviet position regarding the non-European socialist states is very different. These countries, except for Mongolia and North Korea, could not be cowed into obedience by Soviet military action. China is too big, while North Vietnam and Cuba are too distant. The smaller Asian countries are open to the influence of both Communist great powers. They can choose any of three possible policies: either to side with either of these powers, or to try to assert their own autonomy by counterbalancing the influences of the two great powers. Mongolia wisely opted for Russia. The acceptance of the Chinese protectorate would have carried with it the great risk of a mass Chinese immigration that could have reduced the Mongolians to the position of a minority in their own homeland. From the Mongolian point of view, Russia represents a barrier against the Chinese tide and a guarantee of the survival of national identity.

Another non-European Communist state, Cuba, has made an original contribution to the movement. Fidel Castro, who seems to be a recent convert to Communism, has merged the old Communist party with his own movement of the 26th of July and with the students' Revolutionary Directorate and has placed this newly formed Marxist-Leninist party, temporarily called the Integrated Revolutionary Party, under his own leadership. This origin of the Cuban party is without precedent in the history of the Communist movement and may be the source of unorthodox policies not always to Moscow's liking.

The very fact that one can now talk about the choices open to the Communist parties indicates that the Communist victory in China brought about a fundamental change in the patterns of inter-party relations. Several factors make for the difficulties which the Soviet and Chinese parties have experienced in their relations with each other. The two countries have a different geographical perspective. The frontier dispute with India, the Taiwan issue, the probable future of Laos and generally of Southeast Asia take on a different aspect depending on whether they are viewed from Moscow or from Peking. Even if the two points of view coincided, the sense of urgency would vary. It is obvious from the history of NATO that no two allies can possibly have identical national interests and that the relative importance of international problems varies from one capital to another. The same is necessarily true of the two Communist great powers. The elimination of American influence from Turkey, for example, would have a much greater significance for Russia than an American retreat from Taiwan. Peking would view these two events in the opposite order of importance.

Their levels of development are altogether different. Russia is the second industrial nation in the world. China still remains an economically backward country. Their economic and social problems are different. The two nations belong to different civilizations. Culturally, the Russians are Europeans. The Chinese have built their own civilization, one which, however remarkable, has failed to produce a modern society. Like all other nations which are now called underdeveloped, China is confronted with the overwhelming problem of borrowing patterns of modern society from the European civilization. This process subjects the Chinese, as it does the other underdeveloped countries, to psychological and social strains which Russia has not experienced. The Chinese sense of cultural superiority is outraged by the need to borrow from the European civilization. Since Russia, as the only European country which has successfully combined the patterns of modern society with a collectivist economy, acts as the standard-bearer of that civilization, it is understandable that their national pride should cause the Chinese to feel some irrational animosity toward the Russians. The frantic Chinese efforts to discover their own road to socialism (the egalitarian communes and the Great Leap Forward) and to oppose their innovations to the Soviet system ended in a failure which could not but intensify this animosity.

The national interests of the two countries are far from identical. The image of the former Chinese empire, which is not forgotten either in Peking or in Hopei, contains the territories of neighboring countries, including Russian territory. There is no self-evident reason why Mongolia, formerly a part of China, should now be a Soviet rather than a Chinese protectorate, or why Korea should be dominated by China instead of Russia. Which of the two parties should have the dominant voice in the formulation of Asian policies? Which should exercise leadership among the Communist parties of Asia? These and similar questions, unless resolved by mutual concessions, are bound to breed competition. If the Chinese ever seriously press their claim to vast portions of Soviet territory in Asia (formerly parts of the Chinese Empire), which their press raised in 1963, this competition may change into open conflict.

Each leadership has an equal right to interpret Marxism-Leninism, because both are independent. Either interpretation reflects the historical experience, present problems, and future objectives of the regime concerned, and is therefore bound to differ from the other interpretation. This does not exclude the possibility of reaching mutually acceptable compromises which would be reflected in joint statements such as the two adopted in Moscow in 1957 and 1960.

It seems that one of the most important issues which divide China from Russia is the size of Soviet and Eastern European economic assistance. This assistance, which could accelerate Chinese development, has been reduced and now seems to be nil or almost nil. If the Russians intended to force Peking to follow Soviet policy by withholding aid, they have been disappointed. The Chinese party publicly challenged Soviet authority at the time of the Albanian schism and has accused the Russians of being weak-hearted revisionists, to which Moscow has replied by reproaching the Chinese for being dogmatic and warlike. The Chinese gauntlet was thrown down at the time of China's greatest economic difficulties, after the bankruptcy of the Great Leap Forward.

The Twenty-second Congress cannot be forgotten either in Moscow or in Peking. A China that was still weak had the stamina to insult the Soviet leaders in their own capital. At times, the Chinese delegation significantly remained silent and seated, while all the other delegates, Soviet and foreign, were giving Khrushchev a standing ovation; they brought a wreath of flowers to Stalin's tomb in the Lenin Mausoleum although they must have known at that time that the Russians were about to remove Stalin's body; they sharply criticized Khrushchev for bringing the Albanian problem into the open; finally, they unceremoniously left Moscow in the middle of the Congress session. The Soviet leaders may well imagine that a future China, fully industrialized and powerful, will be a difficult customer for their successors. The Chinese leaders will find it difficult to forget the harsh Soviet indifference at the time of their economic disaster when they were compelled to buy grain for cash from the capitalist states. Mutual resentment and distrust will remain even if the differences between the two parties are patched up. The Twenty-second Congress is in this sense a landmark.

The problem of Soviet and Eastern European economic assistance to China is aggravated by the economic aid which these European Communist states have been offering to the non-Communist underdeveloped countries. Every piece of equipment exported to the non-Communist countries is seen by the Chinese as an equivalent reduction in the capacity of their European allies for extending aid to China. The Russians believe that it is worthwhile to win the sympathy of the "national bourgeois" governments in the Third World, which they visualize as an immense arena for their political struggle with the West. The Chinese believe that a more effective way of undermining Western influence is to help the foreign Communist parties to seize power at once through revolutions. It is too early to say who is right in this controversy. Certainly, the Soviet Union has complicated the Western problems in all continents by its policy, inaugurated in 1955, of friendliness toward the underdeveloped countries, but it has suffered a few setbacks and disappointments in the Near East and in western Africa. The Chinese can point to the postwar emergence of several Communist states in Europe, Asia, and the Western Hemisphere; these states do not owe their origin to the Communist flirtation with local national bourgeoisie but to a Communist victory won in a civil war or to military intervention by a Communist great power, or to both. They probably feel that Southeast Asia is particularly vulnerable to this more direct strategy.

These two approaches to the problem of the underdeveloped countries reflect different calculations of risk. Both regimes are hostile to the survival of non-Communist systems of government in the advanced and underdeveloped countries alike, but the Chinese are more impatient. They believe that the Communist bloc can run more risks without inviting a nuclear catastrophe, while the Russians prefer to be cautious.

This divergence in policy has been clearly revealed in the opposite attitudes which Russia and China have adopted toward India. The Soviet Union has been engaged since 1955 in a strenuous effort to enlist the sympathies of the Indian government. It granted India credits, provided technical assistance, and offered convenient trade terms; it also consistently sided with India on the Kashmir issue. For a number of years, the Chinese followed the same policy. China participated prominently in the Bandung Conference in 1955, that famous festival of Asian-African solidarity. It tried to promote friendship with all Asian "national-bourgeois" governments, including the government of India. This policy was yielding solid returns in the form of sympathy from the nonaligned countries of Asia.

For reasons not yet clear China sharply abandoned this policy a few years ago. It engaged in a short but bitter controversy with Indonesia over discrimination in that country against the Chinese minority. More recently, it opened the border dispute with India and eventually had recourse to arms. Russia was placed in a highly embarrassing position between its ally China and its "bourgeois" friend India. In its hostility to the Indian national bourgeoisie, the Chinese party could not claim to be ideologically purer than the Soviet, for in spite of its enmity toward India it continued to flirt with the no less bourgeois governments of Burma, Nepal, and Pakistan.

In July, 1963, the Soviet and Chinese parties held fruitless talks in Moscow, allegedly to patch up their quarrel. The bitter mutual attacks which preceded, accompanied, and followed those conversations indicated that neither party intended to make concessions. The talks were staged for the benefit of other Communist parties and for the purpose of demonstrating that neither the Russians nor the Chinese were eager to accept responsibility for the schism within the Communist movement. The conversations ended in a deadlock, but the two parties avoided a final rupture, at least for the time being.

On June 14 the Chinese party published the twenty-five points of its ideological creed in the form of a letter nominally addressed to the Soviet party but actually directed to other Communist parties. The Soviet party did not reply until July 14; its open letter, nominally addressed to its own members, was in fact also addressed to foreign Communists. (The Russian text of both letters was published in *Pravda* of July 14, 1963; the English translations were printed in the *New York Times* of July 5 and 15, 1963.)

These two important documents should be read cautiously; they are propagandistic tracts which contain many half-truths, especially with regard to the rival party's views, and the wording is obtuse whenever the disputants wish to conceal the fact that they have taken liberties with

Marxist-Leninist doctrine. Each party was eager to prove its own orthodoxy and the heretical deviation of its opponent. The style of both letters recalls the tone of the medieval theological controversies over religious dogma and practice. The bitter quarrel is in fact partly a theological dispute and partly a struggle between conflicting national interests.

The Chinese party, like the heretical sects of old, claimed in its letter to have remained truly orthodox and accused the Soviet party and all other parties which were faithful to Moscow of all possible deviations; the Chinese accused their opponents of betraying Marxism-Leninism, of revisionism, opportunism, bourgeois pacifism, nationalism, great-power chauvinism, and of degeneration into social-democratic groups dominated by a labor aristocracy (the very reproach which Lenin used to address to the Western socialists). For a Communist, these charges are the worst insults possible. The parties obedient to Russia were said "to parrot the words of others, copy foreign [Soviet] experience without any analysis, run hither and thither in response to the baton of certain persons [Khrushchev] abroad," and thereby to espouse a mere "hodgepodge of revisionism, dogmatism and everything else but Marxist-Leninist principles." By implication, the Chinese party proclaimed itself the only source of true belief and the legitimate heir of the former leader of the Communist movement, the C.P.S.U., which had disinherited itself by betraying the sacred cause. The problem of the location of Communist Rome was posed in its entirety: Was it Moscow or Peking?

The Soviet reply recalled the Chinese slogan "The wind from the East prevails over the wind from the West." The Soviet party seemed to be asking what the word *West* meant in this slogan. Was it the West in the sense of traditional Communist parlance or was it Russia in the new Chinese interpretation? The Russians charged that for the last three years the Chinese had been undermining Soviet prestige within the Communist movement, especially among the Communists of Asia, Africa, and Latin America and also within Communist-controlled international front organizations such as the peace movement, the federation of trade-unions, and the "democratic" international associations of women and young people. The Soviet reply reflected the bitterness of Moscow but was more restrained in its verbal assaults on the "fraternal" party than the Chinese letter, except for such jibes as calling the Chinese leaders "schoolboys" who were not intelligent enough to comprehend modern trends and such name-calling as "slanderers" and "splitters."

However, the Soviet answer contained a very crude joke at the expense of the Chinese. In reply to the Chinese accusation that the Soviet society had become bourgeois (i.e., thought only of its own material well-being), the Russians said that the Chinese seemed to equate Communism with a state of affairs in which "people wear bast-shoes and eat a thin cabbage soup from a common basin." They conveniently forgot that this was the condition of the Russian people while they were building under Stalin the industrial might of their country and that the Chinese could not afford Soviet living standards.

The Chinese challenged the Russian party in the name of the equality of all Communist parties and denied that the decisions and programs adopted by the Soviet party congresses (a reference to the post-Stalinist congresses) should be considered by other parties as generally binding for the whole movement. They openly contested the perennial Soviet claim that the basic decisions of their party congresses should be regarded by all Communists as a guiding beacon. The Chinese complained, not without reason, that the Russians did not consult other parties prior to the formulation of new ideological or political positions and that in particular they had not done so prior to the Twentieth and Twenty-second Congresses. It suffices to recall the Twentieth Congress with its unexpected downgrading of Stalin to realize that the Chinese were right in their resentment.

The Soviet party was accused of betraying the principle of proletarian internationalism and of failing to stand by other socialist countries, a clear allusion to Soviet neutrality in the Chinese-Indian conflict. It was also accused of trying to exploit other socialist countries under the pretext of a socialist division of labor and specialization in production, of treating these countries as its own economic preserve, and of using economic pressure to extort political concessions. The Soviet answer conceded that Soviet-Chinese trade had dropped in three years to one-third of what it used to be and that Soviet supplies of capital equipment to China had been reduced to one-fortieth of the former volume. It also conceded that the trade of China with the Eastern European countries had been cut by half. The Russians maintained that the Chinese themselves had decided on these reductions in assistance and trade, an improbable assertion. The Chinese made a virtue of necessity and said in their letter that every socialist country should, first of all, rely on its own efforts; they admitted in simultaneous domestic statements that unaided effort would require two or more decades to make China a modern nation. The Russian answer was insultingly ironical in saying that "the people of no country can sit with folded arms and rely only on the assistance of other socialist countries." It added that socialism could be built only under "a correct leadership," a clear intimation that the Chinese party lacked this leadership; the Chinese thought the same of the present Soviet leadership. The Russians also accused the Chinese of black ingratitude for former Soviet economic and technical assistance.

Both parties agreed that nuclear weapons were unprecedentedly destructive, but the Soviet party insisted vigorously that these weapons had radically modified the very nature of a general war. This war, the Russians said, would be the hecatomb of hundreds of millions of innocent, ordinary toilers. They cited previous Chinese statements to the effect that after a general war mankind would build a splendid new civilization a thousand times superior to the present one and protested that socialism could not be constructed on hundreds of millions of human corpses. The Chinese no less vigorously defended themselves by denying that they wanted a nuclear war, an assertion which was probably true if China were to be one of the belligerents.

The real issue boiled down to the calculation of risks. The Chinese urged all-out support for all local wars waged by Asians, Africans, or Latin Americans against the "imperialist" West, and for all Communist revolutions. The Russians agreed that "revolutionary wars" (Communist civil wars and the armed struggle of colonial or semicolonial populations against the West) were "just and necessary." But they opposed being involved in these wars to the extent of running the risk of a nuclear war with the West. The same problem could be worded in a different way: Who should bear the risks, Russia or China? Until that summer of 1963 the Chinese did not engage in any adventure which could expose them to the danger of an all-out war with the West. The Russians were once less cautious than their letter would make one expect. In 1963 they gave Cuba a military guarantee against an American invasion and indicated that they would then use nuclear weapons against the United States. Yet they protested in their letter that they would never be the first to use nuclear weapons.

The Soviet party held that a Communist revolution should not be attempted unless the situation were truly ripe for it. It claimed that the Communists might seize power not only by an armed struggle but also in the process of a "peaceful transition to socialism." The Chinese refuted this thesis and rejected "legalism and parliamentary cretinism" as proper tactics for Communist parties. They correctly asserted that there were no historical precedents for a peaceful seizure of power by the Communist party. They implicitly dismissed as farfetched the Russian examples of a peaceful transition to socialism: the Soviet annexation of the Baltic countries in 1940, and the installment in 1944-45 of Communist regimes in Eastern Europe under the protection of Soviet occupation troops. For them, as probably for many other people, these were no precedents at all.

In their letter the Chinese accepted the concept of peaceful co-existence with nonsocialist countries and even admitted the usefulness of limited agreements on specific matters, but interpreted this co-existence as a nonmilitary but fierce political, economic, and ideological struggle. The Russians agreed that peaceful co-existence might not be equated with an ideological truce but insisted that the governments of the "imperialist West" were, after all, rational and also wanted to avoid a nuclear war. Hence, the socialist countries should not be reluctant to conclude agreements useful to both parties, although the Russians agreed with the

Chinese that the West remained "the common enemy" of all socialist countries.

The Soviet government demonstrated, soon after the departure of the Chinese delegation, what they meant by limited but useful agreements. On July 25, 1963, they initialed with the United States and Britain the draft of a treaty on the suspension of nuclear tests in the atmosphere, outer space, and underwater (this allowed for underground tests). This treaty further forbade the contracting parties "to encourage" testing by other powers, a provision which affected only China and France. It could not prevent these two countries from carrying on their own tests, since the treaty has no binding force for the nonsignatories, but it compelled them to rely on their own research. The treaty was open to further accessions by all other states, but it is highly doubtful whether either France or China would ever adhere to it. The Chinese reaction was hostile. They said that the treaty prevented the U.S.S.R. from helping other socialist countries to acquire nuclear weapons and strengthen the over-all military might of the socialist bloc. The Chinese recriminations which followed the signing of the treaty disclosed another vital reason for the quarrel with the Russians. Apparently the U.S.S.R. promised in 1957 to help China acquire a nuclear armory of its own and in 1959 reneged on this pledge, refusing since then to share its nuclear knowledge with its ally. The treaty was interpreted by the Chinese as proof that the Russians were eager to strike a bargain with the United States at the expense of Chinese interests in the Far East and in Southeast Asia. Similar fears existed in West Germany that it would have to pay the cost of an American-Soviet rapprochement if it ever materialized.

The most potent Chinese challenge to the Russians was their undisguised claim to be the leader of the have-not nations of Asia, Africa, and Latin America, while excluding Russia from this community of the poor. The Chinese letter constantly referred to the struggle of the "oppressed nations" (not classes) against the "oppressor countries." The letter emphasized the crucial importance of the three continents where the "oppressed nations" lived as the arena where the fate of the "imperialist West" would be decisively and finally sealed. In another passage of the letter the Chinese accused the Russians of exploiting the other socialist countries and thereby intimated that Russia was one of the "oppressor countries" and shared this sad privilege with the West.

The paradox of this aspect of the controversy was that the Soviet party had begun immediately after Stalin's death to stress the crucial importance of the underdeveloped countries in the Communist struggle against the West and never abandoned this thesis. The U.S.S.R. had been doing its best since 1955 to win the friendship of the "oppressed nations." The Russians could give the Chinese numerous examples of the political support and economic assistance which they were rendering to such nations as Egypt and Cuba. But their weakness lay in the incontrovertible fact that they themselves did not belong to the have-not family. In their letter, the Chinese opposed rule by what they ironically called the "superior nations," and they unmistakably included Russia among those nations. The Russians retorted by accusing the Chinese of racialism. The Soviet answer cited the words of a Chinese delegate at an Afro-Asian conference who told the Soviet delegates that "white people have nothing to do here." It is probable that the Chinese have not scrupled to use the demagogic argument of color to evict their Soviet rivals from the Third World. Their competition for influence is taking place in an environment which is mostly "colored." Lenin would not have believed that his followers would stoop to racialist arguments in their controversies, as he would not have expected that they would be pitted against one other in the name of their own nationalisms.

The Soviet party took a more complex view of the struggle against the West. The battlefield of the Third World is very important for them, but it is not, as the Chinese thought, the *only* important battlefield. The Soviet party believes that the West can also be vanquished in the economic and technological competition. They said in their reply that socialism would prove to be more efficient than capitalism and thus would spell the doom of capitalism as an antiquated social-economic system. The Chinese were less optimistic on this score, an attitude quite understandable in view of their being far behind both Russia and the West.

The Russians were more optimistic in other respects as well. They pointed out that their regime is consolidated and that their society is approaching the threshold of affluence. They could afford to proclaim at the Twenty-second Congress that the era of the dictatorship of the proletariat had been ended in the U.S.S.R. and was being replaced by the leadership of the working class. Translated from ideological parlance, this proclamation evidently means that the stringency of the Stalinist regime can now be relaxed. The Stalinist era, when great sacrifices were exacted from the population by sheer terror for the sake of making Russia an industrial great power, was at an end. In 1963 Russia was one of the two super-powers and no longer needed mass terror as a tool of government. China faces several decades of hardship before becoming a great power of the first magnitude. The Chinese party inevitably upheld the opposite thesis that the dictatorship of the proletariat has to survive in all socialist countries, not excluding Russia, until the remote day when a classless Communist society can be built. This theological hair-splitting was important for Chinese national pride, which could not concede to the Russians that their country was far ahead of China. The Soviet Twenty-second Congress proudly proclaimed that socialism had been completely constructed in Russia, which was henceforth busy with building the ideal Communist society. The Chinese letter energetically refuted this boastful claim and asserted that all socialist countries were "far, far removed from Communism." What they wanted to convey was that the Russians were not so advanced on the road to Communism as they pretended and hence had no valid title for teaching other Communists how to progress on the same road. They objected to the Soviet "paternalistic" attitude, forgetting their own claim at the time of the Great Leap Forward and of the communes that they had found a short cut to Communism. Sobered by the dismal failure of the Great Leap, they became more realistic and were inclined to teach modesty to the Russians.

The two parties disagreed on Stalin, whom the Chinese continued to include among the greatest international leaders. They scored a point in contrasting the Soviet campaign against the cult of personality with the appearance of a new cult of Khrushchev. In fact, the Chinese worship Mao, while the Russians seize every opportunity to acclaim Khrushchev. Both letters agreed that every Communist party must cultivate the prestige of its leaders.

Each of the disputants had his own small whipping boy. For the Chinese, it was the Yugoslav party, to whom they denied the appellation of a Communist party. The Russians denounced the Albanians as a tool of Chinese intrigues but more tolerantly included both Yugoslavia and Albania among the socialist countries.

At the root of the dispute lay a conflict which will be difficult to heal, a collision between two nationalisms. This underlying conflict was admitted by the Chinese when they said in their letter that the quarrel between the two parties adversely affected the relations between the two states. Yet neither dared in July, 1963, to acknowledge that the breach was final. As long as they do not denounce their alliance, outsiders will be well-advised not to take this breach as consummated, even though a reconciliation seems rather improbable.

With respect to the difficulties between China and the Soviet Union, two possibilities exist at the present time: either the two Communist allies will patch up their differences or else their quarrels will grow increasingly bitter and culminate in an open rupture. Common sense indicates that the West should not rely on an open breach. It will always be easier to adjust Western policies to the termination of the Soviet-Chinese alliance than to anticipate it and thereby get caught by all the problems which an unexpected revival of Soviet-Chinese co-operation would entail. Moreover, the two Communist powers do not disagree on who their main enemy is but only on how this enemy should be engaged. The main opponent of the West is not China but the Soviet Union, which is by far the strongest socialist state; the quarrels over Berlin and Cuba were not with China. In any event, the wisest Western attitude would be to wait and see.

An open rupture between the two Communist great powers would certainly change the present pattern of international alignments. Animosity toward the Soviet Union is the common denominator of NATO, while only a few NATO allies are vitally interested in Chinese actions. If the NATO allies were suddenly placed by a Soviet-Chinese schism before the dilemma of revising their policies, it would be far from certain that they would reach the same conclusions. Some of these countries might seek a rapprochement with the U.S.S.R. on a common ground of suspicion of Chinese intentions; others, who belong to NATO only because they fear Russia, might be tempted to become friendly to China.

Russia and China would suffer obvious losses if their alliance were disrupted. The Communist movement, a great asset for both of them, would be greatly weakened. With the official proclamation of the existence of rival Rome and Constantinople, of two hostile centers, the other parties would be compelled to choose their allegiance. Some might elect their own independent road. The schism could produce not only two rival Communist movements but also a proliferation of national heresies. The only beneficiary would be the West, which would enjoy a respite owing to dissensions among the Communist parties. Soviet prestige would suffer from the loss of a major ally in Asia and also from the probable disaffection of a number of non-European parties. The setback for China would be much greater. Separated from its nuclear ally, China would appear to be what it actually is—a sprawling country whose government controls almost a fourth of the population of the world but whose state is still a medium power compared with the two nuclear super-powers.

Whatever the future brings, the Communist movement is already bicentric like medieval Christianity. Moreover, several parties possess greater autonomy than in Stalin's lifetime. If the more autonomous parties were regarded as additional centers, it would be possible to go further and say that the Communist movement has become polycentric.

Whatever the future evolution of the movement, it should not be overlooked that the Communist parties have much in common even if some of them are at loggerheads. They agree on the basic tenets of Marxism-Leninism understood as a philosophy of the universe and of human destiny, they share a hostility to all "obsolete" regimes and ideologies, they espouse collectivization of the means of production, and they all consider that the Communist party must play the central role in a socialist revolution and later in the construction of a socialist regime. They can quarrel on the best ways of extending the Communist realm but not on whether it should be extended at all.

Even a truncated movement, if centered around a nuclear great power, would retain a great and dynamic potential. Moreover, a less centralized movement offers certain advantages, although these advantages would not compensate for the losses that a schism would cause. Each party is in a better position to adjust its policies to local circumstances. Freed of rigid instructions emanating from an alien party, the leaders of other parties can more freely devise their tactics and thus score successes in the theater of their own operations. After all, the Chinese, the Vietnamese, and the Cuban revolutions did not reproduce the patterns of the October Revolution; yet it cannot be said that these revolutions did not inflict defeats on the West, which was compelled to retreat from these areas. Greater autonomy for the Communist parties would not preclude further successes, especially in the underdeveloped countries. The greatest revolution of our time, the revolution of modernization, opens a long and hazardous chapter in the history of mankind. This chapter of change and instability will not be closed for several decades. If in several countries the revolution of rising expectations becomes a revolution of rising frustrations, the Communist parties may well have a chance to extend their influence.

At this critical stage of the Communist movement it is wise to watch events with an open mind, not to prejudge future developments, to be ready to adjust one's former views to new facts, and, above all, to avoid forecasts. The road of history is paved with the bones of false political prophets.

THE TENETS OF CONTEMPORARY COMMUNISM

The fundamental tenets of contemporary Communism have twice been codified in recent years, first at an assembly held in 1957 and later at a meeting which took place in 1960. In spite of the subsequent Russian-Chinese disputes over the interpretation of these two statements, which they both adopted together with all other Communist parties, these two texts merit close attention as authentic expressions of Communist views and aspirations. The Declaration of 1957 listed the following points:

1. Marxist dialectical materialism is "a world outlook reflecting the universal law of development of nature, society, and human thought. It is valid for the past, the present, and the future." This is a reaffirmation of Marxism as an absolute truth.

2. The socialist revolution must take place everywhere in the world and should be carried out under the leadership of the Communist party. This "leading role" of the party must be upheld after the revolution, in the new socialist society.

3. The revolution should bring about a total socialization of all the means of production.

4. The development of a nationalized economy should be planned and directed by the state, which should regulate the production and distribution of goods.

5. The "socialist revolution in the sphere of ideology and culture" must be effected in every socialist state. In other words, the party must set

up a single correct line in the social sciences, literature, the arts, and music.

6. All Communist parties should always remain committed to "proletarian internationalism."

The Statement adopted in 1960 is all-important for an understanding of the objectives and tactics of the movement. This Statement "unanimously confirmed" the ideological Declaration of 1957 but also formulated its own guiding ideas for the benefit of all Communist parties.

The adoption of the Statement by the Communist parties from the non-Communist countries and by the parties which at that time governed twelve states, and their mutual reaffirmation of solidarity, are crucial for an understanding of the contemporary ideological conflict. The solidarity of the parties means no less than that the twelve governments, controlled by their respective parties, are officially and publicly committed to support the remaining seventy-eight Communist parties which no less openly reaffirmed in the Statement their intention to carry out a revolution in their countries and to install there regimes modelled after the systems which prevailed in the Communist-ruled states. In effect, the Statement notified the non-Communist states that the conflict between them and the Communist countries was not limited to the issue of national interests but included the whole issue of the survival or extinction of the non-Communist regimes and ways of life. The Statement says: "Every Communist party which has become the ruling party in a state bears historic responsibility for both the fate of its own country and the fate of the entire socialist camp." This camp includes not only all Communist states but also all Communist parties. The ultimate ideological objective was affirmed with the deep conviction peculiar to those who imagine that they represent the wave of the future: "The complete victory of socialism is inevitable." The Statement was not diffident about Soviet and Chinese intentions to export their ways of life to all other countries: "The peoples of the socialist countries who build up the road to Communism are creating the prototype of a new society for all mankind."

The Statement reaffirmed the Leninist thesis that this prototype could be extended to all countries only through revolutions. It distinguished between two types of revolutions: the peaceful and the violent. The neo-Leninist concept of a "peaceful" revolution was elaborated for the first time at the Twentieth Congress of the Soviet party, held in 1956. The Congress speakers made this concept quite unequivocal by adducing past examples: the annexation of the Baltic countries in 1940 after their occupation by Soviet troops; the installation of Communist regimes in Eastern Europe after the Soviet military occupation of that area in 1944-45; and the Communist coup in Czechoslovakia in 1948. In other words, a peaceful seizure of power by the local Communists is expected to take place if their action can be supported either by an open military intervention on the part of the neighboring Communist power or by the threat of that intervention. In either case, opponents would be paralyzed by fear and would surrender without attempting a resistance that would seem futile. If this type of peaceful revolution cannot take place and if the opponents are prepared to offer resistance, the Statement recommends violent revolution: "In the conditions where the exploiting classes use violence against the people [the non-Communists resist the Communist attempt at the seizure of power] it is essential to keep another possibility in sight, the nonpeaceful transition to socialism." The Statement adds in a realistic vein: "Lenin teaches, and historical experience confirms it, that the ruling classes do not cede power voluntarily." The non-Communists are thus offered two alternatives, both leading to the same result—either to surrender without resisting, or to resist and be crushed. The Statement advised the Communist parties to be practical in choosing between these two methods of winning power: "In each country the real possibility of using one or the other method of transition to socialism is determined by concrete historical circumstances."

Communists divide mankind into two hostile camps: the socialist and the capitalist. The Statement offers the following interpretation of our historical era: "Our epoch, which is marked basically by the transition from capitalism to socialism and which began with the Great October Socialist Revolution, is an era of struggle by the two opposing social systems, . . . an era of transition to socialism for more and more peoples, of the worldwide triumph of socialism and communism." The essence of contemporary international relations is logically reduced to a nutshell formula: "The development of international relations is determined in our time by the struggle of the two social systems." This division of mankind into two irreconcilably hostile camps excludes the hypothesis of eventual reconciliation. All the non-Communist regimes, democratic and authoritarian alike, all forms of social organization, both the advanced forms of the West and the tradition-bound forms of the underdeveloped countries, are included in this declaration of war.

However, the Statement subdivides the capitalist camp into two groups. One of these groups is the "imperialist" West, which is singled out for an immediate and particularly intense hostility. It is the strong link of the enemy chain. The underdeveloped countries form the other group, which is invited to join forces with the Communist camp in a common struggle against the West. The Statement insists in several passages on this necessity of splitting up the capitalist camp by aligning the underdeveloped countries on the Communist side:

"Life insistently demands still closer unification of the forces and decisive actions of the socialist countries, the international working class, the national anti-imperialist movements, of all peace-loving states. . . .

"The peoples building socialism and communism, the revolutionary movement of the working class in capitalist countries, the national liberation struggle of the oppressed peoples, the common democratic movement —all these great trends of our day are merging in one single current which undermines and destroys the world imperialist system.

"The Conference expresses its solidarity with all the peoples of Asia, Africa, Latin America, and Oceania who wage a heroic anti-imperialist struggle."

This truly Leninist concept of a common anti-Western front calls for the co-operation of the Communist states, the Communist parties in the non-Communist states (the international working class), the anti-colonialist movements in the still existing Western dependencies (the national anti-imperialist movements), and all non-Communist states which have some accounts to settle with the West (the peace-loving states). This concept of combining all anti-Western forces, whatever their ideology might be, has been stressed in Communist literature with great vigor since 1953. Stalin distrusted the non-Communist nationalist leaders in the underdeveloped countries too much to believe that they could become useful temporary allies; he feared that they would betray the Communist camp on the first opportunity. He thus condemned Soviet foreign policy toward the newly independent states to utter sterility, while he concentrated his attention on Europe, where he had, however, no effective means at his disposal for changing the status quo. His successors were quick to understand that the issues which divided the underdeveloped countries from the West could be usefully exploited to undermine the Western political and economic positions in the non-Western lands. The record of Soviet successes in Asia, the Near East, Africa, and Latin America has since proved that they were right in this new approach to international politics. The unavailing direct movement against the Western positions in Europe has been replaced by a more effective enveloping movement.

This Statement leaves no doubt that the West is the main enemy. The code name for this enemy is "imperialism." As the most powerful Western nation, it is not surprising that the United States has been singled out for the fiercest hostility. The Statement characterizes the United States in the following manner:

"The United States, more than any other capitalist country, is pumping out the wealth of the Asian countries and of the Latin American countries even more so; it thus retards their development. The penetration of American capital into Africa is increasing. American imperialism has become the biggest international exploiter."

"Recent international events have provided much new evidence that American imperialism is the backbone of world reaction and is the international gendarme, the enemy of the peoples of the entire world."

"The chief force of aggression and war is United States imperialism."

"The main stronghold of present-day colonialism is the United States."

It is not surprising that the Communist bloc and in particular the Soviet Union level the bitterest accusations against the United States on the score of the military bases which form a ring around the bloc. These bases are a thorn in the Communist flesh. The Statement reiterated the familiar Soviet threat of nuclear destruction against the states committed to the United States:

"The existence of these blocs and bases threatens the general peace and security and not only tramples on the sovereignty of, but also imperils the very survival of, those states which grant their territory for the bases of the United States militarists."

The Soviet Union has frequently announced that it will unleash its nuclear rockets upon any state accommodating United States bases if it feels that those bases constitute a grave threat to Soviet security. These reiterated menaces are in a sense meaningless. A nuclear attack launched against an American ally and American personnel garrisoned on the base would probably bring about an American nuclear retaliation against the Soviet Union itself. The latter country, by giving local provocation, would foolishly yield to the other nuclear power all the advantages of the "first strike," including the chance of crippling the Soviet retaliatory force. Common sense indicates that no nuclear power, neither the Soviet Union nor the United States, would ever use its nuclear force for a limited attack of this type. If a general nuclear war were to break out, all Soviet and American bases would be in danger of destruction regardless of their location. American bases would be equally exposed to the risk of attack whether situated on American or foreign territory. The country which provides its territory for American bases buys American military protection at the price of risks which would be no greater than the American risks in a general nuclear war. The Soviet allies assume the same risks. That these allies accommodate Soviet military bases and garrisons is no secret; in 1956-57 the Soviet Union officially acknowledged the existence of at least some of these bases by concluding agreements with Poland, Rumania, Hungary, and East Germany concerning the legal status of its troops permanently garrisoned in those four countries.

Communist propaganda, including the Statement described above, constantly denounces Western alliances such as NATO, the Central Treaty (the former Baghdad Pact), SEATO, and other American mutual security treaties, as a grave menace to the general peace. The policies of the Communist bloc have not been different, however, from Western policies. The Soviet Union has concluded bilateral treaties of mutual assistance with the Eastern European states, China, North Korea, and Mongolia. The regional Warsaw Treaty, a replica of NATO, covers the whole Eastern European area; its signatories are the Soviet Union and all European Communist states, including East Germany but excluding uncommitted Yugoslavia. China is linked to the Warsaw Treaty by its bilateral alliance with Russia and also by its frequent promises of support in case its European friends become engaged in a war against "the imperialists." Finally, Cuba obtained in 1963 a unilateral Soviet guarantee against the United States.

Soviet propaganda makes a contradictory use of the widespread fear of nuclear war. On the one hand, the allies of the United States are threatened with destruction by Soviet rockets; this menace seems to imply a Soviet readiness to assume the risk of a general nuclear war in response to the slightest provocation. If these threats were to be taken seriously, they would be symptomatic of a reckless policy. On the other hand, the same Soviet propaganda accuses the United States of pursuing a reckless policy of "brinkmanship" and of lightheartedly running the risks of nuclear catastrophe. The Soviet Union and its allies are pictured as the only solid guarantee of the general peace of the world, a peace-loving bloc. This contradiction between the two themes of Soviet propaganda seems to escape general notice.

In spite of its threats, the Soviet Union seems to understand the risks involved in a general nuclear war as well as the United States. Communists share with non-Communists the fear of unprecedented devastations; this fear is reflected in the Statement: "Monstrous means have been created for mass destruction and annihilation. The application of these means in a new war would cause unprecedented destruction to entire countries and could turn the large centers of world production and world culture into ruins. Such a war would bring death and suffering to hundreds of millions of people, including those in the nonbelligerent countries." This description of the consequences of nuclear hostilities makes it clear that no great power can be sure of retaining its former rank after an all-out war and that no regime can confidently expect to stand amidst the radioactive ruins inhabited by the embittered survivors of the catastrophe. This much seems to be understood even by the Chinese party, which signed the Statement.

The invention of nuclear weapons forced the Communists to revise one of the fundamental Leninist dogmas. Lenin taught that wars were inevitable as long as capitalism survived. He saw two reasons for wars: rivalry between the imperialist governments for the sources of raw materials and for markets, and ideological conflict between the capitalist and the socialist states. The Soviet party, fully aware of all the aspects of the nuclear problem, was the first to reject this dogma in 1956 at its Twentieth Congress. The new thesis was approved by the other eighty-nine parties in the following sentence of the Statement: "There is no fatal inevitability of war." When the same Statement added that wars were nevertheless possible, it enunciated a truism. A nuclear war could break out by sheer error in the warning system or be forced on one nuclear power by the rash policy of the other if this policy left no choice but the surrender of its most vital interests. A local war, in which the nuclear powers would not be directly involved, a guerrilla war, a civil war, are all possible. But both parties to the ideological conflict agree that they have no interest in unleashing a general nuclear war.

The Communists have been caught in a dilemma: their ideology compels them to work for a complete change in the international status quo, but they confess their unwillingness to assume nuclear risks in the process. They have solved this dilemma by devising a foreign policy which is called that of peaceful co-existence, a policy of gradually undermining the status quo by every means short of nuclear risks. The Statement makes it clear that peaceful co-existence does not mean an acceptance of the status quo: "Peaceful co-existence among states does not mean . . . a rejection of the class war. Co-existence between states with differing social systems is a form of class struggle between socialism and capitalism. . . . Peaceful co-existence of states with different social systems does not mean a reconciliation between the socialist and the bourgeois ideologies. On the contrary, it implies an intensification of the struggle waged by the working class and by all the Communist parties for the triumph of socialist ideas." It is a fierce competition, which includes the following methods:

1. Revolution, peaceful or violent, each Communist party having the mission of carrying out a revolution if domestic and international circumstances are propitious.

2. Undermining the Western positions by exploiting the conflicts of interests between the Western countries themselves but, above all, between the Western and the underdeveloped countries.

3. Bettering the West in economic competition by overtaking it both in respect to total production and in respect to scientific and technological achievements. The Statement confidently predicts: "Capitalism will be defeated in the decisive field of human activities, the field of material production." The goal is ambitious: ". . . to outstrip the world capitalist system in the absolute volume of industrial and agricultural production and, following this, to outstrip the economically most developed capitalist countries in the level of per capita output and of living standards."

This ambitious goal is to be achieved not only by the individual efforts of Communist countries but also by their economic and technological co-operation: "This requires a constant perfection of the international division of labor thanks to the co-ordination of economic plans and the specialization and co-operation in production within the world socialist system." The objectives are somewhat contradictory. Surpassing the West in respect to living standards would demand a rapid expansion of light industries and a great increase in agricultural output. However, agriculture is the chronic headache of all Communist states, in particular of the Soviet Union and China, and there seems to be no reasonable prospect of rapidly overtaking the West in agricultural labor productivity, i.e., in the output per person and per acre. A forceful race to expand industrial production will require, as it has required in the past, investing as much as possible in the heavy industries and as little as possible in the light industries. Judging from the past record, it is probable that the Communist states, especially Russia, will maintain a high rate of growth of heavy industries but, as before, at the price of slow progress in agriculture and in the industries producing consumer goods. Even a Communist party cannot achieve all the goals, if some of these must be sacrificed to attain others, and have its cake while eating it.

THE PROSPECTS

The foreign objectives of the Communist states have been publicly stated and restated year after year, day after day. They always include an ideological crusade for the conversion of the entire world to their own "self-evident truths" and ways of life. The anti-imperialist, i.e., anti-Western orientation is not a secret. Even a casual look at the record of Soviet policies in the underdeveloped countries brings forth abundant evidence of this orientation. The inclusion of ideological considerations within the foreign objectives of Russia or China certainly complicates the task of both governments and requires a greater expenditure of national energy than purely national goals would have demanded. If the Soviet or the Chinese leaders really did not care about the future expansion of their creed, they could greatly simplify their task, but they refuse to do so. Ideological devotion has, however, its practical advantages; it forms a common bond among the Communist states and parties, a not unimportant consideration.

The ideological commitment of the Communist powers precludes the settlement of international problems within the framework of national interests as they used to be defined in the nineteenth century. However, it would be a mistake to suppose that Russia and China could easily be brought to a compromise settlement with the Western Powers if the ideological conflict did not exist. The entire problem of conflicting national interests would remain. The rise in power of both Russia and China makes it imperative from their point of view that their greater influence in several areas of the world be recognized by the Western powers. For this reason a reconciliation of national interests, even divorced from all ideological considerations, would be difficult to achieve unless the Western powers were ready to accept a redistribution of political influence among the great powers in the Near East, the Far East, Southeast Asia, and perhaps also in Africa.

As a matter of fact, ideological considerations but also the national interests of both Communist great powers make them antagonistic to the international status quo, which seems to them a relic of a bygone age. Moreover, there is another reason why the Soviet leaders might be disinclined to accept a maintenance of the status quo. The Soviet Union has been unusually lucky in its foreign policy during the last few decades. The Second World War provided it with an excellent opportunity to extend its national territory and build a vast zone of influence in Eastern Central Europe. After the termination of this period of expansion (1939-45), the establishment of Communist regimes in China, North Korea, and North Vietnam made the Soviet Union much stronger in the Far East. Since 1953 its political offensive in the Third World has yielded notable results. Its external influence has been extended far afield, including the areas where Russia was never very active before. History records no examples of governments which, having been successful in foreign policy, have suddenly renounced the prospect of further advances for no better reason than to please other great powers. There is little probability that the Soviet Union will be the first power to display such magnanimous moderation. Moderation in international politics is not a moral but a political virtue and consists in maintaining a balance between objectives and available means. The Soviet Union has not so far pursued a policy beyond its means.

Whenever the Soviet Union and the Western powers engage in a discussion of a general nature, the Soviet government never fails to make clear its attitude toward the international status quo. There are certain topics which the Soviet Union categorically withdraws from the agenda of international transactions. One of these topics is the relations between the member-states of the Communist bloc. For example, the West has been repeatedly told that it has no business to be concerned with the Soviet intervention in Hungary or with conditions in East Germany although the existence of the Democratic German Republic is not recognized by the Western powers. The West is urged to acknowledge that the status quo in the Communist part of the world is frozen forever or at least that there is no room there for any active Western policy. The second topic which the Soviet government has persistently declared not to be a subject for diplomatic discussions is its open support for the Communist parties which operate in the non-Communist part of the world. The fact that foreign governments may consider this support an interference in their domestic affairs does not impress the Soviet government, which resents, however, any Western verbal sympathy for the non-Communists who live in the various Communist states. The U.S.S.R. does not accept any reciprocity in this respect. These two reservations restrict the matters open to discussion between the West and the U.S.S.R. to the problems of the non-Communist part of the world. Even so, these discussions should, from the Soviet point of view, convince the West of the necessity of retreating from one or another of its positions. The Berlin issue provides a striking illustration. East Berlin, located within the Soviet zone of influence, has been excluded from all discussions, which have been restricted to West Berlin, located within the Western zone of influence, from which the West has been invited to withdraw.

A current Soviet concept reflects their view of the proper behavior of the Communist states vis à vis the Western states. According to this concept, the Communist states have a moral obligation to support all "wars of national liberation." These wars include all civil and local wars in which the West is directly or indirectly concerned. Specifically, they include civil wars in which the Communist or any other anti-Western faction is one of the contending parties, local wars in which one of the belligerents is a Communist state or an anti-Western state or any state engaged in hostilities against a Western power, and, finally, any anti-Western colonial uprising. All these wars of national liberation should be supported by the Communist states, though within the limits of acceptable risks—i.e., without running the risk of a major war with the West. But the other leaf of this Soviet diptych is the claim that the West has no right to "export counter-revolution." This means that the West should not actively support a party to a civil war or a belligerent in a local war who is opposed to the party or to the belligerent favored by the Communist states.

This Soviet concept is too biased to be seriously examined. But it illuminates the Soviet image of the two contending camps: the dynamic Communist states, which claim the moral right to promote change in foreign countries, are contrasted with an inert West, which is doomed to watch helplessly the gradual, inexorable retrogression of its external influence.

A Western retreat that has already taken place is registered as final and irrevocable. The Soviet attitude toward Hungary and Cuba is a case in point. The Soviet Union considered it perfectly legitimate to intervene in Hungary because that country was included in its zone of influence. But it fiercely denounced every attempt by the United States to restore its position in Cuba, which is as manifestly within the traditional American zone of influence.

This dual attitude toward the international status quo makes it particularly difficult for the two blocs to reach a lasting *modus vivendi*. The history of past ideological conflicts is not very encouraging. The parties to these conflicts desisted from their attempts to convert opponents by force only after having been exhausted by a protracted and finally fruitless struggle and after having been diverted from the ideological issue by the appearance of new problems. Toleration came only after a long period of fierce struggle. The Christians and the Moslems intermittently fought each other for a thousand years, if the Arab and Turkish periods are added together; the Religious Wars between Catholics and Protestants lasted for a hundred years.

Judging from these historical precedents, the two blocs will not reach a durable *modus vivendi* until the Communists conclude that all their missionary efforts have been in vain and that their evaluation of the opportunity in the underdeveloped countries has been mistaken. Repeated failures would have to compel them to admit, at least in secret, that Lenin was wrong when he prophesied:

> The outcome of the struggle depends, in the inescapable analysis, on the fact that Russia, India, China, etc., form the gigantic majority of the population [of the world]. This majority is being dragged, as a matter of fact, with unusual speed in recent years into the struggle for liberation. There cannot be, in this sense, a shadow of doubt as to what the final outcome of the world-wide struggle will be. The final victory of socialism is in this sense fully and unconditionally secured.

Subsequent events have not yet disproved this thesis. But if future developments demonstrate that Communism has no further opportunity for expansion, the Communist governments will eventually tire of their crusade and reluctantly conclude that non-Communist ideologies and regimes will continue to exist. That time would be a modern 1648, a time when the ideological conflict ends and an era of mutual toleration begins, though toleration that is nothing but a reluctant admission that different ideologies are bound to survive. At the present time the Communist leaders appear to be far from this state of mind.

The existence of nuclear weapons has a dual effect on the ideological conflict. On the one hand, it immensely increases the risks of ideological strife. But on the other hand, it has a sobering influence. The prospect of a "heroic" collective suicide of mankind in the name of conflicting ideals does not lure either ideological party. The risks undertaken in the ideological warfare must be carefully calculated, much more carefully than in any former ideological age. One can indulge in verbal insults and threats directed against ideological enemies, but one must be cautious in his acts. It is a peculiarity of our age that governments can practise verbal assaults, often violent and tasteless, but their fear of nuclear catastrophe compels them to react calmly to incidents which in former times would have been an immediate cause of war. Firing upon foreign planes over the open seas, launching illegal flights over foreign territory, or insults addressed by one head of state to another have become "normal" occurrences in the international relations of today, but these occurrences do not endanger a peace which is guaranteed, in spite of ideological passions, by a fear of nuclear war.

Declarations of mutual good will will not reduce international tension. The ineffectiveness of former declarations of this type should be a sufficient warning. Since the early fifties, however, both Russia and China have waged a vigorous campaign for bilateral treaties in which the five principles of peaceful co-existence would be proclaimed. These five principles are as follows:

1. Respect for territorial integrity and sovereignty.
2. Nonaggression.
3. Noninterference in domestic affairs for any reason, economic, political, or ideological.
4. Equality and mutual benefits.
5. Peaceful co-existence.

These five principles were for the first time enshrined in a Chinese-Indian treaty signed in 1954. They have since been reproduced in several declarations adopted by Russia or China and various uncommitted Asian states.

They add nothing to the customary duties of states. Moreover, the Soviet and Chinese records are not very encouraging in this respect. The Soviet Union solemnly promised in regional and bilateral treaties with its neighbors to respect their national independence and territorial integrity, not to commit an aggression against them, and not to interfere in their domestic affairs. Treaties to this effect were signed in the twenties and thirties. However, its neighbors, one after another, were to be bitterly disappointed. Poland, while defending itself against Nazi Germany, was attacked from the rear in September, 1939, by Soviet troops. Its territory was divided between the two great powers. The three Baltic republics were invaded in 1940 by Soviet troops and annexed. Rumania was compelled to cede a part of its territory under the threat of a Soviet ultimatum. Turkey was faced in 1945-46 with Soviet demands to cede two of its provinces and yield control over the Turkish Straits. In 1945-46 Iran barely escaped territorial amputations at the time of the Soviet military occupation of its northern territories; Soviet promotion of the Azerbaijani and Kurdish autonomous movements, which were developing under the protection of Soviet troops, ended only with the withdrawal of Soviet regiments, a withdrawal due, among other reasons, to Western pressure. Outer Mongolia was detached in the twenties from China following Soviet military occupation of that territory.

The Chinese signed their treaty with India in 1954; soon after, they began to occupy several border areas of Indian territory which they claimed as their own and began to build there strategic roads along the northern Indian frontier. The Indian government reminded China of the five principles of peaceful co-existence and of the 1954 treaty but to no avail. The Indian government learned the useful lesson that international tensions cannot be reduced by solemn promises.

The present lack of Communist interest in seeking a global understanding with the West does not preclude limited agreements which both parties might find very useful. A well-known example is the Austrian State Treaty signed in 1955. Both the Soviet Union and the Western powers agreed to evacuate their troops from Austria, to settle with it all remaining outstanding questions, and to recognize its permanently neutral status. Austria recovered its full independence. Another example is the treaty for the demilitarization of the Antarctic, which was signed by all the states concerned, including the United States and the U.S.S.R. A third example is the series of treaties, concluded in recent years by the United States and other Western nations with the Soviet Union and the Eastern European countries, providing for the exchange of scientists, other specialists, students, and musical and theatrical performers and for the exchange of motion pictures. Limited agreements of this type, useful as they are, do not remove the basic causes of conflict between the two blocs.

The question whether ideology or national interests dictate the foreign policies of the Communist great powers seems to be rather academic. Granted the not unreasonable assumption that Khrushchev is a sincere Communist and a Russian who loves his native country and that Mao Tse-tung is an equally sincere Communist and a Chinese who cherishes his own people and its future, is there a necessary conflict between ideology and national interests? As a rule, the two considerations, the ideological and the national, strengthen each other. An expansion of the Russian or Chinese territory or zone of influence would entail a victory for the Communist ideology, because it would bring about an extension of the realm in which the Communist "self-evident truths" and system of government reign. By the same token, the conversion of a foreign people to Communism means the appearance of a new Russian or Chinese friend and the addition of another member-state to the Communist bloc. The creation in 1944-45 of the Russian zone of influence in Eastern Europe resulted in the expansion of the Communist realm. The Eastern European countries were compelled to become Russian allies but also to adopt the Communist system of government. The victory of the revolution in Cuba and the merger of the Fidelists with the Communists in one Leninist organization had the same dual effect. Cuba became a close political friend of the Communist bloc but also another Communist country. If Communism were to conquer the Near East, it would be an ideological victory but also a fulfillment of traditional Russian aspirations. If it were to expand in Southeast Asia, this great ideological success would also yield immense national benefits for China, which could then protect the overseas Chinese and enjoy access to local primary commodities.

The usual concordance between the ideological and national objectives of the Communist great powers does not exclude divergencies of views between one of them and a foreign Communist party. For instance, the Soviet Union may consider that it is more important to cultivate friendly relations with the non-Communist Arab states than to encourage a local Communist party to seize power in one of these states. This seizure could frighten other Arab governments and could throw them into the arms of the West. The local party may feel that an equally propitious opportunity will not arise for many years. The Communist great power may answer with an argument which only the future can prove true or false. It may tell the leaders of the foreign party that the cause of the whole international movement is best served by the continuous extension of its external influence and that the present loss of a local revolutionary opportunity would be amply compensated later by its becoming the paramount power in the world and being able to impose Communist regimes everywhere.

The Communist great powers encourage neutrality in the non-Communist states but reject neutrality for the Communist states. They advocate a complete change in the political and social regime of all non-Communist states but are firmly opposed to any change in the regime of the Communist countries. This attitude was fully demonstrated in 1956. The Hungarian revolution pursued two objectives: the establishment of a multiparty system of government, and withdrawal from the Warsaw Treaty obligations and the proclamation of Hungarian neutrality. The Soviet Union found both objectives completely unacceptable and settled the matter through armed intervention. Since 1948 the perennial quarrels with Yugoslavia have gravitated around two issues: can a small Communist country be allowed to have its own interpretation of Marxism-Leninism, and can it pursue a policy of noncommitment? The Soviet and other Communist parties have been giving a negative answer to both questions. The Yugoslav party has been repeatedly denounced for its "revisionism" (i.e., its ambition to formulate its own doctrinal interpretations which deviate widely from the doctrines accepted by other parties) but also for threatening the solidarity of the socialist camp through its policy of neutrality. Finally, the Soviet-Albanian dispute concerns the same issue of the right of a small party to its own interpretation of Marxism-Leninism.

CHAPTER VIII

International Community, Public Opinion, Morality, and Law

THE FALSE ANALOGY BETWEEN THE NATIONAL AND INTERNATIONAL COMMUNITIES

One of the most common and serious errors in thinking about international politics is to look upon the international community as though it were an imperfect replica of the national society. Many ill-starred projects for the salvation of mankind are founded on this false analogy. The state (i.e., the organized national community) is rooted, in the last analysis, in a deep and shared feeling of national solidarity. Unless this feeling were stronger than centrifugal or sectional loyalties and stronger than intergroup competition, the state would disintegrate. The consciousness of supreme loyalty to the state is the psychological cornerstone of this modern political structure. The population of the state or, at least, the nationality which controls a multinational state must have this consciousness of solidarity. When tested, this loyalty must override all other allegiances—religious, ideological, provincial, or professional. The modern nation-state rests on the compatibility of its citizens' interests and beliefs.

If sectional interests and aspirations prove to be incompatible with, and stronger than, national solidarity, the state is on its way toward revolution, territorial secession (for instance, by the dependent nationality which wants to form its own state), or disintegration. If a revolution occurs, the new regime will restore national solidarity on the basis of a new consensus. If the state disintegrates, as the Austrian-Hungarian Empire did, or if a part of its territory secedes, new states will emerge; if they are to survive, these new states must be founded on a sense of national solidarity.

This solidarity makes the members of the national community accept legal and moral rules and abide by them. Moral and legal rules are enforced primarily by the individual's feeling that they are valid and should be obeyed and by the fear of censure from his neighbors, friends, and colleagues. This inner conviction that national law should be complied with is reinforced by the fear of state coercion. Yet it is interesting to observe that state coercion is not often used; the mass of citizens seldom carry disobedience to the point where it provokes force. The actual use of domestic coercion on a large scale proves that a national society is in the process of transition and hence that the feeling of solidarity is weakened from within by conflicting interests and beliefs. This will be true of a pre-revolutionary regime on its way out or of a post-revolutionary regime which is not yet certain that the mass of citizens accept it as the new spokesman for national solidarity.

The feeling of solidarity makes the citizens accept the priority of state interests over their own individual or group interests; it makes them accept the state system whereby a number of citizens wield public authority in their capacity as state agents, including the right to formulate policies and to apply coercion; it makes them concede the power of these agents to enact general rules of conduct (law) enforceable, if necessary, by coercion and thereby to adjudicate group conflicts, as well as the power of other agents to settle individual disputes (courts); and it makes them acknowledge the right of state agents to use coercion when necessary. Because it assumes that state interests are superior to sectional and individual interests and that the will of the state should ultimately prevail, the same feeling of solidarity supports the state monopoly of coercion.

If a section of the population takes a different view of the matter (for instance, a controlled nationality in a multinational state or in a colonial empire, or a part of the main nationality who are dissatisfied with the present political regime), it has two alternatives. It can openly challenge the existing government in a revolution or a secessionist insurrection. If it feels that an open revolt would be successfully disciplined by state coercion, it can do nothing but accept with resignation the national solidarity which prevails in the country.

All this does not mean that each citizen analyses his feelings toward the state and deliberately chooses to subordinate all other loyalties. He takes this loyalty for granted and acts accordingly; his behavior makes the state's use of coercion a rare occurrence.

The modern state is organized under one government, which formulates and implements all policies, foreign and domestic, and monopolizes external and domestic coercion. Revolution, i.e., an unauthorized collective use of force against the government, is a symptom of national sickness.

By contrast, one hesitates to use the words *international community* to describe the present condition of mankind, which is rent by so many conflicting interests and aspirations and which lacks the precondition of a community, namely a widely shared feeling of solidarity. Modern man gives his supreme loyalty to the nation-state. When his loyalties conflict, he habitually favors the state. Even if he distinctly felt (which he usually does not) an allegiance to mankind as a whole, he is not likely to favor the international community when his loyalty to that community conflicts with his loyalty to the state. The shift of the supreme loyalty from the nation-state to mankind would be a revolution in modern concepts which is not yet announced by any visible signs.

The world is becoming one in two respects but at the same time it is fragmented into several "worlds" in all other respects. It is one scientifically and technologically. There is only one science and technology, the common treasure-house of the whole of mankind. The same treasure-house is also a Pandora's box which can release mass destruction. This consideration should be the basis for a solidarity higher than any other, including national or ideological solidarity. Yet there is no serious indication that this higher solidarity is emerging in human minds.

The world is becoming one in another sense. The revolution of modernization is spreading the influence of the European civilization to the four corners of the earth. The very fact that the European elements are becoming an integral part of the non-European cultures will make for a world less heterogeneous than the present one. There will be a common European denominator.

Yet the same world which is being united by science and technology and by the widespread influence of the European civilization remains deeply divided in all other respects. The ideological conflict between Communism and the West divides not only the realm of European civilization but also, by repercussion, the rest of the globe. Moreover, ideologies other than democracy and Communism do exist and further aggravate the disunity of the world.

The underdeveloped countries have interests and aspirations which are very different from those of the advanced countries. The citizen of an underdeveloped country, whether he is a Communist or not, would not object to lower living standards for the advanced countries or at least to a much slower rise of these standards, if he could at this price receive greater foreign aid and thus hasten the economic development of his own country. He will always consider that the assistance supplied by the advanced nations falls short of his needs, if not of his expectations. A Western citizen wants to live in ever-greater material comfort and does not jubilate over the fact that he is expected to earmark a part of his income for aid to his less fortunate fellow-men in the non-Western lands. The Soviet citizen is eager to taste the fruits of the toil and privation which the drive for rapid industrialization imposed on him; now, he wants a constant improvement in his living standards. He is not overjoyed by the fact that his government reduces the reward due to him by its policy of assistance to the less developed socialist countries and even to the non-Communist underdeveloped states.

The conflict over national interests has not evaporated; on the contrary, it has been intensified. It is impossible to separate ideological from national goals in the foreign policies of today, and the ideological conflict sharpens the competition between national interests. Mass nationalism is no longer a specifically European phenomenon. The number of independent states has multiplied since the last war. Each independent state is a distinct monopolistic center of force and of the formulation of policies. Each government considers itself a trustee for its own countrymen, but certainly not for the whole of mankind. The claim advanced by the Communist governments that they possess the only key to a better future for mankind does not make for one world but reduces the chance of finding compromise solutions for conflicting national interests.

When the chips are down, the citizen of the modern nation-state stands by his country. No state is ready to sacrifice its sovereignty (its power of using force and of formulating its own policies) on the altar of a supranational organization. Even the Communist states, united as they are by the same dynamic ideology, have not tried to form one federation with a common government although this socialist federation was a part of Lenin's program. The Chinese do not want to take orders from the Russians, the Russians are afraid of being swamped by the Chinese, and the less powerful Communist governments prefer to retain a modicum of autonomy. The only successful limitation of national sovereignty which the postwar world has seen is the European Economic Community. But the motivation underlying this economic union indicates the strong national feelings of the participating countries; it is the desire to form together a new world power, a status which none of them can hope to achieve separately.

The analogy with the nation-state would require the existence of a well-organized international community which would possess powers superior to those of member-states. There should be an international government which would hold a monopoly of force and have the authority to formulate policies binding on all states. The present states would have to be downgraded to the position of several members of a universal union, a situation similar to that of the states of the American union. How could this sort of world government be formed and how would it be able to function? Its Western members would presumably like to uphold democracy in their own countries and if possible to extend its realm to other peoples; its Communist members would want "to bury" the regimes of their democratic colleagues. Since their "self-evident truths" are diametrically opposed, how could they formulate common policies for the whole of mankind? Could the participating nations trust one another to the extent of surrendering to this hybrid government exclusive control over the use of force? Since the nations would be divided among themselves by ideological concepts and by national interests, this world government would have to be composed of a nonexisting human species who, like IBM machines, would be perfectly agnostic and indifferent to conflicting ideals and interests.

Probably an international community organized like a state would have to be guided by the modern law of numbers. It would then have to give precedence to the interests of the vast majority of mankind, the underdeveloped countries. This would entail an international redistribution of wealth, not a tempting prospect for the advanced nations. By the same token, the doors of countries with a lower population density would have to be opened to mass emigration from the overpopulated Asian lands. The trends of prices for industrial products and for primary commodities would have to be reversed by the action of this super-state to favor the underdeveloped majority of mankind. The equalization of living standards would have to be the signpost for an organization claiming to serve the interests of the whole of mankind. The citizens of opulent societies (even the Soviet society is opulent by comparison to the underdeveloped countries) would have to accept a heavy contribution, imposed by the world government, from their incomes for the sake of their fellow-men disinherited by history. It is self-evident that the super-state remains a dream in the present condition of mankind although it seems to be a logical salvation from the nuclear nightmare.

The actual picture of present-day mankind is very different. It is divided, and the lines of division crisscross. The only universal organization is the United Nations, a loose association of independent states. The history of this organization, which hardly limits the freedom of action of the member-states, demonstrates that the contemporary national societies have no intention of shedding their supreme national allegiance and are deeply divided by their ideologies and by their national interests and aspirations.

A comparison between the international community as it actually exists and any nation-state proves that there is no analogy between the two. The state is organized to carry out its main functions: legislative, executive, and judicial. Group conflicts are settled through the mediation of the executive or by legislation which is enforced, first because the population takes it for granted that it should be obeyed and secondly because the state is authorized to use coercion against recalcitrant groups or individuals. The legislative power allows the state to adjust the domestic status quo to constant changes in the fluid equilibrium of group interests and aspirations and thus to adjudicate collective conflicts in a peaceful and orderly manner. As long as this function is effectively discharged, it is immaterial from the point of view of the survival of the state which particular agency discharges it. It might be a freely elected legislature or the executive acting as a legislator or a docile legislative assembly manipulated by a monopolistic party as in the Communist states.

The executive function can be performed in various ways: within a system of checks and balances, with or without effective control by the legislature, or by a state administration which implements instructions issued by a monopolistic party. It consists, however, in each case in the formulation and implementation of policies which aim to promote the external interests of the state and to ensure public order (domestic peace) and the welfare of the population, whatever "public order and welfare" might mean in each particular state. Unless a state is in chaos, there is only one foreign and domestic policy, which the citizens might or might not have the right to criticize but which they must accept until it is changed. The courts help to maintain public order by their criminal jurisdiction and by settling private disputes through civil judgments; both types of judicial decisions are enforceable, if necessary, by state coercion.

The international community has no organization even remotely comparable to that of the state. The status quo cannot be altered by any legislative action, because no international institution has the power to make enforceable decisions in conflicts between states over the maintenance or the modification of the status quo. The United Nations can make recommendations, but its recommendations are not binding on the member-states and cannot be enforced without their consent. The international status quo can be changed but only in other ways: by agreements between the states concerned, by a decision of the great powers if they are able to agree and if the state to whom their decision is addressed is not itself a great power, and by the successful foreign policy of individual states. This last mode of revising the status quo is the most frequent but also escapes orderly procedure and international control.

There is no international executive which can formulate policies binding on the states and implement them in spite of their resistance. The last word on the formulation of domestic and foreign policies (sovereignty) is reserved for the state, as is the power of using force domestically or externally.

Each state is free to agree with another state to submit a dispute to the International Court of Justice or to an arbitral tribunal but is also free not to do it. The history of international arbitration amply proves that no state is likely to submit a dispute which involves its vital interests to a judicial or arbitral settlement (see Chapter 9).

All these shortcomings, unknown to the modern state, could be to some extent obviated by the concerted action of the great powers. If they were able from time to time to agree on modifications of the international status quo or on the settlement of those international disputes which the parties refuse to resolve by negotiation or by arbitration, their joint decision would be enforceable by their superior and combined power, which they would seldom need to use. They could police the international community by controlling the actions of its less powerful members. They could not police themselves, it is true, but if they were able to undertake concerted actions regarding the less powerful states, they would probably be inclined to settle their own disputes by compromise arrangements. This would not be the reign of immanent justice, since the great powers would be motivated by their own interests, but at least a semblance of international order and peace would be maintained. This condition existed for several decades during the nineteenth century owing to the Concert of Great Powers. The fundamental conflicts between the great powers of today preclude this arrangement, as the record of the United Nations abundantly proves. The centralized organization of the state has no international counterpart. The international peace rests precariously on two foundations: the general fear, shared by the great powers, of the risks of nuclear war, and the expectation that the governments of the big and the small states are fully aware of these risks and formulate their foreign policies accordingly. This precarious situation is but a symptom of an age of instability in which several revolutionary trends are constantly changing the international environment. An age of revolutionary transition is hardly favorable for the emergence of an effectively organized international community founded on the supreme allegiance of men to mankind as a whole.

INTERNATIONAL PUBLIC OPINION

During the heyday of the League of Nations it was fashionable to speak of the power of international public opinion, which presumably restrained nations from violating the peace and order of the world. The sad story of the totalitarian violations in the thirties and forties apparently was not instructive enough to destroy the myth of international public opinion, which survives to the present day.

The reality and efficacy of international public opinion presupposes certain conditions:

1. That the essential data on international politics are easily accessible, that all or the majority of men are interested in, and sufficiently informed about, international problems, and that they not only care to express their views but also express them only after cautiously weighing the pros and cons of each issue.

2. That it is possible to ascertain at any moment the content of international public opinion and to distinguish it from the opinions expressed by a vocal and more or less influential minority.

3. That human beings are sufficiently detached from their national "self-evident truths" and immediate interests to be able to make fair judgments on the basic international issues, so that no honest and reasonable man could doubt that the voice of the people is the voice of God.

4. That this voice is quasi-unanimous regarding the vital issues, that nations can overcome their divergencies if faced with at least those clear-cut situations which should evoke the same reaction in all of them, and that the serious international issues look clear-cut to mankind, who have no difficulty in distinguishing right from wrong.

5. That international public opinion is self-enforcing or carries with it the threat of compulsory enforcement.

All these assumptions are patently false. Full information on international events is unavailable even to the governments of great powers, which can afford to maintain a large network of intelligence agencies. A number of facts, for instance regarding military preparedness and foreign policy plans, are more or less successfully sheltered behind a wall of official secrecy. A well-administered government does not share these secrets even with its own public. Other facts can escape diplomatic and intelligence observers as well as press correspondents; their relative or potential importance can be overlooked. Each professional observer transmits facts together with his interpretation of them; this interpretation might distort the facts themselves. Thus, the information available to governments is neither complete nor absolutely reliable.

But international public opinion refers, not to governments, but to private citizens. Their range of information is much narrower than that of their governments. They have no access to classified information, which includes not only foreign but also certain national matters. The governments cannot disclose the following data:

1. Information pertaining to foreign countries if the disclosure would compromise the position of its official representatives abroad (for instance, because their reports on developments in the country where they are accredited might not necessarily be favorable to the foreign government or people and, if disclosed, could cause a request for the recall of the representatives) or would imperil the security of its secret agents, national or foreign, or would needlessly warn the foreign government that its secrets and intentions are known.

2. Information relating to the national defense and its own foreign policy intentions; when such information is released to the national public, it necessarily becomes known to foreign governments.

The existence of official secrets makes the government more knowledgeable of foreign developments than its private citizens are. The man in the street, if he is eager to learn, is handicapped in gathering complete information.

However, sufficient data are available to enable the public to acquire a solid background of knowledge. The most significant events cannot remain secret for long, if at all. The private citizen can form sensible opinions for himself, founded on adequate if incomplete information, regarding the main international issues. Yet two persons in possession of the same amount of information often disagree on the meaning of current events and deduce opposite conclusions. The same amount of knowledge does not necessitate agreement. If this is true within the national community, how much more true it is of two men of different nationalities. Men are not computing machines; different men can take the same data to different, or even opposite, conclusions.

One must be seriously interested in international affairs to take the time and the trouble required not only for obtaining the background knowledge but also for keeping abreast of swiftly moving events. Investigations carried out in the Western countries and knowledge of conditions in the underdeveloped and in the totalitarian states indicate that only a small fraction of mankind is seriously and constantly interested in foreign affairs and sufficiently informed to have opinions which might pass for rational. Several governments regularly publish the treaties which they have contracted; the United Nations, like the League of Nations, issues its own Treaty Series. How many people have perused at least the political treaties which are easily accessible and can have far-reaching consequences for the lives of ordinary people? How wide is the circulation of periodicals and daily papers which devote extensive space to international events?

The truth is that the average man in a democratic country, who is literate and free to gather his information from various sources, is not eager to master even a modicum of knowledge in this particular field. Small knowledge of complex international problems might be even more harmful then no knowledge at all, because a half-ignorant man lacks the humility of his ignorant fellow-man, is not prone to feel those doubts which assail the mind of a more fully informed person, and is apt to believe that he has ready answers for every difficult question. An average citizen cannot afford the great expenditure of time which the acquisition of substantial knowledge in international affairs requires. His profession and his daily life do not offer him any incentive for this sustained effort and do not leave him enough spare time. After a strenuous day of work he wants to live a family life, to follow his hobbies, to talk with friends about matters which directly affect them and which they understand, and, finally, to seek relaxation in entertainment.

All this does not mean that he is unaware of the international environment. The two world wars and the threat of nuclear annihilation have not permitted him to forget that external problems exist. The bits of information which he receives from the mass media remind him daily that the main source of trouble is usually located somewhere abroad. But international problems are complex. He trusts that his government knows enough about them and does its best; he leaves them to the government and those other countrymen whom he considers experts in this particular field. He vaguely knows that an everpresent danger lurks behind the headlines, but he feels as helpless as a man living at the foot of a volcano. His interest in foreign affairs flares up from time to time if he discovers from the daily news that his country is facing a major and dramatic threat or has suffered a no less major and dramatic defeat.

The mass media (the popular daily press, radio, and television, which of necessity must be popular because they cater to a large public mainly composed of uninformed people) notice this feeling of resignation among their customers and their lack of sustained interest. They devote little of their space or time to foreign news. This scant information is disjointed and often out of focus. It confuses rather than informs the reader or listener and may well give him the impression that foreigners are either reckless fools or malicious evil-doers whose incomprehensible actions usually result in some trouble for the innocent average man at home. This average man is deeply embedded in his national ethnocentrism; his own countrymen are rational because he understands them and shares their "self-evident truths" and aspirations; foreigners seem irrational for the opposite reasons.

He has no informed opinion for lack of adequate information and sufficient background knowledge. But the daily reminder by the mass media of the existence of foreign affairs makes him *feel* about these matters. His reactions are emotional and offer little resistance to manipulation by a public speaker, a local civic leader, a journalist, or a radio or television commentator. He has no means for rebutting their arguments.

The average man in an advanced country is intellectually imprisoned within the frontiers of his native land. His relative affluence (radio and television at home) and his literacy give him easy access to more knowledgeable countrymen but only countrymen. He seldom travels abroad, he knows no foreign languages, he reads and listens to people who are his fellow-countrymen. Even if he occasionally hears a foreign lecturer or reads a foreign paper or listens to the foreign radio, the wall does not crumble; it is made of an instinctive distrust of foreign sources of information. Beginning with his parents' home and the school, he never escapes the pressure of the national environment. Even a democratic state does not allow its future citizens to imbibe at school ideas which are subversive of the principles on which it is founded. The child is taught in a democracy to cherish the individual freedoms and to cultivate toleration, in a totalitarian state to admire social discipline and obedience to the ruling party, and in both, as well as in all other countries, to love his native country, its institutions and basic beliefs. In all countries the effect of formal education is a widespread conviction that one's own nation is morally superior. If later in life the individual is exposed to foreign propaganda, he instinctively recoils from all foreign views that do not coincide with opinions prevailing in the national environment; to agree with a different foreign opinion would entail the admission that his own country may be wrong or even that its foreign policy may be immoral.

With respect to domestic issues, his daily experience and the divergent views of those around him remind him constantly that every coin has two sides, but with respect to foreign issues he is seldom given an opportunity to see the other side of the national coin. Thus, millions of democratic citizens succumb to conformity in their emotional reactions to foreign events.

Their ballots can elect a new political team for the formulation of foreign policy, but they cannot formulate it themselves for the simple reason that ideas are born in human minds, not in ballot boxes. The government misrepresents itself or deceives itself when it claims to conduct a foreign policy which the general public has already formulated. Moreover, this general public, who elect and remove the government, seldom cast their ballots one way or another for reasons which relate to foreign affairs. The electoral decisions are dictated by domestic considerations, party loyalties, the personalities of competing politicians, and other considerations which the voter can grasp because he is familiar with them. Foreign policy issues are too remote or too difficult to understand to play an important role in elections.

The government is compelled by this situation to communicate with the mass of citizens through slogans and capsule formulas which do not illuminate the problems but encourage the citizen's self-deception by simplifying complex international issues. The average citizen is a captive of fictions or half-truths. This modern need for slogans in mass communication carries with it a danger that the government itself may be tempted to seek the solution of complex international problems in capsule formulas and attractive slogans.

To sum up, the emotional reactions of millions of uninformed democratic citizens do not make for knowledgeable and rational opinions but generate a mass mood which is unstable because it lacks intellectual structure and factual content. This mood may help or hinder the government in the pursuit of foreign policy depending on its ability to manipulate and extract mass support for its views. If national public opinion on foreign affairs means an informed opinion of the majority of citizens, it does not exist.

It is self-evident that this informed public opinion cannot exist in the underdeveloped countries where the average citizen is illiterate or semiliterate. The radio can reach him but it is usually government-controlled. His own experience is limited to his village or the slum district of his city. He often lacks sufficient knowledge even to understand domestic issues. The names of foreign countries are for him empty sounds totally without meaning. This vast majority of the population of the underdeveloped countries must be written off as a source of "international" public opinion.

The average citizen in an advanced or semideveloped Communist state is literate. His capacity for understanding international problems is equal to that of his counterpart in the democratic countries. But his country is sealed off by government censorship. The nonconformist who dares to listen to foreign radio broadcasts or secretly reads foreign newspapers is rare, and his image of the outside world can easily become distorted. If he refuses to believe his government, he may be inclined to accept every foreign interpretation of events as true. He is prone to trust the wildest rumors. Thus, his information is not necessarily more exact than that of his conformist co-citizen.

The mass of citizens in the Communist states do not have the time to secure information from foreign sources and do not want to run the risks involved. The same factors which operate in the democratic countries to discourage this effort are also present in the nondemocratic states where the fear of penalties acts as an additional deterrent. The mass of citizens have access only to information derived from national sources which the government tightly controls. The voice of dissidents, always audible in the democratic countries, cannot be heard. All the sources of information (schools, libraries, lecture halls, printing presses, radio, and television) are subject to strict state supervision. The citizen can hear only what the government wants him to hear. National solidarity on foreign issues is ensured even more effectively than in the democratic societies.

National public opinion on foreign affairs, if this term means an informed opinion, is everywhere the opinion of a minority. The voice of this minority is imputed to the whole country, because the majority have no informed view at all. This minority is proportionately larger in an advanced than in an underdeveloped country, because the ratio of educated people is much higher. It can influence the power elite in a totalitarian state if its members act in an advisory capacity, but its actual role in influencing the formulation of national foreign policy is much greater in a democratic country where the government is subject to open criticism and is liable to the ultimate sanction of elections. But even there this role is that of a minority.

The various groups which form together this articulate minority can be classified according to the particular interest they have in foreign affairs. Certain groups are interested in all principal international issues; others are concerned only with certain matters, such as all or some economic aspects of foreign policy, the ideological or humanitarian aspects, the welfare or security of a particular foreign state or of a particular geographical area. Another way of classification is to follow the pattern established by Professor Gabriel A. Almond and divide the population into groups depending on the intensity of their general interest in foreign affairs. His classification is meant to apply to the United States, but it could be extended with appropriate adjustments to other democratic and advanced nations. He divides the population into three concentric circles: the general public, the attentive public, and the elite. The general public is the majority of the population, who are composed of uninformed citizens. The attentive public are those college-educated people who are better trained in the process of abstract thinking and have a more precise image of the external world than does the general public. Not all college-educated people belong to this attentive public nor is this public exclusively composed of persons with a higher education. Foreign affairs are not their main preoccupation, but their interest in them is permanent though intermittent. They do not originate ideas but are apt to understand basic issues and to listen intelligently to conflicting arguments. The views which they support are referred to as trends in public opinion.

These trends originate within a much smaller inner ring, the elite. The elite in foreign affairs is only one of several elites which exist in every modern society. These elites are the product of the division of labor and of the specialization of knowledge. Each branch of knowledge and each distinct social activity has its own elite: the scientists, the musicians, the historians, and so forth. A member of any elite is only an average man in those fields of knowledge where he knows as little as another average man. There exists also an elite in foreign affairs composed of persons who are permanently interested in these matters, who help to formulate or who influence the formulation of foreign policy, and who initiate the trends in the attentive public. Professor Almond divides this elite as follows:

1. The political elite of professional politicians.

2. The administrative elite composed of civil servants of the executive class who influence foreign policy not only by the decisions which they make by virtue of their delegated powers but also by their advice and implementation. The present complexity of foreign affairs places in this administrative elite not only professional diplomats but also those numerous officials in the military and civilian agencies who operate abroad or whose activities affect the relations with foreign countries.

3. The interest groups or rather the executive personnel of various private organizations interested in foreign matters. Business corporations and their representative organizations, farmers' organizations, labor unions, civic and church groups, exemplify those interest groups which for various reasons take a permanent interest in all or some foreign problems. This interest might be economic, religious, humanitarian, ideological, or any other.

4. The communication elite composed of those people who control or

manage the mass media or who are their public spokesmen and address the reading or listening audience. A process of consolidation has placed the ownership—and therefore the control—of these media in the hands of a small number of individuals or corporations. These men must be included within the elite because their views have an influence on the opinions voiced by the mass media. Insofar as journalists and radio and television commentators are given a free hand in expressing their own views, they too belong to the same elite. If the mass media are controlled by the government, as radio and television are in several countries of Western Europe, the officials who manage the media and influence their policies belong to the same communication elite. The reading and listening public, with few exceptions, should be classified as either the attentive or the general public.

5. Local elite composed of influential leaders of local communities.

One is tempted to add a sixth group, namely the intellectual elite composed of unorganized teachers, lecturers, and writers who take a professional interest in foreign affairs and often originate ideas which, once these are digested, influence the other elites.

The open debates within these elites are watched by the attentive public; its acceptance of certain views rather than others is reflected in the so-called trends in public opinion. The general public does not participate in this process as a permanent and knowledgeable listener, but it has the last word concerning the choice of the government. It is vain to expect that the whole general public will be transformed into the attentive public, but the spirit of democratic processes demands a maximum effort in every democratic country to encourage the growth of both the elite and the attentive public.

The important role played by the elite does not endanger the democracy as long as the elite is open to everyone who qualifies and as long as social mobility guarantees a fluid composition of the elite. By contrast, the totalitarian political elite is noncompetitive, closed, and recruited through co-optation. There is no rival team of politicians who could offer an alternative policy. There is no public and free debate on foreign issues. The only important elite other than the political is the administrative. It influences foreign policy by the information it conveys to the government, by advice, and by implementation. The attentive public is expected only to support the policy already adopted by the political elite and to serve as a channel of communication to the general public.

In every country an important function is performed by the expert if he is a specialist in a problem (a remote and unfamiliar country, a difficult scientific problem) which even the elite does not know or cannot easily grasp. His opinion can be challenged only by another expert.

Polls which sample public opinion on international issues might be misleading for several reasons. First, the person who answers, especially if he belongs to the general uninformed public, might be prompted by personal pride to say "yes" or "no" rather than "I do not know." Secondly, an arithmetical addition of "yeas" and "nays" does not reflect the relative weight of the persons who have supplied the answers. Some of them may belong to the elite, others to the informed public, and the remainder to the general and uninformed public. The counting of noses overlooks the most important factor, the relative influence of each respondent on the actual formulation of national foreign policy. If a distinction is made between these various groups of the population, the results of the poll can still be incorrect. The questions asked are usually fairly simple, while international problems cannot be reduced to elementary propositions of Euclidian simplicity or be answered by a simple yes or no. A short and unqualified answer is seldom truly meaningful. There is, moreover, no assurance that the persons interviewed are sincere or entirely serious in answering the poll questions.

The concept of international public opinion rests on the assumption that people who are well-informed always act rationally. If this bold assumption were true, it would still overlook the fact that two equally informed men can visualize not one but two rational courses of action. But the assumption is not quite correct. It is the legacy of the Age of Enlightenment, of its unbounded faith in human rationality and in the perfectibility of human nature owing to the progress of knowledge and of its optimistic expectation of a continuous moral progress. The history of international relations suffices to supply many examples of folly. Human nature does not seem to have changed throughout recorded history. The record of our own century does not evidence any parallel between the progress of human knowledge, confined mainly to natural sciences and technology, and an improvement in human nature. The notion of moral progress has various and often conflicting connotations for different men; what is an evil for one ideological sect might be a virtue for another.

Although the majority of mankind are not informed on international problems, this does not prevent many uninformed persons from expressing definite views. They are encouraged to do so by the fact that international politics is not an exact science; one is not inhibited from expressing opinions as one would be in nuclear physics. These self-appointed "experts" are not the spokesmen for public opinion, but they can add to the confusion of the general public. Their number grows with the expansion of tourism; a hasty tour of several foreign countries seems to make the tourist an "authority" on all international questions.

If the views prevailing within the articulate minority were regarded as equivalent to national public opinion, the sum of all these national opinions would still not make for one voice of mankind. These opinions of national articulate minorities form a discordant chorus of many voices. A glance at different comments on the same event in the *New York Times*, the *London Times*, and *Le Monde* reveals how different national environments give rise to divergent views. A look at *Pravda* would be enough to destroy all faith in the existence of international public opinion.

Moreover, it is not easy to ascertain whether a group that claims to speak in the name of the country truly represents the opinions prevailing within the articulate minority. It is officially assumed that the government is the authorized and authentic spokesman. But is it true? A totalitarian regime provides no means for testing the veracity of this claim, in the absence of free debate and free elections. Does a military dictator reflect the views of national public opinion? Does a democratic government reflect the opinion of its public when it reaches urgent decisions without having the time to consult the articulate minority or when it acts on the basis of data which are unknown to the public? The democratic government often hopefully anticipates that its decision will be *ex post facto* ratified by the articulate minority and, by implication, by the whole country. The conduct of international relations would become impossible without this assumption that each government speaks on behalf of the country, but the assumption is rather tenuous if it is taken to mean that each governmental policy reflects the views of the articulate minority of the population, let alone of the whole population.

The frequent reference to "international public opinion" (in Communist parlance, this term is replaced by "progressive mankind") is a handy propaganda device but it usually refers to carefully selected foreign voices which support or sympathize with the policy of the state concerned. International public opinion is equated with the views of a number of allied or friendly governments, with the opinions of the mass media in the same foreign countries, and with the attitudes of equally friendly groups and individuals. This careful choice of supporting foreign views authorizes the claim that a given foreign policy enjoys the backing of "international public opinion." The dissenting views are either ignored or dismissed as being distorted by ignorance, irresponsibility, or the evil propaganda of an unfriendly foreign power. This propaganda image of international public opinion should not be taken for the reality.

If one wanted to detect the voice of mankind in the United Nations, he would be baffled by the many discordant voices with which this organization speaks. Its most representative agency, the General Assembly, is a body of delegates appointed by the various governments; these delegates are not free agents who speak according to the dictates of individual conscience. They are expected to defend their national interests according to instructions issued by the governments which have appointed them (see Chapter 9).

The final flaw in the concept of international public opinion is the absence of any effective machinery for the enforcement of its decisions even if this opinion actually existed.

INTERNATIONAL MORALITY

The human mind is not divided into several tight compartments, each capable of operating independently of the others. The cliché images of the political man, the economic man, the scientific man, the moral man, all of them living in the same human mind, convey the false impression that human personality can be conveniently compartmentalized for the purpose of academic analysis. In fact the whole man acts, although certain motivations can be stronger than others depending on the subject of his action. This is also true of international politics, composed as they are of all possible elements: political, military, economic, scientific, moral, cultural, and ideological. To conceive of the man who participates in international politics as a species of *homo politicus* would amount to a misleading simplification of his motives.

Assuming that the world of international politics is inhabited by real men, not by the imaginary species *homo politicus* or *homo economicus*, the motives for their actions must be as complex as their national and international environments. They are guided by their concept of national interests, a concept which includes political, economic, and military interests as well as the priority of the national "self-evident truths" and ways of life; they might also be inspired by a missionary zeal if they have a blueprint for the happiness of mankind; in addition, they can be motivated by personal ambition but usually in the sense that they consider themselves the best men to promote national interests or the ideological cause. They cannot escape the totality of their minds, including the consciousness of moral rules which they honor in their personal relations with other individuals. The moral man cohabits with the political man in the same human mind.

To what extent do these moral rules influence decisions relating to foreign affairs? History indicates that morality has much less influence in international relations than it does in national politics and certainly much less than in personal relations. This century alone has a dismal record of acts which ordinary morality forbids in personal relations: violations or arbitrary denunciations of solemn treaties of alliance, nonaggression, and neutrality, the betrayal of foreign friends for the sake of national interests, political transactions entered into in flagrant violation of formerly proclaimed principles. This record includes acts not only of the totalitarian states, such as Nazi Germany or the Soviet Union, but also of the democratic nations. The neutrality of Iran, guaranteed by customary international law, was grossly infringed in 1941 by military occupation not only by the Soviet Union but also by Great Britain. The Yalta Far Eastern Agreement, which violated a pledge to respect Chinese territorial and administrative integrity, a pledge that was a part of the Washington Treaty of 1922, was signed by the United States and Great Britain. Moreover, China was an ally of both nations. In personal relations, if an individual were similarly unfaithful to his word and to his friends, he would have an uneasy conscience and would be censured by his neighbors. Why is it that the rules of personal morality are much less frequently observed in international politics than in relations between individuals?

The fact itself is not denied by anyone familiar with the history of international relations. An easy answer to this question would be to repeat after David Hume:

"There is a maxim very current in the world, which few politicians are willing to avow, but which has been authorized by the practice of all ages, that there is a system of morals calculated for princes, much more free than that which ought to govern private persons. . . ."

This assumption that there is a particular morality for inter-state relations, less rigid than personal morality, is consistent with historical evidence that the habitual rules of individual morality are not religiously observed in international relations. But the same assumption implies the existence of more or less specific rules binding on states in their mutual relations. So far no one has successfully deduced from the actual practice of states the exact contents of these rules or demonstrated that they are founded on universal assent. This universal assent has never existed because there has never been a fundamental concordance between the "self-evident truths" and between the interests of the various national societies. It is true, however, that those nations which have been satisfied with the international status quo have been inclined to think that this international harmony exists or at least that it would exist if a few international trouble-makers could be removed from the stage.

The existence of a special morality for princes presupposes a concensus among men concerning what is good and what is bad, what is just and what is unjust. But disagreement on this score has never been absent from human history. As recently as before the Second World War the Western nations considered the international division of labor between them and the underdeveloped lands a part of international harmony and a perfectly just and reasonable arrangement. The nationals of the underdeveloped countries could not share this view; the present drive for economic development among the underdeveloped countries is nothing but an aspiration for a different international harmony. A nation defeated in war feels that the restoration of the *status quo ante* would re-establish international harmony, but the victorious nation no less strongly believes that the territories it has annexed are an integral part of the existing harmony. The Nazis held that the destruction or the decimation of "inferior" races such as the Jews and the Slavs promoted international harmony, but their victims took a different view of the matter. The Communists hail every achievement of their fellow-believers as an advance toward the harmony of universal socialism, but the Western democrats denounce these "achievements" as symptoms of moral regression. The issue of whether to preserve or revise the status quo has deeply divided men and nations in every historical period, but this issue is especially divisive in our time when men and nations hold exactly opposite views on the political and moral meaning of international events. This conflict of values precludes the moral consensus without which there can be no morality for princes.

In a century which is inclined to have a Manichean image of mankind, it is somewhat extravagant to speak of an international morality founded on general consensus. Whether the international community is divided between the Nazi-Fascist camp and the camp of their adversaries or between the Western and Communist camps, for the protagonists the struggle is a heroic battle between Good and Evil, between the angels and the devils. Every action of the ideological enemy is immoral by definition. Under these circumstances, it would be vain to seek a consensus on the rules of international morality, rules which the princes of one camp would consider binding in their relations with the princes of the opposite camp.

The concept of a morality for princes only weakens the restraining influence of ordinary morality. It encourages daily departures from this ordinary morality by affirming that international relations are governed by a special morality, one that is vague and lax. Since the actual practice of states has established no clear rules, the vagueness of this alleged morality can excuse any action.

In the absence of convincing proof that a distinct morality exists for princes, it must be assumed that human beings, whether they act as private individuals or as agents of the state (princes), do not compartmentalize their personality and consult different moralities depending on whether their acts refer to other individuals as such or to the organized groups of individuals called states. State agents know in fact only one morality, the one which their national environment has inculcated, and are unaware in conscience of any other morality which should supposedly govern their external acts. The problem is complicated for them by the fact that the personal morality of their national society usually claims to have universal validity and be applicable to personal relations with both countrymen and aliens. Why is it that this moral code, the only one known to human beings whatever the nature of their actions, the morality recognized by their national society, has much less effect on their international behavior, and why is it that behavior in relation to foreign states has even prompted the claim that there is a different morality for princes?

There are several reasons. The moral sense is most alert when the individual deals directly with another individual. The agent of the state acts on behalf of an organized community which he represents in relations with another organized community. Direct human contact is broken by the interposition of two collective images. One does not deal with an individual Japanese but with Japan, a collective concept in which individual Japanese are diluted and lost sight of. The same statesman who would recoil in horror from inflicting any harm on an innocent Japanese as an individual does not recoil from issuing an order to kill millions of Japanese. He does not war against millions of individuals but against a collective image. He would not starve a child, but he enforces a naval blockade or a trade embargo against a foreign country that might result in the starvation, not of one, but of hundreds of thousands of foreign children. He would never abandon a friend to his enemies in order to advance his personal interests, but he abandons an ally to promote national interests. He does not spend sleepless nights in the process and he is not tormented by remorse, because he has made his decision in terms of collective images which conceal from his sight actual human beings. The effect of collective symbols on moral sensitivity can also be observed in national life. The agent of a corporation, of a labor union, of an association, often feels less inhibited morally because he operates within the realm of relations between organized groups. But domestic morality and law control his acts much more effectively than if he were dealing with foreign states.

The fact that the state agent does not act in his own or his family's interest also relaxes the restraining influence of personal morality. The state agent, whether he is elected or has acquired power in any other way, usually has a strong feeling of responsibility for the fate of his own countrymen. He feels that he acts as an elected or self-appointed trustee of his nation and as a guardian of its interests. Although his understanding of the interests of the people may be imperfect, he feels certain, if he is truly a statesman, that he is the best man to serve these interests and thus identifies himself with the people. But he does not feel that he is an appointed guardian either of the whole of mankind or of any foreign nation. His own countrymen, whose future depends so much on his official decisions, can rely on him alone; they are close to his heart because they are his countrymen. They become in his mind a *moral* value. If he promotes their interests, he performs what he considers to be his primary duty and therefore, in his own mind, acts morally. He serves them, not himself. If he is devoted to a dynamic ideology, he adds another image to that of his own country—the image of the whole of mankind, whom he wants to make happy according to his blueprint and by his official actions. Nations and individuals who reject his blueprint are immoral for him and an evil which should be subdued in the name of mankind.

This superior moral value—the nation or mankind—might require actions which his personal morality would not condone. He is faced with a choice between two moral values. This is not a problem confined to politics; every individual has experienced the same dilemma in his personal relations with other individuals whenever he has been faced with the necessity of sacrificing one moral value to another. Lincoln's famous letter of

August 22, 1862, illustrates this conflict between moral values: the national interest and the requirements of ordinary morality:

"If I could save the Union without freeing any slave, I would do it, and if I could save it by freeing all the slaves, I would do it; and if I could save it by freeing some and leaving others alone, I would also do that. . . . I have here stated my purpose according to my view of *official* duty; and I intend no modification of my oft-expressed *personal* wish that all men everywhere could be free."

He clearly distinguished between his wishes, founded on his personal morality, and his duties as the trustee of the American union. This is a frequent dilemma for men who have to make international decisions. They feel the compelling force of the morality which is honored in their country and know that certain acts are forbidden by this morality. Yet the other moral value, their nation and perhaps also their blueprint for the happiness of mankind, requires no less compellingly an action which cannot be reconciled with ordinary morality. They have to make a choice. David Hume's dictum does not offer them any clear advice on what is permissible in international politics, but the idea of a special morality for princes might help them to remove quicker the restraining hand of ordinary morality. On many occasions they will be lucky enough to find a compromise which will safeguard both moral values: the national interests, and the pertinent rule of ordinary morality. But a serious international emergency will leave no escape; they will have to make a decision which sacrifices one value to the other. Should they abandon an allied country or instead lose a war or, at least, cause an additional loss of a million casualties among their countrymen? Should they tolerate an alien regime which carries out domestic reforms necessary for its country or instead undermine that regime because its foreign policy imperils their own country? Should they expose their countrymen to nuclear risks in order to remain faithful to the promise of an alliance or instead leave the ally to his own fate? If these dilemmas are inescapable, as they are in the most dramatic international situations, the interests of the nation triumph in this competition between the two moral values, because the state agent considers himself a trustee for his own nation, and that nation therefore represents for him a superior moral value.

Does it follow that ordinary morality is of no significance in international affairs? An affirmative answer cannot be accepted by anyone who is skeptical of the existence of a special morality for princes or who rejects the unrealistic image of a pure "political man," one allegedly guided in his decisions by political considerations alone. Conscience, the guardian of ordinary morality, is not silent when international decisions are made, but it can be appeased by an invocation of the higher moral value, the nation. Ordinary morality acts as a brake, although a rather ineffective brake whenever the most vital national interests are at stake.

This restraining function of ordinary morality is quashed if the power elite in a country is openly guided by two moral codes: one for personal relations between "loyal" citizens, and the other for relations with domestic and foreign "enemies." The totalitarian power elites of our century have erected their avowed fundamental objectives into supreme moral values which are supposed to sanctify all the means. For the Nazis this objective was the greatness and might of the German "superior race." For the Leninists the supreme moral value is the universal victory of socialism; any means which furthers this victory is moral by definition (see Chapter 7). These two moralities resemble the Machiavellian outlook as expounded in *The Prince*. The restraint of ordinary morality is deliberately removed in dealing with foreign countries and a great flexibility in the choice of means is ensured.

The breach of an international treaty illustrates the point. A politician who knows of one morality only (the one which is currently observed in the personal relations of his countrymen) will do his best to avoid the violation of a treaty and will repudiate it only when he feels that there is no other way of preserving the most vital national interests. He will do it with an uneasy conscience. Another politician, one who deems it moral to use any means in dealing with countries which he considers hostile to his nation or his ideology, will feel no moral qualms about violating an international treaty when this course seems to be practical, safe, and profitable. This is why the list of broken international pledges is incomparably longer for the totalitarian states than for the others.

The modern erection of the nation into the supreme moral value can encourage the belief that what is good for one's country is also good for mankind. There are perhaps in our time more men who think, "My country is always right," than there are who humbly say, "My country, right or wrong." The cultivation of national loyalty and the national seclusion of modern men make for this frequent identification of one's national interests with universal human welfare. Politicians do not escape this particular bias. For a Russian or a Chinese Communist politician what is good for his country is also good for the international Communist movement and, therefore, for the blessed future of mankind. A democratic politician is often no more innocent of confusing national interests with universal human good; the ideological phraseology of democracy and freedom encourages this identification of one's nation with the presumed aspirations of all men.

This sincere identification of national interests with the general welfare of mankind should not be confused with diplomatic overstatements which are not meant to be literally believed. The diplomatic language of all countries abounds in moralistic slogans about universal peace, international justice, the right of peoples to be free, and the sanctity of the pledged word, regardless of whether actual policies are always consonant with these ideals. Even a government which deliberately violates its pledges pays its tribute to virtue by justifying its actions in the name of a "higher" morality —honor, self-defense, the interests of humanity—or at least by blackening the reputation of its victims who are represented as immoral or foolish people unworthy of pity and deserving the rough treatment which is meted out to them.

Moral judgment in international affairs has an unfortunate tendency to be conditioned by the interests involved and by other considerations which are morally irrelevant. President Eisenhower refused in November, 1956, to use two different yardsticks to evaluate the actions of enemies and friends. He condemned the use of force in violation of the United Nations Charter in both the Soviet armed intervention in Hungary and the British-French attack on Egypt. This condemnation prompted several Americans to criticize his political naiveté. While they condoned the British-French resort to force, they indignantly denounced the Soviet Union for the use of force against Hungary. President Eisenhower, who had condemned Britain and France for their unilateral use of force in November, 1956, used a somehow different yardstick a few months later when he thought that American vital interests were threatened in the Near East. Although he had held that the British-French-Israeli action threatened to destroy "the best hope of establishing a real world order," he requested the Congress on January 5, 1957, to grant him the authority to use force unilaterally in the Near East, and in 1958 actually sent troops to Lebanon while Britain, by agreement with the United States, did the same in Jordan. Moral judgments fluctuated with the political evaluation of each situation. For political reasons, the Western powers and the Soviet Union have sometimes reversed their positions on the issue of human rights. The Western powers took a strong stand in defending human rights in Bulgaria, Hungary, and Rumania, while the Soviet Union no less strongly tried to prevent the discussion by invoking the domestic jurisdiction of these three states, which allegedly forbade any examination of their domestic policies. The discussion of racial discrimination in South Africa made the great powers change places. This time it was the Soviet Union that warmly defended human rights, and most of the Western powers objected to the debate in the United Nations on the grounds of South African domestic jurisdiction.

Not only national interests but also national self-righteousness influences moral judgments. The Western powers needed an image of Imperial Russia in 1914-17 and of Soviet Russia in 1941-45 which was attractive from the point of view of their values; Russia was their ally. Both times Russia was pictured as only one step removed from a democracy. Racial affinity is another distorting factor. It certainly affected the moral judgment of Westerners, Asians, and Africans in November, 1956. The morally irrelevant fact that Europeans (Hungarians) in one case and non-Europeans (Egyptians) in the other were the victims of the use of force, and that force was used in one case by the Western powers and Israel and by the Soviet Union in the other, had a marked effect on the moral evaluation of two events which coincided in time.

Moral judgment can be distorted by various other factors. Power and success influence this judgment. An international action which is dubious from the point of view of ordinary morality is more readily excused if its author is a powerful nation or if it is, at least, crowned with success. For instance, the discrimination by the weak Eastern European governments against their national or religious minorities during the inter-war period caused waves of indignation in Western countries which saw nothing objectionable in their own racial discrimination in their Asian and African colonies. The Egyptian nationalization of the Suez Canal was denounced as immoral subversion of the principles of international intercourse, but its eventual success brought the critics around to a more mellowed view of the matter.

The story of the Soviet intervention in Hungary is very instructive in this respect. The U.S.S.R. considered that its dominant position in Eastern Europe and the prestige of the Communist movement would have been seriously impaired by the victory of the Hungarian anti-Communists. It intervened although it knew that this brutal operation would provoke an outcry of indignation. Its reputation was at its lowest during several consecutive months. However, its action was entirely successful; a pro-Soviet government rules in Budapest. The wave of international indignation gradually subsided. Two and a half years later the British Prime Minister paid an official visit to the Soviet Union, and barely three years later the Soviet Premier enjoyed a friendly reception in the United States. A great power cannot be quarantined for long. A mood of moral indignation never survives the first few waves of outrage. People reconcile themselves to unpleasant facts if they cannot change them. Soviet prestige has fully recovered from the shock of events in 1956. If British and French prestige has never been fully restored after the Suez expedition, this is due not to moral causes but to the abysmal failure of the venture. Britain and France unintentionally demonstrated that they were no longer world powers, and the other governments took due notice. It is interesting that the prestige of Israel has been enhanced by the events of 1956. A small country, Israel proved by its lightning military success and its quick occupation of a large part of Egyptian territory that it was more than a match for its Arab neighbors.

History does not offer much comfort in this respect, because the judgment of later generations is also influenced by success rather than by moral criteria. The Romans are admired for their imposing career although the means which they used to build up their empire were not particularly moral, at least by later Christian standards. A rebel comes to occupy a very honorable place in history if he or his followers achieve their ends. Otherwise he is either forgotten or remembered as a man who disturbed the peace. Victory transformed the American rebels of the War of Independence into the Founding Fathers, as it ensured the transfiguration of the prisoners of British colonial jails into the internationally popular leaders of independent India. President Nkrumah is hailed as a statesman because he successfully graduated, as he says, from the political prison; if he had failed the "test," many of the people who now admire him would pay no attention to him.

History does not countenance the belief that Nemesis always overtakes the evildoer and that evil does not pay. In fact, the evildoers and their peoples are sometimes punished but often thrive on their deeds, and their descendants piously invoke the statute of limitation to defend their enjoyment of the fruits of evil.

There is also a relation between moral judgment and the status quo. A state which is satisfied with the status quo does not disturb international peace, not because it is necessarily more moral, but because it has no strong incentive for doing so. People admire it for its peacefulness, but do not enquire into the justice of the status quo. Its opponent, dissatisfied with the status quo and apt to take actions to change the existing situation, does not wear the same cloak of international respectability because it appears in the unwelcome role of an international trouble-maker. Moral judgment tends to favor the states which are satisfied with the status quo.

It is affected by political and cultural sympathies. It is rather to be expected that actions by political friends would be evaluated with much greater indulgence than those of political enemies. Cultural affinity has a similar effect. For instance, the American press tended to take a sterner view of the French policy in Algeria than of the British in Central Africa although both situations involved the African claim to self-determination and the vested interests of European settlers.

International life has its own fashions. Ideas which are popular in a particular period give a moral or immoral flavor to foreign policies. It was fashionable in Europe at the time of the French Revolution and for several decades later to uphold in the upper social circles the "moral" principle of legitimacy of princes against the revolutionary aspirations of their subjects. Nowadays national self-determination is fashionable, and the morality of foreign policies is judged from this point of view.

The conflict between ordinary morality and the duty to protect national interests is well-known to those state agents who have to make international decisions. Its existence or its complexity can easily escape the attention of those people who have never borne direct responsibility for national foreign policy.

Frequent contacts between the nationals of two countries might either promote mutual understanding or deepen already existing animosity. Such contacts certainly increase mutual knowledge, but a better acquaintance does not necessarily promote sympathy if the two nations are at odds. European nations, especially immediate neighbors, knew each other rather well owing to many centuries of constant intercourse. Their interests, however, often collided. A proverb was born out of this checkered experience: "My neighbor is my enemy, but my neighbor's neighbor is my friend because he is also my neighbor's enemy." By the same token, a distant and less known nation was given the benefit of a doubt and was readily credited with an attractive image which lacked any factual foundation.

The frequency of contacts, including cultural exchanges, may give rise to mutual sympathy and dispel former prejudices if the two countries concerned sincerely intend to forget their disputes and to live henceforth in amity. For instance, the postwar cultural exchanges between the Western European countries have proved beneficial because they have derived from a trend toward organized co-operation. The exchanges between the West and the Communist states might have the same effect but only if and when the two parties decide to resolve their conflicts.

This does not mean that cultural exchanges between unfriendly states are useless. Such exchanges may help to efface the image of the other nation as an evil people bent on destroying the visitors' country, but only if these visitors are allowed, on coming home, to depict their impressions truthfully. This is not yet true of the Soviet Union; as recently as 1963 Soviet writers were severely castigated by the party for their not unfriendly accounts of the West. One of them, Nekrasov, was even threatened with expulsion from the party by Khruschev himself. In any event, these cultural exchanges are useful for other reasons. They increase the knowledge of the foreign country and of its achievements, encourage the spread of scientific and technological progress, and provide a wider framework for an intelligent formulation of foreign policy. It may also be hoped that visitors from the Communist countries cannot be completely silenced and that their impressions somehow reach their countrymen, thereby reducing the credibility of the official propaganda image of a West irremediably rotten and animated only by evil intentions.

In conclusion, it can be said that there is no convincing proof of the existence of a special morality for princes (states), that ordinary morality has some influence, though a decidedly limited one, on international relations, and that moral judgments in international affairs can easily be distorted by several factors and are not likely to coincide when the moralists belong to different nationalities or profess different ideologies.

STATUS QUO, PEACE, AND JUSTICE

Three words are frequently used together in international discussions: *status quo*, *peace*, and *justice*. The term *status quo* can simply refer to the contemporary political boundaries between states. It can be used in the much larger sense of the contemporary distribution of power on a regional or global scale. The status quo in the latter sense is rapidly changing and will continue to change. All the revolutionary trends of our era ceaselessly work for change, and each change produces a new status quo as unstable as that of yesterday. The nuclear status quo was drastically altered by the Soviet acquisition of nuclear weapons. The present nuclear balance, which rests on the mutual neutralization of the two massive deterrents, might be upset by a spectacular breakthrough accomplished by one nuclear power or by the emergence of new nuclear powers. The vertiginous progress of science offers no comforting reassurance on this score.

The political status quo has been changing rapidly since the last war for two main reasons: the territorial expansion of the Communist realm in Europe and Asia from some 170 million Soviet citizens in 1939 to the present billion people in the fourteen Communist states, and the Western colonial retreat, which brought about the emergence of some fifty newly independent states in Asia and Africa. The political alignments of these states will certainly continue to shift as they have in the past. The external influence exerted by a great power fluctuates constantly as a result of three factors: the changes in its relative power, its foreign policy, and the policies of other states. New centers of power are arising. West Germany and Japan are again becoming important regional great powers. The European Community may gradually evolve into an integrated center of power which could claim to be a world power. China and India are destined to become great powers. Economic development will bring to the fore other new centers of power. Each new major center of power will reduce by its emergence the relative weight of the present dominant great powers. The status of the distribution of political influence among nations will constantly change.

The revolution of modernization is a negation of the status quo. It is a revolt against the domestic status quo and also against the present international division of labor.

Any nation which would try desperately to uphold the status quo of any given moment would undertake a hopeless task. The true problem is how to ride on the crest of the wave which alters the status quo and which no human force can prevent from rolling on.

In the pre-nuclear age peace was never considered a value of the highest order. Any nation which was dissatisfied with the status quo and felt strong enough to change it by arms, preferred peace only if it could obtain by negotiations what it expected to win by war. But nuclear peace tends to become a value of high order. This suddenly accrued attractiveness of peace is due neither to moral progress nor to general satisfaction with the status quo but to the fear of the consequences of a nuclear war.

This does not mean, however, that peoples and governments are ready to subordinate all other values, including their most vital national interests, their "self-evident truths" and ways of life, and their concepts of good and evil, to this consideration alone and to sacrifice these cherished values for the sake of avoiding at any price a threat to biological survival. Peace has not become, even in our nuclear age, a generally recognized supreme value.

Peace does not and cannot mean a petrification of the status quo. It did not have this meaning even in the relatively stable nineteenth century. The map of Europe was redrawn several times; the European powers were nevertheless able to restore a kind of equilibrium at each stage in the redistribution of their political influence.

Peace does not mean justice. One of the hollowest slogans is "peace with justice." International justice is a relative notion which signifies different things to different nations, but even if most of the governments of the world were able to agree on one definition of justice, it still could not be obtained without endangering peace. This situation is not peculiar to our time. The Vienna peace settlement, to take one out of many examples, gave to the world a hundred years of general peace but was considered unjust by many peoples. Asians and Africans could not like the status quo of the nineteenth century, which entailed their colonial servitude. Germans, Italians, and several Eastern European nationalities, who wanted either to be united within one nation-state or to become independent, certainly did not hail the Vienna settlement as a masterpiece of justice. The authors of the settlement did not intend to establish a just status quo but to found peace on a balance of power. The national aspirations of their subjects were of no concern to them.

The present offers only too many examples of the relativity of international justice. The Communist bloc would consider it a triumph of historical justice if the whole world were converted to their creed. The democratic countries would see the same triumph in the end of all totalitarian and authoritarian regimes and in the advent of a universal reign of individual freedoms. The Fascist, who has not yet become an extinct human species, holds a still different image of justice. A Western businessman might think that low prices for primary commodities and high prices for his industrial products are a part of international justice; the producer of these commodities in an underdeveloped country would support the opposite proposition. Communist China claims Taiwan in the name of justice, but the Nationalist Chinese government would see the fulfillment of justice only in a return to the mainland. The Japanese would say that their recovery of both the Ryukyu and the Kurile islands would be a victory for justice. The Americans would share their view with respect to the Russian-annexed Kurile islands, but the Russians would sympathize with their claim to the American-administered Ryukyu islands.

The Egyptians thought that the Suez Canal should become theirs as a matter of justice, but obviously neither Britain nor France agreed. The nationalization of foreign assets seems just or unjust depending on the point of view; the losing foreigners can hardly agree on its justice with the nationalizing government and its supporters. India keeps Kashmir and feels righteous about it, while Pakistan claims Kashmir and charges India with blatant injustice. Every territorial dispute anywhere in the world brings forth these contradictory interpretations of what is just, and each party honestly feels that its interpretation is the only right one. One nation wants to preserve its frontiers, the other aspires to change them. One nation wants to get rid of foreign domination, but another refuses to relinquish its overseas possessions. Justice carries an altogether different meaning for the Africans and the white settlers in British Central Africa. So the story goes.

There usually exists in domestic affairs a certain basic consensus on what is just at a given time. Moreover, there are procedures for defining justice in particular situations: the legislative process defines justice with respect to social problems, and the judicial process defines it in private disputes. The international community has no similar procedures. No state can be sued before international tribunals without its free consent. The Security Council and the General Assembly of the United Nations may only recommend solutions, which the parties have the right to reject. Moreover, the member-states are guided in their voting by many considerations but other than the search for immanent justice (see Chapter 9). At least one major consideration would take precedence over justice, namely that the preferred solution would promote general peace better than any other. Any recommendation by the United Nations is bound to reflect political expediency much more than justice. However, the member-states which cast their votes for the recommendation might be inclined to hail it as an embodiment of international justice.

As a matter of fact, peaceful changes in the status quo have seldom if ever been carried out for the sake of justice. In the past the great powers were able to agree on certain changes in the status quo and enforce their decision by the pressure of their combined power, but they were motivated by their own national interests, not by a preoccupation with justice. Russia, Prussia, and Austria carved up Poland in the eighteenth century without war; they thereby effected a peaceful change in the status quo but did not claim that they acted as international dispensers of justice. The same was true of Britain and Russia in 1907 when they agreed to divide Iran into their respective zones of influence for the sake of better mutual relations, and of Britain and France in 1904 when they allocated Morocco to France and Egypt to Britain in order to lay the foundation for their co-operation against Germany. Britain and France believed that they were buying peace for themselves in Munich but certainly did not feel that they promoted justice by delivering Czechoslovakia to Nazi Germany. The present partitions of Germany, Korea, and Vietnam seem to be accepted by other nations as a necessary price for the general peace and as an unavoidable part of the status quo, but no one claims that these partitions are just. Today, nuclear risks make people more ready than ever to sacrifice what they consider to be justice on the altar of peace and survival.

INTERNATIONAL LAW

International law is a body of rules which define the mutual rights and obligations of states and whose legally binding force is acknowledged by states. These rules first emerged from the practice of states. Whenever states consistently followed the same pattern of conduct for a reasonably long period of time, a usage, i.e., a habitual behavior, was the result. If states, in addition, implicitly or explicitly acknowledged that this pattern of behavior was obligatory for them and that different conduct would have been a breach of law, the usage became a custom. A custom is a usage (habitual conduct) which states recognize as legally binding on them. Custom is the oldest source of international law. For instance, the rules concerning diplomatic immunities or the rules which govern the jurisdiction of coastal states within territorial waters are parts of customary law and the results of the actual practice of states.

Customary international law, like all customary law, is unwritten. If the existence of a custom is contested, it must be proved by recourse to such subsidiary sources as writings of international lawyers of high repute, decisions of national and international courts, domestic legislations, and pertinent diplomatic documents published by the various states. Since it is unwritten, customary law can easily give rise to controversies between states not only concerning the existence of a rule but also concerning its scope and exact meaning.

The lively tempo of daily relations among modern states has produced in the last hundred years, especially in this century, an ever-increasing number of multilateral and bilateral treaties. Treaties are another principal source of international law. They are of two types: law-making treaties and contract treaties. A law-making treaty is an agreement which regulates a matter of general if not necessarily universal concern. It is usually signed by all or almost all the states which are interested in the subject covered by the treaty. If the signatories are only a few states but include the great powers principally concerned, the rules of general conduct which the treaty creates have a good chance of being followed by other states as well. Eventually this treaty, originally bearing only a few signatures, becomes a law-making treaty if the other states have followed its rules for a reasonably long period of time or have expressly accepted them as having the force of law. In this case, the treaty produces customs which are in content identical with the written rules of the treaty. In 1856 only the principal maritime European powers of the time adopted in Paris the Declaration which outlawed privateering and defined certain rights of neutrals in a maritime war. The other maritime states, which had never signed the Paris Declaration, nevertheless followed it in practice, thus making it a part of customary law. If the treaty creating new rules of international conduct is concluded between practically all the states concerned, it is from the start a law-making treaty. One of the earliest examples of this sort of law-making agreement is the classification of ranks of diplomats adopted in 1815 by the Congress of Vienna and immediately followed by all states; this classification eliminated one of the causes of international disputes, the bitter quarrels over diplomatic precedence among the ambassadors accredited in the same capital.

The last hundred years have seen a multiplication of law-making treaties adopted at the start by almost all states. These treaties are usually open to accession by the remaining nonsignatory states and thus favor their universal acceptance. Treaties establishing nonpolitical universal unions among states and defining the rules of conduct for the member-states of these unions are examples of universal law-making treaties. Such are the treaties which founded the Universal Postal Union and the World Health Organization; agreements of this type are the constitutional charters of the specialized agencies concerned but they also prescribe the rules of conduct for the member-states. Such also are the treaties which organize the co-operation of as many states as possible in the struggle against certain social evils such as trade in women and children, slavery, or illegal traffic in harmful drugs.

Law-making treaties are somewhat analogous to domestic statutes. They have the general effect of creating new rules of conduct which are accepted by all the states concerned. Like statutes in common-law countries, they fill the gaps in customary law and amend or replace existing customs.

A contract treaty is not designed to create a new rule of general conduct. Its aim is to define the specific rights and obligations of the contracting parties within the framework of existing international law. A treaty of this type solves a problem of direct interest only for its signatories. It resembles a private contract, in which the specific rights and obligations of private parties are defined within the framework of domestic law. The private contract cannot alter domestic law; in the same way, the contract treaty cannot modify general international law. The signatory states, like parties to a private contract, may add to, renounce, or modify *inter se* those rights which they derive from general international law, but they may not impose the same provisions on the nonsignatory states.

This general principle holds true for all treaties. Any treaty is binding only on the contracting parties and cannot *ipso jure* produce any legal effects for the nonsignatory states. In the case of a law-making treaty, its legal force can be extended beyond the range of its signatories in either of two ways: either by later accessions if the treaty is open to accessions, or by the actual practice of other states, practice which may make the treaty a part of customary international law.

The mutual rights and obligations of all states are thus regulated by three types of legal devices: general customary law, law-making treaties, and contract treaties insofar as the *inter se* relations of their signatories are concerned. An alliance, a treaty of nonaggression, a treaty of commerce are examples among various types of contract treaties.

Article 38 of the Statute of the International Court of Justice lists the following sources of international law:

"1. International conventions [treaties] whether general [law-making] or particular [contract treaties], establishing rules expressly recognized by the contesting states;

2. International custom, as evidence of a general practice accepted as law;

3. The general principles of law recognized by civilized nations;

4. . . . judicial decisions and the teachings of the most highly qualified publicists of the various nations, as subsidiary means for the determination of rules of law."

This is not a haphazard listing. The order of priorities is clearly indicated. The treaty which is applicable to particular disputes between two of its signatories has the highest priority. If no pertinent treaty has been concluded between them, customary law becomes applicable. If even customary law offers no rule which can be used in the particular controversy, the "general principles of law" may be explored. These are the general principles which can be deduced from the various domestic legislations and from international law itself. For instance, *res judicata,* the principle that a final and valid judgment cannot be any longer contested, is an example of a general principle recognized by all domestic legislations except for certain aspects of Soviet judicial procedure. Another example is the universally accepted principle that after the lapse of a certain period of time a situation which has not been contested during that period may not be challenged by any legal claim (the statute of limitations). If the existence of a general principle of law is proved, the principle, if pertinent, may be used as a basis for the settlement of the dispute. Thus, general principles help fill the gaps in the existing treaty and customary law.

The fourth source is only subsidiary. If the existence or meaning of a custom or of a general principle is contested, the controversy may be settled by having recourse to subsidiary sources, which are more numerous than those listed in the Statute. They include writings of international lawyers of high repute and of various nationalities, judicial decisions by national and international courts, and also various pertinent national legislations and official documents published by various states. These subsidiary sources may be used as evidence of the existence and meaning of a customary rule or of a general principle of law on the strict condition that they represent a consensus among the states of the world. Judicial decisions by the courts of one country or the legislation and official views of one nation do not suffice as a valid proof. The writings of international lawyers may be used as a subsidiary source on two conditions. First, these lawyers must be of various nationalities. Secondly, the writings quoted must consist in the accumulation of abundant proofs derived from the actual practice of states. Whenever a writer of even the highest scholarly caliber writes about what international law *should be*, his views might open the path for new developments but may not be cited as evidence of what international law *actually is*.

International law, which regulates several though not all aspects of relations between states, is usually called an imperfect law by comparison to domestic law. The defects of this imperfect law, if measured by the yardstick of domestic law, are several: there are no courts with a general and compulsory authority to interpret law and to settle disputes, no legislature with the right to modify law in response to the changing equilibrium of social forces, no international agency of enforcement, and, last but not least, no feeling of supreme loyalty to the international community.

The defect of international law which is stressed most often is the lack of a central coercive agency to enforce law on the states. It is true that no such agency exists; nevertheless, international law can be enforced by coercion used by one state against another. This sort of enforcement is sometimes compared with the self-help which a primitive tribal society allows its members. An individual, usually supported by his clansmen, uses physical force to compel a recalcitrant member of the tribe to abide by tribal law. This analogy is not valid because the tribal individual acts with the moral approval of his community; moreover, the most primitive tribe, even if it delegates the power of coercion to its individual members, has some generally recognized authority (the chieftain, the council of elders) who defines customary law in cases of doubt and decides whether the individual has remained within the bounds of legitimate self-help defined by the same law. Self-help by states is left to their discretion tempered only by considerations of power and expediency. If the plaintiff state is much more powerful than the defendant state (discrepancy in power is incomparably greater between states than between tribal individuals), it can use force to sustain a claim of dubious legality.

The remedy of self-help, if self-help means the use of force or the threat of its use, is not so readily available as it seems. It cannot be used to enforce a legal claim against a great power or even against a small country which is protected by a great power. Resort to self-help entails nowadays much greater risks than it did in the nineteenth century because the use of force even on a limited scale may lead to international complications involving the nuclear powers. It has also become less popular because of the United Nations prohibition against the use of force in all circumstances except for self-defense against an armed attack. Forms of self-help which do not consist in the use of force, such as embargoes on trade or on credits, may be rendered ineffective in our time by the discords among the great powers. The coercive measures taken by the plaintiff state to enforce its legal claim may well be neutralized by the help extended by other states to the defendant country. For all these reasons, it is difficult to regard self-help as a substitute for a central agency of enforcement of international law.

The dispersal of power among the several states is sometimes compared to the polycentric distribution of power under the medieval feudal system; the modern state is compared with the feudal lord as a center of effective power. This analogy is used in support of the optimistic expectation that the present decentralization of power will end in a centralization around a future world state, just as the feudal system evolved into the nation-state. Such an expectation may be realized, but the historical analogy is an unconvincing proof. The analogy implies that the evolution of the feudal system into the centralized nation-state was predetermined and inevitable; like all deterministic interpretations of history, it assumes events to have been inevitable because they took place. Just as it seems natural to modern man that power should be centralized in the nation-state, it seemed natural to medieval man that it should be centralized in the feudal lord or the autonomous city, that each lord should enforce domestic order in his own domains, protecting his and his vassals' rights against other lords, and that within a feudal hierarchy each lord should owe definite obligations to his overlord. The first attempts of the king, the highest overlord, to monopolize coercion seemed no more natural and inevitable to medieval man than a world government seems to modern man. Those who confidently expect our decentralized state system to evolve necessarily into a world state forget, whenever they invoke the medieval analogy, that history looks predetermined only when viewed retrospectively. The future is pregnant at any time with many contingencies, only one of which becomes the reality which later seems to have been predestined. Moreover, there is no law of history which compels mankind to evolve toward higher forms of centralization of power.

The feudal system was preceded by the Roman Empire, while the present disintegration of the colonial empires is nothing but a process of decentralization of the power of coercion. There is no certainty either way that the future will or will not bring a centralized agency of coercion which will make international law as effective as domestic law.

Self-help in the feudal society, as in the tribal society, was limited by customary law; it was more or less effectively supervised by the feudal hierarchy and by the Church, which was the generally recognized spiritual authority. In neither society was self-help left entirely to the discretion of the interested parties.

However, the problem of decentralization of power within the international community, as crucial as it is for the maintenance of peace, is not so important as it seems for the observance of international law. The historical record proves that international law has usually been observed in the practice of states. Like domestic law, it owes its existence, first of all, to the conviction that it is binding, a conviction which is shared by the state agents who have to apply it. An equally compelling reason for the existence of international law is that it is deeply rooted in the reciprocity of national interests. As long as this reciprocal interest in the existence of international law subsists, respect for international law does not collide with national interests.

International law emerged out of the actual practice of states, not from the heads of legislators. It is founded on the assumption that it serves the interests of all states; if it did not serve their interests, the states would not have consistently observed those practices out of which international law has grown. If its prohibitions sometimes interfere with the pursuit of national objectives, this short-term disadvantage is usually outweighed by the consideration that one breach may encourage other violations until the entire structure would collapse to the prejudice of all states. Its usefulness enables it to survive its various imperfections, including the lack of a centralized agency of enforcement. It is interesting to note in this regard that the Communist states, as much as they are divided ideologically from other states, do not deny the binding force of international law. Yet this law was built up by the practice of "capitalist" states, and its observance by the socialist states can hardly be squared with the Marxist doctrine which claims that each law is the product of a specific economic base and dies out with the destruction of this base to be replaced by a new law born of a new economic base. Soviet lawyers have not been able to solve this theological puzzle as to why the socialist states abide by an international law which was derived from precapitalist and capitalist economic bases. The Soviet and other Communist governments are not hindered by these doctrinal difficulties; they simply accept international law as it was constructed before the October Revolution. Reciprocity of interests proves to be more compelling than purity of doctrine. The new states, which did not participate in the creation of international law, accept its binding force for the same practical reason. Reciprocity of interests was the midwife of international law and remains its most effective guardian in spite of the lack of an international policeman who could enforce it by coercion. Only when this reciprocity is contested does the observance of international law by a state become a moot question.

The record of compliance with international law during the last one hundred and fifty years is impressive. The exceptions are significant not because they are numerous but because they involved the most vital interests of states and were therefore accompanied by spectacular events on the international stage. It has been said that virtue does not make news. It is understandable that the layman's attention is attracted by these fairly rare but politically important violations of international law rather than by the less spectacular general observance of most of its rules.

Most treaties do not conflict with the national interests of the contracting parties. If they are quasi-universal treaties, they protect the concordant interests of all, or almost all, states; common interests are served by the treaties, which protect copyright or patents or provide for common action against illicit trade in harmful drugs. If the treaties are limited to several states, they promote their joint and specific interests, such as their common interest in defending fisheries against depletion. Bilateral treaties, such as treaties of commerce, are the result of a negotiated compromise. Several simple devices can be used to protect treaties against a change in the national interests of the contracting parties; they may be concluded for a limited period of time, may provide for negotiated revisions, or may stipulate certain conditions under which the treaty can be denounced. The treaty can thus be terminated or its provisions revised without any breach of international law. Rarely is there any urgent reason for violating a treaty. An important exception must be made to this general rule, however, in the case of those treaties which embody obligations that affect the most vital interests of the contracting parties. The record of these treaties proves that, while they usually survive the test, their survival is surrounded with uncertainty. These treaties include the following types: general or specific prohibitions of war or of the use of force (the Covenant of the League of Nations, the Kellogg Pact, and the Charter of the United Nations, as well as bilateral treaties of nonaggression); treaties of mutual assistance (alliances); unreciprocated guarantees of the security of other states; peace treaties and unequal treaties; treaties on the limitation of armaments; and, finally, treaties which control important international seaways such as straits and canals. These types of treaties are fragile for two reasons: (1) they affect the security or the other most vital interests of the contracting parties or their international status, and (2) the distribution of power on which they are founded at the time of their signing may change radically after a number of years. If this change occurs and favors one of the contracting parties, the latter party may conclude that the treaty has become a troublesome burden. The treaty may have been imposed by the superior strength of the other contracting parties and may not have been founded, even at the time of its signing, on the interests of all the states concerned. The contracting party which was too weak to refuse its signature and whose relative power has in the meantime greatly increased may be tempted to denounce the treaty. There is no international procedure for the revision of treaties which one of the parties considers politically obsolete. This party can try to abrogate or revise the treaty through negotiations with the other contracting parties, but if it encounters a refusal to modify or to terminate the treaty and if it is favored by international circumstances, it will have recourse to a unilateral denunciation.

This unilateral denunciation, unauthorized by the treaty, may be rationalized in one or both of two ways. Either the denouncing state accuses the other contracting parties of alleged breaches of the same treaty and thus justifies its own action, or it invokes the so-called *clausula rebus sic stantibus.* (The contracting party may also, of course, simply perform some action forbidden by the treaty; for example, it may conclude another treaty whose provisions conflict with the obligations contained in the former treaty. The practical result is the same.) *Clausula rebus sic stantibus* is a theory which affirms that each treaty contains an implicit though unwritten clause to the effect that the treaty will lapse in the case of a radical change in circumstances since its signing. International lawyers have always been divided on the reality of *clausula rebus sic stantibus,* some denying the theory and others urging its necessity as a political safety valve. In practice, a state which is favored by circumstances and bent on ending a treaty is inclined to invoke this debatable theory, while its opponents, who wish to maintain the status quo, no less energetically protest in the name of the sanctity of treaties. The fact remains that several treaties of the types described above have been unilaterally denounced or violated.

A general treaty which restricts the right of waging war (the Covenant of the League of Nations) or which prohibits war (the Kellogg Pact) or even goes so far as to forbid the use of force or the threat of its use except in self-defense against an armed attack (the Charter of the United Nations) attempts to rule out the forcible modification of the status quo but also makes illegal the forcible protection of the status quo against actions that do not consist in the use of force. This is particularly true of the Charter, which forbids any use of force whatsoever except in self-defense, which is given the strict sense of defense against an armed attack. The Charter widens the scope of self-defense in one respect only: it allows states to come to the rescue of a state which has been attacked.

It does not permit forcible self-defense against an action which is not an armed attack, even though this action threatens the most vital interests of the state concerned. At the same time, the Charter does not offer any effective procedure either for a peaceful revision of the status quo or for the redress of a wrong caused by a nonmilitary action. It is one of the main weaknesses of the Charter that it prohibits the use of force but provides no alternative means of revising the status quo or redressing wrongs. This defect proves equally frustrating to the states which want to change the status quo and those which have an interest in preserving it against nonmilitary actions. The history of the United Nations has already proved that either cause for frustration may incite the member-states to transgress the prohibition and resort to force. They are encouraged by the lack of any effective sanction against violations.

Fortunately, these breaches remain limited in scope, for general war is forbidden more effectively by the fear of nuclear devastations than by the Charter. "Minor" transgressions may occur when a state which wants to revise the status quo is frustrated in its efforts to effect the change through negotiations with other states and knows that the United Nations lacks the means to enforce a recommendation approving its claim. This was the situation of India which had no reasonable hope of obtaining from Portugal a peaceful cession of Goa. After several years of fruitless agitation for a peaceful settlement of the dispute, India used force in an open violation of the Charter.

In 1956 France and Britain fully realized the inconvenience of the absolute prohibition of force for the states which want to maintain the status quo but whose vested interests are threatened by the nonmilitary action of another state. The nationalization of the Suez Canal certainly was not an armed attack and, according to the Charter, did not authorize forcible countermeasures. Yet Britain and France felt, rightly or wrongly, that this Egyptian move would imperil their most vital interest: the steady flow of the Near Eastern oil and profits from the oil concessions. The United Nations had no means to redress what both powers considered a wrong. Frustrated by this inability to enforce a peaceful settlement upon Egypt, they resorted to force in defiance of the Charter.

If Sudan were to retain a greater share of the waters of the Nile than allocated by its agreements with Egypt, it would threaten Egypt with starvation. Its action would not be an armed attack but would have consequences perhaps far more serious for Egypt. Egypt would study the Charter in vain for an effective remedy.

The Soviet Union disregarded the Charter prohibition in 1956 because it wanted to restore the *status quo ante* in Hungary and knew that the sympathies of the members of the United Nations were with the Hungarian revolutionaries.

The ineffectiveness of the Charter prohibition has its precedents in the inter-war period. Japan and Italy disregarded the Kellogg Pact and the Covenant of the League of Nations when they felt that the international circumstances of the thirties favored a forcible change in the status quo. No one remembered the existence of these two solemn documents in September, 1939, when the Second World War broke out.

It is never certain that all states will discover their interests in a general and unconditional prohibition of the use of force.

The same is true of regional or bilateral treaties of nonaggression and neutrality whereby the contracting parties promise never to attack each other and always to remain neutral in case one of them is attacked by a third state. The list of broken nonaggression treaties, which were very popular during the inter-war period, is only too long. The weaker contracting parties learned between 1939 and 1945 that these treaties could not protect them against armed aggressions, territorial annexations, or even wholesale conquest by the stronger co-signatories.

An alliance or a guarantee of security involves the most vital interests of the contracting states. Its implementation might expose them to immense dangers, including in our time the danger of total biological extinction. It is not surprising that a signatory is assailed by stronger misgivings when called upon to meet the obligations of an alliance than when it has to implement a treaty of commerce. The distribution of power which favored the allies at the time of its signing may have changed radically and the risks involved may have increased enormously beyond expectation. The course of international events may have disrupted the reciprocity of interests between the allies. Moreover, the alliance is sometimes founded, even on the day of its signing, on very different interests of the allies. For instance, the United States entered SEATO and supported the Baghdad Pact in order to check the Communist bloc. Pakistan joined both alliances less for this reason than in the hope of receiving a flow of American military supplies and thus maintaining a good security posture vis-à-vis India. An alliance may be signed in the expectation that the combined power of the allies will deter the common adversary from embarking on a military venture; if this hope is frustrated, some of the allies may be reluctant to participate in a joint armed action.

Although it would be entirely false to say that alliances have not been observed as a general rule, there are several examples of their fragility. The treaty of alliance with France, concluded in 1778, forbade the conclusion of a separate peace; yet four years later the United States entered into secret negotiations with Britain for ending the war. Article 11 of the same alliance contained a mutual guarantee of American and French possessions in the Western Hemisphere against all other powers. In 1793, however, the United States proclaimed its neutrality in the war between France and Britain, Austria, and Prussia, a war which clearly threatened the French possessions in America. In 1798 the alliance was unilaterally denounced by the United States. The reciprocity of interests which had existed at the time of signing disappeared after American independence had been achieved.

The Italian alliances with Germany and Austria-Hungary did not fare better in the First World War. Italy considered that its interests required it to remain neutral and eventually in 1915 to side with the enemies of its former allies for the price of a share in the spoils of victory. France, obligated not to conclude a separate peace and still able to continue the resistance from its overseas possessions, chose in 1940 to conclude an armistice with Germany rather than stand by its British ally. Italy changed sides in 1943, abandoning its German ally.

Treaties of unreciprocated guarantees are concluded between the great powers and small nations. Typical are the treaties of permanent neutrality. The Swiss neutrality survived both world wars. But the permanent neutrality of Belgium (guaranteed by treaties concluded in 1831 and 1838) and that of Luxemburg (guaranteed by a treaty of 1867) were both violated by one of the signatories, Germany. Another signatory, Austria-Hungary, fought the First World War as a German ally. At the time of the German violation of the neutrality of Belgium and Luxemburg the two other signatories, Russia and France, were already at war with Germany. Britain, the only signatory to be still neutral, invoked the violation of the treaties of permanent neutrality as a reason for its declaration of war on Germany, but it would be a gross overstatement to say that this was *the* reason for the British decision.

In 1846, the United States guaranteed the sovereignty of Colombia. This treaty was disregarded in 1903 when the United States abetted the secession of Panama by preventing the Colombian military action to restore its territorial integrity and when it hastily recognized the Panamian independence.

A peace treaty, unless concluded after a military stalemate, is imposed by the victor and hence always is an unequal treaty. Most of its provisions are carried out within a short period of time. The permanent provisions, such as the territorial provisions or those which limit the sovereignty of the vanquished state, have a more uncertain life. They constantly remind the state of its defeat. The territorial losses are especially painful; they are felt to be an amputation of the national body and regarded as unjust because imposed by the superior force of the victor. If later the international distribution of power changes radically, the defeated nation is tempted to recover the lost territories by war or the threat of war.

Unequal treaties and the unequal provisions of a peace treaty are bound to be denounced by the disadvantaged state as soon as international circumstances permit. Unequal treaties may disadvantage the weaker state by establishing an enclave of foreign jurisdiction in its territory, by placing resident aliens outside its criminal jurisdiction, or by imposing foreign control over its customs as a guarantee for the repayment of foreign debts; such treaties were often imposed by the European powers on weak Asian and Near Eastern states. The unequal provisions of a peace treaty may demilitarize a part of the territory of the defeated state or limit its armaments. The unequal treaty may be abrogated by negotiations if the states favored by its provisions feel that the treaty will be terminated in any case. Germany was compelled to agree in the Versailles Peace Treaty to accept a limitation of its armaments and the demilitarization of the Rhineland. Both provisions were unequal. It was easy to predict that a powerful Germany would not eternally abide by these unilateral limitations of its sovereignty. Both were denounced in 1935 and 1936.

Treaties of reciprocal limitation of armaments, such as those which were concluded during the inter-war period concerning naval armaments, affect the most sensitive national interest—external security—and reflect the distribution of power at the time of signing. Their life is threatened not only by a change in the distribution of power but also by new technological developments. One or another of the contracting parties may discover that an open armaments race would better serve its interests or that advances in military technology undermine the balance of armaments which the treaty attempted to ensure. It may conclude that the treaty has become "obsolete" from the point of view of its interests.

Treaties controlling the vital seaways are vulnerable to changes in international circumstances because they involve important interests of the riparian states and of all maritime nations. The eventful history of changing regimes in the Turkish Straits (open or closed to non-Turkish fleets, supervised by Turkey or by an International Commission, demilitarized, or guarded by Turkish fortifications, etc.) reflects changes in the interpretation of their interests by Turkey and the great powers. The new distribution of power, in particular the split among the great powers, has shifted control of the Suez Canal from Britain to Egypt.

Because the interpretation of national interests is fluid, the dividing line between those parts of international law which have a precarious life and those which are solidly grounded in a reciprocity of interests is also fluid. A rule such as the three-mile limit for the width of territorial waters seems solid at one time and is challenged at another. It is self-evident that the uncertain part of international law is proportionately smaller in an era of relative stability and increases in a period of marked instability. It suffices to compare the different fortunes of international law in the nineteenth century (until 1914) and in our time. The nineteenth century witnessed a flourishing development of international law. However, even that century saw one spectacular denunciation of unequal treaty provisions. Russia denounced in 1870 the provisions of the Paris Peace Treaty of 1856 concerning the demilitarization of the Black Sea. As a great power Russia bitterly resented this unequal situation which the victors in the Crimean

War had imposed. Once international circumstances had changed (one of the signatories of the Paris Treaty, France, was engaged in a war with Prussia and other German states, while another, Britain, could not enforce these provisions alone), Russia no longer felt obliged to observe the demilitarization of the Black Sea.

The greater number of breaches of international law in our time is due to the instability of the international environment, not to a declining respect for law in general. Domestic law is now respected as much as in the past century.

Law performs the function of maintaining stability and protecting the existing framework of social relations. Hence, a domestic revolution directed against this framework always results in a profound transformation of domestic law. For the same reason states which are dissatisfied with the international status quo show less respect for those rules of international law which stand in their way. The number of such states is always greater in an unstable period such as ours.

Customary law, the product of the long practice of states, is obviously founded on a reciprocity of interests. Its main weakness is its rigidity, i.e., its inability to adjust itself quickly to changing circumstances. It usually takes many years before a new general practice is accepted as proof of the revision by consensus of a part of customary international law. Theoretically, the solution is to reform customary law by a law-making treaty generally accepted by states. In fact, governments find it very difficult to agree on a new rule during this period of transition when the old rule is losing its hold but the new one is not yet clearly established. This is especially true in our time of sharp conflicts of ideologies and national interests which make the codification and revision of customary law a very difficult if not hopeless process. The several attempts made since the First World War to codify certain parts of customary international law have all ended in failure. It is interesting to observe, however, that whenever national interests coincide it is easy, even in our time, for states which are otherwise unfriendly to agree on a new rule of international law, as evidenced by the general acceptance of the concept of the continental shelf and by the Antarctic Treaty of 1960.

If the states cannot agree on a new rule, the old customary rule will be upheld by some states while its validity will be contested by others. The binding force of international law, reciprocity of interests, is lacking in this situation. There is no analogous problem in the domestic society, where the legislator decides whether a rule of statutory or common law has ceased to correspond to the needs of the society. Whatever the legislator decides, whether he upholds the validity of the old rule or enacts a new one, his decision is binding on courts and citizens and is enforced, in the last analysis, by state compulsion. There is neither an international legislator nor an international agency of coercion.

Law in general but customary law in particular lags behind social and political changes. These changes always precede law, which can only reflect them. Domestically, the legislature can quickly adjust law to new circumstances; if it obstinately fails in this duty, a revolution will make the necessary adjustment. Customary international law cannot follow new developments quickly. Rules which lag seriously behind will not be observed by those states which no longer find an interest in abiding by them. This does not mean that customary international law has been invalidated, even in our revolutionary era. Most customary rules continue to correspond to common national interests and are observed by states some of which are diametrically opposed to each other in other respects. The customary law on diplomatic privileges and immunities is an obvious illustration of this general reciprocity of interests. Nevertheless, a few important sections of customary law are now of doubtful effectiveness.

Customary international law is mainly the product of practices long followed by the formerly dominant Western nations. They ruled the world, and their practice moulded customary law. Practices which were founded on a reciprocity of interests among the Western nations did not always respect the interests of non-Western peoples. For instance, the concepts of national sovereignty and of domestic jurisdiction protected the Western states against undue interference by another Western state in their own domestic affairs. But the same concepts did not protect the non-European countries against Western interventions. The colonial expansion was a negation of respect for the sovereignty of the non-European peoples; unequal treaties interfered with the domestic jurisdiction of the same peoples. These two concepts, vital in inter-Western relations, had very little practical meaning for, say, China of the nineteenth century.

The world of today is no longer dominated by the Western nations. Certain rules of customary international law, which evolved from Western practice, might not be considered convenient by the non-Western states, which now have the power to challenge their validity on ideological or national grounds. The progress of science and technology has created problems unknown in the nineteenth century, a second reason why certain rules of customary international law have become obsolescent. New technological developments call for the revision of certain rules and also for the creation of altogether new rules for which there was no need in the past century.

A few examples will illustrate how change can affect several elements of customary law. All states recognized until 1917 the sanctity of private property, and this attitude was reflected in international rules for the protection of foreign property. These rules were fashioned by the Western states whose nationals were engaged in large-scale business in foreign countries. The United States, for instance, could protect the assets of its nationals in Latin America by insisting on the international obligation of states to respect foreign property. The European powers did the same in other parts of the world unless they preferred to impose their colonial rule and assume direct jurisdiction over the lands where their investments were located. In both cases, the ultimate sanction was coercion by the Western powers, either through naval demonstrations and marine landings or through colonial courts and administrations.

Today the same rules of customary law are undermined by the practice of several non-Western states. The Communist states contest the very principle of private ownership of the means of production. They feel that they can confiscate foreign assets just as they confiscate the private property of their own nationals. If sometimes they consent to pay a partial indemnity, they do so not because they recognize the binding force of customary rules but because this sort of contractual arrangement with a foreign state is mutually beneficial. The Communist state agrees to pay a partial indemnity in exchange either for foreign credits or for the unfreezing of its own assets in the territory of the other contracting party. The underdeveloped countries face a decision which they resolve in either of two ways. If they strongly hope to attract new foreign investment, they will carefully respect foreign property; if they prefer to assert control over the economic life of their country or to take revenge on a foreign country, they will nationalize foreign assets.

The dispute gravitates around the problem of fair compensation. A Communist state does not feel that it can be obligated by international rule to pay any compensation at all. An underdeveloped country is inclined to pay an inadequate compensation. The very concept of fair compensation is moot. For instance, how much weight should be given the fact that foreign corporations sometimes get back several times their original investment in the form of exported profits?

The nineteenth-century practice of expropriation by right of eminent domain can hardly be compared in scope with twentieth-century nationalizations of foreign assets. Although both procedures have their roots in the same concept of the supreme jurisdiction of the state, their extent is so different that it would be misleading to consider modern nationalization as a simple extension of the institution of eminent domain. Nationalization is not a sharply limited and exceptional measure undertaken for the purpose of building a railroad or widening a city street; it involves a total expropriation of large foreign holdings. It takes various forms: confiscation without indemnity; partial confiscation because the indemnity is much lower than the market value of the property or because it is paid in state bonds of uncertain future value; unilateral abrogation of rights granted to a foreign corporation to exploit national resources or to manage public utilities (transportation, power) of national or international concern.

The reasons for the nationalization of foreign assets vary from case to case. The government might be guided by its conception of the best society, a conception which requires that all the means of production be socialized. To carry out a badly needed land reform it may have to expropriate foreign plantations but it may lack sufficient means to pay an adequate compensation to foreign and national landowners alike. It might feel that the full implementation of its plan for economic development demands the nationalization of certain key industries which are, however, owned by foreigners. In each case, its point of view will be different from that of the state whose nationals have paid the price for the operation. If accused of violating the human rights of aliens, it will answer that it does not acknowledge private ownership of the means of production as a right and that it treated foreigners in the same way that it treats its own nationals. Another government will oppose to the human rights of foreign owners the human right of its own nationals to order their own society for their greater welfare. A third will say that foreign concessions for the operation of public utilities or for the exploitation of natural resources were wrested from the weak or corrupt governments of the past and are nothing but mortgages on national freedom.

This sort of discussion is fruitless because the contracting parties cannot understand each other's arguments, arguments which are derived from entirely different "self-evident truths." As proved in the case of several Eastern European Communist states, this does not preclude useful bargaining over the actual amount of compensation.

Another example of the present lack of consensus is the controversy over the width of territorial waters. It was almost generally agreed before 1914 that the limit was three miles. This rule was convenient for the Western maritime nations. It allowed them to use the open seas freely, even near the coasts of other states; to exploit ocean resources anywhere except in this narrow coastal belt; and to wage naval war near the coasts of neutral states on the condition of respecting their neutrality within territorial waters. The relative decline in power of the Western maritime nations, the concern to protect coastal fisheries, and security considerations have resulted since the First World War in the claims of numerous states, including the Soviet Union, to a belt wider than three miles but usually not exceeding twelve miles. Today, it is obvious that the three-mile limit is no longer generally accepted, although there is no agreement on any other width. The matter is complicated by various claims to adjacent zones where the jurisdiction of the coastal state extends beyond territorial waters but only for the specific purposes of enforcing customs control, guarding national security, or protecting the national monopoly of coastal fisheries. This part of international law is in flux.

The rapid progress of science and technology has also affected customary law. States are sometimes quick to discover their common interest in defining a new rule to meet the new development. This has been true, for instance, of the new rule concerning the continental shelf. The right of the coastal state to the exclusive exploitation of the natural resources of the bed and the subsoil under the shallow coastal waters (where the depth of the sea, measured from the coast outward, does not exceed 200 fathoms) is now generally recognized. The new rule, announced in 1945 by the United States, eventually met with the approval of other states.

The rule that thc sovereign jurisdiction of the state extends upward to include the air space above its territory does not provide any reasonable answer to the problem of outer space. Science has progressed beyond international law. The problem is extremely important because it involves the satellites orbiting in outer space for all sorts of purposes, including the observation of foreign territories. The security of all states is or will be affected by the unrestricted use of outer space. The practice of the two states competing for control of outer space, the United States and the Soviet Union, has so far suggested an analogy with the unrestricted use of the open seas, but the concept of an open outer space might lead to dangerous consequences for all states if this free use is associated, as it will be, with the capacity to bombard foreign territories. Attention is presently centered on this legal problem of outer space, but the rapid progress of science will occasion other problems of this type. Scientific control over weather is one of the probable developments for which existing international law has no answer. Since the advanced countries cannot be reasonably sure of retaining this lead in science and technology, they and all other states seem to have a common interest in the treaty regulation of these potentially dangerous problems.

Another interesting development is that intervention in the domestic affairs of another state has acquired a different meaning in our time. Before 1914 such intervention usually had a limited objective; states interfered in the domestic affairs of other states in order to protect the rights of their nationals, to open a foreign country to international trade, or to compel a nation to pay its debts. The intervention took the form of a limited use of force (the landing of marines, naval blockades, or naval bombardments) or consisted only in the threat of using force (a naval demonstration, for example). The intervening state was usually a Western great power which thus enforced its claim on what we would now call an underdeveloped country. Sometimes the objective was not limited; the intervention, formally justified by the desire to protect the lives or property of the nationals of the intervening power or by another limited objective, was actually a prelude to the establishment of a colonial regime.

The national awakening of the non-European countries has made intervention, even for limited purposes, unpopular. Yet it is sometimes undertaken, as evidenced by American indirect interventions in Guatemala and Cuba, the British-French intervention in Egypt for the dual purpose of restoring the international regime of the Suez Canal and overthrowing President Nasser, and the Soviet intervention in Hungary. All four actions had the same objective of overturning a government inimical to the intervening great power.

Intervention has acquired new scope for ideological reasons. The Communist states, committed in their foreign policy to a universal ideological crusade, intervene in the domestic affairs of other states by barely disguised support to their foreign co-believers. If a country is rent by civil strife, both the Western and the Communist powers usually intervene by supporting the party with which they sympathize.

Foreign aid and technical assistance are not, strictly speaking, interventions in domestic affairs, at least not in the older sense of this word. The foreign state is invited to supply economic and technical assistance and does not attempt to impose its will by force. But this modern "intervention" in the domestic affairs of the recipient country will have wider and more lasting results than any intervention of the last century. The foreign state actually participates in the economic development and the social transformation of the recipient country; its aid and advice contribute to reshape the assisted nation. Its role is nothing less than to be the leaven of the revolution of modernization.

International law leaves to the exclusive jurisdiction of each state certain matters which are traditionally considered as being mainly of domestic concern. These reserved matters might, however, affect, at least indirectly, the interests of other states. Domestic jurisdiction extends for example, to immigration laws, the regulation of external trade (the state monopoly of trade, tariffs, quotas, currency regulations, import licenses, subsidies to national exporters, etc.), naturalization and expatriation laws, the form of government, and the treatment of nationals. Legally, each state can regulate these matters as it pleases, but its policies can nevertheless interest other states politically. An immigration law that bars foreign immigrants will certainly be read with concern by the governments of overpopulated countries. Any new restriction on foreign imports will worry the states which used to export their products to that particular country. Every state may regulate as it likes the conditions under which its nationality may be acquired or lost. But if a state suddenly denies its nationality to a sizable number of its citizens residing abroad, it creates a problem for the countries where these citizens, now declared stateless persons, reside. These countries are no longer free to expel the foreigners, if they prove to be undesirable aliens, to the country of their nationality, because they have, legally, no country of their own. A form of government adopted in one country might be in our ideological era heartily disliked by another country. Domestic discrimination against certain categories of citizens because of their race, religion, or language might cause a wave of indignation in another nation which is of the same or similar race or religion or speaks the same language. Nevertheless, international law firmly prohibited intervention until the founding of the United Nations; it denied any legal title to the interest of one state in matters reserved for the domestic jurisdiction of another state. The only exception to this general rule was the case of a state which contracted an express treaty obligation regarding a matter habitually reserved for domestic jurisdiction. For instance, several Eastern European states were bound by international agreements not to discriminate against their citizens because of race, religion, language, or nationality. These agreements made it legitimate for the members of the League of Nations to be legally concerned in any case of discrimination that occurred in one of those states. But cases of similar discrimination in other countries could not be brought before the League; the general rule of domestic jurisdiction excluded those cases from the competence of the League. Satisfactory or not, the concept of domestic jurisdiction was clear before the last war and its boundaries were not blurred by political expediency.

Debates in the United Nations on such issues as overseas colonialism and racial discrimination in South Africa have eroded the concept of domestic jurisdiction by effacing the dividing line between matters of reserved domain and matters of legitimate international concern. That South Africa was compelled to quit the Commonwealth because of its domestic racial discrimination is another proof of this erosion of domestic jurisdiction. Today, any issue once limited to domestic jurisdiction can be discussed in the United Nations if a sufficiently large number of states desire it. The opportunity to discuss any domestic policy in an international forum of states would be a welcome development if the concept of domestic jurisdiction had been replaced by a new rule of international law. This is not, however, the case. A matter formerly excluded from international debate is now discussed in the United Nations on the arbitrary condition that this debate suits the political convenience of the majority of member-states of the United Nations. Each member-state is guided in this decision by political expediency, not by a rule of law. For instance, the United States might assent to a debate on the Portuguese policy in Angola or on racial discrimination in South Africa, but certainly would object on the grounds of domestic jurisdiction to a similar debate on discrimination in its own southern states or to an enquiry into conditions in Puerto Rico. The Soviet Union gladly participates in debates on colonial policies and racial discrimination, but would firmly protest in the name of domestic jurisdiction against any attempt to discuss its policy toward the non-Russian nationalities of the U.S.S.R. or its discrimination against religious believers. India or Ghana, always ready to lead the way in a debate on colonial policies, would feel most indignant if a majority could be found to examine the Indian policy in Kashmir or the denial by the government of Ghana of equal political rights to the opposition. The concept of domestic jurisdiction has been thrown into the cauldron of political experimentation.

It was generally recognized before 1914 that a new government brought to power by unconstitutional means (a coup, a revolution) should abide by the international obligations which the former government of the same state had contracted. This principle of the continuity of international obligations was useful in maintaining stability in international relations regardless of domestic upheavals. It was beneficial for the great powers which were thereby insured against the risk that a small country would repudiate its foreign debts or other contractual obligations by using a revolutionary change of government as an excuse. This principle was challenged in 1917 by the Soviet government of Russia which simply repudiated all foreign debts contracted by the former Russian governments and claimed the right to denounce wholesale all the treaties concluded before the October Revolution. The Western protests were of no avail. The Chinese Communist government adopted the same policy in 1949 at the end of the Civil War.

The principle of the continuity of international obligations has been somewhat crippled by these two revolutions. It is an aspect of a wider principle: *Pacta sunt servanda* (i.e., the principle of the sanctity of treaties). Both principles have the same enemy in a radical change of international circumstances. The international record proves that states share a common interest in upholding the sanctity of international obligations when a change in government, although unconstitutional, does not affect the basic social and economic structure of the nation; the same record shows, however, that a true social revolution may introduce a new regime whose policies are not compatible with respect for *all* the international obligations assumed by the pre-revolutionary government. Can one reasonably expect that a revolutionary regime will pay the debts of its hated predecessor; that it will repay, for instance, the private and public credits for foreign supplies of weapons to the pre-revolutionary government? Can one hope that it will honor an alliance concluded by its predecessor if this alliance contradicts its new orientation in foreign affairs? Can one further expect that it will abide by the provisions of formerly concluded treaties of commerce if it has introduced a state monopoly of foreign trade?

Foreign states, if they cannot remove the revolutionary regime, are placed in this respect in the same situation as its defeated domestic enemies. They must write off their political and financial losses as the inevitable cost of the revolution. Protests are fruitless, as the Western powers learned after the October Revolution. Self-help might be more effectual, but if the revolutionary regime is compelled by force to abide by former international obligations or if it is overthrown by foreign action, the question is no longer one of legality but of power.

Except for the successful use of force, the aggrieved states have no remedy but negotiations. The principal aim of these negotiations should be to disinguish between those foreign credits which clearly benefited only the pre-revolutionary regime and those which brought lasting advantages to the economy of the country, and between the treaties which the new regime cannot honor without repudiating its ideology and its new orientation in foreign affairs and other treaties which it can observe in the mutual interest of both contracting parties.

This issue is similar to the one involved in the *clausula rebus sic stantibus*. The *clausula* refers to a radical change in international circumstances; the problem of the continuity of international obligations relates to a radical change in domestic circumstances.

The international law of peace, though incomplete and in several respects fragile, is founded on a reciprocity of national interests and enjoys a rather secure life. The same cannot be said for the international law of war and neutrality, for this law is applied when nations are divided by their most vital interests and fight for the highest stakes. They are then strongly inclined to brush aside all obstacles, legal or otherwise, which might hamper their military operations. The uncertain effectiveness of the international law of war and neutrality is reflected in the old proverb: "Inter armas silent leges" (see Chapter 2).

The commonly discussed question of the legal equality of states is obscured by polite diplomatic language which pays lip service to this concept so popular among the weaker countries. However, diplomatic ceremonial bows to the principle of the equality of states cannot obliterate the fact that the states which form the international community, of which there are more than a hundred, are drastically unequal in power. The "sovereignty" of states is in fact wider or narrower depending on their relative power. A state can be formally independent and theoretically have the last word concerning the formulation of its foreign and domestic policies, but it may be an open secret that it cannot pronounce even the first word without the preliminary approval of the great power within whose orbit it gravitates. There is no equality between the two.

The factual inequality of states has a necessary bearing on their legal equality. Legal equality has the following aspects: (1) an equal capacity to acquire rights; (2) equal rights which the society considers fundamental; (3) equal protection by law of rights whether these rights are equal or not; (4) equal participation in the formulation of laws; (5) equally binding force of law.

The independent states have an equal capacity to acquire rights. However, the factual differences between states prevent some of them from actually using certain of the rights to which international law entitles them. For instance, a land-locked state does not use the rights which the maritime law confers on all states. The same is true of the domestic situation. Every citizen of a capitalist state has the same legal capacity to acquire the rights of a stockholder but not all of them actually acquire those rights; every citizen of a Communist state has the legal capacity to become a party member but only a small fraction of them are actually party members.

States recognize the existence of their fundamental rights; their definition varies but the basic concept is not contested. Such are the rights to foreign respect for the state's independence, territorial integrity, domestic jurisdiction, and so forth. These fundamental rights, which actually reflect the most vital interests of states, are of unequal actual value, because their enforcement depends on the power relations among states. A great power feels secure that other states will respect its fundamental rights, but a weak nation is exposed to the risk that its rights may be infringed by a stronger power.

Theoretically, the rights of states receive equal protection from international law. In fact, the international situation is altogether different from the domestic situation, in which the state guarantees equal protection by law for the rights of its individual citizens. States have no recourse to a super-state institution for the protection of their rights. The state which infringes the rights of another state cannot be sued before an international tribunal without its consent and cannot be restrained by an international policeman who does not exist. The equal protection of the rights of states, which international law recognizes, cannot be enforced against the bad faith of a strong lawbreaker.

The equal protection of rights never means that the rights are identical. In no country do all citizens have identical rights (except for the fundamental rights); their rights vary depending on the contracts which they have concluded and on their social functions. The rights of an employee are different from those of an employer, the rights of a tax collector are different from those of a taxpayer, and so on. The rights of states are the same under the customary international law although natural differences (for instance, geographical location) make some of these rights inoperative for certain states, as indicated in the example of the landlocked countries. Treaties, like contracts in the domestic society, add and subtract rights. As a consequence, states have unequal rights and duties under treaty law. For instance, a treaty of commerce confers on the signatories the right to import their goods after the payment of lower customs duties than those which the nonsignatories must pay; at the same time, it mutually restricts their freedom of tariff regulation, which they retain regarding other states. Each treaty makes for an inequality of rights between the signatories and the nonsignatories. Moreover, the treaty can create unequal rights and duties for the signatories themselves. For instance, a treaty which establishes a military base of one state on the territory of another state confers different rights on the contracting parties. A treaty which legally bestows equal rights on the signatories may, in fact, place them in unequal positions. For example, a treaty of commerce concluded between an advanced and an underdeveloped country might guarantee the national treatment of their respective citizens and corporations in the territory of the other contracting party. In reality, this "equal" provision yields an important concession to the advanced country whose business firms operate in the underdeveloped country and are guaranteed the same rights which local business firms have. Legally, the underdeveloped country is given full reciprocity by the treaty, but it has no business firms in the territory of the advanced state.

The domestic society does not ensure the equal participation of its citizens in the formulation of laws. The citizens of a democratic state elect the legislators to whom they delegate the power to formulate laws. Only in a popular referendum do they directly participate in the legislative process, and even then they only approve or reject a bill submitted for their vote. While there is no equal participation in the formulation of laws between the legislator and the rank-and-file citizen, states, technically speaking, participate equally in the drafting of the treaties which they sign and in the practices from which customary laws emerge. In fact, the actual situation falls short of this ideal. A strong state leaves a much deeper imprint on a treaty than its weaker partner. A multilateral treaty is mainly the product of compromises among the major powers. Customary law is derived from general practice, but this practice is considered general if most of the states, including *all* great powers, accept it.

Domestically, law is equally binding on all citizens. The same is true internationally except that respect for this principle rests on a more fragile foundation, on the expectation of a reciprocity of interests rather than on the compulsion which is the final sanction of domestic law.

Discussions of international topics sometimes disclose an attitude which may be called "legalism." This attitude may be defined as the expectation that legal symbols (treaty obligations) can by themselves solve the basic and most controversial international problems regardless of power considerations and in spite of the conflicting policies of states toward the central question of the status quo. The legalistic approach to international politics is characteristic of nations which enjoy in their domestic life a general respect for law on the part not only of individuals but also of the government. It is also characteristic of those nations which are satisfied with the international status quo or, at least, do not intend to exert themselves for its modification. Their habitual respect for domestic law leads them to suppose that respect for international obligations of any kind must also be general. Those nations which are satisfied with the status quo find it convenient to think of international issues in legal terms, because law is the guardian of the status quo. A legalist is inclined to see the solution of the problem of war and peace in a general or bilateral treaty forbidding recourse to arms; since the status quo does not displease him, he is not likely to be troubled by the fact that he offers no procedures for adjusting the status quo peacefully.

The legalistic approach usually goes hand in hand with a belief in the effectiveness of international public opinion as the supreme guardian of solemn treaty obligations. It places high hopes in those political treaties which are the most precarious part of international law. A solemn political treaty provides a psychological escape from the unpleasant contemplation of harsh international realities and seems to offer an easy way out of the most dangerous situations. It is believed to have the power to exorcise international evils by the magic force of its printed words.

Legalism rests on the assumption that the most controversial international problems exist only because no one has been ingenious enough to contrive a legal solution to them. This legalistic approach to international politics diverts attention from a serious search for the solution of difficult problems and from useful debate on foreign policy to a sterile and never-ending discussion of legal contraptions which have no chance of being accepted by governments or, if accepted, of being respected. Legal formulas are useful not before but toward the end of the process of diplomatic bargaining.

The legalistic approach can give the law-abiding nation a feeling of false security. It can be persuaded that a solemn international treaty will provide it with security against evildoers. The Kellogg Pact, for example, made many Europeans feel secure behind the screen of its prohibition of all wars. The many nonaggression treaties are another example. The so-called Maginot Line mentality in prewar France was due not only to the unfinished line of fortifications of this name but also to confidence in the Treaty of Locarno, which guaranteed France against a German aggression. In 1945 the legalistic approach to international politics generated fantastically high hopes derived from the Charter and its promise of harmonious international co-operation, and the same approach later contributed to the proliferation of Western alliances with militarily weak non-European nations. The ring of mutual assistance treaties that now surrounds the Communist bloc is in large part a paper Maginot Line.

In conclusion, it can be said that international law is an effective regulating factor in international relations but that its effectiveness, which is much less than that of domestic law, varies with the subject-matter it regulates and is highly doubtful in the case of the most important political treaties.

CHAPTER IX

International Organizations

GENERAL OBSERVATIONS

No association can succeed fully unless its members share a community of purpose and are decided to make a concerted effort to achieve their stated objectives. An international association of independent states cannot escape this self-evident rule.

The origin of the League of Nations and of the United Nations, each founded in the aftermath of a world war, indicates that both organizations were formed for the same basic purpose—to maintain international peace and to promote co-operation among states. Since this is the main purpose, three conditions must be fulfilled to ensure the success of this type of universal association of states:

1. It should be as universal as possible in its membership and certainly should include all the great powers as a minimum requirement.

2. The member-states, in particular the great powers, must have the same desire to maintain the general peace of the world and the same conviction that this is the best way of serving their national interests.

3. They can work fruitfully together if they accept the basic framework of the international status quo and are therefore willing to pursue limited and moderate objectives in their foreign policies. Otherwise member-states cannot help working at cross-purposes within the international organization, and their fundamental disagreement concerning the preservation or radical transformation of the status quo must necessarily exert a paralyzing effect on the functioning of the organization.

It is paradoxical that the last two of these conditions could have been more readily fulfilled in the nineteenth century than they can in our own time. The great powers shared a desire to maintain the general peace and pursued limited objectives within the framework of the status quo. It was understood that any changes in that status quo should not seriously upset the balance of power among the great powers. None of these powers intended to transform the status quo radically or to subvert the most vital national interests of the other great powers. Their competition did not threaten the survival of other great powers as great powers. Smaller nations, at least those located in Europe, enjoyed a security which was the consequence of the moderation of great powers. Ideological crusades by governments were unknown. In spite of differences in the political regimes of the time, the governments spoke a language of common social and economic convictions, and none was interested in converting foreign peoples to its own "self-evident truths."

Actually the seeds of the future international organization were planted then and there. The European Concert of great powers was the ancestor of the League Council and of the Security Council. The larger international conferences, held with the participation of smaller states, notably the two Hague Peace Conferences (1899 and 1907), were the heralds of the League and the United Nations General Assemblies. It would not have been politically difficult to formalize these international proceedings and found a league of states. This league would not have been universal in the geographical sense because of European colonialism, but it would have included all the great powers of the time and those smaller states which were considered "civilized" according to European standards of the nineteenth century. An international organization was not founded simply because the need for it was not felt. The great powers demonstrated during these lucky hundred years their capacity for maintaining general peace. Their political moderation and their ability to reach negotiated solutions for international problems precluded the emergence of any acutely felt need for the formalization of international proceedings and the foundation of a chartered association of states.

The traumatic experience of the two world wars produced a deeply felt need for some arrangement which would offer the hope of averting a new catastrophe. The founders of the League of Nations thought that the First World War had been a temporary aberration and did not realize that 1914 marked the dividing line between two entirely different historical epochs. There was a general expectation during the years immediately following the First World War of a gradual return to the "normalcy" of the pre-1914 period. The victors, who were the founders of the League, hoped to restore this normalcy on the basis of the postwar status quo which they imposed on the vanquished. The League of Nations was to help in restoring pre-1914 normalcy by reviving the nineteenth-century methods of international intercourse in a new and formalized shape and by becoming the guardian of peace and the status quo.

People who detected in the very methods of nineteenth-century international politics one of the main causes of the First World War (hence their denunciation of the balance of power) and who enthusiastically saluted the League as the way of salvation for mankind overlooked the fact that the outbreak of the general war in 1914 was due, among other causes, to the breakdown of the mechanism of the balance of power. This mechanism could no longer function satisfactorily after the great powers had coalesced into hostile blocs and had proved unable to find working compromises for the reconciliation of their growing and incompatible ambitions. The severe critics of the balance of power founded their hope for peace on the formalization of international proceedings and were sure that the new mechanism would work better than the old one without asking themselves whether any mechanism of international intercourse could function properly if the great powers, supposed to manipulate the mechanism, were at odds.

The League of Nations failed for two reasons. First, it never became a universal organization because it did not convene all the great powers. The United States was never a member; Germany, Russia, Japan, and Italy participated for periods and not always for the same periods. Hence, many important political transactions, involving the great powers who were nonmembers, had to be carried on outside Geneva. Moreover, political agreements arrived at in Geneva had a precarious future because their viability had to be measured by the intentions and actions of the nonparticipating great powers.

Secondly, the great powers were split, throughout the history of the League, into those who accepted the postwar status quo and those who rejected it. Germany, Japan, Italy, and Russia felt, for different reasons, unhappy about the peace settlements of 1919-20. This conflict among the great powers was aggravated by the new international phenomenon of acute divergencies in ideological outlook. The totalitarian ideologies of Germany, Italy, and Soviet Russia hindered these three nations in reaching diplomatic accommodations with the democratic Western powers. Soviet Russia and Nazi Germany believed that they had a historical mission to convert mankind to their concepts of a better future. Only two great powers, Britain and France, remained members throughout the whole period of the League, but their actions were poorly co-ordinated and their combined power was insufficient to ensure the survival of the League.

The League was practically dead by the outbreak of the Second World War. It failed in its original mission to maintain general peace. Revulsion from the horrors of the Second World War produced a new version of the international organization, the United Nations. The conflict between the great powers has so far prevented this new association from having a much happier history than its predecessor. The basic aim remains the same: to maintain international peace and promote international co-operation.

The United Nations is luckier than the League in two respects. First, it is closer to being a universal organization. However, two important nations are not represented. No one in his senses would claim that the Nationalist government speaks for the Chinese mainland while the Communist government controls its resources, or would deny that Western Germany, though truncated, is a regional great power. Yet their voices are not heard in the United Nations.

Secondly, all nations, including the great powers, members or non-members, have at least one interest in common, namely to avoid the outbreak of a general nuclear war. The fear of a nuclear catastrophe does not, however, preclude fundamental conflicts among the great powers; it merely compels them to use non-nuclear means in their bitter competition.

The United Nations, like the League, is not a super-state which can formulate policies binding on its members and enforce its decisions on recalcitrant states. It is only an association of independent states, each formulating its own policy. An association of states cannot achieve more than the member-states, in particular the great powers, are willing to do. This basic truth is sometimes forgotten. Individuals and at times even the governments gloss over the fact that the United Nations cannot act independently of its members. To submit a matter to the United Nations is not to refer it to an organization which can settle problems otherwise unsolvable for the member-states. It is merely to transfer the negotiations from the diplomatic chanceries to another forum where the same protagonists are to be found.

THE THREE STAGES IN THE HISTORY OF THE UNITED NATIONS

The United Nations has passed so far through three stages in its history. Its founders believed that the political governance of the world should rest in the hands of the great powers, permanent members of the Security Council. The Council was to become the principal organ of the new association of states. It was politically wise to condition all the substantive decisions of the Security Council on the unanimous agreement of its permanent members. A decision adopted by the majority of permanent members would not have much meaning if stiffly opposed by one of them, especially regarding matters of general concern or problems pertaining to the sphere of influence of that member. The veto power of permanent members of the Council was a necessary and realistic arrangement. It certainly was not the cause of the paralysis of the Security Council. The true reason for the stalemate was the fundamental disagreement among the permanent members and their inability to work out compromise solutions.

This paralysis of the Security Council ushered in the second stage in the history of the United Nations, a stage distinguished by the growing political significance of the General Assembly. The Uniting for Peace Resolution of 1950 transferred the main political role from the Security Council to the General Assembly. The growing importance of the General Assembly mirrored a situation in which the great powers could not agree among themselves and vied for the sympathies of the smaller countries. The emerging triangular shape of international relations, created by competition between the two blocs for the support of the underdeveloped countries, further buttressed the prestige of the Assembly, where the underdeveloped countries were fully represented. The General Assembly became the forum for the political battles between the two rival blocs, battles which were staged mainly for the benefit of the underdeveloped peoples. Its constantly increasing membership made the General Assembly truly representative of the governments of almost all independent countries. Taking into account the absence of Communist China and of the divided nations, such as Germany, Vietnam, and Korea, it can be said that the General Assembly gathers together the delegates of countries which form three-fourths of the population of the world.

With the admission of several new members to the United Nations, the Western powers could no longer be sure of a two-thirds majority for any resolution they wanted to sponsor. Now neither bloc can be certain which way the two-thirds majority will vote and even less certain whether a resolution will be blocked by the one-third-plus-one-vote minority. This collective veto can assert itself only if several underdeveloped countries vote against a resolution. Lack of agreement between the great powers has given the underdeveloped countries a vicarious power which, within the United Nations, is displayed in the General Assembly. Since it is vicarious, this power is divorced from the reality of the international distribution of material power, especially military power.

Here lies the weakness of the General Assembly. The underdeveloped countries, if they combined and were unwise enough to overlook international realities, could pass a resolution equally unacceptable to all great powers. This prospect is purely academic because the underdeveloped countries could hardly overcome pressure from the great powers and challenge all of them at the same time and also because they are divided among themselves. But this theoretical possibility dramatizes the divorce between the voting potential of the General Assembly and the international distribution of actual power.

What is not theoretical is the need for the two blocs to argue their cases before an audience which in its majority is composed of the underdeveloped countries and to win as many of their votes as possible. Thus the underdeveloped countries have risen to a dominant position in the General Assembly. Yet the actual reality of the distribution of power cannot be voted away. The great powers remain the great powers. By their pressure and maneuvering they split the front of the underdeveloped countries.

The present enlarged membership and the rivalry between the great powers make it uncertain whether a resolution on an important matter will be supported by the required majority of two-thirds. If this majority cannot be otherwise ensured, the resolution must be watered down to become almost meaningless. A controversial resolution adopted by the votes of one of the two rival blocs and of a sufficient number of underdeveloped countries cannot be enforced if its implementation requires the co-operation of the other bloc. In any area which is accessible to both blocs a meaningful resolution of the General Assembly would require the support of one bloc and at least the abstention of the other bloc; otherwise it would remain a dead letter. The Near East is such an area. In areas where one bloc has a preponderant or exclusive influence a resolution would be meaningless if adopted against the votes of that bloc. The Hungarian affair in 1956 clearly demonstrated this truth. Geography indicates that resolutions relating to Latin America or Tropical Africa would have no better chance of enforcement if adopted against the stiff opposition of the Western bloc, which has easy access to these areas and could take effective action to prevent enforcement. The policy in the Congo which the Communist bloc favored, even if supported by a two-thirds majority in the General Assembly, would have failed because the West had the military capacity to prevent the enforcement of resolutions to which it was adamantly opposed. If the Western powers had submitted the problem of Laos to the General Assembly, they could perhaps have obtained the passage of resolutions satisfactory from their point of view (even this was far from certain), but these resolutions would have been in fact annulled by the actions which Russia, China, and North Vietnam were capable of taking in the Indochinese peninsula. This was probably why the Western powers preferred to negotiate a settlement directly with the Communist powers at a conference held outside the United Nations and unaffected by the votes of the General Assembly.

Since the underdeveloped countries play a role incommensurate with their actual power, the transfer of the center of political gravity from the Security Council to the General Assembly has not enhanced the political effectiveness of the United Nations. Its inherent weakness, due to the discord between the great powers, has not been thereby remedied but only confused by the noisy debates of the General Assembly.

The General Assembly was at times unable to give clear instructions to the Secretary General on the controversial issue of the Congo, its members being split into several groups. Even the African states did not take a unified stand, divided as they were by their own rivalries and by their different concepts of African welfare. The Near Eastern crisis of 1956 and the Congo affair in the 1960's introduced the third stage in the history of the United Nations, a stage characterized by executive actions undertaken largely on the authority of the Secretary General. This stage cannot last forever because it lacks any power foundation. It cannot be expected that the political effectiveness of the United Nations will be provided by the efforts of one individual, however sincere and devoted he may be, while neither the great powers nor the General Assembly are able or willing to give him full support. No individual can for long perform miracles of this kind on behalf of an association which is, after all, an association of states, not of individuals. The enhanced responsibility of the Secretary General is a symptom of the crisis of the United Nations rather than a remedy for this crisis.

THE SECRETARY GENERAL

The Secretary General of the League of Nations was its chief administrative officer who had no right to assume political initiatives publicly. He ensured the smooth working of the executive machinery of the Secretariat, a heavy duty in itself, and if he were a man of great stature, as Sir Eric Drummond was, he acted as a behind-the-scenes mediator whose discreet activities were appreciated by the member-states. Having no right to take any public initiative of a political nature, he was never in danger of sticking his head out and being caught in a whirlwind of conflicting national interests. The situation was clear. Since the League was an association of states, only a state had the right to initiate action by the League and a state had to assume the responsibility for doing so.

The Secretary General of the United Nations is placed in an infinitely more difficult position. Article 99 of the Charter empowers the Secretary General to ". . . bring to the attention of the Security Council any matter which in his opinion may threaten the maintenance of international peace and security." This Article gives him a right, but it also burdens him with a heavy duty. It says by implication that if no state wants to bring to the attention of the United Nations a matter which may threaten the maintenance of international peace and security and if, therefore, this matter is of a highly delicate or grave nature, the Secretary General is expected to do so on his own responsibility. Moreover, the conflict between the great powers catapulted him into a position of responsibility which had not been foreseen when the Charter was drafted. He was forced by events to make decisions, for instance in the Congolese situation, largely on his own responsibility in the absence of clear instructions either from the Security Council or from the General Assembly. The perennial crisis of the United Nations, occasioned by the radically different views of its members, placed an unusually heavy burden on the shoulders of the Secretary General. How long can an association of states function on the basis of this subterfuge?

If the individual holding this post chose to remain as inconspicuous as possible, the subterfuge would not work for long. Such an individual would prefer to follow in the footsteps of the Secretaries General of the League and would refuse to assume any political initiative publicly; he would carry out executive actions only if given clear instructions by the Security Council or the General Assembly. His tenure of office would be longer and personally less trying. His public effacement would enable him to act privately as a discreet mediator behind the scenes, because no member-state would have any strong reason for resenting his activities or for distrusting him. His main job would be to head the administration of the Secretariat. He would be open to the criticism of neglecting his duties under Article 99. But he could retort that no individual can be expected to perform tasks on his own responsibility which neither the Security Council nor the General Assembly is able to define in clear terms.

The first two Secretaries General of the United Nations chose the harder road and did not hesitate to state their views publicly on matters which deeply divided the great powers and other member-states. The frequently inconclusive nature of the deliberations on the Congo in the General Assembly induced the second Secretary General to assume responsibility personally for executive decisions of a highly political character. The present Secretary General follows in the footsteps of his predecessors; however, he has been more cautious in assuming the political responsibilities of his office. His political actions have been carefully planned in order to have the support of the majority but also not to alienate either of the two principal powers, the United States and the Soviet Union.

Whatever the Secretary General does on his own places him closer to one rival bloc than to the other. It is more probable that he will find himself in conflict with the Communist bloc. The Secretary General who takes a political initiative is compelled by the letter and the spirit of the Charter to seek the consolidation or restoration of order in international affairs as a guarantee of general peace. The Communist bloc, opposed on principle to the status quo, may consider that a certain amount of international disorder helps in the transformation of this status quo. Secretary General Hammarskjöld remained faithful to the concept of an orderly and peaceful international community in his persistent efforts to ensure the internal stability of the Congo. His policy highly displeased the Soviet Union but had the support of the Western powers insofar as it prevented an upheaval in Central Africa and thus kept the door closed to a broad Soviet infiltration. Different concepts of what the international community should be resulted in a head-on collision between him and the Soviet Union.

Although it is more probable that a Secretary General who assumes political initiatives on his own responsibility is going to alienate Soviet sympathy, it is far from certain that he will never run afoul of the

Western powers. Mr. Lie learned this in 1950 when he favored the seating of the Chinese Communist delegation. Neither Mr. Hammarskjöld nor Mr. Thant gained popularity in influential circles in Great Britain, France, Belgium, Southern Rhodesia, Portugal, or South Africa, when they tried to bring about the reintegration of the Katanga within a unified Congo by direct military action of the United Nations. This aspect of their Congolese policy did not evoke enthusiasm in several Western countries but was the only one that pleased the Soviet Union. The very existence of the conflict between the two blocs might lead the Secretary General, if he formulates his own policies on highly controversial issues, into a situation where he will antagonize one or the other bloc.

The Soviet Premier said in 1961 that countries could be neutral but that there were no neutral individuals. There is a grain of truth in this statement. Any individual is the product of his environment and holds certain truths to be "self-evident," usually the truths of his cultural environment. A Westerner acting as Secretary General may struggle to take a detached view of current international controversies and should do so, but he cannot help sharing the Western "self-evident truths." This in itself makes him suspect in Communist eyes. In 1961 the Soviet Premier used a rather pertinent argument against a Westerner always being the Secretary General; he asked the rhetorical question whether the citizen of a Communist country would be acceptable to the West as the holder of the same post.

The fact that individuals can never achieve perfect neutrality is one of the reasons why the Soviet Union proposed to replace the single Secretary General with a "troika" of three Secretaries General, one representing the West, a second the Communist bloc, and a third the underdeveloped countries. The other reason was also self-evident. This "troika" could do nothing without the agreement of all three Secretaries, each holding the power of veto. The Soviet Union would be protected against any action by the Secretary General which it would disapprove of. The replacement of the single Secretary General by a three-man directorate would require an amendment of the Charter and could not be accomplished without Western assent. The West and the Soviet Union cannot impose on each other a candidate for the post of the single Secretary General whom the other party is unwilling to accept.

The appointment of Mr. Thant is symptomatic of this situation; it was the only way out of the impasse. The Soviet Union knew that its proposal for a "troika" had no chance of being accepted. The West could not compel the Soviet Union to approve another Westerner as Secretary General. The choice of a citizen from an uncommitted Asian country was the only solution acceptable to both antagonists. Mr. Thant's appointment creates a precedent; in all probability his successors will also be citizens from the uncommitted countries of Asia or Africa.

It is a vain expectation that the officials who form the Secretariat of the United Nations, who are of various nationalities, could shed their national loyalties altogether and suddenly acquire on the day of their appointment a new supreme allegiance to the international organization. They all know that their international careers will not be eternal and that the day will come when they will go back to their respective countries. Many of them know that their government expects them to remain, first of all, its own agents within the international organization; they can hardly resist this pressure for fear of unpleasant consequences on returning home after the end of their contract with the United Nations. Many who are not subject to this pressure will certainly do their best to serve only the United Nations and to leave the protection of the national interests to their respective governmental delegations. But they cannot repudiate the "self-evident truths" which they share with their nationality, and these truths will influence their actions as international civil servants. Moreover, they are liable to powerful emotional stress in any serious emergency involving their own country. Would they be capable of remaining scrupulously faithful to the policy of the United Nations if they discovered an irreconcilable conflict between this policy and the most vital interests of their own country?

As a matter of fact, allegiance to the United Nations is itself subject to various interpretations; any two individuals can honestly disagree on which of several possible courses corresponds most closely to the basic purposes of the United Nations. An international official may well be inclined, perhaps unconsciously, to favor the course which his own country prefers.

The Secretariat is not an administration analogous to the national civil service whose functionaries are bound together by the same supreme loyalty. It is a body of officials with various and often conflicting national loyalties; at best, they may be expected to try to prevent a conflict between their national loyalties and their international duties. The international character of the Secretariat is guaranteed by its multinational composition, which brings about an approximate balance among the national inclinations of its members.

COLLECTIVE SECURITY

During the short existence of the League of Nations the issue of peace was usually subdivided into three interrelated problems: collective security, the peaceful settlement of international disputes, and the limitation of armaments. The main political tasks of the United Nations can usefully be discussed under the same three headings.

The concept of collective security was born out of domestic and international experiences. Domestically, it was clear that an individual or a group of individuals who disturbed the public peace could be effectively checked by the overwhelmingly superior power of the state; this superior power also acted as a deterrent against the commission of crimes. Internationally, the operation of the balance of power seemed to offer a clue to the problem of peace. A power bent on an ambitious expansion could be either deterred or defeated by the coalition of other powers. The cases of Louis XIV, Napoleon, William II, and Hitler were used as illustrations of this principle. The concept of collective security was a practical deduction from these domestic and international facts. Why not apply the superior power of all other states against the nation that breaks the peace, just as the superior power of the state is applied against the individual criminal? Why not institutionalize the ephemeral coalitions formed for a period of emergency and found a permanent coalition of states which would be ready to act against any state which in the future committed an act of aggression? This permanent coalition of states would presumably represent an overwhelming force and its very existence would perhaps suffice to deter the prospective aggressor.

This attractive concept is founded on several misconceptions. First, it assumes that all the member-states prefer the status quo to its modification by force. This assumption is obviously untrue in any historical period. Even now, when states are unwilling to face the risks of a nuclear war, a limited use of force is not only possible but has occurred several times since the foundation of the United Nations. It may be a peripheral and non-nuclear war or a civil war in which foreign powers interfere, but whatever the particular form of the use of force, at least one of the contending parties is motivated by its dissatisfaction with the status quo.

Secondly, if the member-states could not agree at all times on the justice or expediency of upholding the status quo, they could still condemn the use of force for its modification if they had at their disposal an effective international procedure for changing it peacefully. But there is no such procedure in existence. Those states which find the status quo unjust or which are uncertain whether it is just cannot be expected to condemn outright the use of force if there is no other effective way of changing the status quo.

Thirdly, the theory of collective security assumes that the member-states agree on what constitutes an aggression which calls for collective sanctions. So far, all attempts to define aggression *in abstracto* have failed although this problem has preoccupied in turn the League and the United Nations. May aggression be defined merely as the commencement of hostilities? This definition would usually be satisfactory but not always. Let us assume that a state takes an action which is not an armed attack but which nevertheless threatens the most vital interests of another state. The military reoccupation of the Rhineland by German troops in March,

1936, was certainly a most serious challenge to the security of the Western powers. The fortifications built there later effectively paralyzed France by discouraging it from offensive military operations and helped to destroy the effectiveness of its alliances in Eastern Europe. Would France have been an aggressor if in 1936 it had ordered its troops into the Rhineland? Would the Western powers have become aggressors in 1948 if they had responded to the Soviet blockade by sending an armed convoy to Berlin? If one state deprives another of access to sources of water or to fuel resources indispensable to the survival of its economy and if no international procedure offers an effective remedy, should the threatened state have no alternative to the choice between denunciation as an aggressor and economic strangulation?

The problem of aggression cannot be reduced to the simple proposition that a state which initiates open military hostilities is necessarily an aggressor. There are other forms of aggression which can be termed indirect. Military aid provided to a party engaged in a civil war against the established government, or any action calculated to deprive a state of vital supplies, are forms of indirect aggression which may have no less serious effects than a direct and open military attack. The Charter oversimplified the problem by outlawing any use of force or any threat of its use except in individual or collective self-defense against an armed attack (see also Chapter 8).

Moreover, a state which intends to begin military hostilities usually takes care to accuse its victim of having started the war. This was done in 1939 by Germany in its armed attack on Poland and by the U.S.S.R. in its armed action against Finland. In 1950 the Communist bloc accused South Korea of having attacked North Korea. Future claims of this sort may seem more plausible and result in a great amount of confusion. At any rate, those member-states of the United Nations who are not eager to participate in a collective action will justify their inactivity by pleading that they are unable to identify the true aggressor.

Finally, the national interests of the members of a temporary coalition coincide because all these members feel that the same enemy threatens their existence. But the member-states of a permanent coalition like the United Nations cannot be sure that they will all have the same vital interest in checking a future aggressor. To make such certainty possible, international solidarity would have to attain the intensity of national loyalties. The growing trend toward the policy of noncommitment points in the opposite direction; an uncommitted state intends to disengage itself in advance from any obligations which could involve it in a military struggle between other states. The policy of noncommitment contradicts the very concept of collective security.

The prospect of collective action against the aggressor raises the problem of the risks which would face the participating states. If a small nation were to attack another small nation, and the two rival blocs were, against all probability, not greatly interested in the outcome of this local conflict, the collective action could be easily undertaken but would hardly be necessary. The pressure by the great powers, for once in agreement, would suffice to restore peace. This was proved during the Near Eastern crisis of 1956. If the combined pressure of the two nuclear powers, the United States and the Soviet Union, supported by other members of the United Nations, compelled two great powers, Britain and France, to desist from their armed action against Egypt, how much more effective would this pressure be in a case involving two small protagonists? How probable is it, however, that this situation, where the two nuclear powers co-operated, will arise again?

It is more probable that the armed action which threatens collective security will be undertaken by a great power or by a small nation shielded by a great power. If a nuclear great power were directly involved, the collective action would be no less than the beginning of a third world war. If the same power decided to give indirect support to a small nation, its ally or friend, collective action could escalate into a third world war. This risk was feared by several member-states during the Korean War.

Collective action assumes the willingness of member-states always to form a united front against any aggressor, however powerful it may be. However, the governments of member-states cannot be reasonably expected to assume unlimited risks under any and all future circumstances. Britain and France refused to endorse effective sanctions against Italy in 1935-36 for fear of a war with the country guilty of aggression against Ethiopia. The United Nations General Assembly passed on October 7, 1950, an ambitious resolution which defined the aim of its collective action as follows: ". . . the establishment of a unified, independent and democratic government of the sovereign state of Korea." At that time the American and South Korean troops were successfully advancing toward the northern border of the country. After the Chinese military intervention in December of the same year the political purpose of collective action was modified in the light of the Western setbacks and limited to the restoration of the *ante-bellum* status of a Korea divided along the 38th parallel. In 1956 the General Assembly did not consider the question of sanctions against Britain, France, and Israel, because the United States and other friends of these three states did not allow it. It did not dare in the same year to envisage the prospect of sanctions against the U.S.S.R. because this reaction to the Soviet military aggression against Hungary could have meant the beginning of the third world war. In other words, member-states carefully calculate the risks involved in each particular case from the point of view of their own national security. The nuclear risks make this calculation even more circumspect than it was at the time of the League of Nations.

If a great power, a permanent member of the Security Council, were directly or indirectly involved in an armed action, its veto would prevent the Council from adopting any valid resolution. The Uniting for Peace Resolution intended to provide a solution by transferring the matter to the General Assembly. It is ironical that this resolution was adopted at the Western initiative and over the vociferous opposition of the Soviet Union. The Western powers were at that time convinced that the General Assembly would always be docile and responsive to Western wishes and that a collective action would be authorized by the Assembly in spite of the Soviet veto in the Security Council. This calculation explains the Soviet opposition. Yet the same resolution was turned against two Western powers, Britain and France, in November, 1956, and the Soviet Union was only too glad to co-operate in the General Assembly after the British and French vetoes had been cast in the Security Council. The present composition of the General Assembly makes it uncertain against whom the same resolution could be turned the next time; in any event, this resolution has ceased to be a Western weapon exclusively. If the case of an aggression were now submitted to the General Assembly, its members would be split up into three groups: two groups committed to either of the rival blocs and the third group composed of states wishing to stay aloof without incurring the wrath of either bloc. The combined votes of one of the blocs and the states which would prefer not to take sides might result in a collective veto which would preclude the passage of any valid resolution by the required two-thirds majority.

The peace of the world depends in the last analysis on the great powers. If they want to stop an aggression for fear of being involved themselves, their joint action would suffice and the collective sanctions would hardly be required. If they did not stop on the brink of disaster, collective action would not rescue mankind from destruction.

Even in the case of a local conflict which does not involve the immediate risk of an armed clash between the great powers, the member-states are apt to react differently depending on their estimation of the significance of the conflict for their own national interests. A state remote from the area of conflict, for example, might not wish to participate in a collective action to defend a distant member if this participation could antagonize one or the other power bloc.

The history of collective security in the League of Nations and in the United Nations is not encouraging. Immediately after the formation of the League several of its members succeeded in diluting Articles 10 and 16 of the Covenant which together provided for collective action in the defense of the political independence and territorial integrity of member-states. They wanted to limit their future liabilities and reserve for themselves the ultimate decision in each particular case. Some of them were doubtful of the merits of the postwar status quo and did not feel that they should defend it against an armed attack. Mild economic and financial sanctions were applied in 1935-36 against Italy after its open aggression against Ethiopia. They were intentionally ineffective and were meant as a means of pressure, not as an attempt to break the military might of Italy. Effective sanctions (an embargo on oil or the closure of the Suez Canal) were deliberately avoided because they could have involved Britain and France in armed hostilities with Italy. These two great powers, which had a decisive influence on the policies of the League, were uncertain about the best course to follow. On the one hand, they pressured the other members of the League into adopting mild sanctions in the hope that Italy would retreat. On the other hand, they feared that the sanctions would drive Italy into the arms of Nazi Germany. After the adoption of sanctions Britain and France secretly engaged in negotiations with the Italian aggressor and reached an agreement which amounted to a hardly concealed surrender of Ethiopia to Italy. The outcry of public opinion in Britain prevented this agreement, called Hoare-Laval Agreement after the names of the chief Western negotiators, from entering into force. But its conclusion made a farce of the sanctions, and other member-states lost interest in enforcing them. The net result of this unlucky venture in collective security was the repeal of sanctions, the conquest of Ethiopia, and the German-Italian alliance. The machinery of sanctions could not make up for the absence of any clear policy on the part of Britain and France. These two powers neither taught a telling lesson to all prospective aggressors by forcing Italy to its knees nor dissuaded it from joining Germany by condoning its conquest of Ethiopia. Both the League and the two powers paid with the loss of prestige.

The League, already moribund, applied the sanction of expulsion against the Soviet Union after its attack on Finland. By that time (December, 1939) no country considered membership in the League especially important. In any case, the expulsion of the U.S.S.R. did not help Finland, which was compelled a few months later to conclude the peace of the vanquished. Britain, which together with France promoted the adoption of this sanction, was only too glad two years later to hail the Soviet Union as its "gallant ally."

The collective action in Korea seems to offer an entirely different lesson. But the success of this collective action does not vindicate the concept of collective security. The United Nations had at that time its own investigating commission in South Korea, which immediately certified the fact of an unprovoked North Korean aggression. The fact of aggression was not liable to any honest disagreement. The only great power which was both interested in maintaining the status quo in Korea and had its own armed forces in the immediate vicinity, the United States, immediately reversed its former policy according to which Korea was not included within the American perimeter of defense. This was the decisive event. If the United States had continued to abide by its former view, South Korea would probably have been overrun in a few days and the United Nations would have registered the accomplished fact in an indignant resolution condemning the successful aggressor. The Soviet Union, which supported North Korea, was at that time boycotting the meetings of the United Nations in protest against its refusal to accept the credentials of the Chinese Communist delegation. Its delegate did not attend the crucial initial meetings of the Security Council, which was thereby able to pass its resolutions without fear of invalidation by the Soviet veto. After the Soviet Union had revised its tactics and its representative reappeared at the Security Council, the Uniting for Peace Resolution made it possible to shift the matter to the General Assembly, where the Western powers were at that time sure of controlling a two-thirds majority.

However, the whole operation was basically an American and South Korean venture. Only sixteen out of the then sixty members participated with their armed forces in the "collective" action. Thirty members made nonmilitary contributions such as food, clothing, hospital units, and transport facilities. Twenty members did not take part at all. Ninety per cent of the land forces was composed of either Americans (50 per cent of the total) or South Koreans trained and equipped by the United States (40 per cent of the total). Ninety per cent of the air and sea power was supplied by the United States. The so-called United Nations Command in Korea, which directed the military operations, was in fact the United States Far Eastern Command. The military outcome of the action would have been the same had there been no United Nations but if the United States had taken the same military measures with or without the support of allied states. On balance, it can be said that the use of the United Nations flag for a basically American action had one advantage and one disadvantage. The advantage was psychological. The American action could not be termed a unilateral intervention in Korea but acquired the character of a vindication of the principles of the Charter. This was no mean asset in our era of Asian suspicions of Western imperialism. But since the American action was taking place under the flag of the United Nations, the other member-states acquired the right to control the American activities carried on in their name. For better or worse, they tried, after the Chinese intervention, to restrain the United States for fear of extending the conflict. The American armed forces had to fight in Korea under the handicap of respecting the Chinese territory, the strategic base of their main enemy, the Chinese divisions. The result was a stalemate which did not reflect at all the true relation of forces between the United States and China.

The particular circumstances of the Korean War cannot be reproduced in the future. First, the risk for the United States would be much greater now than in 1950; the American nuclear monopoly has since been replaced by a nuclear parity with the Soviet Union. Secondly, the Soviet delegate would certainly veto any resolution in the Security Council. Thirdly, the increased membership in the General Assembly could make the Uniting for Peace Resolution inoperative if the West were unable to muster a two-thirds majority for its proposals.

The ineffectiveness of collective security in a world divided by the hostility of two rival blocs compelled the member-states to adopt either of the following two policies. The first policy had recourse to the old system of alliances. The Western powers surrounded themselves with regional pacts (the Rio de Janeiro Treaty, NATO, the Baghdad or CENTO Pact, and SEATO) and with tripartite or bilateral treaties of mutual assistance. The Communist states followed the same policy (the Warsaw Regional Treaty and a network of bilateral alliances concluded by the Soviet Union with China, Mongolia, North Korea, and its Eastern European friends). The other policy is that of noncommitment, which the third group of states chose as a shield against involvement in the military and political conflicts between the two enemy coalitions. Both policies prove how little faith the member-states have in the collective security of the United Nations. As a matter of fact, the founders of the organization were not much more optimistic. They knew that collective security, as understood at that time, depended on the Security Council whose initiatives could be blocked by any one of the permanent members. They demonstrated their scepticism by inserting in the Charter Article 51 which conceded to the members not only the right of individual self-defense in case of an armed attack against them but also the right of collective self-defense, which meant that each member of the United Nations had the right to use force in order to assist another member against an armed attack. The right of collective self-defense entailed the additional right of the members to conclude alliances which would later protect them in case collective security failed.

It is important not to confuse the problem of collective security with executive actions by the United Nations or to confuse the concept of an international army with that of a United Nations policing task force. Collective security is a system whereby the members of an international organization undertake to participate in military and/or other sanctions (for instance, economic and financial) against a state whose aggression they wish to check. If military sanctions alone will force an aggressor to obey the injunctions of the organization, collective action becomes in fact a war jointly waged by the member-states against the recalcitrant nation.

An international army would be a contingent of armed forces always on the alert to undertake a coercive action against any aggressor. It would form a truly international force fully separated from the national armed forces, completely integrated, and placed under the exclusive command of the United Nations. To be effective it would have to be drastically more powerful than the armed forces of any single great power. For instance, it should have a monopoly of nuclear weapons. This concept is unrealistic in our time because it requires the fulfillment of several preconditions which cannot be met. The member-states would have to relinquish to the international organization ultimate control over their policies. The organization itself would have to be transformed into a super-state, and the present national states would have to be downgraded to the position of several units of a federal world state. The commanders and members of the international army would have to possess supreme loyalty to the international organization, and be ready to fight against their own countrymen if they revolted against the orders of this world state. The high command of the international army would need to have its military tasks defined by a superior political body; hence an international army is inconceivable without a world government that would formulate the policies which the army would have to uphold. One can hardly imagine a world government and an international army composed of Communists, democrats, and Fascists, all of them expected to act in the general interest of mankind while unable to agree on what that interest is.

The United Nations police forces in the Near East and the Congo have nothing in common with this unrealistic dream. Their task is not to apply military sanctions against a state guilty of aggression but to perform certain policing functions with the consent of the states directly concerned. These policing functions serve the following purposes among others: to allow states engaged in hostilities to interrupt them without losing face and to disengage their troops after the interposition of United Nations military units; to safeguard the observance of an armistice by keeping watch over the armistice line; to prevent or to stop a local or a civil war by interposing international detachments between the contending parties; to police a territory threatened with chaos and to help the state in question to restore public order; to control a territory where an international plebiscite is to be held.

The United Nations Emergency Force allowed Britain and France to save face, because their withdrawal from Egypt was staged as a process of handing over the Egyptian territory occupied by their troops not to the Egyptians but to the United Nations contingents. But Britain and France were not forced by these contingents to withdraw; the decision was reached by the two powers for other reasons. The Israeli withdrawal in the same year of 1956 was also due to reasons unrelated to any action by the U.N.E.F.; Israel was not the object of any collective sanctions. Only after the Israeli decision to retreat from Egyptian territory and after obtaining Egyptian assent, could the U.N.E.F. be interposed between the two enemy armies and entrusted with the mission of controlling the observance of the truce. In all these cases the U.N.E.F. acted with the preliminary assent of the states concerned. The U.N.E.F. was not an international army sent to the Near East to fight an aggressor but a police detachment dispatched to perform certain functions with the agreement of the states directly involved.

The sending of military units to the Congo followed the request by the Congolese government of the time. Their task has been to maintain a minimum of public order in a territory bordering on chaos. Moreover, the United Nations has been compelled, by the progressive disintegration of the Congolese public authority, to assume certain governmental functions which normally would have been beyond the jurisdiction of the international organization. If the Congolese were able to restore an effective national government and requested the United Nations to withdraw, this request could not be ignored. In any case, the military units of the United Nations are in the Congo not to fight an aggressor but to police the territory. The three armed actions undertaken by the United Nations military contingents against the separatist government of Katanga (September and December, 1961, and January, 1963) were considered police actions by the majority of the member-states for whom the extension of the authority of the central Congolese government to the Katanga entailed the strengthening of public order in the Congo. Only a minority of member-states, those who had an interest in preserving the independent existence of the separatist province, felt that the Secretariat of the United Nations was engaged in fighting its own war against an independent state.

The police force of the United Nations is composed of distinct military contingents supplied by the various members of the organization and unified under one command organized by the United Nations. Each contingent obeys this international command by the order of its own government and can be withdrawn at any time by the same government, as actually happened in the Congo. The members of this police force have not abandoned their supreme allegiance to their respective states but accept the orders of the international organization only because so commanded by their governments in the name of their national loyalty. The United Nations police force is not an international army.

The executive actions of the United Nations in both the Near East and the Congo included the tasks which normally would be performed by the national administration. The United Nations, for instance, undertook the mission of clearing the Suez Canal, which had been blocked and damaged during the 1956 hostilities. The collapse of an effective public administration in the Congo compelled the United Nations to perform certain administrative functions which normally would exceed the jurisdiction of the organization. These types of executive actions bear no relation to the mechanism of collective security but rather are akin to technical assistance.

PEACEFUL SETTLEMENT OF DISPUTES

The problem of peace cannot be reduced to a negative restatement of the same proposition: the prevention of war and of the use of force. Force has been used in international relations, not for the wicked pleasure of killing and maiming people, but as the ultimate means for achieving political objectives and settling inter-state conflicts. This is why Clausewitz could say that war is the continuation of politics by other means. The outlawing of force would have the prospect of success in either of the following two situations. First, the states might not feel strongly enough about their mutual disputes or might pursue limited objectives which could be reached by political compromises; they would then have no incentive for assuming the risks of the use of force. This is not the temper of present-day governments, whose conflicts of interests are aggravated by the quasi-religious ideological warfare. Secondly, it is possible to imagine an international organization which would provide truly effective international procedures for the settlement of international disputes, procedures which would make the use of force unnecessary. The political moderation of states would nevertheless remain the condition of a successful functioning of these international procedures. However, the mechanism of the United Nations does not offer any effective procedures for settling all or at least the most important international disputes. The procedure is effective if the party to any dispute can be sued before courts or equivalent institutions without the need to obtain its consent and if the decision can be enforced on the recalcitrant party in spite of its resistance. The international situation is altogether different:

1. The legal framework of the international community is far from complete and sometimes does not provide a generally accepted rule that would be pertinent for a particular controversy (for instance, have the two nuclear powers an unlimited right to use outer space for their experiments, or should the other states have some restraining right?).

2. No state is legally bound to submit any dispute to the International Court of Justice or to an arbitral tribunal.

3. A dispute which involves the claim by one party to a change in the existing law cannot be settled by an international legislature, which does not exist.

4. There is no superior coercive power which could compel states to follow any procedure of peaceful settlement and to abide by an international decision.

5. While states cannot be forced to seek a peaceful settlement of

their disputes, they often have an interest in avoiding any settlement. An unresolved dispute might provide handy propaganda arguments for blaming the other party for the tension existing between the two states if the tension itself is a part of the general policy directed against the other state. By keeping several disputes open, a state may be able to gain wider room for diplomatic maneuvering and for over-all bargaining with another state; the intention in this case is to settle all the pending disputes in one package deal. The policy of keeping several disputes unresolved might pursue another objective: it might prevent the opponent from concentrating his attention on one issue and force him to divide his attention among several neuralgic points. A state which possesses the object of the dispute (for instance, a contested territory or nationalized foreign assets) and which does not fear countermeasures by the other party has no interest in seeking a settlement if it does not mind the friction that an open dispute is causing.

6. The power of the parties to a dispute plays a minor role in the national courts. It is true that a powerful individual or corporation has various means of pressure which might dissuade a weak opponent from submitting his claim to the courts; legal advice is more readily available to the rich than to the poor, and in a corrupt society the judge himself might not be inaccessible to bribes. Yet the principle of equality before the law retains its basic significance in every modern society. This same does not hold true in international affairs. The identity of the parties to a dispute is as important as the object of their dispute. The disparity in their relative power has no effect on the International Court of Justice or an arbitral tribunal, but a powerful party can decline to submit the case to adjudication and instead obtain the settlement on its own terms by applying pressure to the opposite party. The superior power of one party frequently inclines the third states to attach greater weight to its arguments, however weak, than to the stronger arguments of the weaker party. The same type of dispute between the United States and Nicaragua and between the United States and the Soviet Union is not, politically, the same type of dispute. The similarity or even the identity of the subject-matter of the two disputes is blurred by the factor of power. A powerful state has an incomparably greater latitude in using nonlegal means of pressure on the weaker party than a powerful individual has in a modern society. Short of war, the strong state can wrest a favorable settlement by trade discrimination, by refusing access to its financial market, by freezing the assets of the other party, by a limited use of force, such as a naval blockade, and so forth. Its last argument might be the full-scale use of force.

If they wish, states may avail themselves of the following procedures for the settlement of their disputes:

1. *Diplomatic negotiation* between the states which are parties to the

dispute. This is the most usual manner of finding a compromise solution agreeable to both parties. The procedure consists in a give-and-take bargaining.

2. *Good offices.* A third state may offer to the parties its friendly services for the initiation of diplomatic negotiations. The role of the third state ends with bringing the parties to the negotiating table. In 1962 the United States and Britain acted in this capacity when they advised India and Pakistan to undertake direct negotiations on matters dividing these two countries, in particular on Kashmir. This example shows that the third state, which has no direct stake in the dispute itself, is motivated by the desire to promote a better understanding between the parties and considers that this understanding is in its own interest. The reconciliation between India and Pakistan, for which both great powers have friendly feelings, and the formation of their united front against China, the enemy of both powers, corresponded to British-American interests in Asia. The offer of good offices, like other external actions of states, is motivated by the national interests, even if indirectly involved, of the states which make the offer.

3. *Mediation.* The third state may go further and offer to participate in the negotiations between the parties in the capacity of a "neutral" party which is not directly interested in the merits of the dispute. The mediating state takes part in the diplomatic conversations between the parties and suggests solutions. Either of the two parties or both of them may decline the offer of good offices or of mediation, or reject the solutions suggested by the mediating state.

4. *Enquiry.* This procedure consists in finding an "objective" version of the facts which are at the origin of the dispute and which are contested by the parties. The fact-finding mission is entrusted by the parties to an international commission, composed of nationals of third states and usually also of two other persons, each representing a party to the dispute. The enquiry commission proceeds with its mission, for instance with an investigation at the places where contested actions occurred, and submits a report with its own version of the facts. The parties are free not to accept the report.

5. *Conciliation.* This procedure was very popular at the time of the League of Nations, and the provisions for its use were often included in the bilateral and multilateral treaties concluded during the inter-war period for the peaceful settlement of disputes. However, these provisions remained a dead letter. A conciliation commission has a wider task than an enquiry commission. It is called upon to investigate all the aspects of the dispute, to hear the pleadings by both parties, and eventually to submit a report in which it proposes a definite settlement. The conciliation commission is composed, like the enquiry commission, of an uneven number of commissioners, usually two of the nationality of the parties and three, including the president, of the nationality of third states. The

commissioners who do not belong to the nationality of the parties form the majority and are therefore able to adopt the report by a majority vote if necessary over the opposition of one or both of the commissioners who are nationals of the parties. However, the settlement which the commission suggests is only a recommendation, which the parties may reject.

6. *Arbitration.* This is a judicial procedure which leads to the settlement of the dispute by the application of international law. While the former procedures are not limited to legal considerations and may be guided by political elements in the controversy, the arbitrators are bound by international law unless the parties expressly authorize them to mitigate their findings by motivations inspired by equity. The procedure before an arbitral tribunal is somewhat similar to that which national courts follow. The final decision (arbitral award) is legally binding for the parties, which are expected to abide by it. The usual composition of an arbitral tribunal is similar to that of an enquiry or conciliation commission. The total number of arbitrators is uneven (usually, though not always, five). Two members of the tribunal are nationals of the parties. The remaining three, including the president, who has the deciding vote in case of a tie-vote, are nationals of third states. All five are appointed by agreement of the parties or, if they fail to agree, according to a procedure which they themselves have accepted in advance. The arbitral award is adopted by a majority vote if necessary over the opposition of the arbitrators of the nationality of the parties. Thus, two states which choose to submit their dispute to arbitration are no longer free to prevent the rendering of the award and must comply with it.

An arbitral tribunal can be established by the parties for the settlement of only one case or of several disputes of the same type (for instance, all claims by their nationals against the other state) or of all controversies arising out of the application or interpretation of a given treaty (the treaty will then contain an article, called the compromissory clause, which will provide for the obligatory submission to an arbitral tribunal of all disputes arising from its application) or of all or most legal disputes which might arise between the parties for any reason whatsoever (this obligation is undertaken in a treaty called a treaty of general arbitration).

Arbitration was popular prior to the foundation of the Permanent Court of International Justice. Since that time the states wishing to submit their legal disputes to a judicial settlement have preferred to have recourse to the Court. Even now, however, states sometimes wish to have certain disputes examined by an arbitral tribunal of their choice; this is especially true if they consider that certain recurrent disputes would be better handled by arbitrators who have become familiar with the problems involved in these disputes than by the judges of the Court, who do not specialize in any particular kind of international dispute.

An arbitral tribunal, always called to life by the parties themselves, might have a short life if it is requested to decide one single dispute, or a fairly long existence if the mission requires it.

7. *Judicial settlement.* This is a procedure practically identical with arbitration except for the body to whom the dispute is submitted. Since the foundation in 1921 of the Permanent Court of International Justice, now renamed the International Court of Justice, a permanent international court has existed, open to all states. The Court resides in The Hague and is one of the organs of the United Nations (formerly of the League of Nations). It is composed of fifteen judges, each of a different nationality. A party which has no judge of its own nationality on the permanent bench has the right to add a judge who is its own national. Thus, the bench may be composed of sixteen or seventeen judges if both parties are not represented on the bench and designate their national judges. The Court decides by a majority vote. The fifteen permanent judges are concurrently elected by the Security Council and the General Assembly, each for nine years. If the parties wish to submit their dispute to the Court, they accept in advance that it will be solved on the basis of international law and that its decision (judgment) will have to be complied with.

The United Nations Charter provides for other procedures of peaceful settlement. The Security Council may offer to the parties its good offices or mediation or may send its own commission of enquiry on a fact-finding mission. It also may act as a commission of conciliation and recommend a settlement of the dispute. The General Assembly may also examine an international dispute and recommend a solution. The recommendations of the Security Council or of the General Assembly are not binding on the parties.

To sum up, it may be said that the parties to an inter-state dispute almost always remain masters of their decisions. They may refuse to follow any of the existing procedures. The only exception—but an important one—is the procedure before the United Nations. The Security Council and the General Assembly both have the right to examine any international dispute, not only at the request of both parties, but also at the request of one of them or at the request of any other member of the United Nations or of the Secretary General. The parties are, moreover, free to reject the suggestions of a mediating power or the recommendations which a commission of conciliation or the Security Council or the General Assembly proposes. Only if they agree to submit their controversy to an arbitral tribunal or to the International Court of Justice is their freedom of action terminated, because they may neither halt the proceedings nor refuse to carry out an arbitral award or judgment.

International disputes are usually divided into legal and political disputes. A legal dispute is a controversy concerning the existence or the exact meaning of the rights of the contending parties. It is formulated in legal terms within the framework of international law. A political dispute is a controversy in which one or both of the parties claim that their interests require a change in the status quo regardless of whether this status quo is or is not founded on international law. This classification is not particularly helpful because the same subject-matter can be regarded as legal or political. The parties can couch their claims in legal terms or in the political language of interests, depending on their convenience and aspirations. For instance, a party to a territorial dispute can question the legal validity of the settlement which established the boundary line or challenge the political fairness of the same settlement without disputing its validity.

Any dispute can be called legal in the sense that, if submitted to judges, it can be settled by the application of international law or by a judgment of *non liquet* (i.e., the court can dismiss the case for lack of any legal foundation for the plaintiff's claim). But the same dispute becomes political if at least one party refuses to settle it by the application of international law or seeks its settlement in a change of the existing legal situation. The classification itself is not an abstract academic distinction but a political issue which the governments concerned decide according to their convenience. If they want to settle their dispute on the ground of international law, this fact will make the dispute a legal one. In the contrary case the dispute becomes political and hence nonjusticiable. A government may prefer to classify a dispute as political because if it consented to view it as legal and to submit it to the International Court of Justice, its superiority in power over the opposite party would not affect the contents of the settlement. The same superiority in power will affect the solution of a dispute which is held to be political and which is therefore handled through diplomatic channels or is examined by the United Nations.

If the two states are parties to a dispute which does not affect their vital interests and if they cannot solve it through negotiations, they might find it expedient to eliminate this minor cause of mutual friction by submitting it to an international tribunal. They will carry out the decision of the tribunal for two reasons. First, they were aware at the time of submitting the case to the international tribunal that its decision would necessarily be adverse to one of them, and they accepted this risk in advance. Secondly, they accepted the risk of an adverse decision because the subject-matter of the dispute did not affect their most vital interests. If the risk is not acceptable, the state will refuse to submit the case to arbitration or judicial settlement.

The disputes which both parties consider legal can be solved by existing international procedures. As noted before, there are two such procedures: either adjudication by the International Court of Justice or arbitration by an arbitral tribunal.

Under the Statute of the International Court of Justice, states can do more than agree in each particular case to submit their dispute to the Court. The so-called Optional Clause of Article 36 of the Statute provides all the states with the opportunity to declare in advance that they accept the jurisdiction of the Court in legal disputes which might arise between them and other states which accept the same obligation.[1] This opportunity is facultative in several senses:

1. No state is bound to undertake this obligation; if it refuses to do so, it cannot be sued before the Court unless it gives its assent in each particular case.

2. It can limit the obligation to a specified period of time—five years, for instance—and then refuse to renew it.

3. It can circumscribe the jurisdiction of the Court by any reservation it chooses to make, thus excluding certain legal disputes from its competence. Usually, the declarations in which states accept the jurisdiction of the Court in virtue of Article 36 are made for a limited period of time and are surrounded by all sorts of reservations.

One of the reservations made in the United States declaration of acceptance of the compulsory jurisdiction of the Court is indicative of a limited trust in the fairness of international judges. This reservation not only excludes, as several other declarations do, disputes relating to matters which are essentially within domestic jurisdiction, but adds that the United States, not the Court, will determine whether a matter is or is not within domestic jurisdiction. Theoretically at least, the United States could refuse to appear as a defendant in any international dispute, in spite of its declaration of acceptance of the compulsory jurisdiction of the Court, simply by stating that the subject-matter is within its own domestic jurisdiction. This American reservation was reproduced in the declarations by other states such as France, Mexico, Pakistan, Liberia, India, and the Union of South Africa. If several states refuse to abide by the generally recognized principle of law that no one should be the judge in his own case and if they reserve for themselves the right to deny the competence of the Court by their own unilateral decision, it is clear that the Court is regarded with somewhat limited trust.

---

[1] Article 36, paragraph 2 of the Statute reads: "The states parties to the present Statute may at any time declare that they recognize as compulsory *ipso facto* and without special agreement, in relation to any other state accepting the same obligation, the jurisdiction of the Court in all legal disputes concerning:

a. the interpretation of a treaty;

b. any question of international law;

c. the existence of any fact which, if established, would constitute a breach of an international obligation;

d. the nature or extent of the reparation to be made for the breach of an international obligation."

Paragraph 3 of the same Article adds: "The declarations referred to above may be made unconditionally or on condition of reciprocity on the part of several or certain states, or for a certain time."

The reluctance of states to accept in advance the compulsory jurisdiction of the Court and to abandon their right to refuse altogether any judicial settlement of legal disputes is reflected in the fact that only about one-third of the states have so far made the declarations under Article 36 of the Statute. This reluctance is due to one or all of the following reasons:

1. The governments cannot foresee the future circumstances under which an international dispute might arise. They might prefer in certain cases to avoid any judicial settlement if the opposite party is helpless in effectively pressing its claim through diplomatic channels and cannot compel a serious consideration of its point of view. In other cases, they might expect that they would be stronger in a diplomatic bargaining and thus could gain a more profitable settlement than by pleading before the Court in purely legal terms. In still other cases, it might be more convenient to combine two or several disputes and gain greater leeway in the negotiations, a tactic which cannot be followed before the Court, where each dispute is examined separately and on its own merits. A state might be willing to assume the risks of compulsory jurisdiction of the Court regarding certain states but not others; yet Article 36 extends the validity of declarations to all states which have accepted or will in the future accept the same obligation. In other words, a state which accepts the compulsory jurisdiction of the Court can never be sure to which states it will find itself bound in the future by this reciprocal obligation.

2. The present gaps in international law and the uncertainty of some of its rules make future judgments more unpredictable than those of national courts.

3. The states might feel reluctant to submit matters which involve their interests to a group of fifteen or sixteen judges among whom only one is their own national. The judges are of the highest personal and scholarly caliber, but they are foreigners.

This particular aspect of the question is aggravated by ideological considerations. First, the Communist states refuse, as a matter of principle, to submit disputes to which they are parties to the Court or to any arbitral tribunal. They feel that the majority of the judges or arbitrators would be prejudiced against them. They do not impugn their personal honesty but think that the judges hold the "capitalist" values as self-evident truths and cannot possibly share the Communist values. This difference in fundamental outlook would give the Court a biased view of the claims and arguments submitted by a Communist government. Secondly, a somewhat similar problem might affect the attitude of the underdeveloped countries, at least with respect to disputes involving the obligations of states toward alien property and the related matter of nationalization. They might believe that the Court or an arbitral tribunal, bound by international law formed through Western practice, would be inclined to protect the vested interests of the advanced countries.

These suspicions may be ill-founded, but if a state has them, it will be reluctant to accept the judicial settlement.

The important disputes, those which cause deep irritations, are the political disputes. Since they are not couched in legal terms and call for a political adjustment of the existing situation, they cannot be solved by a judicial or an arbitral decision. For instance, a state might not question at all the legal validity of a territorial settlement but nevertheless claim a part of the territory of its neighbor. The Court or an arbitral tribunal would have to dismiss the case by pointing out the existence of a valid treaty. A state suffering from overpopulation might ask another country with a much lower population density to open its gates to immigration. The Court or an arbitral tribunal could only rule that immigration falls within the exclusive domestic jurisdiction of the defendant state and would dismiss the case. A state bound by the imposed obligations of a peace treaty to observe certain ceilings in its armaments could not appeal to the court for the abrogation or revision of those obligations.

Political disputes transcend international law. They can, however, be submitted to either the Security Council or the General Assembly. The efficacy of this procedure is severely limited by several considerations:

1. The most the Security Council or the General Assembly can do is to adopt a recommendation regarding the terms of proposed settlement. It can do less: it can mediate between the parties and try to find a compromise solution which both parties are willing to accept. A recommendation is not binding on the parties, which are free to follow or reject it. There is no way to enforce the recommendation unless the parties for some reason cannot withstand the political pressure by the United Nations.

2. Both bodies of the United Nations are composed of delegates of governments which are not guided by abstract justice but by political expediency. These governments might favor one party rather than the other for reasons which are foreign to the merits of the case: their political friendships, the *quid-pro-quo* promised by one of the parties, the fear of establishing a precedent unfavorable for their own national interests, power considerations (the not unusual tendency to favor the stronger party because it is stronger and can cause more international trouble), and, finally, the desire to safeguard international peace even at the price of justice. The parties cannot be expected to have an unlimited trust in the impartiality of either the Security Council or the General Assembly.

Of course, if the great powers agree in advance to promote a solution of a political dispute between two minor states or between a minor state and one of them or, finally, between the two of them, the recommendation of the United Nations will have almost every chance of being enforced. But this concerted action of the great powers is not very probable in our time. Moreover, the great powers, if they can agree among themselves, are fully able to achieve the same result outside of the international organization, as evidenced by the Munich agreement in 1938 or by the Indochinese settlement which was reached in 1954 at the Geneva Conference.

The division of disputes into legal and political disputes overlooks a third category which is especially important in our troubled time, the category of political antagonisms. While a legal or political dispute has a definite object of contention, a political antagonism is a condition of tension which exists in the relations between two states owing to a fundamental conflict of interests, values, and aspirations. An antagonism usually involves the two protagonists in a number of definite disputes but transcends the sum of these particular disputes. It is a condition of mind or, from another point of view, a total conflict over the status quo in all its aspects. It exists if one state wants to eliminate altogether the other state, or if it intends to extend its hegemony to the whole world or a large part of it, or if it aspires to impose its own "self-evident truths" and ways of life on the other peoples of the world.

The antagonism has no circumscribed object of contention; hence, the states concerned cannot eliminate it by negotiation or by submitting it to any of the various international procedures. In 1938 Nazi Germany was interested, not in the particular dispute over the Sudetenland, but in the total absorption of Czechoslovakia; this was an antagonism, not a dispute which the two states concerned could solve by negotiations. The conflict between the Western powers and the Axis states was really not over any particular issue but over the fundamental question whether the United States and Great Britain would retain any influence in the Eastern Hemisphere.

The present conflict between the Western and the Communist powers is of the same nature. The current disputes over Berlin, Laos, the Congo, Cuba, Taiwan, and other problems have definite subject-matters but are also the symptoms of a deep and underlying antagonism. As long as the Communist powers persist in their proclaimed intention of converting the whole world to their "self-evident truths," the settlement of a particular dispute can alleviate a local situation but cannot eliminate the antagonism itself, which will continue to produce new disputes. The antagonism places one party before the dilemma of either abandoning its intention to annex another state, to extend its hegemony, or to convert the world to its ideological creed, on the one hand, or accepting the antagonism as a necessary part of its foreign policy, on the other. Its opponents face a concomitant dilemma of either accepting the antagonism as the price of their struggle for independence or political influence or fundamental values, or of surrendering to the adversary.

History teaches that antagonisms are terminated either by the victory of one party or by the renunciation by the same party of those aspirations which are the cause for antagonism. The progressive conquests by Rome were the cause of a constant antagonism in its relations with other city-states and tribes of the ancient world; the final formation of the Roman Empire ended the antagonism by establishing the total Roman victory over its former opponents. The antagonism between Christianity and Hellenistic paganism was similarly terminated by the total victory of the former. The forcible or voluntary abandonment of the aspirations which were the source of the antagonism is another way to eliminate it. The defeat of the Axis powers ended the antagonism that arose from their extravagant ambitions. The fatigue caused by a protracted and fruitless struggle might induce the parties to accept a *modus vivendi.* Then the bitter antagonism is succeeded by a resigned acceptance of the prospect of mutual survival. The opponents accept the regime of the mutual toleration of their conflicting values. In 1648 this state of mind allowed the Catholics and the Protestants to end their inconclusive religious war.

Political antagonisms are more dangerous than political disputes because they transcend a clearly defined subject-matter, acquire highly emotional overtones, and are hardly susceptible to rational analysis. They invest every dispute between the contending parties with an unduly heightened importance. The negotiations for the settlement of any particular dispute raise such questions as the effect of the negotiating attitudes and of the settlement itself on the prestige of the parties and on their relative power positions, and involve the apprehensions that one party might interpret concessions made by the other party as a sign of its weakening resolve in the over-all struggle between them. Particular disputes tend to be viewed, not in themselves, but in the context of the general tension which exists between the parties; finding a compromise, restricted to the subject-matter of the dispute, becomes difficult under these conditions.

An antagonism which arises from incompatible national interests and from ideological conflict always takes a moral coloring. Accommodations and concessions are likely to appear as immoral transactions with evil itself.

The United Nations cannot solve international antagonisms because the object of controversy cannot be precisely defined and also because the parties cannot accept any solution that would entail surrender for one party or renunciation for the other.

In short, the United Nations is not equipped to ensure the peaceful settlement of all legal disputes, much less the solution of political disputes, and certainly not the elimination of international antagonisms.

The problem of ensuring the peaceful settlement of all international disputes is not a legal one which can be solved by ingenious formulas invented by able lawyers, but a political one which can be resolved only by a general renunciation of ideological crusades and schemes for hegemony and by the acceptance of a *modus vivendi* founded on ideological toleration and on moderation in foreign policy.

DISARMAMENT

The problem of disarmament began to interest the world seriously at the time of the convocation of the First Hague Conference in 1899. It figured on its agenda as well as on the agenda of the Second Conference in 1907. The reason for this initial interest was the rapid progress in military technology and the apprehension that wars would henceforth be much more destructive than they had been in the nineteenth century. The two conferences produced in this respect no results worth mentioning. The cruel experience of the First World War added a new stimulus to the search for some sort of limitation and reduction of armaments. The Covenant made this problem one of the principal tasks of the League of Nations. Yet several years of preparatory work and the two years (1932-33) of the Disarmament Conference itself ended in complete failure. The inter-war period witnessed only a limitation of naval armaments agreed upon by the principal maritime powers, but even this limitation did not survive the crisis of the late thirties.

The Second World War inevitably revived public interest in disarmament. The terrible destructiveness of nuclear weapons added a new dimension to the problem, which has since been subdivided into two interrelated questions: the question of nuclear weapons and the question of conventional weapons. Uninterrupted negotiations, within and without the United Nations, have so far produced no results. The political reason for this lack of success remains the same as at any former time, namely the bitter rivalries among the great powers. The armaments race increases their mutual distrust and fear, but it is the consequence rather than the cause of their hostility.

The protracted postwar disarmament negotiations have produced so far only one limited agreement, the American-British-Soviet Treaty of July 25, 1963, on the prohibition of nuclear tests. This treaty is open to accession by all the states of the world. It is not, strictly speaking, a disarmament agreement, because it neither limits nor reduces the existing armaments.

The contracting parties are forbidden to carry out nuclear weapon test explosions or any other nuclear explosions in the atmosphere, outer space, or underwater. They are permitted to continue the underground explosions which have a practical military significance for the development of tactical weapons. Moreover, the parties have undertaken "to refrain from causing, encouraging, or in any way participating in the carrying out of any nuclear weapon test explosions." This obligation does not seem to preclude the sharing with other states of such nuclear knowledge as might help those states to produce nuclear weapons without the need for tests, or the sale to other states of ready-made nuclear weapons. Another moot question, left open by the drafting of the Treaty, is whether the prohibition of nuclear explosions extends to wartime or is limited to peacetime.

The Treaty is of unlimited duration, but each contracting party may withdraw from it if it decides that "extraordinary events . . . have jeopardized the supreme interests of its country." A three-month advance notice of withdrawal is then required. Presumable reasons for withdrawal might be the following:

1. The suspicion that the suspension of nuclear tests militarily favors the other contracting parties.

2. The breach of the Treaty by another party.

3. The fear that the tests carried out by a state that has refused to accede to the Treaty might upset the nuclear balance of power.

It would be equally unwise to underestimate or to oversell the Treaty. It certainly protects human health from a further pollution of the air and the waters. It might be a first step toward an improvement in relations between the West and the Soviet Union. However, its objective is narrowly circumscribed. It does not in any way stop or reduce the armaments race, in particular regarding the means of delivery of nuclear weapons, the perfection of antimissile missiles, and conventional armaments. It does not prevent the nonsignatories from carrying out nuclear tests; France and China made this crystal clear by refusing to accede. Finally, it leaves intact the major controversial issues such as the future of Germany, the close Soviet association with Cuba, and Western-Soviet rivalry in the underdeveloped areas.

At the time of the Hague conferences the great powers were already aligned into two hostile coalitions (Great Britain finally joined France and Russia in the Triple Entente before the Second Conference). The split among the great powers was clear-cut by the time of the opening of the Geneva Disarmament Conference convoked by the League of Nations. Japan had already begun its venture in China with the military seizure of Manchuria, and Hitler had been appointed Chancellor of Germany at the beginning of the second year of the Conference. Disarmament negotiations have been conducted since the last war in an atmosphere of sharp political struggle between the two power blocs.

The lessons which can be deduced from this long but discouraging record are as follows:

1. There is a close relation between the willingness to consider a limitation and a reduction of armaments and the feeling of political trust among the states concerned. If they think that their hostility cannot

be eliminated in the foreseeable future, they fear that a limitation on armaments will wrap them in a rigid strait jacket which will not permit them to adjust rapidly to technological progress and to retain the relative strength which they possessed before accepting the obligation. It is curious that this limitation on freedom of action seems to the states to be, for some reason, more favorable to their rivals than to themselves. This attitude stems from a feeling of insecurity which is due to the mutual hostility of the prospective signatories of the disarmament convention.

2. A disarmament agreement acceptable to the signatories would have to ensure that their power relative to one another would remain unchanged. It is extremely difficult, however, to find a common denominator for the various types of armaments: the number of men serving in the armed forces versus the quality and quantity of weapons; land armaments versus air and naval armaments; nuclear weapons versus conventional weapons; nuclear rockets versus long-range planes; submarines versus surface warships; bases on foreign territory versus the ICBM; and so forth. Yet the limitation of armaments must somehow be balanced. No state would sign a disarmament treaty which reduces the types of weapons in which it excels while not reducing other types in which co-signatories excel. For instance, the elimination at the present time of foreign bases for airplanes and for the IMBM would reduce the relative power of the United States, while the elimination of the ICBM would probably have a discriminating effect on the relative power of the U.S.S.R. The abolition of nuclear submarines would perhaps favor the Soviet Union, while a sharp reduction of land armies would have the opposite effect.

For the same reason, it is difficult to single out one type of weapon and apply the limitation and reduction only to this type. This kind of selective and partial disarmament might favor some states and discriminate against others, because it would not be balanced within a general framework of armaments of all types.

A major power might feel, rightly or wrongly, that it has achieved a temporary military superiority over the other major powers; it might then be reluctant to abandon this military asset (for instance, more effective weapons of mass destruction or a better means of intercontinental delivery) by concluding a disarmament treaty. By the same token, other major powers might be equally reluctant to forego the chance of improving their military position by the eventual acquisition of these more advanced weapons. They will refuse to conclude a treaty which the other power might be willing to sign if it were to freeze the present imbalance and perpetuate its superiority. A situation in which the major powers believe that they have achieved a balance of various armaments is more propitious for disarmament negotiations than the situation in which they think that one of them enjoys a definite, though temporary, superiority.

3. A viable treaty would have to be signed by all the great powers.

Otherwise, a balance realized through carefully calculated limitations and reductions of the armaments of the signatory states would run the constant danger of being upset by the uncontrolled armaments of the nonsignatories. For instance, a nuclear agreement between the United States, Britain, and the Soviet Union would not have a long life without the participation of the actual or potential candidates for membership in the nuclear club, such as France and China.

4. The implementation of an agreement to limit and reduce armaments would have to depend on a modicum of good faith and mutual confidence among the signatories. At the present time, when a complex military technology is closely related to the whole scientific and economic life of the advanced nations, a foolproof international control is out of the question. Perfect control of nuclear and conventional weapons would require a constant supervision of all the economic, scientific, and technological activities on the territories of the signatory states to discover or prevent any concealed breach of the disarmament convention. It would be impossible to recruit the specialists who would have to operate this kind of near-total international surveillance; their number would probably have to run into six figures. Without this foolproof control, there could be no reasonable guarantee against all secret violations. The democratic states would not be eager to yield their commercial and scientific secrets to an international body of control. The nondemocratic states would be even less willing to open their closed societies to permanent international inspection. They would see in this type of international control a surrender of the advantage they now possess of concealing behind a veil of state secrecy several activities which are public in the democratic societies. Any feasible international control would therefore have to be intermittent and incomplete. It would allow for gaps in surveillance which the prospective signatories might consider too great a risk for their security. The risk of undiscovered breaches would be less regarding those weapons whose existence can be detected by modern means of intelligence without the need for constant supervision. For instance, most though not all nuclear tests can be detected by devices installed outside the territory of the state concerned. The problem of international control cannot be solved to the point of absolute technical perfection, but it could be resolved politically if its technical imperfections were offset by mutual trust among the signatories, a condition sadly lacking in our time.

5. No treaty can stop the progress in military technology which is only a by-product of general scientific progress. An all-embracing treaty, which would limit all the armaments known at the time of its signing, would become obsolete with the lapse of time because of the invention of new weapons and military techniques. Unless immediately supplemented by a limitation on these new weapons, it would not survive a major invention which would upset the former balance of armaments on which the treaty

was originally founded. If there had been a binding convention of disarmament prior to the invention of nuclear weapons, would it have remained acceptable to those signatories who would continue to be bound by its limitation on conventional weapons but who would not yet be in possession of nuclear bombs? If a disarmament treaty were signed today, would it survive the new military techniques which will be derived from the exploration of outer space unless an additional treaty were immediately concluded to cover the new aspect of warfare? In our age, which has witnessed the impact of air power on the relative significance of traditional land and naval forces, the technological revolution caused by nuclear weapons, and the partial eclipse of the military importance of the airplane due to the development of the rocket technique, it must be expected that technological progress will either make a disarmament treaty obsolete with the lapse of time or else require its periodic modernization.

An atmosphere of political stability and trust is the main condition of successful disarmament negotiations. Our time does not offer great hopes in this respect. Yet negotiations will go on as they did before the Second World War and as they have gone on since, because people all over the world fear the prospect of mass destruction and are inclined to seek refuge in disarmament rather than in the termination of the dangerous political struggle among the great powers, the true cause of the armaments race. The prospect of mass destruction is so real that no one has the moral right to discourage negotiations regardless of how much probability he attaches to their success.

Whether or not the participating states seriously intend, at any given time, to reach an agreement, disarmament negotiations provide them with an excellent opportunity for psychological warfare. They can exploit for political purposes the fear of mass destruction widely felt in every country. Insofar as disarmament negotiations are a propaganda tournament for the competitive display of peace-loving and humanitarian impulses, the scores go to the government which offers the most radical schemes. The more radical the disarmament proposal, the greater its chance of attracting popular support. Moreover, it is safe to advance a very radical proposal, such as total disarmament, because there is no risk that it will be accepted by other states. If the other states reject a radical proposal, which may make no sense to experts but seem attractive to the general public, they will be blamed for sabotaging the negotiations. A proposal which is technically simple and hence easily grasped by nonspecialists offers the same propaganda advantage. Disarmament negotiations have a twofold purpose: the limitation and reduction of armaments, but also propaganda by the participating states. It is not always easy for an outsider to be sure which of these two objectives predominates in the thinking of the negotiating governments.

THE GENERAL ASSEMBLY

The General Assembly will probably remain the main political organ of the United Nations. It is worthwhile to analyze its working in order to understand better the political nature of the organization. The decisions of the General Assembly are the result of the two factors: its voting system, and the foreign policies of the member-states. These decisions are not dictated by lofty moral considerations, because each delegate casts his vote in accordance with the instructions sent by his government. In turn, this government formulates its instructions in the light of its objectives and of its relations with other governments. Governments do not become more or less moral simply because they make their voice heard in the hall of the General Assembly rather than through the usual diplomatic channels.

The fact that many vital and controversial issues come up for debate in the General Assembly is a diplomatic handicap unknown before 1914. At that time, a government which was not directly involved in a controversial issue could remain discreetly silent and thus continue on friendly terms with the states vitally concerned with the issue in question. Even a great power enjoyed this privilege, though to a lesser extent because great powers were supposed to take an interest in all important international issues. Today, the inscription of a controversial question on the agenda of the General Assembly compels every member to take a stand. Even silence in the debate and abstention in the vote will be interpreted by other states as expressing a policy friendly or unfriendly to them. The debate and the vote force governments to lay their cards on the table, not always the most pleasant obligation.

The system whereby every member-state has one vote is an almost unavoidable consequence of the concept of the equality of states, a concept dear to the smaller nations. The great powers cannot challenge the system, especially when they are divided among themselves and compete with one another for popularity with the smaller countries. However, the system is a distortion of the realities of international power and a denial of a modern democratic principle—one man, one vote. Four hundred million Indians, 215 million Soviet people, and 180 million Americans are each represented by one vote, as are 170,000 Icelanders or 1,150,000 Costa Ricans. The military, economic, and scientific potentials are overlooked in this numerical "equality" although they are decisive in the real world. Cultural levels do not count; a highly civilized Belgium or Sweden has the same single vote as a backward Yemen or Saudi Arabia. A truly independent state casts one vote, as does each of the two Soviet provinces, the Ukrainian and the Byelorussian Republics.

In other words, the General Assembly, with its two-thirds majority of single votes for each state, does not speak in the name of mankind (even if one were to make the bold assumption that the delegations faithfully reflect the views of their respective populations), because it cannot claim to be the voice of even the numerical majority of human beings. It does not speak in the name of international power, which is concentrated in a few of its members and which cannot be equated with a numerical majority of states. The haphazard division of mankind into many large and small states, itself the result of historical developments, cannot but be reflected in the United Nations membership, which includes all kinds of states: those with a long record of national history and those which emerged only yesterday, those which are buttressed by a strong national consciousness and those which have no coherent national background and might not survive the test of the next international crisis, those which are powerful and those which are desperately weak, those which have contributed greatly to human civilization at one time or another and those which have contributed nothing yet or next to nothing. The voting system is the result of this haphazard collection of modern states which history has brought to life.

The naked figures of votes (the ayes, the nays, and the abstentions) look very impressive until they are carefully analyzed and until each individual vote is properly weighted with the power it actually represents. Then the vote of one single state, like the United States or the Soviet Union, suddenly casts a long shadow behind which several votes of small states dwindle into insignificance. This should be borne in mind in order to avoid the mistake of equating the votes in the General Assembly with the voice of mankind or the expression of actual international reality.

For the purpose of analyzing the political meaning of votes, the General Assembly can be divided into several groups of uneven coherence. The Communist bloc usually votes as one unit and follows the Soviet lead. The Western countries tend to vote together on the main issues affecting their competition with the Communist bloc. The Latin American countries no longer automatically follow the lead of the United States. It can be expected that they will gradually be split into three groups: those voting against the United States (Cuba is so far the only example); those invariably supporting the United States; and those which will cast their votes at variance with either power bloc depending on the merits of each case. The British Commonwealth does not vote as one unit, because its members are not obliged to pursue the same type of foreign policy. A frequent dividing line between them follows the color line; the "white" members side with the Western powers, while the "colored" members, who are also members of the Afro-Asian bloc, often differ with the West. The Afro-Asian bloc, sometimes reinforced by several Latin American votes, is a bloc of votes only with regard to certain issues of common interest, such as economic assistance, antiracialism, and anticolonialism. The solidarity of the same bloc cannot be sustained with regard to other issues. Each Asian or

African state decides the question of its vote on these other issues depending on its interpretation of its national interests, an interpretation which might be at variance with the views of other Asian or African states. These national interests (for instance, the need for military or economic assistance expected from either or both power blocs) make some of them side more frequently with one power bloc than with the other or carefully avoid giving offense to either bloc. The African states, although most of them are of recent creation, are already divided by their own rivalries and suspicions and also by their different attitudes toward the two power blocs. The issues raised by the Congolese problem have demonstrated the lack of a Pan-African solidarity except on one point on which they are unanimous, namely the desire to remain independent and the aversion to being treated by the great powers as mere black pawns in the cold war. The same is true of the Asian and Near Eastern countries, whose national interests and policies are often at odds; they also want to be independent and not to serve as pawns in the great-power game. Beyond this minimum and their common interest in the three basic issues of economic development, anticolonialism, and antiracialism, their solidarity is rather fictitious.

The arithmetical control by the underdeveloped countries of the majority in the General Assembly can be undermined by the great powers through their pressures and promises as well as through their exploitation of conflicts of national interests among the same countries. However, this arithmetical majority reflects an international reality in one respect: these underdeveloped countries form the main political battleground for the two hostile blocs. The two blocs have to court the underdeveloped countries in and out of the United Nations. The rival great powers are highly attentive to what the delegates of the underdeveloped countries have to say and how they cast their votes.

The vicarious power of the underdeveloped countries has a visible effect on the policies of the contending great powers. They cannot help adjusting these policies, especially within the United Nations, to the aspirations and emotions which prevail in the Third World. It is highly embarrassing for a great power not to vote for the United Nations economic assistance fund or for a resolution denouncing a case of racial discrimination or a colonial regime; its negative vote or abstention will not only be resented by most of the underdeveloped countries but will be exploited by the rival great power. The vacillation of the United States on those issues to which the underdeveloped countries attach great political and emotional importance has been resented by the Third World and used by the Soviet Union as evidence that the United States is selfish, indifferent to the needs of the underdeveloped countries, and a champion of colonialism and racialism. The two great powers are placed in this respect in very different situations. The Soviet Union has no allies among the Western colonial or former colonial powers, which are all the friends of the United States, the main Soviet adversary. It can always outbid the United States in the game of anticolonialism and antiracialism. The United States must take into account both aspects of the question: the undeniable need to remain on good terms with the Third World and the no less real requirement to maintain its political friendships with the colonial or former colonial powers who are its associates in NATO.

The rule of the two-thirds majority, which replaced in the United Nations the diplomatic rule of unanimity, makes the adoption of resolutions easier. But it does not promote a spirit of moderation and an inclination to seek generally acceptable compromises. The resolutions on very controversial issues are not expected to solve problems but to provide a platform for subsequent propaganda. From this point of view, what is important is to get the required majority and make the General Assembly adopt a resolution which will be useful for outside propaganda. Whenever the member-states want to resolve a difficult problem, however, the mere two-thirds majority will not make the trick. They will have to negotiate among themselves to reach a compromise acceptable to all states concerned. A resolution of this kind will require its actual implementation by the same states; hence, the two-thirds majority will have to include the assenting votes of these states directly interested.

The voting system, combined with the expanded membership, which has now reached 110, has produced other results. It is no longer certain that either rival bloc can muster the two-thirds majority for its proposals. Any resolution can be blocked by the collective veto of one-third plus one vote. This collective veto would be composed of the votes of either bloc and of a certain number of votes cast by the uncommitted states. It is therefore possible that resolutions on the most controversial issues may sometimes be unobtainable for lack of the required majority or may have to be watered down, until they become almost meaningless, in order to obtain the required two-thirds vote.

If the resolutions of the General Assembly are regarded, not from the point of view of their propaganda value for one or another group of states, but from the point of view of their chance of being implemented, the following conditions would have to be met in order to make a resolution effective in spite of opposition from one or several states:

1. It must be supported by states which together possess sufficient power to enforce the resolution on the recalcitrant member-state.

2. Those states must not only vote for the resolution but be willing to apply their pressure to that recalcitrant member.

3. The state against which the resolution is directed must possess insufficient power to resist the pressure, must be isolated psychologically, and must be morally unable to withstand the shock of international unpopularity and isolation.

4. If the resolution refers to an area of the world where only one or a few great powers have the preponderant influence and if this power or powers sponsor the resolution, it can be enforced without the co-operation or even in spite of the protests by the other great powers.

5. By the same token, a resolution concerning an area within the zone of influence of a great power cannot be implemented against its will. The outvoting of that great power has only psychological value.

A resolution which is not directed against any particular state but which calls for the joint action of member-states is devoid of meaning if opposed by the states which will have to play a major role in this concerted effort. For instance, no amount of resolutions calling for a substantial United Nations fund of economic assistance to the underdeveloped countries can force the advanced states to make the contributions needed to implement the project.

The fate of the resolutions adopted by the General Assembly during the 1956 crisis is very instructive. The resolutions on the Near East were effective. The overwhelming power of the two nuclear great powers supported these resolutions. The power of the incriminated states, Britain and France, was much less. The discreet embargo by the United States on supplies of oil from the Western Hemisphere helped to convince Britain and France that they should yield. Their usual oil supplies from the Near East were temporarily disrupted. The United States and the Soviet Union supported the resolutions to gain favor with the Asian and African states for whose approval they were eagerly competing. Britain itself could not disregard the views of the same states, some of which were represented in the Commonwealth or were otherwise friendly to Britain. This unusual combination of circumstances made the Near Eastern resolutions completely effective. One should not overlook the poor planning of the British-French military expedition. If this expedition had speedily resulted in the overthrow of President Nasser, its main objective, the resolutions of the United Nations would not have reversed events.

One of the main reasons for the frequent political ineffectiveness of the United Nations is revealed by the circumstances that attended the Suez crisis in 1956 and the Congolese crisis in January, 1963. In both cases, the success of the United Nations was due to full support by the United States and the support or neutrality of the Soviet Union. In both cases, opposition from the two lesser great powers was either overcome or disregarded. American-Soviet co-operation in November, 1956, created conditions under which a United Nations executive action in the Near East was possible and could be carried out. American support of Secretary General Thant's military action against the secessionist government of Katanga turned the scales in January, 1963, in favor of a unified Congo. The Soviet Union, a vocal enemy of the secessionist government, could not but tolerate the military action by the Secretary General. The unconcealed displeasure of Britain, France, and Belgium could neither prevent nor stop the action.

The support, or at least the neutrality, of the United States and the Soviet Union regarding the United Nations actions in the Near East (1956) and in the Congo (1963) disclosed by implication the triangular shape of contemporary international politics. Both great powers were mainly motivated by their competition for influence in the Third World. They favored these policies of the United Nations which were apt to win the applause of all or most of the Asian and African states. In both situations the United States did not hesitate to oppose the wishes of its European allies, notably Britain and France. It is evident, *a contrario,* that the American-Soviet conflict is one of the major reasons for the political ineffectiveness of the United Nations. The Hungarian problem, which deeply divided the two major powers, provided a pertinent illustration.

The Hungarian resolutions voted in 1956 proved to be ineffective; the required conditions were not met. Hungary was located within the range of Soviet military power. Neither the United States nor any other member of the United Nations intended to run the risk of a general war for the sake of Hungarian liberty. The nuclear stalemate meant that the resolutions could not be supported by a combined power overwhelmingly superior to Soviet power. The U.S.S.R., supported by its own bloc, did not feel isolated. The Asian and African states were less outraged by the Soviet attack on the "white" Hungarians than they were by the British-French action against the non-European Arabs. The Soviet Union was ready to lose, temporarily, some of its popularity in the Third World for the sake of maintaining its hold on Hungary and Eastern Europe, and calmly withstood international pressure. The resolutions had a propaganda value in the battle between the two blocs but only for a fairly brief span of time.

In addition, the two Western powers were more responsive to the international injunctions. British public opinion was split, and the opponents of the Suez Canal action freely voiced their vigorous dissent. If in the Soviet Union there were any opposition to the intervention in Hungary, the nature of the regime precluded its public expression.

A country which is not a great power can flout the resolutions of the General Assembly if the great powers do not insist on compliance and if the government concerned possesses steady enough nerves to withstand the wave of foreign indignation. This has been proved more than once, but the most telling example is that of South Africa. The oft-repeated resolutions of the General Assembly, calling either for the termination of racial discrimination against South Africans of Indian descent or for some kind of international control over the administration of Southwest Africa (formerly a mandated territory which had been placed after the First World War under South African administration but was supervised by the League of Nations) have been totally disregarded by South Africa. Yet this small country is neither a great power nor particularly popular in the world. Another example was provided by Spain immediately after the foundation of the United Nations. The authoritarian Spanish regime, although isolated at the time, did not bow to the hostile resolutions of the new international organization, survived a short period during which the world was almost unanimously unfriendly, and eventually found its way back to normal relations with other states owing to the Western-Communist conflict. The United Nations resolutions have been forgotten. The third example has been supplied by India, which ignored the resolutions on Kashmir.

The resolutions of the General Assembly, if they censure a particular state or recommend a specific joint action by all members, have only a psychological sanction. Since no state, whether a great power or a small nation, can be compelled to heed such resolutions, the psychological ability of the recalcitrant state to withstand the moral pressure from other governments is a major factor in their effectiveness or ineffectiveness. In this respect, the democratic countries are more vulnerable than the totalitarian or authoritarian regimes. Since the mass media of information are not controlled by a democratic regime, the tenor of the debates in the General Assembly will be widely known in a democratic country. The articulate public opinion becomes immediately cognizant of the criticisms leveled at the government. This public opinion is not always united on matters of foreign policy; agreement on the main objectives does not preclude sharp divergencies regarding the choice of means. A section of this articulate public opinion might use the debates in the General Assembly as arguments against the policy of the government. The resolution of the General Assembly might become the focus of a domestic debate. Hence, the will of the government to resist international pressure and to ignore the United Nations recommendations may be undermined. This kind of domestic controversy took place in Britain (though not in France) in November, 1956, although it is impossible to evaluate to what extent it contributed to the retreat by the British government.

By contrast, a totalitarian or authoritarian regime controls the domestic sources of information, prevents the country from being fully informed on the nature of debates in the United Nations, and does its best to give its population a conception of the international situation which invariably justifies its own policies. Domestic critical opinions, if they exist, cannot be expressed or are ruthlessly silenced. The regime has a greater capacity to withstand foreign pressure, as the Soviet Union convincingly demonstrated in 1961 when it suddenly and unilaterally terminated the moratorium on nuclear tests and proceeded with a long series of nuclear explosions in spite of the outcry in foreign countries and in total disregard of its former denunciations of nuclear testing.

International pressure does not last long; it ceases with the passage of time. The unpleasant reality continues to exist; international life goes on.

The censured government recovers its international standing, while other governments cannot ignore its existence. A censured government needs steady nerves for a relatively short period of time.

Reactions within and without the United Nations reveal nowadays another pattern. Governments and people interested in foreign affairs are inclined to make their moral judgments on international behavior according to two different standards. One of them is more exacting and applies to the democratic states; the other is more lenient and is reserved for the totalitarian regimes. There are two reasons for the existence of these two standards. First, governments, especially those of the uncommitted countries, are afraid that the totalitarian states will react sharply to public criticism, while they know that a democratic government, used to constant criticism at home, will be more patient and forebearing when it hears critical words coming from a foreign capital otherwise not unfriendly. Secondly, it is expected that the democratic states should act with greater restraint in international affairs; this expectation is deduced from their actual foreign policy, which does not intend to upset the status quo and is in fact moderate in its objectives. A ruthless action by a totalitarian regime does not surprise, because one expects bold policies from states which are opposed to the status quo.

This situation has domestic analogies. If two individuals perform equally reprehensible acts, one of them an otherwise law-abiding citizen but the other a generally unruly person, the reputation of the first individual will be ruined while that of the second will merely be confirmed.

In the same way, the counsel of moderation is habitually offered to the democratic states, whose foreign policy is expected to be moderate. To offer the same counsel to the totalitarian state not only seems useless but also involves the risk of offending that state, which never concedes that its policy is anything but moderate.

These two yardsticks, frequently used by the uncommitted nations, might have two undesirable consequences. First, the public statements by the governments of these nations mold the images of the Western and the Communist powers in the minds of their populations. Frequent criticisms of Western actions and sober silence regarding Communist actions abet the Communist propaganda which contrasts the "imperialist and warlike" West with the "peace-loving" Communist bloc. This result is certainly unwanted by the uncommitted governments.

Secondly, these uneven reactions might eventually cause an irritated revulsion in the West. This might have its repercussions both on the Western attitude toward the United Nations and on the Western policies toward the uncommitted nations. The double-standard judgments of the General Assembly in November, 1956, aroused bitter resentment in large sections of public opinion in Britain and France. They certainly contributed to General de Gaulle's critical view of the organization. Similar discrimination might cause resentment in other Western countries. Yet Western support for the United Nations is indispensable if that organization is to remain a factor in international politics. The United Nations cannot exist as a truncated body without Western and Communist participation. Moreover, the uncommitted nations share with the West the same interest in orderly proceedings within the organization, as proved by the frequent coincidence of views between the Western powers, in particular the United States, and most of the uncommitted countries regarding the policies in the Congo.

The underdeveloped countries and the weak nations in general have a much greater interest in preserving the United Nations than the great powers have. It is true that the United Nations provides the great powers with an excellent forum for propaganda and a constant opportunity for diplomatic contacts among themselves and with other countries. But they could manage without the United Nations. The smaller countries derive greater advantages. The noble principles of international behavior enshrined in the Charter might not be generally observed, but their embarrassing existence does serve to restrict the freedom of action of the great powers. The publicity of debates makes it possible for the voice of a small country to be heard all over the world. Strong actions against weak states are not impossible but are more difficult. The same is true of deals between the great powers at the expense of weaker nations. The United Nations provides no certain guarantee against the perils of international life, but its value to the weaker members should not be underestimated. The United Nations offers them a forum in which to display the vicarious power they derive from the discord among the great powers and gives them an opportunity to moderate this discord by their combined efforts. The international organization renders them important technical assistance and might in the future supply them with a measure of economic assistance.

The other danger involved in the use of this double standard is the possibility of a hostile reaction in the West to foreign aid free of political strings. Exasperated by one-sided criticism the Western governments might be led to condition their assistance on a definitely friendly attitude on the part of the receiving state.

The most telling among several illustrations of this double standard has been provided by the Asian and African attitudes toward the French and the Soviet atomic tests. The Asian and African countries raised a storm over the first French explosions, which were, however, measured in kilotons. They did not care to censure the Soviet Union with the same severity in October, 1961, when it carried out a series of tests that included explosions beyond the 50-megaton range; yet at that time the uncommitted nations were holding their Belgrade Conference, where they could have concerted their reaction to the Soviet breach of the nuclear moratorium.

The public debates in the General Assembly and in the Security Council are anything but a serious negotiation. They are a sequence of speeches calculated to impress foreign governments with the soundness of the foreign policy pursued by the state in whose name the speech is given. Speeches are addressed to foreign and domestic audiences in order to captivate their sympathies and support. This is a tournament in propaganda. There is a great temptation to use strong, if not abusive, language that would hardly help in a true negotiation. The large membership in itself makes negotiation impossible. Usually only two or several countries have truly vital stakes in the issue discussed or have the capacity to influence its course. Yet they do not address the other delegations directly concerned, as would be the case in diplomatic negotiations, but a host of delegations only indirectly interested in the issue or having no interest at all.

It could be said that the members who are not directly concerned might play the helpful role of disinterested mediators. This is partly true, but disinterestedness in an issue does not necessarily amount to higher wisdom or impartiality. The lack of intimate knowledge of the merits of the case does not generate political wisdom. The lack of interest in a particular issue cannot be equated with the absence of national interests in general. A disinterested member, who runs no risks related to the controversy, might be inclined to deliver moralistic sermons which it would avoid in controversial disputes which affect it directly. This does not help the parties. The unconcerned member's general national interests and its ideological "self-evident truths" may lead it to interpret the debate as an excellent opportunity to promote its own foreign policy. The content of its speeches might not be influenced by the merits of the case but by other considerations which are not disinterested. It might favor one party rather than another in exchange for benefits promised or might take a stand entirely dictated by its "self-evident truths," such as anticolonialism. These considerations obviously prevent the "disinterested" member from acting as a true mediator.

But the frequent, public meetings of the United Nations indirectly offer a notable advantage in diplomatic relations. Public debates serve for propaganda, but confidential conversations among the delegates held in the lobbies or at the social gatherings can become serious negotiations. Actually, the resolutions themselves are the products of these private contacts. The voting is also influenced by them. Moreover, matters which do not figure on the official agenda can be usefully canvassed behind the scenes. These informal contacts supplement the embassies in foreign capitals as very useful channels for gauging the feelings of other governments. The United Nations is in this respect even more useful than the League, not only because its membership is closer to being universal but also because the risks of misunderstanding the intentions of other states, especially of great powers, are infinitely greater today. The nuclear age demands as many channels of communication between governments as possible. The United Nations is one of these channels and not the least convenient.

The forum of the General Assembly is particularly useful for psychological warfare. Its debates are public and attract general attention. Practically all states are represented and can be reached at one and the same time. The mass media of communication supply excellent coverage.

The member-states are, however, unequally favored by these conditions. The principle of equality gives all of them equal access to the tribunal, but their unequal power gives a different volume to their voices. A statement made by the delegate of a great power is listened to with much greater attention than a speech by the representative of a small nation and is assured of being covered by the media of information in foreign countries. However, if the delegates of several smaller countries state the views which prevail in their particular area or if almost all the underdeveloped countries voice their grievances and aspirations in unison or if a small state, party to an important dispute, speaks out, they also are assured of due attention, and the foreign media of information cannot afford to ignore them.

The Communist bloc enjoys a certain advantage over the West in this war of words. The Western speeches cannot indulge in the same amount of demagogy as the Communist statements do, because the Western governments must bear in mind the possibility of the sharp domestic criticism which an irresponsible speech would cause. But a demagogic speech usually attracts greater attention than a sober one. The world watches with close attention the statements made by the delegates of the Communist bloc for an obvious reason. The intentions of the Communist states are shrouded in a degree of secrecy which is unimaginable in a democratic country. Their dynamic policies have accustomed the other nations to expect surprise moves at any moment. Their speeches are certain to make the news which the mass media of information cannot overlook and often splash on the first page. The non-Communist (foremost Western) press, radio, and television give a worldwide resonance to the Communist speeches and proposals. The Communist media of information complete the effect by supplying attractive comments. Hence, the Communist views reach far afield. By contrast, the Communist mass media of information only briefly, if at all, mention the Western statements and usually supply only distorted excerpts and summaries. Finally, the unsettled situation in the underdeveloped countries, their expectations and frustrations arising out of the revolution of modernization, their anti-Western resentments, their sensitivity to colonial and racial issues, their difficulties experienced in economic relations with the West, provide the Communist bloc with a wealth of sensational themes for psychological warfare.

The speaker in the General Assembly or, as a matter of fact, at any international conference addresses one or all of the following audiences: the other delegates and their governments, the public in his own country, and the public in all or selected foreign countries. He realizes that his eloquence will not sway his fellow-delegates, who are bound by their instructions. But his arguments might convince their governments and make them modify the instructions, especially if the public speech is accompanied by confidential discussions where the point of view of his own government is more soberly but also more fully explained. His government wants him to remember domestic public opinion, which must be duly impressed. As to the foreign populations, the statement in the General Assembly might be addressed to all or some of them.

Hence, the delegate in the General Assembly must always remember that his words will be listened to by a great variety of audiences and not merely by the one which he sees in the hall.

One can better understand the speeches and what the Western press qualified as the "antics" of the Soviet Premier at the 1959 and 1960 General Assemblies if he realizes that Khrushchev did not address the Western public but spoke to his own countrymen, to fellow Communists all over the world, and to the underdeveloped countries. His defiant and occasionally insulting behavior was calculated to evoke the image of an indomitable and fearless leader who had the will and the power to challenge the enemies of Russia, the capitalists, and the former political and economic masters of the Third World, i.e., the West.

The opportunity which the United Nations offers for propaganda is too tempting to be overlooked by governments. However, the higher the dosage of propaganda injected into the deliberations, the lower the level of the debate, which becomes a kind of shadow-boxing. The orator does not argue with other delegates in search for an acceptable compromise but addresses invisible audiences over their heads. The temper of our time favors this trend.

THE REORGANIZATION OF THE SECURITY COUNCIL. CONCLUDING REMARKS.

Sooner or later the much expanded membership of the United Nations might compel the organization to follow in the footsteps of its predecessor, the League of Nations, and increase the numerical composition of the Security Council. Like the League Council, the Security Council was originally conceived as a body in which the great powers (the permanent members) would have the decisive voice. It was expected to inherit the mantle of the Concert of Europe and to serve as a kind of international executive. The idea of entrusting the Council with the main responsibility for the preservation of peace and for the enforcement of international order was sound, because this task cannot be lifted from the shoulders of the great powers if it is to be carried out at all. But the idea proved unrealizable both times because of discords among the great powers.

The Security Council, much more than the League Council, became an arena for battle instead of a forum for co-operation. Eventually, the great powers found that they could fight the same propaganda battles much more effectively before the whole gallery of the General Assembly. They also recognized that their own disputes forced them to seek the support of the smaller nations. The aspirations of these smaller nations were therefore bound to receive greater attention.

Small nations have a limited trust in the great powers and can cite from the historical record several agreements which these powers concluded at various times at the expense of weak countries. Moreover, they are sensitive about their international status and are not fond of being relegated to a second-rate position in an international organization. It is a matter of prestige for them to acquire a representation on the Council larger than originally planned by the great powers.

The Council of the League was gradually expanded until it became a miniature Assembly. It was most numerous at the time when the League came to an end, but by then only two great powers were still sitting on it, the others having quit the League. The expanded Council was a symptom of the League's weakness and of its decline.

The United Nations is more fortunate because the great powers find it useful to remain in the organization. But the expansion of the Security Council to make room for a larger number of smaller nations will reflect, not the strength, but the weakness of the United Nations. It might become a second, smaller General Assembly, a deliberative body without political power for taking executive actions. The discords among the great powers make this process very probable. At least, the present ratio of five permanent members to six elective could be maintained if the member-states were wise enough to increase simultaneously the numbers of both types of Council members and thus not neglect the factor of power in the composition of this body.

The permanent membership could be expanded by including all the great powers, those with worldwide influence and those with a predominately regional ascendancy. Thus, Japan, India, possibly Brazil, and one day Germany would qualify for a permanent seat. This would reflect the actual distribution of power around the world. The elective seats would be increased to provide better representation for various regions. The present situation, in which two out of six seats are in fact reserved for Latin America, is abnormal. Fair representation should be given to various areas, such as Southeast Asia, the Near East, Africa, Western and Eastern Europe, and Latin America, according to realistic divisions of the world into regions with similar cultural backgrounds and political interests.

A change in the composition of the Security Council involves an amendment of the Charter and could be prevented by any present permanent member if it refused its ratification.

Attention to the political activities of the United Nations should not obscure the important role of the organization and of its Specialized Agencies in promoting the multilateral co-operation of states in such areas as economics, finance, trade, the resettlement of refugees, social welfare, control over illicit trade in narcotics, the peaceful use of atomic energy, labor problems, food and agriculture, education, science, culture, health, civil aviation, telecommunications, postal exchanges, and meteorology. All those problems can usually be better handled on a multilateral basis and some cannot be effectively solved by bilateral agreements. These activities of the United Nations and of the Specialized Agencies are fruitful in reverse proportion to their political implications. The less a particular question is related to the power struggle and to the ideological conflict, the greater the likelihood that the member-states will be able to conclude working agreements. The work of the Universal Postal Union is practically unrelated to the explosive contemporary issues and hence can be smoothly carried on. The United Nations Educational, Scientific and Cultural Organization cannot always avoid hitting the rocks of ideological conflict. The problem of the Palestinian refugees seems at first glance to be a humanitarian question, but it cannot be divorced from the bitter Israeli-Arab animosity. The International Labor Organization has been confronted with such political issues as the meaning to attach to traditional notions of employer and labor union if these familiar notions must be placed within the new context of a fully nationalized economy.

Co-operation in these "nonpolitical" fields has, on the whole, been fruitful and has justified in itself the existence of the United Nations. But it would be a mistake to imagine that any matter pertaining to the relations between states, which are political units, is entirely free of political implications. No abstract and arbitrary line can be drawn between political and nonpolitical problems. "Nonpolitical" co-operation does not take place in a vacuum. Its framework is our divided world in which national interests often differ sharply, in which an ideological war is raging, in which cultural patterns and "self-evident truths" cannot be reduced to a common denominator by a simple formula or a miracle-working incantation. Yet states find it possible, even in our divided world, to co-operate whenever they feel that co-operation is in their mutual interest and does not prejudge the outcome of the political struggle.

The political value of the United Nations can be generalized as follows:

1. The organization is not a super-state and cannot achieve more than its members want to achieve. Since these members give the highest priority to national objectives and since these objectives are wide apart in our time of strife and rapid change, the chances for fruitful political co-operation on a universal scale are narrowly circumscribed.

2. The United Nations cannot guarantee peace or provide for an effective collective security, and its members must seek a precarious safety in their own armaments and in treaties of military assistance.

3. It can sometimes help, through mediation, to induce the parties to a dispute to seek a peaceful settlement, but it cannot compel them to do so. The existence of the International Court of Justice offers an excellent opportunity to the willing states for resolving their less important disputes by means of an impartial judgment. But the most dangerous political disputes and especially the political antagonisms, particularly insofar as they affect the great powers, escape the capability of the United Nations. The ideological strife and the power conflict between the two rival blocs are beyond the means of the organization and undermine its effectiveness as an institution for peace and co-operation.

4. As long as these antagonisms persist, disarmament negotiations have a slim chance for success.

5. The frequent meetings of the Security Council and of the General Assembly, as well as the existence of permanent embassies accredited to the organization, multiply the channels of diplomatic contact and offer a permanent occasion for confidential negotiations. This aspect of the United Nations is politically more important than its public debates insofar as the constructive work is concerned. All the smaller nations can easily contact one another at the seat of the United Nations, even if they cannot afford to maintain embassies in their respective capitals, and can co-ordinate their actions if they so wish. Great powers can reach small nations just as easily and can maintain contact with one another. The fact that the chief executives of the great powers and smaller nations sometimes attend the meetings of the General Assembly is useful for the same reason.

6. The public forum of the United Nations offers a resounding loudspeaker for worldwide propaganda. This is useful for the member-states although it has little in harmony with the official purposes of the organization.

7. The United Nations can organize executive actions, as evidenced in the Near East and in the Congo, if the member-states so desire. If a great power does not support this kind of action but tolerates it or if its opposition concerns an area where it cannot effectively intervene, the executive action can still be carried out over its protests. Otherwise, the opposition of a great power would preclude this undertaking from consideration or success.

8. The smaller nations derive distinct advantages from the United Nations. It is an ideal forum for displaying their vicarious power and influencing the policies of great powers. The principles of the Charter and the publicity of proceedings discourage, but do not always prevent, the great powers from taking actions harmful to small nations.

9. No revision of the Charter could improve the prospects of the organization, because these prospects are inextricably tied up with the whole complex of political relations among its members. The immediate future of the organization cannot look brighter than the total vista of our unsettled and troubled world. As President Kennedy said, the United Nations is not perfect but neither is the world of today.

10. The United Nations represents, by its very existence, a restraining factor due to the influence which the member-states can exert on the contending parties. Moreover, the General Assembly produces a kind of collective psychology which is peculiar to all deliberative assemblies. The ideas and trends popular in the General Assembly have an impact on the participating delegations, which in turn communicate this impact to their own governments. Collective psychological pressure, reflected in the reports which the delegations send back to their governments, may sometimes moderate the policies of the instructing governments. The practical importance of this collective mood, called the spirit of Geneva at the time of the League of Nations, should not be overrated, but its existence cannot be denied by anyone who has participated in international assemblies.

The Cuban crisis in the fall of 1962 brought spectacularly into focus the limitations and the usefulness of the United Nations as a political institution. The great adversaries, the United States and the Soviet Union, largely disregarded the United Nations and preferred the quick procedure of bilateral conversations in order to eliminate the risk of nuclear conflagration and to come to an understanding. Neither the Secretary General nor any member-state thought it appropriate to transfer the problem to the public forum of the General Assembly. Everyone, including the nonaligned states, understood that they could not be of any help in the sharp confrontation between the two principal nuclear powers.

However, both antagonists publicly presented their cases (in the debate in the Security Council, for example) with an eye to the reactions of other governments represented in the United Nations. Moreover, the United Nations proved its usefulness in two ways. First, it provided a convenient meeting ground for the American and Soviet delegations, which could confidentially work out a solution within the framework of a bilateral exchange of letters between the President of the United States and the Soviet Premier. Secondly, the Secretary General tactfully acted as a behind-the-scenes mediator trusted by both parties. For a short time, the two powers thought of using the United Nations machinery for an international inspection of the withdrawal of Soviet weapons; the Cuban veto prevented this procedure from being carried out.

The crisis threw a revealing light on the discrepancy between the influence of the underdeveloped countries within the United Nations and their incapacity to alter in any way the policies of the principal great powers in a moment of ominous crisis. The difference between the numerical majorities in the General Assembly and the actual distribution of power in the outside world was once again demonstrated. Even the close allies of the two powers had no opportunity to influence the decisions which these powers reached without consulting anyone, whether individual states or the United Nations. Yet these decisions, if they had been different, could have plunged the world into the greatest catastrophe of its history.

REGIONAL ORGANIZATIONS AND EUROPEAN INTEGRATION

A universal organization, even if it were perfect, could not solve all the problems arising out of the relations between states. There would always be room for bilateral treaties which are the framework for co-operation between any two states as well as for concerted efforts by any limited number of several states. If these several states are located within a definite geographical area and if they set up permanent machinery for carrying out their collaboration, the result is a *regional* organization. This organization may or may not function more efficiently than the universal organization; its success depends on the intentions and the actual performance of the participating states. The advantages and the weaknesses of the regional organization derive from the geographical proximity of its members. States situated in the same area usually have many cultural similarities because of their common roots and because of the influence which they have exerted on each other throughout their histories; they are also aware of the geographical features which make their region a recognizably distinct area. Their economies may be intertwined by mutual trade; at least, the whole region has a wealth and a variety of resources greater than any one state and, if integrated, would form a large economic market. The combined military power would be more effective than the arithmetical sum of the armed forces of individual states. The national loyalties could find a common denominator in familiar regional landmarks, in cultural affinities, and in a common history which is made up of the intertwined histories of the component nations. This common denominator is more tangible and easier to comprehend than the common denominator of the universal organization which seems a more remote abstraction.

However, geographical proximity is also an obstacle on the road to co-operation. The neighbors know each other better than any of them know distant lands. This knowledge has usually been acquired in mutual quarrels and wars. Their memories are haunted by the ghost of the past. The mutual hatreds and prejudices are alive. National independence and territorial integrity have usually been defended against one of the neighbors rather than against a distant country. The patriotism of each nation has been nourished by these struggles with its neighbors; it has asserted its vigor in opposition to them. The same struggles have made each nation jealous of its sovereignty, which would have to be restricted to make room for the jurisdiction of the regional organization.

The problem of the regional organization can be reduced to the question whether its advantages are attractive enough to outweigh the objections rooted in the historical past. The neighbors can be lured into the regional organization if it becomes obvious to them that this is the best way to serve their national interests. If their security is threatened by the same distant country, if their relative international status could not otherwise be preserved or restored, and if their economic growth were imperilled by the slow rate of progress of their unco-ordinated economies, they might be able to repress their animosities, try to forget their hatreds and prejudices, and begin to lay the foundations for a higher regional loyalty arising out of their national allegiances.

The secret of success of a regional organization consists in not attempting to suppress national loyalties, which are rooted in the hearts of modern men so deeply that any such attempt would be doomed to failure. It consists in building a regional allegiance as a projection and sublimation of national loyalties, in convincing people that they can become wiser patriots by uniting and providing a better and safer future for each of their individual countries. As a matter of fact, if mankind ever develops a common interest in an international super-state, the common allegiance without which this super-state cannot be realized will have to be built up in the same way, by proving that international co-operation is the highest expression of national loyalty and the best safeguard of individual national interests. Those who think that universal allegiance can take root only in the grave of national loyalties are profoundly mistaken, because they underestimate the intensity and vitality of national feelings.

While mankind has not yet been confronted with a common enemy (except perhaps the threat of nuclear suicide) who would compel it to unite and while it is rent by deep conflicts, the states located within the same region are placed in a more favorable situation for discovering a community of interests. So far the European Economic Community has been the only truly serious and successful attempt to achieve a viable regional organization founded on the national loyalties of six peoples. The success or failure of this Community will have wide repercussions in Europe and elsewhere, because it will prove whether the regional organization can produce results more tangible and more lasting than the universal organization.

The decline of Western Europe from the dominant position which it held before 1914 is due to several causes:

1. The rise of the two giant states, the United States and the Soviet Union, to positions of strength incomparably greater than that which any individual Western European state, including the United Kingdom, now has or might expect to have.

2. The two world wars, which were mainly waged in Europe and for which Europe paid the highest price in human and material losses.

3. The colonial retreat in Asia and Africa, which has deprived the European colonial powers of the freedom to dispose of the resources of those two continents.

In spite of the vigorous economic expansion of Western Europe since the last war, the fact remains that its international influence has greatly declined. Yet the same economic expansion proves that Western Europe is not a senile part of the world, but, on the contrary, a dynamic area destined to continue to play an important though no longer a dominant role on the international stage. While the individual Western-European states, including those which were once world powers, cannot hope to recapture their former position, they represent in combination a human and economic force which is at least equal to that of either the United States or the Soviet Union. In other words, Western Europe as a whole can reassert its international influence on a par with the two giant states, but only if its component states join forces. The political argument in favor of Western European integration can be reinforced by economic and social arguments; the example of the United States is there to prove that a large market stimulates production and leads to high living standards.

Co-operation requires a political reconciliation among nations which in the past were often divided from each other by bitter rivalries and disastrous wars. This, first of all, is the problem of the French-German reconciliation after a long period of mutual hostility that lasted for 150 years. This reconciliation was made possible after the last war by several factors. The French victory in 1918 was bought at the exorbitant price of millions of Frenchmen killed and was annulled by the defeat in 1940. Germany twice lost the war, in 1918 and in 1945. Insofar as the two world wars were German-French wars, they left the two nations with a feeling of frustration. The Nazi regime of occupation in France was much milder than in Eastern Europe and Russia and did not leave behind the same bitter resentment. Germany, reduced to its Western part, is no longer cutting the figure of a powerful partner who would leave France with only a second-rate role within a scheme of co-operation; the two countries will be more or less equal partners as long as Germany remains divided.

It cannot be said that the Second World War miraculously produced a European patriotism in Western Europe and that Frenchmen, Germans, and the others suddenly placed their loyalty to Western Europe above their allegiance to their own countries. To be a good European does not entail feeling a deep emotional attachment to the European Community but involves a rational recognition that each participating country will be best served economically and politically by co-operating closely with the others. A Frenchmen, a West German, an Italian, feels that he is even a better Frenchman, German, and so on if he is also a good European, i.e., favors Western European integration. General de Gaulle's formula "Europe of the Fatherlands" reflects a reality; European integration is intended to promote the various national interests, which are no longer deemed incompatible.

Only the future can answer several questions. Will the habit of co-operation eventually create an emotional attachment, a Western European patriotism comparable in intensity to the present national patriotisms? If this European patriotism were to emerge, would it become stronger than the national patriotisms, just as national feelings came to exceed in intensity feelings of attachment to province or city? Will the desire to co-operate survive the test of a serious emergency? The crisis may take either of two forms. One would be a sudden and deep conflict between the national interests of the partners. The other type of crisis would materialize if one of the members of the Western European Community were faced with a threat by a third state and the others had to decide whether they would assume the risks of declaring that the interests of one of them are the interests of all. Another question, rather academic under the present circumstances, concerns the consequences of German unification. If the unexpected happened and the 70 million Germans were again united within one state, would Frenchmen and others consent to remain in the Community, which could then be dominated by one partner who would be much stronger than each of the other members? The final question concerns the impact of the internal evolution of the member-states on the fate of the Community. Would it be possible to maintain an integrated community of states if some of them remained democratic while others came to espouse a different ideology? What is clear is the necessity for the member-states to pursue similar foreign policies toward the third states; obviously, if one of them quit NATO and chose a policy of neutrality or of friendship with the U.S.S.R., the Community could hardly continue to exist. Also, if the member-states were to adopt irreconcilably different attitudes toward the other Western powers, the United States and Britain, the cohesion of the Community would be subjected to dangerous strains.

The Western European integration follows the Swiss and American precedents, because it is founded on free acceptance by the participating states, not on overwhelming pressure from the strongest partner, as was the case in 1871 with the German unification under Prussian aegis.

The concept of Western European integration is accepted by the elites in all six countries, while the people at large either approve it or do not oppose it. The Communists alone disapprove, because they see in this integration an anti-Soviet combination. The controversial question is no longer whether there should be a Community of Six but rather what form the integration should take, that of a gradual limitation of national sovereignties in favor of the supranational organs of the Community or that of progressively closer co-operation among the governments, each of them retaining a final veto. The crux of the current quarrel between the adherents of de Gaulle's Europe of the Fatherlands and the followers of a supranational European Union can be summarized in the question whether the decisions of the European Community on important matters should be made unanimously or by a majority vote.

Fear of the Soviet Union and the desire to become less dependent on the United States have been motives shared by all six partners. The West Germans hope that one day they will be placed in a more advantageous position vis-à-vis Russia by enjoying the support of the 115 million other Western Europeans. The European Community prevents any renewal of the French-Russian understanding at German expense. The Germans and all the others expect that the vast market of 165 million will stimulate their expansion and make possible the continuation of the welfare state. Frenchmen see in the Community a consolidation of the German-French reconciliation and such an enmeshing of their economies that a German-French war becomes unthinkable. They also hope that Germany will help, through public and private investment, in the development of former French Africa and ensure the achievement of the Western European-African economic association, an association which would safeguard French economic and cultural influence in the former French colonies in spite of political decolonization. For both Frenchmen and Germans, the Community is the only hope to secure for their countries a voice in international affairs equal to the voices of the United States and the Soviet Union. For the Italians, the Western European Community offers an opportunity to recapture the international role lost in the last war, good prospects for investment by the other partners in the economic development of Italy, and a gradually freer emigration of Italian "surplus" labor to the more developed countries of the Community. The remaining three partners, Belgium, Holland, and Luxemburg, have learned from their Benelux customs union that a wider economic market would benefit them. The national interests of the Six are not sacrificed to the Community; on the contrary, these interests are furthered by its existence.

The success of the Community should not conceal the fact that Western Europe can never become a self-contained unit comparable to the United States or the Soviet Union. It is poor in natural resources and must import fuel and raw materials to survive economically. It might eventually become independent of Near Eastern oil, thanks partly to the Sahara oil fields (Algeria and Libya) and partly to atomic energy. But it will have to import raw materials. An economic association of French-speaking Africa with the Community would relieve Europe, at least partly, of its dependence on primary commodities imported from the other continents.

The economic success of the EEC and the prospect of closer political ties among the six states do not warrant the expectation that the EEC will ever become politically a true equal of the United States or the Soviet Union. The two principal powers have each only one center for the formulation of external policies. The six member-states of the EEC may in time improve their methods for co-ordinating foreign policies (this co-ordination was ineffective during the 1963 crisis over the British accession and over the nature of their relationship with the United States). However, as long as each of the six national governments reserves to itself the ultimate decisions concerning foreign policy, the members do not form one great power. To become a world power in the true sense, they would have to form a federal state, a prospect that seems very remote at best.

The three great powers outside the Community of Six have taken widely different attitudes toward it. The Soviet Union is hostile. It cannot welcome the association of Germany, its principal continental antagonist, with the other European countries or generally any integration of the "capitalist" states which necessarily strengthens them. By contrast, the United States has consistently supported the Community for three main reasons. A united Western Europe could one day relieve the United States of a good part of the burden of protecting the Atlantic community against the Communist bloc. A strong and prosperous Western Europe is welcome as a partner in financing the economic development of the Third World. Finally, the European Community is an attractive place for American private investments, which find there a safe market similar in size to the American market. However, the future support of the United States will depend on whether the common tariff wall, which will surround the Community, will hamper American imports; this question can be settled within the organization to which all Western European countries and the United States belong, the Organization for Economic Co-operation and Development.

Britain has not been particularly elated by the success of the Community of Six. It fears a continental association without its own participation but has found it extremely difficult to join. Traditionally, Britain has been opposed to any continental integration. It has been threatened in the past by integrations imposed by one country on the others (Napoleon's France and Hitler's Germany), but the other continental countries have looked upon Britain as their natural ally against the prospect of hegemony by one of them. The Community of Six, however, is a viable proposition, founded on voluntary acceptance. If successful, the Community will become a political and economic center comparable to the United States and the Soviet Union and far stronger than the United Kingdom. The British position as the closest ally of the United States could be lost to the Community. Economically, as the second industrial producer after the United States and the first importer of raw materials in the world, the Community would take Britain's position as the second Western power. Yet British hostility toward the Community of Six has not brought about its disintegration. Britain was faced with the clear-cut problem of either remaining outside the Community and being gradually outdistanced or joining it but paying a rather high price for doing so. In 1961, after much hesitation, the British Government decided in the face of a divided public opinion to enter into negotiations for adhesion to the Community. The French veto put an end in January, 1963, to these protracted negotiations, at least for the time being.

The difficulties encountered in negotiations between Britain and the Six were due not only to French reluctance to make concessions but also to the understandable insistence of the British on a special arrangement that would have facilitated their joining the EEC. These difficulties related to the need for a new orientation of the British people, to close British economic relations with the Commonwealth, to the British agricultural policy that would have to be adjusted to that of the Six, and to British obligations toward other members of the Free Trade Association which Britain had founded to counterbalance the EEC.

To have returned to the continent, which Britain had abandoned after the Hundred Years War, would have amounted psychologically to a major revolution in British political thinking. Could Britain become European and still retain its role as the center of the Commonwealth?

Preferential tariffs open the British market to the products of the Commonwealth (mainly primary commodities) but also greatly help British industries to sell on the Commonwealth markets by limiting Western European competition. It is true that preferential tariffs will gradually lose their significance for British industries, because the process of industrialization will compel the other members of the Commonwealth to protect their own industries against the British imports as well. If Great Britain were to abandon the preferential system by joining the European Community, the Commonwealth markets would be as open to the other members of the Community as they now are to Britain. British industries would be forced to keep pace with continental industries, not only because the tariffs between Britain and its continental partners would be eliminated, but also because preferential tariffs would disappear from the Commonwealth markets. This could eventually prove to be a healthy stimulus for British industries, just as the Common Market has been for the industries of the Six. But the close economic ties between the United

Kingdom and the Commonwealth would disappear, at the risk of weakening the structure of the Commonwealth. This could in turn undermine the traditional British position as the Commonwealth center for banking, shipping, insurance, and other services which Britain renders to its associates in return for large foreign earnings. The other members of the European Community could in time share this role with Britain.

If Britain joined, several other European countries would follow suit, notably some, if not all, members of the British-sponsored European Free Trade Association, which includes Britain, Sweden, Norway, Denmark, Austria, Switzerland, and Portugal. The avowed aim of this association is to create a preferential trade area, but the main objective is to apply joint pressure to the Community of Six in any reciprocal negotiations. Some of these states could not become full-fledged members of the Community for fear of compromising their neutrality in Soviet eyes; this is the case with Switzerland, Sweden, Austria, and Finland, which is an associated member of the Free Trade Area. However, it is possible that the Community could accommodate them through some intermediate association. This sort of half-membership (the status of an associated state) the EEC has already granted to Greece and is considering for the benefit of Turkey.

The relative importance for British trade of the various areas of the world can be visualized by glancing at the distribution of British imports and exports. In 1961 the percentages pertaining to those areas which are most important for the discussion of British participation in the EEC were as follows:

Area	British Imports from	British Exports to
The EEC	14.72	17.00
The EFTA	12.60	12.85
The U.S.A.	11.00	7.80
The Commonwealth	37.80	39.00

The above percentage for the EEC does not include either the African states associated with the Common Market or the French and Dutch dependencies.

During the last few years, the trend of British trade with EEC countries has been toward a constant increase in its relative importance.

The French government fears, not without reason, that expanding the membership of the Community may loosen the ties which bind its present members. The concessions which would have to be made to accommodate each new candidate would have this effect. Other Europeans regretfully conceded that British adhesion would impede the evolution toward a supranational form of union and would strengthen the concept of a Europe of the Fatherlands in which each Fatherland would retain an ultimate veto. Yet the other five seemed to be ready to pay this price for British admission.

The European Community owes its beginnings to the initiative of the French Foreign Minister Robert Schumann, who on May 9, 1950, launched the idea of a European Coal and Steel Community. Five other European countries responded favorably, and the European Coal and Steel Community Treaty was signed in 1951 and entered into force in 1952. This Treaty was destined to become the nucleus of the European Economic Community, which took shape in 1957. The approach taken in 1950 by the French government and since followed by the Six wisely avoided a frontal assault on the problem of European integration and placed economic co-operation at the top of the agenda. If the six governments had tried to draft a constitutional charter for a United States of Europe, a charter which would have limited the political jurisdiction of the member-states, and if they had produced the impression that they were founding a super-state, the reaction in their own countries would probably have been hostile and the whole venture would have collapsed in the initial stage. Schumann's functional approach did not offend national susceptibilities. The authority of the Coal and Steel Community did not extend to such ticklish matters as foreign policy or national defense, although the very existence of this Community could not but influence both. National sovereignty seemed to have been left intact in its most visible manifestations. "Only" a few aspects of economic life were to be regulated by the new Community. Yet the process of gradually enmeshing the lives of the six countries began then and there.

The main purpose of the Treaty of 1951 was to establish one market for coal and steel with the free circulation of these products across the borders of the member-states. Politically, it was hoped by its authors that the close co-operation of these two essential industries and their production for the whole market of the Six instead of for the national market alone would so entangle the economies of the member-states, in particular the economies of France and Germany, that none of them would retain enough economic autonomy to adopt a hostile policy toward any of the remaining five countries or to wage war on them.

The main powers of regulating the production and ensuring the free circulation of coal and steel were vested in a supranational organ, the High Authority, composed of nine members, eight appointed by their governments and the ninth elected by his eight colleagues. The advisory function was entrusted to a Consultative Committee composed of fifty-one representatives of producers, workers, distributors, and consumers; these representatives are appointed by the Council of Ministers from among competent persons in the six countries. The third organ was the Common Assembly of seventy-eight members elected by their national parliaments.

The Common Assembly could not legislate but could discuss the policies pursued by the High Authority and pass a motion of censure by a vote of two-thirds majority. If the Assembly were to approve a motion of censure, the High Authority would have to resign and its successor would have to be approved by the Assembly. The fourth organ was the Council of Ministers, composed of delegates appointed by their governments and charged with co-ordinating the policies of the High Authority and the national governments. The fifth body was the Court of Justice, composed of seven judges elected for six years. The national governments and private firms can appeal to it when they consider that the High Authority has exceeded its jurisdiction. The Court may quash the decisions of the Authority.

The next step toward European integration was less judicious because it confronted the problem from the most controversial political angle. A treaty signed in 1952 established a European Defense Community, a sort of European Army of the six countries. In effect, the six nations were asked to relinquish jurisdiction over their own armed forces. The treaty raised another delicate question: the rearmament of Western Germany seven years after the Second World War. The European Army was to be a clever device for the incorporation of German detachments in mixed European divisions; the German soldiers were to serve the Western cause without the German government having any authority over their employment. The treaty was approved by five parliaments but the sixth, the French, rejected it. The opposition came from two quarters: those who opposed German rearmament, and those who resisted any limitation on French military sovereignty. Paradoxically enough, the same French parliament which had killed the EDC approved soon after the Paris agreements on German rearmament in the form of an independent German army.

The setback was only temporary. In 1957, two important treaties were signed by the six governments in Rome: one for the formation of the European Economic Community (which merged some of the organs of the Coal and Steel Community with those of the new Community), and the other for the establishment of the European Atomic Agency (Euratom). Nineteen hundred and fifty-seven marked the turning point; since that time it has become gradually more probable that the European Community will survive and take deep roots in the soil of the six countries.

The treaty relating to the European Economic Community intended, first of all, to establish a customs union (a zone free of all governmental restrictions on free trade, such as customs duties, importation quotas, and currency regulations). The complete abolition of all these restrictions was to be effected within twelve or fourteen years beginning on January 1, 1959. The transitional period was divided into three stages: (1) four to six years for a 30 per cent reduction of customs duties from their 1957 level; (2) the next four years for a further reduction of 30 per cent; and (3) the last four years for the abolition of the remaining 40 per cent. At the same time, restrictive import quotas were to be eliminated. The first few years of the application of the treaty have been so encouraging that the six governments plan to cut down the transitional period to eight years and to achieve a fully free trade by the end of 1966. A uniform common tariff will then surround the six countries. The free trade will include all goods, including agricultural products which will be protected against foreign competition by an all-European tariff. The Common Market is expected to promote economic expansion at an annual rate of growth equal to from 4 to 5 per cent of national income and to bring about a rapid rise in living standards.

The European Community is, however, much more than a customs union. Its other features are as follows:

1. The free trade between the six countries could become, in effect, discriminatory against some of them, because the cost of production can be affected by factors beyond the control of an enterprise. Differences in taxation, in laws relating to wages, in national statutes on working conditions and social security, in state credit and monetary policies, are typical factors which escape control by a private enterprise but influence its cost of production. The Treaty of Rome obligates the signatories to co-ordinate their taxation, social, credit, and monetary policies in order to safeguard fair competition between their producers.

2. Free competition could favor those European areas which are most advanced industrially. The less developed areas of the Community could remain economically backward; their chances for development could be effectively killed by free competition with the existing industries and by the superior attraction which these industries hold for private investment. To prevent this development, the Treaty of Rome provides for joint action to promote an influx of funds to the less developed areas. The European Bank of Investment grants loans to governments and private enterprises for national and inter-state development projects and for the modernization or conversion of enterprises or for the founding of new ones.

3. Free competition promotes the growth of the most efficient industries and results in the elimination of less efficient enterprises; at the same time, it creates the social problem of unemployment by closing enterprises and undermining entire regional industries which cannot compete with more efficient enterprises and industries. The Community has its own European Social Fund which helps the governments to provide the financial assistance which must be given to the workers affected. This assistance usually takes the form of transferring workers from one region to another but within the same industry or of retraining them for new industrial occupations.

4. The European Economic Community is planned to become what its name indicates. The Treaty of Rome not only foresees the formation of a common market in which goods would circulate freely as they now circulate within each national territory, but it also envisions a common economy in which all obstacles would be gradually removed and a free circulation of men, capital, and services ensured. By the end of this decade or earlier, the territories of the member-states will be open for the mutual investment of capital, for the free migration of labor, and for the no less free exchange of services such as banking, insurance, and transportation. The free circulation of labor will be guaranteed by the national treatment offered to workers who are nationals of any of the six countries (the same wages, working conditions, social insurance benefits, and pensions as those which the citizens of the country of immigration enjoy).

5. Euratom, which is the third European Community, aims to promote the use of atomic energy for peaceful purposes, through research and through the joint effort of the six countries. The final objective is to make the European Community independent of imported energy.

6. The Treaty of Rome faced another problem of great importance for France and for French-speaking Africa. Since the last war, France has been investing large public funds in its African overseas territories to help in building up the social-economic substructure. It also offers to those African territories a preferential tariff for imports of agricultural products, notably coffee, bananas, cocoa, and vegetable oil, which face stiff competition from other producers on the international market. Especially now, when the former French colonies have become independent states, these financial and economic ties are important for France because they help to maintain French influence in Africa. But the Treaty of Rome, with its concept of one tariff for all the six countries, raised the question of future economic relations between France and French-speaking Africa. France solved the question by favoring the extension of its close relations with Africa to the whole European Community. This is being achieved in two complementary ways. First, the Community has a Fund of Overseas Investment which provides public funds derived from the contributions by the six states for the development of the economic-social substructure of the African countries which used to be the dependencies or trusteeships of France, Belgium, or Italy. Secondly, the EEC has assented to the extension of the preferential trade system from France to the whole Community, which now acts jointly as an economic partner of French-speaking Africa.

This twofold economic co-operation between the EEC and the African states, inaugurated by the Treaty of Rome, was extended into the future by a treaty of association signed on July 20, 1963, in Yaoundé, the capital of Cameroon. The eighteen African signatories, all of them former French, Belgian, or Italian colonial dependencies, were Burundi, Cameroon, the Central African Republic, Congo (Brazzaville), Congo (Leopoldville), Ivory Coast, Dahomey, Gabon, Upper Volta, Madagascar, Mali, Mauritania, Niger, Ruanda, Senegal, Somalia, Chad, and Togo. Among the former French dependencies only four remain outside the association with the EEC: Algeria, Morocco, Tunisia, and Guinea. However, the three North African states have bilateral agreements with France concerning trade and French economic and technical assistance.

The Treaty of Yaoundé concedes to the African states three important advantages:

1. The offer of $730 million which the six European countries will invest over the next five years in the development and diversification of the African economy. These public funds will be transferred to the African governments in the form of grants and loans.

2. The preferential access of tropical African commodities to the markets of the Six. In exchange, the African states will open their markets to the imports of the Six, all of which will enjoy the preferential treatment formerly reserved for the colonial power. They retain, however, the right to defend their infant industries against Western European competition with protective tariffs. Moreover, they may form customs unions or free trade zones with other African states, even those which have not signed the treaty of Yaoundé, for example the former British dependencies.

3. Technical assistance which the Six will step up in order to increase the absorptive capacity of African economies. The training of Africans in Europe and the sending of European experts to Africa will be the principal means.

The guiding idea of the treaty consists in the gradual reduction of tariff preferences now enjoyed by the eighteen African states and the compensating progressive increase in financial assistance. The Six would like to terminate the tariff discrimination against the other producers of tropical commodities who are their customers for industrial products. They hope that this discrimination will eventually become superfluous without endangering the interests of their African associates thanks to the transfer of European funds and the resulting increased diversification of African economies. If these hopes are realistic and if the African associates consent to the gradual removal of preferential treatment, the beneficiaries of this change will be the other African states, mainly former British dependencies, and Latin American exporters of tropical commodities. They already benefit from the first steps taken in the treaty in this direction of equal treatment, namely by the removal of preferences for tea and tropical woods, by a 40 per cent reduction of these tariff preferences for coffee and cocoa beans, and by a 25 per cent reduction for pineapples, vanilla, and spices.

The eighteen African signatories of the treaty do not seem to be enthusiastic about British accession to the EEC. They know that if Britain accedes the English-speaking African states will submit their claim to Western European financial assistance. The fund would have to be distributed not only among the 50 million people living in the present eighteen African associates but also among over 70 million people in English-speaking Africa. This simple arithmetical calculation seems to be more persuasive than all the talk about Pan-African unity and solidarity.

The European Economic Community is the largest importer of raw materials in the whole world. Its present and its future depend on free access to the sources of raw materials. A close economic co-operation with Africa might be of considerable importance in ensuring greater European independence of the remaining continents. The paucity of geological surveys of Africa results in two current opinions. The pessimists believe that Africa is not very rich in raw materials, while the optimists think that it is a treasure-house whose full wealth has not yet been discovered and point to the already known resources and the recent discoveries of oil and minerals in the Algerian Sahara. In any case, close European-African co-operation should be mutually beneficial. The Treaties of Rome and of Yaoundé opened the road toward this co-operation.

Britain remaining outside, the close economic co-operation between the European Community and French-speaking Africa results in cutting Africa in two, just as Western Europe is divided by the Community itself. The former French and Belgian colonies revolve within the economic orbit of the Community, while the former or present British Africa remains the economic satellite of the United Kingdom. The British accession would not only have reunified Western Europe but would also have helped to bring the African states together regardless of their former colonial allegiances. In this respect, the Europeans will once again decide the fate of Africa.

7. These various aspects of the Community indicate that it is destined to become an association much wider in its implications than a customs union. The governments of the member-states are compelled to co-ordinate their policies, domestic and external, insofar as these policies can affect the functioning of the Community. A venture which seems at first glance to be purely economic is in fact political. If a further transfer of powers to the supranational organs is at present improbable, the close co-operation will be the result of a constant co-ordination of policies by the participating governments. The former ideal of a European federal state is being replaced by that of a confederation of European states which is nevertheless a highly coherent organization because of the dovetailing of the economies of its partners. The member-states are thinking of formally organizing their political co-operation by superimposing on the three existing communities a political confederation with joint councils which would, probably by unanimity, co-ordinate their external policies toward third states.

The total population of the Community is 165 million, not significantly less than the population of the United States or the Soviet Union. The Six together are the first importer and the second exporter (after the United States) in the world. They import about the same amount of raw materials as the United States and Britain together. Their total steel production in 1960 was equal to over 20 per cent of the world's output, i.e., amounted to 72.8 million tons.

Even if the ties of the Community are further strengthened and if it is able to speak with one voice in the international arena, Western Europe will not recapture its former dominant position; but it will command an influence comparable to that of the two giant powers, a prospect well beyond the reach of any of the six partners acting alone.

The European Community will be a third great economic complex existing side by side with the two other, the United States and the Soviet Union. The other states in Europe and in the other continents, which do not want to be associated with any of these three economic complexes, will find themselves in a decidedly awkward situation; their greatly reduced bargaining power will put them at a serious disadvantage in commercial negotiations with any of the three economic giants, and their economic isolation will not enhance their political stature.

The organization of the European Economic Community is as follows:

1. The Commission is the executive body, comparable to the High Authority of the Coal and Steel Community. It is composed of nine members appointed by agreement between the six governments. Not more than two members may be of the same nationality, and their mandate is for four years but renewable. Its decisions are made by a majority vote. It is a supranational organ, but its decisions can be abrogated by a unanimous vote in the Council of Ministers. The Commission watches over the application of the Treaty of Rome and administers the Social and Overseas Development Funds of the Community.

2. The Council of Ministers is composed of six Ministers, each designated by his government. It makes its most important decisions unanimously; less important decisions require only a qualified majority vote.

3. The European Parliamentary Assembly is a consultative body composed of 142 deputies elected by the six parliaments. Its resolutions are adopted by a majority vote. It performs its consultative function for all three communities, having replaced for the Coal and Steel Community its own Common Assembly. It may censure the Coal and Steel High Authority, the EEC Commission, or the Euratom Commission; each must then resign and be replaced by new members. It may not, however, censure the Councils of Ministers.

4. The Court of Justice is also now the same for all three Com-

munities. It is composed of seven judges appointed by agreement between the six governments. It rules in disputes between the member-states concerning the alleged nonfulfillment of their obligations and also in other disputes brought before it by the governments, private firms, or individuals and involving complaints that due jurisdiction has been exceeded by one of the three Commissions or of the three Councils of Ministers.

5. The Economic and Social Council is composed of 101 representatives of various economic organizations (industrial producers, workers, farmers, merchants, liberal professions, consumers, etc.) who are selected by the Council of Ministers to represent fairly the economic interests of the six national societies. This Committee has replaced a similar one of the Coal and Steel Community and now performs this advisory function for all three communities by addressing its views to their Commissions and Councils of Ministers.

Euratom has its own executive Commission of five members and its own Council of Ministers.

The existence of rival economic associations (the European Economic Community [EEC] and the European Free Trade Association [EFTA]) divides Western Europe and therefore weakens the ties of the North Atlantic community. However, all members of the EEC and most members of the EFTA are bound together by other ties which might prove stronger than the economic and political disagreements between the two competitive associations. Political friendships and trade cut across the boundary line between the two economic organizations. They belong to NATO, which links Western Europe to North America and which is the ultimate bulwark of their security. They can co-operate economically, not only through bilateral and multilateral agreements, but also through their membership in organizations larger than Western Europe—GATT, which is a universal platform for tariff reductions, and the Organization for Economic Co-operation and Development, where they find themselves in the company of the United States and Canada. It is not out of the question that some *modus vivendi* will be found between the EEC and the EFTA.

If the Western Europeans chose to do so, they could make better use of an existing European organization for their political co-operation and for resolving their differences. The name of this organization, founded in 1949, is the *Council of Europe*. Fifteen states are members: Western Germany, France, Italy, Belgium, Netherlands, Luxemburg (the Six of the EEC), Britain, Denmark, Norway, Sweden, Austria (members of the EFTA), Iceland, Ireland, Greece, and Turkey. Of the members of the EFTA, only Portugal and Switzerland do not belong to the Council, Portugal because of its undemocratic regime and Switzerland because of its permanent neutrality (in this respect Switzerland follows a more cautious policy than Austria, which is also permanently neutral). Except for uncommitted Austria, Ireland, and Sweden, all others are NATO members.

The purpose of the Council is aptly expressed in its Statute, which refers to the "need of a closer unity between all like-minded countries of Europe." *Like-minded* refers to the democratic regimes of the member-states and excludes the Communist and authoritarian states.

The Council has three organs: the Committee of Ministers, on which all the participating states are represented by their Foreign Ministers; the Consultative Assembly; and a permanent secretariat located in Strasbourg, France. The Committee may recommend to member-states a common policy concerning any matter of mutual interest. It is self-evident that the Foreign Ministers may agree only on those recommendations which their governments have accepted in advance. The Consultative Assembly is meant to be a meeting ground for the national parliaments. Its delegates are nominated by their political parties and then elected by their parliaments. The 135 seats in the Assembly are distributed among the various countries roughly in proportion to their populations; in turn, the composition of each national delegation reflects the parliamentary strength of its national parties. This composition is deemed to mirror the various political shades of opinion in non-Communist Europe. However, the national parliaments exclude from their delegations the Communist deputies who represent in France and Italy large sections of the electorate. Moreover, the delegates have no mandate for speaking in the name of their governments, parliaments, or political parties. Once sent to Strasbourg, they are free to express any opinion within the limits traced by their party discipline and the national interests of their countries. They know that they do not commit anyone, and their speeches tend to be much more "European" than they would be if made in their own parliaments. A delegate might be an enthusiastic "European" at the Assembly, but if he later becomes a member of his national government, he might take a less sympathetic attitude toward European unity. An old-timer of the Assembly was not off the mark when he summarized his experience in Strasbourg in one word, "frustration." Participation in the Assembly is frustrating because its deliberations have a discouraging lack of effect. The Assembly may adopt, by a two-thirds majority, recommendations addressed to the Committee of Ministers, who may quietly put them on the shelf. Judging from the actual policies of the governments, the annual sessions of the Assembly have so far made no major difference. The visible results in integration have been achieved elsewhere, in the EEC. However, the Council of Europe exists and would be available if the rival European groups wanted to make good use of it as a common means for understanding and co-operation.

Finally, if circumstances were to favor a renewed search for mutual understanding, Britain and the Six could revive the now dormant Western European Union. This association is founded on the Brussels Treaty signed in 1948 by Britain, France, Belgium, the Netherlands, and Luxemburg. West Germany and Italy acceded to it several years later. The Treaty provides for mutual military help in case of aggression committed by a third state but also for political consultation. It is this latter provision in the Treaty that could be used for closer political co-operation between the Six and Britain. So far, the Treaty has not played a major role in Western European politics. It has been overshadowed in its military and political aspects by a larger association, founded on the North Atlantic Treaty, and in its political aspects also by a more restricted association among the Six based on the solid economic integration of the EEC. However, this paper bond between the Six and Britain might become another useful device for bridging their differences.

THE COMMONWEALTH

The Commonwealth of Nations is not a regional organization, because it is not organized and does not cover a well-defined geographical area. The heir to the British Empire, it is composed of member-states located in all the continents, separated by the vast stretches of the ocean, and often culturally unrelated. It is a conglomeration of peoples whom the hazards of European wars and British political skill, military conquests, geographical discoveries, trading interests, and maritime power had placed under the jurisdiction of the British Crown. Their emancipation gave these peoples political independence; the British Empire has been transformed into the Commonwealth, which no longer bears the qualification *British*. The process of transformation is not yet complete, because each of the remaining British dependencies will join the Commonwealth on the day of its emancipation. The Commonwealth defies definition; it is a loose and voluntary association of independent states without any common organs of overall jurisdiction. Each member may withdraw from the association on its own decision, as Ireland and South Africa have done. Yet the concordant interests of its members make it a living reality. What are those interests which persuade the United Kingdom and its former colonial possessions to remain in the association?

1. Each member is fully independent in its external and domestic policies and does not feel that its sovereignty is in any way restricted by participation in the Commonwealth. Each freely formulates its own foreign policy, including issues of war and peace. The absence of any common federal organs makes the bonds of the Commonwealth light to bear. Actually, the foreign policies of member-states differ from each other. Ireland, at that time a member, was free to remain neutral in the Second World War which was deciding the fate of both the United Kingdom and the whole Commonwealth. Several members now follow the policy of noncommitment, while the others belong to the Western military system. However,

each member knows that usually, though not always, it can count on the residue of solidarity which ties the Commonwealth together. None, therefore, feels lonely in an unsettled world.

The power structure of the United Kingdom is enhanced by this constellation of states grouped around it as the main center. Owing to the existence of the Commonwealth it can claim to have remained a world power, although it would be more exact to say that the Commonwealth itself is a sort of world power insofar as it is able to exert the combined influence of its members on the course of international politics. The other members, if they left the Commonwealth, would assume the figure of what they are separately, namely, medium or small nations. Even India is only a prospective great power, its graduation depending on its success in the process of modernization. Membership does not entail a diminution of national independence but enhances the international status of each member.

The members' only mutual obligation is to consult each other on matters of common concern. Consultation consists of a continuous exchange of information, comments and opinions, but does not impose the obligation to agree. The principal channels of communication are: the Prime Ministers' conferences, the daily contacts between the British Office of Commonwealth Relations and the Departments of External Affairs of other member-states, the less frequent contacts between these departments, and the messages exchanged between the members' High Commissioners, who are ambassadors adorned with a different title, and the government of another member to whom the High Commissioner is accredited. The purpose of these exchanges is to communicate to each other information on foreign affairs, as well as to seek the views of other members on those matters which a member-state is called upon to decide but which might affect the interests of other members or of the whole Commonwealth. These views, confidentially expressed, are duly taken into consideration, but the final decision rests with the member concerned. Consultation does not even mean that a member who has concurred in a political decision taken by another member shares the responsibility for the consequences of that decision. The members greatly benefit by the information on foreign affairs supplied by the United Kingdom and sometimes have the occasion to reciprocate.

2. The industrially advanced members, such as the United Kingdom, are able to provide military equipment to other members. Conversely, the industries developed in the Commonwealth countries serve the British purpose of strategic dispersal which cannot be achieved within the small territory of the United Kingdom. The dispersal of sources of supplies and of the location of vital stocks also has a military significance for Great Britain. The far-flung overseas territories would allow Britain in case of war to use them as military bases and as training grounds for the British

military personnel with the consent of the member-states concerned. Scientific research of military significance can be shared with or jointly carried on by the member-states. Commonwealth co-operation in intelligence activities is mutually profitable. Finally, there is a strong possibility that a member engaged in a war with an outsider might be militarily or at least politically supported by all or most of the other members. The security of member-states is, in other words, increased by the existence of the Commonwealth in spite of the lack of any obligation of mutual military assistance.

3. There are close economic relations between the members, especially between the United Kingdom and the others. Preferential tariffs favor British industrial exports, and also open the British market to the primary commodities of other members. London remains the banking, shipping, insurance, and monetary center of the Commonwealth. Except for Canada, all members are included within the sterling area, which in itself stimulates their mutual trade.

4. The educated elites in the Commonwealth use English either as their native language or as the *lingua franca.* Out of the total population of the Commonwealth and the British Empire about 12.5 per cent know English and for 11 per cent it is their native language. Thus, English is the cultural bond between these elites, who exert the decisive influence on the policies of their countries. British publications, news agencies, radio broadcasts, and other media of information have, therefore, an impact on the formulation of opinion on international affairs throughout the Commonwealth.

5. The newly independent member-states in Africa need, for the time being, the services of the British "expatriates" (military officers, civil servants, and other specialists) to help them in operating the state machinery. This ensures the survival of the British influence after the political emancipation.

The fact that the members follow divergent foreign policies actually helps Britain to maintain a footing in various international groupings to which it cannot belong, such as the Asian-African bloc.

For these and other reasons the Commonwealth is a solid structure although the bricks of which it is made are almost invisible. However, there are also enervating centrifugal forces, of which the following are the strongest.

1. The members are sharply divided into advanced and underdeveloped countries. Their individual political, economic, and social problems are altogether different. The underdeveloped members are beset with all the difficulties which they share with other underdeveloped countries. Moreover, their independence is new and they face the grave problem of national integration. They all may survive the pressure of sectional interests

and the centrifugal aspirations of their linguistic, religious, or tribal groups, or some of them may succumb to these adverse forces. In other words, the political stability of the United Kingdom, Canada, Australia, and New Zealand has no counterpart in the new member-states.

2. The old members are all united by the same European civilization, while the new members are the products of different cultural histories, even though all of them were influenced by European civilization during the former British rule. The present elites among the Asian and African members are in the cultural sense Anglicized, but their successors will be educated at the native schools and may no longer feel culturally close to the United Kingdom.

3. The color line divides the Commonwealth. The fact that South Africa was compelled in 1961 to quit the Commonwealth is indicative of the high importance of the racial problem for the Asian and African members. The same problem might produce other frictions in the future. The "colored" people form almost 90 per cent of the total population of the Commonwealth.

4. At least one but a very important member, India, will one day attain the strength of a great power and then may feel that it no longer needs the additional security provided by the Commonwealth.

5. The solidarity of the Commonwealth is being undermined by conflicts of national interests among its members. The perpetual discord between India and Pakistan, the problem of Indian Tamils in Ceylon, the precariously held balance between the Malays, Chinese, and Indians within the Federation of Malaya or between the Greeks and Turks in Cyprus, the uncertain future allegiance of the Chinese majority in Singapore, the rivalries between the leaders of the newly independent African states, could become serious divisive forces. These intra-Commonwealth disputes can place Great Britain in a very delicate position. Britain would always try to act as a moderating and mediating factor, but the quarrelling members might want it to take sides and be bitterly disappointed if it refuses to do so. Actually Asian-African pressure compelled the United Kingdom to choose in 1961 between those members and South Africa. This might not be the final case for choosing between the contending members. Unequal density of population might give rise to future conflicts. India and Pakistan are overpopulated, but Canada, Australia, and New Zealand continue to close their doors to colored immigration. Free immigration from the Caribbean possessions has confronted the United Kingdom itself with the new problem of race riots and of the co-existence of two racial communities.

The future of the Commonwealth, like that of any international association, ultimately depends on the moderation of its members and their conviction that their participation serves their national interests.

THE ORGANIZATION OF AMERICAN STATES (OAS)

This is another regional organization. Its enthusiasts trace its beginnings to Simon Bolivar's letter of June 12, 1818, in which he urged the need for an American pact uniting the newly independent republics into a "single body politic." However, he thought of the unity of Spanish American republics only; a conference, held through his initiative, gathered together in 1826 in Panama the representatives of several of those republics but ended in a complete failure.

In reality the first modest beginning of organized multilateral inter-American co-operation took place in 1889-90 at a conference of American states held on the initiative of the United States. This conference established the International Union of American States; the purpose of this Union was clearly reflected in the name of its only permanent institution called the Commercial Bureau of the American Republics. This first Inter-American organization planned to promote trade by the exchange of commercial information. During the following two decades the name of the Bureau was changed to the International Union of American Republics, and finally in 1910 the name Pan American Union was adopted. These alterations in the name of the Bureau corresponded to the gradual amplification of the tasks which the American states entrusted to it. The Pan American Union and its association of states, called at that time the Union of American Republics (this name also was subject to small variations), had an uneventful history in the inter-war period. The solidarity of the Western Hemisphere during the Second World War and the need felt for closer co-operation brought about in 1948 the adoption of a formal constitutional Charter at a conference held in Bogota. This regional organization of the Western Hemisphere, renamed in 1948 the Organization of American States, has the following structure:

1. The territories of member-states cover the whole Western Hemisphere except for Canada, which so far has declined to join, and the British, French, and Dutch possessions, which cannot become members as long as they are dependent. The present members are, therefore, the United States and the Latin American republics.

2. The Inter-American Conferences are the policy-making body. They meet once every five years but can be convened at any other time with the approval of two-thirds of the member-states. All members are represented at the conferences and have one vote each. Decisions are made by a two-thirds majority.

3. At the request of any member-state a Meeting of Consultation of Foreign Ministers may be called to consider urgent problems, particularly cases of armed attack against one of the American states or of a threat to the peace of the Hemisphere. The request must be addressed to the Council

of the OAS, which decides on it by a majority vote; if the Council accepts the request, the meeting is convoked. The Meeting of Consultation makes decisions by a two-thirds majority.

4. The Council is the permanent executive body of the Organization with its headquarters in Washington, D.C. It performs the following functions: It deals with any question referred to it by the Inter-American Conference or the Meeting of Consultation; it may recommend matters for consideration either by the Conference or the Meeting; it serves as a permanent committee of liaison for the member-states; it may, in cases of utmost urgency, provisionally perform the functions of the Meeting of Consultation until such time when the Meeting is actually assembled; it supervises the activities of the Pan American Union. Its decisions are made by a two-thirds majority. Unlike the Security Council of the United Nations, the Council of the OAS, as well as the Meeting of Consultation of Foreign Ministers, is composed of representatives of all member-states, of whom none has the veto power.

5. The Pan American Union, located in Washington, is headed by a Secretary-General who is appointed for a term of ten years. It performs the functions of the secretariat of the OAS.

6. The OAS has its own regional Economic and Social Council, an Inter-American Council of Jurists, an Inter-American Cultural Council, a Pan American Institute of Geography and History, an American International Institute for the Protection of Childhood, a Pan American Sanitary Organization, an Inter-American Institute of Agricultural Sciences, an Inter-American Indian Institute, and since 1959 an Inter-American Development Bank. These specialized regional agencies parallel to a large extent the organization of the United Nations and its Specialized Agencies. Members of the OAS can hold, if they want, Inter-American Conferences on special matters of hemispheric significance, such as the Conference of Punta del Este in 1961 which launched the program of the Alliance for Progress (see Chapter 5).

The mutual political obligations of member-states are defined in two important instruments, the Rio de Janeiro Treaty of Mutual Assistance signed in 1947 and the Charter of the Organization signed in 1948 in Bogota. These obligations are as follows:

1. "An act of aggression against one American state is an act of aggression against all other American states . . ." (Article 5, paragraph F of the Charter which repeats the formula of the Rio Treaty). This obligation to assist each other extends to all acts of aggression whether committed by an outsider or by an American state.

2. Controversies between the American states should be peacefully settled by submission to any of the existing international procedures (Article 5, paragraph G of the Charter). If the parties so wish, they may refer their case for mediation to the Inter-American Peace Committee which is

composed of five persons usually selected from among the members of the Council of the OAS.

3. Article 15 of the Charter contains an important obligation: "No state or group of states has the right to intervene, directly or indirectly, for any reason whatsoever, in the internal or external affairs of any other state. The foregoing principle prohibits not only armed force but also any other form of interference or attempted threat against the personality of the state or against its political, economic, or cultural elements." This sweeping obligation is reinforced by Article 17, which reads: "The territory of a state is inviolable; it may not be the object, even temporarily, of military occupation or of other measures of force taken by another state, directly or indirectly, on any grounds whatsoever. . . ." This prohibition of intervention and of using force is somehow moderated by a reservation in Article 19 which says that measures adopted for the maintenance of peace and security, in accordance with the existing treaties, do not constitute a violation of the principles of non-intervention and of the inviolability of territories.

4. Economic co-operation is declared in Article 5, paragraph I, to be "essential to the common welfare and prosperity of the peoples of the continent." This provision has been given practical meaning by the foundation of the Inter-American Bank for Development and by the Alliance for Progress.

The OAS has helped, since the adoption of the Charter, in handling several controversial issues such as the cases of Costa Rica and Nicaragua in 1948-49, the Caribbean situation in 1950, the problems arising out of the overthrow of the pro-Communist government in Guatemala in 1954, the dispute between Costa Rica and Nicaragua in 1955, the quarrel between Honduras and Nicaragua in 1957, and the oft-recurring problem of the Communist regime in Cuba.

The vitality of the OAS, like any other regional organization, is dependent, in part, on the co-ordination of policies regarding matters of common concern and those related to nonmembers. In view of the disparity of power between the United States and the other members, this condition amounts to the expectation that Latin American foreign policies toward the Eastern Hemisphere would follow the guiding lines of the policy practised by the United States, the only member to have vital stakes in both hemispheres. This expectation rests on the assumption that national interests of all member-states coincide with those of the United States. This assumption has been challenged by Cuba, which follows a foreign policy diametrically opposed to that of the United States. The new trend among several Latin American countries toward a foreign policy more independent of the United States, including an inclination toward noncommitment, might make the co-ordination of policies more difficult than formerly. Open hostility on the part of any nation against the most important member of the OAS makes it practically impossible for that nation to participate in the Organization, as the Cuban case has proved. A policy of noncommitment regarding U.S.-Soviet or Sino-U.S. confrontations would be hard to reconcile with the obligations of mutual military assistance which are an integral part of the Rio Treaty and of the Bogota Charter.

The OAS, if analyzed in terms of distribution of power, has one analogy with the Warsaw Treaty organization and the Soviet-East European Council for Mutual Economic Aid. It also is made up of one mighty great power, which occupies the dominating position in the area, and of several weak states which depend in their economic lives mostly on their trade with the same power. This contrast between the United States and other members is heightened by the fact that the former power is economically the most advanced state in the whole world, while the other members of the OAS are at best unevenly developed and most of them simply underdeveloped. This key factor in the Western Hemisphere indicates that the OAS may effectively function in either of two situations: a heavy and constant pressure by the United States "to keep in line" the Latin American republics, or a great restraint on the part of the United States (a "good neighbor" policy) and a painstaking effort to devise together with the Latin American republics a joint compromise policy to be carried out through a truly voluntary co-operation. Neither attitude is easy.

The OAS, if understood as a true forum of regional collaboration, can effectively function if member-states are able and willing to find a common denominator for their interests. The Alliance for Progress is an attempt at finding this common denominator in mutual collaboration for the economic and social modernization of Latin America.

Cuba's military, political, and economic commitment to the Soviet bloc is the most serious challenge in the whole history of the Monroe Doctrine, but it also is the most crucial test of inter-American solidarity vis-à-vis outside powers. The question which the Latin American republics will have to answer is whether the Soviet presence in Cuba is a matter of vital significance to the United States only or to the whole Organization, and whether the Western Hemisphere should remain closed to political penetration by outside great powers or should the outside influence be welcomed as a counterweight to the United States? The problem for the United States lies in another question, namely, whether the economic and social modernization of Latin America will progress under political flags friendly to the United States or, as in Cuba, under a hostile banner?

THE ARAB LEAGUE

This is still another regional organization founded in 1945 to co-ordinate the policies of the Arab states. It is a loose association, each member-state having the right to formulate its own policies according to its own judgment. The Council of the League may adopt its decisions only by unanimity. The obligation of member-states to assist each other in case of outside aggression is not very meaningful, because the statutes of the League do not specify what measures of assistance should be taken and because the implementation of this obligation is contingent on the unanimous agreement of member-states. Each member-state is obliged to respect the domestic regime of another member, a duty too often forgotten by the Arab states in their mutual relations. The seat of the League is in Cairo, and a Secretary General heads its permanent secretariat.

The record of the Arab League is far from impressive. The first major test of its cohesion in 1948-49, the joint war against Israel, was a disastrous failure. The second, at the time of the British-French-Israeli attack on Egypt, was not a show of true solidarity except for eloquent words of support showered on Egypt. The third potential test, namely the ability of member-states to co-operate in their economic development by a joint use of profits from oil, has not so far been passed. The main weakness of the League consists in the rivalries and quarrels among its members. Its only cementing tie is the hostility to Israel, but the League members have been unable to synchronize their attitudes toward the great powers which compete within the Arab world.

Finally, another embryonic regional organization should be mentioned. In 1963, at a conference held in Addis Ababa by their heads of state, the independent African states founded the Organization for African Unity (OAU). This organization is intended to be a loose association of the African continent and a means for the co-ordination of African external policies.

APPENDIX I: STRUCTURE OF THE UNITED NATIONS

Membership. Members are either those states which founded the United Nations at the San Francisco Conference in 1945 or states which were subsequently admitted by the General Assembly upon recommendation of the Security Council. Recommendation by the Security Council requires a majority decision by seven members of the Council, including the five permanent members who have the power of veto and may prevent admission by casting a negative vote. The General Assembly admits by a two-thirds majority vote. Total membership has already exceeded 110; the large increase is due mainly to the admission of newly independent states. The division of Germany, Vietnam, and Korea into two states each precludes their admission. A member-state may be expelled by the General Assembly on the recommendation of the Security Council.

The General Assembly is composed of representatives of all member-states. All important decisions, including elections to the other organs of the United Nations, are made by a two-thirds majority. Other matters are decided by a simple majority. The General Assembly may discuss any matter within the scope of the Charter and make appropriate recommendations. It may in particular examine disputes between states and recommend a settlement. It also approves the budget of the United Nations and exercises a general supervision over the activities of other organs of the United Nations; the Security Council, however, is a co-equal organ and is not subordinate to the General Assembly. The Uniting for Peace Resolution of 1950 granted to the General Assembly a jurisdiction originally reserved by the Charter for the Security Council. This resolution authorized the General Assembly to examine threats to or breaches of international peace, and to make recommendations concerning the measures to be taken by the United Nations if the Security Council were prevented from taking any action because of veto by a permanent member.

The Security Council consists of eleven members, five permanent (the United States, the Soviet Union, Britain, France and the Republic of China) and six nonpermanent members, elected by the General Assembly for two-year terms. The terms of office of elective members overlap, because half of them are elected each year. The General Assembly is guided in these elections by the principle of equitable geographical representation of the membership of the United Nations.

The Security Council adopts its resolutions on substantive matters by the votes of at least seven of its members, but a resolution is not valid if one of the permanent members votes against it. This is the so-called veto power of the permanent members, who nevertheless may permit adoption of the resolution not only by voting for it but also by abstaining. Procedural matters are decided by a vote of any seven members. Therefore, a permanent member cannot prevent any matter from being placed on the agenda of the Council. A member of the Council, even a permanent one, must abstain from voting on resolutions related to any international dispute to which it is a party. A non-member of the Council, if a party to a dispute, has the right to be represented on the Council but may not vote. Any non-member may be invited by the Council to participate, without vote, in the discussion of any matter which, according to the Council, affects its interests.

The Security Council's primary responsibility is the maintenance of international peace. Consequently, it has the task of promoting peaceful settlement of international disputes and taking appropriate action to prevent breaches of peace as well as ordering the coercive action of the United Nations against a recalcitrant state, particularly an aggressor. The Security Council may advise parties to have recourse to any available procedures of peaceful settlement, investigate any dispute or situation which might lead to international friction, and recommend definite terms of settlement. Any state involved in a dispute has the right to submit its case to the Council. Alternatively, a party to a dispute may submit it to the General Assembly, unless it is already under the Council's consideration.

The Council determines the existence of any threat to peace or an act of aggression and decides on measures to be taken. It may ask the parties to comply with such provisional measures (a truce, for example) as it deems necessary to maintain or restore peace. It may decide to apply sanctions against a recalcitrant state, including complete or partial interruption of communications and economic relations as well as severance of diplomatic relations between that state and members of the United Nations. The Council may order a collective military action against the same state, if other measures of coercion are judged inadequate. The veto power of the permanent members of the Council, however, might preclude it from adopting any valid resolution concerning the settlement of a dispute or from its ordering the application of sanctions. The United for Peace Resolution allows then the transfer of the matter to the General Assembly, where the permanent members have no veto.

The Economic and Social Council has eighteen members elected by the General Assembly. Six members are elected annually for a term of three years. They may be re-elected. This Council supervises and co-ordinates all economic, social, cultural, educational, health, and similar functional activities of the United Nations and its Specialized Agencies. It annually reports to the General Assembly which in turn may make the recommendations to the Council and to member-states. The Council adopts its resolutions by a majority vote.

The Trusteeship Council is composed ex officio of the representatives of states which administer trust territories and of the delegates of the five permanent members of the Security Council. The General Assembly also elects other members of the Council. However, the total number of members of the Council who do not administer Trust Territories (the elective members, and the representatives of permanent members of the Security Council who do not administer any Trust Territory) must be equal to the total number of the representatives of powers which administer Trust Territories. A Trust Territory is a dependent country (in fact, a former German, Italian or Japanese possession) which is placed under the administration of a member of the United Nations and is governed under the supervision of the organization. The decisions are taken by a majority vote, but the composition of the Council makes it impossible for members to outvote the trust administrative powers. The Council supervises the administration of the Trust Territories in the interest of the native population by examining the annual reports which the administering powers submit to it, by investigating petitions sent by private individuals and organizations concerning the Territories, and by sending visiting missions to the Territories.

The territorial jurisdiction of the Council has been constantly shrinking because of the rapid political emancipation of the Trusteeship Territories which have been granted independence. The remaining Territories are as follows: Western Samoa (administered by New Zealand), Nauru (jointly administered by Britain, Australia and New Zealand), New Guinea (Australia), and the Pacific Islands (the United States). Since only Britain and the United States are administering powers among the permanent members of the Security Council, the total membership of the Trusteeship Council is reduced.

The Secretariat is the executive office of the United Nations. Its head, the Secretary General, is appointed by the General Assembly on recommendation by the Security Council. The permanent members of the Security Council, each having the veto, must agree on a candidate before a valid recommendation can be submitted to the General Assembly. The Secretary General serves as the secretary for the General Assembly, the Security Council, the Economic and Social Council, and the Trusteeship Council. He may bring to the attention of the Security Council any matter which he believes may threaten international peace and security. He appoints all the employees of the Secretariat but he is expected to pay due attention both to their competence and a fair distribution of posts among the nationals of member-states.

The International Court of Justice is composed of fifteen judges, no two of whom may be of the same nationality. They are jointly elected by the General Assembly and the Security Council, voting separately and by majority vote. The term of office of a judge is nine years, but he may be re-elected. Every three years one-third of the judges are elected. If a party to a dispute submitted to the Court has no national of its own on the permanent bench, it may designate its own national judge who has all the rights of the permanent judge except that he sits only during the proceedings for which he has been appointed.

The seat of the Court is in The Hague. United Nations headquarters are in New York.

The Court has two functions: 1. To decide by majority vote international disputes submitted by the parties. (The judges have the right to formulate separate or dissenting opinions if they disagree with majority decision.); and 2. to provide at the request of the General Assembly, the Security Council or other organs of the United Nations and the Specialized Agencies, its advisory opinions on any legal question; these opinions may be accepted or rejected by the requesting body.

Amendments. The Charter of the United Nations, which defines the structure and the jurisdiction of the organization as well as the rights and obligations of its members, may be amended. An amendment must be adopted by at least a two-thirds majority of member-states voting in the General Assembly, and ratified by two-thirds of the member-states, including all the permanent members of the Security Council. Thus each power, a permanent member of the Security Council, may prevent the enactment of any amendment by withholding ratification.

APPENDIX II: SPECIALIZED AGENCIES OF THE UNITED NATIONS

International Atomic Energy Agency (IAEA)

The Agency was established in 1957. Its *functions* are: to assist research on and practical application of atomic energy for peaceful purposes, including the production of electric power, with special consideration being given to underdeveloped areas; to act as an intermediary for the purposes of obtaining services or materials, equipment or facilities by one member of the Agency from another; to foster the exchange of scientific and technical information on peaceful uses of atomic energy; to encourage the exchange and training of scientists and experts in the field of peaceful uses of atomic energy; to establish standards of safety in the use of atomic energy.

IAEA headquarters are in Vienna, Austria. Its *organization* is as follows: a General Conference of all member-states, a Board of Governors, and the permanent secretariat headed by a Director-General. Authority is divided between the General Conference, which meets once a year, and the Board of Governors, consisting of twenty-three members. The Board is composed in such a way as to create a balance between producer and consumer countries and to ensure that it always includes the five member-states most advanced in atomic energy technology. The Board carries out the Agency's functions, subject to its responsibility to the General

Conference. The Director-General and the permanent secretariat work under the control of the Board of Governors.

International Labor Organization (ILO)

Established in 1919, the *function* of the ILO is to promote social justice through co-operation between member-states. Its concerns are: hours of work, including a maximum working day and week; prevention of unemployment; provision of an adequate living wage; protection of workers against illness and injury arising out of their employment; protection of the interests of workers when employed outside their own countries; recognition of the principle of equal pay for equal work; upholding of the principle of freedom of professional association; technical assistance to underdeveloped countries on matters relating to the jurisdiction of ILO.

Organization: an International Labor Conference, a Governing Body, and an International Labor Office headed by a Director-General. The Conference, which meets once a year, is the policy-making body. It is composed of national delegations of member-states comprising two government delegates and two delegates representing employers and workers. Each delegate has one vote; the delegates of employers and workers do not need to cast their votes in the same sense as the official delegates of their government do. This tripartite structure of the organization, reflecting the separate interests of governments, employers, and employees, is unique among the international official organizations. The principal function of the Conference is to establish international social standards in the form of international labor conventions and recommendations. If a member-state ratifies an ILO convention, it is binding on that state like any other treaty. ILO recommendations set up targets, but member-states are not legally bound to achieve those targets. The Conference elects members of the Governing Body, which is the executive council of ILO. The Governing Body is composed of forty members: ten representing employers, ten representing labor, and twenty representing governments. Each of the three groups at the Conference elects its own representatives to the Board; however, ten governmental seats are permanently held by an equal number of member-states of chief industrial importance, and only ten other seats are elective. Elections are held every three years. The Governing Body elects the Director-General and supervises the work of the International Labor Office, which functions as a permanent secretariat of the ILO. ILO headquarters are in Geneva, Switzerland.

Food and Agricultural Organization (FAO)

FAO came into being in 1945. Its *functions* are: to provide an intelligence service, including not only facts and figures relating to nutrition, agriculture, forestry and fisheries, but also appraisals and forecasts of production, distribution and consumption in these industries; to promote national and international action toward the improvement of production, marketing, processing and distribution of the products of agriculture, as well as conservation of natural resources, and to further policies concerned with credit and with commodity arrangements; to furnish technical assistance to member-states in any of the above fields of operation.

The *organization* of FAO is as follows: a biennial Conference of all member-states, a Council, and a secretariat headed by a Director-General. The Conference is the policy-making body. The Council consists of representatives of twenty-four governments elected by the Conference. It supervises the work of FAO and makes recommendations to member governments and other international organizations on measures to improve the food and agricultural situation. The Director-General is chosen by the Conference. FAO headquarters are in Rome, Italy.

United Nations Educational, Scientific, and Cultural Organization (UNESCO)

UNESCO was established in 1946. Its *functions,* as defined in its Constitution, are designed to "contribute to peace and security, by promoting collaboration among the nations through education, science, and culture in order to further universal respect for justice, for the rule of law, and for the human rights and fundamental freedoms for all." UNESCO's program is carried out in the territories of member-states only with their consent and co-operation. The organization may make recommendations, but no government is required to follow them. It promotes international cultural and educational exchanges in various ways, such as meetings of creative thinkers and leaders of various nationalities, the distribution of books, pamphlets, documents, newspapers, films, and phonograph records. UNESCO headquarters, located in Paris, France, serves as a clearinghouse of information.

Organization: UNESCO works through a General Conference, an Executive Board, and a secretariat. The Conference, consisting of representatives of all member-states, is the policy-making body; it meets every two years and elects the Executive Board of twenty-four members. The Board oversees the carrying out of the UNESCO program. The secretariat is headed by a Director-General appointed by the Conference on the recommendation of the Board.

World Health Organization (WHO)

WHO was established in 1948. Its *functions* are as follows: to act as the directing and co-ordinating authority in international health projects; to assist governments in strengthening health services; to furnish appropriate technical assistance and, in emergencies, necessary aid upon the request of governments; to stimulate and advance work to eradicate epidemic, endemic and other diseases; to promote improved standards of teaching and training in the health, medical, and related professions; to establish and stimulate establishment of international standards with respect to biological, pharmaceutical and similar products, and to standardize diagnostic procedures; to promote international agreements with respect to health matters; to promote co-operation among scientific and professional groups which contribute to the advancement of health; to contribute to the improvement of nutrition, housing, sanitation, and other aspects of environmental hygiene.

Organization: the main organs of WHO are the World Health Assembly, the Executive Board, and the secretariat. The World Health Assembly, which meets each year and is composed of delegates of all member-states, is the policy-making body. The Executive Board is made up of eighteen persons elected by the World Health Assembly. It carries out the decisions of the Assembly with the assistance of the secretariat which is headed by a Director-General, who is appointed by the Assembly. The headquarters of WHO are in Geneva, Switzerland.

International Monetary Fund (IMF)

The IMF was founded in 1945. Its *functions* are: promoting international monetary co-operation and exchange stability, and giving confidence to member-states by making the Fund's resources available to them under certain safeguards. Operations of the Fund are made possible by assets of approximately $10 billion; these assets come from contributions by member-states. The Fund may conclude exchange transactions with its member-states which purchase, if necessary and within certain limitations, currencies of other member-states from the resources of the Fund. The Fund also maintains an extensive program of technical assistance and provides studies of monetary and related problems to the member-states.

Organization: the Fund works through a Board of Governors, Executive Directors, a Managing Director, and his staff of assistants. All powers of the Fund are vested in the Board of Governors, consisting of one Governor and one alternate appointed by each member-state. Voting power of the Governors is approximately in proportion to the size of the contribution quotas of the states which they represent. The Executive Directors are responsible for the conduct of the operations of the Fund and exercise the powers delegated to them by the Board of Governors. Five of the Executive Directors are appointed by states having the largest quotas, and the twelve others are elected by the Governors representing the remaining member-states. Each Director casts all the votes of the state which appointed him or all the votes combined of states which elected him. The Executive Directors appoint the Managing Director. The Fund is based in Washington, D.C.

International Bank for Reconstruction and Development

Established in 1945, the principal *functions* of the International Bank are: to assist in the development of its member-states by facilitating the investment of capital for productive purposes; to promote private foreign investment by guarantees of and participation in loans and other investments made by private investors; and, when private capital is not available on reasonable terms, to make loans for productive purposes out of its own resources or from funds it borrows. The authorized capital of the Bank is $10 billion; it is divided into shares which member-states purchase by subscription. Only 20 per cent of the capital may be used for loans. Loans can be made only to member-states, their political subdivisions, or to private enterprises located in the territories of members. The Bank may encourage private investment by participating in or guaranteeing loans by private investors, and also provides advisory assistance to its members. For example, it sends its missions, on request, to make comprehensive surveys of the economies of member-states. The main objective of these missions is to help the state concerned formulate a program of investment priorities based on the important sectors of the economy, to suggest measures for improving productive efficiency in existing enterprises, and to recommend improvements in the government's economic and financial policies.

Organization: The Bank is administered by a Board of Governors, Executive Directors, a President, and a permanent staff. All powers of the Bank are vested in the Board of Governors, which consists of one Governor and one alternate by each member-state. Each member-state has a number of votes approximately proportionate to its share of the Bank's capital stock. The Board of Governors, which meets annually, delegates most of its powers to the Executive Directors, of whom there are eighteen. Five of the Executive Directors are appointed, one by each of the five member-states having the largest number of shares of capital stock; the thirteen others are elected by the Governors representing the remaining member-states. Each Executive Director is entitled to cast as many votes as are allocated to the member-state or states by whom he was appointed or elected. The President of the Bank is appointed by the Executive Directors. He is ex officio chairman of the Executive Directors and the chief executive officer of the Bank. The headquarters of the Bank are in Washington, D.C.

International Finance Corporation (IFC)

The IFC was organized in 1956. Its *functions* consist of: investing in productive private enterprises in cases where sufficient private capital is not available on reasonable terms; serving as a clearinghouse to bring together investment opportunities, private capital and experienced management; helping to stimulate the productive investment of private capital, both domestic and foreign. The Corporation is an investing and not a lending institution. In order to be eligible for IFC investment an enterprise must be essentially privately owned. The project to be financed must be located in a member-state. The IFC concentrates mainly on projects located in underdeveloped countries. The IFC may sell its investments as soon as they prove sufficiently successful to attract private investors. Member-states contribute to the capital stock of the IFC.

Organization: IFC administration is vested in a Board of Governors, a Board of Directors, a President, and a permanent staff. All powers of IFC are vested in the Board of Governors, each member-state appointing one Governor and one alternate. Each Governor has a number of votes approximately proportionate to the number of shares held by his country. The Board of Directors is composed of those Executive Directors of the International Bank who represent states which are also members of the Corporation. The Board supervises the operations of IFC. The President of the International Bank serves ex officio as Chairman of the Board of Directors who appoint the President of the Corporation. IFC headquarters are in Washington, D.C.

The International Development Association (IDA)

The Association was established in 1960 as an affiliate of the International Bank. This new international agency for the promotion of economic growth in the underdeveloped countries has the following *functions:* to provide financial resources for the development projects on terms which are more flexible and bear less heavily on the balance of payments than those of conventional loans, including the loans granted by the International Bank. IDA supplements the activities of the International Bank, whose loans are calculated on the usual banking terms, and, therefore, are not flexible enough for the underdeveloped countries. The resources of IDA come from the subscriptions of member-states. The guiding idea is to channel funds from the wealthier nations to the underdeveloped countries. Projects that IDA helps to finance need not be economic; they may be of a social nature, such as housing or public sanitation. Loans may be made for long periods of repayment, at low interest rates or interest-free, and with repayment wholly or partly in local currency. IDA may provide financing to member-states and to public or private enterprises located in their territories.

Organization: the structure of IDA is adapted to administration by the International Bank. Its Board of Governors, Executive Directors, and President are the holders of the same positions in the Bank, serving ex officio in the Association. The staff of the Bank serves IDA.

International Civil Aviation Organization (ICAO)

ICAO was established in 1947 and performs the following *functions:* to ensure the safe and orderly growth of worldwide civil aviation; to encourage the arts of aircraft design and operation for peaceful purposes; to encourage the development of airways, airports and air navigation facilities for international civil aviation; to promote safe, regular, efficient and economical air transport; to prevent unreasonable competition; to prevent discrimination among member-states; to promote safety of flight in international air navigation; and generally to encourage the development of international civil aeronautics.

ICAO has established patterns for meteorological services, traffic control, radio beacons and other facilities for safe international flights. It has formulated recommendations with respect to uniform standards and practices, such as requirements for licensing aircrews, uniform specifications for aeronautical maps and charts, meteorological codes, rules of airworthiness of transport planes, measures for the simplification of customs, immigration and health inspection regulations at border airports, and so on.

Organization: ICAO operates through an Assembly, a Council, a President of the Council, a Secretary-General and a secretariat. The Assembly consists of all the member-states and meets twice in a three-year period. It is the policy-making body. The Council, composed of twenty-one states designated by the Assembly, carries out the program of activities which the Assembly has adopted. It also elects its President and the Secretary-General. ICAO is based in Montreal, Canada.

Universal Postal Union (UPU)

The first attempt to develop a universal postal agreement was made by an international conference held in 1863 in Paris. Eleven years later the first International Postal Congress met in Berne, Switzerland. It established the General Postal Union, which began operations in 1875. Three years later the name was changed to the present one.

The *functions* of UPU consist of working for the improvement of various postal services and in promoting the development of international collaboration in this field. The members of UPU are united in a single postal territory for the reciprocal exchange of correspondence. The Universal Postal Convention regulates the conditions under which the member-states co-operate through their postal services.

Organization: UPU is composed of the Universal Postal Congress, the Executive and Liaison Committee, and the International Bureau. The Universal Postal Congress, which usually meets every five years, reviews the Universal Postal Convention. The Executive and Liaison Committee consists of twenty members elected by the Congress on an equitable geographical basis. The Committee maintains relations with the national postal administrations and exercises control over the International Bureau. The Bureau, which is the permanent secretariat of UPU, is headed by a Director. The seat of UPU is in Berne, Switzerland.

International Telecommunication Union (ITU)

The International Telegraph Union was established in 1865. The first regulations affecting international telephone services were formulated in

1885 and the first international radio-telegraphic co-operation inaugurated in 1906. The International Telecommunication Union was founded in 1934 to ensure international collaboration for all telecommunication services.

ITU *functions* are as follows: to maintain international co-operation for the rational use of telecommunication; to promote the most efficient operation of technical facilities and, as far as possible, to make them generally available to the public; to harmonize the actions of governments in the attainment of these common ends. In particular, ITU allocates radio frequencies suitable for providing the channels of communication required by the various radiocommunication services and for minimizing harmful interference between the radio stations of various states; it seeks to establish the lowest rates possible; it promotes the adoption of measures for ensuring the safety of life through telecommunication; it makes studies and recommendations, and collects and publishes information for the benefit of member-states; it also offers technical assistance in telegraphy, telephony and radio.

Organization: The ITU structure consists of a Plenipotentiary Conference, Administrative Conferences, an Administrative Council, and a General Secretariat. The Plenipotentiary Conference, at which each member-state has the right to be represented, meets every five years. It is the policy-making body. There are two administrative conferences: the Telegraph and Telephone, and the Radio Conference; they meet periodically to revise pertinent international regulations. In addition, regional administrative conferences are convoked, if necessary, to deal with questions concerning one region only. The Administrative Council, composed of eighteen members elected by the Plenipotentiary Conference, supervises the work of ITU between the sessions of the Plenipotentiary Conference. It appoints the Secretary General of ITU, who is the head of the permanent secretariat. Headquarters are in Geneva, Switzerland.

World Meteorological Organization (WMO)

An international meteorological co-operation program began in 1853. The first union was established in 1878 under the name of International Meteorological Organization. It was reorganized in 1947 under the new name of World Meteorological Organization.

Its *functions* are as follows: to facilitate international co-operation between the national meteorological services; to promote the establishment of systems for the rapid exchange of weather information; to promote standardization of meteorological observations and ensure uniform publication of observations and statistics; to further the application of meteorology to aviation, shipping, agriculture and other activities; to encourage research and training in meteorology.

Organization: A World Meteorological Congress, an Executive Committee, regional associations, and a permanent secretariat headed by a

Secretary-General. The Congress, composed of delegates of all member-states, meets every four years. Each state designates as its principal delegate the director of its meteorological service. The Congress is the policy-making body. The Executive Committee is composed of the President and Vice-Presidents of WMO, the presidents of regional associations, and an equal number of directors of meteorological services of member-states. It supervises the implementation of Congress decisions. Regional associations are composed of those member-states with meteorological stations situated in a definite region (Africa, Asia, South America, North and Central America, Southwest Pacific, and Europe). The secretariat is the executive office of WMO. The headquarters of WMO are in Geneva, Switzerland.

Inter-Governmental Maritime Consultative Organization (IMCO)

Established in 1958, IMCO *functions* are: to provide machinery for co-operation among governments in the field of governmental regulation and practices relating to technical matters, including safety at sea; to consider any matters concerning shipping that might be referred to it by any organ or Specialized Agency of the United Nations; to provide for the exchange of information among governments on matters within the jurisdiction of IMCO; to provide for the drafting of international agreements and to convene conferences for the adoption of these agreements.

Organization: IMCO has an Assembly of delegates of all member-states, a Council of sixteen members, a Maritime Safety Committee, and a permanent secretariat headed by a Secretary-General. The Assembly, which is the policy-making body, meets every two years. The Council performs all the functions of IMCO between the sessions of the Assembly. Six of the Council's sixteen members represent countries having the largest interest in providing international shipping services; six represent countries with the largest interest in international seaborne trade; two are elected by the Assembly from among countries having a substantial interest in providing international shipping services; and two are elected by the Assembly from among countries having a substantial interest in the international seaborne trade. The Council's members are elected for a term of two years. The Maritime Safety Committee is elected by the Assembly; its fourteen members should represent nations with the largest shipping tonnage or with an important interest in maritime safety (such as those which supply large numbers of crews or large numbers of maritime passengers). The composition of the Committee should also provide a fair representation of major geographical areas. IMCO headquarters are in London.

General Agreement on Tariffs and Trade (GATT)

Attempts to establish an International Trade Organization have so far failed to produce results. However, a General Agreement on Tariffs and

Trade was drafted in 1947 and entered into force in 1948. GATT is primarily an international treaty. Its purpose is to remove, as far as possible, restrictions on trade between the contracting parties. These parties are the non-Communist states, advanced and underdeveloped, but three Communist countries, Czechoslovakia, Cuba, and Yugoslavia also participate in GATT. Tariff concessions made between two parties to GATT extend to all other contracting parties by virtue of the most-favored-nation principle. Tariff concessions mutually agreed upon at the periodical GATT conferences are incorporated into the schedules attached to the agreement. These schedules refer to approximately 60,000 articles which together represent more than one-half of the world's international trade. Internal taxes must be applied equally to national and imported goods. Restrictions on trade, which could in effect nullify the tariff concessions, should be eliminated. In particular, this applies to the quantitative restrictions (import quotas) which may be retained or introduced only in case of serious balance-of-payment difficulties. The combined foreign trade of GATT members amounts to about four-fifths of the world's trade. Disputes, arising out of the application of GATT, if not settled in the negotiations between the states concerned, are submitted to a conciliation panel composed of representatives of countries with no direct interest in the case. The panel recommends a settlement. One of the difficult problems facing GATT is the question of regional economic unions, such as the European Economic Community. The common tariff of the EEC is on the average lower than the highest tariff which any of its members previously had, but it might be higher than the former tariff of some of its members. Third states, parties to GATT, might run the risk of paying higher customs duties for their imports to those members of the EEC to whom they have usually exported certain of their products.

Conferences among GATT signatories have met from time to time to consider problems arising out of its application and complaints of violations of its rules; conferences also deal with any other problem relating to trade which a government wishes to submit.

GATT has its Council of Representatives, which meets between the Conferences, and a permanent secretariat, whose seat is located in Geneva, Switzerland.

Specialized Agencies are also normally open to non-members of the United Nations.

CHAPTER X

Diplomacy

THE FORMULATION OF FOREIGN POLICY

The word *diplomacy* has two distinct meanings. It is used as a synonym for foreign policy itself. To condemn or praise the diplomacy of a country is, in this sense of the word, to point out the failures or achievements of its foreign policy. The same word is just as often used as a collective name for the officials who implement governmental decisions and carry out the foreign policy which the government has formulated. The dual significance of *diplomacy* suggests the existence of two aspects of foreign policy, its formulation and its implementation.

The formulation of foreign policy is the prerogative of the government, i.e., those state agents who are empowered by the written or unwritten constitution of the country to commit the collective responsibility of the nation in relation to other states. It is another prerogative of the government to select and appoint those subordinate state agents who will carry out its decisions, i.e., implement its foreign policy. In actual practice the line of demarcation is blurred. Although normally the government leaves the implementation to its subordinate officials, the contemporary habit of personal diplomacy frequently makes the chief executive or the foreign minister combine in his person the two functions; he formulates foreign policy, as it is his political role to do, but he also implements it through his personal contacts and negotiations with the member of a foreign government of the same rank.

By the same token, the implementing officials have never been confined to this important but subordinate function. The chief executive or the foreign minister or whoever else in the government has the authority to formulate foreign policy cannot himself make all the decisions concerning the relations with other states. He has to delegate his powers. The implementing official who is thus empowered to make decisions in the name of the state formulates foreign policy within the limits of his delegated powers whenever he takes steps which commit his country. A negotiator, for example, who is usually given by governmental instructions a certain leeway for exercising his own judgment, formulates foreign policy to the extent of concessions to the foreign country which he makes during the process of diplomatic bargaining. As a matter of fact, the sheer volume and complexity of foreign matters which must be taken care of every day compel governments to delegate the power of decision in most cases to their subordinate officials.

The formulation of foreign policy is inconceivable without information and expert advice; both are provided by the same subordinate officials. They inevitably influence the tenor of foreign policy by the information and advice which they supply to the government. Thus, even if the government does not delegate the power of decision (it should never do so regarding the crucial decisions which delineate the main course of foreign policy), the implementing officials still participate in the decision through the information which they provide and through advice which usually limits governmental decision-making to a choice between two or several courses of action which the advising officials consider best.

As blurred as the line of demarcation is in actual practice, it is politically useful not to confuse these two aspects of foreign policy. First, the distinction between the two, if present in the mind of the chief executive or his foreign minister, might act as a restraint on the modern proclivity to spend too much time on personal implementation at the expense of time which should be devoted to the study of the substance of foreign policy. Secondly, the participation of implementing officials in the formulation of foreign policy (through information, advice, and delegated powers of decision) can never dilute the political responsibility of the government for the external policy. This responsibility is solidly founded under any regime on the power of the government to appoint and dismiss the officials who provide information and advice and to determine when and to whom powers of decision will be delegated.

Whatever the constitutional regime of a country might be, the blame for a faulty foreign policy attaches to the government. It is a political error to criticize the implementing officials (the State Department, the Foreign Office, the Ministry of Foreign Affairs, or whatever the collective name might be). Their responsibility is of a different type. They are responsible to the government, which can inflict on them all sorts of disciplinary penalties, including dismissal. It is the government itself which is responsible to the nation. The criticism of foreign policy should always be addressed to whom it politically concerns—the chief executive, his foreign secretary, and that body of politicians called the government.

The formulation of foreign policy consists of two types of decisions:

the strategic and the tactical. The strategy of foreign policy is determined by several basic decisions which provide a quasi-permanent framework for the tactical decisions. These basic decisions are as follows:

1. The choice of an interpretation of contemporary historical trends and of their relation to the national interests of the state. The interpretation which the government selects from among two or several possible interpretations will guide the course of foreign policy.

2. The definition of long-term objectives which will be consistently pursued unless an unexpected and fundamental change in external circumstances should justify their modification.

3. The clarification of the long-term objectives of other states. Once their objectives have been clarified, other states can be divided into three categories: (1) those whose national interests coincide with one's own interests and with whom a close co-operation should be maintained; (2) those whose national interests are not diametrically opposed to one's own interests and with whom one should try to reach limited and temporary understandings; (3) those whose long-term objectives clash with one's own and who probably will constantly counteract one's foreign policy.

4. The general plan of action. This general plan is the framework for planning particular actions regarding a specific problem or a particular area or country. Both general and particular plans should be founded on contingency forecasts. Any forecast of future events must necessarily be contingent because those events are the composite result of one's own policy and of the policies of other states. Any cautious planning will outline two or more desirable and possible policies. The one which is considered the best under the present circumstances will be carried out. If the premises upon which it has been founded prove to be false because of new developments, the alternative policy, better suited to those developments and prepared in advance, will replace the former one now discarded. All alternative policies, elements of contingency planning, must be keyed to the eventual achievement of strategic objectives.

The strategic objectives, if wisely defined, should not be modified in midstream for any lesser reason than a radical transformation in the international environment, a very substantial rise or decline in the relative power of the state, or the seizure of power by a regime which is inspired by an ideology altogether different from the one which guided its predecessor. The stability of long-term objectives will result in a continuity of foreign policy in spite of such domestic changes as the replacement of one government by another in consequence of democratic elections or the death of an authoritarian leader. If an opposition party feels that it would inaugurate a totally new foreign policy after its electoral victory, it will soon discover, once it forms the government, that it cannot perform miracles, that it faces external problems with which the former government already had to cope, and that it can only alter the tactics in the pursuit of the same strategic objectives. The smooth continuation of foreign policy, in spite of changes of governments, is facilitated by the existence of a strong professional diplomatic service such as the one that exists in Britain. These civil servants, who owe their loyalty to the country but not to any particular party and who together represent a great capital of knowledge and experience, are keenly aware of the long-term objectives of national policy. They are the guardians of the continuity of foreign policy since the government never lightly rejects their advice.

Tactics consist in a never-ending stream of particular decisions which should all be oriented toward the eventual achievement of the long-term objectives. Since external circumstances are constantly changing, partly because other states are taking their own actions, tactics should be flexible and rapidly adjusted to new circumstances but should never lose sight of the strategic goals of the entire foreign policy.

EXTERNAL AND DOMESTIC LIMITATIONS ON FREEDOM OF DECISION

No power is omnipotent, able to do whatever it wants. Decisions concerning foreign affairs are always reached within certain limits which circumscribe the freedom of choice. One of these limiting factors is geography: the location of the country, its natural resources, its transportation problems, and so forth. For instance, Russia, whatever the character of its regime, has a vital interest in safe access to the oceans. It cannot remain indifferent to the regimes which control the exits from the Baltic Sea and the Black Sea, and its concern with the Danish and the Turkish Straits and beyond them with the Suez Canal and the Gibraltar Straits is understandable. The United States must remain alert to developments on the opposite coasts of the two oceans which form its frontiers and must vigilantly watch events in Latin America, where vital mineral resources are located. Britain is compelled by its location to scrutinize events on the continent; the channel which intervenes is now passable, as D-Day proved. Poor in natural resources, Britain must keep open the channels of its maritime trade, which supplies indispensable foodstuffs, raw materials, and oil. It is forced by its economy to consider the Near East almost as vital as the continent itself. Its small territory and the unusually heavy concentration of the population in a few metropolitan areas compels Britain to follow a very cautious policy in the nuclear age; the threat of obliteration is much more real for Britain than for a country with a very large territory and a better dispersed population, such as the United States, the Soviet Union, or China. India would not tolerate, if it could be avoided, the transfer of Singapore, the Andamans Islands, and Aden to an unfriendly power; China would always consider Korea and Southeast Asia as zones of vital interest. The geography of the continental nations gives them neighbors that might be friendly or hostile, powerful or weak, but also neighbors' neighbors who might become allies against the common neighbor. The range of power (except for strategic nuclear weapons borne by the ICBM) decreases in inverse ratio to distance. For instance, a land power can more easily reach the peripheral areas of its continent than a distant maritime nation whose centers of power are separated by the seas from the same areas.

History is another limitation. It is the mold of national self-evident truths, ways of life, and habits of thought. Each generation is born in a national environment fashioned by its predecessors and cannot escape the impact of this legacy. American reactions to foreign events are influenced by psychological traces of isolationism, such as a proclivity toward moralistic interpretations of foreign developments. Russian history, with its heritage of distrust of the West, reinforces the ideological hostility of the Soviet leaders. The nineteenth century, a great and happy period in British history, has left its legacy in the British belief that a steady negotiation with other powers will always result in a gradual reduction of tension and will eventually bring about a stable *modus vivendi.* This method was successful in the past century when no great power was revolutionary or intended to subvert the whole status quo and when continental great powers counterbalanced each other and thus gave Britain a comfortable space in which to maneuver. Britain was safe because of its naval superiority and because there was no danger that the continent would unite against it. Britain could quietly and patiently watch events and effectively negotiate while maneuvering between the contending European powers, none of which had exorbitant objectives. This situation created a habit of thought which is not always helpful in an epoch of turmoil. The initial search for a compromise did not yield a *modus vivendi* with Napoleon. The method of gradual negotiation with Nazi Germany did not produce the results hoped for by the British government of the time, because Nazi Germany pursued objectives which were almost unlimited and hence unnegotiable. The search for a lasting *modus vivendi* with the Communist powers may prove equally unsuccessful unless these revolutionary powers abandon their unlimited objective of the universal conversion of mankind. One should, however, make a clear distinction between a hopeful search for a lasting *modus vivendi* with a revolutionary power, and the necessary maintenance of contacts or the negotiation for a settlement of limited issues which the two parties want to solve but which do not affect the basic antagonism between them.

The philosophical outlook of a country (its self-evident truths, the nature and hierarchy of its fundamental values) is also a limitation insofar as external events are interpreted within this ideological framework. A militant ideology coupled with a missionary zeal cannot but influence the objectives of foreign policy.

Another limitation are the emotions and prejudices prevailing in the country. The dislike of a foreign nation or of its regime, the popularity of another, the cliché image of the character of a foreign population, and other nonrational factors might strongly influence those who formulate foreign policy and distort their judgment.

The morale of the country (its willingness to bear the costs of foreign policy and to face the risks that it involves) is still another limitation which it would be unwise to disregard.

The relative national power is a self-evident limitation. This limitation is external because the power of a nation is measured by comparison with that of other nations.

Freedom of decision is further circumscribed by external commitments such as alliances and other treaty obligations. The foreign policies of other states are still another limitation. If these states are hostile, they reduce freedom of action; if friendly, they extend this freedom by acting in support.

DECISION-MAKING

In actual practice, foreign-policy decisions are often improvised on the spur of the moment. However, the process of decision-making should follow certain stages. The first stage is that of collecting information through open and secret channels. Most of this information comes through open channels, such as reports of the embassies accredited to foreign governments and research on the foreign press and other public sources of information. It is never possible to have all the desired information, because some data are successfully kept secret by foreign governments. Other facts, which are not secret, can be overlooked or their importance underestimated by the diplomatic and intelligence agents in charge of collecting information.

Data concerning foreign states are necessarily abundant. The second stage, that of analysis, calls for a choice of facts which are deemed relevant. This choice depends on the frame of reference of the person who performs the analysis and on his criteria of the importance of analyzed facts for the subject-matter which he studies. We have mentioned in Chapter I the role of the subjective factor in the apprehension and interpretation of facts. We meet the same factor in the process of selection of facts deemed relevant. In both cases, the views of any two individuals may differ regarding the "true" version of facts, their significance, and their relevance for the matter under consideration. These views are unavoidably colored by their "self-evident truths" and by the amount of knowledge and the degree of experience each of them possesses.

The analysis of data which have been selected as relevant cannot stop with the conclusion concerning their significance for one's own government. One must try to find out whether these data are equally relevant for the foreign government concerned or whether other facts might not be more relevant for it. Neither an intelligent formulation of foreign policy nor a skillful implementation is possible without following the wise advice which de Callières, a French diplomat, offered at the beginning of the eighteenth century:

> This consideration must ever be in the mind of the good negotiator who should, therefore, strive to divest himself of his own feelings and prejudices, and place himself in the position of the [foreign] King so that he may understand completely the desires and whims which guide his actions. And when he has done so he should say to himself: "Now, if I were in the place of this prince, wielding his power, subject to his passions and prejudices, what effect would my mission and my arguments have upon me?"

This important question should be asked at each stage of the formulation and implementation of foreign policy. It can meaningfully be asked only by a person who knows a given foreign country well, understands its "self-evident truths," is familiar with its interpretation of its national interests, and is acquainted with the personalities of those politicians who formulate its foreign policy. The question itself can be subdivided into several subquestions: What meaning can the data which the investigator takes into consideration have for the foreign government? How might these facts affect its future decisions? How will his own government's decision, founded on its interpretation of the same facts, influence the process of thinking of that foreign government? How may that government react to protect its national objectives? What are the arguments which his own government should advance to explain its actions in a manner that would ensure that these actions produce the desired effect on the foreign government?

The third stage consists in defining the rational courses of action which the government can undertake. These courses are rational if they are directed toward the strategic objectives of foreign policy and if they can be implemented within the limits of the national ratio of power.

The fourth stage is the choice of one from among two or several courses of action and the instructing of implementing agents who will carry out this selected course.

Every decision relating to foreign affairs is a choice between two or several courses of action. Each of these alternative courses will commend itself by the advantages it offers but will also discourage choice by the disadvantages which its implementation involves. No move in international relations can be perfect and yield only unmixed blessings. Each will produce undesirable effects which are foreseen but accepted in advance as the cost of an operation otherwise beneficial. The art of international politics consists in weighing the pluses and minuses of all rationally possible courses, in comparing their balances of pluses and minuses, and finally in selecting one course rather than the others because it is the least imperfect.

As no particular move and no foreign policy can possibly produce only excellent results without any drawbacks, nothing is easier but also more sterile than merely to point out the disadvantages of a policy undertaken by the government. Helpful criticism consists in proposing an alternative policy which offers a better balance-sheet of pluses and minuses.

The foreign-policy decision should be well-integrated in space. A move in one area or regarding one particular country might and usually will produce repercussions elsewhere. These repercussions should be foreseen; a balance-sheet of expected advantages and disadvantages should include these indirect consequences. A decision which seems locally beneficial should be reversed or modified if its indirect repercussions in other parts of the world or on the relations with other states would be more harmful than the immediate benefits expected locally.

Integration in space is easy by comparison with integration in time. The latter integration consists in foreseeing, as far as humanly possible, the distant consequences of a decision taken today. This sort of forecast, which must include a prediction of probable future changes in international circumstances, is liable to many errors which only a prophet could avoid. It should be attempted, however, as a necessary precaution. Two factors can help in this necessarily hazardous forecast. The one is the history of international relations, in which one can find analogous situations and discover their later developments. The other is the knowledge and understanding of contemporary historical trends and of the changes which they produce in the international environment.

Foreign policy must be planned; a mere reaction to the moves by other states is no foreign policy at all. A government which is conscious of its objectives must constantly move forward toward the achievement of these objectives. The so-called pragmatic method, if it is understood as coping with events as they happen, is actually the lack of any method. It is especially defective in our world, which is changing at a rapid pace and which is inhabited by powers intending to transform the existing status quo radically. This intention compels those powers to pursue a dynamic and long-term policy, to plan it for decades ahead and to assume a constant initiative. If they fail to take the initiative, the international situation will not be modified in the way that they passionately desire. The status-quo powers are therefore constantly confronted with new and often unexpected moves to which they are forced to react as best as they can. This carries with it a peculiar implication, namely that the revolutionary power might indirectly (by its own constant and repeated initiatives) determine the formulation of policies by the status-quo powers.

Demosthenes aptly denounced in 351 B.C. the defects of a reactive policy which leaves to the adversary the privilege of initiative and thus enables him to influence indirectly the formulation of one's own decisions:

> Shame on you, Athenians . . . for not wishing to understand that in war one must not allow oneself to be at the command of events, but to forestall them. . . . You make war against Philip like a barbarian when he wrestles. . . . If you hear that Philip has attacked in the Chersonese, you send help there; if he is at Thermopylae, you run there; and if he turns aside, you follow him to right and left, as if you were acting on his orders. Never a fixed plan, never any precautions; you wait for bad news before you act.

The other inconvenience of the pragmatic method is that events move fast in the rapidly changing world of today and that merely reactive moves can never catch up with the multitude and the quick succession of events. The status-quo power is constantly in danger of being left behind events. The revolutionary power will do its best to take two or more initiatives simultaneously and thus prevent the status-quo power from concentrating its attention on reacting to one initiative at a time.

Finally, another defect of this method is that it discourages the effort which is necessary to understand the international environment and the principal trends that modify it. The pragmatic method encourages its practitioners to view events as unconnected phenomena and to lose sight of their interrelation. It inhibits the attempt to interpret the patterns which relate events to each other and consequently to lay out a long-term policy. The lack of a long-term foreign policy leads to incoherent improvisation in decision-making; on the other hand, the presence of such a policy provides the incentive for initiating events.

It goes without saying that each country should have only one foreign policy. If decision-making is not co-ordinated at the national center, the various agents of the same state may be pursuing different policies. This situation leads to dangerous confusion and a tragic waste of effort. The co-ordination of activities by various official agencies is much easier than a co-ordination between governmental foreign policy and the activities abroad of private organizations of the same country. This problem does not confront the totalitarian state, which controls all the activities, domestic and foreign, of its citizens. Its official and "private" spokesmen carry out the same foreign policy, formulated by the government, in all their external activities. The monopoly of foreign trade and the nationalization of the means of production allow the state always to act as one unit in trade negotiations. The cultural exchanges with other states are directed by a centralized state agency. A democratic state finds itself in an altogether different position. Its very nature makes it tolerate the conflicting views among its private organizations and citizens who are free to express any opinion at home and abroad on all domestic and external matters and to disagree openly with the official policy. The discrepancies between the words and acts of the democratic government and the words and acts of its citizens are unavoidable but can be mitigated insofar as contacts with foreign nations are concerned by the citizens' feeling of national solidarity and by close contacts maintained between the government and the leaders of various private organizations.

Foreign policy is judged by its results, not by its intentions. It is not a popularity contest and does not aim at gaining the love of foreign peoples. The individual usually loves only his own country but may sometimes have personal reasons for loving a foreign nation as well. But millions of individuals, a nation, cannot be expected to feel a strong collective emotional attachment for any particular foreign country and never do. Foreign policy should be calculated to inspire the respect of other nations, not their love. It is obviously defective if it results in a universal dislike of the country concerned. Respect means, in this context, the foreign conviction that the country is guided in its external relations by well-defined ends, that it is absolutely serious in the pursuit of these ends, and that it has the means for carrying out its foreign policy.

George Washington wisely said in his Farewell Address: "There can be no greater error than to expect, or calculate upon, real favors from nation to nation. It is an illusion which experience must cure, which a just pride ought to discard. . . ." In particular, gratitude, rare in personal relations, never lasts in international relations. The country which has benefited from the actions of another country, usually and not without reason, believes that these actions were dictated by the interests of the foreign nation, not by any disinterested sympathy. This argument was invoked by the first generation of independent Americans to justify their policy of neutrality in the French wars in spite of the French alliance and the decisive role which French assistance had played in the War of Independence. They were right: Royalist France certainly did not assume the risks of war with Britain out of sympathy with the ideas of the Declaration of Independence but because it wanted to weaken its traditional British enemy. This same argument is equally valid for other times and other nations.

Foreign policy is a never-ending business. Certain problems are solved; others might remain unsolvable for a long period of time; the solution of others might breed new problems; and problems now unexpected will arise in due time. Obviously, patience is one of the principal virtues required for the successful conduct of foreign relations.

Those who formulate foreign policies choose among several possible courses of action. They act in the realm of contingencies which are made of other men's actions. Their decisions are not the result of mathematical equations which a computer can solve. There are too many unknown and unknowable factors. This is why the skillful formulation of foreign policy requires, in the last analysis, not a learned expert but a man who has that indefinable quality called political talent. It is true that this talent cannot function in a void. It must be buttressed by experience and knowledge which the advisers can partly supply. But the best advisers cannot guarantee that the actions which they propose will produce the desired results, or they might suggest two or more alternative courses of action. Political talent is the intuition which enables a politician to make the right decision in spite of the fact that the equation includes several unknown factors. Only the future will tell whether the decision has been right. This talent remains barren without historical opportunity, which is often created by the errors of other participants in the international game.

The personality of the man who formulates foreign policy is important because, while many people can influence him, the final decision is his own. He is placed in a situation altogether different from that of his ordinary countrymen, not only because he holds the power of decision but also because he has at his disposal incomparably better information which he cannot always share with his country. His view of what foreign policy would best serve the nation might for this and other reasons differ from the opinions of his countrymen. His greatness of mind and character depends on the answers his actions give to the following questions:

Is he ready, if necessary, to risk his political career for the sake of upholding a foreign policy which he deems desirable? Has he the capacity to swing his countrymen to his side? Is he hopelessly ethnocentric and incapable of understanding the motivations of other governments? Is he capable of telling his own people what he knows will displease them? Is he oblivious to changes in external circumstances or is he able to adjust national policy to these changes? Is he disposed to remain blind to those facts which contradict his expectations or rather to change his mind if necessary? Has he the courage to assume responsibility for the consequences of his decisions or does he prefer to avoid the risks? As he must, in the last analysis, rely on the support of his own people, is he a leader who inspires trust and whom his own nation will follow even if it does not fully understand his motivations? Is his will-power equal to the policy-making authority which is vested in him? Does he combine patience, wisdom, foresight, imagination, and consistency in pursuing his objectives? Is he a good judge of other men and is he able to select his advisers and main implementing agents wisely? Does he know how to distinguish between very important decisions which he himself must make and the decisions which he should delegate to others?

This combination of qualities is rare. Thus, the stage of international politics has always been crowded with mediocre actors, and the true statesmen who leave a permanent imprint on history have rarely made their appearance.

INFORMATION AND ADVICE

The tasks of those state agents who help the government in the formulation of foreign policy and who implement it by their actions are three: (1) to gather and assess the information; (2) to offer advice; and (3) to carry out the decisions of the government in their personal contacts with the representatives of foreign governments. These three essential functions of the diplomatic agents have been defined and gradually refined throughout the long history of diplomatic practice and have not declined in importance at the present time. They constitute the heart of the so-called old diplomacy, which is old if judged by the ancientness of its history but which remains young as long as we live in a multistate system. This century added new methods of international intercourse, such as personal diplomacy, the use of mass propaganda as a weapon of conflict, economic and technical assistance as a new means of foreign policy, and the multiplication of nondiplomatic agents of implementation. However, the three traditional functions of diplomacy remain as important as ever.

Information, without which there can be no sensible foreign policy, comes from various sources: direct observation by embassies and consulates; the no less direct observation by nondiplomatic state agents, such as the technical advisers dispatched to help a foreign government, and by those private citizens who are willing to share their experience abroad with the governmental agencies of their country (they range from journalists, missionaries, and employees of business corporations to intelligent tourists); the analysis of data collected from foreign sources publicly accessible to official and private research agencies; and, finally, secret intelligence agents. Information includes the reporting not only of particular events but also of political and other trends in a foreign country.

The embassy, which is permanently located in a foreign capital and continuously observes developments, is the most reliable source of balanced information. The information which it supplies should be checked and supplemented by other information coming from other sources. Eventually, the Ministry of Foreign Affairs (State Department, Foreign Office) should sift and place in perspective the total information which is available regarding a given country. The embassy is close to events and is well-situated for detecting the first signs of new developments. However, its own perspective is limited to the particular country where it is located. The meaning of an event can change or acquire wider significance if the central office, which has at its disposal worldwide information, analyzes the report submitted by the embassy against the background of its own wider perspective.

The gathering of information through personal contacts is not a simple affair in our time. In former times it sufficed to be aware of what the sovereign and his immediate advisers had in mind and be familiar with the trends of thought prevailing within a narrow upper class. Now and then it is and was vitally important to discover where the real center of power is located; this center is not necessarily the official government, or the Foreign Minister might not in fact be the main adviser of the chief executive. Regardless of where the real center of power is located, the first duty of an embassy is to maintain close contacts with the persons who form this center.

Nowadays the embassy cannot limit its contacts to the upper class. Our time is one of great social mobility, political instability, and the multiplication of social groups which influence the formulation of domestic and foreign policies. The proportion of people who count politically has greatly increased. The man in the street cannot be disregarded, because his moods and his morale limit the government's freedom to maneuver. The task of those who gather information has been greatly increased over the last hundred years or even since 1914.

It is necessary in a democratic country to maintain contacts with the lawfully existing opposition which might form the next government. A steady contact with the agents of the mass media of information, in particular with the journalists, is extremely useful and should be founded on an exchange of information. They often know almost as much as the officials but are less discreet. The embassy offers information which is not its own state secret in exchange for information which the journalist possesses. The journalist in the foreign capital either is a national of that country and works for the local newspaper or is a citizen of a third country who resides in the same city as the embassy and serves his newspaper as a foreign correspondent. Contacts with both are useful, but the journalist who works for a foreign newspaper is naturally less reluctant than a local journalist to give out information concerning the local country. Contacts with journalists and other agents of the mass media of information provide the opportunity to influence their views. Generally speaking, the process of gathering information should be combined with a subtle "sale" of one's government's views.

The embassy should pay close attention to the leaders of various social groups (churches, business organizations, labor unions, civic associations, etc.), because they initiate or influence public opinion on foreign affairs. One can also learn from them about the emotional currents in the population at large. The intellectuals, whose ideas eventually affect the views of politicians, cannot be neglected. This list of useful contacts could be extended, but it suffices to say that the embassy faces an immense task.

The ambassador himself should maintain contact with the members of the government, his foreign colleagues residing in the same capital, and the upper stratum of influential people. This upper stratum is no longer identical with the upper class. In this respect, a labor leader is as important as a big businessman, a high-ranking churchman as an influential publicist. The ambassador cannot "specialize" in his personal contacts and should remain in touch with the persons who are "the summits" of all sections of the foreign population. The other members of the staff are well-advised, if they are sufficiently numerous, to divide the foreign population into its characteristic segments and to assign to each member of the embassy the task of maintaining close contacts with one particular segment. This "specialization" enables the diplomat to look at the problems of the foreign country from the point of view of a particular social group, to understand much better its professional or ideological interests, to speak its conceptual language, and almost to be accepted as one of the members of the group. It is not psychologically possible for the same diplomat to be thought of simultaneously by the leaders of an association of manufacturers and by those of labor unions as a kindred spirit, but he can win this position for himself with either group and thus gain insight into its interests and aspirations.

De Callières, the wise French diplomat of the reign of Louis XIV, wrote: "The better his [ambassador's] relations are with his countrymen living abroad, the more surely will he discover how large are the reciprocal benefits to be gained thus, for it will often happen that unofficial persons receive information as if it were by accident which may be of the utmost importance to the ambassador. . . ." This advice is as useful now as it was in the eighteenth century. The information obtained directly by embassy personnel should be supplemented by data which are supplied by nondiplomatic state agents and by private co-citizens residing in the same foreign country. The information which they receive "as if it were by accident" is always useful for the embassy and sometimes can be "of the utmost importance."

The press correspondent is one of those countrymen who should be an important source of the embassy's information. He is usually a keen observer, agile in collecting information, and unrestricted by any protocol requirements in his moves and the choice of his local friends. He might have resided in the foreign country much longer than the senior members of the embassy, and his knowledge of that country might be more intimate and more profound. He might be able to detect new developments quicker than the embassy. His published dispatches are in themselves a valuable source of information for his government, but he might be willing to communicate to the embassy off-the-record information which he cannot, for one reason or another, send to his newspaper.

The diplomat should remember that he must never tempt his friends among the journalists, whether they are foreigners or countrymen, by telling them state secrets off the record; the temptation to publish interesting news might be too great for the most reliable journalist. However, a diplomat who does not know how to handle his personal relations with journalists and is afraid of their possible indiscretions disqualifies himself, because he himself lacks discretion, judgment, and tact in dealing with other people.

The personal contacts of the embassy in an authoritarian state are restricted by the nature of its regime. Opposition of any kind might be unlawful or hardly tolerated. An embassy is accredited to the government in power and should never give offense through contacts with the opposition. Such contacts could be interpreted by the government as an encouragement for its overthrow. It is not the business of the embassy to help in overturning the existing government. If a power believes that its interests require an action aiming at the overthrow of an alien government, it should use its secret agents for this purpose; it can, if circumstances permit, intervene directly or indirectly. But this is not the task of the embassy whose main mission consists in maintaining contact with the government in power. Contacts with the illegal opposition cannot be shunned, because it might become the future government of the country, but they should be carried on by secret agents or by private citizens who reside in the country, if these contacts are not unnecessarily dangerous for them. These unofficial contacts might forewarn of an impending coup or revolution and provide some insight into the policies which the future regime will inaugurate.

The most arduous task of the embassy is in the totalitarian state. Its government ruthlessly limits opportunities for contact by such measures as restricting the travel of foreign diplomats or discouraging its own citizens, officials or private persons, from seeking or welcoming personal friendships with foreigners. These restrictive measures usually extend to foreign private residents and casual visitors. However, no society is hermetically closed because each is made up of human beings whatever mask they want or must wear. Citizens of a totalitarian state are no exception; some of them are talkative by nature, others can be ingratiated through their hobbies or foibles, and still others might, out of personal or national vanity, say more than their government would like. Moreover, much valuable information can be gathered from the domestic publications of the totalitarian state and interesting clues can be found between the printed lines.

The second function of the diplomatic service is to give advice on desirable courses of action. The Department of State or the Foreign Office should be the repository of accumulated professional knowledge and experience. A government is ill-advised if it frequently seeks counsel from nonprofessional "geniuses" who are apt to believe that they can remedy all international ills and who tend to oversimplify problems by coining attractive slogans. However, diplomatic advice is not sufficient. If a decision depends upon military capacity for its execution, the military expert must be called in. Other decisions will require the opinions of experts in other fields, such as international commerce.

In the past, military and naval advisers exerted the greatest influence on the most vital decisions of their government, because their expert opinion regarding the probable consequences of a particular course of action for national security could not be disregarded. Today, they share this role not only with the professional diplomat, as was true in the pre-nuclear age, but with the scientist as well. A small group of people who have the required scientific knowledge and enjoy the political trust of their government offer advice on matters which might determine the future of their country. For instance, this advice might prejudge the choice of new weapons which will be produced or the selection of scientific research projects which the government will finance in the hope of increasing military preparedness. The present responsibility of the scientist is much greater than that of the military adviser in the pre-nuclear age. Not only are the stakes of international politics incomparably greater, but the statesman of that bygone age could, if he wanted, master the basic concepts of military strategy and intelligently follow the arguments of his military advisers. The contemporary member of government can rarely achieve a comparable scientific proficiency and is accordingly more dependent on the advice of his scientists. This advice, although liable to error, might predetermine the most vital decisions. The government cannot protect itself against the professional misjudgments of its scientific advisers and might be faced with conflicting views among which it is not competent to choose. The statesman of today should at least possess a modicum of scientific knowledge to be able to understand the gist of the scientists' arguments. Even so, the scientists wield a tremendous power over the future of their own people and carry an equally tremendous responsibility.

IMPLEMENTATION AND NEGOTIATION

The third function of the diplomatic service is to implement foreign policy. Implementation has two facets: the building abroad of a favorable image of one's country and its foreign policy, and negotiations with foreign governments.

The image which foreign governments and peoples have of another nation, its regime, its ideology, and its external objectives, is extremely important. It might be true or false but it always remains one of the capital premises on which foreign governments will base their own foreign policy. They will construct this image primarily from materials supplied by their own sources of information. But other factors will try to influence the shape and color of this image. The third governments and their propaganda services will certainly have an interest in shaping this image. They will try to embellish it if they are friendly and deface it if they are hostile. Above all, each government does its best to influence the foreign image of its own country. Its efforts are directed at making this image as attractive as possible for foreign onlookers. This can be achieved if those national values are stressed which have an important place in another nation's hierarchy of values. A great effort should be made to convince other countries that the objectives of one's foreign policy coincide with their own national goals. Naturally, the actual behavior of the state in its relations with another country is the main factor in shaping the image of that state in the minds of the foreign government and population. If the foreign policy seems ill-defined, self-contradictory, and lacking in a sense of direction, or if it is unsupported by adequate means, or if the will and persistence in striving for the achievement of announced objectives are manifestly deficient, no amount of spoken or printed words can make the national image attractive or respectable. The image of a country can be made more attractive by the activities and behavior of its nationals resident in foreign countries: the personnel of the embassy, civilian and military advisers and other experts, missionaries, press correspondents, businessmen, and a multitude of others who all, intentionally or unintentionally, contribute to the foreign image of their country. If they are willing to make the effort and if their efforts are co-ordinated, their attitudes will play a very important role in forming the image of their country.

Negotiations are not the only business of the embassy but a very important one. Negotiations can be carried elsewhere, for instance at a specially convoked conference or in the lobbies of the United Nations. They can be conducted by nondiplomatic experts (for instance, if they aim at the conclusion of a treaty of commerce or of an agreement on a special matter such as extradition), but each negotiation between any two or several states is, in the last analysis, a political transaction and should be supervised by professional diplomats. Negotiations aim at gradually promoting the achievement of national objectives by reducing or eliminating friction and establishing closer co-operation with foreign governments. Their result is a mutually acceptable compromise. Of course, compromise does not necessarily mean a settlement which is equidistant between the initial positions of the states concerned. First, the factor of power works against this ideal. A powerful state is usually "more right" in its original claims than a weak one. Secondly, the initial positions might have been so extreme for the purpose of future bargaining that the final compromise cannot be found in a middle-of-the-road arrangement. Thirdly, the personal skill of the negotiator can tilt the balance of compromise in favor of his country.

Unless distorted by the overwhelming power of one party, whether this preponderance of power is actually used as a telling argument or remains in the background of negotiations, an international agreement is the result of a bargaining process which is not radically different from the bargaining procedures in an oriental bazaar. The outcome falls short of the positions assumed by the two parties at the beginning of the negotiation. The negotiation is a gradual exchange of concessions until some mutually agreeable balance is achieved. It is also a constant effort to convince the other party that the agreement is desirable from its point of view and would favor its interests. If a particular concession cannot be made but the true reasons for refusal must be concealed, the unlikely reasons which are given will be understood by the other party as a more or less polite refusal.

It is self-evident that it is safer and more intelligent to reach national objectives by agreements with other states than by the use of force. This is why war with its inherent unpredictability was called the *last* argument of kings. Negotiation, if possible, is a better alternative. Its difficulty increases in reverse ratio to the friendliness between the two states. If they are hostile to each other, negotiation becomes very awkward but is not impossible. Agreements on limited subjects can still be reached without affecting the basic objectives of the parties if these objectives collide head on.

Negotiations are a full-time job. The plenipotentiary who is in charge of them must be thoroughly briefed and familiar with the subject-matter. He must be aware not only of the particular objectives which his government wants to achieve through this negotiation but also of the basic goals of its foreign policy; he must also be cognizant of the interests of the opposite party because they will determine the attitudes of his counterpart. If he cannot be briefed in advance on the personality of his foreign colleague with whom he will sit for days or perhaps months at the same negotiating table, he should find out for himself what kind of man he is dealing with. He must never forget that he does not talk to an automaton but to a human being who cannot help having his own personal interests, foibles, and preoccupations. Once he discovers a human being in his diplomatic opponent, he will be able to establish personal contact and begin to enjoy the arduous game of bargaining. His power of resistance to fatigue and boredom will be increased and hence also his negotiating ability, if he truly enjoys the company of the other man who interests him as an individual and if he patiently listens to the arguments which that man must advance on behalf of his government.

Insofar as possible, the instructions should be flexible and leave room for maneuvering between the initial position and the minimum beyond which the negotiator is forbidden to make concessions unless otherwise instructed by new orders from his government. The personal skill of the negotiator is deployed within these upper and lower ceilings defined in his instructions.

If the process of bargaining results in an agreement, the latter should be couched in clear terms to avoid future misunderstandings and to prevent the other party from implementing the agreement in a manner which was not originally intended. One should not rely on the good faith of the other party, because this might result in grave disappointments. Imprecision is desirable only in two cases: when the two governments (for instance, two allies) want to conceal from the third states the lack of true understanding behind the vague terms of their agreement, or when one party intends to reserve freedom for its future actions by making the agreement unclear and liable to diverse interpretations.

Negotiation is never a venture in charity; both parties must be prepared to give and take. The timing of the beginning of negotiations might not be unimportant, because one party might lose international prestige or a part of its bargaining power by accepting the date of negotiations at the other party's choosing and at a moment inconvenient for itself.

One should never ask the question whether another government intends to negotiate, because every government, unless controlled by fools, is always ready to negotiate, at least on its own terms. Even before the nuclear age it was more sensible and cheaper to negotiate than to use force. If the other party was hopelessly weaker and could not offer effective resistance, a negotiated treaty was a better instrument for extorting from it a large part of its territory or even the surrender of its independence, because the new status quo was more acceptable to the third states if achieved "legally" and also because the blood of one's countrymen was not shed in this kind of peaceful conquest. Even an aggressive conqueror would rather obtain what he wants on a silver platter tendered to him across the negotiating table than on the battlefield.

The questions to be asked are as follows:

1. What are the matters which the other government is prepared to make the object of negotiations?

2. Do these matters leave enough room for mutual bargaining and the conclusion of an acceptable agreement?

3. If not, is the other government likely to accept a widening of the agenda to include other matters in order to build up a balanced framework for future bargaining at the negotiating table?

4. What are the assets of the two parties for sustaining their bargaining positions and for avoiding a situation in which one party would be able to dictate the terms of settlement to the other?

If the answers to these four questions are unfavorable for the government concerned, it should avoid negotiation if it is strong enough to afford it.

There is no virtue in negotiation for its own sake although negotiation may serve some purpose other than reaching agreement on the stated subject. Its real purpose may be to provide a convenient forum for propaganda directed against the other party, or to gain time until one's country is prepared for a showdown, or to mislead the opponent state regarding one's true intentions, or, finally, to postpone a crisis which could lead to armed hostilities. The latter consideration is especially important in our time. Sir Winston Churchill was right when he said that in the relations between the nuclear powers it was infinitely better to jaw-jaw than to war-war.

Propaganda helps to prepare the ground for negotiations and to influence their development by bringing pressure to bear on the opponent state from the third countries and from its own domestic public opinion, thereby compelling it to make concessions which it would not otherwise be prepared to make. Kite-flying is another technique related to negotiations. A government inspires a private source to voice a suggestion for which it officially does not assume responsibility. The reaction of foreign governments provides it with an estimate of whether the suggestion is acceptable or not. Accordingly, the trial balloon becomes an official proposal or is simply forgotten after an official denial that it originated with the government.

The lack of clarity in modern international agreements is due, if unintentional, to various reasons. One of them is the use of nonprofessional negotiators, a not unusual practice. The other is personal diplomacy. A chief executive or foreign minister who negotiates himself can spare only a few days for the negotiation and is always pressed for time. If the chief executives or foreign ministers come to a definite agreement, its terms have to be drafted in a haste which does not favor the selection of the clearest and most appropriate words. The third reason is the use of more than one language for the drafting of international agreements. The use of Latin and later of French as the general diplomatic language has been replaced by the insistence of the contracting parties on having as many authentic texts as there are languages which they consider their official languages. Each language is the product of its own distinct cultural history; a word which seems to be perfectly translated may acquire an altogether different connotation in another language. This linguistic difficulty is aggravated in our time by deep differences in values; the same universally familiar word may have various meanings for the contracting parties, each meaning defined by their different values. Identical terminology can often conceal opposite or at least divergent meanings, as the Western powers have discovered in their relations with the Soviet Union.

Threats, if they precede or accompany a negotiation, can be useful if they are believed. Otherwise, they are not only ineffective, but the state which proffers them loses international prestige after its bluff has been called.

The chief business of diplomacy is to strive for the achievement of national objectives by peaceful means, i.e., by negotiations with other states. Its task is not, however, terminated with the outbreak of hostilities. War is the use of force for political ends, and the diplomat should constantly remind his government of this simple truth, which is easily forgotten in the din of military hostilities. The government might be fascinated by the pursuit of hostilities and might be inclined to subordinate all other considerations to the one goal of the military victory. The diplomat should remind his government that the enemy of today might become an ally on the day after his defeat and that the ally of today might become the principal adversary after the common victory. Diplomacy must strive without respite to detach allies from the main enemy, to keep one's own allies together, and to influence the attitudes of the neutral states. These considerations might be obsolete in a nuclear war, but they still hold good for non-nuclear wars.

THE DIPLOMATIC PROFESSION

There are people who naively believe that an ambassador is only a messenger-boy waiting at the other end of the telephone line to carry the messages of his government to the government to which he is accredited. The truth is that the role of the diplomat continues to be very important but less so than in former times before the invention of railroads, planes, the telegraph, the telephone, and other means of telecommunication. The other reason for the decline in the importance of the diplomat is the contemporary fashion of personal diplomacy by the chief executives and foreign ministers as well as the practice of using the "trouble-shooters."

Prior to the era of these modern developments, the ambassador could receive instructions only occasionally and at rare intervals; he was a very important international figure. The lack of frequent instructions compelled him to make crucial decisions on his own in the hope that they would later be ratified by his government. He therefore had a hand in formulating the policy of his country toward the foreign state to which he was accredited. His government provided him before his departure for a new post with general instructions which determined the basic lines of his future conduct and usually supplied him with an orientation on the overall policy of his state not only toward the particular country in which he was going to reside but also toward other important countries. He arrived at the foreign capital fully familiar with the objectives of his government. By the same token, his own government was forced to take stock from time to time of its whole foreign policy; occasion was provided by the need to issue general instructions to a departing ambassador. It was also an opportunity for planning long-term policies. The planning of foreign policy was not invented in this century.

Today, the ambassador should also receive this sort of general briefing paper before joining his new post. But he can be instantly reached by telegraph and telephone. (The usual way of communicating is by telegram in cipher or by messages sent through diplomatic messengers. The code can be deciphered by foreign states and sometimes has been. The most secret messages are better delivered orally if time permits.) The embassy can be immediately instructed on the attitude which it should take in view of new and unexpected developments. This is true at least in technological theory. In fact, the embassy must sometimes rely on its own judgment if the instructions are ill-defined or if the government cannot make up its mind and fails to send instructions on time. Moreover, even detailed and clear instructions can be implemented in an adroit and intelligent manner or otherwise. The reaction of the foreign government might depend partly on this implementation.

Personal diplomacy, increased by the existence of air transportation, further reduces the importance of the embassy. The most difficult questions might be reserved for personal meetings between the chief executives or foreign ministers. A similar development, peculiar to the United States, consists in dispatching a "trouble-shooter" to a country or an area and entrusting him with the mission of ferreting out the true meaning of local events or of negotiating an important matter with the foreign government.

This method rests on the doubtful assumption that the "trouble-shooter" will be able in a few days to reach a more exact interpretation of local developments than the one which the embassy can supply although the permanent diplomatic mission has been familiar for years with local conditions. The parallel assumption is that he is capable, also in a few days, of overcoming difficulties which have proved too much for the embassy and reaching an agreement with the foreign government for which the embassy has striven in vain. Both assumptions presume that the "trouble-shooter" is necessarily incomparably more intelligent and more adept at diplomacy than the professional personnel of the embassy. The results obtained from this method might prove disappointing, but one consequence is unavoidable, the loss of prestige by the ambassador. If he is implicitly considered by his own government as a man of inferior quality, the foreign government cannot treat him as a representative fully authorized to speak on behalf of his country.

The modern diplomat continues to perform important functions. He can influence the tenor of the instructions by the reports which he sends back home. His advice cannot be lightly discarded. He is the most reliable source of information. His personal skill in building up a favorable image of his country and in carrying out the instructions of his government makes a great difference in the final results. An able diplomatic service makes an intelligent foreign policy effective. But it cannot achieve anything if the policy itself is inept or uncertain of its goals.

International relations is one of these rare fields of human knowledge in which few people are inclined to confess their ignorance and in which many people are always ready to offer their own ingenious recipes. This produces the conviction that diplomacy is not a professional occupation. No one would ask a medical doctor to draw the plan for a new house or an architect to carry out a surgical operation. No one would fancy a businessman acting as the commander of an army, but there is no lack of people who are inclined to think that any nice man can handle diplomatic business although he lacks the professional knowledge and experience. Today, one can echo de Callières' complaint: ". . . one may see often men who have never left their own country, who have never applied themselves to the study of public affairs, being of meagre intelligence, appointed to speak overnight to important embassies in countries of which they know neither the interests, the laws, the customs, the language, nor even the geographical situation. . . ." A government which is inclined to engage in this deplorable practice would do well to ponder this anecdote recounted by de Callières:

> The late Duke of Toscany, who was a remarkably wise and enlightened prince, once complained to the Venetian ambassador, who stayed overnight with him on his journey to Rome, that the Republic of Venice had sent as resident at his court a person of no value, possessing neither judgment nor knowledge, not even any attractive personal quality. "I am not surprised," said the ambassador in reply; "we have many fools in Venice." Whereupon the Grand Duke retorted: "We also have fools in Florence, but we take care not to export them. . . ."

One can conclude with the same author:

> The diplomatic genius is born, not made. But there are many qualities which may be developed with practice, and the greater part of the necessary knowledge can only be acquired by constant application to the subject. In this sense diplomacy is certainly a profession itself capable of occupying a man's whole career, and those who think to embark upon a diplomatic mission as a pleasant diversion from their common task only prepare disappointment for themselves and disaster for the cause they serve. . . . All are agreed that military command must be earned by long service in the army. In the same manner it should be regarded as folly to entrust the conduct of negotiations to an untrained ambassador unless he has conspicuously shown in some other walk of life the qualities and knowledge necessary for the practice of diplomacy. . . .

Lord Strang, a distinguished British diplomat, has said: "Most problems of foreign affairs are so difficult and full of ramifications that even the expert who spends his life in dealing with them is seldom as knowledgeable as he should be."

This statement is not an invitation for amateurs to meddle in diplomacy, which is assuredly a profession and a very difficult one at that. It requires from its adepts certain qualities of mind and character, knowledge, and experience that can only be acquired gradually, through long years of actual practice. As de Callières remarks, there are people who have not practised this profession and yet have the required qualities of mind and character and have obtained the necessary knowledge and experience in another walk of life. For instance, a domestic politician, who has been assigned by his government to oversee all or certain aspects of international affairs and to represent it in an international organization, might become an excellent ambassador. The telling question is whether these appointments form the rule or are rare deviations from it.

THE DIPLOMATIC IDEAL

The diplomatic profession, like any other profession, needs its ideal. The ideal is never a pattern of behavior which all the people concerned follow without deviation. If it were, it would be the common practice, not an ideal. In actual practice, human beings always fall short of the ideal, but its image provides them with a yardstick for measuring their successes and failures and with a goal to strive for. The ideal of the diplomat is exacting and requires certain traits of mind and character as well as professional knowledge. Several of its features should be of interest, not only to foreign service officers, but also to those nondiplomatic agents who have multiplied since the last war and play a considerable role in the inter-state relations.

Experience comes gradually while playing the game. The diplomat deals with politics and, like the domestic politician, should have the same indefinable political gift. Whether this aptitude for politics is called intuition or flair, certain people are deaf to political music and cannot catch its rhythm and others possess a musical ear. The political gift of the diplomat can be discovered only by observing him for a time in action.

The diplomatic profession is a vocation. One must love it to be successful. It is also a public service of the utmost importance to the country. National interests must be placed, without reservations, above everything else, including personal comfort and career. It requires certain traits of character and of mind. De Callières says that the diplomat must "possess the patience of a watchmaker." This patience not only helps him in living among foreign people whose beliefs and ways of life might be shockingly different from his own, not only makes possible his persistent ploughing through the ups and down of a negotiation, but also enables him to suffer gladly the fools who abound in every country and who might hold important positions. He should be courageous in both the physical and the civic sense. He is one of the most important builders of the foreign image of his people; if caught in the midst of street riots in a foreign country, he should not give the impression that his nation is made up of cowards. But civic courage is more important and more difficult to display. He must tell his own government the whole truth even if very unpleasant and even if it flatly contradicts his superiors' wishful thinking. They might dislike it. This duty to be truthful to one's government is infrequently rewarded with promotion; more often it hinders careers. The true wisdom of the government consists in giving its representatives complete freedom of expression in the reports they send home. Freedom of public expression should be denied to all the implementing agents (diplomatic, military, and other), because the state should speak with one voice only, that of the government itself. Whatever a diplomat or another implementing agent says regarding his official business cannot but be treated by foreign states as the reflection of official views. If they can be convinced that this is not true, they will discover a great weakness, a lack of discipline in the implementing agencies and of a proper co-ordination of national policies. Every public word uttered by a diplomat or a general or an admiral or any other ranking official should be spoken only with the government's assent and reflect its views, never his own personal opinion. The reminiscences which a diplomat accumulates during his career do not become his personal property after retirement, because he has acquired them only as a result of his public service. His memoirs should never be published without the consent of his government, because they can contain clues valuable to foreign countries and can cause unnecessary irritation in the relations with another nation. Freedom of expression for diplomats has these two facets: it should be complete in the confidential communications which they address to their government but should be denied to their public statements.

An essential feature of the diplomatic career is its anonymity. The diplomat's advice might have determined a crucial decision by the government or his skill in negotiations might have resulted in a very notable achievement. Yet the public and usually the historian will crown with laurels the president, the prime minister, or the secretary of state. This is not unjust, because the government, not the diplomat, bears ultimate responsibility for the external actions of the state. The power of the final decision is vested in the government, which might approve or reject the advice received from the professional diplomat. By the same token, the diplomat must implement any decision of his government even if he disapproves of it; his business is to advise and to implement, not to formulate the policy.

There are other unattractive features of this career which is far removed from the popular image of glamor and ease. The diplomat's place of residence depends on the government's assignment. Living an itinerant life, he cannot long enjoy the company of the same friends. Each new assignment begins a new chapter in his personal life. His children wander from one foreign school to another or must be separated from their parents and left behind in the home country at a boarding school. His professional work is not only a full-time job but often nerve-wracking. The frequent official meals and receptions are not a mere entertainment but a part of the painstaking task of gathering information and negotiating. One must really love this career to embrace it.

The diplomat must combine a lively curiosity (he is the source of his government's information) with the utmost discretion. Laymen are apt to take seriously the inept witticism in which Sir Henry Wotton, James I's ambassador, once indulged: "An ambassador is an honest man who is sent to lie abroad for the good of his country." Every experienced diplomat would rather agree with de Callières: "The use of deceit in diplomacy is by its very nature limited, since there is no curse that comes quicker to roost than a lie that has been found out." The reputation of being a liar would pursue the diplomat from one post to another and make him useless to his own government. His success in dealing with foreign people depends on his being trusted, respected, and liked even if the same people are disinclined to grant the same credit to his government. De Callières wisely adds: ". . . he should share freely with others everything except what it is his duty to conceal." There is no contradiction between being truthful and being careful to conceal state secrets which are not the personal property of the diplomat.

The Greek story about the lies and mischiefs of Hermes as a child throws clearer light on this problem. Hermes, a very naughty though divine boy, once stole a fine herd of cows from his elder brother Apollo. After many denials by Hermes, Apollo finally discovered his guilt and brought him for judgment before Zeus, their father. Hermes at first tried to plead not guilty, but his lies were of no avail. He had to confess. Zeus ordered him to take an oath never to lie again. Hermes obeyed but after making a cautious reservation that he would not be obliged to tell the whole truth. Zeus graciously agreed and granted him patronage over those human beings who make treaties. Thus, Hermes became the diplomats' patron. Unlike a witness before the court, the diplomat should imitate his divine protector—tell only the truth but not the whole truth.

Everyone who deals with foreign problems and foreign countries must possess the capacity to concede that foreigners have the right to their own self-evident truths and ways of life. One does not need to share their beliefs (this is often impossible, because these beliefs contradict one's own self-evident truths) or inwardly like their ways of life, but one must recognize that there is no valid reason for their having the same values and the same interests as one's nation. A diplomat or another implementing agent must go a step beyond cultural empathy; he must adjust himself to the local ways of life, including good manners. He must be aware that good manners are not a universally identical code of behavior but variable human conventions which are conceived to make life easier and more pleasant in a given cultural environment. The same behavior might be polite in one country and very rude in another. The implementing agent abroad must be polite by the standards of the country in which he resides.

De Callières was fully cognizant of cultural empathy although he did not know the words; he said:

> He must fall into the ways and customs of the country where he lives without showing repugnance or expressing contempt for them, as is frequently done by diplomatists who lose no opportunity of praising their own country and decrying all others. The diplomatist must bear in mind once for all that he is not authorized to demand that a whole country shall conform to his way of living, and that it is more reasonable, and in the long run greatly to his comfort, to accommodate himself to foreign ways of living. He should be beware of criticising the form of government or the personal conduct of the prince to whom he is accredited. On the contrary he should always praise that which is praiseworthy without affectation and without flattery, and if he properly understands his own function he will quickly discover that there is no nation or state which has not many good points, excellent laws, charming customs, as well as bad ones; and he will quickly discover that it is easy to single out the good points, and that there is no profit to be had in denouncing the bad ones, for the very reason that nothing the diplomatist can say or do will alter domestic habits or laws of the country in which he lives. . . .

These words point out, by their modern implication, the difficulty of the task assigned to a foreign expert. He temporarily resides in a foreign country for the express purpose of assisting in its economic development or the reform of its social institutions. He is invited by the foreign government to evaluate critically certain aspects of local life and to offer advice for reforming them. His task in this respect is more difficult than that of the diplomat, whose only obligation is to accept the foreign country as it is. He must reconcile a constructive criticism with the utmost respect for the country itself.

It is an anachronistic prejudice still entertained in the United States, the richest country in the world, that the ambassador in an important foreign capital should be a man of considerable personal means, able to defray the cost of representation from his own pocket. This obsolete view derives from the European practice of past centuries. Social mobility was then circumscribed by the privileges of the upper class. Education as a rule was accessible only to children of wealthy parents. Persons with the educational background required for the ambassadorial position were to be found in the upper class, i.e., among the people usually provided with considerable personal wealth. The state budget was a modest affair, and the sovereign was only too glad if he could shift the financial burden of maintaining an embassy to a wealthy subject who had the ambition to become an ambassador.

Modern conditions are altogether different. Education is widely open to people who have no wealth of their own. The available talents from among whom diplomats can be recruited have been greatly increased by this factor and by modern social mobility. The state budget is now computed in astronomical figures, while the expenses of an embassy are by comparison a tiny affair. The fashion of lavish receptions is gone. Each economically advanced country can easily pay the cost of its representation abroad. The United States, more than any other country, can afford to follow de Callières' advice:

> . . . a wise prince will not fall into the fault common to many princes, namely that of regarding wealth as the first and most necessary quality in an ambassador. Indeed he will serve his own interests much better by choosing an able negotiator of mediocre fortune than one endowed with all the wealth of the Indies but possessing a small intelligence, for it is obvious that the rich man may not know the true use of riches, whereas the able man will assuredly know how to employ his own ability. And the prince should further remember that it is within his power to equip the able man with all the necessary means, but that it is not in his power to endow with intelligence one who does not possess it. . . .

It is self-evident that the diplomat should not be a security risk and should be able to control any inclination which might make him the victim of foreign blackmail. Governments are alert to this consideration but are apt to forget the problem of security regarding the lower personnel employed abroad. Yet a locally recruited clerical employee, messenger-boy, telephone operator, chauffeur, or domestic servant might very well be in the service of the foreign intelligence. This risk exists not only in the totalitarian states. A true security would require that all personnel on the premises of an embassy be composed of well-screened nationals.

It is obvious that the diplomat should have an observant mind and sound judgment, be quick in his mental reactions, resourceful, able to combine discretion with curiosity. It is much less obvious that a good diplomat should never be so "sophisticated" as to speculate endlessly on matters on which there is no adequate information, to spin fantastic and barren hypotheses, and to reject commonsense explanations of events in favor of "subtle" refinements which create confusion and lead nowhere. Lord Strang offers useful advice: ". . . if he is wise and conscientious, will he wish to appear either quite as well-informed or quite as quick-witted as he actually is; for people seldom open out in conversation when they are made to feel that they are confronted with profound knowledge or intellectual pre-eminence."

The United Nations is a very good practical school for diplomats provided they bear in mind that it is a mirror but a distorted mirror of international reality and do not take the speeches and resolutions literally. They can learn there how to address a self-restrained audience which cannot be swayed by easy eloquence, how to attune their speeches to foreign arguments, and how to debate in public discussions and private conversations. They can establish personal contacts with politicians, diplomats, and journalists of practically all nationalities; these contacts will prove useful in their later career. All these assets are important, because the diplomat must be not only a good dialectician in confidential negotiations but also an able public speaker; his government might assign him to represent it at an international conference and, if he is a member of the embassy, he is expected to make speeches to various private audiences in the country where he resides.

The professional knowledge of the diplomat should include such subjects as universal history and geography (not only his national history or the history of his own civilization, and not only the geography of his area of the world), international politics, contemporary ideologies, the customs and rules of diplomacy, international law, economics, and so on. Moreover, he should have a good background of general culture, including a sufficient understanding of science, which is essential for the evaluation of the power of modern states. He is expected to meet well-educated foreigners and should be capable to sustain conversations on nonprofessional topics. This will protect him from the reputation of being a professional bore who never allows people to relax and forget international worries. He must be able to remain silent on those matters which he prefers not to discuss and yet to carry on a lively conversation on nonpolitical subjects. Finally, a man with versatile interests can build a bridge to meet the opposite negotiator on the noncontroversial ground of mutual interest and establish this personal contact which frequently makes an enjoyable game of the most arduous negotiations.

The diplomat assigned to a foreign country should possess or acquire a good knowledge of its "self-evident truths" and ways of life, its history and geography, its economic and social problems, its literature, which is the key to the foreign mentality, and its language. Language is the necessary tool of work. To take one example, it opens direct access to the foreign media of information. Native interpreters cannot always be trusted. Two members of the same embassy are apt to discover different news in the same local press or at least to interpret its meaning differently. An effort to speak in the local language, even with faulty pronunciation and grammatical errors, is always appreciated as a sign of interest and respect.

It is obvious that the implementing agent assigned abroad cannot be a gloomy introvert; he must like people and enjoy their company. Yet he must be aware of the imperfections of human nature.

Assignment to a foreign country should be neither too short nor too long. A diplomat becomes fully useful only after the lapse of one year, the period of his acculturation to the foreign environment and of his establishing a circle of useful personal contacts. A long sojourn will produce one of two possible effects. Either he will accumulate grudges against the country in which he resides or he will begin to feel a true sympathy. At this point his reports might become biased and less useful to his government.

The wives of diplomats and other implementing agents posted abroad face their own responsibilities. They also create an image of their country. Their ethnocentric behavior is sure to cause great harm to the reputation of their nation. They should also remember that people believe that the hidden thoughts of the husband are expressed by the wife, which is often true.

Should women be recruited for the foreign service? Two considerations, related to surviving prejudices, militate against it. First, there are a number of countries in which a woman ambassador would cut a strange figure either because of their customs (Moslem countries, for instance) or because they do not favor an active role for women in domestic politics. The appointment of a woman to any of these countries would be an ethnocentric error. The range of possible assignments for women diplomats is more restricted than for men although it is steadily becoming wider with the emancipation of women in the non-European countries. The second objection is practically more important. Universal prejudice singles out the man as the main provider for the family. A married woman ambassador raises the question of the social position of her husband. Lord Strang says: ". . . the idea of an unemployed husband of Her Excellency hovering somewhere in the domestic background is still not easily acceptable."

The image of the diplomat which emerges from the writings of de Callières and his disciples in the following centuries might mislead the inexperienced reader. He might imagine the diplomat as a sort of Christian knight without blemish, above all careful to observe the rules of the diplomatic tournament, or as a mild-mannered and meticulously polite gentleman, disenchanted with human nature and averse to ruthless deals. The history of diplomacy during the two centuries which followed the publication of de Callières' book does not support the accuracy of these portraits. Diplomats did not and could not aspire to sainthood any more than the professional politicians could. Politics, international or domestic, are not a competition for moral prizes. These diplomats placed the interests of their country above everything else and were not reluctant to conclude deals which could hardly be reconciled with Christian virtue. If there was a favorable opportunity, they gladly partitioned weak nations or carved out better frontiers or bargained for overseas possessions, disregarding in the process the aspirations of the populations concerned. Their professional restraint did not fetter them if the opponent was weak and helpless, especially if he was not a "civilized" European. Polite manners like a kid glove not infrequently covered a hard fist.

Yet the rosy image contains a grain of truth. If one restricts one's retrospective horizon to Europe only, as the historians of diplomacy often do while they paint its alluring portrait, if one eliminates from sight the several European nationalities who were foreign-controlled in the past two centuries, if one forgets the treatment which the same diplomacy meted out to the Asian countries, if one shares the then generally accepted division of mankind into civilized and uncivilized peoples, the image looks true in its narrow frame. Except for the intermezzo of the French Revolutionary and Napoleonic wars, the moderate objectives of the great powers made the diplomat the instrument of amiable negotiations for limited goals which the parties could achieve by bargaining concessions against concessions. The survival of his "self-evident truths" and ways of life and the independence of his country were not at stake. His deepest emotions were not stirred by the process of negotiation except on the rare occasions when his country, defeated in a limited war, was compelled to cede to the victor a province or an overseas territory. The refined manners of the upper and upper-middle classes from which he was recruited were an integral part of his nature. He was as impeccably polite with his foreign colleagues as he was with his social equals at home. He was not an ideological fanatic, but his fundamental social "self-evident truths" were never challenged by his diplomatic opponents. The historical circumstances of the time favored his being a polite and reasonable gentleman at home and abroad.

Even if one views with some skepticism the attractive classical image of the diplomat which emerges from the pages of de Callières, Sir Ernest Satow, Sir Harold Nicolson, and Lord Strang, he cannot deny that this diplomat had excellent manners. His choice of words was exquisitely courteous although his argument or maneuver could have been as sharp as a duellist's sword. Good manners do not make people more virtuous but help in making their mutual intercourse more pleasant. Good manners in diplomacy made the bargaining process more amiable if not less hard.

The manners of today's diplomats and statesmen are visibly of a lower quality. The discreet and indirect language of the past centuries, observed without deviation until 1914, has given place, at least in the relations between mutually unfriendly states, to rude overstatements and half-truths calculated to impress people who are not well-versed in international affairs, to bolster national morale, or to appeal to one's ideological followers or prospective sympathizers. The diplomatic notes and statements resemble the tone of war propaganda rather than the polite pronouncements which were directed at persuading the foreign government but not at converting the foreign public.

Even the declarations of war and ultimata were couched prior to 1914 in cold but polite words. Today, international sensitivity has been blunted. Notes exchanged between two powers which maintain peaceful relations and do not intend to begin military hostilities often include not only accusations of evil designs and of bad faith but also insults which would not be tolerated in private personal relations. The foreign policy of the other state is sometimes characterized as "banditism" or "gangsterism," and yet messages of this sort are accepted and answered. The former diplomatic usage of returning a note because of its incorrect or impolite phraseology seems to be forgotten. The change in diplomatic style can best be measured by comparing the American reactions in 1960-61 to insulting Soviet statements addressed to two successive presidents of the United States with the reaction to the famous indiscreet letter which the Spanish minister in Washington wrote in 1898. He called President McKinley "a bidder for the admiration of the crowd" and "a would-be politician . . . who tries to leave a door open behind himself while keeping on good terms with the jingoes of his party." This letter was not addressed to the President and was published in the American press because of an indiscretion and against the intention of its author. The Spanish government immediately disavowed the letter and recalled its minister. Yet this letter infuriated the American public and contributed to the warlike atmosphere.

Actually, two diplomatic styles co-exist. The one, reminiscent of the past century if less elaborate, survives in the relations between friendly nations. The other, tough, often brutal, rarely polite, is reserved for the exchange of views between unfriendly governments. The same governments currently speak two entirely different languages depending on whether they address their friends or neutrals or send messages to the opponents.

There are several reasons for this undeniable deterioration in diplomatic manners:

1. The present struggle is for stakes infinitely higher than anything known prior to 1914. The continuous tension makes people more impatient. Their self-control might not always withstand the pressure of the foreign challenge. Good manners are not easy to observe in this turbulent world.

2. The political emancipation of the common man has immensely widened the scope of foreign propaganda. Propaganda, i.e., the building of images in foreign minds, has always existed, but its scope was narrowly limited to the upper and later also the middle classes. The proportion of well-educated people and even of merely literate people was small by comparison with their present proportion. Today, foreign propaganda must address itself to the vast masses. Even illiterate people can be reached by radio broadcasts. Politically, the common man counts, and the proportion of educated people has greatly increased. These masses, inexpert in international affairs, must be confronted with images of striking simplicity, because only these images can be absorbed and digested within their limited frame of reference. The simplification of issues demands black and white pictures and calls for strong words which stir human emotions. Good manners suffer from the use of strong words.

3. Ideological warfare inevitably acquires a moral connotation. Its protagonists see themselves as Angels incarnate and view their adversaries as the embodiment of the Devil himself; they are inclined to regard the uncommitted nations with a certain contempt, as Pontius Pilates guilty of moral indifference. Moral indignation, if sincere, does not choose gentle or polite words for expressing itself and inhibits good manners toward those who are held to be the servants of Evil.

4. The social recruitment of statesmen and diplomats has changed profoundly. The social and colonial upheavals have brought to power new elites often of humble origin. The good manners of the former upper-class elites may often seem to them only ridiculous relics of a hated past. All economically advanced countries, even those which have not experienced any violent revolution, have been transformed by modern social mobility and by more equal access to education. Men of any social background can now formulate or implement foreign policies.

Statesmen and diplomats, like all men, are the products of their social environment. This environment has changed radically since the beginning of this century. It does not recall either the eighteenth or the nineteenth century. The society of the eighteenth century was dominated by the landed nobility and in several countries also by the upper bourgeoisie. Their privileges and vested interests were not challenged until the French Revolution. Social mobility was effectively limited not only by the legal privileges of the nobility but also by the narrow access to higher education, which was restricted to the scions of noble and upper bourgeois families. If a man of humbler descent had the luck to acquire this education and by his exceptional ability raised himself to the level of the ruling classes, he conformed to the pattern of upper-class behavior and could not be distinguished from the other members of this class. Members of the upper classes were not faced with a deadly competition, because the number of competitors was restricted by the social conditions of the time. They did not need to push very hard in order to forge ahead. The notion of personal honor dominated the life of the nobility and fixed a clear boundary line between what could or could not be done. Manners were refined, and the atmosphere was relatively relaxed. The humanistic education favored a keen sense of intellectual humor. Ridicule could kill as effectively as the sword. To be rude was to be ridiculous. The governmental and diplomatic personnel was not numerous; they could easily make personal friendships with their no more numerous foreign counterparts. The political struggle was confined to competition between state interests, or, as it was the fashion to say in those days, between the interests of sovereigns mutually related by family ties. The diplomatic game could be played without giving offense to good manners.

The eighteenth century left its imprint on the manners of the following century. The recruitment of statesmen and diplomats was progressively widened as a result of the increasing role of the middle classes, but these classes tried to imitate the manners of the nobility. The style was somewhat simplified but was not very different from what it had been in the eighteenth century. Social mobility was no longer hampered by legal privileges but continued to be restricted by wealth. The competition was sharper but still confined to a smaller number of competitors than now.

Today, social mobility and more equal access to education have opened the gates to all professions, including those of statesman and diplomat. The competition has become sharp, because anyone with adequate education can participate in it. The ideal of the gentleman is being replaced by that of the skillful operator who knows how to move up in a complex and highly organized society. The tempo of modern society leaves little time for good manners. Modern man is inclined to excuse his fellow-men for being rude; he himself can be unintentionally rude under the tension of sharp competition and the pressure of too little time. His family background is not necessarily one in which good manners are valued. This is the type of man who now becomes a member of the government or a diplomat. He is apt to be a rougher specimen than his predecessor of past centuries.

5. The criteria of good manners were practically uniform throughout the diplomatic world prior to 1914. The standard was set by the European manners of the dominant social classes. Today, the world arena has been expanded to include all the continents. What is polite for a European might be rude for an Asian or an African. Hence, the concept of good manners has been blurred.

The statesman or diplomat of our time is not the exemplar of excellent manners that his predecessor was. Overstatement is more popular than understatement. His rude attitude toward a foreign country evokes the applause of his countrymen and his ideological followers as a heroic pose of defiance. Ridicule does not kill, because people no longer agree on what is ridiculous or sublime. The deterioration in manners does not make international life easier, but this life is difficult for additional and more important reasons.

Another new feature, the suspicion which surrounds the embassies of the rival powers, is less of a novelty than one would suppose from glancing at nineteenth-century practices. It is rather a sharp return to the usages of the sixteenth, seventeenth, and eighteenth centuries. Diplomats were not infrequently instructed at that time to foment domestic opposition against the government to which they were accredited if that government pursued an unfriendy policy. Social contacts with foreign diplomats were sometimes discouraged as a measure of precaution. For instance, an English statute of 1653 forbade members of Parliament to speak to any foreign ambassador under the penalty of losing their parliamentary seat. The movements of foreign diplomats and their social contacts were supervised and sometimes hampered, as they are now in the Communist countries. The second half of the eighteenth and the nineteenth century put an end to those inhospitable practices. This century has revived and magnified them.

NONDIPLOMATIC AGENTS

Another new development has taken place since the last war. Until that time diplomats were the only implementing agents of foreign policy. This is no longer true. The revolution of modernization brought forward an increasing demand for economic and technical assistance which is now an integral part of the foreign policy of all economically advanced states (see Chapter 5). The military assistance granted to the less developed and committed countries has become another regular feature. The advanced countries send legions of nondiplomatic agents, who perform functions entrusted to them by their own state but by agreement with the receiving state. Military instructors, other military personnel stationed on foreign soil, and a multitude of technical experts and "expatriates" (civil servants leased by one state to another) live abroad and have a direct bearing on relations between the two states concerned. They often deeply affect the domestic patterns of life of the receiving country, something that would be called an illegitimate foreign intervention if a diplomat tried to do it. These foreign experts and advisers are protected against this accusation by the fact that they have come on the express invitation of the host government. However, they all contribute to refashion economic and social institutions and to reorganize state machinery, including the armed forces, and might have an influence on the future of the host country which is much greater than any embassy could ever hope to have. This cannot be of slight consequence to the state of their nationality.

The daily contacts which nondiplomatic agents have with local people influence the opinions which these foreigners will have of their country. They can make friends or enemies of the people they meet. Their work must be measured, insofar as the interests of their own nation are concerned, by two standards: have they accomplished their technical mission, and have they helped to create a favorable image of their own country?

These nondiplomatic activities should, in the last analysis, serve the same political objectives as the diplomatic activities. The foreign policy should be unitary, and its implementation by diplomatic or nondiplomatic agents should be carefully co-ordinated at the center by the Department of State and on the local level by the principal representative, the ambassador. This task of co-ordination is new insofar as technical assistance is concerned and requires from the diplomats of our age a very versatile knowledge which would allow them to understand the political, economic, and social implications of the work which their own countrymen perform in foreign lands. These countrymen, fascinated by the technical aspect of their job, might not always realize these various implications and might need some guidance from the embassy.

An expert sent by the United Nations or one of its Specialized Agencies is regarded by the inhabitants of the host country not only as an international agent but also as an individual of a definite nationality. His behavior affects their views of both the international organization and his country.

The governments of the advanced countries, as well as the international agencies, are confronted with the problem of what kind of preliminary training they should give their technical experts who are going to be sent to an underdeveloped country. It is obvious that no amount of purely professional knowledge guarantees that these experts will assume proper attitudes in a foreign country presumably very different from their own. They should be briefed about the main problems of the country where they are going to reside temporarily but they should also be reminded that they must never depart from an attitude of respect for the values and ways of life of the people whom they are to help with their advice.

PERSONAL DIPLOMACY

Summit or personal diplomacy, i.e., negotiations between chief executives, is more common in our time than in previous periods. It was practised in the ancient, medieval, and later periods, but meetings between the principals were rare. They were rare for various reasons, such as the slow means of transportation, the hazards of travel, and the cost involved in the lavish display of princely pageantry. Their frequency varied between the beginning of the nineteenth century and the outbreak of the First World War. Napoleon, as sure of his political as of his military genius, favored personal diplomacy. He personally negotiated the Peace Treaty of Campo Formio and carried on important conversations with Alexander I at Tilsitt in 1807 and with several foreign sovereigns in 1808 at the assembly held at Erfurt. His practise survived his fall. Several congresses of sovereigns, prime ministers, and foreign ministers were held by the European great powers beginning with the Congress of Vienna (1814-15) and ending with the Verona Conference in 1823. The practise later lapsed to be revived by Napoleon III, who undertook two important personal negotiations, with Cavour in 1858 and with Bismarck in 1865. The Paris Peace Conference for the termination of the Crimean War (1856) was attended by prime ministers and foreign ministers. The understanding among the emperors of Russia, Germany, and Austria was kept alive by the personal meetings of these three sovereigns. The Berlin Congress of 1878 for the settlement of the Near Eastern question was again attended by prime ministers and foreign ministers. However, the conclusion of the alliances which eventually aligned the great powers into the two hostile blocs was achieved by patient negotiations through the usual diplomatic channels.

The First World War revived the practice of direct contact between the principals because the allied powers felt that their war efforts could be more efficiently co-ordinated in this way. Since that time summit diplomacy has been a regular feature of international intercourse. The meetings of the League of Nations were frequently attended by prime ministers and foreign ministers. The crisis of the late thirties spurred them to meet even more frequently. The Munich conference was one of these summit meetings. Hitler, Mussolini, and Stalin liked to negotiate directly with other chief executives or foreign ministers.

The Second World War revived the practise of the First, and again the two or three heads of the allied great powers met frequently. The most famous summit conferences of that time were held in 1943-45 at Teheran, Yalta, and Potsdam; the political and military decisions reached at these three conferences largely predetermined the postwar situation in Europe and the Far East.

Persons with actual international experience have always been almost unanimous in agreeing with Philippe de Comines, whose oft-quoted statement was made in the second half of the fifteenth century: "Two great princes who wish to establish good relations should never meet each other face-to-face but ought to communicate through good and wise ambassadors." However, to enumerate the disadvantages of personal diplomacy is mainly an academic exercise; its frequent modern use has established a custom which probably no amount of argument can eradicate.

The reasons for the popularity of summit diplomacy are as follows:

1. The rise of dictatorial rulers who are more free than their democratic colleagues to make personal decisions. The prominence of the United States as an active world power has produced similar effects because of the great constitutional powers vested in the president.

2. The development of quick transportation, in particular air transportation. This in itself seems to be a standing invitation to hop on a plane and visit foreign capitals or to go to the appointed rendezvous with other principal leaders.

3. The meetings of the League and now of the United Nations, which provide frequent opportunities for personal diplomacy.

4. The widespread fear of a nuclear catastrophe, which is constantly nourished by ever-recurring crises and which generates pressure for personal meetings between chief executives.

Although people think of personal diplomacy as the practice of great powers, this method of international relations is also favored by the chief executives of other states. The usual expectation is that the men who hold the power of final decision regarding the external actions of their states should be able, if they meet personally, to achieve what cannot be done through diplomatic channels. This expectation is founded on the false assumption that, if the same leaders stay in their capitals, formulate policies there, and issue instructions to their diplomatic representatives, they cannot possibly understand what the stakes are, will be inadequately informed on the intentions of their foreign counterparts, and will be poorly served by their ambassadors, who will fail to implement their instructions faithfully. People hope that insurmountable difficulties which have refused to yield to years of patient negotiations will melt away in the warm atmosphere of personal conversations between the top men held for a few days.

The chief executives might be inclined to take an equally optimistic view. A successful political leader is sincerely convinced that he is the man to solve the problems which other men have failed to solve. His domestic success confirms him in the conviction that he is endowed with unusual political sagacity. He knows how to manipulate his countrymen whether he is a democratic or a totalitarian leader; otherwise, he would not have become the chief executive. There is but one short step to take to become sure that he can twist any foreign leader around his finger as he has done with his own countrymen. But this foreign leader is, by definition, also an able manipulator of men and might, in fact, have greater talent in this respect.

It is true that the totalitarian leaders have a very great discretionary power and do not need to look over their shoulders to watch the maneuvers of the opposition. But they, too, are limited in their freedom by their own understanding of national interests and cannot improvise quixotic decisions on the spur of the moment. If they are wise men, they will not depart from positions taken prior to the summit meeting, because these positions have been defined after long reflection, and will not disregard the opinions of trusted advisers. If they truly want to reach an agreement with another state, they have only to issue appropriate instructions to their diplomatic representatives, who will carry out their orders through the usual channels without the need for a summit meeting. If they insist on a summit conference, they might just as well want the conference for reasons which are unrelated to the topics on the agenda, such as an accretion of their international prestige, an excellent platform for international propaganda, or an opportunity to impress their opponents with their will-power or the military might of their country.

The disadvantages of personal diplomacy have often been listed. The chief executive's main function in foreign affairs is to formulate policy, a function which no one can perform for him. He has many other obligations, such as initiating domestic policies and leading his own party. He is hard put for time. The several days which he devotes to the summit meeting or the innumerable hours which he spends in conferring with important foreign visitors leave him with less time for his other vital duties. He must concentrate during a summit meeting on a few issues, which are beyond any doubt important, but life will not stand still. Domestic problems and other foreign issues will not patiently await his return. The national administration is decapitated for a number of days, not because he cannot communicate with his capital but because he has temporarily no time to attend properly to the other business. Moreover, he should carefully husband his time and reserve a good part of it for his own thinking and for discussions with his closest advisers.

The same pressure for time can prevent him from mastering all the data of the problems to be negotiated at a summit meeting. Yet these data might be of vital importance. The history of summit conferences held during the last three decades does not prove that all the principal participants were well-briefed and fully understood the implications of the issues discussed. The reason was not that information was lacking but that they did not have enough time to consult the files.

A summit conference cannot last long. The participants are in a hurry to go home and hence are inclined to patch up agreements which are either unclear or fall short of the national requirements of their countries. The one who can outsit the others and is a hard bargainer, impervious to fatigue and boredom, finds an excellent advantage in the haste of his colleagues if he knows exactly what he wants.

By contrast, a plenipotentiary has all the time demanded by the negotiation. He may sit there for weeks and months, because this is his only job at the time. He knows by heart all the aspects of the issue. Personal factors, such as fondness or dislike for his opposite partner, cannot greatly influence his tactics because he is bound by governmental instructions.

The chief executive has no comparable protection because he is the fountainhead of foreign policy and cannot issue instructions to himself. Personal factors (his sympathy or antipathy for the other chief executive, his trust or its lack in his reliability, his depressed or buoyant mood, or his condition of health) can irremediably alter the outcome of the conference. His word is final. But his representative's word does not need to be final. If he oversteps his instructions, diplomatic usages allow him to withdraw his former statements by pleading misinterpretation of governmental instructions. The same usages permit his being instructed to withdraw a statement which he made on his government's orders, if the government has changed its mind in the meantime. Since the instructions are secret, it cannot be proved whether he made an error in their interpretation or whether they have been subsequently modified. This sort of retreat is closed to the man who is himself the supreme source of all instructions.

The plenipotentiary, if he is a professional diplomat, is used to the techniques of negotiations, while the chief executive, whose personal experience has been different, might lack the required skill.

The summit meeting, like any international conference, should at least be well prepared in advance. The agenda should be agreed upon before its convocation to give an equal bargaining chance to all participants. The issues should be narrowed down to a few important points left for settlement by the chief executives. This prior diplomatic preparation guarantees that the participants in a summit conference will know exactly the framework of their discussions and will have a reasonable hope of reaching an agreement. It is an illusion to think that a summit meeting can be only an occasion for the chief executives to get acquainted with each other. A meeting between chief executives cannot remain a social visit. They cannot help talking about current issues and thus defining in the process their own positions. This is a negotiation even if they fail to agree.

The summit meeting raises great hopes. If two or four main actors on the international stage meet together, the public, alarmed by the immense risks of our time, is naturally inclined to expect some relief from them. Yet these leaders cannot perform miracles. The political antagonism between their states arises from deep causes, not from their personal hostility to each other. Their brief display of amiability and their smiles produced for the press photographers cannot suddenly remove these deep causes. There is a risk that disappointment will replace great hopes if the summit conference leaves matters basically unchanged. The public feels frustrated, and the net result might be greater international tension.

The wartime and postwar record of summit conferences is not particularly encouraging. The Teheran, Yalta, and Potsdam conferences were guided in Western thinking by the desire and hope that the wartime unity of the three great powers would survive the common victory and would become the cornerstone of a lasting peace and of orderly international relations. The United Nations was to be the common bond. These hopes, entertained in spite of the known history of all previous great coalitions which had disintegrated on the morrow of victory and of the many disappointing moments experienced during the wartime co-operation among the three powers, were frustrated in 1945-46. The former allies began their "cold war."

The Geneva summit conference of 1955 met under auspices which were interpreted by most contemporary observers as very promising. Stalin was dead. There was an eager expectation in the West that the cold war had died with him. Public Soviet pronouncements seemed to promise a more conciliatory foreign policy. The Conference produced, however, no visible results except for a wave of Western optimism that did not last long. One of the participants, Khrushchev, stopped on his way back in East Berlin and made a speech there which finally quashed Western hopes for a negotiated settlement of the German question. He said that unification could not entail the sacrifice of "the political and social achievements" of the German Democratic Republic, i.e., that the Communist ways of life would have to survive in East Germany even after unification. As two diametrically opposed political and social systems cannot co-exist within the same state, Khrushchev thus intimated that the U.S.S.R. was opposed to unification. Soon after the Geneva Conference the Czechoslovak-Egyptian arms deal became known. The Western powers were notified in this way that the Soviet Union and its allies would henceforth represent a new and able competitor in the Near East.

The summit conference which was to be held in 1960 in Paris was preceded by the usual great expectations. In the months prior to the date of the conference, the Soviet premier had received the British prime minister and the American vice-president and had himself paid an official visit to the United States. The high hopes were quashed by the U-2 incident. The conference never formally met; instead, its would-be participants held press conferences in Paris at which they exchanged acrimonious accusations. Mutual feelings were certainly not improved by the miscarriage of that summit meeting.

The Vienna meeting in 1961 between the Soviet premier and the new president of the United States was not, judging from the comments after the conference, an auspicious beginning of their relations with each other. No summit meeting held in our time, from the Munich conference to the present, has produced the results which the participants or the public expected.

The informality of the proceedings might prove hazardous; it might well encourage the less cautious participants to relax as though they were taking part in a private social gathering and to forget that they are engaged in the business of hard international bargaining. It is difficult enough to conceal the fact that negotiations are going on between two or several states, but the summit meeting is preceded, accompanied, and followed by the loudest publicity. The meeting of principal executives attracts a great crowd of journalists and agents of other media of information. The secrecy of conversations is subject to continuous assault. Official communiqués, issued by the chief executives either jointly or separately, provide only meager news, but leaks usually tear off a good part of the veil of secrecy. The conversations tend to become semi-secret, with the result that discordant versions of what is happening are circulated by the press and sometimes become the source of no less discordant historical accounts.

Modern diplomacy, including personal diplomacy, has brought to the fore two new specialists: the interpreter and the press officer. The disappearance of the international diplomatic language, in which members of government and diplomats were formerly proficient, makes the interpreter's function imperative, especially at the meetings of the chief executives, who rarely know foreign languages well. If a negotiator knows the language of his foreign counterpart only imperfectly, he is well-advised to use his own language and the services of an interpreter. Otherwise, he will be unable to express himself with the desired clarity and to catch all the fine points in the other man's argument. The interpreter is also a very useful witness if the principal negotiators decide to closet themselves without their advisers, a procedure which is rather unwise under any circumstances. In this case, each chief executive should be accompanied by his own interpreter, who should be experienced enough to follow the discussion intelligently.

The press officer who accompanies the chief executive to a summit meeting has a very difficult assignment which requires great tactical skill. He must keep the press fairly happy and yet avoid any damage to the national interests that could be caused by his indiscretion. He distills the propaganda of his government and protects his chief from pressure by the journalists. If the chief executive wants the conversations to be truly secret, the press officer must supply enough interesting but trivial news to fill the press dispatches; if the principal desires a leak, the press officer must find the journalist who will be discreet enough to keep secret the source of his information but is "indiscreet enough" to publish the "secret" on the next day.

Summit meetings take various forms: the official visit of the chief executive to a foreign capital; a specially arranged meeting of two or several chief executives at a place mutually agreed upon; a meeting of two, three, four, or more heads of government; a conference convoked for the stated purpose of negotiating on certain definite topics, or a meeting without any formal agenda and characterized by free-wheeling conversation; meetings with allies, neutrals, or opponents.

The only advocate of personal diplomacy who has had long and rich international experience, Lord Hankey, had in mind negotiations among allied governments. He was an eyewitness of the summit meetings during the First World War. These meetings of the allied chief executives were successful because the existence of common enemies provided grounds for a basic unity of purpose and spurred the participants into an earnest search for mutually agreeable decisions. The reason for these conferences was the urgent need for a speedy co-ordination of military and political actions which could not be achieved so rapidly through normal diplomatic channels. The informality of the proceedings and the personal contact between the participating statesmen helped them to arrive at joint decisions; they reached these decisions, however, for a more important reason than their personal contact, namely the same desire to win the war.

The wartime experience which left such favorable recollections with Lord Hankey could be invoked in favor of peacetime personal diplomacy in the relations between allied states. They have a basic unity of purpose which should allow for a degree of frankness that would be unthinkable at a summit conference attended by the chief executives of unfriendly powers. If the allied states face an urgent problem in their relations with their common adversary and must speedily devise a joint policy, the summit meeting might be a handy method. However, their unity of purpose will never be felt as strongly as in wartime, because the survival of their countries does not appear to be at stake. A summit meeting between allied powers on matters which divide them from each other might be as unproductive as a summit conference held with their adversary.

A no less experienced person than Dean Acheson, who looked at a different type of summit conference from the type favored by Lord Hankey, warned of the risks involved in personal diplomacy between the chief executives of mutually unfriendly powers. According to him, the dynamic (anti–status quo) power uses the summit meeting for the following purposes:

1. To disrupt the unity of its opponents. The favorite technique is to meet separately each of the chief executives of the states allied in the opposite coalition. The head of the dynamic power tries to widen the existing divergencies of views among his adversaries and thus to undermine their common diplomatic front. The same technique is used at a multilateral summit conference but there the allies can compare notes daily so that their separation from one another is much more difficult.

2. The dynamic power uses the summit conference as a propaganda platform from which to convince international bystanders that the "peaceful and reasonable" settlement which it offers is blocked by its opponents' inflexibility. The dynamic power is in a favorable tactical position for hurling these accusations. Because it wants to change the status quo, the revolutionary power appears to be flexible; the status-quo powers resist

this change and thus appear to be stubborn and inflexible. The chief executives of these powers are placed in an embarrassing position. Their own countries and certainly the uncommitted nations are apt to get impatient and mistake their firmness for unreasonable rigidity; the feeling might grow that a settlement would be just around the corner but for their obstinacy and lack of imagination.

Dean Acheson says:

> The makers of ultimate decisions must be insulated a little from the negotiators themselves. They must remain more detached. Neither their prestige nor their judgment should be caught up by the ebb and flow of the struggle in the negotiating chamber. Any commander-in-chief would be unwise to put himself in a forward command post in personal charge of the first assault columns. In particular, this is unwise when the metaphor gains added force by reason of the almost exclusive use of conferences for political warfare. It becomes triply unwise when, as in the United States, the offices of chief of state and head of government are combined.

The temptation to use personal diplomacy is even greater for the foreign minister than for the chief executive. Foreign policy is his business, and the fashion of the day almost compels him to visit foreign capitals and attend diplomatic conferences. Yet his time is also limited. The days which he spends abroad in personal negotiation with his foreign counterparts are days lost for other duties of his office which are also important. The Secretary of State (foreign minister) has large powers delegated to him either by the chief executive or by the cabinet for the formulation of foreign policy. He is the principal adviser to his government on international matters and the head of the Department of State. He is the channel of communication between the government and the Department of State. During his absence abroad, these other functions cannot be properly attended to. The decisions which he should have made are left to others or are not made. The government as a collective body and the chief executive (the president or the prime minister) has to seek advice from other people. The Department of State cannot easily channel its views to the government or the chief executive and be constantly informed of their intentions. An important cog in the state machinery is absent, while it is far from certain that he is a better negotiator than his subordinate professional diplomats.

CONFERENCE DIPLOMACY AND PUBLICITY

Whenever more than two states engage simultaneously in the same negotiation and consider that the parallel use of their bilateral diplomatic channels would be awkward and inexpedient, they assemble their representatives at a conference table. The participation of several delegations changes the character of the negotiation. It is no longer an informal conversation *à deux* but becomes a formal debate at an assembly which cannot operate except by following quasi-parliamentary rules. There must be a chairman and other officers elected from among the delegates, rules of procedure, a voting system, possibly committees which assist the plenary session in expediting matters by allocating each particular topic or each particular aspect of the same topic to a different committee, and so forth. The conference is nevertheless a negotiation, and its success depends on the capacity and willingness of the parties to reach a compromise solution. The conference can conduct its deliberations in secret or be fully or partly public (for instance, its plenary meetings might be public but its committee or subcommittee sessions remain secret). Public or secret, the proceedings are necessarily more formal than a bilateral conversation because they consist of a succession of statements made by the delegates; these statements are listened to without interruption and are answered if need be in the following speeches by the other delegations.

The first condition of the success of the conference is its thorough preparation. The topics to be debated should be delineated in advance, and the divergencies between the positions of would-be participants narrowed down to make it possible, if not probable, that the conference reach an agreement. If the parties do not expect to find a mutually acceptable agreement and yet are willing to convoke a conference, their purpose is obviously not negotiation but propaganda; the publicity of debates then becomes a necessary medium for oratorical performance. Informal negotiations accompany the formal proceedings of the conference which, if meant to be a serious bargaining operation, cannot progress unless the delegates meet in the lobbies and discuss their differences there in an atmosphere free of rigid rules of procedure and of the noise of publicity.

The participants in a diplomatic conference usually feel the pressure of time more acutely than the two plenipotentiaries who are engaged in a bilateral negotiation. The conference can last for days, weeks, or even months, but the assembled delegations are too numerous to think that they should proceed at a leisurely pace and retain scores if not hundreds of people at the conference table for long. Nevertheless the conference saves time. A multilateral agreement can be reached much more quickly if all the states concerned bargain simultaneously with each other than if each two of them negotiate separately and need to adjust their bilateral agreements with other states in the same bilateral manner until a general multilateral agreement is finally achieved. This is the reason why the conference is an indispensable tool of diplomacy.

The criticisms often leveled at conference diplomacy are directed, not against the method itself, but against certain of its modern aspects, such as the voting system (see Chapter 9) or the publicity of debates. The voting system, whether it rests on unanimity or on a two-thirds majority, would not in itself make much difference in the final outcome of debates if the great powers were able to find a compromise solution acceptable to all of them. The sheer combined weight of their political power would usually suffice to ensure the required majority or even unanimity.

Publicity is a different matter. It would be a hindrance in the negotiations even if the great powers were not, as they are, deeply divided among themselves. It is customary to place the blame for modern publicity in international transactions on two countries, the United States and Soviet Russia. Both made themselves its apostles toward the end of the First World War. Their motivations were different. President Wilson thought that European secret diplomacy was one of the major reasons for that war and was dismayed by the discovery of the secret agreements concluded by the Allies before the American entry into the war. These agreements could not be squared with his publicly announced war aims. His democratic convictions led him to believe that popular control over foreign affairs was impossible without the fullest publicity of international transactions and that only this popular control could guarantee general peace. This somewhat academic view of international politics was possible against the background of American detachment. The United States of the time was the only belligerent to feel secure and strong enough to afford to forego any territorial or other expansionist ambitions; its isolationist history nourished the conviction that it was morally above "power politics and the game of the balance of power" of the Eastern Hemisphere.

The Soviet leaders did not attribute war to secret diplomacy but to the capitalist system itself. They believed that wars could be eliminated forever only by the universal destruction of capitalism. Publicity meant to them constant appeals to the supposedly discontented masses over the heads of their capitalist governments, which were expected to be forced by popular pressure to adopt a more conciliatory policy toward the new socialist regime. Publicity was also to become the means for "unmasking" the rapaciousness and duplicity of capitalist diplomacy. The Soviet publication of secret treaties for the division of spoils from the first World War, which the Tsarist regime had concluded with its Western allies, was a device for exposing the "wicked" nature of capitalism and for embarrassing the Western powers.

It is interesting to note that both protagonists of publicity very soon learned that secrecy was an integral part of the international transactions which no amount of moralistic preaching or Marxist propaganda could exorcise. The loud appeals broadcast to the German and Austrian "proletarians" did not save the fledgling Soviet government in 1918 from the offensive by the German and Austrian armies, composed of these "proletarians" in uniform, from the accompanying ultimatum, and from the eventual signing, under duress, of the ruthless Brest-Litovsk Peace Treaty. After this harsh lesson the Soviet government fully acknowledged in its practice that the secrecy of negotiations could not be dispensed with if one was compelled or wanted to make an international deal. In 1939, secret diplomacy won a signal victory when the Soviet Union engaged in ultra-secret negotiations with Nazi Germany and concluded in consequence a treaty of neutrality and an accompanying secret agreement for the division of Eastern Europe between the two powers.

President Wilson learned the lesson in a less harsh but no less realistic way, when he conducted negotiations with the Allied statesmen for the peace settlement. An eyewitness, Sir Harold Nicolson, thus describes the President's negotiating method:

> Not only were Germany and her allies excluded from any part in the discussion; not only were all the minor Powers kept in the dark regarding the several stages of the negotiation; not only were the press accorded no information beyond the most meagre of official bulletins; but in the end President Wilson shut himself up in his own study with Lloyd George and Clemenceau, while an American marine with fixed bayonet marched up and down in order to prevent the intrusion of all experts, diplomatists or plenipotentiaries including even the President's own colleagues on the American delegation.

The pendulum swings from one extreme to the other. The President kept his negotiations secret even from his own Secretary of State. The Soviet government conducted its secret negotiations with Nazi Germany for a treaty of neutrality under the cover of public conversations with Britain and France for the conclusion of an anti-German alliance.

President Wilson defined his objective in the first of his famous Fourteen Points of January, 1918: "Open covenants openly arrived at, after which there shall be no private international understandings of any kind, but diplomacy shall proceed always frankly and in public view."

He thus announced two distinct ideas. The first was to demand the full publicity of international treaties (open covenants). In this respect, his view was a logical outcome of the democratic system of government. The people cannot control the foreign policy of their government if they are kept in the dark concerning the foreign commitments entered into by their government on their behalf. The publicity of treaties is less relevant for other regimes in which the public has little if anything to say about foreign or domestic policies. However, it is historically untrue that states have wanted at any time to keep all treaties secret. They have seldom done so and only when they felt that a particular agreement should not become known to the third states, which would otherwise have been forewarned of the intentions of the contracting parties. Actually, several wealthier countries began long ago to print their national series of treaties concluded with other states. These treaty series were meant to facilitate implementation by their own administration and courts and also to make the treaty stipulations known to private citizens whom they could concern. Today, these national treaty series are supplemented by the international treaty series which the League of Nations began to publish and the United Nations continues to publish. The knowledge of almost all international treaties is easily accessible to the literate public.

The fact that the average person does not care to read them does not detract from the political significance of publicity. The actual control over foreign policy is exercised by an articulate minority on behalf of the majority (see Chapter 8). This minority is usually cognizant of the contents of important political treaties. Particular groups within the minority are aware of the stipulations of other treaties which are of special interest to them; for instance, a treaty of commerce will not pass unnoticed by the leaders of various economic interest groups. Their knowledge of treaties allows the articulate minority to alarm the country if they disapprove of an agreement and to exert pressure on the government and the legislature; in extreme cases, they can prevent the ratification of the treaty, and in other cases, they can at least warn the government against similar commitments in the future.

While Wilson, as the president of a democratic country, was right in vindicating the publicity of treaties, he failed to mention any exceptions. The exceptional situation will seldom arise and only in a national emergency, but then the government might feel the pressing need to conclude a secret treaty. It faces a choice between exposing the most vital interests of the country to a great danger and concluding a secret agreement; it might have no choice if the other prospective party to the agreement refuses to commit itself unless the treaty is kept secret. The need for this type of secret agreement occurs especially during war. Secrecy protects the contracting parties from unintentionally forewarning their common enemy. The secret treaties concluded by the Allies during the First World War aimed at consolidating their unity of purpose by dividing the spoils of victory in advance. President Wilson was right in denouncing their immorality, but they were not meant to be moral. They certainly collided with his own ideals, but these treaties, if the parties wanted to conclude them, could not but be secret. Otherwise, their knowledge would have given the enemies an additional reason for offering stiff military resistance. The treaty which Britain, France, and Russia concluded in 1915 with Italy, then still a neutral country and but recently an ally of Germany and Austria-Hungary, promised Italy various territorial gains at the expense of Austria and Turkey; this was the price to be paid for its entry into the war on the Western-Russian side. Obviously, the Italians would have never agreed to the publication of the treaty; their former allies, thus forewarned of Italian intentions, would have attacked first. This secret treaty and other inter-allied treaties concluded during the First World War, if published, would possibly have alienated neutral public opinion, including public opinion in the United States, because they were not consonant with the high ideals which Allied propaganda associated with the war aims of the Allied powers.

The Soviet Union, then a neutral in the Far Eastern war, would never have assented to the immediate publication of the Yalta Far Eastern Agreement, which was similar in purpose and content to the Allied-Italian treaty of 1915. The United States and Britain agreed to pay Russia for its entry into the war against Japan with territorial and political concessions made at the expense of Japan and China. One can dispute the need at that time for Soviet participation in the Far Eastern war or the morality of a deal at the expense of the Chinese ally, but obviously the Yalta Agreement, which seemed desirable at the time, would have been inconceivable unless kept secret. The Soviet Union, which still faced Germany on its European front, could not have been asked to forewarn Japan by allowing the publication of the agreement. At that time, Russia entertained correct neutral relations with Japan, which kept a large army on its Eastern border. It wanted to attack by surprise and only after the termination of hostilities in Europe.

President Wilson's truly controversial proposal was to have international diplomacy proceed "in the public view." He did not stop to think that even domestic interest groups will not always consent to bargain openly. Yet national interests are incomparably greater than those of any domestic group and more difficult to reconcile with those of other countries than the interests of any two domestic corporations. Any bargaining requires for its success the informal and confidential atmosphere which only secrecy guarantees.

International bargaining begins with the issuing of secret instructions to the plenipotentiary. These instructions must be kept secret because they define the limits within which the negotiator can move and the minimum stand beyond which he cannot make any further concessions. If these instructions were known to the opposite side, bargaining would be made either impossible or infinitely more difficult. Publicity also means that the public at home is immediately acquainted with the maximum position which the government initially assumed. What this opinion is apt to ignore is that this initial position has been expanded to provide some leeway for the exchange of concessions. Hence, it might indignantly tax every concession which the government makes in the further stages of the negotiation as a betrayal of national interests. This is particularly true in our time when every important international controversy acquires a moral connotation and each change in the governmental position is liable to be exploited, sincerely or not, by the opposition, various interest groups, and patriotic organizations, against the party in power. Publicity might eliminate the freedom of the government to maneuver.

The publicity of negotiations provides an almost irresistible temptation to resort to propaganda. The government engaged in public negotiations will tend to impress its domestic opinion with its inflexibility in defending national interests, to reassure its allies of the utmost devotion to the common cause, to convince neutrals that their countries' happiness is not forgotten, and to make a show of unshakable resolve for the other party's benefit. The public negotiation ends by becoming a dialogue of the deaf, each party paying attention only to its own monologue. If, however, the negotiating states do not intend or do not expect to arrive at a settlement, the full publicity becomes most desirable for them, because their debates are no longer a negotiation but a propaganda tournament. Secrecy and propaganda are an antinomy.

Yet publicity cannot be eliminated from modern international transactions. The reasons are deeper than President Wilson's First Point or the Soviet government's early appeals to the toilers of the world. One of these reasons is the rapid expansion of the mass media of information. These media create their own need for a broad coverage of news. Secondly, the same media offer a wide forum for public propaganda. Thirdly, the circle of people seriously interested in foreign affairs has greatly increased since the nineteenth century. Finally, the average person, who is not particularly conversant with international problems, is nevertheless ready to absorb daily a small dose of foreign news; the memory of the two world wars, the atmosphere of continuous international crisis, and the fear of nuclear catastrophe make him apprehensive that the press, radio, and television might suddenly bring him foreign news of ominous significance for his own life and well-being. This pervasive feeling of international insecurity creates a demand for foreign news which can be supplied only by publicizing international transactions. It is next to impossible for the governments to resist this pressure.

The contemporary negotiator, if he sincerely desires to seclude himself with his foreign colleague in order to carry on a serious negotiation, is constantly exposed to the risk of being discovered by the agents of the mass media of communication and pushed by them to the highly illuminated forefront of the stage.

Publicity is meaningful if it refers to broad access to international information by the mass media which relay such information to the widest public in the world. It is meaningless if it relates to the admission of the public to an international conference. The public gallery at the United Nations, unlike the press gallery, is politically without significance because it is filled by haphazard visitors who cannot claim to represent anyone but themselves.

PROPAGANDA

Propaganda—i.e., deliberate action undertaken to implant in human minds certain images and ideas—is as old as international relations. It suffices to read the speeches which Thucydides places in the mouths of the representatives sent by one Greek city to another to discover that these Greeks were trying to create in the minds of their listeners an appealing or convincing image of the superiority of their own political ideology or form of government, of their impressive military and naval strength, of the justice of their cause, or of the coincidence of interests between their native city and the city whose popular assembly they were addressing. The Romans used the image of the invincibility of their city to secure their hold on the conquered provinces and to impress foreign cities, states, and tribes. The medieval Christians and Moslems owed their successes to the propagation of their religious beliefs which added new followers by conversion. Catholics and Protestants appealed during the Religious Wars to their fellow-believers in foreign countries to rally their support. Revolutionary France owed the expansion of its influence in Europe not only to its military victories but also to widespread sympathy with the ideology which it energetically propagated abroad. A man sent to represent his country in a foreign capital has always had the duty to create there an attractive image of his own government and its foreign policy.

The intensity of propaganda has varied from one epoch to another. At a time of ideological conflicts which involve the deepest human beliefs and most fervently held conceptions of the best society, when a militant doctrine is bent on converting foreign peoples, this intensity is at its peak. Whenever, by contrast, ideological differences play a minor role in international politics, propaganda continues to serve as a tool of foreign policy but loses its fervor. Its purpose is not to convert people but only to convince them of the superior power of the state on whose behalf it is emitted, of the coincidence of national interests between this state and the foreign state to which the propaganda is directed, of the futility of resisting the foreign policy of the same state or of the interest to be found in supporting it, and, finally, of the justice of the cause defended by the propagandistic arguments.

It is natural that the intensity of propaganda is high in our time of ideological warfare and irreconcilable philosophies of life. As was true in similar ages, its scope is immensely widened by the intention, not only to gain support for national policy, but also to convert aliens to national "self-evident truths."

The propaganda of our epoch has a new aspect derived from technological progress. Wide masses can be easily reached by inexpensive books, pamphlets, newspapers, and leaflets, by radio, which can communicate with people at practically any distance, by motion pictures, and by television. This wide opportunity secured by technology has its counterpart in the ever-growing number of people who are ready to listen and to read. The expansion of prospective audiences is due to the growing emancipation of the common man even in the backward countries and the increasing proportion of literate and educated people. It is no longer a question of convincing a small group of the upper class, because the converts made in the ranks of the gray crowd look politically insignificant today but might in a number of years become the government of their country. These two factors, new techniques of communication and expanding audiences, give modern propaganda an extraordinary political importance.

Propaganda is no longer carried on merely by the nationals of the state concerned. It is much more effective if the same state has secured a number of devoted converts among the citizens of the foreign country and speaks henceforth with their voice. With the sincere zeal of their new convictions, they take over the task of the apostolate among their own countrymen and work to secure popular support for the policies of the state which is the bastion of their ideology.

The propaganda by the nationals of the foreign state faces certain difficulties which do not confront the native convert speaking to his countrymen. First, an instinctive distrust greets the words of the foreigner. Secondly, the foreigner finds it difficult to discover a language which is easily understood by an audience alien to him. He has not lived their lives, his problems are different from theirs, his outlook is not identical with theirs. Yet if he wants to be listened to and believed, he must overcome these obstacles and advance his propositions against the background of actual experience, present interests and aspirations, and prevailing ideas of the foreign audience. These difficulties do not exist for the native convert to a foreign ideology; his arguments are intimately related to the problems of utmost interest to his countrymen, problems which he fully understands because they are his own. The handicap of the convert is his apostolate for an ideology whose Rome is located in a foreign country; he is open to the accusation of being an agent of that foreign country.

Propaganda operates with simplified images and concepts, because modern audiences are large and are not composed of highly sophisticated intellectuals only. It should speak with several voices. Each voice should be attuned to a different country, because each country has its own problems; moreover, propaganda should be adapted to more than one intellectual level in order to reach the various strata of the foreign population, each with its own preoccupations and its own educational background. To grip the imagination, it must disseminate a somewhat accentuated image of the message to be conveyed. This message is seldom the whole truth, but effective propaganda must use the truth as the core of its themes. The foreign audience which discovers that the core of the statements is true will be more inclined to believe the rest of the story.

Propaganda aims at undermining the confidence of the population of the opponent state in their own government and in the righteousness or wisdom of its policies; it expects to arouse a domestic pressure for a change in these policies in the sense desired by the authors of foreign propaganda. To undermine the morale of a foreign nation means to loosen the bonds of its social solidarity. One can try to subvert the trust of the population in their nation's military capacity, in the efficiency of their system of government, and in the ability of their leadership. One can appeal to the various social groups, such as national or other minorities, or social classes, and try to oppose these sectional interests to over-all state loyalty.

Propaganda also pursues the objective of winning as much sympathy as possible in the countries which are not involved in the struggle and of fortifying whatever sympathy already exists in other countries which are inclined to be friendly. The true or alleged community of ideals and interests will be stressed. The opponent state or its ruling elite will frequently be presented as ill-intentioned and obdurate, and the center of gravity of difficult international problems will be shifted from the merits of the case to the bad faith or ill will of the adversary. The adversary will be accused of having evil designs on the country of the foreign audience, friendly or uncommitted. The image of a common enemy will be created.

Whatever the political complexion of the audience addressed, the issues must be simplified to make them understandable to an average person. It is unfortunately true that the appeal to human prejudices, aspirations, and emotions is often much more effective than a rational analysis of the merits of the case. Above all, issues must be related to problems of direct interest for the foreign audience in order to arouse their attention and make them listen to the argument. A presentation which does not apply to the daily experience of the alien audience and does not appeal to their hopes, fears, and grievances will fall on deaf ears.

Propaganda, if successful, is the most inexpensive method of winning foreign support, certainly less expensive than economic aid and less risky than the use of military force. Yet it is only a tool of foreign policy. It supports it but cannot replace it. Slogans can reflect the policy but cannot make it.

SOVIET TECHNIQUES

Soviet and generally Communist techniques in international relations are well adjusted to modern conditions, but several of their features are only up-to-date versions of techniques used in past epochs of ideological conflict and political turmoil. These techniques are typical of a revolutionary power, i.e., a power which intends to transform the international status quo radically, and also of a power which is the center for a widespread and dynamic ideological movement. For both reasons, these techniques serve an active foreign policy which never rests or relaxes. The important role played by propaganda in Soviet foreign policy is understandable for a regime which wants to convert mankind to its own "self-evident truths" and ways of life and which fully realizes the usefulness of propaganda in domestic and foreign politics.

The means used by Soviet propaganda are many. Official statements (diplomatic notes, speeches made at international conferences, declarations adopted at the meetings of Communist parties, etc.) are one of them. These notes, speeches, or personal messages sent to foreign chief executives are only partly, if at all, addressed to the persons or governments to whom they are delivered. If they are published simultaneously, they are also, or only, destined for a worldwide audience. As they emanate from the government or the prime minister of a nuclear power, they are widely disseminated by the non-Communist media of information and reach, through Communist and non-Communist channels, the four corners of the world.

Soviet propaganda usually conveys a contrast between two images: the West is always entirely wrong in its policies, and its arguments originate either in bad faith or in evil intentions; the Soviet Union is no less invariably motivated only by the desire to consolidate peace and to ensure a brighter future for mankind. If the Soviet note or a personal message addressed to a foreign head of government is frankly insulting, this is not due to any personal aversion felt for the addressee but to the intention of reducing the prestige of his country in foreign eyes. Soviet propagandists expect the foreign onlooker to conclude that, if another great power accepts insulting messages and notes, it must be intimidated by Soviet power.

Khrushchev once said that repetition is the mother of wisdom. This is not true; Khrushchev himself would agree that an oft-repeated lie cannot become the truth. But the repetition of the same argument or statement can convince many people that a view heard often enough must contain a grain of truth and should be given proper attention. Repetition is an important technique in any propaganda, just as it is in commercial advertising. This principle is fully understood by the Soviet propagandists.

Another feature of Soviet propaganda is the use of various channels of communication: books and pamphlets, distributed or sold at a very low price, radio broadcasts, motion pictures, and other media of mass communication. These means are used in European and non-European languages. Another way of winning foreign friendships, if not necessarily ideological conversions, is the constantly expanding program of educating young people from the Third World at the universities of the Communist countries. The native channel is important; it is the local Communist party and its sympathizers who support the Soviet objectives in international affairs for the sake of their ideological affinity with Russia. If possible, this native channel is reinforced by various national and international front organizations in which the vast majority of members are non-Communists but are ready to sponsor a few Communist objectives with which they agree for their own reasons.

Propaganda is so intertwined with Soviet diplomacy that they are rarely separated from each other. Even when the Soviet government seriously intends to make a deal, it seldom dispenses with a barrage of propaganda which aims to "soften" the other party and to win the sympathy of the third countries.

Soviet diplomacy tries to keep several irons in the fire. The first reason is the desire to prevent other governments from concentrating on one important issue at a time or to deflect their attention from one crisis to another. The Berlin blockade in 1948-49 and the Czechoslovak coup in 1948 absorbed Western attention at a time when a much more important development was taking place; the Communist operations in China were entering on their last stage. The Soviet outlook is global, all the areas of the world and all the current problems forming one whole; they attend simultaneously to all the vulnerable spots in the world, sometimes creating alarming tension in one spot in order to make gains in another a thousand miles away.

Secondly, by keeping several irons in the fire the Soviet Union gains greater space in which to maneuver and bargain. A simultaneous offensive on several geographical fronts and in respect to several unrelated issues creates the prospect for scoring successes on one front where the opponent might decide to retreat in order to improve his position elsewhere. These tactics are calculated to score gradual advances at points where the opponents are divided in their intentions or feeble and irresolute or handicapped by local conditions.

The Soviet government tries to hold the initiative in its own hands, an attitude natural for a dynamic power. The issue might be created by its own move, as demonstrated several times in Berlin, or an existing international issue might be made the center of international tension. The initial Soviet claim might be spurious or greatly inflated, but the constant hammering on its reasonableness and justice might eventually convince the opponent that the existing status quo is truly abnormal and should become the topic of negotiation. The Soviet government, whatever the issue might be, always assumes the posture of an injured party which has the right to redress. The opponent is thus placed on the defensive. If he refuses to yield, he is accused of unfairness, bad faith, and an obstinacy which is not only unreasonable but might have grave consequences for the peace of the world. The third states might be convinced that the only way to preserve peace is to exert pressure on the Soviet opponents and to persuade them that they should make concessions. At the same time, the pressure of foreign governments and opinions seems to have little effect on the course of Soviet foreign policy. The waves of indignation which followed the Communist coup in 1948 in Czechoslovakia and the military intervention in 1956 in Hungary or the resumption of nuclear tests in 1961, did not deflect the Soviet government by an inch from the course of action it set for itself.

The Soviet government uses a method which would be convenient for any state in initiating a diplomatic negotiation. It tries to limit the agenda to those issues on which it has greater bargaining assets or with which it is mostly concerned. If this limitation is rejected by the other party, it attempts to place these items at the top of the agenda in order to have a chance to secure an agreement on them before discussing other items of greater interest to the other state.

It is usually expected that a compromise in international negotiations is to be found somewhere in the middle between the initial positions of the parties. The Soviet government knows this and inflates its initial position even more than is customary in hopes that the opponent will be compelled by this tactic to make greater concessions than he would otherwise have made and yet feel that the achieved settlement is a sound one, i.e., located in the middle between the two initial positions. This is why the initial Soviet claims advanced at the beginning of the negotiation often seem preposterous.

Traditional diplomacy has accustomed people to regard negotiation as a continuous business. The concession made today is expected to be reciprocated tomorrow and so on until the last day when the results are summed up and the bargain concluded. This is not necessarily the Soviet view. They regard each day as a separate and closed chapter. The concession made by the opponent is duly accepted as irrevocable but not as something that should be reciprocated on the next day. Tomorrow the bargaining starts afresh from the line reached by the Soviet delegation today. This tactic can be easily counteracted if the opponent makes each of his concessions simultaneously with, and conditional on, the equivalent Soviet concessions.

If several states are interested in the same issue, the Soviet government uses the time-honored method of trying to split the opponents and, if possible, negotiate with each of them separately. The secrecy of its proceedings allows it to use the weapon of surprise in diplomatic maneuvering much more freely than a democratic government, always threatened with press leaks, could afford to do.

The nature of the Soviet regime, with its strict hierarchical discipline, gives the Soviet diplomats less opportunity than their "capitalist" counterparts to display their own initiative and personal talent. Their moves are strictly regulated by rigid instructions. Since every unexpected and new development requires new instructions, negotiations with the Soviet Union are a time-consuming and often tedious business.

The first purpose of Soviet negotiations is to wear down the opposite negotiator, his government, his public opinion, and the third states. This objective explains why the Russians are refractory even when they intend to conclude a deal. The endless haggling over seemingly unimportant matters or merely procedural issues is designed to "soften up" the other party and lower its power of resistance. But the procedural squabbles may have other than psychological objectives. They are a handy device for wrecking a negotiation which the U.S.S.R. does not want to succeed in the first place. At other times the procedural matter might have a bearing on the substance of the controversial issue. At the Geneva Conference of Foreign Ministers in 1959, the Soviet insistence on a particular seating arrangement for the two German delegations was not aimless stubbornness but had a definite political objective. When the Western powers finally consented to seat both German delegations in a manner which proclaimed their equal international status, they were acting at variance with their refusal to acknowledge the German Democratic Republic as another German state. At the Geneva Conference on Laos in 1961, when the Communists insisted on seating the three Laotian delegations (Royalist, neutralist, and Communist) in a way that gave the three equal recognition, they were attempting to prejudge the composition of a future coalition government and prove that even the Western governments did not consider that the Royal government, which they were recognizing at that time, had any legitimate claim to be the only spokesman for Laos.

Soviet diplomacy, like any skillful diplomacy, always tries to clothe its refusal to make concessions in the positive form of clearly formulated, simple, and easily understandable counterproposals which will nevertheless be unacceptable to the other party; the burden of refusal is thus shifted to the other party, which will be blamed by innocent onlookers for the breakdown of negotiations.

THE ECONOMIC TOOLS OF INTERNATIONAL RELATIONS

The material well-being and/or economic might of a nation are an integral part of national interests. Foreign policy is therefore influenced by the need to have unimpeded access to raw materials and sources of fuel necessary for the operation of national industries, to pay reasonable prices for these imports, to possess foreign markets for selling nationally produced goods and for buying abroad those industrial and agricultural products which are required by the national economy, to have foreign places for profitable capital investment, and to be able to use foreign services such as shipping, banking, and insurance. The national economy might need the influx of foreign capital, public and private, to help in its development. Foreign countries might be the source of supply of cheap labor or, vice versa, might serve as a place for the temporary or permanent exodus of national "surplus labor."

The national interest groups ask the government to protect the domestic market against foreign competition or to apply pressure to foreign states in order to open their markets to national exports or to allow the exploitation of their natural resources; the same or other interest groups expect the government to protect national investments abroad against the threat of nationalization or discriminatory legislation. Modern governments acknowledge the obligation to ensure full employment through their domestic and foreign policies. Hence, they must keep out competitive foreign immigrants, do their best to find foreign markets for the exporting industries, and carefully watch over the flow of capital to and from the country. Farmers in the advanced countries expect to share with other economic groups in the benefits of the welfare state, through state-supported prices for agricultural products, tariffs against foreign agricultural imports, and the "dumping" of agricultural surpluses on foreign markets. Certain enterprises, considered vital to the country, such as shipping and air transport lines, want to be subsidized to compete more effectively with foreign companies.

Big corporations have an effect on international politics, not only through their influence on the formulation of national foreign policy, but also through their own foreign operations, whether cartels and other agreements with foreign corporations for the control of markets and prices or the influence which they have in the countries where they pursue their activities. The government might be helped by its national corporations in attaining the objectives of its foreign policy. Banks might refuse to subscribe to an unfriendly state's loan, or an industrial corporation might decline to export its products to that country, or another corporation will refuse to share industrial patents with corporations in the hostile country. Powerful corporations have played an important, even decisive role in the domestic politics of the foreign countries where they operate their plantations, mines, or oil fields. Other corporations, which have infiltrated the economy of a foreign country and do not wish to be dislodged from their acquired positions, might camouflage their presence under indirect ownership of the controlling stock in companies located in that country. They own this controlling stock through the intermediary of one or even several holding companies, each incorporated in a different country.

Since no country is self-sufficient, foreign trade is a vital necessity for all of them. Foreign markets may provide the marginal profit which certain domestic industrial and agricultural producers need for a successful operation of their enterprises. For other producers, foreign exports might represent a very substantial part of their total market. Imports of foreign fuel and raw materials might be a *sine qua non* for national defense industries and for the functioning of the national economy. No country produces all its indispensable raw materials. Imported machinery might be necessary for the economic development of the country or because foreign industrial equipment of certain types is better than that produced nationally. Agricultural surpluses may be sold abroad, or foreign agricultural products might be needed to supplement an insufficient domestic output. Exports are one of the means of payment for imports, foreign services, and credits.

This vital need for foreign trade has led many people to believe that the removal of all governmental restrictions on international trade (free trade) would be an unmixed blessing for the whole of mankind. It would allegedly allow each country to specialize in the type of production in which it excels or in which its cost of production is the lowest or for which it has the necessary human skills and available raw materials. However, national free trade is founded not only on the absence of domestic restrictions on the movement of goods but also on the free circulation of capital and men. Its international replica would have to consist in a free migration of labor from one country to another, a prospect which the most enthusiastic "free traders" are reluctant to accept. Capital does not circulate freely across national boundaries; its movements are often restricted by governmental regulations or directed by governmental advice. Moreover, the vast area of the Third World does not attract private capital for reasons discussed in Chapter 5.

The present division of countries into what might be called three social classes—the advanced (the international upper class), the partly or unevenly developed (the middle class), and the underdeveloped (the proletarian class)—would call for much more than a free circulation of capital, if international "free trade" is to resemble "free trade" within the present welfare-oriented national society. Every social class in the welfare state is assured of a fair opportunity to share in the national wealth. Hence, if the economic relations between countries were to be modeled on the economic relations between individuals in the modern society, the proletarian nations of the world would expect a fair chance to develop and thus to participate in the international wealth. This would require not a free but a directed flow of capital in which governments guided the transfer of investment capital, public or private, from the rich to the poor nations. Economic aid involves such a government-directed transfer of funds, but this aid certainly does not constitute a free and spontaneous migration of capital.

International free trade, if its consequences were not corrected by the free circulation of labor and a planned transfer of funds for the development of poorer nations, would help to ensure full employment in the advanced nations but would only aggravate the concealed rural unemployment in the underdeveloped countries. The advanced and underdeveloped nations are unequally armed for free-trade competition. Free trade would be a means for achieving a fair international division of labor if all countries were on a comparable level of economic development. It would be equitable among equals. Otherwise, it would become, as the German economist Friedrich List said more than a hundred years ago, "the weapon of the strongest." The present international division of labor between the advanced and underdeveloped nations indicates that its perpetuation through unrestricted trade would doom the producers of primary commodities to remain forever the have-not nations, because foreign competition on their own domestic markets would hamper the development of a balanced economy. Free trade cannot be a "paying" proposition for them because of the downward secular trend of prices for primary commodities and also because they must industrialize to provide nonagricultural jobs for their "surplus" rural population (see Chapter 5). Their budding industries will have to be protected until they acquire the vigor needed for unrestricted competition with the industries of the advanced nations. For the time being, the restrictions on foreign imports also serve another purpose: by keeping out luxury goods they reserve the meager fund of foreign currencies for the purchase of equipment which their development needs.

The advanced countries protect their national producers by placing restrictions on foreign imports to ensure full employment or to safeguard strategically important industries. It is true, however, that under pressure from national interest groups, governments also extend tariff protection to industries which are neither vital nor give employment to a large manpower and which could disappear without causing any upheaval. All in all, probably all the countries have not been wrong all the time if none of them have ever practised foreign trade unhampered by any restrictions. International trade and international economic relations in general have always been subject to restrictions for economic, political, and national security reasons. The period of "free trade" in the nineteenth century was a time of low tariffs but also a time when vast colonial possessions subserved the economic requirements of the European colonial powers.

The influx of American investment capital to Britain and the EEC countries in the last several years proves that protective tariffs are not useless even in the relations between advanced countries. Facing European tariffs, the American corporations have bypassed them by building their factories abroad. The net result for Western Europe is a stronger economy and fuller employment.

Freer trade is a different matter from *free* trade in the sense of a total or near-total removal of restrictions. The producers of primary commodities have an interest in low tariffs in the advanced countries for their raw materials and agricultural products and, above all, for their textiles, the first manufactured goods they are able to export because of the low cost of production. This is their means of earning foreign currencies for the purchase of industrial and other equipment. They have, however, a greater interest in the stabilization of prices for primary commodities, but this stabilization would be achieved, not by uncontrolled international competition, but by intergovernmental agreements.

The advanced countries can benefit from a gradual removal of restrictions on their mutual trade, because their comparable economic development enables them to afford a reasonable specialization in production. An increased foreign competition in their own domestic markets would provide them with an additional incentive for encouraging greater productivity of industries, better technological processes, and a more efficient managerial and commercial organization. The experience of the EEC countries has demonstrated the benefits of a gradual removal of mutual restrictions on trade; their industries have become more efficient and more competitive even in trade with the third countries. However, the EEC member-states could accept the risks involved in increased foreign competition because they agreed to invest co-operatively in the weaker economic areas of their countries and to assist one another in bearing the cost of transferring labor from industries and plants which would prove unable to sustain foreign competition to more efficient plants or to other industries. Free trade within the EEC area is being achieved gradually to allow each country to adjust its production to new circumstances and with safeguards for less developed areas. It does not consist in a simple removal of all restrictions without any compensating guarantees. Free trade is being accompanied by a partly concerted policy of capital investment and by a gradually freer circulation of labor.

The example of the EEC proves that freer trade is possible and beneficial for more or less equally developed nations; such trade serves as an incentive for greater productivity and specialization. One should not, however, overlook the fact that this area of free trade is being surrounded by a common tariff wall. The victory of free trade within the integrated EEC territory might not necessarily be a prelude to freer trade among all advanced nations (see Chapter 9).

In addition to the underdeveloped countries, a large area of the world and one-third of the world's population are excluded from participation in unregulated trade. The Communist states cannot be partners in really free international trade, because their foreign trade is an integral part of national economic planning and because their state monopoly on external trade consists in a total control over all commercial transactions with foreign countries.

Restrictions on foreign trade are dictated by political as well as economic considerations. For example, these restrictions can be used to damage the economy of an unfriendly state or to make the national economy less dependent on foreign states.

Governments have several means for controlling international economic relations, including trade relations:

1. *Tariffs* are entry duties which importers of foreign goods must pay. The net effect of custom duties is to raise the price of imported products. The purpose might be purely fiscal, to provide another source of state revenue. The usual reason for tariffs is to protect domestic producers. Tariffs may also be used as a tool of policy against an unfriendly state by discouraging its imports. The most radical form of this policy is the tariff war; it consists in the refusal to conclude any commercial agreement and in the application of the highest tariffs to all imports originating in the country discriminated against.

Commercial agreements have the opposite effect of encouraging mutual trade by reciprocal tariff concessions. Countries which intend to liberalize their foreign trade may insert in their commercial agreements with each other a clause which stipulates that either contracting party will benefit from all tariff concessions which the other contracting party offers to third states. No additional agreement is needed for this extension of tariff concessions. This clause may be unconditional, i.e., all concessions granted to the third states automatically benefit the other contracting party. It may be conditional, i.e., the other contracting party must grant in exchange a concession which is equivalent to the one made by the third state before it may claim the benefit of tariff reductions conceded to that third state. This clause is called the clause of the most favored nation.

States rarely institute taxes on exports of their own products; this may be done if the government seeks another source of revenue or if it prefers to keep a given type of product for the use of its own economy.

GATT (see Chapter 9) is a general agreement for the gradual removal of restrictions on international trade.

2. *Quotas* are government-determined annual amounts of specific goods which may be imported from certain or from all foreign countries. After the annual import quota has been exhausted, no more imports are allowed.

3. *Currency regulations* consist in the state control of all expenditures abroad, including foreign imports and tourism. Each purchase abroad may be paid only with the state license which authorizes a withdrawal from the state fund of foreign currencies. This is a way of protecting the national balance of payments against expenses which the country cannot afford or against superfluous purchases with a hard currency which is in short supply. In other words, the fund of foreign currencies or of hard currencies must be carefully husbanded and used for buying only those goods which are vital for the national economy. Western Europe protected its insufficient fund of dollars in this way during the postwar period. Of

course, currency regulations presuppose the inconvertibility of national currency, which may be exchanged for foreign currency only with the government's permission.

Quotas and currency regulations are harsher in effect than tariffs. A foreign producer might try to lower his cost of production and import in spite of higher custom duties imposed by the purchasing country. He can do nothing against quotas and currency regulations which prohibit his prospective customers from buying at any price.

4. An *embargo* is a partial or total prohibition on trade with the state discriminated against. The U.S. embargo on trade with China and Cuba is an example of *total* embargo. The general Western policy of forbidding the sale of strategic goods to the Communist states is a *partial* embargo. The definition of strategic goods is flexible and varies at the convenience of the Western governments and with their estimation of which goods are strategically useful at a given time for the Communist states. The effects of the embargo might be mitigated by illegal trade, by selling prohibited goods to third countries which resell them to the nation against which the embargo is being enforced (Hong Kong and Portuguese Macao are possibly used to circumvent the U.S. embargo on trade with China), and finally by stepping up trade with the third countries (this is the way in which the Communist and non-Communist states partly moderate the effects of the U.S. embargo on trade with Cuba). If a country is economically strong, the embargo might act as an incentive for developing national production and thereby obviating the need for products which foreign countries refuse to sell.

5. A *boycott* is a refusal to buy goods produced in a given foreign country. It is initiated and enforced, not by the government (it would then be an embargo), but by patriotic organizations. This is the weapon of weak nations whose governments do not dare to take discriminatory measures. Pre-Communist China used this weapon against Japan and those Western powers which encroached on its sovereignty.

6. *Barter* commercial agreements control the trade between two contracting countries which assent to exchange only stated amounts of specified goods. This is one of the favorite devices of the Communist states for tightly controlling the exchange of goods with foreign countries.

7. *Preferential tariffs* are reduced tariffs which are mutually applicable between the countries concerned. They give the participating states easier access to one another's markets than the third countries have. In 1932, the members of the British Commonwealth introduced preferential tariffs for their mutual trade. This arrangement favors their trade to the prejudice of third countries, which are subject to higher customs duties.

8. *Regional economic integration* goes further in favoring the trade between the participating states. An economic union such as the EEC or a customs union results in the elimination of tariffs and other restrictions

on trade within the integrated area. Producers of the participating states freely sell their goods in the whole common market, which remains protected against outsiders. The third countries might discover that the products which they used to sell to some of the members of the integrated area are now subject to higher customs duties imposed by common tariffs for the whole area. Outsiders might make the additional unpleasant discovery that they encounter stiffer competition from the industries of the common market on both the domestic and international markets; this is due to the greater competitive capacity of industries already subjected to free competition on their own common market. In other words, regional economic integration might make foreign trade more difficult for non-participating states, as the United States, Britain, and several other countries have learned in their relations with the EEC. It is true that the existence of the Common Market in Western Europe increases domestic demand by improving general prosperity; it should offer in the long run a larger market for goods produced both within and outside the integrated area.

9. *Subsidies* and other favors granted to national producers are other means for enabling them to compete better on the domestic and international markets. The government may pay outright subsidies or guarantee high prices on the domestic market, concede lower freight rates on its nationalized means of transportation, charge higher internal taxes on foreign-produced goods, or encourage exports by paying subsidies to allow the national producer to sell abroad at a price lower than the domestic price or even lower than his cost of production (the last procedure is called *dumping*). It is unfair, however, to use the term *dumping* when a country with low living standards sells its products abroad at a low price merely because its wages are lower than in the prosperous countries.

10. Countries whose economies are founded on the private ownership of the means of production have various ways of *concerting* their foreign policies with the external operations of their national corporations. The government may encourage or discourage private banks in floating foreign bonds, or the investment of private capital abroad, depending on its own foreign objectives and the nature of its relations with particular foreign nations. It may recommend private investment in the exploitation of foreign raw materials and fuel resources if these materials and resources are needed by the national economy; it will extend its diplomatic protection to defend these investments against foreign encroachment. Private investment may infiltrate the economy of a foreign country and thus help the government to apply pressure to that country. The co-ordination of foreign activities between the government and its national corporations is mutually beneficial.

11. The *assets* of a foreign state, located on the national territory of another state, may be "frozen" in reprisal for its unfriendly policy, such as

the nationalization of property owned by the nationals of the state which takes this measure. A government may *nationalize* foreign assets or cancel a concession for the exploitation of natural resources or public services (railroads, power stations, etc.) in order to win greater economic independence.

12. The government may advise its national corporations (or do it itself if it is engaged in economic activities) to place orders for foreign goods in a friendly country rather than another country. This *preferential allocation of orders* for foreign purchases is another way to foster national interests.

13. A greater independence of foreign vital imports might be achieved by encouraging and financing the domestic production of *substitutes,* such as synthetic rubber or fuel.

14. *Devaluation* of national currency might be undertaken in order to stimulate exports to foreign countries which will pay lower prices than previously because of the reduced value of the currency of the exporting country.

15. Goods might be deliberately sold at *a price lower* than the international market price in order to disrupt the exports and production of foreign countries. Western producers fear from time to time that the Soviet Union might resort to this practice on a large scale to cause confusion in the Western world. This policy cannot be excluded as a possibility, but so far the fear has not been confirmed by any important dumping of Soviet products on the international market.

16. *Foreign aid* is another deliberate governmental intervention in international economic relations. Whatever the specific motivation, the government which offers grants or convenient loans or favorable trade terms and which encourages private investment by its nationals does so for political reasons. Credits might be granted on the condition that they are spent for goods produced in the lending country; this is a roundabout way of assisting the national economy. In any case, it is expected that foreign aid will be repaid in the form of a not unfriendly policy on the part of the receiving state. The surplus of national production might be expended as economic aid. The receiving country is helped if it suffers from a shortage of the goods which are shipped to it, while the assisting state is relieved of its surplus. The grants and sales for soft currency of American agricultural surpluses to foreign countries are an example of this procedure.

17. The Communist complete *nationalization of all means* of production and the adoption of *planning* for production, distribution, and consumption have produced a *state monopoly on foreign trade.* The Communist state exercises a total control over its economic relations with other states. A private corporation which is interested in exports to or imports from a Communist state does not bargain with another private corporation,

as it does in relation to a capitalist country, but with a governmental agency. The Communist government determines not only the kind and quantity of goods imported and exported and the geographical distribution of its foreign trade, but also negotiates directly with foreign firms on prices and on all other terms of each commercial transaction. Because of its monopoly on trade, the Communist state enjoys several advantages: (1) the state has a greater bargaining power than a private corporation; (2) foreign trade may be perfectly adjusted to the political objectives of foreign policy; and (3) foreign trade may be planned not only with a view to securing external political objectives but also in order to make it contribute to the national military and economic might.

A capitalist state can assume a somewhat similar complete control over its external economic relations only under wartime conditions. Otherwise, its free-enterprise economy precludes full governmental control over any commercial transactions.

Its nationalization of the means of production and its monopoly on foreign trade sometimes enable the Communist state to price its exported products below the international market price or below its own cost of production (a moot notion in a nationalized economy) if, for instance, it intends to undercut the prices offered by other countries or to bestow a favor on the purchasing state, usually an uncommitted and underdeveloped country.

The national planning of the European Communist states is now supplemented by their inter-state planning which their Council for Mutual Economic Aid promotes and co-ordinates (see Chapter 7). This joint planning of production, as imperfect as it still is, cannot be undertaken without the co-ordination of their trade with other states (capitalist and those Communist states which are not members of the Council—China, North Korea, North Vietnam, and Cuba) and of their economic assistance to the non-Communist underdeveloped countries.

As important as the *balance of trade* (the annual total of exports and imports) is, it is only one element in the *balance of payments*, i.e., in the total of foreign earnings and disbursements in a given year. The balance of payments includes principally the following items:

A. *Earnings*

1. Exports of goods.

2. Foreign payments for services rendered to other countries, such as shipping, banking, or insurance.

3. Expenditures by foreign tourists and other alien visitors.

4. Remittances of money from foreign countries, such as from nationals working abroad who send their savings to their families back home. For instance, the Algerian economy is greatly helped by remittances sent home by the half million Algerian workers employed in France; it is said that these remittances account for the subsistence of two million Algerians.

5. The repayment by foreign countries of loans and interests on loans.

6. The repatriation of capital invested abroad or of profits made on these investments.

7. The off-shore procurements which a foreign power makes in order to maintain its troops stationed on foreign soil or to maintain its foreign bases.

8. Grants and loans which foreign countries provide through economic assistance programs. Any other short- or long-term credits obtained from foreign countries.

B. Disbursements

1. Imports of goods.

2. Payments for services which foreign nations have provided.

3. Expenses abroad of nationals who have visited foreign lands.

4. Remittances of money which foreign workers send to their families.

5. Repayment of foreign loans and payments of interest on these loans.

6. Investments abroad of national capital and payment of profits on foreign investments made in the country.

7. Grants and credits offered to foreign nations to help them bolster their military defense or develop their national economies (military and economic aid—see Chapter 5). All other short- and long-term credits granted to foreign countries.

8. Off-shore procurements made in foreign lands.

These and other earnings and disbursements, made across national boundaries by the state, other public institutions, private corporations, and individuals (nationals and resident aliens) form together the balance of payments which provides annually an image of the economic and financial situation of the country in relation to foreign states. The net result consists each year either in a surplus which foreign states owe or in a deficit. The deficit is made good either by increased earnings in the following year or by short- or long-term credits granted by foreign countries or, in the last analysis, by transfers abroad of gold from the national monetary reserve. The last remedy is risky because it cannot be employed infinitely and also because a constant outflow of gold creates the impression that the state spends abroad more than it can afford or that its economy is unsound. In any case, it serves to undermine foreign trust in the worth of that country's currency.

The fluctuations of rates of exchange between the Western currencies, due in part to speculation and to the fears and hopes of foreign investors, do not help to ensure the economic stability of the Atlantic community of nations. They could be terminated by a co-ordinated monetary policy with fixed rates of exchange. The International Monetary Fund (see Chapter 9) or another new agency could become the co-ordinating institution. The Organization for Economic Co-operation and Development, created in 1961, could be used to foster a more orderly economic intercourse between the Western nations. They are NATO allies, but they are frequently divided not only by political differences but also by economic rivalries. The sad spectacle of their quarrels in 1963, after the French veto on British admission to the EEC, was the most glaring illustration of those political and economic disagreements which weaken their Atlantic unity. What they need is not mutual recriminations but understanding, even if achieved at the price of laborious negotiations. In 1963 these recriminations concerned more the alleged motivations of Britain, the United States, and France than the actual issues which were serious enough in themselves.

To sum up, it can be said that economic relations provide strong states with a rich arsenal of means for influencing the conduct of other nations and for fostering their external objectives, while weak states run the risk of being subjected to external economic pressures which might culminate in limiting their independence.

IN PLACE OF A CONCLUSION

This book ends without any general conclusion. The omission is not an oversight. A conclusion which offers a brief summary of the content of a book merely insults the intelligence of the reader; one which recommends sweeping solutions to world problems or definite predictions of the future shape of the world is foolish and presumptuous. Who can honestly predict the look of the world in the next century after it has been shaped and reshaped by the revolutionary trends which have shaken the foundations of the world of our fathers? The process of change that began in 1914 is far from completed. One could perhaps repeat Sir Winston Churchill's words spoken on another occasion: "This is the end of the beginning but not the beginning of the end." It would be bold indeed to prophesy at this moment; one can only say what is self-evident, that the new world, though it may not be "brave," will certainly be altogether different from the one our fathers and we have known.

History has approached a crossroads and may turn into any one of the several highways and lanes which human choices open for it. How unwise it would be to prescribe for present ills when we do not know what the future will bring and when those ills, considered evils by one section of mankind and blessings by another, may be in fact the inevitable birth pangs announcing the advent of a new world. One thing is certain: no single formula will introduce order into international relations and allow everyone to relax when there is neither agreement on what that order should be nor any widespread inclination to relax.

Two counsels could be offered to all nations. The first would be to move cautiously in the midst of nuclear bombs and rockets. The survival of nations is at stake. The other was given by de Callières a long time ago:

"Faults in domestic policy are often more easily remedied than mistakes in foreign policy. There are many factors in foreign affairs which lie beyond the control of the ministers of any given state, and all foreign action requires greater circumspection, greater knowledge, and far greater sagacity than is demanded in home affairs."

Bibliography

CHAPTER I

1. *Basic problems and concepts of contemporary international politics*

ARON, RAYMOND. *Paix et Guerre entre les Nations.* Paris: Calmann-Lévy, 1962.

ASSOCIATION FRANÇAISE DE SCIENCE POLITIQUE. *La Politique Etrangère et Ses Fondements.* Paris: Armand Colin, 1954.

ATWATER, ELTON; BUTZ, WILLIAM; FORSTER, KENT; and RIEMER, NEAL. *World Affairs: Problems and Prospects.* New York: Appleton-Century-Crofts, 1958.

BIBLIOTÈQUE DES CENTRES D'ETUDES SUPÉRIEURES SPECIALISÉES. *Les Affaires Etrangères.* Paris: Presses Universitaires de France, 1959.

BOWLES, CHESTER. *Ideas, People and Peace.* New York: Harper and Brothers, 1958.

———. *The New Dimensions of Peace.* New York: Harper and Brothers, 1955.

BURNS, EDWARD MCNALL. *Ideas in Conflict: The Political Theories of the Contemporary World.* New York: W. W. Norton and Company, 1960.

CARR, EDWARD HALLETT. *The Twenty Years' Crisis, 1919-1939: An Introduction to the Study of International Relations.* London: The Macmillan Company, 1958.

DAWSON, CHRISTOPHER. *The Movement of World Revolution.* New York: Sheed and Ward, 1959.

FOX, W. R. T. (ed.). *The Theoretical Aspects of International Relations.* Notre Dame, Indiana: University of Notre Dame Press, 1959.

FRANKEL, JOSEPH. *The Making of Foreign Policy.* Oxford: Oxford University Press, 1962.

HERZ, JOHN H. *International Relations in the Atomic Age.* New York: Columbia University Press, 1959.

———. *Political Realism and Political Idealism.* Chicago: The University of Chicago Press, 1951.

KIRK, GRAYSON; BROWN, HARRISON S.; BROGAN, DENIS W.; MASON, EDWARD S.; FISHER, HAROLD H.; and THORP, WILLARD L. *The Changing Environment of International Relations.* Washington: The Brookings Institution, 1956.

LASSWELL, HAROLD D.; MERRIAM, CHARLES E.; and SMITH, T. V. *A Study of Power.* Glencoe, Ill.: The Free Press, 1950.

MORGENSTERN, OSCAR. *The Question of National Defense.* New York: Random House, 1959.

MORGENTHAU, HANS J. *Dilemmas of Politics.* Chicago: The University of Chicago Press, 1958.

———. *Politics Among Nations: The Struggle for Power and Peace.* 3rd ed. New York: Alfred A. Knopf, 1960.

———. *Scientific Man vs. Power Politics.* Chicago: The University of Chicago Press, 1946.

OSGOOD, ROBERT ENDICOTT. *Ideals and Self-Interest in America's Foreign Relations.* Chicago: The University of Chicago Press, 1953.

SCHWARZENBERGER, GEORG. *Power Politics: A Study of International Society.* New York: Frederick A. Praeger, 1951.

SETON-WATSON, HUGH. *Neither War nor Peace: The Struggle for Power in the Postwar World.* New York: Frederick A. Praeger, 1960.

STRAUSZ-HUPÉ, ROBERT and POSSONY, STEFAN T. *International Relations: In the Age of the Conflict between Democracy and Dictatorship.* 2nd ed. New York: McGraw-Hill Book Company, 1954.

THOMPSON, KENNETH W. *Political Realism and the Crisis of World Politics.* Princeton, N.J.: Princeton University Press, 1960.

WARD, BARBARA. *Five Ideas That Change the World.* New York: W. W. Norton and Company, 1959.

2. *Balance of power*

GULICK, EDWARD VOSE. *Europe's Classical Balance of Power.* Ithaca, N.Y.: Cornell University Press, 1955.

LISKA, GEORGE. *International Equilibrium: A Theoretical Essay on the Politics and Organization of Security.* Cambridge, Mass.: Harvard University Press, 1957.

TAYLOR, A. J. P. *The Struggle for Mastery in Europe: 1848-1918.* Oxford: Oxford University Press, 1954.

3. *History of international relations (for the recent history see Chapter 10)*

DROZ, JACQUES. *Histoire Diplomatique de 1648 à 1919.* Paris: Librairie Dalloz, 1952.

PRATT, JULIUS W. *A History of United States Foreign Policy.* Englewood Cliffs, N.J.: Prentice-Hall, 1955.

RENOUVIN, PIERRE (ed.). *Histoire des Relations Internationales.* Eight volumes. Paris: Librairie Hachette, 1953-58.

STRANG, LORD. *Britain in World Affairs: A Survey of the Fluctuations in British Power and Influence, Henry VIII to Elizabeth II.* London: Faber and André Deutsch, 1961.

CHAPTER II

1. *Basic concepts*

ARON, RAYMOND. *On War: Atomic Weapons and Global Diplomacy.* London: Secker and Warburg, 1958.

———. *The Century of Total War.* Garden City, N.Y.: Doubleday and Company, 1954.

CLAUSEWITZ, KARL VON. *On War.* New York: The Modern Library, 1943.

EMME, EUGENE M. *The Impact of Air Power: National Security and World Politics.* Princeton, N.J.: D. Van Nostrand Company, 1959.

FURNISS, EDGAR S., JR. *American Military Policy: Strategic Aspects of World Political Geography.* New York: Rinehart and Company, 1957.

KAHN, HERMAN. *The Nature and Possibility of War and Deterrence.* Santa Monica, Calif.: The Rand Corporation, 1960.

KAUFMANN, WILLIAM W. (ed.). *Military Policy and National Security.* Princeton, N.J.: Princeton University Press, 1956.

KISSINGER, HENRY A. *Nuclear Weapons and Foreign Policy.* New York: Harper and Brothers, 1957.

———. *The Necessity for Choice.* New York: Harper and Brothers, 1961.

LIDDELL HART, BASIL HENRY. *Deterrence or Defense: A Fresh Look at the West's Military Position.* New York: Frederick A. Praeger, 1960.

MORGENSTERN, OSCAR. *The Question of National Defense.* New York: Random House, 1959.

TAYLOR, MAXWELL D. *The Uncertain Trumpet.* New York: Harper and Brothers, 1959.

2. *Nuclear warfare*

BRODIE, BERNARD. *Implications of Nuclear Weapons in Total War* (mimeographed). Santa Monica, Calif.: The Rand Corporation, 1957.

———. *Strategy in the Missile Age.* Princeton, N.J.: Princeton University Press, 1959.

———. *The Meaning of Limited War* (mimeographed). Santa Monica, Calif.: The Rand Corporation, 1958.

Inquiry into Satellite and Missile Programs: Hearings Before the Preparedness Investigating Subcommittee of the Committee on Armed Services, United States Senate, Eighty-fifth Congress. Parts I and II (November 25, 1957–January 22, 1958). Washington, D.C.: United States Government Printing Office, 1958.

KAHN, HERMAN. *On Thermonuclear War.* Princeton, N.J.: Princeton University Press, 1960.

MIKSCHE, LT. COL. F. O. *Atomic Weapons and Armies.* New York: Frederick A. Praeger, 1955.

National Security in the Nuclear Age (mimeographed). University of Minnesota, Center for International Relations and Area Studies, 1958.

ROYAL INSTITUTE OF INTERNATIONAL AFFAIRS. *On Limiting Atomic War.* London, 1956.

TELLER, EDWARD and LATTER, ALBERT L. *Our Nuclear Future: Facts, Dangers and Opportunities.* New York: Criterion Books, 1958.

UNITED STATES CONGRESS, JOINT COMMITTEE ON ATOMIC ENERGY. *Summary-Analysis of Hearings May 27-29 and June 3-7, 1957, on the Nature of Radioactive Fallout and Its Effects on Man.* Washington, D.C.: United States Government Printing Office, 1957.

3. *Soviet strategic concepts*

DINERSTEIN, H. S. *War and the Soviet Union: Nuclear Weapons and the Revolution in Soviet Military and Political Thinking.* New York: Frederick A. Praeger, 1959.

GARTHOFF, RAYMOND L. *Soviet Strategy in the Nuclear Age.* New York: Frederick A. Praeger, 1958.

GLUSHKO, COL. A. P., *et al. Atomnoe Oruzhie i Protivoatomnaia Zashchita.* Moscow: Voennoe Izdatelstvo Ministerstva Oborony Soiuza SSR, 1958.

MODELSKI, G. A. *Atomic Energy in the Communist Bloc.* Melbourne, Australia: Melbourne University Press, 1959.

4. *Potential*

KNORR, KLAUS. *The War Potential of Nations.* Princeton, N.J.: Princeton University Press, 1956.

5. *Alliances*

ROYAL INSTITUTE OF INTERNATIONAL AFFAIRS. *Collective Defence in South East Asia: The Manilla Treaty and Its Implications.* London–New York, 1956.

———. *The Baghdad Pact: Origins and Political Setting* (mimeographed). London, 1956.

CHAPTER III

1. *Basic concepts and history*

CARR, EDWARD HALLETT. *Nationalism and After.* New York: The Macmillan Company, 1945.

CHADWICK, H. MUNRO. *The Nationalities of Europe and the Growth of National Ideologies.* Cambridge: Cambridge University Press, 1945.

COHEN, CARL (ed.). *Communism, Fascism, Democracy: The Theoretical Foundations.* New York: Random House, 1962.

DEUTSCH, KARL W. *Nationalism and Social Communication.* New York: John Wiley and Sons, 1953.

FEATHERSTONE, HUGH L. *A Century of Nationalism.* London: Nelson, 1939.

FISHER, HERBERT. *The Common Weal.* Oxford: Oxford University Press, 1924.

HAYES, CARLTON J. H. *Essays on Nationalism.* New York: The Macmillan Company, 1926.

———. *Nationalism: A Religion.* New York: The Macmillan Company, 1960.

———, *The Historical Evolution of Modern Nationalism.* New York: The Macmillan Company, 1931.

HERTZ, FREDERICK. *Nationality in History and Politics.* London: Kegan Paul, Trench, Trubner and Co., 1944.

HUIZINGA, JOHAN. *Men and Ideas: History, the Middle Ages, the Renaissance.* Chapter I: "Patriotism and Nationalism in European History" (pp. 97-155). New York: Meridian Books, 1959.

KOHN, HANS. *Pan-Slavism: Its History and Ideology.* Notre Dame, Indiana: University of Notre Dame Press, 1953.

———. *Revolutions and Dictatorships.* Cambridge, Mass.: Harvard University Press, 1939.

———. *The Idea of Nationalism: A Study in Its Origins and Background.* New York: The Macmillan Company, 1944.

POWERS, GEORGE C. *Nationalism at the Council of Constance: 1414-1418.* Washington, D.C.: Catholic University of America, 1927.

ROYAL INSTITUTE OF INTERNATIONAL AFFAIRS. *Nationalism.* London–New York: Oxford University Press, 1939.

SHAFER, BOYD C. *Nationalism, Myth and Reality.* New York: Harcourt, Brace and Co., 1955.

STURZO, LUIGI. *Nationalism and Internationalism.* New York: Roy, 1946.

WEIL, GEORGES JACQUES. *L'Eveil des Nationalités et le Mouvement Libéral.* Paris: Presses Universitaires de France, 1946.

ZNANIECKI, FLORIAN. *Modern Nationalities: A Sociological Study.* Urbana, Ill.: University of Illinois Press, 1952.

2. *Self-Determination*

COBBAN, ALFRED. *National Self-Determination.* London–New York: Oxford University Press, 1945.

3. *National minorities*

CLAUDE, INIS L. *National Minorities: An International Problem.* Cambridge, Mass.: Harvard University Press, 1955.

MACARTNEY, CARLILE A. *National States and National Minorities.* London: Oxford University Press, 1934.

4. *Communist concepts*

KOHN, HANS. *Nationalism in the Soviet Union.* New York: Columbia University Press, 1933.

LENIN, V. I. *Critical Remarks on the National Question.* Moscow: Foreign Languages Publishing House, 1951.

———. *The Right of Nations to Self-Determination.* Moscow: Foreign Languages Publishing House, 1951.

LIU, SHAO-CHI. *Internationalism and Nationalism.* Peking: Foreign Languages Press, 1951.

STALIN, J. *Marxism and the National Question.* Moscow: Foreign Languages Publishing House, 1950.

———. *The National Question and Leninism.* Moscow: Foreign Languages Publishing House, 1952.

CHAPTER IV

1. *General*

A World on the Move: A History of Colonialism and Nationalism in Asia and North Africa from the Turn of the Century to the Bandung Conference. Amsterdam: Djambatan International Educational Publishing House, 1956.

ALMOND, GABRIEL A. and COLEMAN, JAMES S. (eds.). *The Politics of Developing Areas.* Princeton, N.J.: Princeton University Press, 1960.

EMERSON, RUPERT. *From Empire to Nation: The Rise to Self-Assertion of Asian and African Peoples.* Cambridge, Mass.: Harvard University Press, 1960.

JENNINGS, SIR IVOR. *The Approach to Self-Government.* Cambridge: Cambridge University Press, 1956.

NIEBUHR, REINHOLD. *The Structure of Nations and Empires.* New York: Charles Scribner's Sons, 1959.

PANIKKAR, K. M. *Asia and Western Dominance: A Survey of the Vasco da Gama Epoch of Asian History, 1498-1945.* London: George Allen and Unwin, 1953.

STRAUSZ-HUPÉ, ROBERT and HAZARD, HARRY W. (eds.). *The Idea of Colonialism.* New York: Frederick A. Praeger, 1958.

WINSLOW, E. M. *The Pattern of Imperialism: A Study in the Theories of Power.* New York: Columbia University Press, 1948.

2. *Asia*

BALL, W. MACMAHON. *Nationalism and Communism in East Asia.* Melbourne: Melbourne University Press, 1952.

BOWLES, CHESTER. *Ambassador's Report.* New York: Harper and Brothers, 1954.

DESAI, A. R. *Social Background of Indian Nationalism.* Bombay: Oxford University Press, 1948.

DUTT, R. PALME. *India Today and Tomorrow.* London: Lawrence and Wishart, 1955.

ELSBREE, WILLARD H. *Japan's Role in Southeast Asian Nationalist Movements: 1940-1945.* Institute of Pacific Relations. Cambridge, Mass.: Harvard University Press, 1953.

FIFIELD, RUSSELL H. *The Diplomacy of Southeast Asia: 1945-1958.* New York: Harper and Brothers, 1958.

GOPALAN, A. K. *Kerala: Past and Present.* London: Lawrence and Wishart, 1959.

HARRISON, SELIG S. *India: The Most Dangerous Decades.* Princeton, N.J.: Princeton University Press, 1960.

———. *The Most Dangerous Decades: An Introduction to the Comparative Study of Language Policy in Multi-Lingual States* (mimeographed). New York: Language and Communication Research Center, Columbia University, 1957.

HOLLAND, WILLIAM L. *Asian Nationalism and the West.* New York: The Macmillan Company, 1953.

KAHIN, GEORGE MCTURNAN (ed.). *Governments and Politics of Southeast Asia.* Ithaca, N.Y.: Cornell University Press, 1959.

———. *Nationalism and Revolution in Indonesia.* Ithaca, N.Y.: Cornell University Press, 1952.

———. *The Asian-African Conference, Bandung, Indonesia, April 1955.* Ithaca, N.Y.: Cornell University Press, 1956.

MASANI, M. R. *The Communist Party of India: A Short History.* London: Derek Verschoyle, 1954.

MORAES, FRANK. *India Today.* New York: The Macmillan Company, 1960.

PANIKKAR, K. M. *Hindu Society at Cross Roads.* Bombay–Calcutta: Asian Publishing House, 1955.

———. *India and China: A Study of Cultural Relations.* Bombay: Asian Publishing House, 1957.

SINGH, JITENDRA. *Communist Rule in Kerala.* New Delhi: Diwan Chand Indian Information Centre, 1959.

THAYER, PHILIP W. *Nationalism and Progress in Free Asia.* Baltimore: Johns Hopkins Press, 1956.

3. *The Near East*

ANTONIUS, GEORGE. *The Arab Awakening: The Story of the Arab National Movement.* London: Hamish Hamilton, 1938.

HARRIS, GEORGE L. *Iraq: Its People, Its Society, Its Culture.* New Haven: Hraf Press, 1958.

HOURANI, A. H. *Great Britain and the Arab World.* London: John Murray, 1945.

HUREWITZ, J. C. *Diplomacy in the Near and Middle East: A Documentary Record —1535-1914* (Vol. I) and *1914-1956* (Vol. II). Princeton, N.J.: D. Van Nostrand Company, 1956.

KOHN, HANS. *Nationalism and Imperialism in the Hither East.* London: George Routledge and Sons, 1932.

LAQUEUR, WALTER Z. (ed.). *The Middle East in Transition: Studies in Contemporary History.* New York: Frederick A. Praeger, 1958.

———. *The Soviet Union and the Middle East.* New York: Frederick A. Praeger, 1959.

NUSEIBEH, HAZEM ZAKI. *The Ideas of Arab Nationalism.* Ithaca, N.Y.: Cornell University Press, 1956.

4. *Africa*

AKADEMIIA NAUK SSSR, INSTITUT VOSTOKOVEDENIIA. *Afrika Iuzhnee Sakhary: Voprosy Ekonomiki i Istorii.* Moscow: Izdatelstvo Vostochnoi Literatury, 1958.

AL-FASI, ALAL. *The Independence Movements in Arab North Africa.* Washington, D.C.: American Council of Learned Societies, 1954.

BARTLETT, VERNON. *Struggle for Africa.* London: Frederick Muller Ltd., 1953.

COLEMAN, JAMES S. *Nigeria: Background to Nationalism.* Berkeley and Los Angeles: University of California Press, 1958.

FITZGERALD, WALTER. *Africa: A Social, Economic and Political Geography of Its Major Regions.* New York: E. P. Dutton and Company, 1955.

HAILEY, LORD. *An African Survey Revised 1956: A Study of Problems Arising in Africa South of the Sahara.* London–New York: Oxford University Press, 1957.

HAINES, C. GROVE (ed.). *Africa Today.* Baltimore: Johns Hopkins Press, 1955.

KIMBLE, GEORGE H. T. *Tropical Africa.* Vol. I: *Land and Livelihood.* Vol. II: *Society and Polity.* New York: Twentieth Century Fund, 1960.

PADMORE, GEORGE. *Pan-Africanism or Communism? The Coming Struggle for Africa.* London: Dennis Dobson, 1956.

PARAF, PIERRE. *L'Ascension des Peuples Noirs: Le Réveil Politique, Social et Culturel de l'Afrique au XXe Siècle.* Paris: Payot, 1958.

STILLMAN, CALVIN W. (ed.). *Africa in the Modern World.* Chicago: The University of Chicago Press, 1955.

TEDESCHI, PIERO. *Probuzhdenie Afriki.* Moscow: Izdatelstvo Inostrannoi Literatury, 1952.

5. *Latin America*

DANILEVICH, M. V. and SHUL'GOVSKII, N. A. (eds.). *Problemy Sovremennoi Latinskoi Ameriki.* Moscow: Izdatelstvo Instituta Mezhdunarodnykh Otnoshenii, 1959.

HANKE, LEWIS. *Modern Latin America: Continent in Ferment.* Vol. I: *Mexico and the Caribbean.* Vol. II: *South America.* Princeton, N.J.: D. Van Nostrand Company, 1959.

JOHNSON, JOHN J. *Political Change in Latin America: The Emergence of the Middle Sectors.* Stanford, Calif.: Stanford University Press, 1958.

MACDONALD, AUSTIN F. *Latin American Politics and Government.* New York: Thomas Y. Crowell, 1949.

PIKE, FREDERICK B. (ed.). *Freedom and Reform in Latin America.* Notre Dame, Indiana: University of Notre Dame Press, 1959.

SMITH, T. LYNN. *Current Social Trends and Problems in Latin America.* Gainesville, Florida: University of Florida Press, 1957.

STOKES, WILLIAM S. *Latin American Politics.* New York: Thomas Y. Crowell Company, 1959.

STUART, GRAHAM H. *Latin America and the United States.* 5th ed. New York: Appleton-Century-Crofts, 1955.

VILLOLDO, PEDRO A. *Latin-American Resentment.* New York: Vantage Press, 1959.

WILLIAMS, MARY W.; BARTLETT, RUHL J.; and MILLER, RUSSELL E. *The People and Politics of Latin America.* New York: Ginn and Company, 1955.

CHAPTER V

1. *General*

ALMOND, GABRIEL A. and COLEMAN, JAMES S. (eds.). *The Politics of Developing Areas.* Princeton, N.J.: Princeton University Press, 1960.

BALANDIER, GEORGE (ed.). *Le "Tiers Monde": Sous-Développement et Développement.* Paris: Presses Universitaires de France, 1956.

BAUER, PETER T. and YAMEY, BASIL S. *The Economics of Underdeveloped Countries*. Chicago: The University of Chicago Press, 1957.

CALIFORNIA INSTITUTE OF TECHNOLOGY. *Resources of the World: A Speculative Projection*. Pasadena, Calif., 1956.

COHEN, CARL (ed.). *Communism, Fascism, Democracy: The Theoretical Foundations*. New York: Random House, 1962.

FRANKEL, S. HERBERT. *The Economic Impact on Underdeveloped Societies*. Oxford: Basil Blackwell, 1953.

HOSELITZ, BERT F. *Sociological Aspects of Economic Growth*. Glencoe, Ill.: The Free Press, 1960.

KAUTSKY, JOHN H. (ed.). *Political Change in Underdeveloped Countries: Nationalism and Communism*. New York: John Wiley and Sons, 1962.

LINDSAY, BENJAMIN. *The Modern Democratic State*. New York: Oxford University Press, 1962.

MANDELBAUM, K. *The Industrialization of Backward Areas*. Oxford: Basil Blackwell, 1955.

MYRDAL, GUNNAR. *An International Economy: Problems and Prospects*. New York: Harper and Brothers, 1956.

———. *Beyond the Welfare State*. London: Duckworth, 1960.

NURKSE, RAGNAR. *Patterns of Trade and Development*. Stockholm: Almqvist and Wiksell, 1959.

PERROUX, FRANÇOIS. *La Coexistence Pacifique*. Three volumes. Paris: Presses Universitaires de France, 1958.

ROSTOW, W. W. *The Stages of Economic Growth: A Non-Communist Manifesto*. Cambridge: Cambridge University Press, 1960.

ROYAL INSTITUTE OF INTERNATIONAL AFFAIRS. *World Production of Raw Materials*. London, 1953.

SHANNON, LYLE W. *Underdeveloped Areas: A Book of Readings and Research*. New York: Harper and Brothers, 1957.

STALEY, EUGENE. *The Future of Underdeveloped Countries: Political Implications of Economic Development*. New York: Harper and Brothers, 1954.

THE PRESIDENT'S MATERIALS POLICY COMMISSION. *Resources for Freedom*. (The so-called Paley Report.) Five volumes. Washington, D.C.: United States Government Printing Office, 1952.

Un Défi à l'Occident: l'Avenir des Pays Moins Développés. Nancy-Strasbourg: Berger-Levrault, 1958.

UNITED NATIONS. *Méthodes et Problèmes de l'Industrialisation des Pays Sous-Développes*. New York, 1955.

———. *Statistical Yearbooks*.

WOYTINSKY, W. S. and WOYTINSKY, E. S. *World Population and Production: Trends and Outlook*. New York: The Twentieth Century Fund, 1953.

2. *Foreign assistance*

American Private Enterprise, Foreign Economic Development, and the Aid Programs. A study prepared at the request of the Special Committee to study Foreign Aid Programs, United States Senate, by the American Enterprise Association. Washington, D.C.: United States Government Printing Office, 1957.

BLACK, EUGENE R. *The Diplomacy of Economic Development*. Cambridge, Mass.: Harvard University Press, 1960.

JACKSON, SIR ROBERT G. A. *The Case for an International Development Authority*. Syracuse, N.Y.: Syracuse University Press, 1959.

LISKA, GEORGE. *The New Statecraft: Foreign Aid in American Foreign Policy.* Chicago: The University of Chicago Press, 1960.

MILLIKAN, MAX F. and ROSTOW, W. W. *A Proposal, Key to an Effective Foreign Policy.* New York: Harper and Brothers, 1957.

STANFORD RESEARCH INSTITUTE. *Significant Issues in Economic Aid.* Menlo Park, Calif.: International Industrial Development Center, 1960.

The Objectives of United States Economic Assistance Programs. A study prepared at the request of the Special Committee to study Foreign Aid Programs, United States Senate, by the Center for International Studies, Massachusetts Institute of Technology. Washington, D.C.: U. S. Government Printing Office, 1957.

UNITED NATIONS. *Mésures à Prendre Pour le Développement Economique des Pays Insuffisamment Développés.* Rapport d'un groupe d'experts nommé par le Secrétaire Général des Nations Unies. New York, 1951.

WIGGINS, JAMES W. and SCHOECK, HELMUT (eds.). *Foreign Aid Reexamined: A Critical Appraisal.* Washington, D.C.: Public Affairs Press, 1958.

3. *Asia*

BENHAM, FREDERIC. *The Colombo Plan: An Economic Survey.* London: Royal Institute of International Affairs, 1956.

The Colombo Plan: Co-operative Economic Development in South and South-East Asia. Colombo: Information Unit Colombo Plan, 1954.

4. *The Near East*

ROYAL INSTITUTE OF INTERNATIONAL AFFAIRS. *British Interests in the Mediterranean and Middle East.* London–New York: Oxford University Press, 1958.

———. *The Middle East: A Political and Economic Survey.* 2nd ed. London–New York: Oxford University Press, 1954.

———. *The Western Powers and the Middle East 1958* (mimeographed). Oxford: Oxford University Press, 1958.

SHWADRAN, BENJAMIN. *The Middle East, Oil and the Great Powers.* 2nd ed. New York: Council for Middle Eastern Affairs Press, 1959.

5. *Africa*

BOWLES, CHESTER. *Africa's Challenge to America.* Berkeley and Los Angeles: University of California Press, 1956.

DURAND-REVILLE, LUC. *L'Assistance de la France aux Pays Insuffisamment Développés.* Paris: M.-Th. Génin, 1961.

FITZGERALD, WALTER. *Africa: A Social, Economic and Political Geography of Its Major Regions.* New York: E. P. Dutton and Company, 1955.

HAILEY, LORD. *An African Survey Revised 1956: A Study of Problems Arising in Africa South of the Sahara.* London–New York: Oxford University Press, 1957.

HAINES, C. GROVE (ed.). *Africa Today.* Baltimore: Johns Hopkins Press, 1955.

HANCE, WILLIAM A. *African Economic Development.* New York: Harper and Brothers, 1958.

KIMBLE, GEORGE H. T. *Tropical Africa.* Vol. I: *Land and Livelihood.* Vol. II: *Society and Polity.* New York: Twentieth Century Fund, 1960.

STILLMAN, CALVIN W. (ed.). *Africa in the Modern World.* Chicago: The University of Chicago Press, 1955.

6. *Latin America*

HANKE, LEWIS. *Modern Latin America: Continent in Ferment.* Vol. I: *Mexico and the Caribbean.* Vol. II: *South America.* Princeton, N.J.: D. Van Nostrand Company, 1959.

JOHNSON, JOHN J. *Political Change in Latin America: The Emergence of the Middle Sectors.* Stanford, Calif.: Stanford University Press, 1958.

ORGANIZATION OF AMERICAN STATES. *International Trade, Industrialization and Economic Growth.* Washington, D.C.: Pan American Union, 1956.

———. *Selected Economic Data on the Latin American Republics.* Washington, D.C.: Pan American Union, 1954.

SMITH, T. LYNN. *Current Social Trends and Problems in Latin America.* Gainesville, Florida: University of Florida Press, 1957.

STUART, GRAHAM H. *Latin America and the United States.* 5th ed. New York: Appleton-Century-Crofts, 1955.

UNITED NATIONS. *The Latin American Common Market.* New York, 1959.

VILLOLDO, PEDRO A. *Latin-American Resentment.* New York: Vantage Press, 1959.

CHAPTER VI

BEAUJEUNE-GARNIER, JACQUELINE. *Géographie de la Population.* Vol. I. Paris: Librairie de Médicis, 1956.

BOUTHOUL, GASTON. *La Surpopulation dans le Monde.* Paris: Payot, 1958.

BOWEN, IAN. *Population.* Cambridge: Cambridge University Press, 1954.

COALE, AUSLEY J. and HOOVER, EDGAR M. *Population Growth and Economic Development in Low-Income Countries: A Case Study of India's Prospects.* Princeton, N.J.: Princeton University Press, 1958.

DARWIN, SIR CHARLES. *The Problems of World Population.* Cambridge: Cambridge University Press, 1958.

NOTESTEIN, FRANK W. *et al. The Future Population of Europe and the Soviet Union.* Geneva: League of Nations, 1944.

RUSSELL, SIR E. JOHN. *World Population and World Food Supplies.* London: George Allen and Unwin, 1954.

SAUVY, ALFRED. *Théorie Générale de la Population.* Two volumes. Paris: Presses Universitaires de France, 1952-54.

UNITED NATIONS. *Demographic Yearbooks.*

———. *The Future Growth of World Population: Population Studies No. 28.* New York, 1958.

CHAPTER VII

1. *International Communist movement*

BALL, W. MACMAHON. *Nationalism and Communism in East Asia.* Melbourne: Melbourne University Press, 1952.

BARNETT, A. DOAK. *Communist China and Asia.* New York: Harper and Brothers, 1960.

BASS, R. and MARBURY, E. *The Soviet-Yugoslav Controversy, 1948-1958: A Documentary Record.* New York: Prospect Books, 1959.

BENES, V. L.; BYRNES, R. F.; and SPULBER, N. (eds.). *The Second Soviet-Yugoslav Dispute: Full Text of Main Documents, April-June 1958.* Bloomington: Indiana University Press, 1959.

BORKENAU, FRANZ. *European Communism.* New York: Harper and Brothers, 1953.

———. *World Communism: A History of the Communist International.* New York: W. W. Norton and Company, 1939.

BRZEZINSKI, ZBIGNIEW. *The Soviet Bloc: Unity and Conflict.* Cambridge: Harvard University Press, 1960.

BURKS, R. V. *The Dynamics of Communism in Eastern Europe.* Princeton: Princeton University Press, 1961.

COHEN, CARL (ed.). *Communism, Fascism, Democracy: The Theoretical Foundations.* New York: Random House, 1962.

DRAPER, THEODORE. *Castro's Revolution: Myths and Realities.* New York: Frederick A. Praeger, 1962.

DZIEWANOWSKI, M. K. *The Communist Party of Poland: An Outline of History.* Cambridge: Harvard University Press, 1959.

FISCHER, RUTH. *Stalin and German Communism: A Study in the Origins of the State Party.* Cambridge: Harvard University Press, 1948.

HOFFMAN, G. W. and NEAL, F. W. *Yugoslavia and the New Communism.* New York: Twentieth Century Fund, 1962.

HUDSON, G. F.; LOWENTHAL, R.; MACFARQUHAR, R. *et al. The Sino-Soviet Dispute.* New York: Frederick A. Praeger, 1962.

LATTIMORE, OWEN. *Nationalism and Revolution in Mongolia.* New York: Oxford University Press, 1962.

MONNEROT, JULES. *Sociology and Psychology of Communism.* Boston: Beacon Press, 1960.

ROCA, BLAS. *The Cuban Revolution: Report of the Eighth National Congress of the Popular Socialist Party of Cuba.* New York: New Century Publishers, 1961.

SKENDI, STAVRO (ed.). *Albania.* New York: Frederick A. Praeger, 1958.

The Anti-Stalin Campaign and International Communism: A Selection of Documents. New York: Columbia University Press, 1956.

Yugoslavia's Way: Program of the League of the Yugoslav Communists. New York: All Nations' Press, 1958.

ZINNER, PAUL E. (ed.). *National Communism and Popular Revolt in Eastern Europe: A Selection of Documents on Events in Poland and Hungary, February-November* 1956. New York: Columbia University Press, 1956.

2. *Soviet and East European regimes*

DALLIN, DAVID J. *The New Soviet Empire.* New Haven: Yale University Press, 1951.

DJILAS, MILOVAN. *The New Class: An Analysis of the Communist System.* New York: Frederick A. Praeger, 1957.

FAINSOD, MERLE. *How Russia Is Ruled.* 2nd ed. Cambridge, Mass.: Harvard University Press, 1963.

GSOVSKI, VLADIMIR and GRZYBOWSKI, KAZIMIERZ (eds.). *Government, Law and Courts in the Soviet Union and Eastern Europe.* Two volumes. New York: Frederick A. Praeger, 1959.

HAZARD, JOHN N. *The Soviet System of Government.* Chicago: The University of Chicago Press, 1957.

KULSKI, WLADYSLAW W. *The Soviet Regime: Communism in Practice.* 4th ed. Syracuse, N.Y.: Syracuse University Press, 1964.

3. *Soviet foreign policy*

BELOFF, MAX. *Soviet Policy in the Far East: 1944-1951.* London–New York: Oxford University Press, 1953.

———. *The Foreign Policy of Soviet Russia: 1929-1941.* Two volumes. New York: Oxford University Press, 1949.

DALLIN, DAVID J. *Soviet Foreign Policy after Stalin.* Philadelphia: J. B. Lippincott Company, 1961.

FISCHER, LOUIS. *The Soviets in World Affairs: 1917-1929.* Two volumes. Princeton, N. J.: Princeton University Press, 1951.

KULSKI, W. W. *Peaceful Co-existence: An Analysis of Soviet Foreign Policy.* Chicago: Henry Regnery Company, 1959.

LAQUEUR, WALTER Z. *The Soviet Union and the Middle East.* New York: Frederick A. Praeger, 1959.

STRAUSZ-HUPÉ, ROBERT; KINTNER, WILLIAM R.; DOUGHERTY, JAMES E.; and COTTRELL, ALVIN J. *Protracted Conflict.* New York: Harper and Brothers, 1959.

4. *The Chinese Communist party*

BRANDT, CONRAD; SCHWARTZ, BENJAMIN; and FAIRBANK, JOHN K. *A Documentary History of Chinese Communism.* Cambridge: Harvard University Press, 1952.

ROSTOW, W. W. *The Prospects for Communist China.* New York: John Wiley and Sons, 1954.

CHAPTER VIII

1. *Public opinion*

ALMOND, GABRIEL A. *The American People and Foreign Policy.* New York: Harcourt, Brace and Company, 1950.

BELOFF, MAX. *Foreign Policy and the Democratic Process.* Baltimore: Johns Hopkins Press, 1955.

CARR, EDWARD HALLETT. *The Twenty Years' Crisis, 1919-1939: An Introduction to the Study of International Relations.* London: The Macmillan Company, 1958.

KENNAN, GEORGE F. *Realities of American Foreign Policy.* Princeton, N.J.: Princeton University Press, 1954.

LIPPMANN, WALTER. *Essays in the Public Philosophy.* Boston: Little, Brown and Company, 1955.

———. *Public Opinion.* New York: Harcourt, Brace and Company, 1922.

MEYNAUD, JEAN. *Les Groupes de Pression en France.* Paris: Librairie Armand Colin, 1958.

MILLIS, WALTER and MURRAY, JOHN COURTNEY. *Foreign Policy and the Free Society.* New York: The Fund for the Republic, 1958.

PRICE, JOHN. *Foreign Affairs and the Public.* London: Royal Institute of International Affairs, 1946.

WESTERFIELD, H. BRADFORD. *Foreign Policy and Party Politics: Pearl Harbor to Korea.* New Haven: Yale University Press, 1955.

2. *Morality*

CARR, EDWARD HALLETT. *Op. cit.*

CORBETT, PERCY E. *Morals, Law and Power in International Relations.* Los Angeles: The John Randolph Haynes and Dora Haynes Foundation, 1956.

KENNAN, GEORGE F. *Op. cit.*

LEFEVER, ERNEST W. *Ethics and United States Foreign Policy.* New York: Meridian Books, 1957.

NIEBUHR, REINHOLD. *Moral Man and Immoral Society: A Study in Ethics and Politics.* New York: Charles Scribner's Sons, 1932.

OSGOOD, ROBERT ENDICOTT. *Op. cit.*

POLITIS, NICOLAS. *La Morale Internationale.* New York: Brentano's, 1944.

THOMPSON, KENNETH W. *Christian Ethics and the Dilemmas of Foreign Policy.* Durham, N.C.: Duke University Press, 1959.

3. *International law*

AKADEMIIA NAUK SSSR, INSTITUT PRAVA. *Mezhdunarodnoe Pravo.* Moscow: Gosudarstvennoe Izdatelstvo Iuridicheskoi Literatury, 1957.

BRIERLY, J. L. *Law of Nations.* 4th ed. Oxford: Clarendon Press, 1949.

CORBETT, PERCY E. *Law in Diplomacy.* Princeton, N.J.: Princeton University Press, 1959.

FENWICK, CHARLES G. *International Law.* 3rd ed. New York: Appleton-Century-Crofts, 1948.

HACKWORTH, G. H. *Digest of International Law.* Eight volumes. Washington, D.C.: U. S. Government Printing Office, 1940-44.

HYDE, C. C. *International Law, Chiefly as Interpreted and Applied by the United States.* 2nd ed. Three volumes. New York: Little, Brown and Company, 1945.

KAPLAN, MORTON A. and DE B. KATZENBACH, NICHOLAS. *The Political Foundations of International Law.* New York: John Wiley and Sons, 1961.

LAUTERPACHT, H. *Recognition in International Law.* Cambridge: Cambridge University Press, 1947.

———. *The Function of Law in the International Community.* Oxford: Oxford University Press, 1933.

OPPENHEIM, L. (edited by Lauterpacht, H.). *International Law.* London: Longmans, Green and Co., Vol. I—1955; Vol. II—1952.

VISSCHER, CHARLES DE. *Theory and Reality in Public International Law.* Princeton, N.J.: Princeton University Press, 1957.

CHAPTER IX

1. *United Nations*

ASHER, ROBERT E.; KOTSCHNING, WALTER M.; BROWN, WILLIAM ADAMS *et al.* *The United Nations and Economic and Social Co-operation.* Washington, D.C.: The Brookings Institution, 1957.

BERKES, ROSS N. and BEDI, MOHINDER S. *The Diplomacy of India: Indian Foreign Policy in the United Nations.* Stanford, Calif.: Stanford University Press, 1958.

Documents on Disarmament: 1945-1959. Two volumes. Washington, D.C.: Department of State, 1960.

Everyman's United Nations: The Structure, Functions and Work of the Organization and Its Related Agencies During the Years 1945-58. 6th ed. New York: United Nations, 1959.

GOODRICH, LELAND M. *The United Nations.* New York: Thomas Y. Crowell Company, 1959.

GOODRICH, LELAND M. and SIMONS, ANNE P. *The United Nations and the Maintenance of International Peace and Security.* Washington, D.C.: The Brookings Institution, 1955.

GOODSPEED, STEPHEN S. *The Nature and Function of International Organization.* New York: Oxford University Press, 1959.

LANGENHOVE, FERNAND VAN. *La Crise du Système de Securité Collective des Nations Unies: 1946-1957.* The Hague: Martinus Nijhoff, 1958.

LISKA, GEORGE. *International Equilibrium: A Theoretical Essay on the Politics and Organization of Security.* Cambridge, Mass.: Harvard University Press, 1957.

RAY, JEAN. *Commentaire du Pacte de la Société des Nations selon la Politique et la Jurisprudence des Organes de la Société.* Five volumes. Paris: Librairie de Receuil Sirey, 1930-35.

STONE, JULIUS. *Aggression and World Order: A Critique of United Nations Theories of Aggression.* Berkeley: University of California Press, 1958.

The United Nations Conference on International Organization, San Francisco, 1945: Selected Documents. Washington, D.C.: U. S. Government Printing Office, 1946.

Yearbooks of the United Nations. New York: United Nations, 1946-47 and ff.

2. *European integration*

ARON, RAYMOND *et al. L'Unification Economique de l'Europe.* Neuchâtel: Editions de la Baconnière, 1957.

COUSTÉ, PIERRE BERNARD. *L'Association des Pays d'Outre-Mer à la Communauté Economique Européenne.* Paris: Librairies Techniques, 1959.

European Yearbooks. The Hague: Martinus Nijhoff.

HAAS, ERNST B. *Consensus Formation in the Council of Europe.* Berkeley: University of California Press, 1960.

———. *The Uniting of Europe: Political, Social and Economic Forces, 1950-1957.* London: Stevens and Sons, 1958.

HAINES, C. GROVE (ed.). *European Integration.* Baltimore: Johns Hopkins Press, 1957.

LAWSON, RUTH C. (ed.). *International Regional Organizations: Constitutional Foundations.* New York: Frederick A. Praeger, 1962.

LEFEBVRE, JACQUES. *Afrique et Communauté Européenne.* Brussels: Editions du Treurenberg, 1958.

LINDSAY, KENNETH. *Towards a European Parliament.* Strasbourg: Council of Europe, 1958.

NORTHEDGE, F. S. *British Foreign Policy: The Process of Readjustment, 1945-1961.* London: Allen and Unwin, 1962.

ROBERTSON, A. H. *European Institutions: Co-operation, Integration, Unification.* New York: Frederick A. Praeger, 1959.

———. *The Council of Europe.* New York: Frederick A. Praeger, 1956.

ZURCHER, ARNOLD J. *The Struggle to Unite Europe: 1940-1958.* New York: New York University Press, 1958.

3. *Commonwealth of Nations*

ATTLEE, EARL CLEMENT. *Empire into Commonwealth.* London: Oxford University Press, 1961.

FAWCETT, J. E. S. *The Inter Se Doctrine of Commonwealth Relations.* London: University of London, The Athlone Press, 1958.

HARVEY, HEATHER J. *Consultation and Co-operation in the Commonwealth: A Handbook of Methods and Practice.* London–New York: Oxford University Press, 1952.

JENNINGS, SIR IVOR. *Problems of the New Commonwealth.* Durham, N.C.: Duke University Press, 1958.

———. *The British Commonwealth of Nations.* London: Hutchinson's University Library, 1948.

ROUSSEAU, CHARLES. *Le Commonwealth dans les Relations Internationales* (mimeographed). Paris: Paris University, 1955-56.

4. *Organization of American States*

BLACKMER, HENRY MYRON. *United States Policy and the Inter-American Peace System: 1889-1952.* Geneva: University of Geneva, 1952.

DREIER, JOHN C. *The Organization of American States and the Hemisphere Crisis.* New York: Harper and Row, 1962.

DUPUY, RENÉ-JEAN. *Le Nouveau Panaméricanisme: L'Evolution du Système Inter-Américain vers le Fedéralisme.* Paris: Editions A. Pedone, 1956.

FENWICK, CHARLES G. *The Inter-American Regional System.* New York: The Declan X. McMullen Company, 1949.

The Basic Principles of the Inter-American System. Washington, D.C.: Pan American Union, 1943.

The Organization of American States and the United Nations. 2nd ed. Washington, D.C.: Pan American Union, 1952.

The Organization of American States (OAS): What It Is and How It Works. Washington, D.C.: Pan American Union, 1959.

WHITAKER, ARTHUR P. *The Western Hemisphere Idea: Its Rise and Decline.* Ithaca, N.Y.: Cornell University Press, 1954.

CHAPTER X

1. *Formulation and implementation of policies*

ACHESON, DEAN. *Meetings at the Summit: A Study in Diplomatic Method.* University of New Hampshire, 1958.

———. *Power and Diplomacy.* Cambridge, Mass.: Harvard University Press, 1958.

ALLEN, ROBERT LORING. *Soviet Economic Warfare.* Washington, D.C.: Public Affairs Press, 1960.

BOWLES, CHESTER. *Ambassador's Report.* New York: Harper and Brothers, 1954.

CALLIÈRES, DE. *On thc Manner of Negotiating with Princes.* (Translated from the French by A. F. Whyte.) Boston–New York: Houghton Mifflin Company, 1919.

CARDOZO, MICHAEL. *Diplomats in International Co-operation: Stepchildren of the Foreign Service.* Ithaca, N.Y.: Cornell University Press, 1962.

CHABOD, FEDERICO. *Machiavelli and the Renaissance.* London: Bowes and Bowes, 1958.

CHAMBRUN, CHARLES DE. *L'Esprit de la Diplomatie.* Paris: Editions Corréa, 1944.

CORBETT, PERCY E. *Law in Diplomacy.* Princeton, N.J.: Princeton University Press, 1959.

CRAIG, GORDON A. and GILBERT, FELIX (eds.). *The Diplomats: 1919-1939.* Princeton, N.J.: Princeton University Press, 1953.

DENNETT, RAYMOND and JOHNSON, JOSEPH E. (eds.). *Negotiating with the Russians.* Boston: World Peace Foundation, 1951.

FULLER, C. DALE. *Training of Specialists in International Relations.* Washington, D.C.: American Council on Education, 1957.

GROSS, FELIKS. *Foreign Policy Analysis.* New York: Philosophical Library, 1954.

HALLE, LOUIS J. *Choice for Survival.* New York: Harper and Brothers, 1958.

HANKEY, LORD. *Diplomacy by Conference.* London: Ernest Benn, 1946.

HILSMAN, ROGER. *Strategic Intelligence and National Decisions.* Glencoe, Illinois: The Free Press, 1956.

KAPLAN, MORTON A. *System and Process in International Politics.* New York: John Wiley and Sons, 1957.

KENNAN, GEORGE F. *American Diplomacy: 1900-1950.* Chicago: The University of Chicago Press, 1951.

MARSHALL, CHARLES BURTON. *The Limits of Foreign Policy.* New York: Henry Holt and Company, 1954.

MATTINGLY, GARRETT. *Renaissance Diplomacy.* Boston: Houghton Mifflin Company, 1955.

NICOLSON, HAROLD. *Diplomacy.* 2nd ed. London–New York: Oxford University Press, 1950.

———. *The Evolution of Diplomatic Method.* London: Constable and Company, 1954.

PANIKKAR, K. M. *The Principles and Practice of Diplomacy.* Delhi: Ranjit Printers and Publishers, 1953.

PEARSON, LESTER B. *Diplomacy in the Nuclear Age.* Cambridge, Mass.: Harvard University Press, 1959.

Report of the Committee on Foreign Affairs Personnel: Personnel for the New Diplomacy. Washington, D.C.: The Carnegie Endowment for International Peace, 1962.

SATOW, SIR ERNEST. *A Guide to Diplomatic Practice.* 4th ed. London: Longman's, Green and Company, 1957.

SNYDER, RICHARD C.; BRUCK, H. W.; and SAPIN, BURTON. *Decision-Making as an Approach to the Study of International Politics.* Princeton, N.J.: Princeton University Press, 1954.

STRANG, LORD. *The Foreign Office.* London–New York: Oxford University Press, 1955.

THAYER, CHARLES W. *Diplomat.* New York: Harper and Brothers, 1959.

WRISTON, HENRY M. *Diplomacy in a Democracy.* New York: Harper and Brothers, 1956.

2. *Contemporary American foreign policy*

A Decade of American Foreign Policy: Basic Documents, 1941-1949. Washington, D.C.: U. S. Government Printing Office, 1950.

American Foreign Policy: Current Documents. Volumes for 1956 and ff. Washington, D.C.: U. S. Government Printing Office, 1959 and ff.

American Foreign Policy: 1950-1955, Basic Documents. Two volumes. Washington, D.C.: U. S. Government Printing Office, 1957.

BOWLES, CHESTER. *American Politics in a Revolutionary World.* Cambridge, Mass.: Harvard University Press, 1956.

Foreign Relations of the United States: Diplomatic Papers. The Conferences at Malta and Yalta, 1945. Washington, D.C.: U. S. Government Printing Office, 1955.

LERCHE, CHARLES O. *Foreign Policy of the American People.* Englewood Cliffs, N.J.: Prentice-Hall, 1958.

MORGENTHAU, HANS J. *In Defense of the National Interest: A Critical Examination of American Foreign Policy.* New York: Alfred A. Knopf, 1951.

PERKINS, DEXTER. *Foreign Policy and the American Spirit.* Ithaca, N.Y.: Cornell University Press, 1957.

———. *The American Approach to Foreign Policy.* Cambridge, Mass.: Harvard University Press, 1953.

REITZEL, WILLIAM; KAPLAN, MORTON A.; and COBLENZ, CONSTANCE G. *United*

States Foreign Policy: 1945-1955. Washington, D.C.: The Brookings Institution, 1957.

ROSTOW, W. W. *The United States in the World Arena: An Essay in Recent History.* New York: Harper and Brothers, 1960.

Study of United States Foreign Policy: Summary of Views of Retired Foreign Service Officers Prepared for the Committee on Foreign Relations, United States Senate. Washington, D.C.: U. S. Government Printing Office, 1959.

TANNENBAUM, FRANK. *The American Tradition in Foreign Policy.* Norman, Oklahoma: University of Oklahoma, 1955.

THOMPSON, KENNETH W. *Political Realism and the Crisis of World Politics: An American Approach to Foreign Policy.* Princeton, N.J.: Princeton University Press, 1960.

TRUMAN, HARRY S. *Memoirs.* Two volumes. Garden City, N.Y.: Doubleday, 1955-56.

United States Relations with China, with Special Reference to the Period 1944-49. Washington, D.C.: Department of State, 1949.

UNITED STATES SENATE, COMMITTEE ON FOREIGN RELATIONS. *United States Foreign Policy. Developments in Military Technology and Their Impact on United States Strategy and Foreign Policy.* A study prepared by the Washington Center of Foreign Policy Research, Johns Hopkins University. Washington, D.C.: U. S. Government Printing Office, 1959.

3. *History of contemporary international politics*

CHURCHILL, WINSTON S. *The Second World War.* Six volumes. Boston: Houghton Mifflin Company, 1948-1951.

Conference for the Conclusion and Signature of the Treaty of Peace with Japan, San Francisco, 1951: Record of Proceedings. Washington, D.C.: Department of State, 1951.

DUROSELLE, J. B. *Histoire Diplomatique de 1919 à Nos Jours.* Paris: Librairie Dalloz, 1953.

FEIS, HERBERT. *Between War and Peace: The Potsdam Conference.* Princeton, N.J.: Princeton University Press, 1960.

———. *Churchill, Roosevelt, Stalin: The War They Waged and the Peace They Sought.* Princeton, N.J.: Princeton University Press, 1957.

GATHORNE-HARDY, G. M. *A Short History of International Affairs: 1920-1939.* London: Oxford University Press, 1950.

GAULLE, CHARLES DE. *Mémoires de Guerre.* Three volumes. Paris: Librairie Plon, 1954-1959.

HILGER, GUSTAV and MEYER, ALFRED G. *The Incompatible Allies: A Memoir-History of German-Soviet Relations, 1918-1941.* New York: The Macmillan Company, 1953.

Nazi-Soviet Relations, 1939-1941. Documents from the Archives of the German Foreign Office. Washington, D.C.: Department of State, 1948.

OPIE, REDVERS *et al. The Search for Peace Settlements.* Washington, D.C.: The Brookings Institution, 1951.

Perepiska Predsedatelia Soveta Ministrov SSSR z Prezidentami SShA i Premier-Ministrami Velikobritanii vo Vremia Velikoi Otechestvennoi Voiny, 1941-1945 gg. Two volumes. Moscow: Gosudarstvennoe Izdatelstvo Politicheskoi Literatury, 1957-1958.

The Ciano Diaries: 1939-1943. New York: Doubleday and Company, 1946.

WEINBERG, GERHARD L. *Germany and the Soviet Union: 1939-1941.* Leiden: J. E. Brill, 1954.

4. *International economics*

ELLSWORTH, PAUL T. *International Economy: Its Structure and Operation.* Rev. ed. New York: The Macmillan Company, 1961.

HARROD, ROY F. *International Economics.* Chicago: The University of Chicago Press, 1958.

KILLOUGH, HUGH B. and LUCY, W. *International Economics.* Princeton: D. Van Nostrand Company, 1960.

MEADE, JAMES E. *Theory of International Economic Policy.* Vol. I: *Balance of Payments.* Vol. II: *Trade and Welfare.* New York: Oxford University Press, 1951 and 1955.

MYRDAL, GUNNAR. *An International Economy: Problems and Prospects.* New York: Harper and Brothers, 1956.

SNIDER, DELBERT A. *Introduction to International Economics.* Rev. ed. Homewood, Illinois: Irwin, 1958.

The foregoing bibliography could not possibly be exhaustive of the vast literature devoted to international politics. It is meant only to serve as a useful reference for the various topics discussed in the present book.

The following periodical publications of interest for a study of international affairs are enumerated *exempli modo:*

African Affairs, quarterly. London: Royal African Society.

American Journal of International Law, quarterly. Washington, D.C.: American Society of International Law.

American Political Science Review, quarterly. Washington, D.C.: American Political Science Association.

Annals of the American Academy of Political and Social Science, annual. Philadelphia.

Asia-Africa Review, quarterly. New Delhi: Asian Solidarity Committee.

Australian Journal of Politics and History, semi-annual. Brisbane: University of Queensland Press, Australia.

Australian Quarterly. Sydney: Australian Institute of Political Science.

British Yearbook of International Law. London: Royal Institute of International Affairs.

Central Asian Review, quarterly. London: Central Asian Research Centre.

Chronology of International Events and Documents, biweekly. London: Royal Institute of International Affairs.

Contemporary Japan, quarterly. Tokyo: Foreign Affairs Association of Japan.

Current Digest of the Soviet Press, weekly. New York: The Joint Committee on Slavic Studies, American Council of Learned Societies.

Current History, monthly. Philadelphia: Current History, Inc.

East Europe, monthly. New York: Free Europe Committee.

Eastern World, monthly. London: Eastern World, Ltd.

Foreign Affairs, quarterly. New York: Council on Foreign Relations.

India Quarterly. New Delhi: Indian Council of World Affairs.

International Affairs, monthly. Moscow: Soviet Society for the Popularization of Political and Scientific Knowledge.

International Affairs, quarterly. London: Royal Institute of International Affairs.

International Conciliation, five times a year. New York: Carnegie Endowment for International Peace.

International Journal, quarterly. Toronto: Canadian Institute of International Affairs.

International Organization, quarterly. Boston: World Peace Foundation.

Journal of Politics, quarterly. University of Florida: Southern Political Science Association.

Middle East Journal, quarterly. Washington, D.C.: Middle East Institute.

Pacific Affairs, quarterly. New York: Institute of Pacific Relations.

Pakistan Horizon, quarterly. Karachi: Pakistan Institute of International Affairs.

Political Quarterly. London: Stevens and Sons.

Political Science Quarterly. New York: Academy of Political Science.

Political Studies, three times a year. London: Political Studies Association of the United Kingdom.

Problems of Communism, bimonthly. Washington, D.C.: United States Information Agency.

Review of Politics, quarterly. Notre Dame, Indiana: University of Notre Dame.

The Round Table, quarterly. London: Round Table, Ltd.

Western Political Quarterly. Salt Lake City: Western Political Science Association.

World Politics, quarterly. Princeton, N.J.: Center of International Studies, Princeton University.

World Today, monthly. London: Royal Institute of International Affairs.

INDEXES

Index of Persons

Index of Place-Names

Subject Index